Text and Materials on the Criminal Justice Process

Third Edition

Nicola Padfield

BA (Oxon) Dip Crim (Cantab) DES (Aix-Marseille)
Barrister-at-Law, Senior Lecturer, Institute of Criminology,
University of Cambridge and Fellow of Fitzwilliam College, Cambridge

Members of the LexisNexis Group worldwide

United Kingdom	LexisNexis UK, a Division of Reed Elsevier (UK) Ltd, Halsbury House, 35 Chancery Lane, LONDON, WC2A 1EL, and 4 Hill Street, EDINBURGH EH2 3JZ
Argentina	LexisNexis Argentina, BUENOS AIRES
Australia	LexisNexis Butterworths, CHATSWOOD, New South Wales
Austria	LexisNexis Verlag ARD Orac GmbH & Co KG, VIENNA
Canada	LexisNexis Butterworths, MARKHAM, Ontario
Chile	LexisNexis Chile Ltda, SANTIAGO DE CHILE
Czech Republic	Nakladatelství Orac sro, PRAGUE
France	Editions du Juris-Classeur SA, PARIS
Germany	LexisNexis Deutschland GmbH, FRANKFURT, MUNSTER
Hong Kong	LexisNexis Butterworths, HONG KONG
Hungary	HVG-Orac, BUDAPEST
India	LexisNexis Butterworths, NEW DELHI
Ireland	Butterworths (Ireland) Ltd, DUBLIN
Italy	Giuffrè Editore, MILAN
Malaysia	Malayan Law Journal Sdn Bhd, KUALA LUMPUR
New Zealand	LexisNexis Butterworths, WELLINGTON
Poland	Wydawnictwo Prawnicze LexisNexis, WARSAW
Singapore	LexisNexis Butterworths, SINGAPORE
South Africa	LexisNexis Butterworths, DURBAN
Switzerland	Stämpfli Verlag AG, BERNE
USA	LexisNexis, DAYTON, Ohio

© Reed Elsevier (UK) Ltd 2003

A CIP Catalogue record for this book is available from the British Library.

First edition 1995
Second edition 2000

ISBN 0 406 96382 7

Typeset by Sparks Computer Solutions Ltd, Oxford – http://www.sparks.co.uk
Printed by Thomson Litho Ltd, East Kilbride, Scotland

Visit LexisNexis UK at www.lexisnexis.co.uk

Text and Materials on
the Criminal Justice Process

Preface

Since the first edition of this book, the pace of change in the criminal justice system has not slowed. Nor has the quality of justice obviously improved. The seminal review of the criminal justice process at the time of the first edition was the Royal Commission on Criminal Justice (1993). In the last few years there has been a further flurry of 'official' reviews of the system: the Narey Review of Delay in the Criminal Justice System (1997), the Halliday Review of the Sentencing Framework (2001) and the Auld Review of the Criminal Courts (2001), to name but three. In updating this edition, I have sought to give proper space to such reports and to academic and research critiques of criminal justice: as a result, citation of statutory material as well as government White Papers, now so easily downloaded from the Internet, have been kept to the minimum. The selection of materials remains idiosyncratic: designed to stimulate thought, as much as anything. Readers are warmly invited to let me know what they think of my selection!

The shape of the book continues to emphasise each discrete part of the decision-making process, whereas the government appears committed to 'team working', 'joined-up' criminal justice and inter-agency co-operation in criminal justice. It might therefore be argued that a book divided as this one is, is out of date. I would argue that the opposite is true. The reality is that there are several very different players within the criminal justice process. We should not be seduced into thinking that they all sing from the same songbook. The working relationships between the various agencies must be explored, as must the legal framework within which they function. As Big Brother tightens his grip, are there enough checks and balances within the process?

As ever, my thanks go to many colleagues for their help and advice. Perhaps I might single out Julia Flack, of Cambridgeshire Probation Service.

Nicola Padfield
June 2003

Preface to the First Edition

The criminal justice system has probably never been as much discussed as it has been in the last few years. We all have an interest in understanding the problems associated with crime in our society, whether we are politicians, journalists, students, academics or simply curious citizens. The subject is popular with students, who seek not only to understand, but also to see a way forward out of the penal 'crisis' in which we seem constantly to find ourselves. Yet students cannot be expected to make judgments and to evaluate the process without access to much published material, and this book aims to address that need in a way that brings a touch of real life to the subject. It is hardly surprising that there are few books seeking to provide students with a window on these sources: the subject is vast, and constantly shifting.

The author of a criminal justice text faces a difficult challenge in deciding the angle from which to approach the subject. This book concentrates on a number of discrete stages within the criminal justice process. For this, it may be criticised for reinforcing the fallacy that there is a neat process, made up of self-contained stages, through which a criminal case will pass. However, it is only by looking at the diversity of powers exercised at different stages that one can come to see the unsystematic nature of the criminal justice process.

This is not a subject which should be learnt entirely from books. To maintain a toehold in reality, this book introduces a fictional but, I hope, credible case history. The case history is not pursued too rigorously, since it provides only an example, not a blueprint, of a criminal case. Wherever possible, however, students should try to create their own scenery, their own understanding of the environment, by arranging to 'shadow' police officers, solicitors, barristers, judges, magistrates and probation officers 'on the job'. Visits to police stations, courts and prisons, even brief visits, often open students' eyes and provoke a more critical and analytical response to the subject than can any class discussion.

I have chosen to include a wide variety of sources in order to reflect the depth and variety of ways in which the subject can be approached. Statutes are quoted to illustrate the legal structure behind the decision-making process, and the proliferation of statutes in this area is evidence of continual upheaval. Many of the governing 'rules' are non-statutory, and Prison Rules, Home Office Circulars and National Standards are necessarily included. Increasingly, the boundaries of discretion are being decided by the courts by way of the judicial review procedure, and a number of such cases are therefore annotated in the book. Statutes and cases are perhaps more readily accessible to the student than is the ever-expanding body of academic publications and research studies. A number of these, as well as official and semi-official reports, are therefore extracted, and reference has been made to those which may stand the test of time. I have tried to include a wide selection of material from recent empirical work and academic analyses.

There are several ways of compiling a 'text and materials' book: many link the materials by a continuous commentary. The style adopted in this book is to leave the documents to speak for themselves: my text therefore stands alone at the beginning of each chapter. The text is designed to introduce the materials, highlighting key issues and questions. It is hoped that in this way students will sense that this is a subject with no clear 'right answers', and that no linear approach suffices.

Choosing material was at once a pleasure and a nightmare, perhaps comparable to the exercise of reducing one's favourite music to eight records for *Desert Island Discs*. The selection is not comprehensive. The aim is to whet the student's appetite for more, and to provide a balanced, catholic, grounding. I approach the subject from the perspective of a lawyer; it may therefore be that the book is of most interest to law students.

There are doubtless omissions which may surprise my colleagues: some will be oversights and some deliberate. Material in this edition has been gathered up to the end of November 1994. Whilst the errors in this book are certainly all my own, I am particularly grateful to Professor Andrew Ashworth and to Sir Derek Oulton, who both found time to read through substantial parts of the text within tight time constraints. Dr David Thomas and Mr Philip Brown were also always ready to give advice. Several students taking the MPhil in Criminology in Cambridge in 1994–95 also gave much encouragement and stimulating comments. I hope that the book will be sufficiently attractive to students, that I will have the opportunity to amend the book in a new edition. I would welcome suggestions on material which should be included, and on material which can be omitted.

Because students should be aware of the practical everyday pressures on decision makers, I have accordingly spent some time visiting and talking to those who actually make the kind of decisions discussed in the book. I am grateful to those who kindly tolerated my persistent questioning: in particular, Inspector Bill Giles and Sergeant Simon Cross of Cambridge Police Station; Mr Robert Martin, Area Manager of Cambridge Legal Aid Area Office; Mr Hew Heycock, Branch Crown Prosecutor, and Ms Sue Hemming, Principal Crown Prosecutor, of the Crown Prosecution Service in Huntingdon; Ms Ellen Yahuda, of Matthew, Grosse, & Bullock, Solicitors; and Mr Peter Johnson, Senior Probation Officer with West Yorkshire Probation Service.

Nicola Padfield
December 1994

Contents

Chapter One

Introduction   I

Chapter Two

The Police   55

Chapter Three

The Crown Prosecution Service (CPS)   178

Documents

Chapter Four

Non-Police Investigations   217

Documents

Chapter Five

Defence Lawyers   247

Chapter Six

Magistrates   274

Chapter Seven

Trial Judges   338

Chapter Eight

Juries   385

Chapter Nine

Appeal and Review Decisions   414

Chapter Ten

Sentence Management   460

Acknowledgments

The author and publisher gratefully acknowledge the generosity of copyright owners of the materials extracted in giving permission to reproduce their work. Without this generosity, the book could not have been completed. The publisher would also be pleased to hear from those copyright holders from whom permission has been sought but not yet received.

Blackwell Publishing

Henham, R *'Bargain Justice or Justice Denied? Sentence Discounts and the Criminal Process'* [1999] MLR 515, at page 524

Lord Hoffman *'Human Rights and the House of Lords'* (1999) 62 MLR 159, at page 162

Hoyano, L C H *'Policing Flawed Police Investigations: Unravelling the Blanket'* (1999) 62 MLR 912, at page 920

McKeever, G *'Detecting, Prosecuting and Punishing Benefit Fraud: The Social Security Administration (Fraud) Act 1997'* (1999) 62 MLR 261

Morgan, R *'Magistrates: The Future According to Auld'* (2002) 29 J Law and Society 308, at page 314

Sanders, A *'Class Bias in Prosecutions'* [1985] Howard Journal of Criminal Justice 176, at page 194

Clarendon Press

Genders, E and Player, E *Race Relations in Prisons* (1989), page 117 ff, 124 ff

McConville, M, Hodgson, J, Bridges, L and Pavlovic, A *Standing Accused: The Organisation and Practice of Criminal Defence Lawyers* (1994), at page 126 ff (from Chapter 5), at page 210 ff (from Chapter 8), at page 267 ff (from Chapter 10)

Croom Helm

King, M *The Framework of Criminal Justice* (1981), at page 13

Incorporated Council of Law Reporting

Practice Direction: Crown Court: Bail Pending Appeal [1983] 1 WLR 1292
R v Ensor [1989] 1 WLR 497
R v Smith [1990] 1 WLR 1311

Justice of the Peace

[2:8] Farrington, D and Dowds, E *'Why does crime decrease?'* (1984) Justice of the Peace 506, at page 507

Longmans

James, A and Raine, J *The New Politics of Criminal Justice* (1998), at page 44 ff, 116 ff
Worrall, A *Punishment in the Community: The Future of Criminal Justice* (1997), at page 149 ff

Macmillan

Skyrme, T *The Changing Image of the Magistracy* (2nd edition, 1983), at page 6 ff, 67

Magistrates' Association

Magistrates' Association *Sentencing Guidelines* (2001), at page 14, 43, 49

Open University Press

(Copyright for these Open University Press titles has now reverted to the author of those titles)

Brown, S *Magistrates at Work: Sentencing and Social Structure* (1991), at page 81 ff

Cook, D *Rich Law, Poor Law* (1989), at page 116 ff, 142 ff, 167 ff

Eaton, M 'The Question of Bail' in Carlen, P and Worrall, A (eds) *Gender, Crime and Justice* (1987), at page 106 ff

Worrall, A 'Sisters in Law? Women Defendants and Women Magistrates' in Carlen, P and Worrall, A (eds) *Gender, Crime and Justice* (1987), at page 122 ff

Oxford University Press

Hood, R *Race and Sentencing: a Study in the Crown Court* (1992)

Jones, Carol 'Auditing Criminal Justice' (1993) 33 British Journal of Criminology 187, at page 199 ff

Morgan, R Review of Drakeford, M, Haines, K, Cotton, B and Octigan, M *Pre-trial Services and the Future of Probation* (2002) BJ of Criminology 224

Packer, H *The Limits of the Criminal Sanction* (1968), at page 153 ff

Oxford Centre for Criminological Research

Ashworth, A, Genders, E, Mansfield, G, Peay, J and Player, E *Sentencing in the Crown Court: Report of an Exploratory Study* (1984) Oxford Centre for Criminological Research Occasional Paper No 10, at page 60 ff

Hood, R and Shute, S *Parole in Transition: Evaluating the Impact and Effects of Changes in the Parole System: Phase Two* (1994) Oxford Centre for Criminological Research No 16, at page 46

Routledge and Kegan Paul

Bottoms, A E and McClean, J D *Defendants in the Criminal Process* (1976), at
page 228
McConville, M, Sanders, A and Leng, R *The Case for the Prosecution* (1991), at
page 124 ff, 147

Sweet and Maxwell

Ashworth, A *'Should the Police be Allowed to use Deception?'* (1998) 114 LQR
108, at page 138 ff
*Attorney-General's References (Nos 159, 60 and 63 of 1998) (R v Goodwin and
others)* [1999] 2 Cr App R (S) 128
Attorney-General's Guidelines: Juries: The Exercise by the Crown of its Right
of Stand By (1989) 88 Cr App R 124
Block, B, Corbett, C and Peay, J 'Ordered and Directed Acquittals in the Crown
Court: A Time of Change?' [1993] Crim LR 95, at page 100 ff, 105 ff
Cape, E 'The Revised PACE Codes of Practice: A Further Step Towards
Inquisitorialism' [2003] Crim LR 355, at page 355 ff
Darbyshire, P 'The Lamp that Shows that Freedom Lives – is it Worth the
Candle?' [1991] Crim LR 740, at page 741 ff
Devlin, P 'The Conscience of the Jury' (1991) 107 Law Quarterly Review 398,
at page 402 ff
Hoyano, A, Hoyano, L, David, G and Goldie, S 'A Study of the Impact of
the Revised Code for Crown Prosecutors' [1997] Crim LR 556, at page
557 ff, 564 ff
Monnell and Morris v UK (1988) 10 EHRR 205, at page 217 ff, 223 ff
R v Chalkley and Jeffries [1998] QB 848, at page 98 ff, 107 ff
R v Dosseter [1999] 2 Cr App R (S) 248, at page 252 ff
R v Looseley (Attorney-General's Reference No 3 of 2000) [2002] Crim LR 301,
at page 302 ff
R v McIlkenny and Others (1992) 93 Cr App R 287, at page 310 ff
R v Newton (1982) 77 Cr App Rep 13, at page 15 ff
R v Paris, Abdullahi and Miller (1993) 97 Cr App R 99, at page 109 ff
R v Webbe and Others [2002] 1 Cr App R (S) 82, at page 85 ff
Richardson, G 'Strict Liability for Regulatory Crime: the Empirical Research'
[1987] Crim LR 295, at page 303 ff
Roording, J 'The Punishment of Tax Fraud' [1996] Crim LR 240, at page
240 ff, 248 ff
Seago, P, Walker, C and Wall, D 'The Development of the Professional
Magistracy in England and Wales' [2000] Crim LR 631, at page 648
Stafford v UK (2002) 35 EHRR 32

Thynne, Wilson and Gunnell v United Kingdom (1991) 13 EHRR 666, at page
    693 ff, 695 ff
Uglow, S, Dart, A, Bottomley, A and Hale, C 'Cautioning Juveniles – Multi-
    Agency Impotence' [1992] Crim LR 632, at page 640

Weidenfeld & Nicolson

Richardson, G *Law, Process and Custody: Prisoners and Patients* (1993)

Willan Publishing Ltd

Holloway, K and Grounds, A 'Discretion and the Release of Mentally
    Disordered Offenders' in Gelsthorpe, L and Padfield, N (eds) *Exercising
    Discretion: Decision-making in the criminal justice system and beyond* (2003)
    Willan, at page 158 ff

Table of Statutes

References in this Table to Statutes are to Halsbury's Statutes of England (Fourth Edition) showing the volume and page number at which the annotated text of an Act will be found.

Table of European Legislation

References in the right-hand column are to page. Page references printed in **bold** type indicate where the legislation is set out in part or in full.

Table of Cases

Reference to set out cases are to paragraph number and in **bold** type.

CHAPTER ONE

Introduction

About this book

Imagine walking home one evening, when you come across a young woman lying on the pavement, moaning. On closer inspection, you see that she looks a little drunk, and she is bleeding through her jacket. What do you do? You telephone the emergency services, dial 999. Do you ask for the police or an ambulance? Whatever you do, the matter will soon be safely out of your hands, and the National Health Service and/or the criminal justice system will take over. This book follows the processes that a case such as this will pass through in the criminal justice system.

In our fictional case, you contacted the police. Of course, in many circumstances, the police never hear about a crime. Probably less than half of all crimes are reported to the police. The factors which influence victims in their decision whether or not to report a crime are analysed by Clarkson et al (1994). They include victims' habituation to violence, their reluctance to have their own behaviour scrutinised, their fear of reprisals, their own criminality and hostility toward the police, and the social costs associated with reporting crime. Nor do the police record all incidents reported to them: they may not believe the complainant or they may not consider that the reported behaviour constitutes a criminal act. The British Crime Survey (BCS), which measures crimes against people living in private households by carrying out face-to-face interviews, has been conducted ten times since 1982, and it became an annual event in 2001. It estimates that only about a quarter of crime is recorded and that little more than half of reported crimes are actually recorded by the police (a figure which has changed little in the last few years). For BCS, crimes which can be compared with police statistics, incomplete reporting and recording mean that there are four times as many crimes according to BCS than are recorded by the police. This approximate percentage varies widely from crime to crime: theft and burglary are more likely to be reported than is vandalism, for example. It is worth noting that, as we move through the process – and as we move through the chapters of this book – we are dealing with an ever-decreasing proportion of cases. Of those cases which are reported to the police, not all result in a prosecution; and not all prosecutions end in convictions – perhaps two in every hundred offences committed result in a conviction.

Once an alleged offence is reported, or comes to the attention of the police in some other way, then, as we shall see in Chapter Two, the police have wide discretionary powers. They may record it or they may decide it was just an accident; they may investigate the crime further, using wide common law and statutory powers under the Police and Criminal Evidence Act 1984 (PACE); they may eventually charge an arrested person with an offence. Many criminals are never charged: they will either be summonsed to appear before a magistrates' court or be cautioned (or, in the case of young offenders, subject to a more formal reprimand and warning scheme).

Let us go back to our story. Our victim recovers from the attack and tells the police that her name is Rosa Bottles. She says she went to the pub with the usual group of friends, they all drank heavily, and on the way home she was involved in a fight with a man with whom she had earlier had an argument, Gerry Good. She is prepared to see the police proceed against him. The next day Gerry is arrested. What goes on in the police station between the time he is arrested and the time he is charged is perhaps the most crucial of all to a successful prosecution. It is also in the police station that the seeds of most miscarriages of justice are likely to be sown. In Chapter Two we examine police powers and the safeguards for the suspect held in a police station. The police then choose, after discussion with the Crown Prosecution Service (CPS), whether Gerry should be charged with a minor assault or a more serious wounding offence. The police do not conduct the prosecution in court – the prosecution is taken over by the CPS – and we will discuss the complex relationship between the police and the CPS in Chapter Three.

But not all prosecutions are initiated by the police. Non-police and non-CPS agencies, such as the Inland Revenue and the Health and Safety Executive, deal with many criminal offences, often in very different ways. Chapter Four thus offers a rather different perspective on the criminal justice process.

Another influence which is often neglected is that of the lawyer. The suspect's solicitor and barrister, in particular, may play a significant role in the process, since their advice about such matters as the plea, whether to give evidence and whether to appeal may have a significant impact on the way in which the case is finally dealt with. Chapter Five, on the role of defence lawyers, will attempt to assess the appropriateness of the legal advice given to suspects at all stages in the criminal process.

When the alleged offender reaches the magistrates' court, more decisions are taken. The court may have to decide whether the accused should be remanded in custody or released on bail, or whether the accused should be tried on indictment by a judge and jury in the Crown Court or summarily before the magistrates. If the case remains before the magistrates, they may have to decide on sentence as well as on guilt. Since most prosecutions begin and end in the magistrates' court, they clearly merit a chapter (Chapter Six).

Our fictional case is a serious one and the police may well charge the accused with an indictable crime, one which can only be tried in the Crown Court. The roles of judge and jury at the trial stage are clearly different, and each merits separate examination (Chapters Seven and Eight).

If convicted, Gerry will be sentenced. The role of the judge or magistrate in sentencing (why does the jury have no role here?) will be examined in their respective chapters (above). But the story, of course, does not end there – perhaps Gerry will appeal or seek some other review of his sentence and/or conviction, so the powers of appellate bodies must be considered (Chapter Nine). In any event, the process continues beyond Gerry's conviction – he has a sentence to serve – and in Chapter Ten we look at how various bodies exercise their wide discretionary powers in relation to sentenced offenders.

The emphasis of the book is on the decisions made by the key actors in the process, stressing the wide discretionary powers exercised. As Davis (1969) pointed out, the greatest and most frequent injustices occur where discretion is unfettered, where rules and principles provide little or no guidance. Since consistency and certainty are important objectives of the criminal justice system, it might seem that the system should be governed by clearer, pre-determined rules. Why have such wide discretionary powers been delegated to different individuals and bodies? The answer is simple: rules can be inflexible, and decisions based on purely legal criteria would be unduly rigid and harsh. But even if it is generally accepted that a certain degree of flexibility is necessary, has the English criminal justice system gone too far? We have moved into an age of 'multi-agency co-operation'. Can shared decision making work in practice? The danger is that as decision making passes away from the courts, control is lost. Decisions are difficult to challenge and lines of accountability are often blurred. Much of this book is descriptive, painting a picture of decision making in the criminal process today (see also Gelsthorpe and Padfield (eds) (2003)). It does not seek to concentrate on the principles behind the process, but the student should nonetheless consider a number of preliminary issues.

Is there a criminal justice *system*?

Since different parts of the criminal justice system often appear to pull in different directions, working within different (and competing) budgets, it probably should not be called a system at all. For example, we will see that whilst a judge uses 'proportionality' in fixing the length of a sentence, the Parole Board does not do so in deciding on release from prison. But a system is simply, according to the Oxford Reference Dictionary, a 'set of connected things or parts that form a whole or work together'. Remember, too, that we are looking at a 'snapshot' of the system taken at one particular moment in time and that the different elements in the process are constantly evolving. This can help you digest some of the inconsistencies. Norrie (1993) puts English criminal law in its nineteenth-century context, and a similar historical approach to criminal procedure and evidence is also useful. No central planning at one point in history went into drawing up the skeleton of the system. Indeed, if you were inventing a criminal justice system from scratch today, how closely would it resemble our present system?

Feeney [1:1] explains clearly the way in which 'systems concepts' came to be applied to criminal justice. Perhaps because the different parts may clash and sometimes work against each other, we should call it a process and not a system, but even this might imply a neat 'conveyor belt' operation. Is this system really little more than a series of decisions? Each agency is interdependent, as Feeney makes clear, but each is not necessarily working consistently with the others. It is one of the purposes of this book to look at the different stages of the criminal justice process in order to see the impact on the process as a whole of different decisions taken at different stages.

Characteristics of the English criminal justice process

The criminal justice system is not just a stream of unrelated decisions – there are some central themes. Two key characteristics have traditionally been singled out as running throughout the English criminal justice system. Particularly important at the trial stage in the process, they necessarily affect decision making at all stages.

(i) The system is accusatorial, or adversarial, rather than inquisitorial. Much has been made of the differences between different legal systems, but the differences can be deceptive. The Royal Commission on Criminal Justice (1993) recommended no fundamental change, and its discussion of the issues is included as a summary of the debate [1:2].

The Royal Commission regarded the principle of the presumption of innocence as fundamental. What does this mean in practice? It certainly doesn't mean that the police actually presume that all suspects are innocent! A visit to a police station – or even to a magistrates' court where the court officials may seem to bark out 'Stand up', 'Sit down' – can give the clear impression of a presumption of guilt. Even the substantive criminal law does not always respect the presumption of innocence: strict liability offences are committed without proof of a guilty mind; and defendants are often required to prove elements of specific defences (see Ashworth and Blake (1996)). The presumption of innocence is simply a procedural safeguard.

Attention should be paid to the resources available to the defence in an adversarial system: the 'equality of arms' argument. After all, a heavyweight boxer is not permitted to box professionally against a puny opponent. Are the dice loaded too heavily in one direction? In an adversarial system, convictions are achieved either by proof (beyond reasonable doubt) or by an admission of guilt. There is strong pressure on defendants to plead guilty, and on the police to secure guilty pleas. If somebody admits their guilt, there may be little 'process' at all. Where does this leave the presumption of innocence?

(ii) There is a strong lay element. Two chapters in this book are devoted to non-lawyers: juries and magistrates. Many foreign lawyers are astonished that the powers of a judge are entrusted to lay magistrates and that lay juries are entrusted to reach verdicts without giving reasons or explanations. Increasing inter-agency co-operation at all levels means a wider range of non-lawyer involvement. The Royal Commission on Criminal Justice (1993), in recommending the creation of a Criminal Cases Review Authority (now the Criminal Cases Review Commission (CCRC) – see Chapter Nine), suggested that 'both lawyers and lay persons should be represented. We recommend that the Chairman should be chosen for his or her personal qualities rather than for any particular qualifications or background that he or she may have' (page 184). The first chairman was indeed a non-lawyer (an engineer), yet the same report concluded that more use should be made of stipendiary (legally qualified) magistrates, thus recognising the strengths of lay involvement at one point and ignoring them at another. Unfortunately the report made no attempt to value the lay element in our criminal justice system. What is its value, and is it worth striving to keep it?

A third characteristic has appeared in the last two decades.

(iii) 'Managerialism'. The language of management and of auditing appear as priorities throughout the criminal justice system. Much of the government's agenda for reform has been led by what are often called the 'three Es' – economy, efficiency and effectiveness (see Jones **[1:3]**). There have been a number of 'official' reports on criminal justice in the last decade or so. Look at who wrote them, and at their terms of reference. First there was the Royal Commission on Criminal Justice, set up in 1991 after the Court of Appeal quashed the convictions of the 'Birmingham Six', six Irishman convicted of murder following a pub bombing in Birmingham in 1974. Its terms of reference are set out at **[1:2]** and it reported in 1993. Many critics have suggested that the Royal Commission wasted its opportunity to suggest a radical overhaul. Thus, Bridges (1994) described its report as 'a sham. It is a document that is slip-shod in its use of empirical evidence, slippery in its argumentation, and shameful in its underlying political purposes'. Is he unduly harsh? The Royal Commission was severely limited by its brief. However, the danger of a managerial perspective is that philosophy and vision may be ignored. The Royal Commission failed to make fundamental evaluations.

Another influential report – *Review of Delay in the Criminal Justice System* – was produced in 1997 by a Home Office team led by civil servant Martin Narey (now Commissioner for Correctional Services and Permanent Secretary in the Home Office), many of whose recommendations were enacted in the Crime and Disorder Act 1998. This emphasis on reducing delays became a key election pledge of the Labour Party in 1997: its manifesto, for example, committed it to halving the time from arrest to sentence for persistent young offenders. Was this emphasis misplaced? Some delays may, after all, be necessary and in the interests of justice.

A flurry of further reports appeared in 2001. There was the government's White Paper, *Criminal Justice: The Way Ahead* (Feb 2001), followed by another Home Office report, *Review of the Sentencing Framework* (the Halliday Report), published in July 2001, and finally the much longer and fuller *Review of the Criminal Courts of England and Wales* by Lord Justice Auld (October 2001) **[1:5]**. Lord Justice Auld's terms of reference were:

'A review into the practices and procedures of, and the rules of evidence applied by, the criminal courts at every level, with a view to ensuring that they deliver justice fairly, by streamlining all their processes, increasing their efficiency and strengthening the effectiveness of their relationships with others across the whole of the criminal justice system, and having regard to the interests of all parties including victims and witnesses, thereby promoting public confidence in the rule of law'.

Add to this the Audit Commission's *Route to Justice: Improving the pathway of offenders through the criminal justice system* (2002), and the White Paper *Justice for All* Cm 5563, published in July 2002. We will have reason to mention each of these in the course of this book: it is worth exploring them, and considering not only their terms of reference but also their authorship.

Running through all these reports is the shift towards managerialism, which can be seen in many of the recent changes mentioned in this book – legal aid, youth justice, magistrates' courts, prisons and the probation service all reflect a new priority. Jones [1:3] suggests that the shift towards managerial justice has led not to more public accountability but to increased central control of criminal justice practice. For Bottoms (1994), there are four themes which lie behind many of the recent changes in criminal justice: just deserts, managerialism (he singles out its systematic, consumerist and actuarial dimensions), community, and popular punitiveness. He explains the rise of these in the context of various aspects of theories of modernity: 'the relative erosion of class and its partial replacement by interest-group and lifestyle differentiators; the decline in intermediate-level social groups and a general disembedding of social relations; and the subjective concomitants of living in a technological world'.

These themes remain relevant to the criminal justice system being 'managed' by the 'new Labour' government since 1997. 'Tough on crime, tough on the causes of crime' was a successful election message. The Crime and Disorder Act 1998, the Youth Justice and Criminal Evidence Act 1999, the Criminal Justice and Court Services Act 2000 [10:5] and the Police Reform Act 2002 are all examples of attempts to 'tighten up' the criminal justice system. One advantage of managerialist practices might be better case management: a better ordering of the 'system'. But the greater the order within the system, the greater the need for checks and balances and for accountability. Those whose priority is justice and fairness must remain vigilant to ensure that the aims of the criminal justice system are not forgotten [1:4].

Evaluating the criminal justice process

Before evaluating the criminal justice system, one should identify what the system is seeking to achieve. At one level the answer is easy: it seeks to reduce the incidence of crime in society. But it is not obvious that the criminal justice system itself is (or is even capable of) actually doing that. Perhaps it seeks merely to convict the guilty and to acquit the innocent. We should then question why, and with what justification, we punish those deemed guilty. Ashworth (2000), Walker and Padfield (1996) and von Hirsch and Ashworth (1998) provide some answers to these questions on crime and punishment. This book seeks merely to assess the process used to convict the guilty and to acquit the innocent.

A useful starting point is Packer's (1968) classic exposition of two models of the criminal process: the Due Process Model and the Crime Control Model [1:6]. No one would suggest today that these models are entirely satisfactory, but they do allow us to recognise the value choices that underlie the details of the criminal process. The assumptions that underlie competing policy claims have to be recognised. McConville and Baldwin (1981) suggested that the English system conforms to the Crime Control Model, pointing out, for example, the lack of due process safeguards in a system where 90% of all defendants plead guilty and trial by jury is so rarely used. Their concerns are as valid today as they were then.

Packer's models are not enough. There are not just two clear-cut alternative value systems competing for priority in the criminal process. Thus, for example, the Royal Commission on Criminal Procedure in its 1981 report (at page 11) – having discussed the 'two main opposing groups, ... those who gave paramountcy to the principles of the presumption of innocence and the burden of proof, and those who saw the purpose of the criminal justice system as being a means to the end of bringing the guilty to justice' – went on to seek the 'fundamental balance'. Bottoms and Maclean **[1:7]** identified a third model – the Liberal Bureaucratic Model – and King **[1:8]** preferred six models, three based on the perspective of the typical participants and three based on the work of social theorists. Students may well find it useful to keep these different perspectives in mind as they attempt to evaluate the different processes at work.

Other writers have sought to move away from the 'model' perspective, to identify other fundamental values and principles. Cavadino and Dignan (2003) argue that the key to what they see as a penal crisis is one of legitimacy. The penal process needs to be reconstructed around the principle of respect for human rights. Ashworth (1998) concentrates on the need to identify fundamental values and principles. He singles out, for example, the right of an innocent person not to be convicted and the right to consistent treatment within declared policies. Ashworth's insistence on a principled approach is particularly important at a time when, as was discussed above, governments are putting increasing emphasis on managerialism and auditing, perhaps at the expense of justice (see also Henham (1998)).

International and European standards play an increasing role in helping to identify basic principles. Thus, the European Court of Human Rights, applying the European Convention for the Protection of Human Rights and Fundamental Freedoms, is frequently asked to rule on criminal justice matters. There are frequent references in this book to judgments of the European Court of Human Rights, illustrating the way in which the court applies the Convention in practice (for example: **[2:5]**, **[7:11]**, **[9:10]** and **[10:14]**). Since the Human Rights Act 1998 **[1:9]** incorporated the Convention into domestic law, the Convention has been used in domestic courts to challenge, for example, police surveillance techniques **[7:11]** and Parole Board decision making **[10:16]**. Also, developed under the aegis of the Council of Europe, the European Prison Rules are a detailed code of standards, although they are not yet mandatory. We will refer in Chapter Ten to the extensive powers of inspection of the European Committee for the Prevention of Torture and Inhuman or Degrading Treatment or Punishment.

The 'other' Europe, the European Union, has only involved itself in criminal justice matters more recently. Most importantly, the Amsterdam Treaty of 1997 gave the Council of Ministers of the European Union the power to draw up a variety of legal instruments to help create an 'area of freedom, security and justice'. The most important legal instruments are Framework Decisions, such as the Framework Decision on the European Arrest Warrant. Driven by concerns for security, many of the Brussels-led initiatives seem authoritarian and prosecution-minded. A lengthy consultation paper in 2003 on 'Procedural safeguards for suspects and defendants in criminal proceedings throughout the European Union' raises important issues about the difficulty of harmonising certain aspects of criminal justice in a union made of up of many different Member States, all with different criminal laws and rules of evidence and procedure which vary enormously. Can we have enhanced police and judicial co-operation without more root-and-branch harmonisation?

At an international level, the Universal Declaration of Human Rights was adopted in December 1948 by the General Assembly of the United Nations. As significant, and perhaps with potentially more impact, is the International Covenant on Civil and Political Rights (ICCPR), which came into force in 1976. The body set up by the ICCPR to monitor compliance is the Human Rights Committee. The United Kingdom has not ratified the Optional Protocol to the ICCPR, which provides for written applications to the Human Rights Committee by individuals who have been victims of violations of the Covenant's provisions. However, the United Kingdom is coming under increasing pressure to recognise a right of individual petition, which it will eventually have to do if it wishes to play a significant role in enhancing the protection of human rights around the world.

One measure of whether the system is working well is whether there is evidence of bias. Section 95 of the Criminal Justice Act 1991 **[1:10]** puts the official seal of approval on the detection of discrimination. The statistics are very worrying: for example, black people are eight times more likely to be stopped and searched by the police than whites; and, whereas 2% of the general population of England and Wales in 2000 was estimated to be black, 12% of the male prison population, and 19% of the female prison population, was black (Home Office (2002)). At several points in this book we will review the evidence as to whether 'the system' in its many parts is biased against, for example, women or people from ethnic minorities. The difficulties in identifying bias are revealed in Home Office research findings **[1:11]** and **[1:12]**, which show that general statistics may not help us answer the question of bias (see also Fitzgerald and Sibbitt (1997), who suggest that ethnic monitoring data should be treated as 'indicators' of areas needing further scrutiny). Partly as a result of the Macpherson Inquiry Report (1999) into the police investigation of the killing of the black teenager, Stephen Lawrence, the Race Relations (Amendment) Act 2000 at last applied anti-discrimination law to public services, including the police. But the over-representation of black people in the criminal justice system cannot simply be explained away by racism. The evidence is far from clear, since the causes of crime are many and complex. Poverty, unemployment, poor education, environmental deprivation may all lead to a higher rate of crime **[1:13]**. Since many women and black people are poorer than average, it is difficult to identify whether any bias is the result of the criminal justice system or merely a reflection of society generally.

The law seeks to impose a universal framework on diverse groups of people: *can* there be justice in an economically unjust society? As Phillips and Bowling (2002) suggest, we need more sophisticated qualitative research, as well as quantitative measures, in order to understand changing patterns in criminal justice. Other forms of bias, defined by wealth and class (see **[4:6]**), and which may reflect either prejudice or merely statistical imbalance, are even more difficult to detect. Hood, Shute and Seemungal **[1:14]** note an important 'cultural shift' in the treatment of ethnic minorities in the last decade but also raise important questions about perceptions of fairness.

A final word of warning: in this book we are following a relatively straightforward case study in order to understand how the system works in practice. Even if the system works quite appropriately in the case of Gerry Good, you should remain alert. Notice when the system fails – a fundamental aim of the criminal justice system must be to reduce injustice.

Further reading

Ashworth, A *Sentencing and Criminal Justice* (3rd edition, 2000) Butterworths
Ashworth, A *The Criminal Process: an Evaluative Study* (2nd edition, 1998) Oxford
Ashworth, A and Blake, M 'The presumption of innocence in English law' [1996] Crim LR 306
Bottoms, A E 'The philosophy and politics of punishment' in Clarkson C and Morgan R, *The Politics of Sentencing* (1994) Oxford UP
Bridges, L 'Normalising Injustice: the Royal Commission on Criminal Justice' (1994) 21 Journal of Law and Society 20
Cavadino, M and Dignan, J *The Penal System: an Introduction* (3rd edition, 2002) Sage

Clarkson, C, Cretney, A, Davis, G and Shepherd, J 'Assaults: the relationship between seriousness, criminalisation and punishment' [1994] Crim LR 4

Davis, K C *Discretionary Justice: A Preliminary Inquiry* (1969) Louisiana State UP

Fitzgerald, M and Sibbitt, R 'Ethnic Monitoring in Police Forces: a beginning' (1997) HORS No 173 HMSO

Gelsthorpe, L and Padfield, N (eds) *Discretion: Its uses in criminal justice and beyond* (2003) Willan

Hawkins, K (ed) *The Uses of Discretion* (1992) Oxford: Clarendon

Henham, R 'Human rights, due process and sentencing' (1998) BJ of Criminology

von Hirsch, A and Ashworth, A *Principled Sentencing* (2nd edition, 1998) Edinburgh University Press

Home Office *Race and the Criminal Justice System* (2002)

Leigh, L and Zedner, L *A Report on the administration of criminal justice in France and Germany* (1993) Royal Commission on Criminal Justice Research Study No 1, HMSO

Maguire, M 'Crime Statistics: the "data explosion" and its implications' in Maguire, Morgan, Reiner (eds) *The Oxford Handbook of Criminology* (3rd edition, 2002) Oxford

McConville, M and Baldwin, J *Courts, Prosecution and Conviction* (1981) Oxford

Norrie, A *Crime, Reason and History* (1992) Oxford

Phillips, C and Bowling, B 'Racism, ethnicity, crime and criminal justice' in Maguire, Morgan, Reiner (eds) *The Oxford Handbook of Criminology* (3rd edition, 2002) Oxford

Stenson, K and Sullivan, R (eds) *Crime, Risk and Justice: the politics of crime control in liberal democracies* (2001) Willan

Walker, N *Why Punish?* (1991) Oxford Paperbacks

Walker, N and Padfield, N *Sentencing Theory, Law and Practice* (2nd edition, 1996) Butterworths

Whittaker, C and Mackie, A 'Managing courts effectively: the reasons for adjournments in magistrates' courts' (1997) HORS No 168 HMSO

A note on free resources

The Internet is a wonderful resource – though one which seems to result in the waste of more paper rather than less, as we all download more and more things which we might previously have read in a library. For government websites a good starting point is www.homeoffice.gov.uk, although it is worth looking at Parliament's website too: www.parliament.uk.

A number of paper publications are also available free of charge from the Home Office. Recommended publications include: a 42-page booklet entitled 'The Criminal Justice System in England and Wales' (1997); 'Digest 4: Information on the Criminal Justice System in England and Wales' (1999), a colourful and glossy, if somewhat out of date, presentation of criminal justice statistics; and, generally, Research Findings and Statistical Bulletins.

Contact: RDS Communications Development Unit, Room 264, 50 Queen Anne's Gate, London, SW1H 9AT. Tel: 020 7273 2084.

Other Home Office publications – for example, on race, gender and costs – may be available free of charge from: Home Office, 50 Queen Anne's Gate, London SW1H 9AT (or via their website).

Annual reports are available (usually for a hefty fee) from: The Stationery Office Ltd, PO Box 29, St Crispins, Duke Street, Norwich NR3 1GN (online ordering: www.tso.co.uk/bookshop). However, you can find them free of charge on the appropriate website. Useful examples include:
- Report of Her Majesty's Chief Inspector of Prisons for England and Wales
- Report of the Parole Board
- Report of the Prison Service
- Report of the Crown Prosecution Service
- Report of Her Majesty's Chief Inspector of Constabulary

Other documents may be available elsewhere. For example, legal aid leaflets should be available from any court or Citizens' Advice Bureau, and the Code for Crown Prosecutors is available free of charge from any Crown Prosecution Service branch office.

Documents

[1:1] *Feeney, Floyd (1985)* 'Interdependence as a working concept' in Moxon, D (ed) *Managing Criminal Justice* (1985) HMSO (at page 8):

There may well have been a time when criminal justice was viewed as a series of separate processes connected neither with each other nor anything else. These times have long since passed, however, and today there is widespread agreement that the work of the various criminal justice agencies is closely related and that together these agencies form some kind of 'system'. There is much less agreement, however, about the nature of this system and the implications of such related concepts as interdependence of the criminal justice system.

The general idea of a system dates back at least to the ancient Greeks, who saw systems as some kind of organised whole. By the eighteenth century the system concept had already assumed great importance in branches of theoretical physics such as mechanics where it appeared in full mathematical garb. In the nineteenth century the term began to be applied to biology, and has since been extended to a wide variety of fields including engineering, physiology, international affairs, political affairs and even language. In the late 1950s and early 1960s the concept was further refined and systems analysis appeared as an 'in' method for analysing complex problems. It became common at this time to think of systems in almost every field of human and scientific endeavour. While some earlier criminal justice studies had taken something of a systems-type approach, it was not until this era that the term 'criminal justice system' first began to be used.

The application of systems concepts to criminal justice which followed these developments bore almost immediate fruit, leading to a much better understanding of the linkages among the various parts of the system and the way that the work of each agency affected the work of the other agencies involved. This knowledge proved to be very useful in thinking about criminal justice problems and 'criminal justice system' rapidly became a standard part of the criminal justice vocabulary.

The explicit application of systems concepts to criminal justice produced a number of other results as well. It exposed a great deal of divergence in the way that agencies approach particular problems and showed that the policies followed by one agency often undermined or were at cross-purposes with those followed by other agencies. It also demonstrated just how complex and interdependent the various parts of the system actually are.

Public drunkenness was an early example used to illustrate the kind of divergences that systems analysis could expose. Enforcement efforts for this crime at this time typically involved a large number of police arrests followed in America by short jail sentences and in England by fines. In both countries the offenders were rapidly back on the street, and the whole process started over again. Calculating the enormous waste of police and court effort in this revolving-door situation, systems analysts sought to devise treatment approaches that would make more productive use of the resources expended. They argued explicitly that there were benefits to be gained in overall system accomplishment by transferring resources from the police and the courts to the treatment end of the system. Experiments with detoxification programmes for street alcoholics were one result of their efforts.

Some of those who first sought to apply systems concepts to criminal justice were less impressed with the linkages among criminal justice agencies, however, than with their fragmentation. They argued that criminal justice was in reality not a system but a 'non-system'. Judged strictly by the formal definitions developed by theorists these analysts made a persuasive case.

A very broad definition, used by some general systems theorists, for example, views a system as a set of entities whose relations are specified so that deductions may be made from some relations to others or from the relations among the entities to the behaviour or history of the system. A more detailed formulation requires that the system under investigation be explicitly distinguished from its environment, the internal elements of the system be explicitly stated, the relationships between the elements of the system and between the system and its environment be explicitly stated, the use of canons of logical or mathematical reasoning in deductions relating to these relationships, and the confirmation of assertions about these relationships through scientific methods.

Even the strongest proponents of the systems approach would be hard-pressed to claim that their efforts meet the precision required by these standards. Despite this, however, most of those involved in criminal justice have come to think of it as a system. There is also considerable agreement that the system includes: the police and the prosecution; the defence; the courts; and corrections, including probation and the prisons. The medical, mental health, welfare, education and private security systems are all seen as closely related systems but not as part of the criminal justice system. As the criminal justice system receives not only clients but also political guidance, financial support, information and personnel from the larger society, it obviously is part of the general political, economic and social systems of the larger society.

One of the central features of all systems is the interdependence of the various system parts. The concept of interdependence is therefore a natural part of the systems idea. In recent years, however, interdependence has taken on special meaning in the criminal justice system, particularly in Great Britain. As this special meaning has a considerable overlap with the more general systems approach, it cannot be defined in ways that sharply distinguish the two concepts. It is perhaps best understood, however, as meaning that what one criminal justice agency does is likely to affect and be affected by other agencies and that a detailed knowledge of the kinds of interactions that are likely to take place is essential for undertaking system improvements. The idea is thus explicitly concerned with the development of improved performance in functions that cross agency lines.

In the criminal justice system interdependence occurs at many different levels – national and local; agency head and working officer; strategic, tactical and mechanical. Strategic level choices include large questions of system design or structure, and in Great Britain are generally made at the national level. Included in such choices would be issues such as whether there should be an independent prosecution service, whether probation resources should be increased in order to provide more sentencing alternatives to prison, and whether the police should receive a much larger share of the system's resources than the courts. Questions such as how the defence function is to be organised and financed and whether greater efforts should be expended on prevention as opposed to apprehension and punishment also involve strategic issues likely to be decided at the national level.

Tactical level choices generally concern use of the resources available to particular criminal justice agencies. Whilst these choices can be made at many different levels within a given organisation, they are generally made locally rather than nationally. Decisions of this kind include such things as the deployment of police forces, the hours of service provided by the courts, and how the duty solicitor rota is to function.

Perhaps the most fundamental sense in which criminal justice agencies are linked together at the tactical level lies in the process of discretionary decision-making by which cases are adjudicated and transferred from one agency to another. Cases typically begin with the discovery of a crime and the apprehension of a suspected offender by the police. After deciding whether to prosecute, the police pass the case on to the courts for adjudication. The courts in turn often secure the services of the probation service to assist in the sentencing decision, and in this decision may pass the case on either to probation or the prison service. This process is rather like an assembly line in which each agency's workload is essentially controlled by the actions of the previous agency. In most instances the decision of the transmitting agency is largely discretionary, but the receiving agency generally has little or no say in the decisions made. Probably the most important of these discretionary decisions are the decisions to arrest, to prosecute and to sentence. Obviously policies such as cautioning and non-charging by the prosecution are of major importance in this system of discretionary decision-making.

[1:2] Report of the Royal Commission on Criminal Justice (Cm 2263) (1993) HMSO (at page iii):

Terms of reference

To examine the effectiveness of the criminal justice system in England and Wales in securing the conviction of those guilty of criminal offences and the acquittal of those who are innocent, having regard to the efficient use of resources, and in particular to consider whether changes are needed in:
(i)   the conduct of police investigations and their supervision by senior police officers, and in particular the degree of control that is exercised by those officers over the conduct of the investigation and the gathering and preparation of evidence;
(ii) the role of the prosecutor in supervising the gathering of evidence and deciding whether to proceed with a case, and the arrangements for the disclosure of material, including unused material, to the defence;
(iii) the role of experts in criminal proceedings, their responsibilities to the court, prosecution, and defence, and the relationship between the forensic science services and the police;
(iv) the arrangement for the defence of accused persons, access to legal advice, and access to expert evidence;
(v)   the opportunities available for an accused person to state his position on the matters charged and the extent to which the courts might draw proper inferences from primary facts, the conduct of the accused and any failure on his part to take advantage of an opportunity to state his position;
(vi) the powers of the court in directing proceedings, the possibility of their having an investigative role both before and during the trial, and the role of pre-trial reviews, the courts' duty in considering evidence, including uncorroborated confession evidence;
(vii) the role of the Court of Appeal in considering new evidence on appeal, including directing the investigation of allegations;
(viii) the arrangements for considering and investigating allegations of miscarriages of justice when appeal rights have been exhausted.

(and at page 3):

Adversarial or inquisitorial?

11   The criminal justice system of England and Wales, in common with other jurisdictions which have evolved with the 'Anglo-Saxon' or 'common law' tradition, is often categorised as 'adversarial'. This is in contrast to the so-called 'inquisitorial' system based on the 'Continental' or 'civil law' tradition. In this context, the term 'adversarial' is usually taken to mean the system which has the judge as an umpire who leaves the presentation of the case to the parties (prosecution and defence) on each side. These separately prepare their case and call, examine and cross-examine their witnesses. The term 'inquisitorial' describes the systems where judges may supervise the pre-trial preparation of the evidence by the police[1] and, more important, play a major part in the

---

[1]   Although in practice this is rare. For example, in France the *juge d'instruction* plays a part in only some 10% of cases. See the Report of the French Commission Justice Penale et Droits de l'Homme, La Mise en Etat des Affairs Penales, Paris 1991.

presentation of the evidence at trial. The judge in 'inquisitorial' systems typically calls and examines the defendant and the witnesses while the lawyers for the prosecution and the defence ask supplementary questions.

12   It is important not to overstate the differences between the two systems; all adversarial systems contain inquisitorial elements, and vice versa. But it is implicit in our terms of reference that we should consider whether a change in the direction of more inquisitorial procedures might not reduce the risks of mistaken verdicts and the need for subsequent re-examination of convictions which may be unsafe. For the reasons set out below we do not recommend the adoption of a thoroughgoing inquisitorial system. But we do recognise the force of the criticisms which can be directed at a thoroughgoing adversarial system which seems to turn a search for the truth into a contest played between opposing lawyers according to a set of rules which the jury does not necessarily accept or even understand. In some instances, such as our approach to forensic science evidence, our recommendations can fairly be interpreted as seeking to move the system in an inquisitorial direction, or at least as seeking to minimise the danger of adversarial practices being taken too far. But we have not arrived at our proposals through a theoretical assessment of the relative merits of the two legal traditions. On the contrary, we have been guided throughout by practical considerations in proposing changes which will, in our view, make our existing system more capable of serving the interests of both justice and efficiency.

13   We have sought information from a wide range of other countries' criminal jurisdictions (both adversarial and inquisitorial) in order to see whether there are lessons to be learned from them that might be applied with advantage to the criminal justice system in England and Wales. In particular, we have during two visits to Scotland looked in some depth at the Scottish system. We have not, however, found, either in Scotland or anywhere else, a set of practices which has so clearly succeeded in resolving the problems which arise in any system of criminal justice that it furnishes the obvious model which all the others should therefore adopt. Every system is the product of a distinctive history and culture, and the more different the history and culture from our own the greater must be the danger that an attempted transplant will fail. Hardly any of those who gave evidence to the Commission suggested that the system in another jurisdiction should be adopted in England and Wales; and of those who did, not argued for it in any depth or with any supporting detail. We have, accordingly, no evidence to suggest that there is somewhere a jurisdiction in which the rights and interests of the various parties involved are so uniquely well balanced as to give the system the best of all worlds. In the relevant chapters of this report, we make occasional reference to the features of other jurisdictions by which we have been influenced in arriving at our conclusions. But we make no attempt to give them either an 'adversarial' or an 'inquisitorial' label.

14   Our reason for not recommending a change to an inquisitorial system as such is not simply fear of the consequences of an unsuccessful cultural transplant. It is also that we ourselves doubt whether the fusion of the functions of investigation and prosecution, and the direct involvement of judges in both, are more likely to serve the interests of justice than a system in which the roles of police, prosecutors, and judges are as far as possible kept separate and the judge who is responsible for the conduct of the trial is the arbiter of law but not of fact. We believe that a system in which the critical roles are kept separate offers a better protection for the innocent defendant, including protection against the risk of unnecessarily prolonged detention prior to trial. Moreover, there are 'inquisitorial' jurisdictions in which the system is moving, or being urged to move in an 'adversarial' direction. For example, Italy has sought to introduce a more adversarial approach, and in France there has been widespread criticism of the role of the *juge d'instruction*.

15   We in no way suggest, as is sometimes done, that 'Inquisitorial' systems presume suspects to be guilty until they are proved innocent. Nor do we suggest, as is also sometimes done, that 'Adversarial' systems are not concerned to unearth the facts on which the guilt or innocence of the suspect depends. Both recognise the principle of the 'burden of proof' – that is, the obligation on the prosecution to establish the defendant's guilt on the basis of evidence which the defence is entitled to contest. We regard this principle as fundamental. This, as will become apparent in later chapters, is not incompatible with changes to our system which would require the defence to disclose the outline of whatever case it intends to put forward at an earlier stage than at present, or remove from the defendant charged with an 'either way' offence the right to choose the mode of trial, or permit the judge to rule before the jury is empanelled on questions of admissibility of evidence or the production of statements of agreed facts. But defendants are always to be presumed to be innocent unless and until the prosecution has satisfied the magistrates or jury of their guilt beyond reasonable doubt.

[1:3]   Jones, Carol 'Auditing Criminal Justice' (1993) 33 BJ of Criminology 187 (at page 199):

I have argued that the auditing process has had a profound impact upon the practice of criminal justice in Britain. Clearly, the process has a good side in so far as it has made more explicit the value preferences underlying the criminal justice system. It has also subjected criminal justice agencies to an unprecedented degree of scrutiny – the hearings of the Public Accounts Committee, which summons top civil servants and officials to answer criticisms made by the National Audit Office, have provided parliamentary accountability of a particularly robust kind.

Officials are frequently placed in 'the hot seat'. Senior law officers have been brought for the first time before a Committee of Parliament to answer criticisms, and their evidence has been published. Arguably, the National Audit Office, the Audit Commission, and the Public Accounts Committee are fulfilling the promise of 'social accounting' to render key organisations more open to public scrutiny.

At first sight, therefore, the traditional structures of accountability appear to be reinforced by the new system. The contrary view argues that auditing undermines these traditional structures. Instead of officials being responsible to ministers for their decisions, ministers are forced to rely upon the professional values of accountants and auditors. Accountants are no longer simply providers of financial information: they are in the forefront of decision-making. Policy-making thus moves outside recognised political channels.

The National Audit Office recommendation of greater liaison between all agencies of the criminal justice system (courts, police, prosecution) also weakens traditional constitutional boundaries. The pursuit of economy and effectiveness thus encourages a more intricate meshing of criminal justice agencies, whose efficiency and effectiveness are increasingly defined in terms of their 'success rate': ie convictions. The auditing process itself also enables central government to penetrate criminal justice agencies more effectively and less obtrusively. Standardisation creeps through the system via a new route. National application of the 'three Es' undercuts local distinctiveness and professional autonomy. It may also cut across national boundaries. For example, procurators fiscal in Scotland were literally 'called to account' because their practices did not accord with a set of criteria formulated in another legal system. What is marketed as a 'hands off' policy may thus actually result in a 'receding locus of power' which masks a more intricate realignment of the forces of law and order and removes existing – if imperfect – channels of accountability.

Cumulatively, there has also been a shift away from a formal commitment to rational justice and 'rule of law' to 'managerial justice'. While managerialism may pay lip-service to all the 'three Es', the 1980s saw the 'ascendancy of economy' over efficiency and effectiveness, resulting in a 'managerial myopia' and a concern with short-term managerial innovation at the expense of a long-term focus. 'Value for money' translated not only into a greater emphasis upon crime control but also into 'more crime control with fewer resources'. This produced a new definition of what the criminal justice system was for; the rights of accused persons were inefficient and uneconomic 'trappings'; due process of law was too expensive, too inefficient, and too ineffective – it 'let too many guilty persons go free'. Thus the tenets of auditing, allied to those of managerialism and devolved control, came to underpin an increasingly 'crime control'-oriented legal system.

I have argued that the construction of the consumer as a participant in the management of his or her own life served as a useful ideological strategy for stabilising this increasing focus on 'law and order' in society. This was particularly crucial at a time when the 'post-war consensus' appeared to be breaking down, where the policy was 'not to integrate the poor and underprivileged but to manage their protest'.[2] I have also argued that despite the rhetoric of consumer power there has in fact been a greater centralisation of control over criminal justice practices. This undercuts the notion of consumers being able to make strategic choices among competitors in a free market.

The increase in managerial discretion is also quite at odds with the tenets of 'rule of law' ideology, though the rhetoric of freely contracting consumers is the epitome of that bourgeois individualism found in rule of law ideology. It provides a gloss of equality where none exists. It legitimises a system of settled – or emerging – inequalities. Managerialism undercuts the distinction between formal legal rationality and technocratic rationality. It also undercuts the 'traditional apparatuses of justice' and increasingly legitimises a 'relatively naked emphasis within the criminal justice system upon criminalisation and the suppression of resistance, and a relative de-emphasising of the formal norms and values of individual justice. Typically, sociologists have predicted that a move away from formal legal rationality will result in a move towards technocratic justice. Managerialism is a hybrid form which intercepts these boundaries. It is pragmatic and instrumentalist but it is also flexible and informal, substituting discretion and 'the right of management to manage' for explicit legal rules, formal procedural norms, the principle of precedent, and due process of law. In this respect, managerialism shares what Heydebrand has termed the 'tendencies of de-juridification and de-stratification' which characterise technocratic decision-making. The 'virtue' of managerialism is that it is divorced from any substantive normative or political value. Indeed, it transforms the absence of principled policy (for example, along lines of justice and fairness) from a vice into a virtue.

[2]   Norrie and Adelman (1989) Journal of Law and Society 16/1 112, at page 123.

[1:4]   James, A and Raine, J *The New Politics of Criminal Justice* Longmans (1998) (at page 44):

The story of the public service managerialist reforms as they affected criminal justice is one of inconsistent and piecemeal direction on the part of ministers and reluctant participation on the part of most agencies. First, in the absence of an agreed purpose for the reform of criminal justice itself (see Chapter 2), the intermediate goals of cost efficiency and service effectiveness became pre-eminent. In the absence of an agreed strategy for change, intervention by government was influenced by size of budget, ease of pickings and ministerial preference. The effort put into resisting the reforms by agencies, perhaps with only the Crown Prosecution Service as the exception, hampered any real potential for imaginative and innovative change driven by services themselves.

Second, it is arguable that the reforms could never have worked in criminal justice in any case where the three prerequisites for their success were absent. There was no market and hence no real consumer in criminal justice, and no real prospect of creating one given the special character of the key 'customer' (the offender) and difficulties for providers around market entry and exit. Without even a quasi-market in place, there was no real basis for competition between providers (Le Grand, 1990).

Together, it is argued, these two factors resulted in managerialism; that is, the introduction of a variety of methods and techniques into practice without a meaningful context. They were management tools introduced without a broad understanding, a theory or a praxis of management, and without consent to or support for the change process within agencies.

Managerialism can be, and was, heavily criticised. Its characteristically extreme rationalism in decision-making was arguably inappropriate within a complex and pluralistic setting; its simplistic conversion of service users into consumers made no sense when the service user was an offender; the use of false competition created inequality and artificiality in the contracting process which, in turn, created a paper-chase of new administrative demands.

At the same time, wrapped up in the reforms were a number of important ideas and developments which had, and have, the potential to progress criminal justice, and which can be all too easily overlooked. Among these was the impetus to needs-driven rather than provider-driven services, propelled by a formulae basis for budget calculation. Important, too, was the demand for transparency and the provision of public information in services and service performance as part of a revised approach to public accountability. There was also an emphasis on service quality which, though not necessarily realised, was to persist. Of on-going significance was the focus on service efficiency and practice effectiveness, known within criminal justice as the 'what works' debate. Above all, the identification of purchasers (or commissioners) and providers of service, though never converted into structural reform in most criminal justice settings, facilitated the realisation that public services did not necessarily need to be publicly provided. This made explicit the potential for a mixed economy of provision (public, private and voluntary).

The immediate effect of the imposition of managerial reforms on a reluctant audience was, first, to drive a deep division between government and agencies normally characterised by their conservatism. Second was the deleterious effect on staff morale, particularly among professional groups. The longer term effect is more difficult to estimate. Certainly at the end of the 1990s, variations on managerialism were embedded in criminal justice, as in the wider public service sector, in the UK and abroad, suggesting a continuing influence. At the same time, Labour's commitment to end the introduction of markets into public services, if implemented, must affect the shape of future reform. Rather than dismantling what limited markets currently exist, a more successful way forward might be to concentrate on growing the mixed economy for which the market was itself simply a tool in a transition process from a paternalistic and bureaucratic model of social welfare to a model more appropriate for the future (James, 1997). Getting beyond the market means getting beyond means to ends in criminal justice. It means actively pump-priming private and voluntary sector initiatives to generate a mixed economy; identifying the needs of offenders in addition to the needs of service providers; and, above all, agreeing an overall purpose and change strategy in criminal justice such that strategy drives behaviour and not the other way around.

(and at page 116):

In discussing the influences which have shaped criminal justice in recent years, Part I of this volume (Chapters 2–5) has argued the presence and interplay of four dynamics (politicisation, managerialism, administrative processing and public voice and participation). In thinking about criminal justice for the future, Part II has rehearsed the key features of a revised approach (Chapter 6) and a set of priorities: informing and educating public voice and participation; addressing the reality of crime as it affects the public; addressing the totality of crime, not just that small proportion which reaches the courts; and redesigning and rebalancing the organisation of criminal justice to address the requirements of an informed public rather than those of the official agencies and government departments. Finally, Chapter 7 has gone on to present a possible way forward in the interests of dialogue and discussion.

The extent to which a revised approach emerges for criminal justice depends on developments with regard to each of the four dynamics. Each has the potential to (a) contribute towards the realisation of a more effective criminal justice process and (b) address the crime problem.

The dynamic of *politicisation* is clearly important; fresh direction from political leaders is necessary to move on from the narrow preoccupation with sentencing and punishment of recent years towards a new vision for tackling crime and for relocating criminal justice firmly in its social policy context. It is also vital in the renegotiation of the 'contract' between the state and its people about a shared responsibility for crime.

The dynamic of *managerialism* – though problematic because of the tendency for management to become regarded as an end in itself rather than part of the means by which criminal justice is done better – is also important for the future. Significant weaknesses about the pre-managerial way of doing things have been highlighted and challenged. Much of the complacency and inertia of the past, particularly regarding the way the agencies have approached their responsibilities, has been driven out. The momentum for change that managerialism has created will remain an important attribute underpinning a revised approach to criminal justice. In particular, a revised approach depends on sustaining and developing those legacies of managerialism: needs-driven rather than provider-driven services, more transparency and stronger public accountability, and a focus on effectiveness and outcomes (on 'what works').

The *administrative processing* dynamic, though also in some ways associated with negative attributes of inertia and resistance to change, of organisational fragmentation, and of undue provider-orientation, is important to the revised approach. It provides the key to the translation of policy into practice. Its focus on the practitioners and on how criminal justice works in practice means that it is potentially a very important dynamic in relation to local communities being empowered to take responsibility for crime and encouraged to participate more actively in tackling the problem. The challenge is for practitioners to reorient their work and their organisational and administrative processes so that a stronger relationship with, and accountability to, local communities is achieved.

This brings us to the *public voice and participation* dynamic, which is perhaps the most important key to realisation of the revised approach. Above all, the revised approach builds upon the notion that tackling crime should begin with the reality of crime as it is experienced by the public and as it affects them. The challenge here is to find ways of capturing and engaging the full complexity of public voice and participation in appropriate ways within the criminal justice policy-making process and in its practice.

What, then, is the contemporary purpose of criminal justice? The conclusion from this volume is that first, it remains that identified in the ancient contract between the people and the state – namely, the provision of security in exchange for allegiance. Second, and relevant to the position of the UK in Europe, it is the protection of individual human rights (as presently represented in the European Convention on Human Rights, and endorsed by the Labour Government in 1997).

Recapturing that ancient purpose, and making explicit that new purpose, is the fundamental prerequisite to the rebuilding of trust in the criminal justice agencies and in government on law and order. It is also a prerequisite to public confidence in the view that crime is not, after all, out of control and that there are constructive approaches to be pursued, based on a partnership between the state and its people, which will make a difference.

[1:5]   Auld, LJ *Review of the Criminal Courts of England and Wales* The Stationery Office (2001) (at pages 23–30):

Chapter 2: summary and recommendations

Introduction (Chapter 1 – pages 7–22, rec 1)

2.   The criminal law should be codified under the general oversight of a new Criminal Justice Council and by or with the support as necessary of the Law Commission. There should be codes of offences, procedure, evidence and sentencing (paras 35–36, rec 1). See also: as to a code of criminal procedure, (Chapter 10 paras 271–280, recs 228–234); as to a code of criminal evidence, (Chapter 11, paras 76–77); and as to a sentencing code, (Chapter 11, para 198, and Chapter 12, paras 110–111).

The Criminal Justice System (Chapter 8 – pages 315–336, recs 121–139)

3.   A national Criminal Justice Board should replace all the existing national planning and 'operational' bodies, including the Strategic Planning Group, and the Trial Issues Group. The new Board should be the means by which the criminal justice departments and agencies provide over-all direction of the criminal justice system (paras 37–66, recs 121–122). It should have an independent chairman and include senior departmental representatives and chief executives of the main criminal justice agencies (including the Youth Justice Board) and a small number of non-executive members (paras 67–72, recs 123–125). At local level, Local Criminal Justice Boards should be responsible for giving effect to the national Board's directions and objectives and for management of the criminal justice system in their areas. Both the national and local Boards should be supported by a centrally managed secretariat and should consult regularly with the judiciary (paras 73–77, recs 126–129). The national Board should be responsible for introducing an integrated technology system for the whole of the criminal justice system based upon a common language and common case files, the implementation and maintenance of which should be the task of a Criminal Case Management Agency accountable to the Board. (paras 92–114, recs 137–139).

4.   A Criminal Justice Council, chaired by the Lord Chief Justice or senior Justice of Appeal, should be established to replace existing advisory and consultative bodies, including the Criminal Justice Consultative Council and the Area Strategy Committees. It should have a statutory power and duty to keep the criminal justice system under review, to advise the Government on all proposed reforms, to make proposals for reform and to exercise general oversight of codification of the criminal law. The Council should be supported by a properly resourced secretariat and research staff (paras 78–88, recs 130–135).

A unified Criminal Court (Chapter 7 – pages 269–314, recs 83–120)

5.   The Crown Court and magistrates' courts should be replaced by a unified Criminal Court consisting of three Divisions: the Crown Division, constituted as the Crown Court now is, to exercise jurisdiction over all indictable-only matters and more serious 'either-way' offences allocated to it; the District Division, constituted by a judge, normally a District Judge or Recorder, and at least two magistrates, to exercise jurisdiction over a mid range of 'either-way' matters of sufficient seriousness to merit up to two years' custody; and the Magistrates' Division, constituted by a District Judge or magistrates, as magistrates' courts now are, to exercise their present jurisdiction over all summary matters and the less serious 'either-way' cases allocated to them (paras 2–35, recs 83–87). The courts, that is those of the Magistrates' Division, would allocate all 'either-way' cases according to the seriousness of the alleged offence and the circumstances of the defendant, looking at the possible outcome of the case at its worst from the point of view of the defendant and bearing in mind the jurisdiction of each division. In the event of a dispute as to venue, a District Judge would determine the matter after hearing representations from the prosecution and the defendant. The defendant would have no right of election to be tried in any division (paras 36–40, recs 88–95). (In the event of the present court structure continuing, the defendant should lose his present elective right to trial by jury in 'either-way' cases; see paragraph 10 below.)

6.   Whether or not the Crown Court and magistrates' courts are replaced with a unified Criminal Court, there should be a single centrally funded executive agency as part of the Lord Chancellor's Department responsible for the administration of all courts, civil, criminal and family (save for the Appellate Committee of the House of Lords), replacing the present Court Service and the Magistrates' Courts' Committees. For the foreseeable future, circuit boundaries and administrations should remain broadly as they are and the courts should be locally managed within the circuits and the 42 criminal justice areas (paras 41–73, recs 96–103). Justices' clerks and legal advisers responsible to them should continue to be responsible for the legal advice provided to the magistrates (para 74, rec 104; see also Chapter 4 – Magistrates paras 50–58, recs 6–7).

Magistrates (Chapter 4 – pages 94–134, recs 2–15)

7.   Magistrates and District Judges should continue to exercise their established summary jurisdiction and the work should continue to be allocated between them as much as at present (paras 1–49, recs 2–5). If my recommendation for the establishment of a new unified Criminal Court with a District Division is adopted, they should also sit together in that division exercising its higher jurisdiction. I do not recommend any further extension of justices' clerks' case management jurisdiction (paras 50–58, rec 7). Steps should be taken to provide benches of magistrates that more broadly reflect the communities they serve (paras 59–86, recs 8–9). In order to strengthen the training of magistrates, the Judicial Studies Board should be made responsible, and be adequately resourced, for devising and securing the content and manner of their training (paras 91–100, recs 11–15).

Juries (Chapter 5 – pages 135–225, recs 16–60)

8.   Jurors should be more widely representative than they are of the national and local communities from which they are drawn. Qualification for jury service should remain the same, save that entitlement to, rather than actual, entry on an electoral role should be the criterion. Potential jurors should be identified from a combination of public registers and lists (paras 21–24, recs 17–18). While those with criminal convictions and mental disorder should continue to be disqualified from service, no one in future should be ineligible for or excusable as of right from it. Any claimed inability to serve should be a matter for discretionary deferral or excusal (paras 27–40, recs 20–24). Provision should be made to enable ethnic minority representation on juries where race is likely to be relevant to an important issue in the case (paras 52–62, rec 25).

9.   The law should not be amended to permit more intrusive research than is already possible in the workings of juries, though in appropriate case trial judges and/or the Court of Appeal should be entitled to examine alleged improprieties in the jury room (paras 76–98, recs 26–29). The law should be declared, by statute if need be, that juries have no right to acquit defendants in defiance of the law or disregard of the evidence (paras 99–107, rec 30).

10.   The defendant should no longer have an elective right to trial by judge and jury in 'either-way' cases. The allocation should be the responsibility of the magistrates' court alone and exercisable where there is an issue as to venue by a District Judge. The procedures of committal for trial and for sentence in 'either-way' cases should be abolished.

Under my recommendation for a unified Criminal Court with three divisions, matters too serious for the Magistrates' Division would go direct either to the District or Crown Division depending on the seriousness. In the meantime 'either-way' cases for the Crown Court should be "sent" there in the same way as indictable-only cases (paras 119–172, recs 32–36). Trial by judge and jury should remain the main form of trial of the more serious offences triable on indictment, that is, those that would go to the Crown Division, subject to four exceptions. First, defendants in the Crown Court or, if my recommendations for a unified Court with three divisions is accepted, in the Crown and District Divisions, should be entitled with the court's consent to opt for trial by judge alone (paras110–118, rec 31). Second, in serious and complex frauds the nominated trial judge should have the power to direct trial by himself and two lay members drawn from a panel established by the Lord Chancellor for the purpose (or, if the defendant requests, by himself alone) (paras 173–206, recs 37–47). Third, a youth court, constituted by a judge of an appropriate level and at least two experienced youth panel magistrates, should be given jurisdiction to hear all grave cases against young defendants unless the charges are inseparably linked to those against adults (paras 207–211, recs 48–50). Fourth, legislation should be introduced to require a judge, not a jury, to determine the issue of fitness to plead. (paras 212–213, rec 51).

The Judiciary (Chapter 6 – pages 226–268, recs 61–82)

11.   The current hierarchy of judges and their jurisdictions should continue, subject to my recommendations for the establishment of a District Division of a new unified Criminal Court and extension of the powers of District Judges and magistrates when sitting in it (paras 1–18). Systems of judicial management and deployment should be strengthened and also made more flexible to enable a better match of High Court and Circuit Judges to criminal cases, proper regard also being given to the arrangements for civil and family justice. In particular, there should be a significant shift in heavy work from High Court Judges to the Circuit Bench, coupled with greater flexibility in the system for allocating work between them. Save in the case of Circuit Presiding Judges, the present rigid circuiteering pattern of High Court Judges should be replaced by one in which they travel out to hear only the most serious of cases (paras 19–56, recs 63–70). In implementing the recent recommendations for reforms in the system of appointing judges, the Lord Chancellor's Department should exercise vigilance to root out any indirect discrimination, hurry forward the substitution of assessment exercises for short interviews and establish and publish a clear policy for the appointment of disabled persons to judicial office (paras 65–88, recs 76–78). There should be a strengthening in the training provided to judges, appropriately enlarging the Judicial Studies Board's role for the purpose (paras 89–97, rec 79). There should be a system of appraisal for all part-time judges, and consideration should be given to the appraisal of full-time judges (paras 98–104 , recs 80–82).

Decriminalisation and alternatives to conventional trial (Chapter 9 – pages 367–394, recs 140–151)

12.   I have found little scope or justification for decriminalisation of conduct that Parliament has made subject to penal sanctions (paras 1–6). There should, however, be greater use of a system of fixed penalty notices subject to a right of challenge in court, for example for television licence evasion and the existing provisions for road traffic offences (paras 7–25, recs 140–142). There is no compelling case at present for the creation of any specialist courts, in particular, drugs or domestic violence courts

(paras 26–40). Consideration should be given to the wider use of conditional cautioning or 'caution-plus' alongside existing and future restorative justice schemes, for which a national strategy should be devised (paras 41–47 and 58–69, recs 143–144 and 150). Once the Financial Services Authority has assumed full responsibility for supervision in the financial services field, consideration should be given to transferring appropriate financial and market infringements from the criminal justice process to the Authority's regulatory and disciplinary control. Consideration should also be given in this field for combining parallel criminal and regulatory proceedings (paras 48–57, recs 145–149). Preparatory work should be undertaken with a view to removal of all civil debt enforcement from courts exercising a criminal jurisdiction (paras 70–77, rec 151).

Preparing for trial (Chapter 10 – pages 395–513, recs 152–235)

13. The key to better preparation for, and efficient and effective disposal of, criminal cases is early identification of the issues. Four essentials are: strong and independent prosecutors; efficient and properly paid defence lawyers; ready access by defence lawyers to their clients in custody; and a modern communications system (paras 1–34, recs 152–153). All public prosecutions should take the form of a charge, issued without reference to the courts but for which the prosecutor in all but minor, routine or urgent cases, would have initial responsibility. It should remain the basis of the case against a defendant regardless of the court which ultimately deals with his case, thus replacing the present mix of charges, summonses and indictments (paras 35–63, recs 154–170). A graduated scheme of sentencing discounts should be introduced so that the earlier the plea of guilty the higher the discount for it. This should be coupled with a system of advance indication of sentence for a defendant considering pleading guilty (paras 91–114, recs 186–193).

14. The scheme of mutual disclosure established by the Criminal Procedure and Investigations Act 1996 should remain, but subject to the following reforms: its expression in a single and simply expressed instrument; a single and simple test of materiality for both stages of prosecution disclosure; automatic prosecution disclosure of certain documents; removal from the police to the prosecutor of such responsibility as the police have for identifying all potentially disclosable material; and encouragement, through professional conduct rules and otherwise, of the provision of adequate defence statements (paras 115–184, recs 194–205). There should be a new statutory scheme for third party disclosure (paras 185–190, rec 206) and for instruction by the court of special independent counsel in public interest immunity cases where the court considers prosecution applications in the absence of the defendant (paras 191–197, rec 207).

15. In the preparation for trial in all criminal courts, there should be a move away from plea and directions hearings and other forms of pre-trial hearings to cooperation between the parties according to standard time-tables, wherever necessary, seeking written directions from the court. In the Crown and District Divisions and, where necessary, in the Magistrates' Division, there should then be a written or electronic 'pre-trial assessment' by the court of the parties' readiness for trial. Only if the court or the parties are unable to resolve all matters in this way should there be a pre-trial hearing before or at the stage of the pre-trial assessment. The courts should have a general power to give binding directions and rulings either in writing or at pre-trial hearings (paras 198–234, recs 208–221). In the Crown and District Divisions and, where necessary, in the Magistrates' Division, following the pre-trial assessment and in good time before hearing, the parties should prepare, for the approval of the judge

and use by him, them, and the jury in the hearing, a written case and issues summary setting out in brief the substances of charge(s) and the issues to be resolved by the court (para 235; see also Chapter 11, paras 15–24, recs 235–236).

The Trial: procedures and evidence (Chapter 11 – pages 514–610, recs 236–300)

16.   In trials by judge and jury, the judge, by reference to the case and issues summary, copies of which should be provided to the jury, should give them fuller introduction to the case than is now conventional (paras 14–24, recs 235–236). The trial should broadly take the same form as at present, though with greater use of electronic aids in appropriate cases. The judge should sum up and direct the jury, making reference as appropriate to the case and issues summary. So far as possible, he should 'filter out' the law and fashion factual questions to the issues and the law as he knows it to be. Where he considers it appropriate, he should require the jury publicly to answer each of the questions and to declare a verdict in accordance with those answers (paras 25–55, recs 237–250).

17.   In trials by judge and magistrates in the District Division, the judge should be the sole judge of law, but he and the magistrates should together be the judges of fact, each having an equal vote. The order of proceedings would be broadly the same as in the Crown Division. The judge should rule on matters of law, procedure and inadmissibility of evidence in the absence of the magistrates where it would be potentially unfair to the defendant to do so in their presence. The judge should not sum up the case to the magistrates, but should retire with them to consider the court's decision, which he would give and publicly reason as a judgment of the court. The judge should be solely responsible for sentence (paras 57–61, rec 251).

18.   There should be a comprehensive review of the law of criminal evidence to identify and establish over-all and coherent principles and to make it an efficient and simple agent for securing justice. Subject to such review, I consider that the law should, in general, move away from technical rules of inadmissibility to trusting judicial and lay fact finders to give relevant evidence the weight it deserves. In particular, consideration should be given to the reform of the rules as to refreshing memory, the use of witness statements, hearsay, unfair evidence, previous misconduct of the dependant, similar fact evidence and the evidence of children (paras 76–128, recs 254–261). There should be reforms to strengthen the quality and objectivity of expert evidence and improve the manner of its presentation both from the point of view of the court and experts, following in some respects reforms made in the civil sphere by the Civil Procedure Rules (paras 129–151, recs 262–275). Urgent steps should be taken to increase the numbers and strengthen the quality of interpreters serving the criminal courts and to improve their working conditions (paras 155–162, recs 276–286). There are a number of ways in which the facilities and procedures of the courts should or could be modernised and better serve the public (paras 163–196, recs 287–295). The criminal courts should be equipped with an on-line sentencing information system (paras 200–211, recs 296–299).

Appeals (Chapter 12 – pages 611–658, recs 301–328)

19.   There should be the same tests for appeal against conviction and sentence respectively at all levels of appeal, namely those applicable for appeal to the Court of Appeal (paras 5–13, and 45–46, recs 300–301). There should be a single line of appeal from the Magistrates' Division (Magistrates' Courts) and above to the Court of Appeal in all criminal matters. This would involve: 1) abolition of appeal from magistrates' courts to the Crown Court by way of rehearing and its replacement by an appeal to the Crown Division (Crown Court) constituted by a judge alone; and 2) abolition of appeal from magistrates' courts and/or the Crown Court to the High Court by way of a case stated or claim for judicial review and their replacement by appeal to the Court of Appeal under its general appellate jurisdiction enlarged if and to the extent necessary (paras 14–44, recs 302–307).

20.   I support the general thrust of the Law Commission's recommendations for the introduction of statutory exceptions to the double jeopardy rule, save that a prosecutor's right of appeal against acquittal should not be limited to cases of murder and allied offences, but should extend to other grave offences punishable with life or long terms of imprisonment (paras 47–65, recs 308–309). There should be provision for appeal by the defence or the prosecution against a special verdict of a jury which on its terms is perverse; see para 16 above (paras 66–67, rec 310).

21.   The Court of Appeal should be reconstituted and its procedures should be improved to enable it to deal more efficiently with, on the one hand appeals involving matters of general public importance or of particular complexity and, on the other, with 'straightforward' appeals (paras 73–101, recs 311–321). The law should be amended: to widen the remit of the Sentencing Advisory Panel to include general principles of sentencing, regardless of the category of offence; and to enable the Court of Appeal to issue guidelines without having to tie them to a specific appeal before it (paras 108–111, recs 324–325).

[1:6]   Packer, H *The Limits of the Criminal Sanction* (1968) Oxford University Press (at page 153):

Two models of the criminal process will let us perceive the normative antinomy at the heart of the criminal law. These models are not labeled 'Is' and 'Ought', nor are they to be taken in that sense. Rather, they represent an attempt to abstract two separate value systems that compete for priority in the operation of the criminal process. Neither is presented as either corresponding to reality or representing the ideal to the exclusion of the other. The two models merely afford a convenient way to talk about the operation of a process whose day-to-day functioning involves a constant series of minute adjustments between the competing demands of two value systems and whose normative future likewise involves a series of resolutions of the tensions between competing claims.

Crime control values

(at page 158):

The value system that underlies the Crime Control Model is based on the proposition that the repression of criminal conduct is by far the most important function to be performed by the criminal process. The failure of law enforcement to bring criminal conduct under tight control is viewed as leading to the breakdown of public order and thence to the disappearance of an important condition of human freedom. If the laws go unenforced – which is to say, if it is perceived that there is a high percentage of failure to apprehend and convict in the criminal process – a general disregard for legal controls tends to develop. The law-abiding citizen then becomes the victim of all sorts of unjustifiable invasions of this interests. His security of person and property is sharply diminished, and, therefore, so is his liberty to function as a member of society. The claim ultimately is that the criminal process is a positive guarantor of social freedom. In order to achieve this high purpose, the Crime Control Model requires that primary attention be paid to the efficiency with which the criminal process operates to screen suspects, determine guilt, and secure appropriate dispositions of persons convicted of crime.

The model, in order to operate successfully, must produce a high rate of apprehension and conviction, and must do so in a context where the magnitudes being dealt with are very large and the resources for dealing with them are very limited. There must then be a premium on speed and finality. Speed, in turn, depends on informality and on uniformity; finality depends on minimising the occasions for challenge. The process must not be cluttered up with ceremonious rituals that do not advance the progress of a case. Facts can be established more quickly through interrogation in a police station than through the formal process of examination and cross-examination in a court. It follows that extrajudicial processes should be preferred to judicial processes, informal operations to formal ones. But informality is not enough; there must also be uniformity. Routine, stereotyped procedures are essential if large numbers are being handled. The model that will operate successfully on these presuppositions must be an administrative, almost a managerial, model. The image that comes to mind is an assembly-conveyor belt down which moves an endless stream of cases, never stopping, carrying the cases to workers who stand at fixed stations and who perform on each case as it comes by the same small but essential operation and brings it one step closer to being a finished product, or, to exchange the metaphor for the reality, a closed file. The criminal process, in this model, is seen as a screening process in which each successive stage – pre-arrest investigation, arrest, post-arrest investigation, preparation for trial, trial or entry of plea, conviction, disposition – involves a series of routinised operations whose success is gauged primarily by their tendency to pass the case alone to a successful conclusion.

What is a successful conclusion? One that throws off at an early stage those cases in which it appears unlikely that the person apprehended is an offender and then secures, as expeditiously as possible, the conviction of the rest, with a minimum of occasions for challenge, let alone post-audit. By the application of administrative expertness, primarily that of the police and prosecutors, an early determination of probable innocence or guilt emerges. Those who are probably innocent are screened out. Those who are probably guilty are passed quickly through the remaining stages of the process. The key to the operation of the model regarding those who are not screened out is what I shall call a presumption of guilt. The concept requires some explanation, since it may appear startling to assert that what appears to be the precise converse of our generally accepted ideology of a presumption of innocence can be an essential element of a model that does correspond in some respects to the actual operation of the criminal process.

The presumption of guilt is what makes it possible for the system to deal efficiently with large numbers, as the Crime Control Model demands. The supposition is that the screening processes operated by police and prosecutors are reliable indicators of probable guilt. Once a man has been arrested and investigated without being found to be probably innocent, or, to put it differently, once a determination has been made that there is enough evidence of guilt to permit holding him for further action, then all subsequent activity directed toward him is based on the view that he is probably guilty. The precise point at which this occurs will vary from case to case; in many cases it will occur as soon as the suspect is arrested, or even before, if the evidence of probable guilt that has come to the attention of the authorities is sufficiently strong. But in any case the presumption of guilt will begin to operate well before the 'suspect' becomes a 'defendant'.

The presumption of guilt is not, of course, a thing. Nor is it even a rule of law in the usual sense. It simply is the consequence of a complex of attitudes, a mood.

If there is confidence in the reliability of informal administrative fact-finding activities that take place in the early stages of the criminal process, the remaining stages of the process can be relatively perfunctory without any loss in operating efficiency. The presumption of guilt, as it operates in the Crime Control Model, is the operational expression of that confidence.

Due process values

(at page 163):

If the Crime Control Model resembles an assembly line, the Due Process Model looks very much like an obstacle course. Each of its successive stages is designed to present formidable impediments to carrying the accused any further along in the process. Its ideology is not the converse of that underlying the Crime Control Model. It does not rest on the idea that it is not socially desirable to repress crime, although critics of its application have been known to claim so. Its ideology is composed of a complex of ideas, some of them based on judgments about the efficacy of crime control devices, others having to do with quite difference considerations. The ideology of due process is far more deeply impressed on the formal structure of the law than is the ideology of crime control; yet an accurate tracing of the strands that make it up is strangely difficult. What follows is only an attempt at an approximation.

The Due Process Model encounters its rival on the Crime Control Model's own ground in respect to the reliability of fact-finding processes. The Crime Control Model, as we have suggested, places heavy reliance on the ability of investigative and prosecutorial officers, acting in an informal setting in which their distinctive skills are given full sway, to elicit and reconstruct a tolerably accurate account of what actually took place in an alleged criminal event. The Due Process Model rejects this premise and substitutes for it a view of informal, non-adjudicative fact-finding that stresses the possibility of error. People are notoriously poor observers of disturbing events – the more emotion-arousing the context, the greater the possibility that recollection will be incorrect; confessions and admissions by persons in police custody may be induced by physical or psychological coercion so that the police end up hearing what the suspect thinks they want to hear rather than the truth; witnesses may be animated by a bias or interest that no one would trouble to discover except one specially charged with protecting the interests of the accused (as the police are not). Considerations of this kind all lead to a rejection of informal fact-finding processes as definitive of factual guilt and to an insistence on formal, adjudicative, adversary fact-finding processes in which the factual case against the accused is publicly heard by an impartial tribunal and is evaluated only after the accused has had a full opportunity to discredit the case against him. Even then, the distrust of fact-finding processes that animates the Due Process Model is not dissipated. The possibilities of human error being what they are, further scrutiny is necessary, or at least must be available, in case facts have been over-looked or suppressed in the heat of battle. How far this subsequent scrutiny must be available is a hotly controverted issue today. In the pure Due Process Model the answer would be: at least as long as there is an allegation of factual error that has not received an adjudicative hearing in a fact-finding context. The demand for finality is thus very low in the Due Process Model.

This strand of due process ideology is not enough to sustain the model. If all that were at issue between the two models was a series of questions about the reliability of fact-finding processes, we would have but one model of the criminal process, the nature of whose constituent elements would pose questions of fact not of value. Even if the discussion is confined, for the moment, to the question of reliability, it is apparent that more is at stake than simply an evaluation of what kinds of fact-finding processes, alone or in combination, are likely to produce the most nearly reliable results. The stumbling block is this: how much reliability is compatible with efficiency?

Granted that informal fact-finding will make some mistakes that can be remedied if backed up by adjudicative fact-finding, the desirability of providing this backup is not affirmed or negated by factual demonstrations or predictions that the increase in reliability will be x per cent or x plus n per cent. It still remains to ask how much weight is to be given to the competing demands of reliability (a high degree of probability in each case that factual guilt has been accurately determined) and efficiency (expeditious handling of the large numbers of cases that the process ingests). The Crime Control Model is more optimistic about the improbability of error in a significant number of cases; but it is also, though only in part therefore, more tolerant about the amount of error that it will put up with. The Due Process Model insists on the prevention and elimination of mistakes to the extent possible; the Crime Control Model accepts the probability of mistakes up to the level at which they interfere with the goal of repressing crime, either because too many guilty people are escaping or, more subtly, because general awareness of the unreliability of the process leads to a decrease in the deterrent efficacy of the criminal law. In this view, reliability and efficiency are not polar opposites but rather complementary characteristics. The system is reliable because efficient reliability becomes a matter of independent concern only when it becomes so attenuated as to impair efficiency. All of this the Due Process Model rejects. If efficiency demands short-cuts around reliability, then absolute efficiency must be rejected. The aim of the process is at least as much to protect the factually innocent as it is to convict the factually guilty. It is a little like quality control in industrial technology: tolerable deviation from standard varies with the importance of conformity to standard in the destined uses of the product. The Due Process Model resembles a factory that has to devote a substantial part of its input to quality control. This necessarily cuts down on quantitative output.

[1:7] **Bottoms, A E and McClean, J D** *Defendants in the Criminal Process*
(1976) Routledge and Kegan Paul (at page 228):

The Liberal Bureaucratic Model is the model of the criminal justice process typically held by humane and enlightened clerks to the justices and Crown Court administrators in this country – as well as by many others. It differs substantially from the Crime Control Model, the model typically held by the police, since it dissents from its underlying central value-position: 'The value-system that underlies the Crime Control Model is based on the proposition that the repression of criminal conduct is by far the most important function to be performed by the criminal process' (Packer, 1969, p 158).

The Liberal Bureaucratic Model holds, rather, that the protection of individual liberty, and the need for justice to be done and to be seen to be done, must ultimately override the importance of the repression of criminal conduct. The liberal bureaucrat here joins with the advocate of Due Process in agreeing that formal adjudicative processes are very important, and moreover that – in the conventional phrase – 'it is better for ten guilty men to go free than for one innocent man to be convicted'.

But the Liberal Bureaucratic Model also differs substantially from the Due Process Model. For the Due Process Model looks very much like an obstacle course. Each of its successive stages is designed to present formidable impediments to carry the accused any further along in the process ... [It] resembled a factory that has to devote a substantial part of its input to quality control. *This necessarily cuts down on quantitative output* (Packer, 1969, pp 163, 165; italics added).

It is precisely this restriction on quantitative output which offends the liberal bureaucrat about the Due Process Model. The liberal bureaucrat is a practical man; he realises that things have to get done, systems have to be run. It is right that the defendant shall have substantial protections; crime control is not the overriding value of the criminal justice system. But these protections must have a limit. If it were not so, then the whole system of criminal justice, with its value to the community in the form of liberal and humane crime control, would collapse. Moreover, it is right to build in sanctions to deter those who might otherwise use their 'Due Process' rights frivolously, or to 'try it on'; an administrative system at State expense should not exist for this kind of time-wasting.

[1:8] King, M *The Framework of Criminal Justice* (1981) Croom Helm (at page 13):

Theoretical Models and Their Features

I	Social Function	II	Process Model	III	Features of Court
1.	**Justice**		Due Process Model	(a)	Equality between parties
				(b)	Rules protecting defendant against error
				(c)	Restraint of arbitrary power
				(d)	Presumption of innocence
2.	**Punishment**		Crime Control Model	(a)	Disregard of legal controls
				(b)	Implicit presumption of guilt
				(c)	High conviction rate
				(d)	Unpleasantness of experience
				(e)	Support for police
3.	**Rehabilitation**		Medical Model (diagnosis, prediction and treatment selection)	(a)	Information collecting procedures
				(b)	Individualisation
				(c)	Treatment of presumption
				(d)	Discretion of decision-makers
				(e)	Expertise of decision-makers or advisers
				(f)	Relaxation of formal rules
4.	**Management of crime and criminals**		Bureaucratic Model	(a)	Independence from political considerations
				(b)	Speed and efficiency
				(c)	Importance of and acceptance of records
				(d)	Minimisation of conflict
				(e)	Minimisation of expense
				(f)	Economical division of labour
5.	**Denunciation and degradation**		Status Passage Model	(a)	Public shaming of defendant
				(b)	Court values reflecting community values
				(c)	Agents' control over the process
6.	**Maintenance of class domination**		Power Model	(a)	Reinforcement of class values
				(b)	Alienation and suppression of defendant
				(c)	Deflection of attention from issues of class conflict
				(d)	Differences between judges and judged
				(e)	Paradoxes and contradictions between rhetoric and performance

[1:9]   Human Rights Act 1998 sections 1–6; 8; Schedule 1

1   The Convention Rights

(1)   In this Act "the Convention rights" means the rights and fundamental freedoms set out in—
  (a)   Articles 2 to 12 and 14 of the Convention,
  (b)   Articles 1 to 3 of the First Protocol, and
  (c)   Articles 1 and 2 of the Sixth Protocol,
as read with Articles 16 to 18 of the Convention.

(2)   Those Articles are to have effect for the purposes of this Act subject to any designated derogation or reservation (as to which see sections 14 and 15).

(3)   The Articles are set out in Schedule 1.

(4)   The Lord Chancellor may by order make such amendments to this Act as he considers appropriate to reflect the effect, in relation to the United Kingdom, of a protocol.

(5)   In subsection (4) "protocol" means a protocol to the Convention—
  (a)   which the United Kingdom has ratified; or
  (b)   which the United Kingdom has signed with a view to ratification.

(6)   No amendment may be made by an order under subsection (4) so as to come into force before the protocol concerned is in force in relation to the United Kingdom.

2   Interpretation of Convention rights

(1)   A court or tribunal determining a question which has arisen in connection with a Convention right must take into account any—
  (a)   judgment, decision, declaration or advisory opinion of the European Court of Human Rights,
  (b)   opinion of the Commission given in a report adopted under Article 31 of the Convention,
  (c)   decision of the Commission in connection with Article 26 or 27(2) of the Convention, or
  (d)   decision of the Committee of Ministers taken under Article 46 of the Convention,
whenever made or given, so far as, in the opinion of the court or tribunal, it is relevant to the proceedings in which that question has arisen.

(2)   Evidence of any judgment, decision, declaration or opinion of which account may have to be taken under this section is to be given in proceedings before any court or tribunal in such manner as may be provided by rules.

(3)   In this section "rules" means rules of court or, in the case of proceedings before a tribunal, rules made for the purposes of this section—
  (a)   by the Lord Chancellor or the Secretary of State, in relation to any proceedings outside Scotland;

    (b)   by the Secretary of State, in relation to proceedings in Scotland; or
    (c)   by a Northern Ireland department, in relation to proceedings before a tribunal in Northern Ireland—
        (i)   which deals with transferred matters; and
        (ii)   for which no rules made under paragraph (a) are in force.

3 Interpretation of legislation

(1)   So far as it is possible to do so, primary legislation and subordinate legislation must be read and given effect in a way which is compatible with the Convention rights.

(2)   This section—
    (a)   applies to primary legislation and subordinate legislation whenever enacted;
    (b)   does not affect the validity, continuing operation or enforcement of any incompatible primary legislation; and
    (c)   does not affect the validity, continuing operation or enforcement of any incompatible subordinate legislation if (disregarding any possibility of revocation) primary legislation prevents removal of the incompatibility.

4 Declaration of incompatibility

(1)   Subsection (2) applies in any proceedings in which a court determines whether a provision of primary legislation is compatible with a Convention right.

(2)   If the court is satisfied that the provision is incompatible with a Convention right, it may make a declaration of that incompatibility.

(3)   Subsection (4) applies in any proceedings in which a court determines whether a provision of subordinate legislation, made in the exercise of a power conferred by primary legislation, is compatible with a Convention right.

(4)   If the court is satisfied—
    (a)   that the provision is incompatible with a Convention right, and
    (b)   that (disregarding any possibility of revocation) the primary legislation concerned prevents removal of the incompatibility,
it may make a declaration of that incompatibility.

(5)   In this section "court" means—
    (a)   the House of Lords;
    (b)   the Judicial Committee of the Privy Council;
    (c)   the Courts-Martial Appeal Court;
    (d)   in Scotland, the High Court of Justiciary sitting otherwise than as a trial court or the Court of Session;
    (e)   in England and Wales or Northern Ireland, the High Court or the Court of Appeal.

(6)   A declaration under this section ("a declaration of incompatibility")—
    (a)   does not affect the validity, continuing operation or enforcement of the provision in respect of which it is given; and
    (b)   is not binding on the parties to the proceedings in which it is made.

5   Right of Crown to intervene

(1)   Where a court is considering whether to make a declaration of incompatibility, the Crown is entitled to notice in accordance with rules of court.

(2)   In any case to which subsection (1) applies—
  (a)   a Minister of the Crown (or a person nominated by him),
  (b)   a member of the Scottish Executive,
  (c)   a Northern Ireland Minister,
  (d)   a Northern Ireland department,
is entitled, on giving notice in accordance with rules of court, to be joined as a party to the proceedings.

(3)   Notice under subsection (2) may be given at any time during the proceedings.

(4)   A person who has been made a party to criminal proceedings (other than in Scotland) as the result of a notice under subsection (2) may, with leave, appeal to the House of Lords against any declaration of incompatibility made in the proceedings.

(5)   In subsection (4)—
  "criminal proceedings" includes all proceedings before the Courts-Martial Appeal Court; and
  "leave" means leave granted by the court making the declaration of incompatibility or by the House of Lords.

6   Acts of public authorities

(1)   It is unlawful for a public authority to act in a way which is incompatible with a Convention right.

(2)   Subsection (1) does not apply to an act if—
  (a)   as the result of one or more provisions of primary legislation, the authority could not have acted differently; or
  (b)   in the case of one or more provisions of, or made under, primary legislation which cannot be read or given effect in a way which is compatible with the Convention rights, the authority was acting so as to give effect to or enforce those provisions.

(3)   In this section "public authority" includes—
  (a)   a court or tribunal, and
  (b)   any person certain of whose functions are functions of a public nature,
but does not include either House of Parliament or a person exercising functions in connection with proceedings in Parliament.

(4)   In subsection (3) "Parliament" does not include the House of Lords in its judicial capacity.

(5)   In relation to a particular act, a person is not a public authority by virtue only of subsection (3)(b) if the nature of the act is private.

(6) "An act" includes a failure to act but does not include a failure to—
   (a) introduce in, or lay before, Parliament a proposal for legislation; or
   (b) make any primary legislation or remedial order.

8 Judicial remedies

(1) In relation to any act (or proposed act) of a public authority which the court finds is (or would be) unlawful, it may grant such relief or remedy, or make such order, within its powers as it considers just and appropriate.

(2) But damages may be awarded only by a court which has power to award damages, or to order the payment of compensation, in civil proceedings.

(3) No award of damages is to be made unless, taking account of all the circumstances of the case, including—
   (a) any other relief or remedy granted, or order made, in relation to the act in question (by that or any other court), and
   (b) the consequences of any decision (of that or any other court) in respect of that act,
the court is satisfied that the award is necessary to afford just satisfaction to the person in whose favour it is made.

(4) In determining—
   (a) whether to award damages, or
   (b) the amount of an award,
the court must take into account the principles applied by the European Court of Human Rights in relation to the award of compensation under Article 41 of the Convention.

(5) A public authority against which damages are awarded is to be treated—
   (a) in Scotland, for the purposes of section 3 of the Law Reform (Miscellaneous Provisions) (Scotland) Act 1940 as if the award were made in an action of damages in which the authority has been found liable in respect of loss or damage to the person to whom the award is made;
   (b) for the purposes of the Civil Liability (Contribution) Act 1978 as liable in respect of damage suffered by the person to whom the award is made.

(6) In this section—
   "court" includes a tribunal;
   "damages" means damages for an unlawful act of a public authority; and
   "unlawful" means unlawful under section 6(1).

SCHEDULE 1 The Articles

Section 1(3)

PART I THE CONVENTION

RIGHTS AND FREEDOMS

Article 2 Right to life

1 Everyone's right to life shall be protected by law. No one shall be deprived of his life intentionally save in the execution of a sentence of a court following his conviction of a crime for which this penalty is provided by law.

2 Deprivation of life shall not be regarded as inflicted in contravention of this Article when it results from the use of force which is no more than absolutely necessary:
    (a)   in defence of any person from unlawful violence;
    (b)   in order to effect a lawful arrest or to prevent the escape of a person lawfully detained;
    (c)   in action lawfully taken for the purpose of quelling a riot or insurrection.

Article 3 Prohibition of torture

No one shall be subjected to torture or to inhuman or degrading treatment or punishment.

Article 4 Prohibition of slavery and forced labour

1 No one shall be held in slavery or servitude.

2 No one shall be required to perform forced or compulsory labour.

3 For the purpose of this Article the term "forced or compulsory labour" shall not include:
    (a)   any work required to be done in the ordinary course of detention imposed according to the provisions of Article 5 of this Convention or during conditional release from such detention;
    (b)   any service of a military character or, in case of conscientious objectors in countries where they are recognised, service exacted instead of compulsory military service;
    (c)   any service exacted in case of an emergency or calamity threatening the life or well-being of the community;
    (d)   any work or service which forms part of normal civic obligations.

Article 5 Right to liberty and security

1 Everyone has the right to liberty and security of person. No one shall be deprived of his liberty save in the following cases and in accordance with a procedure prescribed by law:
  (a) the lawful detention of a person after conviction by a competent court;
  (b) the lawful arrest or detention of a person for non-compliance with the lawful order of a court or in order to secure the fulfilment of any obligation prescribed by law;
  (c) the lawful arrest or detention of a person effected for the purpose of bringing him before the competent legal authority on reasonable suspicion of having committed an offence or when it is reasonably considered necessary to prevent his committing an offence or fleeing after having done so;
  (d) the detention of a minor by lawful order for the purpose of educational supervision or his lawful detention for the purpose of bringing him before the competent legal authority;
  (e) the lawful detention of persons for the prevention of the spreading of infectious diseases, of persons of unsound mind, alcoholics or drug addicts or vagrants;
  (f) the lawful arrest or detention of a person to prevent his effecting an unauthorised entry into the country or of a person against whom action is being taken with a view to deportation or extradition.

2 Everyone who is arrested shall be informed promptly, in a language which he understands, of the reasons for his arrest and of any charge against him.

3 Everyone arrested or detained in accordance with the provisions of paragraph 1(c) of this Article shall be brought promptly before a judge or other officer authorised by law to exercise judicial power and shall be entitled to trial within a reasonable time or to release pending trial. Release may be conditioned by guarantees to appear for trial.

4 Everyone who is deprived of his liberty by arrest or detention shall be entitled to take proceedings by which the lawfulness of his detention shall be decided speedily by a court and his release ordered if the detention is not lawful.

5 Everyone who has been the victim of arrest or detention in contravention of the provisions of this Article shall have an enforceable right to compensation.

Article 6 Right to a fair trial

1 In the determination of his civil rights and obligations or of any criminal charge against him, everyone is entitled to a fair and public hearing within a reasonable time by an independent and impartial tribunal established by law. Judgment shall be pronounced publicly but the press and public may be excluded from all or part of the trial in the interest of morals, public order or national security in a democratic society, where the interests of juveniles or the protection of the private life of the parties so require, or to the extent strictly necessary in the opinion of the court in special circumstances where publicity would prejudice the interests of justice.

2 Everyone charged with a criminal offence shall be presumed innocent until proved guilty according to law.

3 Everyone charged with a criminal offence has the following minimum rights:
- (a) to be informed promptly, in a language which he understands and in detail, of the nature and cause of the accusation against him;
- (b) to have adequate time and facilities for the preparation of his defence;
- (c) to defend himself in person or through legal assistance of his own choosing or, if he has not sufficient means to pay for legal assistance, to be given it free when the interests of justice so require;
- (d) to examine or have examined witnesses against him and to obtain the attendance and examination of witnesses on his behalf under the same conditions as witnesses against him;
- (e) to have the free assistance of an interpreter if he cannot understand or speak the language used in court.

Article 7 No punishment without law

1 No one shall be held guilty of any criminal offence on account of any act or omission which did not constitute a criminal offence under national or international law at the time when it was committed. Nor shall a heavier penalty be imposed than the one that was applicable at the time the criminal offence was committed.

2 This Article shall not prejudice the trial and punishment of any person for any act or omission which, at the time when it was committed, was criminal according to the general principles of law recognised by civilised nations.

Article 8 Right to respect for private and family life

1 Everyone has the right to respect for his private and family life, his home and his correspondence.

2 There shall be no interference by a public authority with the exercise of this right except such as is in accordance with the law and is necessary in a democratic society in the interests of national security, public safety or the economic well-being of the country, for the prevention of disorder or crime, for the protection of health or morals, or for the protection of the rights and freedoms of others.

Article 9 Freedom of thought, conscience and religion

1 Everyone has the right to freedom of thought, conscience and religion; this right includes freedom to change his religion or belief and freedom, either alone or in community with others and in public or private, to manifest his religion or belief, in worship, teaching, practice and observance.

2 Freedom to manifest one's religion or beliefs shall be subject only to such limitations as are prescribed by law and are necessary in a democratic society in the interests of public safety, for the protection of public order, health or morals, or for the protection of the rights and freedoms of others.

Article 10 Freedom of expression

1 Everyone has the right to freedom of expression. This right shall include freedom to hold opinions and to receive and impart information and ideas without interference by public authority and regardless of frontiers. This Article shall not prevent States from requiring the licensing of broadcasting, television or cinema enterprises.

2 The exercise of these freedoms, since it carries with it duties and responsibilities, may be subject to such formalities, conditions, restrictions or penalties as are prescribed by law and are necessary in a democratic society, in the interests of national security, territorial integrity or public safety, for the prevention of disorder or crime, for the protection of health or morals, for the protection of the reputation or rights of others, for preventing the disclosure of information received in confidence, or for maintaining the authority and impartiality of the judiciary.

Article 11 Freedom of assembly and association

1 Everyone has the right to freedom of peaceful assembly and to freedom of association with others, including the right to form and to join trade unions for the protection of his interests.

2 No restrictions shall be placed on the exercise of these rights other than such as are prescribed by law and are necessary in a democratic society in the interests of national security or public safety, for the prevention of disorder or crime, for the protection of health or morals or for the protection of the rights and freedoms of others. This Article shall not prevent the imposition of lawful restrictions on the exercise of these rights by members of the armed forces, of the police or of the administration of the State.

Article 12 Right to marry

Men and women of marriageable age have the right to marry and to found a family, according to the national laws governing the exercise of this right.

Article 14 Prohibition of discrimination

The enjoyment of the rights and freedoms set forth in this Convention shall be secured without discrimination on any ground such as sex, race, colour, language, religion, political or other opinion, national or social origin, association with a national minority, property, birth or other status.

Article 16 Restrictions on political activity of aliens

Nothing in Articles 10, 11 and 14 shall be regarded as preventing the High Contracting Parties from imposing restrictions on the political activity of aliens.

Article 17 Prohibition of abuse of rights

Nothing in this Convention may be interpreted as implying for any State, group or person any right to engage in any activity or perform any act aimed at the destruction of any of the rights and freedoms set forth herein or at their limitation to a greater extent than is provided for in the Convention.

Article 18 Limitation on use of restrictions on rights

The restrictions permitted under this Convention to the said rights and freedoms shall not be applied for any purpose other than those for which they have been prescribed.

PART II THE FIRST PROTOCOL

Article 1 Protection of property

Every natural or legal person is entitled to the peaceful enjoyment of his possessions. No one shall be deprived of his possessions except in the public interest and subject to the conditions provided for by law and by the general principles of international law.

The preceding provisions shall not, however, in any way impair the right of a State to enforce such laws as it deems necessary to control the use of property in accordance with the general interest or to secure the payment of taxes or other contributions or penalties.

Article 2 Right to education

No person shall be denied the right to education. In the exercise of any functions which it assumes in relation to education and to teaching, the State shall respect the right of parents to ensure such education and teaching in conformity with their own religious and philosophical convictions.

Article 3 Right to free elections

The High Contracting Parties undertake to hold free elections at reasonable intervals by secret ballot, under conditions which will ensure the free expression of the opinion of the people in the choice of the legislature.

PART III THE SIXTH PROTOCOL

Article 1 Abolition of the death penalty

The death penalty shall be abolished. No one shall be condemned to such penalty or executed.

Article 2 Death penalty in time of war

A State may make provision in its law for the death penalty in respect of acts committed in time of war or of imminent threat of war; such penalty shall be applied only in the instances laid down in the law and in accordance with its provisions. The State shall communicate to the Secretary General of the Council of Europe the relevant provisions of that law.

[1:10]   Criminal Justice Act 1991 section 95

95   Information for financial and other purposes

(1)   The Secretary of State shall in each year publish such information as he considers expedient for the purpose of—
  (a)   enabling persons engaged in the administration of criminal justice to become aware of the financial implications of their decisions; or
  (b)   facilitating the performance by such persons of their duty to avoid discriminating against any persons on the ground of race or sex or any other improper ground.

(2)   Publication under subsection (1) above shall be effected in such manner as the Secretary of State considers appropriate for the purpose of bringing the information to the attention of the persons concerned.

[1:11]   Hedderman, Carol and Hough, Mike *Does the criminal justice system treat men and women differently?* HORS Research Findings No 10 (1994) HMSO (at page 1):

Academics, pressure groups and journalists have used a variety of criminal justice statistics to argue that the courts systematically discriminate against women. This paper shows that differences do exist in the way men and women are treated by the criminal justice system, but that these largely favour women.

The extent to which men and women offend

Criminal statistics both across time and different cultures show that an overwhelming majority of those caught, convicted and sentenced by the courts are male. Over the last ten years in England and Wales, around five males were cautioned or convicted for an indictable offence for every one female. Such statistics do not account for all crimes committed, of course. Self-report studies – not without problems of their own – ask samples about the extent to which they have committed offences; these indicate that the discrepancy between males and females is more like two males for every one female, although the sex ratio does appear to increase with offence seriousness.

Males are more likely than females to be reconvicted, according both to small-scale research and analysis of the Home Office Offenders' Index (a database which contains details of all offenders convicted of serious offences). Also, the average length of male criminal careers (3.3 years) is three times as long as that for females, although the ratio narrows when those with careers less than one year are excluded, effectively eliminating those convicted of only one offence.[3]

The types of crime men and women commit

On the basis of those convicted and cautioned, the male/female ratio in offending is at its greatest in the late teens and early 20s. This is not because females commit the same offences as males at a later age, but because they are much less likely to commit the sorts of offences committed by younger people, such as burglary, and theft from or of motor vehicles.

Although there has been a rise in the proportion of females dealt with for violence and for drug offences over the last ten years, 71% of their offences in 1992 were theft and handling – in contrast to only 43% of males.

Cautioning

Cautioning is the main disposal used for female offenders. In 1992, 61% of all females convicted or cautioned for indictable offences received a caution, compared with 36% of males. Women had higher cautioning rates across all age groups and most offences, with the exception of drugs.

A statistical exercise carried out by the Home Office examined the criminal histories of samples of those cautioned in 1985 and 1988. This showed that, whilst a majority of both sexes had no criminal history, cautioned males were twice as likely as females to have been previously convicted. They were also more likely to have been cautioned on the previous occasion.[4] The most likely explanation for this difference is the higher offending rate for males. However, without knowing more about these cases, and those in which the police took no further action or prosecuted the offender, we cannot eliminate the possibility that different standards are being applied when deciding whether to caution males and females.

Remands

A smaller proportion of female offenders are remanded in custody than males. One of the few studies to investigate the reasons[5] concluded that this was partly because women were less likely than men to fall into 'high risk' categories, defined as those who had previously failed to appear after being given court bail, or had been charged with a further offence while on bail, or were of no fixed abode. This was only part of the story,

[3]   Tarling, R *Analysing Offending: data, models and interpretations* (1993) HMSO.
[4]   'The criminal histories of those cautioned in 1985 and 1988' (1992) Home Office Statistical Bulletin No 20/92.
[5]   Morgan, P and Pearce, R 'Remand Decisions in Brighton and Bournemouth' Research and Planning Unit Paper No 53 (1989) Home Office.

however; women falling into 'low risk' categories were still less likely to be remanded in custody than their male counterparts.

Though relevant prison statistics are incomplete, they suggest that about 30% of women who were remanded in custody are subsequently sent to prison, compared with 40% of their male counterparts. Women on bail are also less likely to receive a custodial sentence – about 5% compared with 10% of men. Taken together, these findings suggest that men and women may be treated differently both at the remand and the sentencing stage.

Sentencing

There are large overall differences in the sentencing of men and women. In particular women are far less likely than men to receive a custodial sentence for virtually all indictable offences. The only exception is for drugs, for which the proportions are roughly equal (14%).

When women do receive prison sentences, these tend to be shorter than men's: in 1992 the average length of prison sentences awarded for indictable offences at the Crown Court was 17.7 months for women aged 21 or over and 21.1 months for men. The average length was lower for females convicted of burglary, fraud and forgery, robbery, and theft and handling, but higher for criminal damage and drug offences.

According to the National Prison Survey, 38% of women serving prison sentences in 1991 were there for their first offence, but only 10% of men. Prison statistics show that a much larger proportion of the female prison population are serving custodial sentences for less serious crimes. A common statistical fallacy is to infer from these and similar statistics that the criminal justice system discriminates against women. However, nothing can be inferred about discrimination on the part of sentencers from differences between the sexes in the proportion either of first-offenders or of property offenders in prison. One has to compare the proportions sent to prison of men and women who have committed similar crimes and have similar criminal histories.

One of the reasons that women receive fewer and shorter custodial sentences than men is that they are less frequently dealt with at the Crown Court. For example, in 1992, only 14% of the females aged 17 or over who were proceeded against for an indictable offence went to the Crown Court for trial compared with 24% of males. Recent Home Office research[6] has shown that, in comparable cases, defendants who are sentenced at the Crown Court are about three times more likely to get a custodial sentence than those dealt with at magistrates' courts; such sentences also tend to be longer.

Another possible explanation for the apparently more lenient sentencing of women offenders is that, as discussed above, they are less likely to have previous convictions than men. However, analysis of an Offenders' Index sample of 21,000 offenders convicted of a serious offence in 1991 shows that women first-offenders are half as likely to be given a sentence of immediate imprisonment as male first-offenders – 4% compared with 8%; and those with one, two, or three or more previous convictions were all less likely to receive custodial sentences than equivalent men. The same pattern is repeated

[6] Hedderman, C and Moxon, D 'Magistrates' court or Crown Court? Mode of trial decisions and sentencing' (1992) Home Office Research Study No 125 HMSO.

for individual types of crime such as theft and causing actual bodily harm. Given that these two types of offence account for two-thirds of female convictions for serious offences, it is hardly surprising that such offenders constitute a large part of the female prison population.

Hood[7] reached a similar conclusion in his study of the way men and women are sentenced at Crown Court. He found that women were less likely to be sentenced to custody than men when legal and socio-demographic factors were taken into account.

Homicide

Despite recent claims to the contrary, women are at less risk of imprisonment than men even in cases of domestic homicide. An analysis of cases dealt with between 1984 and 1992 shows that 23% of females compared with only 4% of males indicted for homicide were acquitted on all charges. Of those found guilty, 80% of the women compared with 62% of the men were found guilty of the lesser charge of manslaughter; and more than two-thirds of the men convicted of manslaughter received a prison sentence compared with less than half the women. The fact remains, of course, that women are at much greater risk of domestic homicide.

Much of the controversy around recent cases has surrounded the use of the provocation defence, which is said to be less easy for women to deploy. Information on recent cases shows that 36% of the women convicted of manslaughter used this defence, and under a third (32%) of the men. By combining the percentages employing the provocation defence with the percentages of men and women convicted of manslaughter, we can infer that a defence of provocation was accepted in about 29% of cases involving female defendants compared with 20% of cases involving men.

Conclusions

This paper presents available research and statistics which call into question claims that the criminal justice system is systematically more severe towards women than men. If anything, the evidence points to more lenient treatment of women. Some caveats are needed, however. First, there is still insufficient evidence to be definitive: it could be that even when individual offence categories are examined, the statistics mask differences between men and women in the seriousness of their offending. In other words, it is possible that on the face of it, women are being treated leniently – but not as leniently as their less serious offending warrants. However, there is no statistical support for (or against) this hypothesis; and testing it would require analysis within very detailed offence categories.

Secondly, the question remains whether there is equal suitable provision for women as for men throughout the criminal justice system. There are grounds (albeit not fully researched) for believing that, in a system which deals very largely with male offenders, the needs of women offenders are not always effectively addressed. For example, an investigation by HM Inspectorate of Probation[8] found that a limited range of community penalties was available for women in some areas.

[7]   Hood, R *Race and sentencing: a study in the Crown Court* (1992) Oxford: Clarendon Press.

[8]   HM Inspectorate of Probation 'Report on women offenders and Probation Service provision' (1991) Home Office.

Finally, the paper has not considered whether there are disparities in treatment *within* gender. The likelihood that female offenders may overall receive more lenient treatment than males obviously does not rule out the possibility that individual women receive unusually harsh treatment.

[1:12] Hedderman, C and Gelsthorpe, L (eds) *Understanding the sentencing of women* HORS No 170 (1997) HMSO (at page vii):

Summary

A superficial examination of the criminal statistics suggests that, for virtually every type of offence, women are treated more leniently than men. This report describes the results of a two-part study of the sentencing of women. In Part I, sentencing patterns are explored in more detail using samples of men and women convicted of shoplifting, violence and drug offences in 1991. The results of this analysis, which was based on more than 13,000 cases, were then used to inform Part II of the study in which magistrates were interviewed about what they thought were the main influences on their decision-making.

Part I

Statistical tests were used, first, to examine whether an offender's sex appeared to affect the likelihood of a prison sentence once criminal and sentencing history was taken into account; and then, to model the likelihood of various other sentencing outcomes. The penalties that the model *predicted* each offender would receive were compared with the *actual* sentence men and women received.

Women shoplifters were less likely than comparable males to receive a prison sentence. They were also more likely to be sentenced to a community penalty or to be discharged. However, the results should not be interpreted as evidence of a general policy of leniency towards women shoplifters. They suggest rather that sentencers may be reluctant to fine a woman – possibly because they may be penalising her children rather than just herself. This results in many women receiving a discharge but others receiving community penalties which are rather more severe than fines.

Men and women stood an equal chance of going to prison for a first violent offence. However among repeat offenders women were less likely to receive a custodial sentence.

Women first offenders were significantly less likely than equivalent men to receive a prison sentence for a drug offence, but recidivists were equally likely to go to prison.

Among first and repeat offenders, women convicted of violence and drug offences were always more likely to be discharged and men more likely to be fined. But again, this seems to be less a consequence of a policy of leniency than a reluctance to impose one particular sentence – the fine – on women.

Part II

Nearly 200 magistrates were interviewed individually or in groups at five courts using a semi-structured questionnaire and a small sentencing exercise involving two stereotypical cases designed to bring out differences in their thinking about men and women offenders. These interviews, which were carried out between June and December 1995, took account of the findings in Part I.

Magistrates said they found it hard to compare the way they sentenced men and women because they dealt with women offenders far less frequently. However, they broadly distinguished between 'troubled' and 'troublesome' offenders, and tended to locate most women in the former category. In part this was because women tended to be first offenders, facing less serious charges than men and because they behaved more respectfully in court. In addition, magistrates tended to ascribe different motives to them. However, even when men were stealing bacon or coffee rather than alcohol or items to sell, they rarely engaged magistrates' sympathies.

Because they regarded women offenders as troubled, magistrates responded to their offending with measures (a discharge or probation) designed to assist them to lead law-abiding lives rather than punishing them. Fines were regarded as particularly unsuitable for women with children to care for and because they were seen as lacking 'independent means' for paying fines.

While magistrates stressed that 'the facts' of a case were most influential, many made references to 'common sense' or 'gut feelings' determining how they approached issues of motivation, body language or the offender's personal circumstances.

Appearance and demeanour in the courtroom were often commented on by magistrates. Although they denied that this influenced their decision-making, their comments concerning the importance of seeing the offender in court, and anecdotes about those who behaved inappropriately, suggested that these factors were influential.

(and from the conclusion at page 55):

Few people would seriously contest the notion that the criminal justice system should dispense justice fairly, regardless of sex, race, class or any other improper influence. No one is more aware of this need than the magistracy, who already spend a proportion of their training on such (human awareness) issues. But what exactly does fairness consist of in this context? In our view, it lies in consistency of approach rather than uniformity of outcome. In other words, it involves asking the same questions about factors such as employment status, family responsibilities and financial circumstances regardless of the offender's sex, rather than presuming that certain questions will only apply to males or females. From this perspective, to criticise sentencing practices on the grounds that the official statistics show different sentencing patterns would be unfair and, in any case, a futile exercise. These patterns may simply reflect the fact that the men and women who come to court differ across a wide range of factors which sentencers take into consideration when determining an appropriate sentence. In order to look at whether there is disparity in sentencing decisions, one needs therefore to look at the characteristics of those coming to court and at how sentencers say they weigh these and other factors in their decision-making. This research set out to do both these things.

In our view, neither the statistical analysis described by Dowds and Hedderman nor the interviews Gelsthorpe and Loucks carried out support the contention that differences in the way men and women are sentenced by magistrates is a consequence of anything as simple as deliberate discrimination. If that were true one would expect the statistical exercise to show women consistently receiving different sentences to men. But they do not. For example, they stood an equal chance of going to prison for a first violent offence, whereas among repeat offenders, women were less likely to go to prison. And among drug offenders, women recidivists were as likely as man to be imprisoned, but first timers were not.

In fact both parts of this study suggest that sentencing decisions are the outcome of the interactive effect of a number of factors. The most important of these is the nature of the offence. However, the offender's circumstances, the way other participants in the courtroom portray the offence and offender, the offender's appearance and behaviour in court, and how the members of each bench interact are also influential. Together these factors shape the court's perception of an offender as essentially troubled or troublesome, and this in turn determines whether help or punishment is at the heart of the court's response.

Women were more likely to be defined as troubled than men. From interviews with magistrates there seem to be a number of reasons for this. First, five out of every six of the offenders magistrates routinely deal with are male and most are under 30 years of age. Perhaps because of their sheer numbers, young men are likely to be seen as troublesome and are only very rarely viewed as troubled. As we know from the statistics, the majority of the women offenders magistrates try and sentence are charged with shoplifting. Again, from the interviews with magistrates in Part II of this study, we know that magistrates generally believe that such women steal through need rather than greed, they often have sole care of young children, and they are usually living on benefits or are dependent on a partner's income. So how are these perceptions of women translated into sentencing? The most striking consequence is that, as the analyses presented in Part I show, magistrates are reluctant to fine women. Even if this difference was found to be inspired by a desire not to financially penalise a woman's family, it carries the risk that, skipping a step on the sentencing ladder this time round, will lead to an even more severe sentence being imposed in the event of a subsequent conviction. To use probation where a fine would have been appropriate is also an ineffective use of resources (Moxon et al., 1990).

Both parts of the study show that magistrates appear to favour probation or discharges for women. The interviews carried out in Part II suggest that these measures are used with the intention of assisting rather than punishing women. Unless sending women to prison was unavoidable because of the seriousness of their offending, it was usually ruled out on the grounds that it would adversely affect their children.

We know from previous research that female offenders do indeed describe themselves as stealing through need and having responsibility for dependent children (see, for example, Carlen 1988 and Morris et al., 1995). However, neither those studies nor the current research show whether they differ from men in either respect. Examination of court records to see if male and female offenders are matched in these ways has proved difficult because records do not hold such information consistently. This is certainly an issue worth examining in future research, however, as the magistrates interviewed in Part II of this study revealed that, when considering mitigation, they were not simply responding to the fact that women and men appeared in different circumstances. Thus, for example, having family responsibilities was less central to decisions about male offenders, and being employed carried less weight when the offender was a woman. Even when a man is considered to be more troubled than troublesome, this does not necessarily have the same consequences as for a woman. On the occasions when magistrates believed that male offenders merited assistance, this tended to take the form of employment training through Community Service Orders or help with alcohol or drug addiction. These findings are strikingly similar to those reported by Farrington and Morris (1983) and Mary Eaton (1983, 1986). A key difference is that they reflect sentencing in the mid-1990s rather than the mid-1980s and occur in a period when a great deal of attention has been given to notions of fairness and justice and to race and gender issues in the delivery of justice.

Turning to the offender in the courtroom, while some magistrates recognised that body language is open to misinterpretation, most stressed the importance of seeing the offender in court, and a number were confident that they would not themselves misinterpret nonverbal cues. The research also indicated that, based on perceptions of body language and appearance, men – ethnic minority men in particular – may come across as having less respect for the court, while women are generally perceived to be inexperienced, deferential and (therefore) honest.

The internal politics of the courtroom also seem to shape magistrates' decision-making. The same information could be viewed quite differently according to which courtroom player provided it – most weight was accorded to information from prosecutors or the Clerk, who were regarded by magistrates as being impartial. Not only defence solicitors but probation officers were seen as siding with the offender.

Interaction between magistrates was also important, with experience weighing more heavily than training. Moreover, virtually all the magistrates mentioned 'common sense' or 'gut feelings' at some stage of their assessment as to who was respectful or rebellious, remorseful or rancorous; and 'common sense' was what magistrates used to explain any decision that seemed to have no other explanation or, at least, no easily expressed explanation. Yet notions of what is 'common sense' and what are reliable indicators of honesty and remorse differed among magistrates.

Taken as a whole, these findings suggest that there remains a risk that some magistrates will resort to their 'common sense' (and a gendered 'common-sense' at that) as the best arbiter of what is right, despite the fact that new magistrates receive training designed to inform them of the inherent dangers of making decisions on the basis of stereotypes and on the dangers of relying on non-verbal cues.

The difficulty to be addressed is one of finding ways to challenge stereotypical pictures of men and women, without ignoring the fact that they often (but *not* always) do have different needs and responsibilities (and these are often precisely the needs and responsibilities which fuel the stereotypes). It may also be that the time to recognise such differences is in the shape and content of particular sentences rather than in the choice between different levels of sentence, but discussion of this is beyond our remit. A number of changes may be helpful here:
- Increased emphasis on gender issues in training to counteract the fact that so many magistrates have comparatively little experience of dealing with women in the courtroom. This is probably best accomplished through the 'human awareness' element of magistrates' training which encourages them to reflect on how cultural and gender specific stereotypes inform their practices and perceptions

in the courtroom in ways which could lead to unfair sentencing. Currently, such training tends to focus on race issues and it would be unfortunate if combining race and gender in this way masked the importance of either issue. it is also important to note that while 'human awareness' training is popular, it does not appear to have been subject to any large scale or systematic evaluation.

- Training on gender (and race) should be made available to *all* magistrates rather than to new magistrates alone so as to ensure that resistant or reluctant magistrates are exposed to the issues as a matter of routine.
- Where magistrates may feel that their sentencing options are constrained by a (male of female) offender's childcare responsibilities, the Probation Service should use PSRs to draw attention to the fact that suitable childcare arrangements can be made.
- Increased feedback on sentencing patterns in each court – particularly patterns relating to men and women – may also assist magistrates in the general task of achieving consistency in approach.

Finally, we would suggest that there are at least three questions which require further exploration and discussion:
- to what extent does training help to address the tendency to use gender-stereotyping in sentencing?
- to what extent do gender, race and other factors have an interactive effect on sentencing?
- are the decisions of professional sentencers subject to the same influences as those of lay magistrates?

[1:13]   HM Inspectorate of Prisons (England and Wales) *Women in Prison: a Thematic Review* (1997) (at page 16):

Summary

2.20 The results of our survey broadly confirm past research. The majority of women in prison:
- have never been in prison before, are mothers of children aged under 16, the care of whom, in a large number of cases, is unsettled, have accommodation problems, have poor employment and education histories.

2.21 Many report that they:
- have suffered physical and sexual abuse, frequently at the hands of men close to them, are serious drug misusers with long histories of poly-substance abuse, have self harmed or attempted suicide.

2.22 These are striking findings about the nature of the women's prison population.
- They have evident policy and practice implications for the Prison Service.

And from the conclusion (page 55):

Information about women prisoners should be the starting point for policy and planned use of resources. There should be an on-going assessment of the needs of women prisoners which can be identified from their characteristics.

[1:14] Hood, R, Shute, S, and Seemungal, F *Ethnic Minorities in the Criminal Courts: Perceptions of Fairness and Equality of Treatment* (2003) Lord Chancellor's Department Research Series No 2/03

Executive Summary

...

A substantial number (778) of ethnic minority and (for comparative purposes) white defendants were interviewed at the conclusion of the criminal proceedings against them. The study was conducted at both the Crown Court and magistrates' courts in three urban areas with high concentrations of ethnic minority citizens – Manchester, Birmingham, and South-East London. In addition, 150 witnesses were interviewed at the same courts, as well as 112 solicitors and barristers, 125 magistrates, 61 court staff, and 26 judges in the Crown Court. Those working in the courts were asked about their perceptions of how the courts deal with persons from ethnic minorities, and in particular whether this has changed over time. Altogether, 1,252 people were interviewed and the proceedings in more than 500 cases were observed.

Respondents were asked to classify their ethnicity according to the categories used in the national census of 2001 but, so as to make the findings comparable with official data on race and criminal justice, persons have, for most purposes, been classified as black, Asian or white.

It is important to emphasise that this is a study of how defendants and witnesses *interpreted* their experiences in the criminal courts. It is not an *objective* study of whether or not racial discrimination had actually taken place.

The Defendants' Perspective:

- Most of the defendants who were interviewed had just been convicted and sentenced, many to imprisonment, so their feelings may well have been running high. Very few had been acquitted. The sample therefore probably over-represented the kind of defendant who might be most likely to complain of unfair or racially biased treatment. The majority were interviewed by ethnic minority researchers. Defendants were given several opportunities to express any concerns about racial bias. For these reasons it is likely that the findings reflect 'a worst case scenario.'
- Leaving aside complaints which turned out <u>not</u> to be directed at the courts (i.e. mainly at the police and to a lesser extent the Crown Prosecution Service), the proportion of defendants who said their treatment had been unfair in court was *nearly a third* (31 per cent) in the Crown Court, with little difference between the ethnic minority and white defendants (33 per cent of black, 27 per cent of Asian and 29 per cent of white defendants).
- In the magistrates' courts *a quarter* of defendants (26 per cent) said they felt unfairly treated, a rather higher proportion among ethnic minority than among white defendants (26 per cent of black, 31 per cent of Asian and 19 per cent of white defendants).
- However, when ethnic minority defendants were asked whether they thought that their unfair treatment in court had *anything to do with their ethnicity*, a lower proportion said definitely 'YES': *one in five* of black defendants in the Crown Court and *one in ten* in the magistrates' courts, and *one in eight* Asian defendants in both the Crown Court and the magistrates' courts.

- Most of the defendants' complaints about racial bias concerned sentences perceived to be more severe than those they thought would have been imposed on a similarly placed white defendant. Very few perceived explicit racial bias in the conduct or attitude of judges or magistrates – only *three per cent* in the Crown Court and *one per cent* in the magistrates' courts. The majority thought the remarks made when their sentence had been imposed had been fair, and no complaints were made about racist remarks from the Bench.
- Neither age, country of birth, nor previous court appearances affected the propensity of defendants to complain of racial bias. But there were substantial variations between the court areas. These were not explained by the proportion sentenced to custody or the proportion of ethnic minority staff employed in the particular court.

The Witnesses' Perspective:
- *Sixteen per cent* of witnesses in the Crown Court complained of unfair treatment, almost the same proportion amongst black, white and Asian witnesses. But *none* of the 68 ethnic minority witnesses complained of *racial* bias. There were more complaints (mostly about inconvenience and feeling intimidated) in the magistrates' courts: one in five of white and Asian and 45 per cent of black witnesses; but *only seven per cent* of the 41 ethnic minority witnesses perceived the unfairness to have been *racially* motivated.
- *None* of the witnesses in either court complained of ill treatment by a judge or magistrate.

Issues of Confidence:
- In the Crown Court, black (38 per cent) and Asian defendants (34 per cent) were just as likely as white defendants (40 per cent) to say that they would *not* expect to be fairly treated next time they came to court. In the magistrates' courts, a higher proportion of black (39 per cent) and Asian (35 per cent) than white defendants (15%) said this.
- However, a much smaller proportion of all black and Asian defendants (seven per cent in the Crown Court and nine per cent in the magistrates' courts) believed they would be disadvantaged in the future *because of their ethnic origin*.
- Nevertheless, a considerably higher proportion of black (44 per cent in the Crown Court; 49 per cent in the magistrates' courts) than either Asian (33 per cent and 26 per cent) or white defendants (30 per cent and 16 per cent) believed that generally there was *not always* equal treatment of ethnic minority defendants by the courts.

The Perspective of Informed Observers – Court Officials and Lawyers:
- Most white (98 per cent) and Asian (71 per cent) clerks and ushers and white (69 per cent) and Asian (63 per cent) lawyers thought that there was nowadays *always* equal treatment of ethnic minorities by the courts. But the proportion was much lower among the black lawyers (43 per cent) and black staff (28 per cent).
- A higher proportion of black (30 per cent) and either white (13 per cent) or Asian (11 per cent) lawyers said they had personally witnessed incidents in court that they regarded as 'racist.'

The Judicial and Magisterial Perspective:
- All the judges and two-thirds of the magistrates interviewed had received training in ethnic awareness. Only two of the 26 judges and three of the 125 magistrates

said that it had 'added nothing' or been 'unhelpful.' Yet only a few (2 judges and 11 magistrates) thought there was a need for *further* such training.

A Cultural Change?

- Judges mentioned that judicial attitudes and behaviour towards ethnic minority defendants had changed markedly in recent years for the better, and magistrates also reported a substantial decline in the frequency of racially inappropriate remarks. Many lawyers reported that racial bias or inappropriate language in court was becoming 'a thing of the past.'
- These positive findings, taken together with the much lower than expected proportion of defendants complaining of racial bias, may be a reflection of both general social improvements in the treatment of ethnic minorities and the specific efforts begun by the Lord Chancellor's Department in the early 1990s to heighten the awareness of all involved in the system of the need to be aware of, and guard against, racial bias.

What Still Needs to be Done?

- Although this study has revealed that the perceptions of racial bias amongst ethnic minority persons who appear before the criminal courts appear to be less widely held than in the past, the findings should not lead to complacency. The fact that one in five black and one in eight Asian defendants definitely perceived racial bias in the Crown Court, and at least one in ten in the magistrates courts, combined with the fact that black lawyers and staff were more likely to perceive racial bias than others, is sufficient cause to continue the efforts towards eliminating the vestiges of perceived unequal treatment.
- Perceptions of racial bias, more frequently held by black defendants in the Crown Court, may well arise from a belief that the disproportionately large number of black people caught up by the criminal justice and prison systems must, at least to some extent, be a reflection of racism. Every effort therefore should be made when passing sentence to demonstrate and convince defendants that no element of racial stereotyping or bias has entered into the decision.
- Among black defendants and lawyers in particular there was a belief that the authority and legitimacy of the courts, and confidence in them, would be strengthened if more personnel from ethnic minorities were seen to be playing a part in the administration of criminal justice. Indeed, in the Crown Court 31 per cent ethnic minority defendants, and in the magistrates' courts 48 per cent, said they would like more people from ethnic minorities sitting in judgment and amongst the staff of the courts. Many judges shared this view that more could be done to avoid the impression of the courts as 'white dominated institutions.'
- It should be emphasised that this research has been directed at revealing *perceptions of and beliefs about* equal treatment held by ethnic minorities who have found themselves subject to the jurisdiction of the criminal courts. It has shown that the main concern amongst the *minority* who perceived racial bias in their treatment arose from their view that the sentence imposed was more severe than a similarly placed white defendant would have received. Very few complained that they had been subjected by any court official to racist language or conduct. However, given the changing circumstances since an objective study of sentencing practices in the West Midlands in 1989 was carried out (Roger Hood, *Race and Sentencing* 1992), it is not possible to say whether that perception of differential racially biased sentencing has any basis in objective evidence.

- The findings of this study may go some way to dispelling the view that most minority ethnic defendants believe that their treatment by the courts has been racially biased. But, if it could be shown that the 'cultural change' which this study has identified has had a real impact on eliminating differential sentencing of white and ethnic minority defendants, this would further encourage the confidence of ethnic minorities in the criminal courts.

CHAPTER TWO

The Police

In our case study, you rang the ambulance service to tell them that you had found an injured woman in the street. The ambulance crew radioed for the police to attend. This is a fairly typical scenario: in the majority of cases the police rely heavily on members of the public, and in particular on victims, to tell them about crimes. Between 75% and 90% of offences are brought to the attention of the police by victims, bystanders or other members of the public (see Phillips and Brown (1998) for a study of the arrest population in police stations). The preliminary decision of the victim to report a crime may be influenced by many factors, as was mentioned in Chapter One.

The police officer who arrives on the scene has to make several decisions. Wide discretionary powers are exercised by those at the very lowest level in the organisation: in the vast majority of cases, if a police officer chooses not to act, not to intervene, this decision will not be subject to any review. Police officers decide whether to record a crime, whether to arrest someone, whether to initiate a prosecution, whether to release a suspect on bail, whether informally to warn or formally to caution an offender. Much fieldwork has been carried out in recent years to assess 'police culture' and policing in practice. A review of some of this research, and an analysis of the efficacy of the statutory and common law limits on this discretion, will be explored later in this chapter (see also Bowling and Foster (2002)), but it may be useful to start by looking briefly at the accountability of the police in constitutional terms.

(i) Police accountability

The police as we know them are a modern development. Whether you conclude that they have evolved out of community-based consensus policing, or rather as agents of state control, depends on your interpretation of history. Not until the late eighteenth century did the need for a paid police force become widely accepted. The Metropolitan Police Act 1829 gave London its first police force, nicknamed 'Peelers' or 'Bobbies' after Robert Peel, the Home Secretary. In 1856 it became compulsory for every county to have a police force. Today there are still 43 separate police forces in England and Wales. Their function continually evolves: concepts such as community policing, zero-tolerance policing, intelligence-led policing, problem-oriented policing reflect changing police priorities, but our concern here is the governance of the police.

Their 'independence' has traditionally been valued as reflecting the fact that the police are not an arm of government. Strong 'security police' are a feature of dictatorships and totalitarian states; democratic government is seen to require something less centrally controlled. Yet the downside of this independence may be that the police are both inadequately powerful and inadequately accountable. Today they are governed by a curious tripartite structure – what Laws LJ called (in *R v DPP, ex p Duckenfield* [1999] 2 All ER 873) the 'interlocking roles' of three key players: chief constable, police authority and the Home Secretary.

The Police Act 1996 **[2:1]** provides that a police force is under the direction and control of the chief constable. Each police district has a police authority comprising local councillors, magistrates and 'independent members'. The authority appoints the chief constable and has a duty under section 6 of the Act to 'secure the maintenance of an efficient and effective'[1] force for its district. The elected councillor element on police authorities has been reduced from two-thirds to 'a number which is greater by one' than half, reflecting the increasingly centralised control. Five members, or up to one-third of the authority, are 'independent', but appointed from a short-list prepared by the Secretary of State. The Audit Commission's 1994 **[2:2]** analysis of police accountability remains useful, but remember the increased centralisation that has followed on from this.

The highly charged political atmosphere of the miners' strike in the early 1980s, along with modern policing techniques, have led to the creation of such bodies as the National Criminal Intelligence Service (NCIS) and the National Crime Squad (see the Police Act 1997). Increased centralisation of police powers was also recognised in sections 136–141 of the Criminal Justice and Public Order Act 1994, which extended arrangements for police officers to exercise their powers outside their home jurisdictions. More recently, the Police Reform Act 2002 inserted a new section 36A into the Police Act 1996, requiring the Home Secretary to prepare a National Policing Plan and, if necessary, to issue a code of practice for the purpose of promoting the efficiency of police forces. Under section 3 he may require inspections of a police force or of the NCIS.

---

[1]   A subtle change from the words 'adequate and efficient' in the Police Act 1964.

The weakness (some would argue the non-existence) of local accountability was made clear as long ago as the 1989, in the decision in *R v Secretary of State for the Home Department, ex p Northumbria Police Authority* [2:3], where the Court of Appeal held that it was lawful for the Home Secretary to supply equipment to a police force without the approval of the police authority. The police authority today appears only to have as much authority as will be tolerated by the chief constable and the Home Secretary. Yet what is the best way forward? If chief constables are free from control by local or central government, to whom are they accountable? Do we want a national police force?

Another test of police accountability is the way in which complaints are dealt with. If, as it appears, the police are preoccupied with catching criminals (or, to go back to Packer [1:6], if they give a high priority to crime control at the expense of due process), it is vital that an internal disciplinary procedure effectively fights malpractice. The Police Act 1964 required chief officers of police to supervise all serious complaints against the police made by members of the public, and to cause them to be investigated. This procedure was widely criticised, largely for having no independent elements in the investigation process. The Police and Criminal Evidence Act 1984 (commonly known as PACE) replaced the Police Complaints Board with the Police Complaints Authority, in order that internal police investigations should be externally supervised. Nevertheless, public disquiet with a system that is both secret and not wholly independent of the police, and whereby many police officers are able to take early retirement when facing the prospect of disciplinary action, continued.

The Home Affairs Select Committee Inquiry into Police Disciplinary and Complaints Procedures (1998) concluded, depressingly, that 'police complaints and disciplinary procedures are inadequate both to ensure effective management and to command public confidence'. New police discipline procedures took effect in April 1999, incorporating: the civil standard of proof; a 'fast-track' dismissal system for the most serious cases; and measures to prevent the misuse of retirements 'on medical grounds' to evade disciplinary action. This has been followed with the creation, by the Police Reform Act 2002, of a new 'independent' Police Complaints Commission, which will replace the Police Complaints Authority in April 2004. The Home Office Statistical Bulletin publishes annual statistics on police complaints and (in)discipline (see HO Statistical Bulletin 04/03).

Complainants who prefer to bring civil proceedings against the police have found this route equally problematic. Whilst police authorities are vicariously liable for the wrongful actions of police constables, and legal aid may be available for such proceedings, civil proceedings do nothing to reprimand the individual police officer. And even here, as *Hill v Chief Constable of West Yorkshire* [2:4] revealed, the courts remain reluctant to fetter police discretion in policing matters.

There the House of Lords held that the police did not owe a general duty of care to individual members of the public to apprehend an unknown criminal. This attitude may change: in *Osman v United Kingdom* (1998) 29 EHRR 245 the European Court of Human Rights stated that police immunity from negligence claims was only one aspect of the public interest. Note that each of the applicants was awarded £10,000 by way of compensation. Rather than extract the decision itself, the materials here **[2:5] [2:6]** reveal two very different interpretations of the European Court of Human Rights' decision.

(ii)   Recording and enforcing crime

In theory, all laws are enforced, but in practice clearly some are enforced more than others. With limited operational resources, the police are selective in which crimes they pursue. Thus, for example, the police give a fairly low priority to enforcing laws about obscenity – but without going so far as to *refuse* to act in this area – largely because the law itself is unsatisfactory, and the police choose not to waste their resources in an area where they are particularly ineffective. In other areas, the police may choose not to enforce laws which they perceive to be outdated. In effect, this gives them a power to decriminalise. A case brought over 30 years ago is still useful in illustrating the extent of police discretion **[2:7]**. Although he lost several cases, Blackburn achieved a certain publicity for his causes by initiating judicial review proceedings, and this 'political' side-effect of judicial review may sometimes be as useful to applicants as the decision itself. A more recent example is *R v Chief Constable of Sussex, ex p International Trader's Ferry Ltd* [1999] 2 AC 418, in which exporters of live animals were unsuccessful in their attempts to force the police to give them greater police protection. The case was, in the words of Lord Nolan, 'an acceptance of the plain fact that there are limits to the extent to which the police can control unlawful violence in any given situation. If those limits are felt to be too narrow, the remedy lies in increasing the resources of the police. It does not lie in the imposition of further restrictions upon the discretion which the law allows to a chief constable to decide upon the best use of the resources which are in fact available to him'.

To revert to the story with which this book began, PC Jane Green, the police officer called to the scene where the woman is found bleeding in the street, has to decide whether to record this as a crime. Here, she will undoubtedly record the incident. Individual police officers affect crime statistics by their decision to record an incident as an offence or not. A reported theft may be recorded as an incidence of lost property, or not recorded at all. Maybe the police officer does not believe the person who is reporting the crime, or perhaps it happened a long time ago or is considered insufficiently serious. A broken window might be an accident, but it might be recorded as criminal damage or even attempted burglary. The divergence between actual, reported and recorded crime was noted in Chapter One.

What guidance does the police officer have? The police have a statutory obligation to record 'notifiable offences', which broadly cover the most serious offences. The study by Farrington and Dowds [2:8] shows how different police practices can have astonishing results. They established that the high official crime rate in Nottingham in the 1980s resulted largely from differential police recording of crimes. Although much has been done to try to standardise the rules for the recording of crimes by the police – there must be prima facie evidence, in the eyes of the police, that a notifiable offence has been committed, and the case must be sufficiently serious – even the National Crime Reporting Standard of April 2002 is unlikely to iron out regional differences. As the figures are increasingly used as measures of police performance, and indeed are used to inform the distribution of resources, a certain degree of scepticism in your approach to these figures may be warranted.

Once reported and recorded, the likelihood of an offender being caught will be affected by the decision as to how much time and money is spent on an inquiry. Thus, in our case study, if resources allow, a police car will immediately drive around looking for a suspect escaping the scene of the crime. A suspect carrying a knife and wearing bloodied clothes, arrested on the day of the incident, will provide more compelling evidence than one arrested three days later.

(iii) Police powers

The statutory powers of the police in the investigation of crime were largely codified by the Police and Criminal Evidence Act 1984 (PACE) [2:9], which was enacted as a result of the 1981 Report of the Royal Commission on Criminal Procedure. Whilst this has achieved some uniformity in police practice, widespread powers have been given to the police by subsequent Acts, such as the Public Order Act 1986, the Criminal Justice and Public Order Act (CJPOA) 1994 [2:10] and the Proceeds of Crime Act 2002. Thus, PACE cannot be seen as the only code of police powers.

PACE also authorised the Secretary of State to issue codes of practice in connection with the exercise by police officers of their various statutory duties. These cover such areas as the powers of stop and search and the searching of premises. The Criminal Justice Bill 2002 abolishes the necessity for revisions of the codes to be approved by an affirmative resolution of both Houses of Parliament: in future they will be simply laid before Parliament. Revised codes were brought into force in 1991 and 1995 to take account of new police powers contained in the CJPOA 1994. The latest revisions came into force in

April 2003. By way of example, part of Code C (Code of Practice for the Detention, Treatment and Questioning of Persons by Police Officers) is included at **[2:11]**. Brown **[2:12]** reviewed the research into the first ten years of life with PACE, concluding that PACE 'has not yet produced a system in balance'. Bucke and Brown **[2:13]** researched the 1995 changes: note in particular their comments on the quality of legal advice. Cape **[2:14]** explores the changing relationship between suspects and the police as a result of the 2003 changes (and see Zander (2003)).

There has been considerable debate not only about the constitutional status of these codes, but about the capacity of legal rules to influence police conduct. Chapter Seven includes a discussion of the trial judge's discretion to exclude evidence which was unfairly obtained. Proof of a breach of a code of practice does not necessarily lead to the exclusion of the evidence. In *Christou* **[7:9]** – where the Court of Appeal held that the appellants' admissions had been rightly admitted in evidence even though they had not been cautioned or informed of their rights – was the court correct in concluding that the relevant code was 'simply not intended to apply in such a context'? In *Khan* **[7:11]** the House of Lords allowed the bugging of private homes in order to facilitate the detection of serious crime. Are these decisions inconsistent with the right to privacy guaranteed by article 8 of the European Convention on Human Rights **[1:9]** or are they legitimate policing tactics 'for the prevention of disorder or crime'? Ashworth **[2.15]** seeks to test the justifications for the use of deceptive practices by the police. The decision of the European Court of Human Rights in *Teixeira de Castro v Portugal* (1998) 28 EHRR 101 has caused many lawyers to re-assess police practices. A recent application of this case – *R v Loosely; A-G's Reference No 3 of 2000* (2002) **[2:16]** – is extracted not from the full judgment but from the *Criminal Law Review* summary. Covert and intrusive surveillance is now governed by Part III of the Police Act 1997 and the Regulation of Investigatory Powers Act 2000, which distinguishes 'directed surveillance', 'intrusive surveillance' and the use of covert human intelligence sources. The Office of Surveillance Commissioners oversees this hugely important but largely invisible area of police activity: see Chief Surveillance Commissioner (2002) and www.surveillancecommissioners.gov.uk.

Another device used to control police discretion is Home Office circulars, used to advise all chief constables as to how particular policing tasks be performed. *R v Secretary of State for the Home Department, ex p Northumbria Police Authority* **[2:3]** concerned a circular on the use of plastic bullets; and until 1999 the practice of cautioning was governed solely by Home Office circulars. It is important to recognise that such circulars do not have the force of law. Nearly 20 years ago, Baldwin and Houghton (1986) painted a highly critical picture of the growth of 'government by informal decree'. If the 'informal decree' is not obeyed, no sanction for disobedience necessarily follows. Do such documents have any effect on individual police officers? 'Police culture' is not easily changed, certainly not just by a new document from the Home Office.

Before 1984, there were a variety of laws granting powers of stop and search. Most notorious was the Vagrancy Act 1824, which gave parish constables powers to arrest vagabonds, trespassers and loiterers. This 'sus' law was repealed in 1981, largely as a result of increasing evidence that it was being used disproportionately towards black people. The dangers of bias and prejudice within the system are clear – if police officers expect more trouble from certain individuals, the expectation can become self-fulfilling; if more attention is given to a particular section of the community, it is hardly surprising if more offences are detected amongst that group. Also, innocent people within that group will be more frequently stopped and searched. Part I of PACE gave the police wide powers to stop and search, and to carry out road-checks, both of which are forms of detention short of arrest. Section 60 of CJPOA 1994 **[2:10]** gave the police a wide new power to stop and search for offensive weapons in anticipation of violence – officers do not need to have grounds for suspicion against an individual before searching him under this power: a huge discretion to be exercised by junior officers out of the sight of senior officers. Clause 1 of the Criminal Justice Bill 2002 further extends the powers to stop and search by widening the definition of prohibited articles.

Many police powers are dependent upon proof of 'reasonable suspicion'. The classic definition of suspicion is that of Lord Devlin in *Hussein v Choong Fook Kam* [1970] AC 942: 'Suspicion in its ordinary meaning is a state of conjecture or surmise where proof is lacking: I suspect but I cannot prove'. The Royal Commission on Criminal Procedure (1981) concluded that it would be impracticable to formulate standards of reasonable suspicion in a statute or code of practice. It concluded (at page 29) that the requirements of notifying reasons, making records and the monitoring of such records by superior officers would be the most effective way of reducing the risk of random action. For a less complacent view, see Clayton and Tomlinson's comments on the case of *Castorina v Chief Constable of Surrey* [1980] NLJR 180: 'If the police are justified in arresting a middle-aged woman of good character on such flimsy grounds, without even questioning her as to her alibi or possible motives, then the law provides very scant protection for those suspected of crime' (at page 26).

A concept so vague as 'reasonable suspicion' is almost impossible to challenge. Constables are under a duty, imposed by section 3 of PACE, to make comprehensive records of searches, and chief constables are obliged to report annually on how many, and what kinds of, stops and searches have been carried out in their force areas. Yet these figures are not an accurate record of how many people are being stopped, since the records only apply to those who have been searched after having been 'detained'. The Macpherson Report (1999) recommended that all stops should be recorded, but, after consulting widely on the suggestion, the government decided that this would be an unjustifiable waste of limited resources. Nowadays there is concern that, because the exercise of stop-and-search powers can be used as a measure of a constable's industry, the pressure on officers to stop and search poorer/disadvantaged people – rather than the more affluent, who are less likely to be out in the street – will increase.

A detailed analysis of the powers of entry, search and seizure (Part II of PACE), the powers of arrest (Part III), the powers of detention (Part IV) and the powers of questioning and treatment of persons by the police (Part V) is beyond the scope of this book. However, let us apply the rules to our story. It seemed obvious to the ambulance crew that the victim had suffered four or five knife wounds to various parts of her upper body, arms and chest, which necessitated many stitches and a stay in hospital. PC Green was not able to carry out a detailed interview since the ambulance crew wanted to take the woman straight to hospital, but she did establish that the woman's name is Rosa Bottles. She was drinking in the Black Bull pub with a group of friends, and at closing time there had been a fight. She mentions a few names, and says it was Gerry Good who stabbed her. PC Green goes straight to the pub, and asks the landlord, who is just going to bed, some questions. Meanwhile, two other officers in a police car are looking for Gerry Good. However, neither the landlord nor Rosa's friends seem to have witnessed the stabbing. They seem to agree that Rosa and Gerry, two regulars at the pub, had had an argument, and that Gerry had been seen following Rosa home in a fury. Rosa has a reputation as a heavy drinker, and as a 'tough cookie' capable of looking after herself.

The next day the police are able to interview Rosa at length in hospital. They also find Gerry Good, who spent the night with friends. Rather than ask him questions, they arrest him straight away and take him to the police station for questioning. Since wounding is an arrestable offence (see section 24 of PACE [2:9]), they can arrest him without a warrant. They inform him that he is under arrest on suspicion of having committed a wounding. He may be searched on arrest only as authorised within section 17 of PACE [2:9]. If the police are still looking for the knife used in the attack, they may well wish to search Gerry's home under section 18 or 32 [2:9]. If so, since Gerry has not been at his home for some hours, the police officers should obtain authority from an officer of the rank of inspector or above before entering his house.

If Gerry were wanted for a minor non-arrestable offence, the police would have to explain their grounds for arrest, within the terms of section 25 of PACE [2:9]. This power, like the power to stop and search, is drafted in such vague terms that it is very difficult to challenge, and attempts through the courts to challenge the legality of arrests are rarely successful.

What sort of conversation will go on in the police car? There has been some concern, especially since the introduction of taped interviews at police stations, about so-called 'car-seat' confessions. In Moston and Stephenson's study **[2:16]** arresting officers reported having interviewed suspects before arrival at the station in 8% of cases in the sample. In addition, 31% of suspects were reported to have been questioned before their arrest. They saw strong arguments in favour of the provision of portable tape recorders, and the Royal Commission (1993) recommended that a PACE code of practice should cover what is and is not permissible between the time of arrest and arrival at the police station. Brown, Ellis and Larcombe **[2:17]** found that, although the rewording of Code of Practice C in 1991 to discourage interviews outside police stations had had some effect, such interviews still took place in 10% of cases.

As soon as Gerry is brought to the police station, the police must open a custody record. However, the reception area at the police station is a busy, sometimes chaotic, place and he may have to wait before being booked in. The custody officer, a sergeant, is responsible for the accuracy and completeness of the custody record, and all entries must be timed and signed by the maker. It is the custody officer who has the main responsibility for upholding the suspect's rights. Is it appropriate that this person should be a serving police officer? When Gerry eventually leaves the police station, he (or his solicitor) will be given a copy of the custody record if he requests it.

The custody officer will inform Gerry of his rights: he has the right to consult a solicitor; the right to ask the police to notify his arrest to a relative or other named person likely to take an interest in his or her welfare; and the right to consult the PACE codes of practice. Sanders and Young (2000) comment that giving the police the job of 'triggering' legal advice appears to be a major obstacle to the success of the scheme: 'to make the police the main gatekeepers to these rights is plainly illogical' (at page 228). The right to legal advice is, in the words of the Court of Appeal in *Samuel* [1988] QB 615, clear and unambiguous, but it is only effective if the legal profession provides the advice adequately, and we will return to this subject in Chapter Five.

The arrangements for supervising police inquiries were criticised by the Royal Commission on Criminal Justice (1993). In a research study conducted for the Royal Commission, Baldwin and Moloney **[2:19]** found that supervision as such was rare in most of the cases they studied. In the general run of cases, supervision and investigation were inextricably blurred, with supervising officers doing much of the interviewing. As Maguire and Norris (1993) comment, 'In a sense, the actual extent of malpractice, even if it is minuscule, is irrelevant ... what is important is the potential for it to occur, should any officer or group of officers fail to do their job properly, and the soundness of any system designed to prevent it' (at page 3). The Royal Commission (1993) concluded that a new approach to supervision is needed throughout the police service, with improved training in the supervision of inquiries at all levels. The need for close quality control over investigations and effective supervision remains: see Brown [2:12].

The length of time that a suspect can be held in custody without charge is strictly regulated by Part IV of PACE. For lesser offences, the period must not exceed 24 hours. A person suspected of committing a serious arrestable offence can be detained for up to 96 hours without charge, but only beyond 36 hours where a warrant is obtained from a magistrate. A review by the custody officer to check whether the criteria for detention are still satisfied must be made at regular intervals: six hours after initial detention and then at least every nine hours. In any 24-hour period a detained person must be allowed a continuous period of at least eight hours for rest, free from questioning, travel or other interruption arising out of the investigation concerned. Police cells accommodating detainees must be adequately lit, heated, cleaned and ventilated (see Code C: The Detention, Treatment and Questioning of Persons by Police Officers [2:11]). Access to toilet facilities must be provided, as well as suitable food and clothing. Despite these provisions, the student must remember that police cells and custody blocks are often dismal places.

Gerry tells the custody officer that he wants to see his solicitor, and so the custody officer rings Shaw and Co, the solicitors who have represented him in the past, and they agree to send someone. There is often no facility for private telephone calls by suspects. Ian Brown, a legally unqualified clerk from Shaw and Co, arrives soon after one o'clock. In a private interview, Gerry admits that he was in the Black Bull that night, that he had been involved in a fight, but that he hadn't used a knife and hadn't seen anyone else use one either. At three o'clock Gerry is formally interviewed by a different police officer, since the arresting officer has now gone off duty. Ian Brown is present throughout, but says nothing. Detailed rules governing the questioning of persons held in custody are set out in Code C [2:11]. The suspect must be cautioned before any questions are put for the purpose of obtaining evidence. The current caution says:

> 'You do not have to say anything, but it may harm your defence if you do not mention, when questioned, something which you later rely on in court. Anything you say may be given in evidence.'

False confessions and police misconduct are two of the main causes of miscarriages of justice, and much of the Report of the Royal Commission of Criminal Justice (1993) looked at ways to improve safeguards inside the police station. A whole chapter was given over to the 'right of silence' and confession evidence. The discussion of the right to silence is reproduced at [2:20]. The Royal Commission concluded that, because it is the less experienced and more vulnerable suspects against whom the threat of adverse comment at trial would be likely to be more damaging, there should be no adverse comments if they do not answer police questions. In reality, few suspects exercise their right to silence, and Leng's research (1994) found no evidence that the abolition of the right to silence would lead to more convictions. Zuckerman (1994) doubted that the right to silence ever protected the weak or confused: they have always been more likely to succumb to police demands for answers despite the right. Sections 34–39 of the CJPOA 1994 **[2:10]** controversially changed the law on the right to silence, setting out the circumstances when the court or the jury may draw adverse inferences from the fact that a person did not give evidence at his trial or answer questions put to him by the police. In response to the European Court of Human Rights decision in *Murray v United Kingdom* (1996) 22 EHRR 29, section 58 of the Youth Justice and Criminal Evidence Act 1999 prevents such an inference being drawn against a silent suspect who has not yet consulted a solicitor.

An important challenge to the new rules was made in the case of the Condrons, who were convicted of drug-related offences following a direction by the trial judge stating that the jury had the option of drawing an adverse inference from silence during police interviews. Their solicitor, believing them to be suffering from heroin withdrawal symptoms, had advised them to say nothing. They were found guilty and whilst the Court of Appeal in *Condron* [1997] 1 Cr App Rep 185 considered the judge's direction to be flawed, it did not find the conviction to be unsafe. However, Condron complained to the European Court of Human Rights, contending that he had not received a fair trial within the meaning of article 6(1) of the European Convention on Human Rights. The European Court of Human Rights in *Condron v United Kingdom (No 2)* (2000) 31 EHRR 1 allowed his application, stating that Condron had not received a fair trial under article 6(1) as the jury should have been directed that, if the silence could not be attributed to Condron having no answer, or none that would stand up in cross-examination, no adverse inference should be drawn. The reason for the silence, if one is proffered, and its plausibility, should have been taken into account. However, this ruling has not prevented the domestic courts from taking a tough line: a series of cases from the Court of Appeal has confirmed that legal advice to remain silent cannot prevent an adverse inference being drawn under section 34 of the CJPOA 1994. Whilst at one level this makes sense (to have held otherwise would have given solicitors *carte blanche* to advise silence on all occasions, so undermining the change in the law), the current position can be highly problematic. In *Howell* [2003] EWCA Crim 1 [2003] Crim LR 405 the Court of Appeal confirmed that there must always be 'soundly based objective reasons' for silence, which makes the advisory role of the solicitor very difficult.

In our case, Gerry Good is reminded of the caution, and makes admissions to the police similar to those he made earlier to the solicitor's clerk. He admits that he had an argument with Rosa Bottles earlier in the evening, when she had refused to go home with him, but continued to deny using a knife. He is very irritated at the tone of the police questioning, insisting that he is being set up. What is acceptable police practice in interviews remains unclear. There is a classic dilemma here between crime control and due process – tactics that will often effectively uncover the truth will elicit false confessions in other cases. However many due process safeguards are imposed on the police, 'cop culture acts as a powerful crime control engine at the heart of the machinery of criminal justice' (Sanders and Young (2000) at page 77).

It has been standard practice to tape-record interviews since 1991, but the custody officer who makes the decision to charge a suspect, and with what offence, will not listen to the tape. He will rely on the version of events reported to him by the police officer who conducted the interview. At 6 pm Gerry is charged. The custody officer accepts the interviewing officer's view that there is enough evidence that it was Gerry who stabbed Rosa Bottles. A suitable charge must be made. Gerry could be charged with an offence under section 18 (grievous bodily harm with intent), section 20 (reckless grievous bodily harm) or section 47 (actual bodily harm) of the Offences Against the Person Act 1861. There may be a degree of 'over-charging': he may be charged with section 18, in the knowledge that a lower charge can be bargained in return for a guilty plea. The Code for Crown Prosecutors **[3:6]** sets out in paragraph 7 that the charges selected should reflect the seriousness of the offending; give the court adequate sentencing powers; and enable the case to be presented in a clear and simple way.

Charging standards were introduced in 1994 in order to bring more consistency to police charging practice, but it has remained a thorny issue. In his Annual Report for 1999–2000, HM Chief Inspector of the Crown Prosecution Service noted that in some 22% of cases to which charging standards applied the police had selected inappropriate charges. In almost all cases, the inspectors agreed that the CPS had then applied the charging standards correctly, usually to downgrade the charges but sometimes to upgrade them. This led the Auld Review of the Criminal Courts **[1:5]** to recommend that the CPS should assume from the police a greater responsibility for determining the charges at the outset of criminal proceedings. We return to this subject in the next chapter, on the CPS.

Gerry is charged with an offence under section 18 of the Offences Against the Person Act 1861. Once he has been charged, the police may no longer ask him any questions relating to the offence, and will have to decide whether to grant him bail, discussed in section (v) below.

(iv) Cautioning

Until recently the police had four options when dealing with an offender: they could take no further action ('NFA'); they could issue an informal warning (when no official record was made); they could give a formal caution; or they could pass the case to the CPS with a recommendation for prosecution. In recognition of the need for greater consistency in the way police forces and individual police officers decide how to proceed, and of the fact that a court appearance and conviction may have harmful effects, especially in relation to juveniles, Home Office circulars were issued in 1985 and 1990 to encourage greater use of cautioning. As a result of Evans and Wilkinson's (1990) research into the original Home Office Circular 14/85, Home Office Circular 59/90 was issued, which gave clearer guidance to police forces, urging greater use of diversion, and encouraging inter-agency pre-cautioning liaison and greater consistency.

The 1990 Circular introduced national standards. National figures probably still masked wide regional variations, partly reflecting the use of formal rather than informal cautioning in a given force area. Diversion from the criminal courts can have longer-term net-widening effects, in that offenders who would previously have been dealt with informally may now be formally cautioned and so may be pushed more swiftly into the criminal justice system. There is inconclusive evidence on this, since no statistics are kept on cases in which no further action is taken. However, the use of formal cautions attaches a stigmatising label to the suspect, and McConville et al (1991; see also [3:10]) believe they are used on suspects where there is insufficient evidence to prosecute. Most importantly, diversion procedures may usurp the powers of the court. Nearly twenty years ago Light (1987) bemoaned the fact that drunks are now 'processed through the revolving door of the cautioning system with the prospect of any alternative facilities receding further and further into the distance'. The problems facing habitual drunks in our society are thus being effectively swept under the carpet. Due process safeguards can also disappear when vital decisions are taken 'informally'.

By 1994 the tide had turned against cautions. Home Office Circular 18/94 [2:21] tightened up the guidance to the police, resulting in a decline in the number of repeat cautions. Evans and Ellis (1997) pointed to a decrease in the rate of cautioning for juveniles. Whilst the 1994 circular suggested that 'it will often be desirable for the police to liaise with local statutory and voluntary agencies', it also stressed that 'the decision to caution is in all cases one for the police, and although it is open to them to seek the advice of multi-agency panels, this should not be done as a matter of course'. It is worth noting, though, the high number of adults who continue to be cautioned. In 2001, the cautioning rate (ie the percentage of offenders formally cautioned as a percentage of offenders found guilty or formally cautioned) for indictable offences for men aged 21 or over was 19%, and for women over 21 an astonishing 32% (see Criminal Statistics, 2002). This is an extraordinary feature of the English criminal justice system: most European legal systems do not entrust their police with a discretion not to prosecute.

The Crime and Disorder Act 1998 **[2:22]** abolished this system of cautioning for young offenders. Sections 65 and 66 of the Act introduced a system of warnings and reprimands, which result in the child or young person being referred to a Youth Offending Team (a YOT – see section 39). Whilst many welcome this welfarist approach, especially in relation to juveniles, McConville et al **[3:11]** were more sceptical. Is police dominance maintained despite the welfarist rhetoric? See Holdaway et al (2001).

(v)   Bail

Will Gerry be granted bail? His case will not be tried for many weeks. The police will have to decide whether it will be enough merely to give him a date on which he is to appear before the court. The Bail Act 1976 **[6:6]** provides a statutory presumption in favour of bail, but section 38 of PACE (as amended by CJPOA 1994, s 28) **[2:9]** sets out the grounds on which the custody officer may keep Gerry in custody. This involves him in the impossible task of predicting risk. Until section 27 of the CJPOA 1994 inserted a new section 3A in the Bail Act 1976, the custody officer could not release someone on bail subject to conditions. This section adopts the Royal Commission on Criminal Justice (1993) recommendation that the police should have the power to release a suspect on bail subject to conditions (though not a condition that they reside at a bail hostel). This power should have reduced the suspect's liability to attend court, and a person bailed by the police in this way whom it is later decided not to charge or to prosecute may thus avoid altogether a court appearance and its attendant publicity. He is also spared the unpleasant experience of a night in the cells. The disadvantage for the suspect is that he may agree to unwarranted conditions just to get away from the police station. Bucke and Brown **[2:13]** found that the power to attach conditions to police bail is being used in roughly one-fifth of cases in which suspects are bailed after charge, but that there has been little reduction in the proportion detained for court. Rather, conditions are often imposed where the suspect would formerly have been given unconditional bail. The impact of these conditions on levels of offending whilst on bail are difficult to measure. In Gerry Good's case, the police are concerned that he will go back to the Black Bull and 'have a go' at all those who have mentioned him to the police. They decide, to Gerry's fury, to keep him in the cells until the morning and take him to the magistrates' court for a remand hearing. Bail applications are discussed in Chapter Six.

The necessary paperwork must now be prepared for the court. A time-consuming task for the police is the preparation of written summaries of taped interviews. The Police Service estimates that preparing summaries takes the equivalent of some 1,300 to 1,500 officers' full-time working hours (see the Royal Commission (1993) at page 41). Baldwin **[2:23]** questions the accuracy of that estimate, and concludes that there is no satisfactory alternative to lawyers using the record of interview only after having played the tape itself. He suggests that some of the main benefits of tape recording interviews with suspects are being filtered away by too heavy a reliance upon the records of interviews, which are often inadequate. The Royal Commission (1993) recommended that the Home Office explore a number of options to establish the best practicable method of producing interview records for the future, but little has changed in this area.

As far as Gerry is concerned, he has now been 'set up' by the police. He does not think they have any evidence against him. What goes on in the early stages of an investigation is clearly vital to the satisfactory conviction of offenders, but also at the root of many apparently unsafe convictions. The courts have a vital role in preventing inappropriate policing: see Chapter Seven and Ashworth (1998). It was partly a recognition of the wide discretionary powers that are wielded by the police which led to the creation in 1985 of the CPS. In the next chapter, we examine the role of the CPS and the friction that has been generated between it and the police. The police are working under increasing pressure, as the demands on them outstrip any growth in resources. It is clearly essential that legal safeguards are present in the police station and not just in the courtroom: should there be greater independent scrutiny of what goes on in the police station?

Further reading

Ashworth, A *The Criminal Process* (2nd edition, 1998) Oxford
Ashworth, A 'Should the police be allowed to use deceptive practices?' (1998) 114 LQR 108
Bevan, V and Lidstone, K *The Investigation of Crime* (1991) Butterworths
Baldwin, R and Houghton, J 'Circular arguments: the status and legitimacy of administrative rules' [1986] Public Law 239
Bowling, B, and Foster, J 'Policing and the Police' in Maguire, Morgan, Reiner (eds) *The Oxford Handbook of Criminology* (3rd edition, 2002) Oxford
Bucke, T, Street, R and Brown, D 'The Right to Silence: The Impact of the Criminal Justice and Public Order Act 1994' (2000) HORS No 199 HMSO
Chief Surveillance Commissioner Annual Report 2001–02 HMSO
Cotton, J and Povey, D 'Police Complaints and Discipline, England and Wales, April 1997 to March 1998' (1998) HORS Issue 20/1998 HMSO

Holdaway, S, Davidson, N, Dignan, J, Hammersley, R, Hine, J and Marsh, P 'New strategies to address youth offending: the national evaluation of the pilot youth offending teams' (2001) Home Office, RDS Occasional Paper No. 69

Leng, R 'The right to silence in police interrogation' (1993) RCCJ Research Study No 10 HMSO

Macpherson, W 'The Stephen Lawrence Inquiry' (1999) HMSO, Cm 4262-1

Maguire, M and Corbett, C *A Study of the Police Complaints System* (1991) HMSO

Maguire, M and Norris, C 'The conduct and supervision of criminal investigations' (1993) RCCJ Research Study No 5 HMSO

Morgan, D and Stephenson, G *Suspicion and Silence: the Right to Silence in Criminal Investigations* (1994) Blackstone

Phillips, C and Brown, D 'Entry into the criminal justice system: a survey of police arrests and their outcomes' (1998) HORS No 185 HMSO

Report of the Royal Commission on Criminal Procedure (1981) Cmnd 8092

Sanders, A 'The limits to diversion from prosecution' (1988) 28 BJ of Criminology 513

Sanders, A and Young, R *Criminal Justice* (2000) Butterworths

Waddington, P A J *The Strong Arm of the Law* (1991) Oxford UP

Walker, C and Starmer, K *Justice in Error* (chapters 1–4) (1993) Blackstone

Zander, M 'The Revised PACE Codes' (2003) 3 Archbold News 5

Zuckerman, A A A 'Trial by unfair means – the report of the Working Group on the Right to Silence' [1989] Crim LR 855

Zuckerman, A A A 'The inevitable demise of the right to silence' (1994) 144 NLJ 1104

Documents

[2:1]   Police Act 1996 sections 1–12

1   Police areas

(1)   England and Wales shall be divided into police areas.

(2)   The police areas referred to in subsection (1) shall be—
    (a)   those listed in Schedule 1 (subject to any amendment made to that Schedule by an order under section 32 below, section 58 of the Local Government Act 1972, or section 17 of the Local Government Act 1992),
    (b)   the metropolitan police district, and
    (c)   the City of London police area.

(3)   References in Schedule 1 to any local government area are to that area as it is for the time being.

Forces outside London

2 Maintenance of police forces

A police force shall be maintained for every police area for the time being listed in Schedule 1.

3 Establishment of police authorities

(1) There shall be a police authority for every police area for the time being listed in Schedule 1.

(2) A police authority established under this section for any area shall be a body corporate to be known by the name of the area with the addition of the words "Police Authority".

4 Membership of police authorities etc

(1) Subject to subsection (2), each police authority established under section 3 shall consist of seventeen members.

(2) The Secretary of State may by order provide in relation to a police authority specified in the order that the number of its members shall be a specified odd number greater than seventeen.

(3) A statutory instrument containing an order under subsection (2) shall be laid before Parliament after being made.

(4) Schedules 2 and 3 shall have effect in relation to police authorities established under section 3 and the appointment of their members.

5 Reductions in size of police authorities

(1) This section applies to any order under section 4(2) which varies or revokes an earlier order so as to reduce the number of a police authority's members.

(2) Before making an order to which this section applies, the Secretary of State shall consult—
  (a) the authority,
  (b) the councils which are relevant councils in relation to the authority for the purposes of Schedule 2, and
  (c) any selection panel, constituted under regulations made in accordance with section 29(2) of the Justices of the Peace Act 1997, which is responsible, or is represented on a joint committee which is responsible, for the appointment of members of the authority.

(3) An order to which this section applies may include provision as to the termination of the appointment of the existing members of the authority and the making of new appointments or re-appointments.

The metropolitan police force

5A   Maintenance of the metropolitan police force

A police force shall be maintained for the metropolitan police district.

5B   Establishment of the Metropolitan Police Authority

(1)   There shall be a police authority for the metropolitan police district.

(2)   The police authority established under this section shall be a body corporate to be known as the Metropolitan Police Authority.

5C   Membership etc of the Metropolitan Police Authority

(1)   The Metropolitan Police Authority shall consist of twenty-three members (subject to subsection (2)).

(2)   The Secretary of State may by order provide that the number of members of the Metropolitan Police Authority shall be a specified odd number not less than seventeen.

(3)   Before making an order under subsection (2) which reduces the number of members of the Metropolitan Police Authority, the Secretary of State shall consult—
    (a)   the Greater London Authority;
    (b)   the Metropolitan Police Authority; and
    (c)   the person or body responsible for the appointment of members of the Greater London Magistrates' Courts Authority under regulations made under section 30B of the Justices of the Peace Act 1997 (which, by virtue of paragraph 5(b) of Schedule 2A to this Act, appoints magistrates to be members of the Metropolitan Police Authority).

(4)   An order under subsection (2) which reduces the number of members of the Metropolitan Police Authority may include provision as to the termination of the appointment of the existing members of the Metropolitan Police Authority and the making of new appointments or re-appointments.

(5)   A statutory instrument containing an order under subsection (2) shall be laid before Parliament after being made.

(6)   Schedules 2A and 3 shall have effect in relation to the Metropolitan Police Authority and the appointment of its members.

The metropolitan police and forces outside London

6 General functions of police authorities

(1)   Every police authority established under section 3 shall secure the maintenance of an efficient and effective police force for its area.

(2)   In discharging its functions, every police authority established under section 3 shall have regard to—
  (a)   any objectives determined by the Secretary of State under section 37,
  (b)   any objectives determined by the authority under section 7,
  (c)   any performance targets established by the authority, whether in compliance with a direction under section 38 or otherwise, and
  (d)   any local policing plan issued by the authority under section 8.

(3)   In discharging any function to which a code of practice issued under section 39 relates, a police authority established under section 3 shall have regard to the code.

(4)   A police authority shall comply with any direction given to it by the Secretary of State under section 38 or 40.

(5)   This section shall apply in relation to the Metropolitan Police Authority as it applies in relation to a police authority established under section 3.

6A Three-year strategy plans

(1)   Every police authority maintaining a police force for a police area in England and Wales shall, before the beginning of every relevant three-year period, issue a plan ("a three-year strategy plan") which sets out the authority's medium and long term strategies for the policing of that area during that period.

(2)   Before a three-year strategy plan for any period is issued by a police authority, a draft of a plan setting out medium and long term strategies for the policing of the authority's area during that period must have been—
  (a)   prepared by the chief officer of police of the police force maintained by that authority; and
  (b)   submitted by him to the police authority for its consideration.

(3)   In preparing the draft plan, the chief officer of police of a police force shall have regard to the views, obtained in accordance with arrangements under section 96, of people in the police area in question.

(4)   A police authority which has issued a three-year strategy plan for any period may modify that plan at any time during that period.

(5)   It shall be the duty, in issuing, preparing or modifying a three-year strategy plan or a draft of such a plan, of every police authority or chief officer of police to have regard to the National Policing Plan in force at that time.

(6)   The Secretary of State—
  (a)   shall issue guidance to police authorities and chief officers of police as to the matters to be contained in any three-year strategy plan, and as to the form to be taken by any such plan; and
  (b)   may from time to time revise and modify that guidance;
and it shall be the duty of every police authority and chief officer of police to take account of any guidance under this subsection when issuing, preparing or modifying any such plan or any draft plan prepared for the purposes of subsection (2).

(7)   Before issuing or revising any guidance under subsection (6) the Secretary of State shall consult with—
  (a)   persons whom he considers to represent the interests of police authorities;
  (b)   persons whom he considers to represent the interests of chief officers of police; and
  (c)   such other persons as he thinks fit.

(8)   A police authority which is proposing to issue or modify any plan under this section shall submit that plan, or the modifications, to the Secretary of State.

(9)   Where a police authority issues a three-year strategy plan or modifies such a plan, it shall—
  (a)   send a copy of the plan or the modified plan to the Secretary of State; and
  (b)   cause the plan or modified plan to be published;
and the copy of any modified plan sent to the Secretary of State and the publication of any modified plan must show the modifications, or be accompanied by or published with a document which sets them out or describes them.

(10)   If the Secretary of State considers that there are grounds for thinking that—
  (a)   a police authority's three-year strategy plan, or
  (b)   any proposals by a police authority for such a plan, or for the modification of such a plan,
may not be consistent with any National Policing Plan applicable to a financial year wholly or partly comprised in the period to which the strategy plan applies, he shall, before informing the police authority of his conclusions on whether or not it is in fact so inconsistent, consult with the persons mentioned in subsection (11).

(11)   Those persons are—
  (a)   the police authority in question;
  (b)   the chief officer of police of the police force maintained by that authority;
  (c)   persons whom the Secretary of State considers to represent the interests of police authorities; and
  (d)   persons whom the Secretary of State considers to represent the interests of chief officers of police.

(12)   Before a police authority—
  (a)   issues a three-year strategy plan that differs in any material respect from the draft submitted to it by the chief officer of police of the force maintained by that authority, or
  (b)   modifies its three-year strategy plan,
it shall consult with that chief officer.

(13) Any best value performance plan prepared by a police authority under section 6 of the Local Government Act 1999 (c 27) for any financial year must be consistent with any three-year strategy plan which sets out the authority's current strategies for policing its area during any period which includes the whole or any part of that financial year.

(14) The Secretary of State may by regulations make provision for—
    (a)   the procedure to be followed on the submission to him of any plan or modifications for the purposes of this section; and
    (b)   the periods which are to constitute relevant three-year periods for the purposes of this section;
and those regulations may provide for a period of less than three years to be the first period treated as a relevant three-year period for the purposes of this section.

(15) A statutory instrument containing regulations under this section shall be subject to annulment in pursuance of a resolution of either House of Parliament.

7 Local policing objectives

(1)   Every police authority established under Section 3 shall, before the beginning of each financial year, determine objectives for the policing of the authority's area during that year.

(2)   Objectives determined under this section may relate to matters to which objectives determined under section 37 also relate, or to other matters, but in any event shall be so framed as to be consistent with the objectives determined under that section.

(3)   Before determining objectives under this section, a police authority shall—
    (a)   consult the chief constable for the area, and
    (b)   consider any views obtained by the authority in accordance with arrangements made under section 96.

(4)   This section shall apply in relation to the Metropolitan Police Authority as it applies to a police authority established under section 3, but taking the reference to the chief constable for the area as a reference to the Commissioner of Police of the Metropolis.

8 Local policing plans

(1)   Every police authority established under section 3 shall, before the beginning of each financial year, issue a plan setting but the proposed arrangements for the policing of the authority's area during the year ("the local policing plan").

(2)   The local policing plan shall include a statement of the authority's priorities for the year, of the financial resources expected to be available and of the proposed allocation of those resources, and shall give particulars of—
    (a)   any objectives determined by the Secretary of State under section 37,
    (b)   any objectives determined by the authority under section 7, ...
    (c)   any performance targets established by the authority, whether in compliance with a direction under section 38 or otherwise, and
    (d)   any action proposed for the purpose of complying with the requirements of Part I of the Local Government Act 1999 (best value).

(2A) The local policing plan for any financial year must be consistent with any three-year strategy plan under section 6A which sets out the authority's current strategies for the policing of its area during any period which includes the whole or any part of that financial year.

(3)   A draft of the local policing plan shall be prepared by the chief constable for the area and submitted by him to the police authority for it to consider.

(4)   Before issuing a local policing plan which differs from the draft submitted by the chief constable under subsection (3), a police authority shall consult the chief constable.

(4A) It shall be the duty of a police authority and of a chief constable, in preparing, issuing or submitting any plan or draft plan under this section, to have regard to any general guidance given by the Secretary of State with respect to local policing plans and the drafts of such plans.

(4B) Before giving any guidance under subsection (4A), the Secretary of State shall consult with—

- (a)   persons whom he considers to represent the interests of police authorities;
- (b)   persons whom he considers to represent the interests of chief officers of police; and
- (c)   such other persons as he thinks fit.

(5)   A police authority shall arrange for every local policing plan issued by it under this section to be published in such manner as appears to it to be appropriate, and shall send a copy of the plan to the Secretary of State.

(6)   This section shall apply in relation to the Metropolitan Police Authority as it applies to a police authority established under section 3, but taking the references to the chief constable for the area as references to the Commissioner of Police of the Metropolis.

9   Annual reports by police authorities

(1)   As soon as possible after the end of each financial year every police authority established under section 3 shall issue a report relating to the policing of the authority's area for the year.

(2)   A report issued by a police authority under this section for any year shall include an assessment of the extent to which, during that year proposals have been implemented, and things have been done, in accordance with the following plans—

- (a)   the three-year strategy plan issued under section 6A for the period that includes that year; and
- (b)   the local policing plan issued for that year under section 8.

(3)   A police authority shall arrange for every report issued by it under this Section to be published in such manner as appears to it to be appropriate, and shall send a copy of the report to the Secretary of State.

(4)   This section shall apply in relation to the Metropolitan Police Authority as it applies to a police authority established under section 3.

9A General functions of the Commissioner of Police of the Metropolis

(1)   The metropolitan police force shall be under the direction and control of the Commissioner of Police of the Metropolis appointed under section 9B.

(2)   In discharging his functions, the Commissioner of Police of the Metropolis shall have regard to the local policing plan issued by the Metropolitan Police Authority under section 8.

9B Appointment of Commissioner of Police of the Metropolis

(1)   There shall be a Commissioner of Police of the Metropolis.

(2)   Any appointment of a Commissioner of Police of the Metropolis shall be made by Her Majesty by warrant under Her sign manual.

(3)   A person appointed as Commissioner of Police of the Metropolis shall hold office at Her Majesty's pleasure.

(4)   Any appointment of a Commissioner of Police of the Metropolis shall be subject to regulations under section 50.

(5)   Before recommending to Her Majesty that She appoint a person as the Commissioner of Police of the Metropolis, the Secretary of State shall have regard to—
   (a)   any recommendations made to him by the Metropolitan Police Authority; and
   (b)   any representations made to him by the Mayor of London.

(6)   Any functions exercisable by the Mayor of London under subsection (5) may only be exercised by him personally.

9C Functions of Deputy Commissioner of Police of the Metropolis

(1)   The Deputy Commissioner of Police of the Metropolis may exercise any or all of the powers and duties of the Commissioner of Police of the Metropolis—
   (a)   during any absence, incapacity or suspension from duty of the Commissioner,
   (b)   during any vacancy in the office of the Commissioner, or
   (c)   at any other time, with the consent of the Commissioner.

(2)   The Deputy Commissioner of Police of the Metropolis shall not have power to act by virtue of subsection (1)(a) or (b) for a continuous period exceeding three months, except with the consent of the Secretary of State.

(3)   The Deputy Commissioner of Police of the Metropolis shall also have all the powers and duties of an Assistant Commissioner of Police of the Metropolis.

9D Appointment of Deputy Commissioner of Police of the Metropolis

(1)   There shall be a Deputy Commissioner of Police of the Metropolis.

(2)   Any appointment of a Deputy Commissioner shall be made by Her Majesty by warrant under Her sign manual.

(3)   A person appointed as the Deputy Commissioner shall hold office at Her Majesty's pleasure.

(4)   Any appointment of a Deputy Commissioner shall be subject to regulations under section 50.

(5)   Before recommending to Her Majesty that She appoint a person as the Deputy Commissioner, the Secretary of State shall have regard to—
    (a)   any recommendations made to him by the Metropolitan Police Authority; and
    (b)   any representations made to him by the Commissioner.

(6)   In this section—
    "the Commissioner" means the Commissioner of Police of the Metropolis;
    "Deputy Commissioner" means Deputy Commissioner of Police of the Metropolis.

9E Removal of Commissioner or Deputy Commissioner

(1)   The Metropolitan Police Authority, acting with the approval of the Secretary of State, may call upon the Commissioner of Police of the Metropolis to retire in the interests of efficiency or effectiveness.

(2)   Before seeking the approval of the Secretary of State under subsection (1), the Metropolitan Police Authority shall give the Commissioner of Police of the Metropolis an opportunity to make representations and shall consider any representations that he makes.

(3)   Where the Commissioner of Police of the Metropolis is called upon to retire under subsection (1), he shall retire on such date as the Metropolitan Police Authority may specify or on such earlier date as may be agreed upon between him and the Authority.

(4)   This section shall apply in relation to the Deputy Commissioner of Police of the Metropolis as it applies to the Commissioner of Police of the Metropolis.

(5)   This section is without prejudice to—
    (a)   section 9B(3),
    (b)   section 9D(3),
    (c)   any regulations under section 50, or
    (d)   any regulations under the Police Pensions Act 1976.

9F Assistant Commissioners of Police of the Metropolis

(1)   The ranks that may be held in the metropolitan police force shall include that of Assistant Commissioner of Police of the Metropolis ("Assistant Commissioner").

(2)   Any appointment of an Assistant Commissioner shall be made by the Metropolitan Police Authority, but subject to the approval of the Secretary of State and to regulations under section 50.

(3)   Subsections (1) to (3) of section 9E shall apply in relation to an Assistant Commissioner as they apply to the Commissioner of Police of the Metropolis.

(4)   Subsection (3) is without prejudice to—
    (a)   any regulations under section 50, or
    (b)   any regulations under the Police Pensions Act 1976.

(5)   An Assistant Commissioner may exercise any of the powers and duties of the Commissioner of Police of the Metropolis with the consent of the Commissioner.

(6)   Subsection (5) is without prejudice to any regulations under section 50.

9FA Appointment and removal of Deputy Assistant Commissioners

(1)   The ranks that may be held in the metropolitan police force shall include that of Deputy Assistant Commissioner of Police of the Metropolis ("Deputy Assistant Commissioner").

(2)   Any appointment of a Deputy Assistant Commissioner shall be made by the Metropolitan Police Authority, but subject to the approval of the Secretary of State and to regulations under section 50.

(3)   Subsections (1) to (3) of section 9E shall apply in relation to a Deputy Assistant Commissioner as they apply in relation to the Commissioner of Police of the Metropolis.

(4)   Subsection (3) of this section is without prejudice to—
    (a)   any regulations under section 50, or
    (b)   any regulations under the Police Pensions Act 1976 (c 35).

9G Commanders

(1)   The ranks that may be held in the metropolitan police force shall include that of Commander.

(2)   Any appointment of a Commander in the metropolitan police force shall be made by the Metropolitan Police Authority, but subject to the approval of the Secretary of State and to regulations under section 50.

(3)   Subsections (1) to (3) of section 9E shall apply in relation to a Commander in the metropolitan police force as they apply to the Commissioner of Police of the Metropolis.

(4)   Subsection (3) is without prejudice to—
    (a)   any regulations under section 50, or
    (b)   any regulations under the Police Pensions Act 1976.

9H   Other members of the metropolitan police force

(1)   The ranks that may be held in the metropolitan police force shall be such as may be prescribed by regulations under section 50.

(2)   The ranks so prescribed in the case of the metropolitan police force shall include, in addition to the ranks of—
    (a)   Commissioner of Police of the Metropolis,
    (b)   Deputy Commissioner of Police of the Metropolis,
    (c)   Assistant Commissioner of Police of the Metropolis,
    (ca)   Deputy Assistant Commissioner of Police of the Metropolis, and
    (d)   Commander,
those of chief superintendent, superintendent, chief inspector, inspector, sergeant and constable.

(3)   In the metropolitan police force, appointments and promotions to any rank below that of Commander shall be made in accordance with regulations under section 50 by the Commissioner of Police of the Metropolis.

10   General functions of chief constables

(1)   A police force maintained under section 2 shall be under the direction and control of the chief constable appointed under section 11.

(2)   In discharging his functions, every chief constable shall have regard to the local policing plan issued by the police authority for his area under section 8.

11   Appointment and removal of chief constables

(1)   The chief constable of a police force maintained under section 2 shall be appointed by the police authority responsible for maintaining the force, but subject to the approval of the Secretary of State and to regulations under section 50.

(2)   Without prejudice to any regulations under section 50 or under the Police Pensions Act 1976, the police authority, acting with the approval of the Secretary of State, may call upon the chief constable to retire in the interests of efficiency or effectiveness.

(3)   Before seeking the approval of the Secretary of State under subsection (2), the police authority shall give the chief constable an opportunity to make representations and shall consider any representations that he makes.

(4)   A chief constable who is called upon to retire under subsection (2) shall retire on such date as the police authority may specify or on such earlier date as may be agreed upon between him and the authority.

11A   Appointment and removal of deputy chief constables

(1)   Every police force maintained under section 2 shall have a deputy chief constable.

(2)   The appointment of a person to be the deputy chief constable of a police force shall be made, in accordance with regulations under section 50, by the police authority responsible for maintaining that force, but only after consultation with the chief constable and subject to the approval of the Secretary of State.

(3)   Subsections (2) to (4) of section 11 shall apply in relation to a deputy chief constable as they apply in relation to a chief constable.

12   Assistant chief constables

(1)   The ranks that may be held in a police force maintained under section 2 shall include that of assistant chief constable; and in every such police force there shall be at least one person holding that rank.

(2)   Appointments and promotions to the rank of assistant chief constable shall be made, in accordance with regulations under section 50, by the police authority after consultation with the chief constable and subject to the approval of the Secretary of State.

(3)   Subsections (2), (3) and (4) of section 11 shall apply to an assistant chief constable as they apply to a chief constable.

(4)   ...

(5)   ...

(6)   ...

12A   Power of deputy to exercise functions of chief constable

(1)   A deputy chief constable of a police force may exercise or perform any or all of the powers or duties of the chief constable of that force—
   (a)   during any absence, incapacity or suspension from duty of the chief constable,
   (b)   during any vacancy in the office of the chief constable, or
   (c)   at any other time, with the consent of the chief constable.

(2)   A police authority responsible for maintaining a police force may designate a person holding the rank of assistant chief constable in that force to exercise or perform any or all of the powers or duties of the chief constable of that force—

  (a)   during any absence, incapacity or suspension from duty of both the chief constable and the deputy chief constable, or

  (b)   during any vacancy in the offices of both the chief constable and the deputy chief constable.

(3)   Only one person shall be authorised to act at any one time by virtue of a designation under subsection (2).

(4)   The power to act by virtue of subsection (1)(a) or (b) or subsection (2) shall not be exercisable for a continuous period exceeding three months except with the consent of the Secretary of State.

(5)   The provisions of subsections (1) and (2) shall be without prejudice to any other enactment that makes provision for the exercise by any other person of powers conferred on a chief constable.

[2:2]   Audit Commission *'Cheques and Balances: A Framework for Improving Police Accountability'* (1994) HMSO (at page 10):

Exhibit 4

Duties and powers: co-operation or conflict?

The Act seeks to balance duties and powers, but there is a degree of overlap.

	Chief Constable	**Police Authority**	**Home Office**
General duty	Responsibility for the direction and control of the force	To secure the maintenance of an efficient and effective police force for its area	Must promote the efficiency and effectiveness of the police
Finance	Day-to-day financial management within regulations drawn up by police authority. Prepares draft budget	Ultimate responsibility for all expenditure. Its financial regulations determine degree of delegation to chief constable. Agrees budget; issues precept	Issues guidance to encourage grant and capping level. After adverse HMIC report, may direct a police authority as to a minimum budget

	Chief Constable	**Police Authority**	**Home Office**
Personnel	Has direction and control of police officers and civilians whom the police authority wishes to manage directly	Employs all civilians and places them under control of chief constable, except where agreed otherwise. Appoints chief constable; can call upon him to retire	Arbitrates in disputes over management of civilians. Approves appointment of chief constable and can require him to retire
Objectives and targets	Must have regard to national and local objectives and targets in discharging his functions	Must set local objectives and performance targets after consulting chief constable and obtaining the views of the community	Set national objectives and can direct police authority to establish levels of performance for these objectives. Receives a copy of the issues Plan; but does not resolve disputes over the content
Deployment of resources	Has operational control over how resources are depleted.	Local Policing Plan will specify the proposed allocation of resources. Control funding for additional resources	Can issue directions on levels of performance to aim at in relation to national objectives; this may impact upon use of resources

[2:3] *R v Secretary of State for the Home Department, ex p Northumbria Police Authority* [1989] QB 26

The Secretary of State for the Home Department issued a circular (No 40/1986) to all chief officers of police and clerks to police authorities in England and Wales informing them that in future police requirements for plastic baton rounds and CS gas for use in the event of serious public disorder would be met from a central store to be maintained by the Secretary of State. A police authority sought to challenge the issue of the circular on the grounds that the Secretary of State had no power either by virtue of the Police Act 1964 or otherwise to maintain a central supply of such equipment, or to supply the equipment without the approval of the relevant police authority save in a situation of grave emergency. The Divisional Court dismissed the application to quash the decision of the Secretary of Sate to issue and apply the circular.

The Court of Appeal concluded that the Secretary of State had power both under the Police Act and the prerogative to supply the equipment, and the decision of the Divisional Court was affirmed.

Croom-Johnson LJ (at page 39):

It is common ground that the chief constable has complete operational control of his force. Neither the police authority nor the Secretary of State may give him any directions about that. The relationship between police forces and their appropriate local authorities was exhaustively examined by McCardie J in *Fisher v Oldham Corporation* [1930] 2 KB 364. In that case it was held that the police were not the servants of the watch committee of a borough corporation so as to make the corporation civilly liable for wrongs committed by the police. The police perform their duties as constables wholly independently of the watch committee or police authority. McCardie J gave this illustration, at pp 372–373:

> 'Suppose that a police officer arrested a man for a serious felony. Suppose, too, that the watch committee of the borough at once passed a resolution directing that the felon should be released. Of what value would such a resolution be? Not only would it be the plain duty of the police officer to disregard the resolution, but it would also be the duty of the chief constable to consider whether an information should not at once be laid against the members of the watch committee for a conspiracy to obstruct the course of justice.'

The independence of a constable, and *a fortiori* a chief constable, from outside control, whether by a local authority or the executive, has been repeatedly upheld.

This independence of the police goes back a long way, it is not the creation of the Police Act 1964.

The financial provisions of the Act of 1964 are contained in section 8, as amended by section 25 of and Schedule 11 to the Local Government Act 1982. The effect is that all receipts of the police authority shall be paid into the police fund and all expenditure of any such police authority shall be paid out of that fund. That fund is in the exclusive control of the police authority.

Part II of the Act of 1964 is headed 'Central Supervision, Direction and Facilities.' Section 28 sets out the general duty of the Secretary of State. It reads:

> 'The Secretary of State shall exercise his powers under this Act in such manner and to such extent as appears to him to be best calculated to promote the efficiency of the police.'

It indicates the object to be achieved by the exercise of powers conferred on him elsewhere. By section 31 he may make grants to the police authority in respect of expenses incurred for police purposes. By section 33 he has a power to make regulations, none of which are relevant for present purposes. Section 38 provides for the appointment and functions of inspectors of constabulary, who are to inspect and report to the Secretary of State on the efficiency of all police forces. They shall also carry out such other duties for the purpose of furthering police efficiency as the Secretary of State may from time to time direct.

Section 41 is important. It begins a part of the Act subheaded 'Central services'. It was under this section that the circular was sent. Section 41 says:

'The Secretary of State may provide and maintain, or may contribute towards the provisions or maintenance of, a police college, district police training centres, forensic science laboratories, wireless depots and such other organisations and services as he considers necessary or expedient for promoting the efficiency of the police.'

Before the Divisional Court the police authority contended that section 41 did not give the Secretary of State power to supply equipment to the police force without the consent of the police authority. On that point the Divisional Court found in favour of the police authority. In this court the Secretary of State has argued that the Divisional Court was wrong, and that he does have the power. The Divisional Court however accepted an argument advanced by the Secretary of State that alternatively he may supply equipment, without the permission of the police authority, under the Royal prerogative. Against that finding the police authority now appeals.

It is convenient to take the section 41 point first. It is a straight matter of construction of the section, when placed in the context of the statute as a whole. It is not now contended by the Secretary of State that he can, as was stated in the circular, propose that all police requirements for plastic baton rounds and CS gas must be met from his central store. The police authority agreed that section 41 gives the Secretary of State power to maintain a central store – which it was conceded would be an 'organisation' within the meaning of that section – but it was argued that section 4(4) reserves to the authority the exclusive right to obtain equipment in discharge of its duty to secure the maintenance of an efficient police force. That the authority has financial control over the police fund was prayed in aid. The interpretation was said to be consistent with the general scheme of the statute which divides the respective functions for providing an efficient force into three: an authority to maintain, provide and equip; a chief constable to control and operate; and a Secretary of State to supervise and regulate. The authority's case was that the Police Act 1964 sets out a complete and comprehensive code which defines and limits the functions of each of those three entities. It is correct that there is a general scheme as described by the authority. The question is whether the functions are as closely limited and exclusive as is suggested.

Section 4 places a duty on the authority and gives it a discretion how the duty is to be discharged. Section 8 provides it with the funds with which to do so. But section 28 places a duty on the Secretary of State to use high powers so as to promote the efficiency of the police. Those powers include the provision of central services. It is too narrow a construction of section 41 to say, as the authority contended, that the establishments mentioned in the section are only organisations and no more, and that the central store would be another. It ignores the word 'service' in the section. If the Secretary of State gives instruction at a police college, or if a forensic science laboratory examines material sent to it by a force, he is providing services. Similarly, the supply of baton rounds or CS gas from the store is another service. It is not permissible to read into section 41 words which are not there, such as 'with the consent of the police authority'. There is no need to do so. Such services may be asked for by a chief constable in the ordinary course of carrying out his duty of efficient policing. If some payment for the service used is required, it would have to come from the police fund concerned, but if the Secretary of State is willing to make no charge there is no reason why the chief constable may not avail himself of what is available without asking the authority. To read into section 41 the words which are suggested would involve an interference by the authority in the operational discretion of the chief constable. The provisions in section 43 relating to the payment of policemen who are seconded for service under the Crown in providing the central services have no bearing on the point now at issue.

(and at page 42):

Although there has always been what is called the war prerogative, which is the Crown's right to make war and peace, Mr Keene submitted that there is no corresponding prerogative to enforce the keeping of what is popularly called the 'Queen's peace within the realm'. It does, however, contain an extensive section on 'The King as the Fountain of Justice' and courts and gaols. The argument is that if there was no prerogative power to keep the peace in 1820, at which date no organised police force existed, then all police forces exist and are controlled only by the later statutes by which they were created, and there is no residual prerogative power to draw on in cases of necessity ... There were constables long before the establishment of Peel's Metropolitan Police in 1829. At all events, the assumption was early made that keeping the peace was part of the prerogative. The position of the Secretary of State is that he is one of a number of secretaries of state through whom the prerogative power is exercised. In *Harrison v Bush* (1856) 5 E & B 344 at 353, Lord Campbell CJ stated:

> 'In practice, to the Secretary of State for the Home Department ... Belongs peculiarly the maintenance of the peace within the Kingdom, with the superintendence of the administration of justice as far as the Royal prerogative is involved in it.'

By its very nature the subject of maintaining the Queen's peace and keeping law and order had over the years inevitably been dealt with by statute much more than the war prerogative has been ... but I have no doubt that the Crown does have a prerogative power to keep the peace, which is bound up with its undoubted right to see that crime is prevented and justice administered. This is subject to Mr Keene's next submission, which was that any prerogative power may be lost by being overtaken by statute law ...

It is clear that the Crown cannot act under the prerogative if to do so would be incompatible with statute. What was said here is that the Secretary of State's proposal under the circular would be inconsistent with the powers expressly or impliedly conferred on the police authority by section 4 of the Police Act 1964. The Divisional court rejected that submission for reasons with which I wholly agree: namely that section 4 does not expressly grant a monopoly, and that granted the possibility of an authority which declines to provide equipment required by the chief constable there is every reason not to imply a Parliamentary intent to create one.

Mr Keene's last submission was that if there is a prerogative power it can only be used in emergency and that this does not allow its use beforehand in circumstances of peace and quiet. One need only quote and adapt ... passages from the speeches in *Burmah Oil Co Ltd v Lord Advocate* [1965] AC 75. That was a case concerning the war prerogative, but the same point was taken, Lord Reid said, at p 100: 'it would be very strange if the law prevented or discouraged necessary preparations until a time when it would probably be too late for them to be effective.'

The same reason must apply to the provision of equipment to the police, and to their being trained in its use, in times when there is reason to apprehend outbreaks of riot and serious civil disturbance.

Nourse LJ (at page 56):

It has not at any stage in our history been practicable to identify all the prerogative powers of the Crown. It is only by a process of piecemeal decision over a period of centuries that particular powers are seen to exist or not to exist, as the case may be. From time to time a need for more exact definition arises. The present need arises from a difference of view between the Secretary of State and a police authority over what is necessary to maintain public order, a phenomenon which has been observed only in recent times. There has probably never been a comparable occasion for investigating a prerogative of keeping the peace within the realm.

The Crown's prerogative of making war and peace, the was prerogative, has never been doubted. Its origins may not have been fully explored. Here it is important to remember that the Royal prerogative was never regarded as a collection of mere powers, to be exercised or not at the will of the sovereign. The King owed certain duties to his subjects, albeit duties of imperfect obligation whose performance could not be enforced by legal process ... They include a duty to protect the lives and property of the King's subjects ...

[The] scarcity of references in the books to the prerogative of keeping the peace within the realm does not disprove that it exists. Rather it may point to an unspoken assumption that it does.

[2:4] *Hill v Chief Constable of West Yorkshire* [1988] 2 All ER 238

Between 1969 and 1980 Peter Sutcliffe (the 'Yorkshire Ripper') committed a series of 13 murders and 8 attempted murders. The mother of his last murder victim sued under section 48(1) of the Police Act 1964, claiming damages against the chief constable in whose area most of the offences took place. Her claim was struck out on the ground that the police owed no duty of care to a member of the public who suffered injury through the activities of a criminal.

The House of Lords dismissed her appeal. Having held that no duty of care was owed to members of the public, Lord Keith stated (at page 243):

In my opinion there is another reason why an action for damages in negligence should not lie against the police in circumstances such as those of the present case, and that is public policy.

The general sense of public duty which motivates police forces is unlikely to be appreciably reinforced by the imposition of such liability so far as concerns their function in the investigation and suppression of crime. From time to time they make mistakes in the exercise of that function, but it is not to be doubted that they apply their best endeavours to the performance of it. In some instances the imposition of liability may lead to the exercise of a function being carried on in a detrimentally defensive frame of mind. The possibility of this happening in relation to the investigative operations of the police cannot be excluded. Further, it would be reasonable to expect that if potential liability were to be imposed it would be not uncommon for actions to be raised against police forces on the result that he went on to commit further crimes. Whilst such actions might involve allegations of a simple and straightforward types of failure, for example that a police officer negligently tripped and fell while pursuing a burglar, others would be likely to enter deeply into the general nature of a police investigation, as indeed the present action would seek to do. The manner of conduct of such an investigation must necessarily involve a variety of decisions to be made on matters of policy and discretion, for example as to which particular line of inquiry is most advantageously to be pursued and what is the most advantageous way to deploy the available resources. Many such decisions would not be regarded by the courts as appropriate to be called in question, yet elaborate investigation of the facts might be necessary to ascertain whether or not this was so. A great deal of police time, trouble and expense might be expected to have to be put into the preparation of the defence to the action and the attendance of witnesses at the trial. The result would be a significant diversion of police manpower and attention from their most important function, that of the suppression of crime. Closed investigations would require to be reopened and retraversed not with the object of bringing any criminal to justice but to ascertain whether or not they had been competently conducted. I therefore consider that Glidewell LJ, in his judgment in the Court of Appeal in the present case, was right to take the view that the police were immune from an action of this kind on grounds similar to those which in *Rondel v Worsley* were held to render a barrister immune from actions for negligence in his conduct of proceedings in court (see [1987] 1 All ER at 1183, [1988] QB 60 at 76). My Lords, for these reasons I would dismiss the appeal.

Lord Templeman said (at page 244):

My Lords, the appellant, Mrs Hill, is tormented with the unshakeable belief that her daughter would be alive today if the respondent, the West Yorkshire police force, had been more efficient. That belief is entitled to respect and understanding. Damages cannot compensate for the brutal extinction of a young life and the appellant proposes that any damages awarded shall be devoted to an appropriate charity. Damages awarded by the court would not be paid by any policeman found wanting in the performance of his duty but would be paid by the public. The appellant therefore brings these proceedings with the object of obtaining an investigation into the conduct of the West Yorkshire police force so that lives shall not be lost in the future by avoidable delay in the identification and arrest of a murderer.

The question for determination in this appeal is whether an action for damages is an appropriate vehicle for investigating the efficiency of a police force. The present action will be confined to narrow albeit perplexing questions, for example whether, discounting hindsight, it should have been obvious to a senior police officer that Sutcliffe was a prime suspect, whether a senior police officer should not have been deceived by an evil hoaxer, whether an officer interviewing Sutcliffe should have been better briefed and whether a report on Sutcliffe should have been given greater attention. The court would have to consider the conduct of each police officer, to decide whether the policeman failed to attain the standard of care of a hypothetical average policeman. The court would have to decide whether an inspector is to be condemned for being as obtuse as Dr Watson. The appellant will presumably seek evidence, for what it is worth, from retired police inspectors, who would be asked whether they would have been misled by the hoaxer and whether they would have identified Sutcliffe at an earlier stage. At the end of the day the court might or might not find that there had been negligence by one or more.

It may be, and we all hope that the lessons of the Yorkshire Ripper case have been learned, that the methods of handling information and handling the press have been improved, and that co-operation between different police officers is now more highly organised. The present action would not serve any useful purpose in that regard. The present action could not consider whether the training of the West Yorkshire police force is sufficiently thorough, whether the selection of candidates for appointment or promotion is defective, whether rates of pay are sufficient to attract recruits of the required calibre, whether financial restrictions prevent the provision of modern equipment and facilities or whether the Yorkshire police force is clever enough and, if not, what can and ought to be done about it. The present action could only investigate whether an individual member of the police force conscientiously carrying out his duty was negligent when he was bemused by contradictory information or overlooked significant information or failed to draw inferences which later appeared to be obvious. That kind of investigation would not achieve the object which the appellant desires. The efficiency of a police force can only be investigated by an inquiry instituted by the national or local authorities which are responsible to the electorate for that efficiency.

Moreover, if this action lies, every citizen will be able to require the court to investigate the performance of every policeman. If the policeman concentrates on one crime, he may be accused of neglecting others. If the policeman does not arrest on suspicion a suspect with previous convictions, the police force may be held liable for subsequent crimes. The threat of litigation against a police force would not make a policeman more efficient. The necessity for defending proceedings, successfully or unsuccessfully, would distract the policeman from his duties.

This action is in my opinion misconceived and will do more harm than good. A policeman is a servant of the public and is liable to be dismissed for incompetence. A police force serves the public, and the elected representatives of the public must ensure that the public get the police force they deserve. it may be that the West Yorkshire police force was in 1980 in some respects better and in some respects worse than the public deserve. An action for damages for alleged acts of negligence by individual police officers in 1980 could not determine whether and in what respect the West Yorkshire police force can be improved in 1988. I would dismiss the appeal.

[2:5]   Lord Hoffman *'Human Rights and the House of Lords'* (1999) 62 MLR 159 (at page 162):

We have had a very recent example of a decision of the Strasbourg court giving an interpretation to the Convention which, I venture to suggest, it is inconceivable that any domestic court in this country would have adopted. I want to use this decision as an example of the potential conflict between our legal system under the new regime and the jurisprudence emanating from Strasbourg.

On 28 October 1998, judgment was given in the case of *Osman v United Kingdom*. Mrs Osman's husband had been shot and killed by an insane teacher who had formed an obsessional attachment to their young son at school. She sued the police for damages, alleging that they had been warned that the man was a danger to her family but had not taken adequate steps to protect them. The Court of Appeal struck out the action on the ground that the police could not be made liable in negligence for failing to take action in the investigation or suppression of crime. The decision was based upon the

Yorkshire Ripper case, *Hill v Chief Constable of West Yorkshire*, in which the House of Lords held that the imposition of a duty of care in such circumstances would be contrary to public policy. The maintenance of police efficiency was better secured by other methods than having the question of whether they had acted reasonably in a given case expensively investigated in civil proceedings at the instance of a private litigant, with the possibility of compensation having to be paid out of the police budget. The prospect of such an investigation and the payment of compensation might in fact be detrimental to good policing, since it might make the police defensively unwilling to take risks. Furthermore, the efficiency with which the police handled a particular investigation often depended upon the share of their resources which was devoted to that kind of investigation and questions about the allocation of resources by public authorities such as the police were not suitable for determination by judges.

Persons who suffer criminal damage have no claim to compensation solely on the ground that it could have been prevented by more efficient policing. This decision is in line with a number of recent cases on the failure of public authorities to deliver services which could have prevented loss, such as *X (Minors) v Bedford County Council* on social services, *Stovin v Wise* on highway improvements, *Capital and Counties plc v Hampshire County Council* on fire services, *O'Rourke v Camden LBC* on housing the homeless, and *Murphy v Brentwood LBS* on building inspection services. The theme which runs through these cases is that the fact that public services are provided at the public expense to confer benefits or protection on members of the public does not mean that a person who fails to receive those benefits or protection will be entitled to sue for compensation on the ground that the authority acted negligently in failing to provide them. The social justification for such a rule is that, on the one hand, the person who has failed to receive the benefit is no worse off than if it had not been provided in the first place, and on the other hand, the budgetary and efficiency grounds discussed in *Hill v Chief Constable of West Yorkshire.*

Not everyone would agree with such a rule. Some might think that it shows a somewhat niggardly attitude to people who have suffered loss because they had the misfortune not to receive some public benefit which they were reasonably entitled to expect, and that the allocation of funds for public services should budget not merely for providing the services but also for compensating those who did not receive them. It might also be said that the law is inconsistent in excluding liability in such cases but making public authorities liable when they enter into relationships which have long been recognised as giving rise to a duty of care in private law, such as between a doctor or hospital and a patient. For my part, I see no inconsistency, but I recognise that the merits of the rule are open to political debate, the question being essentially one about the obligations of the welfare state.

Mrs Osman, however, petitioned the European Court of Human Rights on the ground that the rejection of her claim was a denial of her fundamental human right under Article 6(1) of the Convention, which provides that 'in the determination of his civil rights and obligations, everyone is entitled to a hearing by a tribunal'. One might be forgiven for thinking that Mrs Osman's rights had been determined, rightly or wrongly, by a tribunal. She had been before the Court of Appeal and they had decided that even if all the allegations in her statement of claim were proved at the trial to be true, she would not be entitled under English domestic law to compensation from the police. But the Court, consisting of 17 judges including one from the United Kingdom, decided unanimously that because her action had not been allowed to proceed to trial, she had not had a hearing. What, you may ask, would be the point of a hearing which, under English law, was bound to end in the claim being dismissed? The answer, according to the European Court, was that it should not have been treated as bound to be dismissed. There should have been the possibility that on the facts alleged, Mrs Osman would win. A rule that in no circumstances should a person be able to claim compensation on the ground that the police failed to protect him from criminal injury was not proportionate to the public policy grounds advanced in its support. In other words, English domestic law failed to provide compensation out of public funds in cases in which the Strasbourg court thought it should do so.

I am not sure, on a reading of the judgment of the court and the concurring judgment of the British judge, whether they had persuaded themselves that they were really dealing with the right to a hearing rather than the merits of the substantive tort law under which the Court of Appeal had held that Mrs Osman was bound to lose. In my view, there is no disguising the fact that the case was about the latter.

I am bound to say that this decision fills me with apprehension. Under the cover of an Article which says that everyone is entitled to have his civil rights and obligations determined by a tribunal, the European Court of Human Rights is taking upon itself to decide what the content of those civil rights should be. In so doing, it is challenging the autonomy of the courts and indeed the Parliament of the United Kingdom to deal with what are essentially social welfare questions involving budgetary limits and efficient public administration. I say the Parliament of the United Kingdom because it must follow from the decision of the Strasbourg court that even if the rule in *Hill v Chief Constable of West Yorkshire* had formed part of the Police Act 1996, it would have been held to contravene the right in art. 6(1) to a hearing before a tribunal. I understand that a petition by the unsuccessful plaintiffs in *X (Minors) v Bedfordshire County Council* is already on its way and no doubt there are other cases in which the same general principle will be challenged. The whole English jurisprudence on the liability of public authorities for failure to deliver public services is open to attack on the grounds that it violates the right to a hearing before a tribunal. And although the Strasbourg court appears to contemplate the possibility that after a hearing of the facts, the court might still come to the conclusion that on grounds of public policy the claim should be dismissed, it ignores one of the principle reasons for the present doctrine, which is to avoid a trial altogether, to avoid the waste of public resources involved in a judicial investigation, usually on legal aid, as to whether the public authority should reasonably have provided the benefit or not.

It may be that the court did not understand the rather formulaic reasoning by which English courts say that no duty of care exists when they mean that the case is one in which the law does not recognise a right to compensation. It may be that they did not understand the principle by which an action is struck out without going to trial if proof of all the facts alleged would not sustain a cause of action. Either way, the case serves to reinforce the doubts I have had for a long time about the suitability, at least for this country, of having questions of human rights determined by an international tribunal made up of judges from many countries.

I would not like anyone to think that this view reflected a vulgar Euroscepticism. When it comes to questions of a common currency and a large number of other economic and social issues, the advantages and disadvantages of a common European position are matters for pragmatic decision on which one has to weigh up the evidence as best one can. I do not regard national sovereignty on every issue as either possible or desirable. But the international adjudication of questions of human rights goes much deeper because it raises an ancient question about the universality of human values. It brings

into focus the conflict between the universalist philosophy of the French enlighten-
ment, who thought that French concepts of *liberté, égalité, fraternité* were derived from
our common humanity and could therefore be applied world-wide, and pluralist views
such as those of that each community had its own set of values, different but not better
or worse than those of other communities.

Voltaire said that morality was the same in all civilised nations. This is a half truth; of
course we share a common humanity and there are some forms of behaviour such as
torture which we all either reject or are unwilling to acknowledge. But even this is not
inherent in civilisation: in the law of ancient Rome, the evidence of slaves was always
taken under torture and none of the great Roman lawyers who developed the elaborate
and sophisticated system, which forms the basis of law through so much of the world,
seems to have thought this inhuman. Of course, I applaud the patient efforts of the
human rights movement since the Second World War to promote the acceptance of
basic human rights throughout the world. I am well aware that there are countries
which deny their citizens basic human rights and which claim to be justified on grounds
of cultural diversity, when the true reasons are the power and greed of their rulers.
Nevertheless, I say that Voltaire's remark was only half true and that in a confident
democracy such as the United Kingdom the other half is important. We do have our
own hierarchy of moral values, our own culturally-determined sense of what is fair
and unfair, and I think it would be wrong to submerge this under a pan-European
jurisprudence of human rights.

The problem about the hierarchy of rights is not the conflict between good and evil
but the conflict between good and good. Free speech is a good thing; justice is a good
thing, but there are cases in which free speech and justice come into conflict with each
other. For example, the law that preserves the anonymity of rape victims is an infringement of the freedom of the press, but it assists justice by encouraging women to make
complaints against rapists. How then are these two desirable objectives – free speech
and justice – to be reconciled with each other? There is no right answer to that question; any choice involves some degree of sacrifice. But in my view, the specific answers,
the degree to which weight is given to one desirable objectives rather than another, will
be culturally determined. Different communities will, through their legislatures and
judges, adopt the answers which they think suit them. So the Supreme Court of the
United States has ruled a State law which gave anonymity to rape victims to be uncon-
stitutional as infringing the First Amendment right to freedom of the press, whereas
such laws exist in the United Kingdom and other countries. The Supreme Court of the
United States attaches what other communities may regard as an exaggerated value
to the First Amendment and no doubt they think we do not respect it enough. But the
difference in the answers given to the perennial conflict between goals which everyone
accepts to be good shows how impractical it would be to subject the United States and
the United Kingdom to a common court of human rights. If this is true of two countries
so closely bound together in culture, law and history, how much more true must it be
of the disparate collection of states, some old democracies, some former police states,
which belong to the Council of Europe.

Of course it is true that to some extent the Strasbourg court acknowledges the fact that
often there is no right answer by allowing what it calls a 'margin of appreciation' to the
legislature or courts of a member State. Within limits, they are allowed to differ. And, as
I have said, I accept that there is an irreducible minimum of human rights which must
be universally true. But most of the jurisprudence which comes out of Strasbourg is
not about the irreducible minimum. These questions tend to come into play at a point
when civil society itself is called into question; they are far from the normal currency

of dispute over competing values in a democracy like the United Kingdom. The *Osman* case, dealing with the substantive civil law right to financial compensation for not receiving the benefit of a social service, is as far as one can imagine from basic human rights. And I have taken it only as a very recent example: it is by no means unusual. It is often said that the tendency of every court is to increase its jurisdiction and the Strasbourg court is no exception. So far as the margin of appreciation accommodates national choices, the jurisdiction of the European court is unnecessary; so far as it does not, it is undesirable.

[2:6]   Hoyano, L C H *'Policing Flawed Police Investigations: Unravelling the Blanket'* (1999) 62 MLR 912 (at page 920):

Lord Hoffmann's critique of the intersection of tort law and the European Convention

Lord Hoffmann has stated in this journal that the *Osman* decision 'fills me with apprehension'. His Lordship contends that the ECHR, under the guise of Article 6 which says everyone is entitled to have his civil rights and obligations decided by a tribunal, has taken it upon itself to decide the content of those civil rights, which here meant the merits of the substantive tort rules governing duty of care. In so doing, His Lordship maintains, the ECHR is 'challenging the autonomy of the courts and indeed the Parliament of the United Kingdom to deal with what are essentially social welfare questions involving budgetary limits and efficient public administration'.

Is this criticism justified? Parliament, exercising its autonomy, has seen fit to require the British courts to adjudicate issues arising under the Convention, and in so doing to take into account any judgment of the ECHR. Parliament has bound neither itself nor the British courts to act on any declaration of incompatibility by the ECHR. If this amounts to an unjustifiable surrender of parliamentary autonomy, then that is a political, not a legal, issue.

The ECHR had also given due warning that while Article 6§1 does not in itself guarantee any particular content for civil rights and obligations in the substantive law of the Contracting States, and so cannot provide a vehicle for their creation by the Convention enforcement bodies, the State does not enjoy unlimited scope to remove issues of civil liability from the jurisdiction of the courts. In *Fayed v UK*, the ECHR observed:

> [It] would not be consistent with the rule of law and democratic society or with the basic principle underlying Article 6(1) – namely that civil claims must be capable of being submitted to a judge for adjudication – if, for example, a State could, without restraint or control by the Convention enforcement bodies, remove from the jurisdiction of the courts a whole range of civil claims or confer immunities from civil liability on large groups or categories of persons.

Parliament must be taken to have known of this interpretation of Article 6(1) prior to incorporating the Convention into English domestic law.

Lord Hoffman argues that the case was really about the merits of the substantive tort law under which the Osmans were 'bound to lose', rather than about the right to a hearing;

viewed from this perspective, the *Osman* case 'is as far as one can imagine from basic human rights'. However, a close examination of the Court's reasoning suggests that this criticism is less persuasive than it may initially appear.

Interestingly, at several points in his critique His Lordship treats *Hill* as conferring blanket immunity upon the police, without addressing the ECHR's crucial point that the English courts themselves had already torn some holes in that blanket, particularly through the recently resurrected 'assumption of responsibility' justification for duty of care, but then had denied the Osman plaintiffs the opportunity or prove that their case fitted within any of these exceptions or justified unravelling the blanket further.

It is of vital importance to note that the ECHR did not require English courts to rescind public policy immunity from tort liability; rather, it said that the courts must permit litigants an opportunity to contend that countervailing public policy considerations dictate that immunity should not apply to their case. This does not mean that defendants can no longer bring cost-efficient interlocutory applications to strike out pleadings on the ground that they are immune from negligence suits, as Lord Hoffmann suggests; it does mean that the court hearing such an application must approach the issue from the perspective that public policy immunity does not automatically provide a 'watertight defence'. The factors which the ECHR indicated might be relevant to an English court in deciding whether to apply the immunity rule in *Hill* – the alleged failure by an agent of the state to protect the life of a vulnerable child due to a catalogue of gravely negligent acts and omissions – brings Ahmet Osman's case much closer to 'basic human rights' as they are commonly conceptualised.

Thus it is strongly arguable that the *ratio* of *Osman* is quite narrow. Viewed in this way, the ECHR has not taken it upon itself to dictate to domestic courts the content of tort law rules but rather, in the best common law tradition, has upheld the principle that the categories of negligence are not closed, and that tort law must be allowed the flexibility to develop incrementally.

Lord Hoffmann stoutly defends the immunity conferred by *Hill* as being in line with other recent cases refusing to permit plaintiffs to sue public authorities for failure to deliver services which could have prevented their loss. But given the extensive police involvement responding to multiple complaints about the activities of Paget-Lewis over a period of 14 months, is *Osman* simply a case of nonfeasance? As the plaintiffs alleged that they, the school and the ILEA had the Osman and Perkins families, can it fairly be said in their case that 'the person who has failed to receive the benefit [of public services] is no worse off than if it had not been provided in the first place', as Lord Hoffmann asserts? Without such assurances, the Osmans might well have left the locality or made other arrangements to provide for their security; without a trial, it cannot be assumed that they did not rely upon the police to their detriment.

His Lordship contends that public authorities are currently exposed to negligence actions only when they enter into relationships which have long been recognised as giving rise to a duty of care in private law, such as between a doctor or hospital and patient. While there may be an emerging trend in that direction, such reasoning does not appear in the seminal cases delineating the applicability of negligence law to public authorities. Indeed the House of Lords expressly eschewed such a limitation in *Dorset Yacht Co Ltd v Home Office*; Lord Diplock pointed out:

To relinquish intentionally or inadvertently the custody and control of a person responsible in law for his own acts is not an act or omission which, independently of any statute, would give rise to a cause of action at common law against the custodian on the part of another person who subsequently sustained tortious damage at the hands of the person released.

It would have been impossible to establish the existence of a free-standing duty of care absent the statutory power to imprison which, at least until the recent advent of privately managed prisons, was vested solely in public authorities. *Dorset Yacht* thus cannot be explained on the basis of Lord Hoffmann's private/public distinction.

Furthermore, it is unlikely that the ECHR ruling in *Osman* will force the English courts to adjudicate policy issues involving the efficiency of public administration and the allocation of limited public resources, as Lord Hoffmann fears ...

In *Osman*, there was no suggestion that the police's failure to arrest Paget-Lewis was due to a paucity of resources to dedicate to the investigation or to a policy decision not to act on the numerous complaints. While the policy/operational divide may sometimes be difficult to discern, it should have been relatively straightforward to apply here: even if the decision to arrest a suspect might conceivably fall within the realm of non-justifiable discretion, surely the inexplicable failure to implement that decision with any zeal would fall at the operational end of the spectrum.

(and at page 934):

Conclusion

I have argued that it is possible to construe *Osman v UK* as standing for no broader proposition than that where the domestic courts have carved out some exceptions to a general rule conferring immunity upon a class of decision-makers, litigants must be afforded the opportunity to bring their cases within those exceptions or (in the case of a judge-made immunity rule) to develop new exceptions. However, some dicta in the ECHR's lead judgment point to a wider implication, that blanket immunity for any class of potential tortfeasors is likely to violate Article 6(1), as the courts must leave themselves free to examine the merits of each case and to weigh the public policy considerations for and against the existence of the duty of care in a particular case ...

The Human Rights Act 1998 may signal a return to the spirit of flexibility which infused *Donoghue v Stevenson*, and to the robust view of the Court of Appeal in *Dorset Yacht* about the salutary effects of negligence law unless, that is, other English judges share the apprehension of Lord Hoffmann, and lack the confidence of Lord Nicholls in their ability to adjudicate duty of care issues on a case-by-case basis ...

How much better it would be if negligence law could draw on these common law concepts to retain its original vigour and flexibility rather than forcing human rights law to do its work.

[2:7] *R v Metropolitan Police Comr, ex p Blackburn (No 3)* [1973] QB 241

The applicant sought an order of mandamus to require the Metropolitan Police Commissioner to secure the enforcement of the law against the illegal publishing and selling of pornography. The Court of Appeal held that, although the evidence disclosed that obscene material was widely available for sale in shops, the applicant had not established that it was a case for the court to interfere with the discretion of the police in carrying out their duties.

Lord Denning MR (at page 254):

In *R v Commissioner of Police of the Metropolis, ex p Blackburn* [1968] 2 QB 118, 136, 138, 148–149, we made it clear that, in the carrying out of their duty of enforcing the law, the police have a discretion with which the courts will not interfere. There might, however, be extreme cases in which he was not carrying out his duty. And then we would. I do not think this is a case for our interference. In the past the commissioner has done what he could under the existing system and with the available manpower. The new commissioner is doing more. He is increasing the number of the Obscene Publications Squad to 18 and he is reforming it and its administration. No more can reasonably be expected.

The plain fact is, however, that the efforts of the police have hitherto been largely ineffective. Mr Blackburn amply demonstrated it by going out from this court and buying these pornographic magazines – hard and soft – at shops all over the place. I do not accede to the suggestion that the police turn a blind eye to pornography or that shops get a 'tip-off' before the police arrive. The cause of the ineffectiveness lies with the system and the framework in which the police have to operate. The Obscene Publications Act 1959 does not provide a sound foundation. It fails to provide a satisfactory test of obscenity: and it allows a defence of public good which has got out of hand. There is also considerable uncertainty as to the powers and duties of the police when they seize articles.

If the people of this country want pornography to be stamped out, the legislature must amend the Obscene Publications Act 1959 so as to make it strike unmistakably at pornography: and it must define the powers and duties of the police so as to enable them to take effective measures for the purpose. The police may well say to Parliament: 'Give us the tools and we will finish the job'. But, without efficient tools, they cannot be expected to stamp it out. Mr Blackburn has served a useful purpose in drawing the matter to our attention: but I do not think it is a case for mandamus. I would, therefore, dismiss the appeal.

[2:8] Farrington, D and Dowds, E *'Why does crime decrease?'* (1984) Justice of the Peace 506 (at page 507):

We do not know why recorded crime in the whole country decreased between 1982 and 1983, but we do know why it has been decreasing in one county – Nottinghamshire. Taken at face value, the Criminal Statistics for 1981 showed that Nottinghamshire was the most criminal area in the country. For several years, Nottingham, the Metropolitan Police area and Merseyside had the three highest recorded crime rates in the country, and in 1981 Nottinghamshire regained the top position it had last held in 1977. Our research into the puzzling case of the high Nottinghamshire crime rate began in 1982. Between 1981 and 1982, whereas recorded crime in the whole country increased by 10%, in Nottinghamshire is stayed virtually unchanged, leading to a decline in Nottinghamshire's position in the 'league table' of crime rates from first to fifth. In 1983, whereas recorded crime in the whole country fell by 0.5%, the decrease in Nottinghamshire was 5%, and in the first quarter of 1984, when crime increased by 5% overall, it decreased in Nottinghamshire by 6%. These decreases will lead to a further decline in Nottinghamshire's relative standing.

The aim of our research was to compare Nottinghamshire with two other counties which were similar in many respects – Staffordshire and Leicestershire. According to the chief constables' reports, there were 87 recorded crimes per 100 population in Nottinghamshire in 1981, in comparison with 44 in Leicestershire and 40 in Staffordshire. We wanted to explain why Nottinghamshire was roughly twice as high as the other two counties.

There were basically four possible explanations:
(a)   more crimes were committed (in relation to population) in Nottinghamshire;
(b)   members of the public were more likely to report crimes to the police in Nottinghamshire;
(c)   the police were more likely to discover crimes in Nottinghamshire; and
(d)   an alleged crime which was discovered by or reported to the police was more likely to be recorded in Nottinghamshire.

In order to investigate (a) and (b), a random sample of about 1,000 adults in each county was interviewed and asked about crimes committed against them in the previous year and about whether these crimes were reported to the police. In order to investigate (c) and (d), police discovery and recording practices in the three counties were studied.

The crime survey (whose methodology was based on the British Crime Survey) indicated that the number of crimes committed in each county was far greater than the number recorded by the police: 405 per 1,000 in Nottinghamshire, in comparison with 326 in Leicestershire and 262 in Staffordshire. (These estimates include crimes against organisations and against persons under 16). The proportion of crimes reported to the police was almost exactly the same in each county, at about 40%. This led to an estimate of crimes reported to the police per 1,000 population of 162 in Nottinghamshire, 136 in Leicestershire and 102 in Staffordshire.

Comparing these figures with the recorded crime rates of 87, 44 and 40 (respectively) led to the conclusion that the ratio of recorded to reported crime was far higher in Nottinghamshire (53%) than in Leicestershire (32%) or Staffordshire (39%). If the probability of a crime known to the police being recorded had been 35% in all counties (the average of the Leicestershire and Staffordshire figures), the recorded crime rates per 1,000 population would have been 57 in Nottinghamshire, 48 in Leicestershire and 36 in Staffordshire. The police figures for Nottinghamshire were therefore about 30 crimes per 1,000 population higher than expected on the basis of the other two counties.

The study of police recording practices analysed a 1% random sample of 1981 crime reports in each county (over 1,600 in all). The main aims of this analysis were to investigate the origin of each recorded crime (eg from citizen reports or police investigatory practices) and the characteristics of each (eg the value of property stolen). The types of crimes recorded in the three counties were quite similar.

Differences – admissions

One major difference between the counties was in crimes arising from admissions, where a person apprehended for one crime admitted others which had not previously been reported to or recorded by the police. About a quarter of Nottinghamshire's crime reports originated in this way, in comparison with 4% in Leicestershire and 8% in Staffordshire. The difference between the counties in crimes arising from admissions amounted to a difference of 18–20 crimes per 1,000 population.

Differences – crime seriousness

The second major difference between the counties was in the seriousness of recorded crimes. Nearly half of the crimes of dishonesty in Nottinghamshire involved property worth £10 or less, in comparison with 29% in Leicestershire and 36% in Staffordshire. Crimes arising from admissions were especially likely to involve property worth £10 or less (72%). It seemed likely that the Nottinghamshire police were more willing to record relatively trivial crimes than the other two forces.

Adding together crimes arising from admissions and those involving property worth £10 or less, the rate in Nottinghamshire for crimes in one or both of these categories was 43 per 1,000 population, or about half the country's crime rate. The corresponding figure for the other two counties was 12 in both cases. Therefore, these two effects together accounted for a difference of 31 crimes per 1,000 population between Nottinghamshire and the other two counties – almost exactly the excess identified in the crime survey.

We therefore concluded that, of the difference in recorded crime rates between Nottinghamshire and the other two counties of about 45 offences per 1,000 population, about two-thirds reflected differences in police recording practices, while about one-third reflected real differences in crimes committed.

Since our research began, and possibly in the light of our results, the Nottinghamshire police have changed their recording practices. In particular, they decided to spend less time questioning apprehended offenders about all their crimes, and so nowadays do not record so many trivial crimes arising on admission. This is one of the major reasons why recorded crime in Nottinghamshire decreased between 1981 and 1984. Police practices in Nottinghamshire are now come comparable to those in Leicestershire and Staffordshire.

[2:9]　Police and Criminal Evidence Act 1984 (as amended) sections 17–19; 24; 25; 28–32; 36–38; 56; 58; 66–67; 76; 78

17　Entry for purpose of arrest etc

(1)　Subject to the following provisions of this section, and without prejudice to any other enactment, a constable may enter and search any premises for the purpose—
　　　(a)　of executing—

      (i)   a warrant of arrest issued in connection with or arising out of criminal proceedings; or

      (ii)   a warrant of commitment issued under section 76 of the Magistrates' Courts Act 1980;

  (b)   of arresting a person for an arrestable offence;

  (c)   of arresting a person for an offence under—

      (i)   section 1 (prohibition of uniforms in connection with political objects) ... of the Public Order Act 1936;

      (ii)   any enactment contained in sections 6 to 8 or 10 of the Criminal Law Act 1977 (offences relating to entering and remaining on property);

      (iii)   section 4 of the Public Order Act 1986 (fear or provocation of violence);

      (iiia) section 163 of the Road Traffic Act 1988 (c 52) (failure to stop when required to do so by a constable in uniform);

      (iv)   section 76 of the Criminal Justice and Public Order Act 1994 (failure to comply with interim possession order);

  (ca)   of arresting, in pursuance of section 32(1A) of the Children and Young Persons Act 1969, any child or young person who has been remanded or committed to local authority accommodation under section 23(1) of that Act;

  (cb)   of recapturing any person who is, or is deemed for any purpose to be, unlawfully at large while liable to be detained—

      (i)   in a prison, remand centre, young offender institution or secure training centre, or

      (ii)   in pursuance of section 92 of the Powers of Criminal Courts (Sentencing) Act 2000 (dealing with children and young persons guilty of grave crimes), in any other place;

  (d)   of recapturing any person whatever who is unlawfully at large and whom he is pursuing; or

  (e)   of saving life or limb or preventing serious damage to property.

(2)   Except for the purpose specified in paragraph (e) of subsection (1) above, the powers of entry and search conferred by this section—

  (a)   are only exercisable if the constable has reasonable grounds for believing that the person whom he is seeking is on the premises; and

  (b)   are limited, in relation to premises consisting of two or more separate dwellings, to powers to enter and search—

      (i)   any parts of the premises which the occupiers of any dwelling comprised in the premises use in common with the occupiers of any other such dwelling; and

      (ii)   any such dwelling in which the constable has reasonable grounds for believing that the person whom he is seeking may be.

(3)   The powers of entry and search conferred by this section are only exercisable for the purposes specified in subsection (1)(c)(ii) or (iv) above by a constable in uniform.

(4)   The power of search conferred by this section is only a power to search to the extent that is reasonably required for the purpose for which the power of entry is exercised.

(5)   Subject to subsection (6) below, all the rules of common law under which a constable has power to enter premises without a warrant are hereby abolished.

(6)   Nothing in subsection (5) above affects any power of entry to deal with or prevent a breach of the peace.

18 Entry and search after arrest

(1)   Subject to the following provisions of this section, a constable may enter and search any premises occupied or controlled by a person who is under arrest for an arrestable offence, if he has reasonable grounds for suspecting that there is on the premises evidence, other than items subject to legal privilege, that relates—
  (a)   to that offence; or
  (b)   to some other arrestable offence which is connected with or similar to that offence.

(2)   A constable may seize and retain anything for which he may search under subsection (1) above.

(3)   The power to search conferred by subsection (1) above is only a power to search to the extent that is reasonably required for the purpose of discovering such evidence.

(4)   Subject to subsection (5) below, the powers conferred by this section may not be exercised unless an officer of the rank of inspector or above has authorised them in writing.

(5)   A constable may conduct a search under subsection (1) above—
  (a)   before the person is taken to a police station; and
  (b)   without obtaining an authorisation under subsection (4) above,
if the presence of that person at a place other than a police station is necessary for the effective investigation of the offence.

(6)   If a constable conducts a search by virtue of subsection (5) above, he shall inform an officer of the rank of inspector or above that he has made the search as soon as practicable after he has made it.

(7)   An officer who—
  (a)   authorises a search; or
  (b)   is informed of a search under subsection (6) above, shall make a record in writing—
    (i)   of the grounds for the search; and
    (ii)   of the nature of the evidence that was sought.

(8)   If the person who was in occupation or control of the premises at the time of the search is in police detention at the time the record is to be made, the officer shall make the record as part of his custody record.

Seizure etc

19 General power of seizure etc

(1)   The powers conferred by subsections (2), (3) and (4) below are exercisable by a constable who is lawfully on any premises.

(2)   The constable may seize anything which is on the premises if he has reasonable grounds for believing—

  (a)   that it has been obtained in consequence of the commission of an offence; and
  (b)   that it is necessary to seize it in order to prevent it being concealed, lost, damaged, altered or destroyed.

(3)   The constable may seize anything which is on the premises if he has reasonable grounds for believing—
  (a)   that it is evidence in relation to an offence which he is investigating or any other offence; and
  (b)   that it is necessary to seize it in order to prevent the evidence being concealed, lost, altered or destroyed.

(4)   The constable may require any information which is stored in any electronic form and is accessible from the premises to be produced in a form in which it can be taken away and in which it is visible and legible or from which it can readily be produced in a visible and legible form if he has reasonable grounds for believing—
  (a)   that—
      (i)   it is evidence in relation to an offence which he is investigating or any other offence; or
      (ii) it has been obtained in consequence of the commission of an offence; and
  (b)   that it is necessary to do so in order to prevent it being concealed, lost, tampered with or destroyed.

(5)   The powers conferred by this section are in addition to any power otherwise conferred.

(6)   No power of seizure conferred on a constable under any enactment (including an enactment contained in an Act passed after this Act) is to be taken to authorise the seizure of an item which the constable exercising the power has reasonable grounds for believing to be subject to legal privilege.

24   Arrest without warrant for arrestable offences

(1)   The powers of summary arrest conferred by the following subsections shall apply—
  (a)   to offences for which the sentence is fixed by law;
  (b)   to offences for which a person of 21 years of age or over (not previously convicted) may be sentenced to imprisonment for a term of five years (or might be so sentenced but for the restrictions imposed by section 33 of the Magistrates' Courts Act 1980); and
  (c)   to the offences listed in Schedule 1A,
and in this Act "arrestable offence" means any such offence.

(2)   Schedule 1A (which lists the offences referred to in subsection (1)(c)) shall have effect.

(3)   Without prejudice to section 2 of the Criminal Attempts Act 1981, the powers of summary arrest conferred by the following subsections shall also apply to the offences of—
  (a)   conspiring to commit any of the offences listed in Schedule 1A;

(b) attempting to commit any such offence other than one which is a summary offence;

(c) inciting, aiding, abetting, counselling or procuring the commission of any such offence;

and such offences are also arrestable offences for the purposes of this Act.

(4) Any person may arrest without a warrant—

(a) anyone who is in the act of committing an arrestable offence;

(b) anyone whom he has reasonable grounds for suspecting to be committing such an offence.

(5) Where an arrestable offence has been committed, any person may arrest without a warrant—

(a) anyone who is guilty of the offence;

(b) anyone whom he has reasonable grounds for suspecting to be guilty of it.

(6) Where a constable has reasonable grounds for suspecting that an arrestable offence has been committed, he may arrest without a warrant anyone whom he has reasonable grounds for suspecting to be guilty of the offence.

(7) A constable may arrest without a warrant—

(a) anyone who is about to commit an arrestable offence;

(b) anyone whom he has reasonable grounds for suspecting to be about to commit an arrestable offence.

25 General arrest conditions

(1) Where a constable has reasonable grounds for suspecting that any offence which is not an arrestable offence has been committed or attempted, or is being committed or attempted, he may arrest the relevant person if it appears to him that service of a summons is impracticable or inappropriate because any of the general arrest conditions is satisfied.

(2) In this section "the relevant person" means any person whom the constable has reasonable grounds to suspect of having committed or having attempted to commit the offence or of being in the course of committing or attempting to commit it.

(3) The general arrest conditions are—

(a) that the name of the relevant person is unknown to, and cannot be readily ascertained by, the constable;

(b) that the constable has reasonable grounds for doubting whether a name furnished by the relevant person as his name is his real name;

(c) that—

(i) the relevant person has failed to furnish a satisfactory address for service; or

(ii) the constable has reasonable grounds for doubting whether an address furnished by the relevant person is a satisfactory address for service;

(d) that the constable has reasonable grounds for believing that arrest is necessary to prevent the relevant person—

(i) causing physical injury to himself or any other person;

(ii) suffering physical injury;

(iii) causing loss of or damage to property;

(iv)   committing an offence against public decency; or
(v)   causing an unlawful obstruction of the highway;
(e)   that the constable has reasonable grounds for believing that arrest is necessary to protect a child or other vulnerable person from the relevant person.

(4)   For the purposes of subsection (3) above an address is a satisfactory address for
service if it appears to the constable—
(a)   that the relevant person will be at it for a sufficiently long period for it to be
possible to serve him with a summons; or
(b)   that some other person specified by the relevant person will accept service
of a summons for the relevant person at it.

(5)   Nothing in subsection (3)(d) above authorises the arrest of a person under sub-
paragraph (iv) of that paragraph except where members of the public going about their
normal business cannot reasonably be expected to avoid the person to be arrested.

(6)   This section shall not prejudice any power of arrest conferred apart from this
section.

28   Information to be given on arrest

(1)   Subject to subsection (5) below, where a person is arrested, otherwise than by
being informed that he is under arrest, the arrest is not lawful unless the person arrested
is informed that he is under arrest as soon as is practicable after his arrest.

(2)   Where a person is arrested by a constable, subsection (1) above applies regardless
of whether the fact of the arrest is obvious.

(3)   Subject to subsection (5) below, no arrest is lawful unless the person arrested is
informed of the ground for the arrest at the time of, or as soon as is practicable after,
the arrest.

(4)   Where a person is arrested by a constable, subsection (3) above applies regardless
of whether the ground for the arrest is obvious.

(5)   Nothing in this section is to be taken to require a person to be informed—
(a)   that he is under arrest; or
(b)   of the ground for the arrest,
if it was not reasonably practicable for him to be so informed by reason of his having
escaped from arrest before the information could be given.

29   Voluntary attendance at police station etc

Where for the purpose of assisting with an investigation a person attends voluntarily
at a police station or at any other place where a constable is present or accompanies a
constable to a police station or any such other place without having been arrested—
(a)   he shall be entitled to leave at will unless he is placed under arrest;
(b)   he shall be informed at once that he is under arrest if a decision is taken by
a constable to prevent him from leaving at will.

30   Arrest elsewhere than at police station

(1)   Subject to the following provisions of this section, where a person—
    (a)   is arrested by a constable for an offence; or
    (b)   is taken into custody by a constable after being arrested for an offence by a person other than a constable,
at any place other than a police station, he shall be taken to a police station by a constable as soon as practicable after the arrest.

(2)   Subject to subsections (3) and (5) below, the police station to which an arrested person is taken under subsection (1) above shall be a designated police station.

(3)   A constable to whom this subsection applies may take an arrested person to any police station unless it appears to the constable that it may be necessary to keep the arrested person in police detention for more than six hours.

(4)   Subsection (3) above applies—
    (a)   to a constable who is working in a locality covered by a police station which is not a designated police station; and
    (b)   to a constable belonging to a body of constables maintained by an authority other than a police authority.

(5)   Any constable may take an arrested person to any police station if—
    (a)   either of the following conditions is satisfied—
        (i)   the constable has arrested him without the assistance of any other constable and no other constable is available to assist him;
        (ii)   the constable has taken him into custody from a person other than a constable without the assistance of any other constable and no other constable is available to assist him; and
    (b)   it appears to the constable that he will be unable to take the arrested person to a designated police station without the arrested person injuring himself, the constable or some other person.

(6)   If the first police station to which an arrested person is taken after his arrest is not a designated police station, he shall be taken to a designated police station not more than six hours after his arrival at the first police station unless he is released previously.

(7)   A person arrested by a constable at a place other than a police station shall be released if a constable is satisfied, before the person arrested reaches a police station, that there are no grounds for keeping him under arrest.

(8)   A constable who releases a person under subsection (7) above shall record the fact that he has done so.

(9)   The constable shall make the record as soon as is practicable after the release.

(10)   Nothing in subsection (1) above shall prevent a constable delaying taking a person who has been arrested to a police station if the presence of that person elsewhere is necessary in order to carry out such investigations as it is reasonable to carry out immediately.

(11) Where there is delay in taking a person who has been arrested to a police station after his arrest, the reasons for the delay shall be recorded when he first arrives at a police station.

(12) Nothing in subsection (1) above shall be taken to affect—
  (a) paragraphs 16(3) or 18(1) of Schedule 2 to the Immigration Act 1971;
  (b) section 34(1) of the Criminal Justice Act 1972; or
  (c) any provision of the Terrorism Act 2000.

(13) Nothing in subsection (10) above shall be taken to affect paragraph 18(3) of Schedule 2 to the Immigration Act 1971.

31 Arrest for further offence

Where—
  (a) a person—
    (i) has been arrested for an offence; and
    (ii) is at a police station in consequence of that arrest; and
  (b) it appears to a constable that, if he were released from that arrest, he would be liable to arrest for some other offence,
he shall be arrested for that other offence.

32 Search upon arrest

(1) A constable may search an arrested person, in any case where the person to be searched has been arrested at a place other than a police station, if the constable has reasonable grounds for believing that the arrested person may present a danger to himself or others.

(2) Subject to subsections (3) to (5) below, a constable shall also have power in any such case—
  (a) to search the arrested person for anything—
    (i) which he might use to assist him to escape from lawful custody; or
    (ii) which might be evidence relating to an offence; and
  (b) to enter and search any premises in which he was when arrested or immediately before he was arrested for evidence relating to the offence for which he has been arrested.

(3) The power to search conferred by subsection (2) above is only a power to search to the extent that is reasonably required for the purpose of discovering any such thing or any such evidence.

(4) The powers conferred by this section to search a person are not to be construed as authorising a constable to require a person to remove any of his clothing in public other than an outer coat, jacket or gloves but they do authorise a search of a person's mouth.

(5) A constable may not search a person in the exercise of the power conferred by subsection (2)(a) above unless he has reasonable grounds for believing that the person to be searched may have concealed on him anything for which a search is permitted under that paragraph.

(6) A constable may not search premises in the exercise of the power conferred by subsection (2)(b) above unless he has reasonable grounds for believing that there is evidence for which a search is permitted under that paragraph on the premises.

(7) In so far as the power of search conferred by subsection (2)(b) above relates to premises consisting of two or more separate dwellings, it is limited to a power to search—

    (a)   any dwelling in which the arrest took place or in which the person arrested was immediately before his arrest; and

    (b)   any parts of the premises which the occupier of any such dwelling uses in common with the occupiers of any other dwellings comprised in the premises.

(8) A constable searching a person in the exercise of the power conferred by subsection (1) above may seize and retain anything he finds, if he has reasonable grounds for believing that the person searched might use it to cause physical injury to himself or to any other person.

(9) A constable searching a person in the exercise of the power conferred by subsection (2)(a) above may seize and retain anything he finds, other than an item subject to legal privilege, if he has reasonable grounds for believing—

    (a)   that he might use it to assist him to escape from lawful custody; or

    (b)   that it is evidence of an offence or has been obtained in consequence of the commission of an offence.

(10) Nothing in this section shall be taken to affect the power conferred by section 43 of the Terrorism Act 2000.

36 Custody officers at police stations

(1) One or more custody officers shall be appointed for each designated police station.

(2) A custody officer for a police station designated under section 35(1) above shall be appointed—

    (a)   by the chief officer of police for the area in which the designated police station is situated; or

    (b)   by such other police officer as the chief officer of police for that area may direct.

(2A) A custody officer for a police station designated under section 35(2A) above shall be appointed—

    (a)   by the Chief Constable of the British Transport Police Force; or

    (b)   by such other member of that Force as that Chief Constable may direct.

(3) No officer may be appointed a custody officer unless he is of at least the rank of sergeant.

(4)   An officer of any rank may perform the functions of a custody officer at a designated police station if a custody officer is not readily available to perform them.

(5)   Subject to the following provisions of this section and to section 39(2) below, none of the functions of a custody officer in relation to a person shall be performed by an officer who at the time when the function falls to be performed is involved in the investigation of an offence for which that person is in police detention at that time.

(6)   Nothing in subsection (5) above is to be taken to prevent a custody officer—
    (a)   performing any function assigned to custody officers—
        (i)   by this Act; or
        (ii)   by a code of practice issued under this Act;
    (b)   carrying out the duty imposed on custody officers by section 39 below;
    (c)   doing anything in connection with the identification of a suspect; or
    (d)   doing anything under sections 7 and 8 of the Road Traffic Act 1988.

(7)   Where an arrested person is taken to a police station which is not a designated police station, the functions in relation to him which at a designated police station would be the functions of a custody officer shall be performed—
    (a)   by an officer who is not involved in the investigation of an offence for which he is in police detention, if such an officer is readily available; and
    (b)   if no such officer is readily available, by the officer who took him to the station or any other officer.

(8)   References to a custody officer in the following provisions of this Act include references to an officer other than a custody officer who is performing the functions of a custody officer by virtue of subsection (4) or (7) above.

(9)   Where by virtue of subsection (7) above an officer of a force maintained by a police authority who took an arrested person to a police station is to perform the functions of a custody officer in relation to him, the officer shall inform an officer who—
    (a)   is attached to a designated police station; and
    (b)   is of at least the rank of inspector,
that he is to do so.

(10)   The duty imposed by subsection (9) above shall be performed as soon as it is practicable to perform it.

37   Duties of custody officer before charge

(1)   Where—
    (a)   a person is arrested for an offence—
        (i)   without a warrant; or
        (ii)   under a warrant not endorsed for bail, . . .
    (b)   . . .
the custody officer at each police station where he is detained after his arrest shall determine whether he has before him sufficient evidence to charge that person with the offence for which he was arrested and may detain him at the police station for such period as is necessary to enable him to do so.

(2)   If the custody officer determines that he does not have such evidence before him, the person arrested shall be released either on bail or without bail, unless the custody officer has reasonable grounds for believing that his detention without being charged is necessary to secure or preserve evidence relating to an offence for which he is under arrest or to obtain such evidence by questioning him.

(3)   If the custody officer has reasonable grounds for so believing, he may authorise the person arrested to be kept in police detention.

(4)   Where a custody officer authorises a person who has not been charged to be kept in police detention, he shall, as soon as is practicable, make a written record of the grounds for the detention.

(5)   Subject to subsection (6) below, the written record shall be made in the presence of the person arrested who shall at that time be informed by the custody officer of the grounds for his detention.

(6)   Subsection (5) above shall not apply where the person arrested is, at the time when the written record is made—
    (a)   incapable of understanding what is said to him;
    (b)   violent or likely to become violent; or
    (c)   in urgent need of medical attention.

(7)   Subject to section 41(7) below, if the custody officer determines that he has before him sufficient evidence to charge the person arrested with the offence for which he was arrested, the person arrested—
    (a)   shall be charged; or
    (b)   shall be released without charge, either on bail or without bail.

(8)   Where—
    (a)   a person is released under subsection (7)(b) above; and
    (b)   at the time of his release a decision whether he should be prosecuted for the offence for which he was arrested has not been taken,
it shall be the duty of the custody officer so to inform him.

(9)   If the person arrested is not in a fit state to be dealt with under subsection (7) above, he may be kept in police detention until he is.

(10) The duty imposed on the custody officer under subsection (1) above shall be carried out by him as soon as practicable after the person arrested arrives at the police station or, in the case of a person arrested at the police station, as soon as practicable after the arrest.

(11)–(14)   ...

(15) In this Part of this Act—
    "arrested juvenile" means a person arrested with or without a warrant who appears to be under the age of 17 ...;
    "endorsed for bail" means endorsed with a direction for bail in accordance with section 117(2) of the Magistrates' Courts Act 1980.

38 Duties of custody officer after charge

(1)   Where a person arrested for an offence otherwise than under a warrant endorsed for bail is charged with an offence, the custody officer shall, subject to section 25 of the Criminal Justice and Public Order Act 1994, order his release from police detention, either on bail or without bail, unless—

    (a)   if the person arrested is not an arrested juvenile—

        (i)   his name or address cannot be ascertained or the custody officer has reasonable grounds for doubting whether a name or address furnished by him as his name or address is his real name or address;

        (ii)   the custody officer has reasonable grounds for believing that the person arrested will fail to appear in court to answer to bail;

        (iii)   in the case of a person arrested for an imprisonable offence, the custody officer has reasonable grounds for believing that the detention of the person arrested is necessary to prevent him from committing an offence;

        (iiia)   in the case of a person who has attained the age of 18, the custody officer has reasonable grounds for believing that the detention of the person is necessary to enable a sample to be taken from him under section 63B below;

        (iv)   in the case of a person arrested for an offence which is not an imprisonable offence, the custody officer has reasonable grounds for believing that the detention of the person arrested is necessary to prevent him from causing physical injury to any other person or from causing loss of or damage to property;

        (v)   the custody officer has reasonable grounds for believing that the detention of the person arrested is necessary to prevent him from interfering with the administration of justice or with the investigation of offences or of a particular offence; or

        (vi)   the custody officer has reasonable grounds for believing that the detention of the person arrested is necessary for his own protection;

    (b)   if he is an arrested juvenile—

        (i)   any of the requirements of paragraph (a) above is satisfied; or

        (ii)   the custody officer has reasonable grounds for believing that he ought to be detained in his own interests.

(2)   If the release of a person arrested is not required by subsection (1) above, the custody officer may authorise him to be kept in police detention but may not authorise a person to be kept in police detention by virtue of subsection (1)(a)(iiia) after the end of the period of six hours beginning when he was charged with the offence.

(2A)   The custody officer, in taking the decisions required by subsection (1)(a) and (b) above (except (a)(i) and (vi) and (b)(ii)), shall have regard to the same considerations as those which a court is required to have regard to in taking the corresponding decisions under paragraph 2 of Part I of Schedule 1 to the Bail Act 1976.

(3)   Where a custody officer authorises a person who has been charged to be kept in police detention, he shall, as soon as practicable, make a written record of the grounds for the detention.

(4)   Subject to subsection (5) below, the written record shall be made in the presence of the person charged who shall at that time be informed by the custody officer of the grounds for his detention.

(5)   Subsection (4) above shall not apply where the person charged is, at the time when the written record is made—
  (a)   incapable of understanding what is said to him;
  (b)   violent or likely to become violent; or
  (c)   in urgent need of medical attention.

(6)   Where a custody officer authorises an arrested juvenile to be kept in police detention under subsection (1) above, the custody officer shall, unless he certifies—
  (a)   that, by reason of such circumstances as are specified in the certificate, it is impracticable for him to do so; or
  (b)   in the case of an arrested juvenile who has attained the age of 12 years, that no secure accommodation is available and that keeping him in other local authority accommodation would not be adequate to protect the public from serious harm from him,
secure that the arrested juvenile is moved to local authority accommodation.

(6A) In this section—
  "local authority accommodation" means accommodation provided by or on be-half of a local authority (within the meaning of the Children Act 1989);
  "secure accommodation" means accommodation provided for the purpose of restricting liberty;
  "sexual offence" and "violent offence" have the same meanings as in the Powers of Criminal Courts (Sentencing) Act 2000;
and any reference, in relation to an arrested juvenile charged with a violent or sexual offence, to protecting the public from serious harm from him shall be construed as a reference to protecting members of the public from death or serious personal injury, whether physical or psychological, occasioned by further such offences committed by him.

(6B) Where an arrested juvenile is moved to local authority accommodation under subsection (6) above, it shall be lawful for any person acting on behalf of the authority to detain him.

(7)   A certificate made under subsection (6) above in respect of an arrested juvenile shall be produced to the court before which he is first brought thereafter.

(7A) In this section "imprisonable offence" has the same meaning as in Schedule 1 to the Bail Act 1976.

(8)   In this Part of this Act "local authority" has the same meaning as in the Children Act 1989.

56   Right to have someone informed when arrested

(1)   Where a person has been arrested and is being held in custody in a police station or other premises, he shall be entitled, if he so requests, to have one friend or relative or

other person who is known to him or who is likely to take an interest in his welfare told, as soon as is practicable except to the extent that delay is permitted by this section, that he has been arrested and is being detained there.

(2) Delay is only permitted—
  (a) in the case of a person who is in police detention for a serious arrestable offence; and
  (b) if an officer of at least the rank of inspector authorises it.

(3) In any case the person in custody must be permitted to exercise the right conferred by subsection (1) above within 36 hours from the relevant time, as defined in section 41(2) above.

(4) An officer may give an authorisation under subsection (2) above orally or in writing but, if he gives it orally, he shall confirm it in writing as soon as is practicable.

(5) Subject to subsection (5A) below an officer may only authorise delay where he has reasonable grounds for believing that telling the named person of the arrest—
  (a) will lead to interference with or harm to evidence connected with a serious arrestable offence or interference with or physical injury to other persons; or
  (b) will lead to the alerting of other persons suspected of having committed such an offence but not yet arrested for it; or
  (c) will hinder the recovery of any property obtained as a result of such an offence.

(5A) An officer may also authorise delay where he has reasonable grounds for believing that—
  (a) the person detained for the serious arrestable offence has benefited from his criminal conduct, and
  (b) the recovery of the value of the property constituting the benefit will be hindered by telling the named person of the arrest.

(5B) For the purposes of subsection (5A) above the question whether a person has benefited from his criminal conduct is to be decided in accordance with Part 2 of the Proceeds of Crime Act 2002.

(6) If a delay is authorised—
  (a) the detained person shall be told the reason for it; and
  (b) the reason shall be noted on his custody record.

(7) The duties imposed by subsection (6) above shall be performed as soon as is practicable.

(8) The rights conferred by this section on a person detained at a police station or other premises are exercisable whenever he is transferred from one place to another; and this section applies to each subsequent occasion on which they are exercisable as it applies to the first such occasion.

(9) There may be no further delay in permitting the exercise of the right conferred by subsection (1) above once the reason for authorising delay ceases to subsist.

(10) Nothing in this section applies to a person arrested or detained under the terrorism provisions.

58 Access to legal advice

(1)   A person arrested and held in custody in a police station or other premises shall be entitled, if he so requests, to consult a solicitor privately at any time.

(2)   Subject to subsection (3) below, a request under subsection (1) above and the time at which it was made shall be recorded in the custody record.

(3)   Such a request need not be recorded in the custody record of a person who makes it at a time while he is at a court after being charged with an offence.

(4)   If a person makes such a request, he must be permitted to consult a solicitor as soon as is practicable except to the extent that delay is permitted by this section.

(5)   In any case he must be permitted to consult a solicitor within 36 hours from the relevant time, as defined in section 41(2) above.

(6)   Delay in compliance with a request is only permitted—
    (a)   in the case of a person who is in police detention for a serious arrestable offence; and
    (b)   if an officer of at least the rank of superintendent authorises it.

(7)   An officer may give an authorisation under subsection (6) above orally or in writing but, if he gives it orally, he shall confirm it in writing as soon as is practicable.

(8)   Subject to subsection (8A) below an officer may only authorise delay where he has reasonable grounds for believing that the exercise of the right conferred by subsection (1) above at the time when the person detained desires to exercise it—
    (a)   will lead to interference with or harm to evidence connected with a serious arrestable offence or interference with or physical injury to other persons; or
    (b)   will lead to the alerting of other persons suspected of having committed such an offence but not yet arrested for it; or
    (c)   will hinder the recovery of any property obtained as a result of such an offence.

(8A) An officer may also authorise delay where he has reasonable grounds for believing that—
    (a)   the person detained for the serious arrestable offence has benefited from his criminal conduct, and
    (b)   the recovery of the value of the property constituting the benefit will be hindered by the exercise of the right conferred by subsection (1) above.

(8B) For the purposes of subsection (8A) above the question whether a person has benefited from his criminal conduct is to be decided in accordance with Part 2 of the Proceeds of Crime Act 2002.

(9)   If delay is authorised—
   (a)   the detained person shall be told the reason for it; and
   (b)   the reason shall be noted on his custody record.

(10)   The duties imposed by subsection (9) above shall be performed as soon as is practicable.

(11)   There may be no further delay in permitting the exercise of the right conferred by subsection (1) above once the reason for authorising delay ceases to subsist.

(12)   Nothing in this section applies to a person arrested or detained under the terrorism provisions.

66   Codes of practice

(1)   The Secretary of State shall issue codes of practice in connection with—
   (a)   the exercise by police officers of statutory powers—
      (i)   to search a person without first arresting him; or
      (ii)   to search a vehicle without making an arrest;
   (b)   the detention, treatment, questioning and identification of persons by police officers;
   (c)   searches of premises by police officers; and
   (d)   the seizure of property found by police officers on persons or premises.

(2)   Codes shall (in particular) include provision in connection with the exercise by police officers of powers under section 63B above.

67   Codes of practice—supplementary

(1)   When the Secretary of State proposes to issue a code of practice to which this section applies, he shall prepare and publish a draft of that code, shall consider any representations made to him about the draft and may modify the draft accordingly.

(2)   This section applies to a code of practice under section 60, 60A or 66 above.

(3)   The Secretary of State shall lay before both Houses of Parliament a draft of any code of practice prepared by him under this section.

(4)   When the Secretary of State has laid the draft of a code before Parliament, he may bring the code into operation by order made by statutory instrument.

(5)   No order under subsection (4) above shall have effect until approved by a resolution of each House of Parliament.

(6)   An order bringing a code of practice into operation may contain such transitional provisions or savings as appear to the Secretary of State to be necessary or expedient in connection with the code of practice thereby brought into operation.

(7)   The Secretary of State may from time to time revise the whole or any part of a code of practice to which this section applies and issue that revised code; and the foregoing provisions of this section shall apply (with appropriate modifications) to such a revised code as they apply to the first issue of a code.

(7A) Subject to subsection (7B) below, the Secretary of State may by order provide that a code of practice for the time being in force is to be treated as having effect with such modifications as may be set out in the order.

(7B) The effect of the modifications made by an order under subsection (7A) above must be confined to one or more of the following—
    (a)   the effect of the code in relation to such area of England and Wales as may be specified in the order;
    (b)   the effect of the code during such period, not exceeding two years, as may be so specified;
    (c)   the effect of the code in relation to such offences or descriptions of offender as may be so specified.

(7C) An order under subsection (7A) above shall be made by statutory instrument and shall be subject to annulment in pursuance of a resolution of either House of Parliament.

(8)   ...

(9)   Persons other than police officers who are charged with the duty of investigating offences or charging offenders shall in the discharge of that duty have regard to any relevant provision of such a code.

(9A) Persons on whom powers are conferred by—
    (a)   any designation under section 38 or 39 of the Police Reform Act 2002 (c 30) (police powers for police authority employees), or
    (b)   any accreditation under section 41 of that Act (accreditation under community safety accreditation schemes),
shall have regard to any relevant provision of a code of practice to which this section applies in the exercise or performance of the powers and duties conferred or imposed on them by that designation or accreditation.

(10) A failure on the part—
    (a)   of a police office to comply with any provision of such a code;...
    (b)   of any person other than a police officer who is charged with the duty of investigating offences or charging offenders to have regard to any relevant provision of such a code in the discharge of that duty, or
    (c)   of a person designated under section 38 or 39 or accredited under section 41 of the Police Reform Act 2002 (c 30) to have regard to any relevant provision of such a code in the exercise or performance of the powers and duties conferred or imposed on him by that designation or accreditation,
shall not of itself render him liable to any criminal or civil proceedings.

(11) In all criminal and civil proceedings any such code shall be admissible in evidence; and if any provision of such a code appears to the court or tribunal conducting the proceedings to be relevant to any question arising in the proceedings it shall be taken into account in determining that question.

(12) In this section "criminal proceedings" includes—
  (a) proceedings in the United Kingdom or elsewhere before a court-martial constituted under the Army Act 1955, the Air Force Act 1955 or the Naval Discipline Act 1957 ...;
  (b) proceedings before the Courts-Martial Appeal Court; and
  (c) proceedings before a Standing Civilian Court.

76 Confessions

(1) In any proceedings a confession made by an accused person may be given in evidence against him in so far as it is relevant to any matter in issue in the proceedings and is not excluded by the court in pursuance of this section.

(2) If, in any proceedings where the prosecution proposes to give in evidence a confession made by an accused person, it is represented to the court that the confession was or may have been obtained—
  (a) by oppression of the person who made it; or
  (b) in consequence of anything said or done which was likely, in the circumstances existing at the time, to render unreliable any confession which might be made by him in consequence thereof,
the court shall not allow the confession to be given in evidence against him except in so far as the prosecution proves to the court beyond reasonable doubt that the confession (notwithstanding that it may be true) was not obtained as aforesaid.

(3) In any proceedings where the prosecution proposes to give in evidence a confession made by an accused person, the court may of its own motion require the prosecution, as a condition of allowing it to do so, to prove that the confession was not obtained as mentioned in subsection (2) above.

(4) The fact that a confession is wholly or partly excluded in pursuance of this section shall not affect the admissibility in evidence—
  (a) of any facts discovered as a result of the confession; or
  (b) where the confession is relevant as showing that the accused speaks, writes or expresses himself in a particular way, of so much of the confession as is necessary to show that he does so.

(5) Evidence that a fact to which this subsection applies was discovered as a result of a statement made by an accused person shall not be admissible unless evidence of how it was discovered is given by him or on his behalf.

(6) Subsection (5) above applies—
  (a) to any fact discovered as a result of a confession which is wholly excluded in pursuance of this section; and
  (b) to any fact discovered as a result of a confession which is partly so excluded, if the fact is discovered as a result of the excluded part of the confession.

(7) Nothing in Part VII of this Act shall prejudice the admissibility of a confession made by an accused person.

(8) In this section "oppression" includes torture, inhuman or degrading treatment, and the use or threat of violence (whether or not amounting to torture).

(9)   Where the proceedings mentioned in subsection (1) above are proceedings before a magistrates' court inquiring into an offence as examining justices this section shall have effect with the omission of
  (a)   in subsection (1) the words "and is not excluded by the court in pursuance of this section", and
  (b)   subsections (2) to (6) and (8).

78   Exclusion of unfair evidence

(1)   In any proceedings the court may refuse to allow evidence on which the prosecution proposes to rely to be given if it appears to the court that, having regard to all the circumstances, including the circumstances in which the evidence was obtained, the admission of the evidence would have such an adverse effect on the fairness of the proceedings that the court ought not to admit it.

(2)   Nothing in this section shall prejudice any rule of law requiring a court to exclude evidence.

(3)   This section shall not apply in the case of proceedings before a magistrates' court inquiring into an offence as examining justices.

[2:10]   Criminal Justice and Public Order Act 1994 sections 34–39; 60

34   Effect of accused's failure to mention facts when questioned or charged

(1)   Where, in any proceedings against a person for an offence, evidence is given that the accused—
  (a)   at any time before he was charged with the offence, on being questioned under caution by a constable trying to discover whether or by whom the offence had been committed, failed to mention any fact relied on in his defence in those proceedings; or
  (b)   on being charged with the offence or officially informed that he might be prosecuted for it, failed to mention any such fact,
being a fact which in the circumstances existing at the time the accused could reasonably have been expected to mention when so questioned, charged or informed, as the case may be, subsection (2) below applies.

(2)   Where this subsection applies—
  (a)   a magistrates' court inquiring into the offence as examining justices;
  (b)   a judge, in deciding whether to grant an application made by the accused under—
      (i)   section 6 of the Criminal Justice Act 1987 (application for dismissal of charge of serious fraud in respect of which notice of transfer has been given under section 4 of that Act); or
      (ii)   paragraph 5 of Schedule 6 to the Criminal Justice Act 1991 (application for dismissal of charge of violent or sexual offence involving child in respect of which notice of transfer has been given under section 53 of that Act);
  (c)   the court, in determining whether there is a case to answer; and

> (d)   the court or jury, in determining whether the accused is guilty of the offence charged,

may draw such inferences from the failure as appear proper.

(2A) Where the accused was at an authorised place of detention at the time of the failure, subsections (1) and (2) above do not apply if he had not been allowed an opportunity to consult a solicitor prior to being questioned, charged or informed as mentioned in subsection (1) above.

(3)   Subject to any directions by the court, evidence tending to establish the failure may be given before or after evidence tending to establish the fact which the accused is alleged to have failed to mention.

(4)   This section applies in relation to questioning by persons (other than constables) charged with the duty of investigating offences or charging offenders as it applies in relation to questioning by constables; and in subsection (1) above "officially informed" means informed by a constable or any such person.

(5)   This section does not—
> (a)   prejudice the admissibility in evidence of the silence or other reaction of the accused in the face of anything said in his presence relating to the conduct in respect of which he is charged, in so far as evidence thereof would be admissible apart from this section; or
> (b)   preclude the drawing of any inference from any such silence or other reaction of the accused which could properly be drawn apart from this section.

(6)   This section does not apply in relation to a failure to mention a fact if the failure occurred before the commencement of this section.

(7)   ...

35   Effect of accused's silence at trial

(1)   At the trial of any person ... for an offence, subsections (2) and (3) below apply unless—
> (a)   the accused's guilt is not in issue; or
> (b)   it appears to the court that the physical or mental condition of the accused makes it undesirable for him to give evidence;

but subsection (2) below does not apply if, at the conclusion of the evidence for the prosecution, his legal representative informs the court that the accused will give evidence or, where he is unrepresented, the court ascertains from him that he will give evidence.

(2)   Where this subsection applies, the court shall, at the conclusion of the evidence for the prosecution, satisfy itself (in the case of proceedings on indictment, in the presence of the jury) that the accused is aware that the stage has been reached at which evidence can be given for the defence and that he can, if he wishes, give evidence and that, if he chooses not to give evidence, or having been sworn, without good cause refuses to answer any question, it will be permissible for the court or jury to draw such inferences as appear proper from his failure to give evidence or his refusal, without good cause, to answer any question.

(3)   Where this subsection applies, the court or jury, in determining whether the accused is guilty of the offence charged, may draw such inferences as appear proper from the failure of the accused to give evidence or his refusal, without good cause, to answer any question.

(4)   This section does not render the accused compellable to give evidence on his own behalf, and he shall accordingly not be guilty of contempt of court by reason of a failure to do so.

(5)   For the purposes of this section a person who, having been sworn, refuses to answer any question shall be taken to do so without good cause unless—

    (a)   he is entitled to refuse to answer the question by virtue of any enactment, whenever passed or made, or on the ground of privilege; or

    (b)   the court in the exercise of its general discretion excuses him from answering it.

(6)   ...

(7)   This section applies—

    (a)   in relation to proceedings on indictment for an offence, only if the person charged with the offence is arraigned on or after the commencement of this section;

    (b)   in relation to proceedings in a magistrates' court, only if the time when the court begins to receive evidence in the proceedings falls after the commencement of this section.

36   Effect of accused's failure or refusal to account for objects, substances or marks

(1)   Where—

    (a)   a person is arrested by a constable, and there is—

        (i)   on his person; or

        (ii)   in or on his clothing or footwear; or

        (iii)   otherwise in his possession; or

        (iv)   in any place in which he is at the time of his arrest,

        any object, substance or mark, or there is any mark on any such object; and

    (b)   that or another constable investigating the case reasonably believes that the presence of the object, substance or mark may be attributable to the participation of the person arrested in the commission of an offence specified by the constable; and

    (c)   the constable informs the person arrested that he so believes, and requests him to account for the presence of the object, substance or mark; and

    (d)   the person fails or refuses to do so,

then if, in any proceedings against the person for the offence so specified, evidence of those matters is given, subsection (2) below applies.

(2)   Where this subsection applies—

    (a)   a magistrates' court inquiring into the offence as examining justices;

    (b)   a judge, in deciding whether to grant an application made by the accused under—

      (i)   section 6 of the Criminal Justice Act 1987 (application for dismissal of charge of serious fraud in respect of which notice of transfer has been given under section 4 of that Act); or

      (ii)   paragraph 5 of Schedule 6 to the Criminal Justice Act 1991 (application for dismissal of charge of violent or sexual offence involving child in respect of which notice of transfer has been given under section 53 of that Act);

   (c)   the court, in determining whether there is a case to answer; and

   (d)   the court or jury, in determining whether the accused is guilty of the offence charged,

may draw such inferences from the failure or refusal as appear proper.

(3)   Subsections (1) and (2) above apply to the condition of clothing or footwear as they apply to a substance or mark thereon.

(4)   Subsections (1) and (2) above do not apply unless the accused was told in ordinary language by the constable when making the request mentioned in subsection (1)(c) above what the effect of this section would be if he failed or refused to comply with the request.

(4A) Where the accused was at an authorised place of detention at the time of the failure or refusal, subsections (1) and (2) above do not apply if he had not been allowed an opportunity to consult a solicitor prior to the request being made.

(5)   This section applies in relation to officers of customs and excise as it applies in relation to constables.

(6)   This section does not preclude the drawing of any inference from a failure or refusal of the accused to account for the presence of an object, substance or mark or from the condition of clothing or footwear which could properly be drawn apart from this section.

(7)   This section does not apply in relation to a failure or refusal which occurred before the commencement of this section.

(8)   ...

37   Effect of accused's failure or refusal to account for presence at a particular place

(1)   Where—

   (a)   a person arrested by a constable was found by him at a place at or about the time the offence for which he was arrested is alleged to have been committed; and

   (b)   that or another constable investigating the offence reasonably believes that the presence of the person at that place and at that time may be attributable to his participation in the commission of the offence; and

   (c)   the constable informs the person that he so believes, and requests him to account for that presence; and

   (d)   the person fails or refuses to do so,

then if, in any proceedings against the person for the offence, evidence of those matters is given, subsection (2) below applies.

(2)   Where this subsection applies—
    (a)   a magistrates' court inquiring into the offence as examining justices;
    (b)   a judge, in deciding whether to grant an application made by the accused under—
        (i)   section 6 of the Criminal Justice Act 1987 (application for dismissal of charge of serious fraud in respect of which notice of transfer has been given under section 4 of that Act); or
        (ii)   paragraph 5 of Schedule 6 to the Criminal Justice Act 1991 (application for dismissal of charge of violent or sexual offence involving child in respect of which notice of transfer has been given under section 53 of that Act);
    (c)   the court, in determining whether there is a case to answer; and
    (d)   the court or jury, in determining whether the accused is guilty of the offence charged,
may draw such inferences from the failure or refusal as appear proper.

(3)   Subsections (1) and (2) do not apply unless the accused was told in ordinary language by the constable when making the request mentioned in subsection (1)(c) above what the effect of this section would be if he failed or refused to comply with the request.

(3A) Where the accused was at an authorised place of detention at the time of the failure or refusal, subsections (1) and (2) do not apply if he had not been allowed an opportunity to consult a solicitor prior to the request being made.

(4)   This section applies in relation to officers of customs and excise as it applies in relation to constables.

(5)   This section does not preclude the drawing of any inference from a failure or refusal of the accused to account for his presence at a place which could properly be drawn apart from this section.

(6)   This section does not apply in relation to a failure or refusal which occurred before the commencement of this section.

(7)   ...

38   Interpretation and savings for sections 34, 35, 36 and 37

(1)   In sections 34, 35, 36 and 37 of this Act—

"legal representative" means an authorised advocate or authorised litigator, as defined by section 119(1) of the Courts and Legal Services Act 1990; and

"place" includes any building or part of a building, any vehicle, vessel, aircraft or hovercraft and any other place whatsoever.

(2)   In sections 34(2), 35(3), 36(2) and 37(2), references to an offence charged include references to any other offence of which the accused could lawfully be convicted on that charge.

(2A) In each of sections 34(2A), 36(4A) and 37(3A) "authorised place of detention" means—

(a)   a police station; or

(b)   any other place prescribed for the purposes of that provision by order made by the Secretary of State;

and the power to make an order under this subsection shall be exercisable by statutory instrument which shall be subject to annulment in pursuance of a resolution of either House of Parliament.

(3)   A person shall not have the proceedings against him transferred to the Crown Court for trial, have a case to answer or be convicted of an offence solely on an inference drawn from such a failure or refusal as is mentioned in section 34(2), 35(3), 36(2) or 37(2).

(4)   A judge shall not refuse to grant such an application as is mentioned in section 34(2)(b), 36(2)(b) and 37(2)(b) solely on an inference drawn from such a failure as is mentioned in section 34(2), 36(2) or 37(2).

(5)   Nothing in sections 34, 35, 36 or 37 prejudices the operation of a provision of any enactment which provides (in whatever words) that any answer or evidence given by a person in specified circumstances shall not be admissible in evidence against him or some other person in any proceedings or class of proceedings (however described, and whether civil or criminal).

In this subsection, the reference to giving evidence is a reference to giving evidence in any manner, whether by furnishing information, making discovery, producing documents or otherwise.

(6)   Nothing in sections 34, 35, 36 or 37 prejudices any power of a court, in any proceedings, to exclude evidence (whether by preventing questions being put or otherwise) at its discretion.

39   Power to apply sections 34 to 38 to armed forces

(1)   The Secretary of State may by order direct that any provision of sections 34 to 38 of this Act shall apply, subject to such modifications as he may specify, to any proceedings to which this section applies.

(2)   This section applies—

(a)   to proceedings whereby a charge is dealt with summarily under Part II of the Army Act 1955;

(b)   to proceedings whereby a charge is dealt with summarily under Part II of the Air Force Act 1955;

(c)   to proceedings whereby a charge is summarily tried under Part II of the Naval Discipline Act 1957;

(d)   to proceedings before a court martial constituted under the Army Act 1955;

(e)   to proceedings before a court martial constituted under the Air Force Act 1955;

(f)   to proceedings before a court martial constituted under the Naval Discipline Act 1957;

(g)   ...

(h)   to proceedings before the Courts-Martial Appeal Court;

(i)   to proceedings before a Standing Civilian Court;

and it applies wherever the proceedings take place.

(3)   An order under this section shall be made by statutory instrument and shall be subject to annulment in pursuance of a resolution of either House of Parliament.

60   Powers to stop and search in anticipation of violence

(1)   If a police officer of or above the rank of inspector reasonably believes—
  (a)   that incidents involving serious violence may take place in any locality in his police area, and that it is expedient to give an authorisation under this section to prevent their occurrence, or
  (b)   that persons are carrying dangerous instruments or offensive weapons in any locality in his police area without good reason,
he may give an authorisation that the powers conferred by this section are to be exercisable at any place within that locality for a specified period not exceeding 24 hours.

(2)   ...

(3)   If it appears to an officer of or above the rank of superintendent that it is expedient to do so, having regard to offences which have, or are reasonably suspected to have, been committed in connection with any activity falling within the authorisation, he may direct that the authorisation shall continue in being for a further 24 hours.

(3A) If an inspector gives an authorisation under subsection (1) he must, as soon as it is practicable to do so, cause an officer of or above the rank of superintendent to be informed.

(4)   This section confers on any constable in uniform power—
  (a)   to stop any pedestrian and search him or anything carried by him for offensive weapons or dangerous instruments;
  (b)   to stop any vehicle and search the vehicle, its driver and any passenger for offensive weapons or dangerous instruments.

(4A) *This section also confers on any constable in uniform power—*
  (a)   to require any person to remove any item which the constable reasonably believes that person is wearing wholly or mainly for the purpose of concealing his identity;
  (b)   to seize any item which the constable reasonably believes any person intends to wear wholly or mainly for that purpose.

(5)   A constable may, in the exercise of the powers conferred by subsection (4) above, stop any person or vehicle and make any search he thinks fit whether or not he has any grounds for suspecting that the person or vehicle is carrying weapons or articles of that kind.

(6)   If in the course of a search under this section a constable discovers a dangerous instrument or an article which he has reasonable grounds for suspecting to be an offensive weapon, he may seize it.

(7)   This section applies (with the necessary modifications) to ships, aircraft and hovercraft as it applies to vehicles.

(8) A person who fails
    (a)   to stop, or to stop a vehicle; *or*
    (b)   *to remove an item worn by him,*

when required to do so by a constable in the exercise of his powers under this section shall be liable on summary conviction to imprisonment for a term not exceeding one month or to a fine not exceeding level 3 on the standard scale or both.

(9) Any authorisation under this section shall be in writing signed by the officer giving it and shall specify the grounds on which it is given and the locality in which and the period during which the powers conferred by this section are exercisable and a direction under subsection (3) above shall also be given in writing or, where that is not practicable, recorded in writing as soon as it is practicable to do so.

(9A) The preceding provisions of this section, so far as they relate to an authorisation by a member of the British Transport Police Force (including one who for the time being has the same powers and privileges as a member of a police force for a police area), shall have effect as if the references to a locality in his police area were references to any locality in or in the vicinity of any policed premises, or to the whole or any part of any such premises.

(10) Where a vehicle is stopped by a constable under this section, the driver shall be entitled to obtain a written statement that the vehicle was stopped under the powers conferred by this section if he applies for such a statement not later than the end of the period of twelve months from the day on which the vehicle was stopped ...

(10A)   A person who is searched by a constable under this section shall be entitled to obtain a written statement that he was searched under the powers conferred by this section if he applies for such a statement not later than the end of the period of twelve months from the day on which he was searched.

(11) In this section—

"British Transport Police Force" means the constables appointed under section 53 of the British Transport Commission Act 1949;

"dangerous instruments" means instruments which have a blade or are sharply pointed;

"offensive weapon" has the meaning given by section 1(9) of the Police and Criminal Evidence Act 1984 or, in relation to Scotland, section 47(4) of the Criminal Law (Consolidation) (Scotland) Act 1995;

"policed premises", in relation to England and Wales, has the meaning given by section 53(3) of the British Transport Commission Act 1949 and, in relation to Scotland, means those places where members of the British Transport Police Force have the powers, protection and privileges of a constable under section 53(4)(a) of that Act (as it relates to Scotland); and

"vehicle" includes a caravan as defined in section 29(1) of the Caravan Sites and Control of Development Act 1960.

(11A)   For the purposes of this section, a person carries a dangerous instrument or an offensive weapon if he has it in his possession.

(12) The powers conferred by this section are in addition to and not in derogation of, any power otherwise conferred.

60AA Powers to require removal of disguises

(1)   Where—
- (a)   an authorisation under section 60 is for the time being in force in relation to any locality for any period, or
- (b)   an authorisation under subsection (3) that the powers conferred by subsection (2) shall be exercisable at any place in a locality is in force for any period,

those powers shall be exercisable at any place in that locality at any time in that period.

(2)   This subsection confers power on any constable in uniform—
- (a)   to require any person to remove any item which the constable reasonably believes that person is wearing wholly or mainly for the purpose of concealing his identity;
- (b)   to seize any item which the constable reasonably believes any person intends to wear wholly or mainly for that purpose.

(3)   If a police officer of or above the rank of inspector reasonably believes—
- (a)   that activities may take place in any locality in his police area that are likely (if they take place) to involve the commission of offences, and
- (b)   that it is expedient, in order to prevent or control the activities, to give an authorisation under this subsection,

he may give an authorisation that the powers conferred by this section shall be exercisable at any place within that locality for a specified period not exceeding twenty-four hours.

(4)   If it appears to an officer of or above the rank of superintendent that it is expedient to do so, having regard to offences which—
- (a)   have been committed in connection with the activities in respect of which the authorisation was given, or
- (b)   are reasonably suspected to have been so committed,

he may direct that the authorisation shall continue in force for a further twenty-four hours.

(5)   If an inspector gives an authorisation under subsection , he must, as soon as it is practicable to do so, cause an officer of or above the rank of superintendent to be informed.

(6)   Any authorisation under this section—
- (a)   shall be in writing and signed by the officer giving it; and
- (b)   shall specify—
  - (i)   the grounds on which it is given;
  - (ii)   the locality in which the powers conferred by this section are exercisable;
  - (iii) the period during which those powers are exercisable;

and a direction under subsection (4) shall also be given in writing or, where that is not practicable, recorded in writing as soon as it is practicable to do so.

(7)   A person who fails to remove an item worn by him when required to do so by a constable in the exercise of his power under this section shall be liable, on summary conviction, to imprisonment for a term not exceeding one month or to a fine not exceeding level 3 on the standard scale or both.

(8)   The preceding provisions of this section, so far as they relate to an authorisation by a member of the British Transport Police Force (including one who for the time being has the same powers and privileges as a member of a police force for a police area), shall have effect as if references to a locality or to a locality in his police area were references to any locality in or in the vicinity of any policed premises, or to the whole or any part of any such premises.

(9)   In this section "British Transport Police Force" and "policed premises" each has the same meaning as in section 60.

(10)   The powers conferred by this section are in addition to, and not in derogation of, any power otherwise conferred.

(11)   This section does not extend to Scotland.

60A   Retention and disposal of things seized under section 60

(1)   Any things seized by a constable under section 60 or 60AA may be retained in accordance with regulations made by the Secretary of State under this section.

(2)   The Secretary of State may make regulations regulating the retention and safe keeping, and the disposal and destruction in prescribed circumstances, of such things.

(3)   Regulations under this section may make different provisions for different classes of things or for different circumstances.

(4)   The power to make regulations under this section shall be exercisable by statutory instrument which shall be subject to annulment in pursuance of a resolution of either House of Parliament.

60B   Arrest without warrant for offences under section 60: Scotland

In Scotland, where a constable reasonably believes that a person has committed or is committing an offence under section 60(8) he may arrest that person without warrant.

[2:11] *Code of Practice C: The Detention, Treatment and Questioning of Persons by Police Officers* (2003) HMSO

1 General

1.1 All persons in custody must be dealt with expeditiously, and released as soon as the need for detention no longer applies.

1.1A A custody officer must perform the functions in this Code as soon as practicable. A custody officer will not be in breach of this Code if delay is justifiable and reasonable step are taken to prevent unnecessary delay. The custody record shall show when a delay has occurred and the reason. *See Note 1H*

1.2 This Code of Practice must be readily available at all police stations for consultation by:
• police officers
• detained persons
• members of the public

1.3 The provisons of this Code
• include the *Annexes*
• do not include the *Notes for Guidance*

1.4 If an officer has any suspicion, or is told in good faith, that a person of any age may be mentally disordered or otherwise mentally vulnerable, in the absence of clear evidence to dispel that suspicion, the person shall be treated as such for the purposes of this Code. *See Note 1G*

1.5 If anyone appears to be under 17, they shall be treated as a juvenile for the purposes of this Code in the absence of clear evidence that they are older.

1.6 If a person appears to be blind, seriously visually impaired, deaf, unable to read or speak or has difficulty orally because of a speech impediment, they shall be treated as such for the purposes of this Code in the absence of clear evidence to the contrary.

1.7 'The appropriate adult' means, in the case of a:
(a) juvenile
    (i) the parent, guardian or, if the juvenile is in local authority or voluntary organisation care, or is otherwise being looked after under the Children Act 1989, a person representing that authority or organisation;
    (ii) a social worker of a local authority social services department;
    (iii) failing these, some other responsible adult aged 18 or over who is not a police officer or employed by the police.
(b) person who is mentally disordered or mentally vulnerable: See Note 1D
    (i) a relative, guardian or other person responsible for their care or custody;
    (ii) someone experienced in dealing with mentally disordered or mentally vulnerable people but who is not a police officer or employed by the police;
    (iii) failing these, some other responsible adult aged 18 or over who is not a police officer or employed by the police.

1.8   If this Code requires a person to be given certain information, they do not have to be given it if at the time they are incapable of understanding what is said, are violent or may become violent or in urgent need of medical attention, but they must be given it as soon as practicable.

1.9   References to a custody officer include those performing the functions of a custody officer.

1.9A When this Code requires the prior authority or agreement of an officer of at least inspector or superintendent rank, that authority may be given by a sergeant or chief inspector authorised to perform the functions of the higher rank under the Police and Criminal Evidence Act 1984 (PACE), section 107.

1.10 Subject to *paragraph 1.12*, this Code applies to people in custody at police stations in England and Wales, whether or not they have been arrested, and to those removed to a police station as a place of safety under the Mental Health Act 1983, sections 135 and 136. *Section 15* applies solely to people in police detention, e.g. those brought to a police station under arrest or arrested at a police station for an offence after going there voluntarily.

1.11 People in police custody include anyone detained under the Terrorism Act 2000, Schedule 8 and section 41, having been taken to a police station after being arrested under the Terrorism Act 2000, section 41. In these cases, reference to an offence in this Code includes the commission, preparation and instigation of acts of terrorism.

1.12 This Code's provisions do not apply to people in custody:
(i)   arrested on warrants issued in Scotland by officers under the Criminal Justice and Public Order Act 1994, section 136(2), or arrested or detained without warrant by officers from a police force in Scotland under section 137(2). In these cases, police powers and duties and the person's rights and entitlements whilst at a police station in England or Wales are the same as those in Scotland;
(ii)   arrested under the Immigration and Asylum Act 1999, section 142(3) in order to have their fingerprints taken;
(iii) whose detention is authorised by an immigration officer under the Immigration Act 1971;
(iv)   who are convicted or remanded prisoners held in police cells on behalf of the Prison Service under the Imprisonment (Temporary Provisions) Act 1980;
(v)   detained for examination under the Terrorism Act 2000, Schedule 7 and to whom the Code of Practice issued under that Act, Schedule 14, paragraph 6 applies;
(vi)   detained for searches under stop and search powers except as required by Code A.

The provisions on conditions of detention and treatment in *sections 8* and *9* must be considered as the minimum standards of treatment for such detainees.

1.13 In this Code:
(a)   'designated person' means a person other than a police officer, designated under the Police Reform Act 2002, Part 4 who has specified powers and duties of police officers conferred or imposed on them;
(b)   reference to a police officer includes a designated person acting in the exercise or performance of the powers and duties conferred or imposed on them by their designation.

1.14 If a power conferred on a designated person:

(a)   allows reasonable force to be used when exercised by a police officer, a person exercising that power has the same entitlement to use force;
(b)   includes power to use force to enter any premises, that power is not exercisable by that designated person except:
  (i)   in the company, and under the supervision, of a police officer;
  (ii)   for the purpose of:
    • saving life or limb; or
    • preventing serious damage to property.

1.15 Nothing in this Code prevents the custody officer, or other officer given custody of the detainee, from allowing civilian support staff who are not designated persons to carry out individual procedures or tasks at the police station if the law allows. However, the officer remains responsible for making sure the procedures and tasks are carried out correctly in accordance with the Codes of Practice. Any such civilian must be:
(a)   a person employed by a police authority maintaining a police force and under the control and direction of the Chief Officer of that force;
(b)   employed by a person with whom a police authority has a contract for the provision of services relating to persons arrested or otherwise in custody.

1.16 Designated persons and other civilian support staff must have regard to any relevant provisions of the Codes of Practice.

1.17 References to pocket books include any official report book issued to police officers or civilian support staff.

...

2   Custody records

2.1   A separate custody record must be opened as soon as practicable for each person brought to a police station under arrest or arrested at the station having gone there voluntarily. All information recorded under this Code must be recorded as soon as practicable in the custody record unless otherwise specified. Any audio or video recording made in the custody area is not part of the custody record.

2.2   If any action requires the authority of an officer of a specified rank, subject to *paragraph 2.6A*, their name and rank must be noted in the custody record.

2.3   The custody officer is responsible for the custody record's accuracy and completeness and for making sure the record or copy of the record accompanies a detainee if they are transferred to another police station. The record shall show the:
• time and reason for transfer
• time a person is released from detention.

2.4   A solicitor or appropriate adult must be permitted to consult a detainee's custody record as soon as practicable after their arrival at the station and at any other time whilst the person is detained. Arrangements for this access must be agreed with the custody officer and may not unreasonably interfere with the custody officer's duties.

2.4A When a detainee leaves police detention or is taken before a court they, their legal representative or appropriate adult shall be given, on request, a copy of the custody record as soon as practicable. This entitlement lasts for 12 months after release.

2.5 The detainee, appropriate adult or legal representative shall be permitted to inspect the original custody record after the detainee has left the police detention provided they give reasonable notice of their request. Any such inspection shall be noted in the custody record.

2.6 Subject to *paragraph 2.6A*, all entries in custody records must be timed and signed by the maker. Records entered on computer shall be timed and contain the operator's identification.

2.6A Nothing in this Code requires the identity of officers or civilian support staff to be recorded or disclosed:
(a) in the case of enquiries linked to the investigation of terrorism; or
(b) if the officer or civilian support staff reasonably believe recording or disclosing their name might put them in danger.

In these cases they shall use their warrant or identification numbers and the name of their police station. See *Note 2A*

2.7 The fact and time of any detainee's refusal to sign a custody record, when asked in accordance with this Code, must be recorded.

...

3 Initial Action

(a) Detained persons – normal procedure

3.1 When a person is brought to a police station under arrest or arrested at the station having gone there voluntarily, the custody officer must make sure the person is told clearly about the following continuing rights which may be exercised at any stage during the period in custody:
(i) the right to have someone informed of their arrest as in *section 5*;
(ii) the right to consult privately with a solicitor and that free independent legal advice is available;
(iii) the right to consult these Codes of Practice. *See Note 3D*

3.2 The detainee must also be given:
• a written notice setting out:
  • the above three rights;
  • the arrangements for obtaining legal advice;
  • the right to a copy of the custody record as in *paragraph 2.4A*;
  • the caution in the terms prescribed in *section 10*.
• an additional written notice briefly setting out their entitlements while in custody, see *Notes 3A and 3B*.

Note: The detainee shall be asked to sign the custody record to acknowledge receipt of these notices. Any refusal must be recorded on the custody record.

3.3 A citizen of an independent Commonwealth country or a national of a foreign country, including the Republic of Ireland, must be informed as soon as practicable about their rights of communication with their High Commission, Embassy or Consulate. See *section 7*

3.4 The custody officer shall:
- note on the custody record any comment the detainee makes in relation to the arresting officer's account but shall not invite comment. If the custody officer authorises a person's detention the detainee must be informed of the grounds as soon as practicable and before they are questioned about any offence;
- note any comment the detainee makes in respect of the decision to detain them but shall not invite comment;
- not put specific questions to the detainee regarding their involvement in any offence, nor in respect of any comments they may make in response to the arresting officer's account or the decision to place them in detention. Such an exchange is likely to constitute an interview as in *paragraph 11.1A* and require the associated safeguards in *section 11*.

See *paragraph 11.13* in respect of unsolicited comments.

3.5 The custody officer shall:
(a) ask the detainee, whether at this time, they:
    (i) would like legal advice, see *paragraph 6.5*;
    (ii) want someone informed of their detention, see *section 5*;
(b) ask the detainee to sign the custody record to confirm their decisions in respect of (a);
(c) determine whether the detainee:
    (i) is, or might be, in need of medical treatment or attention, see *section 9*;
    (ii) requires:
        • an appropriate adult;
        • help to check documentation;
        • an interpreter;
(d) record the decision in respect of (c).

3.6 When determining these needs the custody officer is responsible for initiating an assessment to consider whether the detainee is likely to present specific risks to custody staff or themselves. Such assessments should always include a check on the Police National Computer, to be carried out as soon as practicable, to identify any risks highlighted in relation to the detainee. Although such assessments are primarily the custody officer's responsibility, it may be necessary for them to consult and involve others, e.g. the arresting officer or an appropriate health care professional, see *paragraph 9.13*. Reasons for delaying the initiation or completion of the assessment must be recorded.

3.7 Chief Officers should ensure that arrangements for proper and effective risk assessments required by *paragraph 3.6* are implemented in respect of all detainees at police stations in their area.

3.8   Risk assessments must follow a structured process which clearly defines the categories of risk to be considered and the results must be incorporated in the detainee's custody record. The custody officer is responsible for making sure those responsible for the detainee's custody are appropriately briefed about the risks. If no specific risks are identified by the assessment, that should be noted in the custody record. See *Note 3E* and *paragraph 9.14*

3.9   The custody officer is responsible for implementing the response to any specific risk assessment, e.g.:
- reducing opportunities for self harm;
- calling a health care professional;
- increasing levels of monitoring or observation.

3.10 Risk assessment is an ongoing process and assessments must always be subject to review if circumstances change.

3.11 If video cameras are installed in the custody area, notices shall be prominently displayed showing cameras are in use. Any request to have video cameras switched off shall be refused.

(b)   Detained persons – special groups

3.12 If the detainee appears deaf or there is doubt about their hearing or speaking ability or ability to understand English, and the custody officer cannot establish effective communication, the custody officer must, as soon as practicable, call an interpreter for assistance in the action under *paragraphs 3.1-3.5*. See *section 13*

3.13 If the detainee is a juvenile, the custody officer must, if it is practicable, ascertain the identity of a person responsible for their welfare. That person:
- may be:
  - the parent or guardian;
  - if the juvenile is in local authority or voluntary organisation care, or is otherwise being looked after under the Children Act 1989, a person appointed by that authority or organisation to have responsibility for the juvenile's welfare;
  - any other person who has, for the time being, assumed responsibility for the juvenile's welfare.
- must be informed as soon as practicable that the juvenile has been arrested, why they have been arrested and where they are detained. This right is in addition to the juvenile's right in *section 5* not to be held incommunicado. See *Note 3C*

3.14 If a juvenile known to be subject to a court order under which a person or organisation is given any degree of statutory responsibility to supervise or otherwise monitor them, reasonable steps must also be taken to notify that person or organisation ('the responsible officer'). The responsible officer will normally be a member of a Youth Offending Team, except for a curfew order which involves electronic monitoring when the contractor providing the monitoring will normally be the responsible officer.

3.15 If the detainee is a juvenile, mentally disordered or otherwise mentally vulnerable, the custody officer must, as soon as practicable:

- inform the appropriate adult, who in the case of a juvenile may or may not be a person responsible for their welfare, as in *paragraph 3.13*, of
  - the grounds for their detention;
  - their whereabouts;
- ask the adult to come to the police station to see the detainee.

3.16 It is imperative a mentally disordered or otherwise mentally vulnerable person, detained under the Mental Health Act 1983, section 136, be assessed as soon as possible. If that assessment is to take place at the police station, an approved social worker and a registered medical practitioner shall be called to the station as soon as possible in order to interview and examine the detainee. Once the detainee has been interviewed, examined and suitable arrangements made for their treatment or care, they can no longer be detained under section 136. A detainee must be immediately discharged from the detention under section 136 if a registered medical practitioner, having examined them, concludes they are not mentally disordered within the meaning of the Act.

3.17 If the appropriate adult is:
- already at the police station, the provisions of *paragraphs 3.1* to *3.5* must be complied with in the appropriate adult's presence;
- not at the station when these provisions are complied with, they must be complied with again in the presence of the appropriate adult when they arrive.

3.18 The detainee shall be advised that:
- the duties of the appropriate adult include giving advice and assistance;
- they can consult privately with the appropriate adult at any time.

3.19 If the detainee, or appropriate adult on the detainee's behalf, asks for a solicitor to be called to give legal advice, the provisions of *section 6* apply.

3.20 If the detainee is blind, seriously visually impaired or unable to read, the custody officer shall make sure their solicitor, relative, appropriate adult or some other person likely to take an interest in them and not involved in the investigation is available to help check any documentation. When this Code requires written consent or signing the person assisting may be asked to sign instead, if the detainee prefers. This paragraph does not require an appropriate adult to be called solely to assist in checking and signing documentation for a person who is not a juvenile, or mentally disordered or otherwise mentally vulnerable (see *paragraph 3.15*).

(c)   Persons attending a police station voluntarily

3.21 Anybody attending a police station voluntarily to assist with an investigation may leave at will unless arrested. If it is decided they shall be allowed to leave, they must be informed at once that they are not under arrest and brought before the custody officer, who is responsible for making sure they are notified of their rights in the same way as other detainees. If they are not arrested but are cautioned as in *section 10*, the person who gives the caution must, at the same time, inform them they are not under arrest, they are not obliged to remain at the station but if they remain at the station they may obtain free and independent legal advice if they want. They shall be told the right to legal advice includes the right to speak with a solicitor on the telephone and be asked if they want to do so.

3.22 If a person attending a police station voluntarily asks about their entitlement to legal advice, they shall be given a copy of the notice explaining the arrangements for obtaining legal advice. See *paragraph 3.2*

(d)   Documentation

3.23 The grounds for a person's detention shall be recorded, in the person's presence if practicable.

3.24 Action taken under *paragraphs 3.12* to *3.20* shall be recorded.

...

4   Detainee's property

(a)   Action

4.1   The custody officer is responsible for:
(a)   ascertaining what property a detainee:
    (i)   has with them when they come to the police station, whether on:
- arrest or re-detention on answering to bail;
- commitment to prison custody on the order or sentence of a court;
- lodgement at the police station with a view to their production in court from prison custody;
- transfer from detention at another station or hospital
- detention under the Mental Health Act 1983, section 135 or 136;

    (ii)   might have acquired for an unlawful or harmful purpose while in custody;
(b)   the safekeeping of any property taken from a detainee which remains at the police station.

The custody officer may search the detainee or authorise their being searched to the extent they consider necessary, provided a search of intimate parts of the body or involving the removal of more than outer clothing is only made as in *Annex A*. A search may only be carried out by an officer of the same sex as the detainee. See *Note 4A*

4.2   Detainees may retain clothing and personal effects at their own risk unless the custody officer considers they may use them to cause harm to themselves or others, interfere with evidence, damage property, effect an escape or they are needed as evidence. In this event the custody officer may withhold such articles as they consider necessary and must tell the detainee why.

4.3   Personal effects are those items a detainee may lawfully need, use or refer to while in detention but do not include cash and other items of value.

(b)   Documentation

4.4   The custody officer is responsible for recording all property brought to the police station which a detainee had with them, or had taken from them on arrest. The detainee shall be allowed to check and sign the record of property as correct. Any refusal to sign shall be recorded.

4.5   If a detainee is not allowed to keep any article of clothing or personal effects, the reason must be recorded. …

5   Right not to be held incommunicado

(a) Action

5.1   Any person arrested and held in custody at a police station or other premises may, on request, have one person known to them or likely to take an interest in their welfare informed at public expense of their whereabouts as soon as practicable. If the person cannot be contacted the detainee may choose up to two alternatives. If they cannot be contacted, the person in charge of detention or the investigation has discretion to allow further attempts until the information has been conveyed. See *Notes 5C* and *5D*.

5.2   The exercise of the above right in respect of each person nominated may be delayed only in accordance with *Annex B*.

5.3   The above right may be exercised each time a detainee is taken to another police station.

5.4   The detainee may receive visits at the custody officer's discretion. See *Note 5B*

5.5   If a friend, relative or person with an interest in the detainee's welfare enquires about their whereabouts, this information shall be given if the suspect agrees and *Annex B* does not apply. See *Note 5D*

5.6   The detainee shall be given writing materials, on request, and allowed to telephone one person for a reasonable time, see Notes *5A and 5E*. Either or both these privileges may be denied or delayed if an officer of inspector rank or above considers sending a letter or making a telephone call may result in any of the consequences in:
(a)   *Annex B paragraphs 1* and *2* and the person is detained in connection with an arrestable or serious arrestable offence; or
(b)   *Annex B paragraphs 8* and *9* and the person is detained under the Terrorism Act 2000, Schedule 7 or section 41.

For the purposes of this paragraph, any reference to a serious arrestable offence in *Annex B* includes an arrestable offence. However, nothing in this paragraph permits the restriction or denial of the rights in *paragraphs 5.1* and *6.1*.

5.7   Before any letter or message is sent, or telephone call made, the detainee shall be informed that what they say in any letter, call or message (other than in a communication to a solicitor) may be read or listened to and may be given in evidence. A telephone call may be terminated if it is being abused. The costs can be at public expense at the custody officer's discretion.

(b) Documentation

5.8   A record must be kept of any:
(a)   request made under this section and the action taken;
(b)   letters, messages or telephone calls made or received or visit received;
(c)   refusal by the detainee to have information about them given to an outside en-
quirer. The detainee must be asked to countersign the record accordingly and any refusal recorded.

...

6   Right to legal advice

(a)   Action

6.1   Unless *Annex B* applies, all detainees must be informed that they may at any time consult and communicate privately with a solicitor, whether in person, in writing or by telephone, and that free independent legal advice is available from the duty solicitor. See *paragraph 3.1, Note 6B* and *Note 6J*

6.2   Not used

6.3   A poster advertising the right to legal advice must be prominently displayed in the charging area of every police station. See *Note 6H*

6.4   No police officer should, at any time, do or say anything with the intention of dissuading a detainee from obtaining legal advice.

6.5   The exercise of the right of access to legal advice may be delayed only as in *Annex B*. Whenever legal advice is requested, and unless *Annex B* applies, the custody officer must act without delay to secure the provision of such advice. If, on being informed or reminded of this right, the detainee declines to speak to a solicitor in person, the officer should point out that the right includes the right to speak with a solicitor on the telephone. If the detainee continues to waive the right the officer should ask them why and any reasons should be recorded on the custody record or the interview record as appropriate. Reminders of the right to legal advice must be given as in *paragraphs 3.5, 11.2, 15.4, 16.4* and *16.5* and Code D, *paragraphs 3.17 (ii)* and *6.3*. Once it is clear a detainee does not want to speak to a solicitor in person or by telephone they should cease to be asked their reasons. See *Note 6K*

6.6   A detainee who wants legal advice may not be interviewed or continue to be interviewed until they have received such advice unless:

(a)   *Annex B* applies, when the restriction on drawing adverse inferences from silence
in *Annex C* will apply because the detainee is not allowed an opportunity to consult a solicitor; or

(b)   an officer of superintendent rank or above has reasonable grounds for believing
that:

   (i)   the consequent delay might:
      •   lead to interference with, or harm to, evidence connected with an
         offence;
      •   lead to interference with, or physical harm to, other people;
      •   lead to serious loss of, or damage to, property;
      •   lead to alerting other people suspected of having committed an of-
         fence but not yet arrested for it;
      •   hinder the recovery of property obtained in consequence of the com-
         mission of an offence.

   (ii)   when a solicitor, including a duty solicitor, has been contacted and has
      agreed to attend, awaiting their arrival would cause unreasonable delay to
      the process of investigation.

Note: In these cases the restriction on drawing adverse inferences from silence in *Annex
C* will apply because the detainee is not allowed an opportunity to consult a solicitor:

(c)   the solicitor the detainee has nominated or selected from a list:

   (i)   cannot be contacted;
   (ii)   has previously indicated they do not wish to be contacted; or
   (iii)   having been contacted, has declined to attend; and
      the detainee has been advised of the Duty Solicitor Scheme but has
      declined to ask for the duty solicitor.
      In these circumstances the interview may be started or continued without
      further delay provided an officer of inspector rank or above has agreed to
      the interview proceeding.

Note: The restriction on drawing adverse inferences from silence in *Annex C* will not
apply because the detainee is allowed an opportunity to consult the duty solicitor;

(d)   the detainee changes their mind, about wanting legal advice.

   In these circumstances the interview may be started or continued without delay
   provided that:

   (i)   the detainee agrees to do so, in writing or on tape; and
   (ii)   an officer of inspector rank or above has inquired about the detainee's
      reasons for their change of mind and gives authority for the interview to
      proceed.

Confirmation of the detainee's agreement, their change of mind, the reasons for it
if given and, subject to *paragraph 2.6A*, the name of the authorising officer shall be
recorded in the taped or written interview record. See *Note 6I*. Note: In these circumstances the restriction on drawing adverse inferences from silence in *Annex C* will
not apply because the detainee is allowed an opportunity to consult a solicitor if they
wish.

6.7   If *paragraph 6.6 (b)(i)* applies, once sufficient information has been obtained to
avert the risk, questioning must cease until the detainee has received legal advice unless
paragraph 6.6 (a), (b)(ii), (c) or *(d)* applies.

6.8   A detainee who has been permitted to consult a solicitor shall be entitled on request to have a solicitor present when they are interviewed unless one of the exceptions in *paragraph 6.6* applies.

6.9   The solicitor may only be required to leave the interview if their conduct is such that the interviewer is unable properly to put questions to the suspect. See *Notes 6D and 6E*

6.10 If the interviewer considers a solicitor is acting in such a way, they will stop the interview and consult an officer not below superintendent rank, if one is readily available, and otherwise an officer not below inspector rank not connected with the investigation. After speaking to the solicitor, the officer consulted will decide if the interview should continue in the presence of the solicitor. If they decide it should not, the suspect will be given the opportunity to consult another solicitor before the interview continues and that solicitor given an opportunity to be present at the interview. *See Note 6E*

6.11 The removal of a solicitor from an interview is a serious step and, if it occurs, the officer of superintendent rank or above who took the decision will consider if the incident should be reported to the Law Society. If the decision to remove the solicitor has been taken by an officer below superintendent rank, the facts must be reported to an officer of superintendent rank or above who will similarly consider whether a report to the Law Society would be appropriate. When the solicitor concerned is a duty solicitor, the report should be both to the Law Society and to the Legal Services Commission.

6.12 'Solicitor' in this Code means:
- a solicitor who holds a current practising certificate;
- a trainee solicitor;
- a duty solicitor representative;
- an accredited representative included on the register of representatives maintained by the Legal Services Commission.

6.12A   A non-accredited or probationary representative sent to provide advice by, and on behalf of, a solicitor shall be admitted to the police station for this purpose unless an officer of inspector rank or above considers such a visit will hinder the investigation and directs otherwise. Hindering the investigation does not include giving proper legal advice to a detainee as in *Note 6D*. Once admitted to the police station, *paragraphs 6.6* to *6.10* apply.

6.13 In exercising their discretion under *paragraph 6.12A*, the officer should take into account in particular:
- whether:
  - the identity and status of the non-accredited or probationary representative have been satisfactorily established;
  - they are of suitable character to provide legal advice, e.g. a person with a criminal record is unlikely to be suitable unless the conviction was for a minor offence and not recent.
- any other matters in any written letter of authorisation provided by the solicitor on whose behalf the person is attending the police station. *See Note 6F*

6.14 If the inspector refuses access to a non-accredited or probationary representative or a decision is taken that such a person should not be permitted to remain at an interview, the inspector must notify the solicitor on whose behalf the representative was acting and give them an opportunity to make alternative arrangements. The detainee must be informed and the custody record noted.

6.15 If a solicitor arrives at the station to see a particular person, that person must, unless *Annex B* applies, be so informed whether or not they are being interviewed and asked if they would like to see the solicitor. This applies even if the detainee has declined legal advice or, having requested it, subsequently agreed to be interviewed without receiving advice. The solicitor's attendance and the detainee's decision must be noted in the custody record.

(b) Documentation

6.16 Any request for legal advice and the action taken shall be recorded.

6.17 A record shall be made in the interview record if a detainee asks for legal advice and an interview is begun either in the absence of a solicitor or their representative, or they have been required to leave an interview.

...

8 Conditions of detention

(a) Action

8.1 So far as it is practicable, not more than one detainee should be detained in each cell.

8.2 Cells in use must be adequately heated, cleaned and ventilated. They must be adequately lit, subject to such dimming as is compatible with safety and security to allow people detained overnight to sleep. No additional restraints shall be used within a locked cell unless absolutely necessary and then only restraint equipment, approved for use in that force by the Chief Officer, which is reasonable and necessary in the circumstances having regard to the detainee's demeanour and with a view to ensuring their safety and the safety of others. If a detainee is deaf, mentally disordered or otherwise mentally vulnerable, particular care must be taken when deciding whether to use any form of approved restraints.

8.3 Blankets, mattresses, pillows and other bedding supplied shall be of a reasonable standard and in a clean and sanitary condition. See *Note 8A*

8.4 Access to toilet and washing facilities must be provided.

8.5 If it is necessary to remove a detainee's clothes for the purposes of investigation, for hygiene, health reasons or cleaning, replacement clothing of a reasonable standard of comfort and cleanliness shall be provided. A detainee may not be interviewed unless adequate clothing has been offered.

8.6   At least two light meals and one main meal should be offered in any 24 hour period. See *Note 8B*. Drinks should be provided at meal times and upon reasonable request between meals. Whenever necessary, advice shall be sought from the appropriate health care professional, see *Note 9A*, on medical and dietary matters. As far as practicable, meals provided shall offer a varied diet and meet any specific dietary needs or religious beliefs the detainee may have. The detainee may, at the custody officer's discretion, have meals supplied by their family or friends at their expense. See *Note 8A*

8.7   Brief outdoor exercise shall be offered daily if practicable.

8.8   A juvenile shall not be placed in a police cell unless no other secure accommodation is available and the custody officer considers it is not practicable to supervise them if they are not placed in a cell or that a cell provides more comfortable accommodation than other secure accommodation in the station. A juvenile may not be placed in a cell with a detained adult.

(b)   Documentation

8.9   A record must be kept of replacement clothing and meals offered.

8.10 If a juvenile is placed in a cell, the reason must be recorded.

8.11 The use of any restraints on a detainee whilst in a cell, the reasons for it and, if appropriate, the arrangements for enhanced supervision of the detainee whilst so restrained, shall be recorded. See *paragraph 3.9*

[2:12]   Brown, D *'PACE Ten Years On: a review of the research'* (1997) HORS No 155 HMSO (at pages ix–xx):

The Police and Criminal Evidence Act 1984 (PACE) is the direct outcome of the Royal Commission on Criminal Procedure's (RCCP) recommendations for systematic reform in the investigative process. The provisions of the Act are designed to match up to principles of fairness (for both police and suspect), openness and workability. Overall, they are intended to strike a balance between the public interest in solving crime and the rights and liberties of suspects.

A considerable body of research on the operation of the Act now exists, and this is reviewed in this report. The main areas examined are as follows.

Stop and search: PACE introduced a general power to stop and search persons or vehicles for stolen or prohibited articles. The safeguards include the requirement to keep records and to inform the person stopped of the reasons for police action.

Entry, search and seizure: PACE provides powers to search premises for evidence, to search premises in connection with making an arrest and to seize evidence. Safeguards relate to the level of authority required to search, the keeping of records and provisions of reasons for searches.

Arrest: PACE rationalises police arrest powers. The basis for arrest is reasonable grounds for suspicion. In less serious offences, arrests may only be made where service of a summons is impracticable.

Detention: detention is only permissible where necessary to secure or preserve evidence, or obtain evidence by questioning. Custody officers, independent from the investigation, decide on the necessity of detention and look after the suspect's welfare while in custody. An upper limit of 24 hours is put on detention without charge, other than in a limited group of 'serious arrestable offences'. Officers of inspector rank or above review the need for further detention at specified intervals.

Questioning and treatment of suspects: suspects have statutory rights to legal advice and to have someone informed of their detention under PACE. They may not generally be interviewed until they have received legal advice, if requested. Accurate records of interviews must be made. Juveniles and the mentally disordered or handicapped must not be interviewed in the absence of an 'appropriate adult'. PACE defines circumstances in which interview evidence is liable to be excluded.

Accountability and supervision: PACE emphasises the need for the reviewability of police actions and the importance of internal police supervision. Custody records for each prisoner must record events occurring during detention. Certain decisions – delaying access to legal advice, for example – must be made by senior officers independent from the investigation. External accountability is enhanced through changes to the police complaints procedure, including the formation of the independent Police Complaints Authority, which supervises the investigation of serious allegations. The Act also provides for arrangements to be made to obtain the views of the community about policing.

The main findings of research are summarised below.

Stop and search
- Pre-PACE research points to considerable under-recording of stops and suggests that the decision to stop was often based on hunch or stereotyping, with Afro-Caribbeans more likely to be stopped than white people. Records of stops were rarely inspected by supervisors. Only a small minority of stops led to arrest.
- Frequency of stop and search has increased under PACE, although to some extent this may be an artefact of better recording. Stop/searches occur most frequently in the Metropolitan Police. Around one in eight searches lead to an arrest.
- It is doubtful if stops are always made on the basis of reasonable suspicion. Where the suspect's consent is obtained, this may not always be fully informed,
- Afro-Caribbeans are more likely to be stopped than white people or Asians, more likely to be repeatedly stopped, and more likely to be searched following a stop.

Entry, search and seizure
- Stemming from clearer statutory powers, there has been a rise in the proportion of searches of premises authorised by the police rather than under court warrants. The most frequently used powers are those to search premises upon or after arrest. Around 15% of searches are conducted with the occupant's consent.

- Around three-quarters of searches on warrant and about half of other searches lead to the seizure of property, usually stolen goods. However, it is doubtful whether all searches are conducted on the basis of reasonable suspicion.
- Around half of those whose premises are searched are satisfied with the conduct of the search. Where there is dissatisfaction it is caused by officers' failures to identify themselves, provide a copy of the search warrant or state their search powers.
- PACE powers to obtain access to confidential information are proving a valuable asset, although problems may arise where large volumes of material are sought or where some explanation of the material found is required.

Arrest and detention
- Although PACE was intended to restrict arrest to situations in which it was strictly necessary, suspects are very rarely summonsed instead. However, there are indications of increased police professionalism and that arrests are now made on a firmer evidential basis. Fewer than before are made without independent evidence.
- Black people are arrested at a higher rate than white people, but this does not appear to be because weaker evidence is used to justify their arrest.
- Custody officers rarely scrutinise the necessity for a suspect's detention in any detail and almost all those arrested are detained. Similarly, reviews of detention after 6 and 15 hours are largely routinised procedures lacking any substantial enquiry.
- Under PACE, those arrested for serious offences are generally held for shorter periods than before but in less serious cases several factors (such as waiting for legal advice or the arrival of appropriate adults) have pushed the length of detention up.
- PACE limits on length of detention have not generally created problems for investigating officers.
- There is considerable regional variation in the bailing of suspects after charge, probably reflecting different interpretations of the PACE bail criteria, particularly in relation to the risks of reoffending.

Treatment of suspects
- The effectiveness of custody officers in looking after the suspect's welfare is constrained by pressure of work and lack of direct oversight of some aspects of the detention process. However, they appear able to maintain a viewpoint independent of that of investigating officers.
- Detainees are generally given written and spoken information about their rights, although not always clearly. There is little evidence that rights are systematically denied.
- A large and increasing proportion of suspects are aware of their basic rights although some confusions remain and the written information provided is not always found to be helpful.
- Nearly 20% of detainees ask to have someone informed of their arrest and implementation of requests is rarely formally delayed. Only around 12% of detainees ask to make a telephone call, and only five receive visitors.
- Doctors are called to examine prisoners in about 7% of cases (although in the Metropolitan Police this rises to 25%), usually where detainees are believed to be drunk, but also where mental disorder or mental handicap is suspected.

Legal advice

- The great majority of suspects are given information about their right to legal advice. Improved information has been provided since the first revised PACE Codes of Practice were introduced, raising awareness among suspects that legal advice is free. Custody officers may exercise considerable influence over whether legal advice is sought.
- Requests for legal advice have more than doubled under PACE and have increased further since. Nearly 40% of suspects now request advice, although there are large regional variations.
- Over 80% of those who request legal advice eventually receive it. Cancellation of requests often occur where the chosen adviser is unavailable or where the parents of juveniles consider a lawyer unnecessary.
- In around 70% of cases in which legal advice is given, the adviser attends the police station, but in the remainder advice is given solely over the telephone. A significant proportion of advice is provided by non-qualified solicitors' representatives.
- Legal advisers often obtain only sketchy information about cases from the police, either because they do not ask for it or because the police withhold it. Generally, consultations with clients prior to police interviews are brief. The advice given is usually either neutral in character or to co-operate with police questions. Advice to remain silent is given in around a fifth of legal advice cases.
- In most police interviews legal advisers are passive and do not always intervene to curtail oppressive or repetitive questioning or to allow suspects to present their version of events.
- Access to legal advice was occasionally delayed when PACE was first introduced but this now occurs only exceptionally.

Interviews with suspects

- Under PACE, interviews are rarely conducted with those who are unfit to be questioned. Suspects are also interviewed less frequently. Interviews do sometimes occur with those suffering from psychological conditions due to the difficulties in identifying such disorders.
- Securing a confession remains an important aim of interviewing suspects, although this is now probably more to supplement other evidence.
- Interviewing officers continue to use tactics designed to secure a confession, although unacceptable tactics (for example, exploiting police control over bail and charge decisions) are now used less often.
- Some forms of questioning raise concerns about false confessions. These concerns are mitigated – although not entirely removed – by the fact that in over 90% of cases preceded with by the police independent corroborative evidence is obtained.
- Between 55% and 60% of those interviewed confess – little different from pre-PACE estimates. Confessions are less likely where suspects are legally advised or the evidence is weak; they are more likely in cases involving juveniles or strong evidence.
- Audio-taping of interviews has led to fewer disputes in court about what was said and has improved the flow of questioning. However, there are considerable problems with written records of taped interview prepared by police officers, with up to half suffering from the omission of salient points, prolixity or prosecution bias. Records prepared by civilians are significantly better in terms of quality and cost.
- Video-taping of interviews has raised some technical problems but has proved its value as a supervisory and training tool. It also appears to offer advantages over

audio-taping in a significant minority of cases – some very serious – by clarifying what was taking place in the interview room. However, few videos are presently played at court.

- Little supervision or monitoring of interviewing takes place. One reason is that supervisory responsibility often rests with those who conduct interviews; another is supervisors' reluctance to risk injuring the professional pride of interviewing officers.
- Some questioning of suspects occurs outside of formal police station interviews. Up to 10% of suspects are interviewed after arrest and prior to arrival at the station; up to a third of suspects who are charged may have made admissions prior to reaching the station. Once at the station, a certain amount of unregulated questioning by case officers still occurs.

Right of silence

- Research has provided widely varying estimates of the use by suspects of the right of silence but it would appear that, under PACE, initially around 5% of suspects outside London and up to 9% in London refused to answer all questions, while 5% and 7% respectively refused to answer some questions of significance. This represents little change from the pre-PACE situation.
- Data from recent studies (albeit pre-dating the implementation of the Criminal Justice and Public Order Act 1994) suggest that increasing numbers of suspects are staying silent and that 10% are refusing all questions and 13% some significant questions.
- Suspects detained for more serious offences, those with previous convictions and those who have taken legal advice are more likely to refuse police questions. In the latter instance, this a direct result of legal advice in only a minority of cases. More often, advisers either proffer no such advice, go along with their client's wishes or urge the opposite course.
- Some interviewing officers abandon interviews with silent suspects but others have various techniques – such as increasing the pressure by revealing further incriminating information – to elicit answers.
- Police decisions to take no further action are largely unrelated to whether suspects have exercised their right of silence. There also appears to be no link with CPS decisions to discontinue cases.
- Those who plead not guilty at court are more likely to have refused to answer police questions than those who plead guilty. However, those pleading not guilty who have exercised their right of silence are less likely to be acquitted than other defendants.
- Significant minorities of defendants who plead not guilty raise defences not previously mentioned during questioning. However, few such defences genuinely amount to 'ambushes' because, for example, they relate to matters the suspect could not have raised during police interviews.

Juveniles

- Up to a fifth of suspects detained by the police are aged 16 or under. In around two-thirds of cases parents or relatives act as appropriate adults but, in 20% or more, social workers fulfil this function.
- Parents are often not well-equipped to act as appropriate adults because they may know little about police procedures or what is acceptable in police interviews, may be emotionally upset at their child's predicament, or may take sides with or against

the police. Their role is often not explained to them by the police. They tend to play little part in police interviews.

- Social workers also often lack training in the appropriate adult's role. The quality of their response is related to the organisation of juvenile justice work in social services departments and the extent to which staff specialise in this area. Like parents, they generally remain passive during police interviews.

- Around 60% of juveniles' time in custody is spent waiting for an appropriate adult to attend. Demands on social services mean that waits are often longer for social worker than relatives. On average, however, juveniles are detained for shorter periods than adults.

- Juveniles are given full information about their rights less often than adults and in some cases information is either not given at all or not until an adult is present. There have been recent improvements in this situation.

- Juveniles are less likely than adults to request legal advice and there is far more variation between areas in request rates than for adults. There is evidence that the police sometimes delay or avoid taking forward requests by juveniles for legal advice.

- There is some evidence that juveniles are more likely than adults to provide admissions, although questioning is not often oppressive. Admissions are most often provided where there is strong evidence, the juveniles has no previous convictions and the offence is less serious.

PACE and the mentally disordered and mentally handicapped

- Up to 2% of detainees are treated by the police as mentally disordered or mentally handicapped. Up to one-third are brought to the police station as a place of safety rather than on suspicion of committing an offence. Identifying detainees with mental health problems presents difficulties for custody officers and substantially more detainees may in fact need an appropriate adult.

- Custody officers often summon the police surgeon in the first instance and in many cases, acting on the doctor's advice, do not then call for an appropriate adult.

- Ensuring that detainees with mental health problems understand their rights is problematic. Experiments with simplified versions of the notices currently provided to all suspects have had some success in raising levels of understanding.

- The role of the appropriate adult raises a number of problems. Firstly, there is sometimes confusion as to whether social workers are acting in this role or making an assessment under the Mental Health Act. Secondly, custody officers may not always be right in assuming that professionals know what is expected of them as appropriate adults. Thirdly, there is a lack of clarity about the status of information confided in appropriate adults by detainees.

- The interviewing of those with mental health problems raises dangers of generating false confessions and of over-ready compliance, leading to inaccurate replies. Police officers tend to over-estimate the reliability of the information provided.

- Appropriate adults seldom intervene during interviews with mentally disordered or mentally handicapped suspects and may not always constitute an adequate safeguard against the production of unreliable interview evidence.

Supervision and accountability

Supervision
- Detectives receive relatively little training in the supervision of investigations; in consequence, investigative errors or shortcomings may be overlooked.
- Effective supervision of investigations is impeded by the low visibility of much detective work, issues of professional pride (especially in relation to interviewing skills) and an emphasis on quantity rather than quality of clear-ups.
- The bulk of investigations are supervised by lower-ranking officers, who have their own caseloads to cope with, and not by senior officers. This carried the risk that malpractice or incompetence may pass unnoticed.
- There is tighter supervision by senior officers in major inquiries and in special squads. In major inquiries, supervision is more directive, there are quality control procedures and teams are comprised of officers without established loyalties to each other. In special squads, there is rigorous scrutiny of the evidence before offenders are targeted and tight managerial control over dealings with informants.

Complaints
- No recent research has been carried out in this area. Work carried out in 1987 suggested that, at that time, the Police Complaints Authority (PCA) was less likely to select assault cases than others for supervision. Complaints of assault tend to be particularly difficult to prove and this may have had a bearing on the PCA's decision.
- PCA supervision varied from passive, active or directive, depending on how complex and how high profile cases were. Where investigations were supervised, action was more frequently taken against officers, complaints were less often withdrawn, reports were of better quality and investigation was speedier.
- Most complainants were dissatisfied with the outcome of supervised cases, although they were more likely than other complainants to feel their case had been treated seriously and to receive good feedback and less likely to have experienced pressure to withdraw. Investigating officers felt that the PCA had little impact on the outcome of investigations, although its attention to the case put them on their mettle.
- Informal resolution of complaints were generally not popular with officers subject to complaint since they felt that accepting it was seen as admitting guilt. Officers did not view meetings between officer and complainant as productive.
- Where complaints were informally resolved, most complainants accepted this outcome as satisfactory, despite persuasion to take this course in some cases. Complainants were dissatisfied at not meeting officers subject to complaint and with lack of feedback.
- A third of complainants reported attempts to dissuade them registering a complaint. Of those withdrawing and proceeding, a majority reported attempts to secure a withdrawal.
- Over two-thirds of complainants were dissatisfied with the outcome of their complaint, usually due to the lack of an apology or of an explanation for decisions reached. Those whose complaints were informally resolved were the most satisfied.
- Investigating officers were concerned to be seen by complainants to be taking their grievances seriously, although they accepted that the low chances of substantiation meant that many complainants would ultimately be dissatisfied. The thoroughness of investigations meant that they tended to be slow, and this was the subject of considerable criticism by officers subject to complaint.

- Public attitude surveys show that up to two-thirds of the public know of the PCA, although rather fewer are aware that it is impartial and independent from the police. Levels of awareness are far lower among members of ethnic minority groups.

Police community consultative committees
- Consultation arrangements now exist in most parts of the country. However, there have been difficulties recruiting members representative of local communities, particularly those from minority ethnic groups and younger people. Meetings are infrequent in some areas and, where public, have tended to be poorly attended.
- Agenda are sometimes dominated by police authorities. For their part, the police have not always been willing to share information, especially where it relates to operational matters.
- The effectiveness of consultative groups appears to be constrained by several factors including: lack of formal authority; absence of hard-edged information; ignorance of policing issues; pro-police orientation; and non-representativeness. However, some groups are notably successful in actively involving local people. Others, which contain influential coalitions of representatives from political parties, local government and statutory and voluntary agencies are effective in raising their agendas with the police.

Conclusions

Fairness, openness and workability
- The review concludes that PACE has introduced a greater element of fairness into pre-charge procedures, in that suspects are now more aware of their rights and given the chance to exercise them, although there remain areas in which improvement is required. There are also benefits for the police in terms of clearer and more certain powers, particularly at the station.
- However, both police and suspect may suffer from the lack of clarity in relation to powers outside the station, particularly stop, search and entry powers, while, at the station, the suspect may be at a disadvantage due to the lack of clear delineation of what interview tactics are permissible.
- The extent to which the exercise of police powers outside the police station can be reviewed after the event is limited where officers act with the apparent consent of the suspect. Reviewability of police action, both at the station and outside, is also constrained by dependence on official records, which may be incomplete, unreliable or unverifiable.
- PACE powers are generally more workable than their predecessors, because they provide clarification and certainty, particularly in relation to detention at the station. However, the use of stop and search and entry and search powers remains problematic, and officers often prefer to operate with the subject's consent.

Legal regulation of policing
- Police behaviour appears to be more strongly influenced by PACE rules inside the police station than out. The reason for this difference is probably that insufficient account was taken of the strong informal working rules which determine how the police behave on the street.

- The lessons to be drawn from the experience of implementing PACE are that new legal rules can alter existing working practices provided that: they are clear; their introduction is accompanied by adequate training; there are effective sanctions and supervision; and the public are aware of their rights and of police powers.

Balance in the investigative process

- The review concludes that PACE has not yet produced a system in balance, in the sense that police powers and safe guards for the suspect are generally well matched in key areas.
- In relation to the exercise of stop and search and entry and search powers and the treatment of at risk groups, suspects may be at a relative disadvantage. However, at the police station suspects may be benefiting considerably from the availability of legal advice and use of the right of silence, to the detriment of the public interest in bringing criminals to account.
- The picture is a shifting one, and current initiatives in the criminal justice field may go some way towards producing a balanced pre-charge process.

[2:13] **Bucke, T and Brown, D** *'In police custody: police powers and suspects' rights under the revised PACE Codes of Practice'* (1997) HORS No 174 HMSO (at page 69):

The main aim of this study was to examine changes in the revised PACE Codes of Practice concerning those in police detention. It also sought to investigate other related changes arising from the CJPOA and to monitor a number of aspects in the operation of PACE. In this concluding chapter the main findings of the research are discussed along with their implications.

Appropriate adults

In line with the Codes of Practice appropriate adults were provided in the majority of cases involving juvenile and mentally disordered or handicapped detainees.[2] However, shortcomings were found in the level of guidance provided to appropriate adults. Custody officers rarely gave advice to those acting as appropriate adults about the role, and were unlikely to be asked for any. The implication of this lack of guidance is that a large proportion of those acting as appropriate adults, particular those other than social workers, probably do not know what their role actually is, and could be said to be acting as appropriate adults in name only.

The research also examined the suitability of those acting as appropriate adults for juvenile detainees. Here the reactions of family members on finding a child in police custody could undermine their ability to be an appropriate adult. Notable proportions of family members were found to be distressed or hostile to the juvenile, leading to various reactions including remoteness, antagonism and, in some cases, violence. In slightly more cases family members were described as either supportive or calm. However, such

---

[2] Although the level of provision was much lower for mentally disordered detainees compared to juveniles.

demeanours did not mean that the appropriate adult role was adequately fulfilled. As revealed by other research (see Palmer and Hart, 1996; Evans, 1993) many parents were simply passive observers, making few or no interventions and providing little advice or assistance to the juvenile. The actions of those who became involved revealed their confusion about the role, with some parents advising their children to remain silent and others encouraging them to confess. The effectiveness of parents acting as appropriate adults and providing a safeguard is an important issue. Juveniles represent around *one in five detainees* and parents act as appropriate adults in the majority of cases. The research also raised questions about the suitability of those other than family members acting as appropriate adults.

Concerns about the role of appropriate adults led the RCCJ to recommend a comprehensive review of the role, functions, qualifications, training and availability of appropriate adults. This review was instituted by the Home Office in 1994. The resulting Appropriate Adults Working Group was also asked to consider three other issues. Firstly, the changes to Code C needed to give effect to any recommendations. Secondly, whether the police required clearer guidance about the criteria to be used in considering the need for an appropriate adult. Thirdly, and following another RCCJ recommendation, whether there was a need for a rule governing the status of information passed by suspects to appropriate adults. The Working Group reported in mid-1995 and made a series of wide ranging recommendations which are currently under consideration. A future Home Office circular will provide the police with further guidance on appropriate adults, with associated changes possibly being made to the Codes of Practice.

Legal advice

Studies since the introduction of PACE have indicated rises in suspects requesting legal advice. The current study found a further increase, with four out of ten suspects now making requests. One explanation for this is the increase in requests among juvenile suspects. However, the level of legal advice actually received was only slightly higher than in previous studies, indicating a rise in the attrition rate. Reasons given by suspects for refusing legal advice were rarely recorded by custody officers; in those cases where they were, the majority of suspects simply said that the situation did not merit it.

Comparisons with previous research suggest that legal consultations have increased in duration. The changes to the right of silence mean that suspects in custody require sound legal advice on their position when being questioned by officers. As a result legal advisers need to take time to guide their clients on how to respond to police questions in the context of the inferences that may be drawn from silence. The quality of legal advice received by suspects has been the source of some criticism in the past, notably surrounding the use of unqualified legal staff. As a result the Law Society introduced a scheme whereby those passing a series of tests can become 'accredited representatives' and receive the same status as solicitors. The current study indicates that the proportion of unqualified legal staff advising at police stations has declined, due to a rise in solicitors attending and the introduction of 'accredited representatives'. Whether this development has led to any improvement in the legal advice suspects receive remains unclear.

The right of silence

The extent to which suspects used the right of silence was found to have declined compared to estimates from studies conducted before the new provisions. 'No comment' interviews were found to have fallen by just under a half, while the selective answering of questions had fallen by just under a third. Reductions in the use of silence were found to be greatest among those receiving legal advice. However, confessions by suspects during interviews remained at the same level as before the new provisions. Suspects therefore appear to be responding to police questions without making admissions of guilt any more than before. One possibility is that more suspects are providing officers with statements which, while not admissions of guilt, can be tested against other evidence. The full implications of the new provisions will depend on what happens in the prosecution and trial processes; however these will be addressed in a forthcoming report which will provide further information from this research and other work.

Disposal of juvenile suspects

One of the most pronounced developments found in the study concerned juveniles. Probably as a result of a Home Office circular advising against multiple cautions, juveniles were more likely to be charged and less likely to be cautioned. Furthermore decisions on juveniles were made much earlier in the process than in the past. Consequently, there was a decline in juveniles being bailed for inquiries or reported for summons, with disposal decisions being increasingly made at the end of detention. Finally, once charged juveniles were more likely than before to be refused bail and detained for court.

These developments have a number of consequences. First, juveniles are less likely to be diverted away from prosecution than in the past. This is linked to a decline in the role of juvenile bureaux or panels, with decisions on juvenile cases increasingly the sole responsibility of police officers. Second, changes in the disposal of juveniles together with the rise in their requests for legal advice, means that previous divisions in the treatment of juvenile and adult suspects appear much less distinct. Third, these developments mean that a greater number of juveniles will be at liberty having been charged by the police and bailed pending various court appearances. An unintended consequence of this may be a rise in the levels of offending on bail.

DNA sampling

Alterations to the Code of Practice have provided far greater scope for DNA sampling, with officers now able to take samples from a much larger range of suspects than in the past. However, the study found samples to be taken from a relatively small proportion of suspects. Clearly intimate samples were only taken in very specific cases, while non-intimate samples were also taken selectively. This may be due to ACPO and Home Office guidance advising that non-intimate samples should only be taken for certain types of crime (ie offences against the person, sexual offences and burglaries). Samples were taken for other forms of crime, although it is likely that the suspects concerned had previous links to the offences in the designated categories. The vast majority of samples were taken in order to build up the DNA database and, while the proportion of suspects sampled appears relatively small, it should be noted that approximately 1.5 million people enter police custody every year. Selective sampling therefore is likely to add a substantial number of people to the database over the forthcoming years.

[2:14]   Cape, E '*The Revised PACE Codes of Practice: A Further Step Towards Inquisitorialism*' [2003] Crim LR 355

The third major revision of the Codes of Practice issued by the Home Secretary under powers granted by Part VI of the Police and Criminal Evidence Act 1984 (PACE) came into force on April 1, 2003.[3] This followed a review that started in December 1999, but which was repeatedly delayed as a result of a heavy legislative programme affecting provisions in the codes, a continuing concern with police stop and search powers – particularly their disproportionate use against ethnic minorities – and finally a joint Home Office/Cabinet Office review of PACE which reported, after deliberating for only six months, in November 2002.[4]

Since the last major revision of the PACE Codes in 1995,[5] there have been a number of changes and modifications falling short of a full revision, although a revised version of Code A[6] was issued in 1999. In April 2002 Code D[7] was temporarily modified[8] so that video identification became, in effect, the preferred method of visual identification procedure. It also sought to negate some of the effects of the House of Lords decision in *R. v Forbes*[9] so that an identification procedure would not have to be held if 'it would serve no useful purpose in proving or disproving' a suspect's involvement in an offence. The following month, modifications to Codes C and D that originally applied to three police force areas[10] were extended to six other police areas.[11] These modifications added a new s.17 to Code C and a new Note for Guidance to Code D, reflecting the powers

---

[3]   PACE (Codes of Practice) (Statutory Powers of Stop and Search) Order 2002, SI 2002/3075 and PACE (Codes of Practice) (Codes B to E) (No. 2) Order 2003, SI 2003/703.

[4]   Home Office/Cabinet Office, *PACE Review: Report of the Joint Home Office/Cabinet Office Review of the Police and Criminal Evidence Act 1984*, November 2002 (hereafter 'PACE Review'). For a critical commentary see M. Zander, 'The Joint Review of PACE: a deplorable report' (2003) 153 N.L.J. 204.

[5]   See D. Wolchover and A. Heaton-Armstrong, 'Questioning and Identification: Changes under P.A.C.E. '95' [1995] Crim.L.R. 356.

[6]   *Code of Practice for the exercise by police officers of statutory powers of stop and search*.

[7]   *Code of Practice for the identification of persons by police officers*. Despite its title, much of the code is concerned with identification by non-police officers.

[8]   PACE, s.67 was amended by Criminal Justice and Police Act 2001, s.77 to enable the Secretary of State to modify a code without publishing, and consulting upon, a draft as required by PACE, s.67(1). See PACE (Codes of Practice) (Temporary Modifications to Code D) Order 2002/615. For a review of these and other modifications see E. Cape, 'A PACE in the wrong direction' (2002) August Legal Action 24.

[9]   [2001] 1 All E.R. 686, [2001] Crim.L.R. 649.

[10]   Staffordshire, Nottinghamshire and the Metropolitan Police. See PACE (Codes of Practice) (Modification) Order 2001, SI 2001/2254.

[11]   See PACE (Codes of Practice) (Modifications to Code C and Code D) (Certain Police Areas) Order 2002, SI 2002/1150. Further areas were added by PACE (Codes of Practice) (Modifications to Code C and Code D) (Certain Police Areas) (Amendment) Order 2002, SI 2002/1863. They were also introduced without consultation under the powers noted in n.6.

contained in s.63B PACE[12] to test for Class A drugs people charged with certain offences. The drug-testing modifications have not been incorporated into the revised Codes C and D that came into force at the beginning of April, and presumably will only be incorporated if and when it is decided to extend the drug-testing powers to the whole of England and Wales. Also in May 2002 a new Code F, *Code of Practice on visual recording with sound of interviews with suspects*, was introduced which only applies to interviews conducted in those police stations that are piloting video recording of police interviews.[13] The pilot ends in May 2003 when presumably the Home Office will decide whether to extend visual recording of police interviews to other parts of the country.

The changes to the codes are, broadly, of four types. First, there are technical and stylistic changes designed to improve the layout, and aid understanding, of code provisions. Secondly, there are a large number of changes reflecting statutory changes since the last code revisions, particularly those contained in the Youth Justice and Criminal Evidence Act 1999, the Terrorism Act 2000, the Criminal Justice and Police Act 2001, the Anti-terrorism, Crime and Security Act 2001 and the Police Reform Act 2002. Thirdly, Code A and Code C contain new provisions designed to improve the way in which the police deal with members of the public and suspects. However, the fourth category consists of provisions that were clearly wanted by the police because they enhance their powers over suspects. It should be noted that many of the provisions of the Codes, although not those in Code A, apply to civilians granted certain 'police' powers as a result of designation under Chapter 1 of Part 4 of the Police Reform Act 2002.[14]

(and at page 368):

Conclusions

This review of the revised Codes of Practice is necessarily selective and the effect of the revisions, particularly those provisions designed to improve stop and search practice and the treatment of vulnerable suspects, will depend to a large extent on the resources the police are willing to devote to training custody and other relevant officers. Disappointingly, this issue was largely ignored in the PACE Review.[15] Although there have been efforts to simplify the language and structure of the codes, the fact is that in the past decade successive governments and courts have considerably increased the complexity of the law relating to the investigative stage of the criminal process. The PACE Review partially recognised this but its preferred solutions, to reduce the consultation requirements applying to revision of the codes,[16] and to rework the codes into a 'Three

---

12 Inserted by the Criminal Justice and Court Services Act 2000, s. 57.
13 PACE (Codes of Practice) (Visual Recording of Interviews) Order 2002, SI 2002/1266, issued under PACE, s. 60A(1)(a) as inserted by the Criminal Justice and Police Act 2001, s. 76. For the police stations to which it applies, see PACE (Visual Recording of Interviews) (Certain Police Areas) Order 2002, SI 2002/1069 and PACE (Visual Recording of Interviews) (Certain Police Areas) (No. 2) Order 2002, SI 2002/2527.
14 The powers of designated persons are set out in Sch. 4 of the Police Reform Act 2002. For implementation see The Police Reform Act 2002 (Commencement No. 1) Order 2002, SI 2002/2306, and The Police Reform Act 2002 (Commencement No. 3) Order 2002, SI 2002/2750.
15 Although it did recommend that, depending on the availability of funding, best practice should be promoted 'via the National Centre for Policing Excellence to be established within Centrex and via the Police Standards Unit' and which could be 'linked to the Centrex work on Policing Knowledge Maps'!
16 To be implemented when clause 7 of the Criminal Justice Bill is enacted.

Tier' framework with the codes containing key principle and detailed guidance being moved to National Standards, is unlikely to improve matters.[17] In the recent case of *R v Howell*[18] the Court of Appeal stated that 'the police interview and the trial are to be seen as part of a continuous process in which the suspect is engaged from the beginning', describing this a 'benign continuum'. What the court failed to adequately recognise is that the police have, in recent years, been given considerable inquisitorial powers to deploy at a stage of the criminal process in which the accused is increasingly regarded as the subject of a police inquiry, but the product of which is available for use by the prosecution for adversarial purposes. The revisions of the codes of practice may only properly be understood in this context.

[2:15]　Ashworth, A *'Should the police be allowed to use deception?'* (1998) 114 LQR 108 (at page 138):

There is a long line of judicial authority to the effect that a criminal court may properly exclude evidence which has been obtained by means of a trick, sometimes justified by reference to the privilege against self-incrimination. The aim of this article has been to conduct a deeper examination: rather than relying on judicial authority, and not confining the discussion to the reception of evidence by courts, it has set out to articulate and to test the justifications for the use of deceptive practices by the police and other law enforcement agencies. The conclusions, in brief, are as follows:

(i)　that lying in court is absolutely wrong because it compromises the integrity of the criminal justice system, and any attempt to justify it in terms of convicting the factually guilty is constitutionally and morally unsustainable;

(ii)　that at any earlier stage in the criminal process 'tricks about rights' are wrong for similar reasons, in so far as the rights are recognised in the European Convention on Human Rights, in domestic legislation or in the Codes of Practice;

(iii)　that for this purpose a trick should be defined so as to include any deception, including a failure to inform a suspect when there is a duty to do so; but,

(iv)　that there are distinctly fewer moral objections to the use of disguises, informers or other agents at the investigative stage, so long as this does not involve prompting or questioning a suspect in relation to an incident in a way that undermines rights that should be protected; and

(v)　that there are also fewer moral objections to covert tape recording or electronic surveillance, although the moral objections to 'bugging' private premises remain strong and should only be overcome in situations where the justifications for invading privacy are powerful and properly tested.

In relation to undercover policing and the use of electronic devices, the community's interests in the prevention and detection of crime may justify a judicious use of these practices, subject to appropriate safeguards. There is a need for controls for two distinct reasons – to prevent the abuse of power by law enforcement agencies, and to ensure that any relevant rights of citizens are recognised and protected. Questions of accountability and of the criteria on which the deployment of these policing methods should be justified must be tackled more convincingly than they are in the Police Act 1997. The admissibility of evidence obtained in contravention of the principles is a separate issue, although several of the arguments discussed above are relevant.

17　Of particular concern was an apparent acceptance by the Review of the police view that 'detail ... can be used by solicitors to undermine cases.'

18　[2003] EWCA Crim 1, [2003] Crim LR 405.

In respect of undercover policing, operations ought to be approved at a high level of command within the police service, Customs and Excise, or whatever agency in concerned; and they should be subject to scrutiny by, for example, the Chief Inspector of Constabulary. So far as the criteria are concerned, it must be established the normal methods of gathering evidence would be 'bound to fail', and the reasons for this must be recorded; the police officer(s) involved in the undercover work must be briefed specifically about the rights of others that must be respected, particularly in terms of not trying to prompt admissions.

Turning to electronic, telephonic and other forms of surveillance, this is likely to involve interference with the privacy and/or the property rights of citizens, and it should therefore be taken far more seriously than it has been hitherto. English law is truly in a lamentable state, and requires both greater consistency and firmer principle. The lack of consistency derives not merely from the variety of separate statutory regimes that exist (eg the Interception of Communications Act 1985, the Intelligence Services Act 1994, the Security Services Act 1996, and the Police Act 1997), but also from the failure of these statutes to cover several forms of electronic surveillance and communications equipment. The lack of principle stems from the desire (at least in previous years) to keep to a minimal compliance with the European Convention. Instead, greater attention should be given to principled criteria for determining whether permission should be granted. Five points should be considered. First, the nature of the right of privacy and the reasons for it should be spelt out. Second, there must be a clear and circumscribed indication of the level of seriousness of offence necessary to justify an incursion on the right of privacy: mere references to 'crimes of violence' is much too broad, whereas a criterion of offences serious enough to attract at least three years imprisonment for an adult of good character gives a better indication of the necessary threshold. Third, it must be shown that the use of electronic devices is necessary, and that no less intrusive method would be likely to succeed. Fourth, it must be shown that the electronic device has good prospects of success. Fifth, any curtailment of the right of privacy should be kept to a minimum.

This discussion of accountability and criteria should not distract attention from the central argument that, in principle, the police should recognise a duty not to use deceptive practices in the investigation of crime. In those limited circumstances in which deceptive practices or electronic surveillance can be justified, the reasons for the general duty and the exceptions should form part of police training and re-training, with a view to implanting them in police culture. For so long as the restrictions are regarded as pointless or irritating handicaps to the pursuit of proper goals, law enforcement officers will be tempted to try to circumvent them or simply to ignore them.

[2:16] *R v Looseley; A-G's Reference (No 3 of 2000) [2002] Crim LR 301*

House of Lords; Lord Nicholls of Birkenhead, Lord Mackay of Clashfern, Lord Hoffmann, Lord Hutton and Lord Scott of Foscote: October 25, 2001; [2001] UKHL 53.

L was charged with supplying or being concerned in the supply of heroin to an undercover police officer known as 'Rob' who was part of an undercover operation mounted by the police in 1999 in Guildford because of their concern about the trade in Class A drugs in that area. Rob's evidence was that a man in a public house had provided him with the appellant's first name and telephone number and suggested he should telephone the appellant if he wished to obtain drugs. Rob telephoned the appellant who agreed that he could 'sort him out a couple of bags' and gave him directions to his flat. The appellant drove Rob from the flat to the supplier's home where the appellant left the car taking £30 from Rob. He returned saying he had the 'stuff'. He kept a small quantity for himself and gave the remainder to Rob. On analysis the package was found to contain 152 milligrams of heroin at 100 per cent purity. Four days later a similar transaction took place and a third transaction took place three days after that. At the trial the defence submitted, as a preliminary issue, that the indictment ought to be stayed as an abuse of the process of the court or, alternatively, that Rob's evidence should be excluded under section 78(1) of the Police and Criminal Evidence Act 1984. The judge ruled against those submissions and the appellant changed his pleas to guilty. His appeal against conviction was dismissed by the Court of Appeal on the grounds that although if a person had been incited or entrapped by a law enforcement officer into committing an offence then the officer's evidence should be excluded under section 78, where the officer, as in this case, had done no more that give the appellant the opportunity to break the law and the appellant had freely taken advantage of that opportunity in circumstances where it appeared he would have behaved in the same way if the opportunity had been offered by anyone else, there was no reason why the officer's evidence should be excluded. The Court of Appeal certified the following point of law of general public importance: 'Should the judge have refused to admit the evidence of the undercover police officer 'Rob' because the role played by 'Rob' went beyond mere observation and involved asking the appellant to supply him with heroin, a request to which, on the judge's findings, the appellant readily agreed?'

In the second case, the Attorney-General referred a point of law to the Court of Appeal after the acquittal of an accused charged with supplying or being concerned in the supply to another of a Class A drug. Undercover police officers had asked S if he wanted to buy some contraband cigarettes. S took them to the accused and after conversations about cigarettes, the police officers asked the accused if he could sort them out some 'brown'. After further conversations the police officers persuaded the accused to provide them with heroin. The accused said at one stage 'I'm not really into heroin myself'. He also said, when interviewed by the police, that the officers 'were getting me cheap fags, so as far as I was concerned a favour for a favour'. At the trial the judge ruled that the police officers went further than was permissible and in fact incited and procured this accused to commit an offence which he would not otherwise have committed. On the accused's acquittal, the Attorney-General referred the following point of law to the Court of Appeal for its opinion: 'In a case involving the commission of offences by an accused at the instigation of undercover police officers, to what extent, if any, have: (i) the judicial discretion conferred by section 78 of the Police and Criminal Evidence Act 1984; and (ii) the power to stay the proceedings as an abuse of the court been modified by Article 6 of the European Convention of the Protection of Human Rights and Fundamental Freedoms and the jurisprudence of the European Court of Human Rights?' The Court of Appeal answered the question in the negative and ruled that the trial judge had erred in staying the proceedings. The question of law was further referred to the House of Lords.

Held, that it was a fundamental principle of the rule of law that every court had an inherent power and duty to prevent abuse of its process. It was simply not acceptable that the State through its agents should lure its citizens into committing acts forbidden by the law and then seek to prosecute them for doing so. That would be entrapment and misuse of State power. The role of the courts was to stand between the State and its citizens and to make sure this did not happen. Although entrapment was not a substantive defence, English law had now developed remedies in respect of entrapment:

the court might stay the relevant criminal proceedings or it might exclude evidence pursuant to section 78. The grant of a stay should normally be regarded as the appropriate response in a case of entrapment. Police conduct which brought about State-created crime was unacceptable and improper but if the police conduct preceding the commission of the offence was no more than might have been expected from others in the circumstances it was not to be regarded as inciting or instigating crime, or luring a person into committing a crime. In the latter situation the police did no more than others could be expected to do and did not create the crime artificially. In assessing the propriety of police conduct proportionality had a role to play; the greater the degree of intrusiveness, the closer the court would scrutinise the reasons for using it. Ultimately, the overall consideration was always whether the conduct of the police or other law enforcement agency was so seriously improper as to bring the administration of justice into disrepute. Accordingly, L's appeal would be dismissed since the undercover officer in that case did no more than present himself as an ordinary customer to an active drug dealer. On the Attorney-General's reference, affirming the Court of Appeal's decision in part, the court's power to exclude evidence under section 78 or to stay proceedings were unaffected by article 6. But in this case the trial judge was entitled to stay the proceedings on the ground that the police officer had instigated the drug offence by offering an inducement of a profitable trade in contraband cigarettes, an inducement which would not ordinarily be associated with the commission of that offence.

Sang (1979) 69 Cr.App.R. 282, [1980] A.C. 402, HL; *R. v. Horseferry Road Magistrates' Court, ex p. Bennett* (1994) 98 Cr.App.R. 114, [1994] 1 A.C. 42, HL; *Latif and Shahzad* [1996] 2 Cr.App.R. 92 [1996] 1 W.L.R. 104, HL, *Teixeira de Castro v. Portugal* [1998] 28 E.H.R.R. 101 and *Nottingham City Council v. Amin* [2001] 1 Cr.App.R. 426, [2000] 1 W.L.R. 1071, DC considered.

Decision of the Court of Appeal (Criminal Division) in *Looseley* affirmed.

Decision of the Court of Appeal (Criminal Division) in *Attorney-General's Reference (No. 3 of 2000)* reversed in part.

Commentary. For the comment on the decision of the Court of Appeal in the *Attorney-General's Reference (No. 3 of 2000)* see [2001] Crim.L.R. 645, and for a comprehensive analysis of the House of Lords decisions and its broader implications, see A. Ashworth, 'Re-drawing the Boundaries of Entrapment' [2002] Crim.L.R. 249.

As Ashworth observes, at a general level, the decision is to be welcomed for clarifying the rationale of, and remedies available for, entrapment. The unanimous decision that although there is no defence of entrapment, nevertheless the principal remedy for entrapment is a stay for abuse of process, demonstrates how significant that doctrine has become. Although the remedy of a stay for abuse looks like a defence created through the back door, the House of Lords acknowledged that, on this point at least, *Sang* had been 'overtaken': per Lord Nicholls at paragraph 16.

On narrower issues the decision is welcome for some clarification of definitions: 'incitement' in this context is not to be construed in its technical criminal law sense. The House of Lords is also to be commended for emphasising that the predisposition of the accused is not a key factor. Indeed, Lord Hoffmann reasons that since the court's inquiry is about abuse of process and not about whether D has a defence or is blameworthy, any predisposition is 'irrelevant', otherwise than in the police forming a reasonable suspicion. This approach prevents the potential for abuse of this pro-active policing method which the decision of the Court of Appeal left open. With the central question of entrapment now clearly stated to be whether the police conduct was 'unexceptional', and the House of Lords' endorsement of a need for prior suspicion and even possibly authorisation, the decision puts the law in this area on a more acceptable foundation. Inevitably, there is still some room for clarification of the application of the principles in hard cases. Prime candidates for argument will be the relevance of the vulnerability of the accused and precisely what amounts to 'unexceptional' behaviour in organised criminal activity.

[2:17] **Moston, S and Stephenson, G M** *'The Questioning and Interviewing of Suspects Outside the Police Station'* RCCJ Research Study No 22 (1993) HMSO (at page 46):

This study has shown that in a large number of cases suspects are questioned, interviewed, or have other conversations with police officers prior to their arrival at the police station. In most cases there is no record of the content of these exchanges and even when records are ostensibly kept, they are typically inadequate. Even under ideal circumstances, contemporaneous notes are not suited for encounters outside the police station and there are strong arguments in favour of the provision of portable recorders.

Encounters outside the police station are important for understanding why suspects make admissions inside the police station. Interviews inside the police station, either recorded on audio or video tape, contain only one part of the relevant exchanges between the suspect and police officers. The current legislation, by emphasising the importance of interviews inside the police station has resulted in a situation in which evidence gathered outside the station is seemingly of minimal value. It is widely assumed that the use of tape or video recording equipment inside the station gives a complete picture of the interview with a suspect. This assumption appears to be incorrect. The statement made by suspects on tape are the outcome of a series of conversations with police officers. The interview inside the police station is merely the final part of this process.

[2:18] **Brown, David, Ellis, Tom and Larcombe, Karen** *'Changing the Code: Police Detention under the Revised Codes of Practice'* (1992) HORS No 129 (at page vi):

This report examines the operation and impact of recently introduced revisions to Code C of the Police and Criminal Evidence Act. This Code contains detailed guidance to the police on the detention, treatment and questioning of suspects. Among the revisions, which came into effect on 1 April 1991, are the following:

- More information is to be given to the suspect about the right to legal advice and there is more detailed guidance about putting the right into practice.
- Suspects are to be told of their entitlements over and above their statutory rights.
- Interviews away from police stations may only be carried out in very limited circumstances. There are tighter rules on recording comments made outside of interview and on allowing interviews without a solicitor present.

- For vulnerable groups – particularly juveniles – the Code defines more closely who is suitable to act as an 'appropriate adult' to advise and assist.

The research was conducted in six different forces in two phases, the first before the new Codes were introduced and the second afterwards. The main findings were as follows:
- The great majority of suspects were given written notices about their rights, although custody records tended to over-record that this had been done and compliance varied between stations. The police are not obliged to provide such information to 'non-PACE' prisoners (eg those held on warrant); however, in phase two these groups were given leaflets about their rights more often.
- Very high proportions of suspects were given at least some spoken information about their rights and this increased still further under the new Code. However, the extra information which is now required was not always given: although nearly three-quarters were told the important fact that legal advice was free, only around half were told it was independent and few were told a legal consultation would be in private. Furthermore, there was considerable variation between stations.
- In around a quarter of cases in phase two, rights were not given clearly, despite a stipulation in the new Code. Other features of the way rights were given may also have swayed some suspects against asking for legal advice.
- Inspectors were lax in recording in custody records whether they had reminded suspects at review times of their right to free legal advice.
- Suspects were often preoccupied at the time they were given their rights but very high proportion recalled being given some information. They were more knowledgeable in phase two about the right to legal advice, especially about the fact that it was free.
- Suspects frequently confused the right to have someone informed of their detention and their entitlement to a telephone call. The new notice of entitlements proved a useful source of information about, for example, the availability of medical attention and the conditions of custody.
- About a fifth of suspects asked to have someone informed of their detention. Contact was known to have been made in about 60% of these cases but the outcome of requests was often not recorded, despite the requirement of Code C. The power to delay informing someone was hardly ever used.
- There was a large increase in the proportion of suspects requesting legal advice, from 24% to 32%. There were considerable differences between stations in request rates for legal advice, but all showed increases in demand, particularly among those detained for offences of intermediate seriousness. This is attributed to the increase in information communicated about rights.
- Of those who did not request legal advice or who only requested it at a later stage, nearly half said they would have asked for a solicitor if one had been to hand on their arrival. It is estimated that this would have led to a request rate for legal advice of between 50% and 66%.
- Despite the increase in requests for legal advice, contact was made with a solicitor by custody officers in more cases: 87% of cases in phase two compared with 80% in phase one. However, the time taken to contact solicitors increased and more requests fell to the duty solicitor scheme.
- The proportion of suspects who spoke to a legal adviser increased: a quarter of all suspects in phase two had a legal consultation. Around two-thirds of advice was given in person. However, the situation varied considerably between stations and up to 80% of advice was given over the telephone in some stations.
- The increase in legal advice has meant that far more suspects who are interviewed have talked to a legal adviser beforehand. However, after giving advice, legal advisers are less often remaining to attend police interviews with their clients. The extent to which they attend interviews varied considerably between stations. When they attended, they seldom interrupted the interview to advise their clients.

- The proportion of cases in which police officers asked suspects questions after arrest and before arrival at the station nearly halved, to 10% in phase two. Moreover, relatively little of the questioning in phase two amounted to an interview as defined in the new Code.
- In phase one, 18% of suspects admitted the offence or made some form of damaging statement prior to arrival at the station, whether in response to police questions or volunteered; in phase two this was true of only 9% of cases.
- Social workers rather than parents are more often acting as appropriate adults in juvenile cases. And, where the suspect is mentally disordered or handicapped, specialist or psychiatric social workers are increasingly involved. Parents often appeared unsuited to the role of appropriate adult; custody officers rarely explained what was expected of them, as is required by the new Code C.
- There has been an improvement in the information juveniles are given about their rights and in their implementation, but juveniles remain at a disadvantage compared with adults. For example, rights are not always implemented when requested if an adult has not yet arrived, information about rights is not always reiterated when an adult arrives, and juveniles are often given little option about having anyone other than the appropriate adult informed of their detention.
- Requests for legal advice by juveniles increased in phase two but remained lower than for adults. There continued to be very wide variations between stations in demand for legal advice by juveniles.
- The report concluded that the new Codes have achieved some degree of success in influencing police behaviour – for example, in providing suspects with information about their rights – but there remains scope for improvement in this and other areas. Other areas for concern that are highlighted are the lack of privacy in talking to solicitors on the telephone, and variations in the amount of legal advice given in person, in the attendance of legal advisers at police interviews and in access to legal advice by juveniles.

(and at page 91):

Compliance with the revised Code

In the introductory chapter, it was noted that the regulation of policing by formal rules is by no means unproblematic. A variety of cultural and practical aspects of police work may determine levels of observance and PACE is no exception. However, previous researchers have differed in their views about the effects of PACE on police practice. On the one hand, there are those who believe that there has been radical change. On the other hand McConville et al (1991) argue that little or any significance has altered, claiming that policing is dominated by 'crime control' values, to which PACE and the Codes of Practice are subordinate. In relation to police detention they maintain that custody officers tend to co-operate with colleagues carrying out investigations in denying suspects their rights. The requirement to keep detailed records is seen as an apparent legitimisation of practice rather than ensuring that what takes place is within the spirit of the rules.

There have been both successes and failures in securing compliance with the new provisions.

Successes

If a balance sheet were to be drawn up, the following would rate as, at the least, moderate successes. Firstly, those detained are being given more information about their rights by means of written notices and spoken information. The police may even be playing safe in some cases by giving this information out where the recipient cannot understand it (to those detained as a place of safety, for example). Importantly, a substantial proportion of suspects are told legal advice is free, information which formerly had to be gleaned from a Law Society leaflet which was patchily distributed. And virtually all who are given a notice of rights are also given the notice of their entitlement while in custody; this contains information which before was only available from reading the Codes of Practice – a right few took up.

Secondly, the facility with which the suspect may exercise the right to legal advice has been enhanced. Reminders of this right are being given at the bulk of reviews and police interviews, as the revised Code requires. It also appears that reviews that would have been conducted while suspects were asleep are more often brought forward to enable them to respond to such reminders (or make other representations). Furthermore, delays of access to legal advice, which used to occur in around 1% of cases, are now hardly ever sought. This is probably not a direct consequence of new guidance in the Code; however, it is in accordance with the revised Code, which in turn reflects the substance of prior Court of Appeal decisions.

Thirdly, the frequency with which suspects are questioned outside the police station appears to have declined, reflecting compliance with new restrictions in the revised Code.

Lastly, there have been moves to ensure that the role of appropriate adult is played by persons who are genuinely appropriate. This means calls upon social workers where parents are also victims or witnesses to the crime or have received admissions.

Failures

Turning to the negative side, the following points may be singled out. Perhaps the most important is the frequent failure by custody officers to deliver information – particularly about the right to legal advice – in accordance with various stipulations in the revised Code. Hardly any suspects were told that the right to consult a solicitor involved a private consultation; only just over half were told legal advice was independent; and over a quarter were not told that it was free. Observers categorised the way information was given as unclear or too fast in over a quarter of cases. Mention of the right to consult the Codes of Practice was also omitted in a significant minority of cases. In addition, a variety of other features of the way rights were given may have tended to bias the suspect against asking for legal advice in some cases, for example, reference to difficulties involved in securing a solicitor.

Are these deficiencies part of what McConville et al (1991) would view as an attempt to evade legal controls and to deny suspects their rights? Is there, in effect, some form of implicit agreement between custody officers and colleagues investigating crime? The strong impression of observers in the present study, based on many hours' presence in custody areas in six different forces, is that it is rarely possible to construe custody officers' actions in this way. Probably closer to the mark is Dixon's (1991) view that the way rights are given reflects the routinisation of familiar tasks and performances without appreciation of the suspect's dilemma. However, what is familiar to the custody officer may not be to the suspect.

It is unlikely that Dixon's interpretation reflects the full range of different attitudes of custody officers. Some may issue rights cursorily because they believe that suspects who are clearly 'guilty' and sure to be charged will gain little advantage from them; therefore, it matters not whether they are given full information. Their hope that the suspect will not request a solicitor is not in sympathy with the investigating officer but primarily to save the work involved in contacting a solicitor and having the suspect on their hands for longer. Others may be brief where they believe suspects are already familiar with their rights. These assumptions are probably often correct, but do not excuse the omissions of information required by the Code. Furthermore, they may sometimes be wrong and this alone should justify the provisions of full information even where it seems superfluous. For example, more than one person who had been arrested before and who was interviewed by observers was under the impression that the duty solicitor was a solicitor employed by the police. Certain information may be omitted because custody officers feel it is valueless: for example, that legal advice is in private, when in fact telephone conversations usually occur within the hearing of everyone in the custody area.

Another negative point concerns juveniles. The research suggests that clarifications in the Code respecting the rights to legal advice and to have someone informed of their detention have not entirely removed the problems that may arise with the implementation of these rights. In particular, juveniles do not always have a free choice to exercise either right. Firstly, custody officers tend to treat contact with a person responsible for the juvenile's welfare (who normally then acts as appropriate adult) as notification under s 56 of PACE, despite C 3.7 which points out that these are separate rights. Secondly, juveniles are generally told of their rights to legal advice on arrival, but decisions on contacting a solicitor are still sometimes deferred until an adult arrives, new guidance notwithstanding (C 3G). This can lead to requests initially made being cancelled later. Custody officers also assume in some cases that juveniles are incapable of deciding on legal advice, when comparatively little explanation would enable them to make a decision.

The operation of the revised Code may also be called into question in certain other areas. There are some deficiencies in record-keeping and, in particular with documenting reminders of the right to legal advice at reviews. Although the research found that in a majority of cases such reminders were given, they were rarely recorded. Since this falls to inspectors, who are themselves the supervisors of custody officers and responsible for checking that their record-keeping is correct, it is an important omission.

Remaining with inspectors, there is some doubt about the value of the provision requiring their permission before an interview can be conducted with someone who has asked for legal advice but not received it. In most cases in which this was sought, observers gained the impression that this procedure had become routinised and effectively rubber-stamped decisions already made at a lower level. Similar criticisms have been made of other PACE procedures, and particularly those for authorising and reviewing detention.

Lastly, mention must be made of the confusion between the right to have someone informed and the entitlement to a telephone call. Custody officers must inform suspects of the former; the latter is contained in the new notice of entitlements. Suspects were hopelessly confused by the two and generally did not discern that they were separate. The revised Code does nothing to correct this confusion and custody officers hardly ever sought to explain the difference. The provision in the Code allowing telephone calls to be delayed or denied in arrestable offences led on a few occasions to denial of outside contact where the suspect had in fact only asked for the police to inform someone. This confusion suggests the need for more explicit guidance.

The impact of the revised Code

How successful have the new provisions been in getting the message about legal advice across? The research suggests a modest degree of success. While most suspects were aware in both phases of the study that they had the right to a solicitor, the proportion who were aware that advice was free rose substantially. Reminders at reviews and prior to interviews that this right could be exercised later also appear generally to have sunk in, although few of those who had not requested a solicitor on arrival acted upon them. However, only a minority noticed the new posters advertising free legal advice. These are positioned in the custody area and suspects may have been too concerned with events to read them. Placing such notices on cell walls might have led to an increase in suspects' awareness of their content.

More people detained by the police now request legal advice. With a request rate of 32%, the study showed that the proportion of suspects asking for a solicitor has risen by one-third since the revised Codes were introduced. It cannot be said for certain that the increase in information available to suspects is the sole cause for this rise – awareness of the right to advice may also have grown independently – but it is believed that it is an important factor. Two important issues will be raised here, which arise from this trend. Firstly, the unevenness in demand, particularly among juveniles; secondly, the capacity of the legal profession to respond.

Unevenness of demand for legal advice

Previous studies have drawn attention to the wide variation in requests for legal advice between police stations. Part of the variation has been attributed to different patterns of offending, different populations of juvenile suspects, and the type of duty solicitor scheme in operation. Much of the variation remains explained. In the present study, request rates for solicitors varied widely. It is useful, however, to consider adults and juveniles separately because the pattern of demand for solicitors differed quite substantially.

There was evidence of a reduction in the amount of variation in the demand for solicitors among adults. There was greater clustering of request rates around the mean, and, generally, stations with low rates in phase one tended to experience above average rises in demand for solicitors in phase two. This may suggest that, under present arrangements for providing advice, there is a certain threshold beyond which demand for solicitors is unlikely to rise and that, given the right conditions may amount to the kind of provision of information that is laid down in the revised Code. There was still a difference between the lowest and highest request rates of 14 percentage points. To the extent that this variation is not explained by difference in offence mix, it is likely to be accounted for by local differences in the provision of legal advice and suspects' awareness of these, and differences in the way information about rights was conveyed, which, as was shown in Chapter 2, may still be quite considerable.

The variation in requests for legal advice among juveniles remains extreme. The lower and upper limits were 4% and 42% in phase one, and 7% and 58% in phase two. The research suggests that only a limited amount of this variation is due to differences in the criminal experience of juvenile suspects. Particularly where demand is low, it is likely that this results to some extent from juveniles' choices about solicitors being constrained by the way in which rights are given. This question has been considered above. Clearly, considerations of equity dictate that juveniles at all stations should be offered equal access to the rights to which they are entitled.

The best way of achieving this is a matter of some debate. It may be argued that juveniles are sometime too young to make an informed decision about legal advice and that this should await the arrival of an adult. However, to do so entails delay. When an adult arrives, he or she may be understandably reluctant to involve the juvenile in a further wait while a solicitor is contacted. Under present rules, the correct procedure (unless the juvenile is clearly incapable of comprehending what is said) is to allow him or her a free choice about legal advice on arrival; if a solicitor is requested, effect should be given to this decision straightaway. However, this may work against the juvenile if their decision is not to request a solicitor. It may be the wrong decision in the circumstances, but if presented to the adult on their arrival as the juvenile's wishes, it may create a presumption against obtaining legal advice. Some of these difficulties might be lessened if legal advice were readily available at the police station – an issue considered below.

The section on the capacity of the legal profession to respond is to be found at extract **[5:2]**.

[2:19]   Baldwin, J and Moloney, T *'Supervision of Police Investigations in Serious Criminal Cases'* RCCJ Research Study No 4 (1993) HMSO (at page 74):

Two distinct models of supervision emerge from this analysis of the investigative process. Major inquiries led by senior officers are supervised in the sense that the officer in charge of the investigation directs operations and assumes a full managerial role in the inquiry. By contrast, in investigations involving small numbers of officers, the ethos of teamwork prevails. The formal supervisor is usually no more than a name on the case papers. The dichotomy is such that it could almost be said that in the former case investigations are supervised, whilst in the latter they are not.

Our abiding impression is that too great a responsibility is being placed on the shoulders of junior officers. The cases included in this study were very serious in nature, and, as a detective constable in Birmingham observed of a section 18 assault case we had been discussing, 'If you try to equate the weight or value of that particular job with something in industry, you wouldn't have someone on such a low echelon in a company dealing with that thing because it would be too big a responsibility.' The question that is raised in this research is therefore whether it is appropriate for officers of constable rank to be expected to investigate and supervise offences of this gravity.

We have noted that the detective constables we interviewed were confident about their own abilities to cope with running such investigations, but it is revealing that three-quarters of them voiced reservations about the laxity of supervision in serious investigations within the police service as a whole. Almost all officers to whom we spoke could easily recount horror stories of working with others whose supervision was not highly regarded, and there are of course enough well-publicised instances of miscarriages of justice to indicate that there has been on occasions in the past a total breakdown in standards of supervision.

It is interesting that the criticisms of standards of supervision that were made by the officers who were interviewed were not directed at immediate colleagues but instead at senior officers. The latter were often seen as being out of touch from the hurly-burly of investigations and so in a weak position to comment upon the way they were being conducted, still less to supervise them. However, it is likely that such attitudes reveal more about the prevailing police culture (a basic tenet of which is that officers have confidence in their immediate colleagues) than about how well these officers might have conducted inquiries.

It seems to us that improvements in standards of supervision might best be effected through an enhancement of the role of sergeant. At present the rank of sergeant within the police service tends to be viewed as an incremental promotion from the rank of constable, and, while they are formally senior to constables, this formality belies an everyday reality where, particularly in the CID, sergeants tend often to be treated as equals by junior colleagues.

The sergeant is, then, very much the *primus inter pares* within the CID, and there are powerful structural imperatives within the police service which produce the relative impotence of the rank. Two factors in particular are significant in this context. First, the difference in pay between constables and sergeants is not great (not nearly as substantial as between sergeants and inspectors, for example), and this affects the way that sergeants are viewed and how in turn they view themselves. Second, and more important, the daily realities of police work tend to prevent sergeants from distancing themselves from their colleagues. The workload of the CID as a rule ensures that sergeants are required to become as immersed in the investigation of offences as detective constables. As one inspector put it in interview, 'Detective sergeants become little more than detective constables because it's a question of all shoulders to the wheel.' In such circumstances, sergeants' authority and capacity to supervise are greatly reduced.

Making the rank of sergeant more substantial would provide a viable alternative to the present 'open-door' policy of senior officers to which we have already referred. The sergeant is in a much better position than officers of higher rank to be acquainted with the strengths and shortcomings of investigating officers and is also better placed to find out about any problems which may develop during the course of an inquiry carried out by a junior officer. By increasing the sergeant's authority and opportunities for supervision, effective intervention in the routine inquiry would be greatly facilitated. Needless to say, increasing the responsibility and authority of the sergeant rank would have resource implications. It would entail enhanced training and remuneration, and would therefore be costly to implement.

Seeking to strengthen supervision at ground level by this means seems to us more likely to be effective than alternatives based upon interposing, as has often been suggested, a senior prosecutorial or quasi-judicial figure at the head of major inquiries.

The involvement of outside figures in criminal investigations is a feature of certain inquisitorial systems, but such notions fit uneasily within the adversarial processes which have traditionally operated in this country. Such proposals do nonetheless enjoy certain appeal as mechanisms for countering what are seen by many as unhealthy police tendencies to pursue single-mindedly the conviction of suspects. The problem of police officers becoming psychologically committed to a certain line of inquiry and unwilling to test alternative theories has been recognised in this country for many years, and, when we put to the officers we interviewed the idea that some outside official might be involved in major investigations, we were surprised that it was favourably received by many of them. Some officers have no strong opinion on the subject but it is interesting to note that, of the remainder, as many favoured the idea as resisted it.

Although there would seem to be little advantage in having Crown Prosecutors as supervisors of inquiries, considerable benefit might nonetheless be derived from seeking to involve them early on in the investigative process. Crown Prosecutors already participate at an early stage in some inquiries, and there is in our view much to be gained from extending this practice. One main benefit is that they could examine whatever evidence the police have collected at that stage and more effectively direct that further inquiries be made along lines they seemed appropriate. Earlier involvement of the Crown Prosecution Service would serve in this way to enhance confidence in the integrity of investigations. If all materials collected by the police in the course of an investigation were handed over to Crown Prosecutors, then they would be in a much stronger position than at present to provide some real direction of inquiries.

Although criticisms have been made in this report about aspects of the police investigations we have examined, it is appropriate that we convey the admirable qualities that were evident to us when we spoke to the officers concerned – their enthusiasm, espirit de corps, commitment, sense of fair play, loyalty and the like. We did not conclude that these were officers who were thrusting remorselessly for conviction; nor did we find that they were often uncaring or slipshod about the way that the people with whom they dealt were treated. But the conclusion we draw, after having spoken at some length with officers, is that the procedures that presently operate, as far as supervision of investigations is concerned, contain the potential for laxity, if not abuse. They allow too great a latitude to officers of constable rank in the way that they conduct inquiries, while at the same time imposing heavy responsibilities upon them. As we have noted in this report, supervision is often regarded by officers as an abstract and artificial concept, almost as a figment of the academic imagination. It is time that the idea of supervision, based upon real responsibility and authority and grounded on rank, was resurrected.

[2:20]   *Royal Commission on Criminal Justice* (1993) Cm 2263, HMSO (at page 52):

(iii) Arguments for retaining the right of silence

13   Those opposed to any weakening of the right of silence in response to police questioning include the Bar Council, Law Society and the Criminal Bar Association, who do not accept that it could be right to allow suspects to be threatened with the possibility of adverse comment simply because they refused to answer police questions. They say that not only are the circumstances of police interrogation disorientating and intimidating in themselves, but there can be justification for requiring a suspect to answer questions when he or she may be unclear both about the nature of the offence

which he or she is alleged to have committed and about the legal definitions of intent, dishonesty and so forth on which an indictment may turn. Innocent suspects' reasons for remaining silent may include, for example, the protection of family or friends, a sense of bewilderment, embarrassment or outrage, or a reasoned decision to wait until the allegation against them has been set out in detail and they have had the benefit of considered legal advice. Members of ethnic or other minority groups may have particular reasons of their own for fearing that any answers they give will be unfairly used against them. There is the risk that, if the police were allowed to warn suspects who declined to answer their questions that they faced the prospect of adverse comment at trial, such a power would sometimes be abused. It is now well established that certain people, including some who are not mentally ill or handicapped, will confess to offences they did not commit whether or not there has been impropriety on the part of the police. The threat of adverse comment at trial may increase the risk of confused or vulnerable suspects making false confessions.

14   Those who take this view argue that it would, for all these reasons, be against the interests of justice to weaken the protection afforded to the innocent suspect by the right of silence. They do not agree that the present safeguard against adverse comment necessarily encourages the police to press too hard for confessions. It may indeed be the case that the police do sometimes try too hard and too exclusively to obtain a formal confession; but they maintain that, if silence is not of itself acceptable evidence, the police should thereby be encouraged to look for other evidence by which the prosecution case can be strengthened. If the right not to answer police questions were removed, adverse comment at the trial would enable a prosecution case which was otherwise too weak to secure a conviction to be strengthened in the minds of the jury by the implication that the defendant's silence automatically supported it.

...

(v)   Our conclusions

20   In the light of all the evidence put before us, we have had to weigh against each other two conflicting considerations. One is the prospect, if adverse comment at trial were to be permissible, of an increase in the number of convictions of guilty defendants who have refused to answer police questions. The other is the risk of an increase in the number of innocent defendants who are convicted because they have made admissions prejudicial to themselves through the fear of adverse comment at trial or whose silence has been taken by the jury to add sufficient weight to the prosecution case to turn a not guilty verdict into one of guilty.

21   Two of us take the view that it would be right for adverse comment (as suggested in paragraph 11 above) to be permitted at the trial and for a consequential amendment (on the lines of the example in paragraph 10 above) to be made to the wording of the caution. In the appropriate case the jury could thus be invited to draw its own conclusions as to whether the silence in the case in question supported the evidence pointing to guilt. The two of us who take this view believe that it is amply justified by the arguments set out in paragraphs 6 to 12 above. They accept that the majority of us are reluctant to take this step for, among other reasons, fear of weakening the safeguards that exist for the vulnerable suspect. The minority would, however, strengthen those safeguards in other ways and in any case believe that the right of silence offers little or no protection to the vulnerable. There is some evidence, as well as the experience of the police service, which in their view implies that it is not the vulnerable but the experienced criminal who shelters behind the right of silence.

22   The majority of us, however, believe that the possibility of an increase in the conviction of the guilty is outweighted by the risk that the extra pressure on suspects to talk in the police station and the adverse inferences invited if they do not may result in more convictions of the innocent. They recommend retaining the present caution and trial direction unamended. In taking this view, the majority acknowledge the frustration which many police officers feel when confronted with suspects who refuse to offer any explanation whatever of strong prima facie evidence that they have committed an offence. But they doubt whether the possibility of adverse comment at trial would make the difference which the police suppose. The experienced professional criminals who wish to remain silent are likely to continue to do so and will justify their silence by stating at trial that their solicitors have advised them to say nothing at least until the allegations against them have been fully disclosed. It may be that more defendants would be convicted whose refusal to answer police questions had been the subject of adverse comment; but the majority believe that their number would not be nearly as great as it popularly imagined.

23   It is the less experienced and more vulnerable suspects against whom the threat of adverse comment would be likely to be more damaging. There are too many cases of improper pressures being brought to bear on suspects in police custody, even where the safeguards of PACE and the codes of practice have been supposedly in force, for the majority to regard this with equanimity. As far as silence at the police station is concerned, therefore, the majority find themselves taking the same stance as the majority of the Royal Commission on Criminal Procedure (RCCP) which said, at paragraph 4.50 on its Report that, if adverse inferences could be drawn from silence, 'It might put strong (and additional) psychological pressure upon some suspects to answer questions without knowing precisely what was the substance of and evidence for the accusations against them ... This in our view might well increase the risk of innocent people, particularly those under suspicion for the first time, making damaging statements ... On the other hand, the guilty person who knew the system would be inclined to sit it out ... If the police had sufficient evidence to mount a case without a statement from him, it would still be to the guilty suspect's advantage to keep to himself as long as possible a false defence which was capable of being shown to be such by investigation. It might just be believed by the jury despite the fact that the prosecution and the judge would be able to comment.'

24   In the majority's view, therefore, in accordance with the recommendations which are argued more fully in chapter six, it is when, but only when, the prosecution case has been fully disclosed that defendants should be required to offer an answer to the charges made against them at the risk of adverse comment at trial on any new defence they then disclose, or on any departure from the defence which they previously disclosed. They may still choose to run the risk of such comment, or indeed to remain silent throughout their trial. But if they do, it will be in the knowledge that their hope of an acquittal rests on the ability of defending counsel either to convince the jury that there is a reasonable explanation for the departure or, where silence is maintained throughout, to discredit the prosecution evidence in the jury's eyes. As argued below, it should be open to the judge, as now in serious fraud cases, to comment on any new defence or any departure from an earlier line of defence.

25   In reaching this view the majority have considered whether there may be a special category of case where a different approach is needed. This is where a crime may have been committed, more than one person is present, and it is impossible to say who has committed the offence. This typically happens when one of two parents is suspected of injuring or murdering a child but it is impossible to say which one. It must not, however, be supposed that removing the right of silence would be the solution in such cases. It would not enable the prosecution to establish which of them had committed the offence if both nevertheless

insisted on remaining silent. Nor would the possibility of adverse comment at the trial enable a court or a jury to determine in respect of which of them the silence should be taken as corroboration. We have every sympathy with the public concern over such cases but it seems to us that they need approaching in a different way, perhaps, where children are the victims, by extending the concept of absolute liability for a child's safety.

[2:21] Home Office Circular 18/94: *The Cautioning of Offenders*

1   The purposes of this Circular are to provide guidance on the cautioning of offenders, and in particular—
* to discourage the use of cautions in appropriate cases, for example for offences which are triable on indictment only;
* to seek greater consistency between police force areas; and
* to promote the better recording of cautions.

2   This Circular, the terms of which have been discussed with the Association of Chief Police Officers and the Crown Prosecution Service, replaces Circular 59/1990 which is hereby cancelled. Some amendments have been made to the national standards for cautioning established by Circular 59/1990; the revised standards, which should be read in conjunction with this Circular, are attached. The general principles underlying those standards are unchanged: properly used, cautioning continues to be regarded as an effective form of disposal, and one which may in appropriate circumstances be used for offenders of any age.

3   Circular 59/1990 left cautioning decisions to the discretion of the police; there is no intention of reducing this discretion, which in the vast majority of cases is properly used. The decision to caution is in all cases one for the police, and although it is open to them to seek the advice of multi-agency panels, this should not be done as a matter of course. It is important that cautions should be administered quickly, and where such advice is sought it must not lead to unnecessary delay.

4   It is apparent that there is some inconsistency between forces about the circumstances in which they consider it appropriate to administer a caution. It is impossible to lay down hard and fast rules such as that first-time offenders must be cautioned, or that certain minor offences should attract only a caution regardless of the offender's record. Nor does the presumption in favour of diverting juveniles from the courts mean that they should automatically be cautioned, as opposed to prosecuted, simply because they are juveniles. Ultimately the proper use of discretion is a matter of common sense: the questions to be asked in each case are –
* whether the circumstances are such that the caution is likely to be effective, and
* whether the caution is appropriate to the offence.

Serious offences

5   Previous guidance discouraged the use of cautioning for the most serious offences, especially for those triable only on indictment. Statistics indicate, however, that cautions are administered in such cases – there were 1735 in 1992. Cautions have been given for crimes as serious as attempted murder and rape: this undermines the credibility of this disposal. Cautions should never be used for the most serious indictable-only offences

such as these, and only in exceptional circumstances (one example might be a child taking another's pocket-money by force, which in law is robbery) for other indictable-only offences, regardless of the age or previous record of the offender.

6   Other offences, less grave in themselves, may nevertheless be too serious for a caution to be appropriate. The factors which will be relevant in making this judgment are too varied for it to be practicable to list them, but they include the nature and extent of the harm or loss resulting from the offence, relative to the victim's age and means; whether the offence was racially motivated; whether it involved a breach of trust; and whether the offence was carried out in a systematic and organised way. Comprehensive lists of such 'gravity factors' have been drawn up by several forces, and these can help in assessing the seriousness of an offence.

7   Efforts should be made to find out the victim's view about the offence, which may have a bearing on how serious the offence is judged to be. It should not, however, be regarded as conclusive. Where a caution has been given and the victim requests the offender's name and address in order to institute civil proceedings, the information should be disclosed, unless there is good reason to believe that it might be used for an improper purpose such as retaliation.

The offender's record

8   Research into a sample of offenders who were cautioned in 1991 indicates that 8 per cent had already received two or more cautions. Multiple cautioning brings this disposal into disrepute; cautions should not be administered to an offender in circumstances where there can be no reasonable expectation that this will curb his offending. It is only in the following circumstances that more than one caution should be considered:

• 	where the subsequent offence is trivial; or
• 	where there has been a sufficient lapse of time since the first caution to suggest that it had some effect.

Consistency

9   There are significant variations between forces – and indeed between stations within forces – in the number of offenders who are cautioned as a proportion of those who are either cautioned or convicted. In 1992 this figure for indictable offences varied, as between forces, from 27 per cent to 57 per cent. This discrepancy may result from differing perceptions of the boundary between informal warnings and formal cautions (see below), or of that between formal cautions and prosecutions. Either way, this degree of variation is undesirable. Accordingly, forces which caution a disproportionately high or low number of offenders should ensure that their force guidelines on cautioning are sound and are being interpreted sensibly.

10   Where there is doubt about whether a prosecution should be brought or a caution given in a particular case, it will often be useful to seek the opinion of the Crown Prosecution Service at an early stage in order to avoid disagreement (and in particular the undesirable outcome of an offender escaping without censure of any kind through being considered to be suitable neither for a caution nor for prosecution). If it is the offender's history, rather than the nature of the offence, which renders the case in the view of the police unsuitable for a caution, the Crown Prosecution Service's attention should be drawn to the fact.

Recording

11   The accurate recording of cautions is essential in order both to avoid multiple cautioning and to achieve greater consistency. This will be made easier when computerised national criminal records are introduced, which will permit a brief description of the offence to be recorded. In the meantime, existing recording systems should be improved, where possible, particularly so as to provide a central force record where this does not already exist. It is essential that records should be checked before a caution is given. When an offender is cautioned on the same occasion for more than one offence, he should be counted as having received one caution only.

12   If a person who is initially suspected of a serious offence is found to have committed a less serious one for which he is then cautioned, it is important that the caution should be recorded as having been given for the lesser offence.

'Informal cautions'

13   There is no intention of inhibiting the practice of taking action short of a formal caution by giving an oral warning, but this should not be recorded as a caution in the criminal statistics nor (unlike a caution) may it be cited in subsequent court proceedings. The expression 'informal caution' used in Circular 59/1990 is confusing and is not recommended.

Supporting cautions

14   Circular 59/1990 made it clear that police officers should not become involved in negotiating reparation or compensation, although these were features which might properly support the use of a caution. In several areas 'caution plus' schemes, incorporating voluntary arrangements of this kind have been developed, apparently to the satisfaction of victims. Since caution plus needs further evaluation before a decision can be made on its future, it would be helpful if forces participating in such schemes would monitor the results.

15   In the case of juvenile offenders, it will often be desirable for the police to liaise with local statutory and voluntary agencies about the ways in which assistance might be offered to the juvenile and their families to prevent reoffending. Such support can be especially valuable if a young person is cautioned for a sexual offence.

National standards for cautioning (revised) – aims

1   The purposes of a formal caution are–
- to deal quickly and simply with less serious offenders;
- to divert them from unnecessary appearance in the criminal courts; and
- to reduce the chances of their re-offending.

Decision to caution

2   A formal caution is a serious matter. It is recorded by the police; it should influence them in their decision whether or not to institute proceedings if the person should offend again; and it may be cited in any subsequent court proceedings. In order to safeguard the offender's interests, the following conditions must be met before a caution can be administered –

- there must be evidence of the offender's guilt sufficient to give a realistic prospect of conviction;
- the offender must admit the offence;
- the offender (or, in the case of a juvenile, his parents or guardian) must understand the significance of a caution and give informed consent to being cautioned.

Note 2A Where the evidence does not meet the required standard, a caution cannot be administered.

Note 2B A caution will not be appropriate where a person does not make a clear and reliable admission of the offence (for example if intent is denied or there are doubts about his mental health or intellectual capacity).

Note 2C If an offence is committed by a juvenile under the age of 14, it is necessary to establish that he know that what he did was seriously wrong.

Note 2D In practice consent to the caution should not be sought until it has been decided that cautioning is the correct course. The significance of the caution must be explained: that is, that a record will be kept of the caution, that the fact of a previous caution may influence the decision whether or not to prosecute if the person should offend again, and that it may be cited if the person should subsequently be found guilty of an offence by a court. In the case of a juvenile this explanation must be given to the offender in the presence of his parents or guardian, or other appropriate adult. The special needs of other vulnerable groups should also be catered for, in accordance with the Code of Practice for the Detention, Treatment and Questioning of Persons by Police Officers.

Public interest considerations

3   If the first two of the above requirements are met, consideration should be given to whether a caution is in the public interest. The police should take into account the public interest principles described in the Code for Crown Prosecutors.

Note 3A There should be a presumption in favour of not prosecuting certain categories of offender, such as elderly people or those who suffer from some sort of mental illness or impairment, or a severe physical illness. Membership of these groups does not, however, afford absolute protection against prosecution, which may be justified by the seriousness of the offence.

Note 3B Two factors should be considered in relation to the offender's attitude towards his offence: the wilfulness with which it was committed and his subsequent attitude. A practical demonstration of regret, such as apologising to the victim and/or offering to put matters right as far as he is able, may support the use of a caution.

Note 3C The experience and circumstances of offenders involved in group offences can vary greatly, as can their degree of involvement. Although consistency and equity are important considerations in the decision whether to charge or caution, each offender should be considered separately. Different disposals may be justified.

Views of the victim

4   Before a caution can be administered it is desirable that the victim should normally be contacted to establish –
• his or her view about the offence;
• the nature and extent of any harm or loss, and their significance relative to the victim's circumstances;
• whether the offender has made any form of reparation or paid compensation.

Note 4A If a caution is being, or likely to be, considered its significance should be explained to the victim.

Note 4B In some cases where cautioning might otherwise be appropriate, prosecution may be required in order to protect the victim from further attention from the offender.

Note 4C If the offender has made some form of reparation or paid compensation, and the victim is satisfied, it may no longer be necessary to prosecute in cases where the possibility of the court's awarding compensation would otherwise have been a major determining factor. Under no circumstances should police officers become involved in negotiating or awarding reparation or compensation.

Administration of a caution

5   A formal caution should be administered in prison by a police officer, and wherever practicable at a police station. A juvenile must always be cautioned in the presence of a parent, guardian or other appropriate adult. Members of other vulnerable groups must be treated in accordance with Code of Practice C.

Note 5A The officer administering the caution should be in uniform and normally of the rank of inspector or above. In some cases, however, a Community Liaison Officer or Community Constable might be more appropriate, or in the inspector's absence the use of a sergeant might be justified. Chief Officers may therefore wish to consider nominating suitable 'cautioning officers'.

Note 5B Where the person is elderly, infirm or otherwise vulnerable, a caution may be administered less formally, perhaps at the offender's home and in the presence of a friend or relative or other appropriate adult.

Recording cautions

6   All formal cautions should be recorded and records kept as directed by the Secretary of State. The use of cautioning should also be monitored on a force-wide basis.

Note 6A Formal cautions should be cited in court if they are relevant to the offence under consideration. In presenting antecedents, care should be taken to distinguish between cautions and convictions, which should usually be listed on separate sheets of paper.

Note 6B Chief officers may also wish to keep records of cases in which action short of a formal caution has been taken, and the reasons for it. But care should be taken not to record anything about an individual which implies that he is guilty of an offence when the evidence is in any doubt. Offences dealt with by action short of a formal caution may not be cited in court.

[2:22]   Crime and Disorder Act 1998 sections 51, 65–66

51   No committal proceedings for indictable-only offences

(1)   Where an adult appears or is brought before a magistrates' court ("the court") charged with an offence triable only on indictment ("the indictable-only offence"), the court shall send him forthwith to the Crown Court for trial—
- (a)   for that offence, and
- (b)   for any either-way or summary offence with which he is charged which fulfils the requisite conditions (as set out in subsection (11) below).

(2)   Where an adult who has been sent for trial under subsection (1) above subsequently appears or is brought before a magistrates' court charged with an either-way or summary offence which fulfils the requisite conditions, the court may send him forthwith to the Crown Court for trial for the either-way or summary offence.

(3)   Where—
- (a)   the court sends an adult for trial under subsection (1) above;
- (b)   another adult appears or is brought before the court on the same or a subsequent occasion charged jointly with him with an either-way offence; and
- (c)   that offence appears to the court to be related to the indictable-only offence,

the court shall where it is the same occasion, and may where it is a subsequent occasion, send the other adult forthwith to the Crown Court for trial for the either-way offence.

(4)   Where a court sends an adult for trial under subsection (3) above, it shall at the same time send him to the Crown Court for trial for any either-way or summary offence with which he is charged which fulfils the requisite conditions.

(5)   Where—
- (a)   the court sends an adult for trial under subsection (1) or (3) above; and
- (b)   a child or young person appears or is brought before the court on the same or a subsequent occasion charged jointly with the adult with an indictable offence for which the adult is sent for trial,

the court shall, if it considers it necessary in the interests of justice to do so, send the child or young person forthwith to the Crown Court for trial for the indictable offence.

(6)   Where a court sends a child or young person for trial under subsection (5) above, it may at the same time send him to the Crown Court for trial for any either-way or summary offence with which he is charged which fulfils the requisite conditions.

(7)   The court shall specify in a notice the offence or offences for which a person is sent for trial under this section and the place at which he is to be tried; and a copy of the notice shall be served on the accused and given to the Crown Court sitting at that place.

(8)   In a case where there is more than one indictable-only offence and the court includes an either-way or a summary offence in the notice under subsection (7) above, the court shall specify in that notice the indictable-only offence to which the either-way offence or, as the case may be, the summary offence appears to the court to be related.

(9)   The trial of the information charging any summary offence for which a person is sent for trial under this section shall be treated as if the court had adjourned it under section 10 of the 1980 Act and had not fixed the time and place for its resumption.

(10)   In selecting the place of trial for the purpose of subsection (7) above, the court shall have regard to—
  (a)   the convenience of the defence, the prosecution and the witnesses;
  (b)   the desirability of expediting the trial; and
  (c)   any direction given by or on behalf of the Lord Chief Justice with the concurrence of the Lord Chancellor under section 75(1) of the Supreme Court Act 1981.

(11)   An offence fulfils the requisite conditions if—
  (a)   it appears to the court to be related to the indictable-only offence; and
  (b)   in the case of a summary offence, it is punishable with imprisonment or involves obligatory or discretionary disqualification from driving.

(12)   For the purposes of this section—
  (a)   "adult" means a person aged 18 or over, and references to an adult include references to a corporation;
  (b)   "either-way offence" means an offence which, if committed by an adult, is triable either on indictment or summarily;
  (c)   an either-way offence is related to an indictable-only offence if the charge for the either-way offence could be joined in the same indictment as the charge for the indictable-only offence;
  (d)   a summary offence is related to an indictable-only offence if it arises out of circumstances which are the same as or connected with those giving rise to the indictable-only offence.

65   Reprimands and warnings

(1)   Subsections (2) to (5) below apply where—
  (a)   a constable has evidence that a child or young person ("the offender") has committed an offence;
  (b)   the constable considers that the evidence is such that, if the offender were prosecuted for the offence, there would be a realistic prospect of his being convicted;

    (c)   the offender admits to the constable that he committed the offence;

    (d)   the offender has not previously been convicted of an offence; and

    (e)   the constable is satisfied that it would not be in the public interest for the offender to be prosecuted.

(2)   Subject to subsection (4) below, the constable may reprimand the offender if the offender has not previously been reprimanded or warned.

(3)   The constable may warn the offender if—

    (a)   the offender has not previously been warned; or

    (b)   where the offender has previously been warned, the offence was committed more than two years after the date of the previous warning and the constable considers the offence to be not so serious as to require a charge to be brought;

but no person may be warned under paragraph (b) above more than once.

(4)   Where the offender has not been previously reprimanded, the constable shall warn rather than reprimand the offender if he considers the offence to be so serious as to require a warning.

(5)   The constable shall—

    (a)   where the offender is under the age of 17, give any reprimand or warning in the presence of an appropriate adult; and

    (b)   explain to the offender and, where he is under that age, the appropriate adult in ordinary language—

        (i)   in the case of a reprimand, the effect of subsection (5)(a) of section 66 below;

        (ii)   in the case of a warning, the effect of subsections (1), (2), (4) and (5)(b) and (c) of that section, and any guidance issued under subsection (3) of that section.

(6)   The Secretary of State shall publish, in such manner as he considers appropriate, guidance as to—

    (a)   the circumstances in which it is appropriate to give reprimands or warnings, including criteria for determining—

        (i)   for the purposes of subsection (3)(b) above, whether an offence is not so serious as to require a charge to be brought; and

        (ii)   for the purposes of subsection (4) above, whether an offence is so serious as to require a warning;

    (aa)   the places where reprimands and warnings may be given;

    (b)   the category of constable by whom reprimands and warnings may be given; and

    (c)   the form which reprimands and warnings are to take and the manner in which they are to be given and recorded.

(7)   In this section "appropriate adult", in relation to a child or young person, means—

    (a)   his parent or guardian or, if he is in the care of a local authority or voluntary organisation, a person representing that authority or organisation;

    (b)   a social worker of a local authority social services department;

    (c)   if no person falling within paragraph (a) or (b) above is available, any responsible person aged 18 or over who is not a police officer or a person employed by the police.

(8)   No caution shall be given to a child or young person after the commencement of this section.

(9)   Any reference (however expressed) in any enactment passed before or in the same Session as this Act to a person being cautioned shall be construed, in relation to any time after that commencement, as including a reference to a child or young person being reprimanded or warned.

66   Effect of reprimands and warnings

(1)   Where a constable warns a person under section 65 above, he shall as soon as practicable refer the person to a youth offending team.

(2)   A youth offending team—
    (a)   shall assess any person referred to them under subsection (1) above; and
    (b)   unless they consider it inappropriate to do so, shall arrange for him to participate in a rehabilitation programme.

(3)   The Secretary of State shall publish, in such manner as he considers appropriate, guidance as to—
    (a)   what should be included in a rehabilitation programme arranged for a person under subsection (2) above;
    (b)   the manner in which any failure by a person to participate in such a programme is to be recorded; and
    (c)   the persons to whom any such failure is to be notified.

(4)   Where a person who has been warned under section 65 above is convicted of an offence committed within two years of the warning, the court by or before which he is so convicted—
    (a)   shall not make an order under subsection (1)(b) (conditional discharge) of section 12 of the Powers of Criminal Courts (Sentencing) Act 2000 in respect of the offence unless it is of the opinion that there are exceptional circumstances relating to the offence or the offender which justify its doing so; and
    (b)   where it does so, shall state in open court that it is of that opinion and why it is.

(5)   The following, namely—
    (a)   any reprimand of a person under section 65 above;
    (b)   any warning of a person under that section; and
    (c)   any report on a failure by a person to participate in a rehabilitation programme arranged for him under subsection (2) above,
may be cited in criminal proceedings in the same circumstances as a conviction of the person may be cited.

(6)   In this section "rehabilitation programme" means a programme the purpose of which is to rehabilitate participants and to prevent them from re-offending.

[2:23]   Baldwin, J *'Preparing Records of Taped Interviews'* RCCJ Research Study No 2 (1993) HMSO (at page 21):

The picture that has emerged from this study is bleak. Even the most progressive forces in the country are failing to produce good quality records of interview in a sufficiently high proportion of cases. Furthermore, the guidance from the Home Office on the subject appears to be unpromising. In tackling the difficulties of compiling balanced records of interview, there is no easy solution and, after years of endeavour, one must surely now be pessimistic about the ability of the police service consistently to prepare records of interview up to the standard required.

The results of this study, which closely parallel those of the author's earlier study in the West Midlands, indicate that there is about a 50% chance that any record of interview will be faulty or misleading – a proportion that increases with the length of interviews. In this study, assessments of the quality of records of interview have been made with a certain charity, and this means that, if anything, it presents the summaries in an unduly favourable light. Yet even when imaginative approaches are examined, records of interview remain dangerously flawed in a high percentage of cases. There seem to be fundamental and inherent difficulties that undermine the usefulness of the records of interview prepared by police officers.

There are, however, some crumbs of comfort. If police officers are to continue to be required to produce the records of interview, then one might derive some consolation from the fact that the approaches adopted both in Bitterne and in Northamptonshire probably indicate the best ways of going about it. If the deficiencies noted in this report that arise in these areas were remedied, then standards could be significantly raised. It is easy to see how improvements could be made if greater care were taken in identifying relevant passages for transcription and if the records of interview did not focus on narrowly defined parts of an interview. Even so, it must be recognised that the main attractions of both approaches – that they will produce savings in police manpower – tend to encourage this kind of corner cutting.

There is unlikely to be any final solution to the problems that have been identified in compiling balanced and fair records of interview. Police officers' summaries are for a variety of reasons almost inevitably flawed in a substantial proportion of cases. It seems unrealistic to expect that police officers, who possess a wide range of literary abilities, will be able to produce the type of balanced and succinct summary that is needed. It is too tall an order for any group, and it is clear that police officers are not well suited to it. It became increasingly evident in carrying out the present study that police officers, because of their temperament, aptitude, educational background, tradition and training, are unlikely to be predisposed to summarise complex materials in a way that can safely be relied upon by other parties. The solution seems not to lie in more police training, and it is unlikely that Circulars from the Home Office, however carefully drafted, can do much to improve matters.

The inherent difficulties of preparing an accurate précis are compounded by the need to exercise sound judgment about what can be left out without distortion, and, the more summaries that one examines, the more convinced one becomes that police officers suffer from an understandable, and probably ineradicable, tendency to view matters through a prosecution prism. The compilation of summaries is not a neutral fact-gathering exercise but one that depends on intuitive judgment. In consequence the scope for conscious and unconscious bias (not to mention more subtle attempts at distortion) is infinite.

While the task remains the responsibility of the police service, it seems inevitable that such problems will arise. Where the interview forms an important part of the prosecution case – and in many cases it is the crux – it is surely unprofessional for lawyers (particularly defence lawyers) to take police officers' summaries on trust. It is not simply that officers may not have the aptitude or the ability to prepare such documents adequately or that they may seek to slant them in favour of the prosecution: it is rather a matter of lawyers in an adversarial system performing their own roles professionally. It is surely incumbent upon defence lawyers, particularly where they have not themselves been in attendance at the police station, to play the tape.

There is in the author's view no effective substitute for the lawyers involved in criminal cases taking the time to do this in a much higher proportion of cases than happens at present. As noted earlier in this report, most interviews are relatively short, and the tapes provide the best picture available of what has taken place in the interview room. It has to be recognised that such a move would have important resource implications, and it is extremely doubtful whether an overstretched Crown Prosecution Service would be able to cope with the added burden of playing tapes without an increase in manpower. Yet, if Crown Prosecutors are to carry out their most critical function effectively – that of case review in order to decide on the appropriate cause of action – then playing the tape must be regarded as a central and unavoidable part of that function.

The compromise of involving civilians in the process, as happens in Bitterne and Northamptonshire, indicates a possible direction for progress, although this solution is unlikely to be one that appeals to all police forces. Even when adopted, more determined efforts will need to be made in the future to ensure that the civilians concerned are themselves adequately trained, and, no less important, that they have fully absorbed the legal significance of what is required in these documents. An ability in the art of précis is a necessary, but not a sufficient, qualification for this work. And it is important to remember that, whether civilians or police officers carry out the work, active supervision and monitoring need to be provided within the police service.

The message of this report is clear: there is no satisfactory alternative to lawyers using the record of interview only after having played the tape itself. This should not be looked on as a purist's solution or as impractical and prohibitively expensive: it is rather the only sure way of avoiding the high risk strategy of taking the records of interview on trust – and the odds at present are greatly inferior to those that apply in Russian roulette. If this conclusion is justified in the four police forces which have made the greatest effort to overcome the problems, then it surely applies even more strongly elsewhere. The expenditure of lawyers' time will mean that records of interview can return to being genuine summaries rather than transcripts, and there will be substantial savings of police officers' time as a result. More important, the lawyers can then be confident – in a way that is certainly not possible at present – that their decision making is soundly based.

CHAPTER THREE

The Crown Prosecution Service (CPS)

Gerry Good has now been charged with 'causing grievous bodily harm with intent', contrary to section 18 of the Offences Against the Person Act 1861 (an offence triable on indictment only – ie before a judge and jury in the Crown Court). But he will still not necessarily be prosecuted. His file passes to the CPS, which has responsibility under the Prosecution of Offences Act 1985 **[3:1]** for the whole conduct of the case in court. Because the CPS may drop or amend charges, it has a veto over prosecution. It also has a significant influence on the distribution of cases between the Crown Courts and magistrates' courts, and in indictable crimes will be involved in the transfer of the case to the Crown Court. In other cases, the CPS may be involved in bail applications and in appeals against decisions by magistrates to grant bail. The CPS will prepare the case for trial, brief counsel to prosecute where appropriate, and prepare the documents for the Crown in the event of an appeal.

(i) Background

Until 1986, the police were responsible for initiating criminal prosecutions, and bringing cases to court. Of the 43 police forces, 31 had their own prosecution departments, and the rest used private firms of solicitors to carry out prosecutions. The Director of Public Prosecutions Department in London dealt with all murder prosecutions and certain other cases, such as those involving national security or public figures. A Royal Commission on Criminal Procedure, set up in 1977 and reporting in 1981, concluded that the traditional police role in investigating crime was incompatible with the objectivity required in prosecution. The police were not in a position to take a sufficiently broad view when applying public interest criteria to prosecution decisions. They criticised the inconsistent policies pursued by different police forces, especially in relation to the decision whether or not to prosecute, and concluded that too many weak cases were being pursued, resulting in a high percentage of trials in which the judge directed a verdict of not guilty at the close of the prosecution case. They therefore recommended a new prosecution service. In 1983 the Home Office published a White Paper, The Investigation and Prosecution of Criminal Offences in England and Wales, which favoured a national organisation with strong local features.

The Prosecution of Offences Act 1985 **[3:1]**, which was brought into force in 1986, still lays down the framework for prosecutions. The CPS is headed by the Director of Public Prosecutions (DPP), under the Attorney-General, and has its headquarters in London. It has two main functions: to provide an objective assessment of the results of police investigation; and to prosecute those cases which pass the tests laid down in the Code for Crown Prosecutors. The CPS ran into serious problems at birth. Many of its initial problems were financial: in 1987–98, the CPS cost £134m, almost double the estimated £70m. Moreover, the managerial structure proved unworkable and had to be reorganised in September 1989 and again in 1993. Until 1993 the CPS was organised into 31 areas covering England and Wales, usually aligned with one, or sometimes two, police force areas, but in that year the 31 areas were reduced to 13 in order to rationalise area administration and to delegate more responsibility to the areas. The financial problems were exacerbated by the difficulty of recruiting enough well-qualified staff, which meant that the service had to use numerous agency lawyers, who were both expensive and, since they worked only occasional days, unable to see cases through consistently.

The problems did not disappear: in 1998 Sir Iain Glidewell was asked to review the CPS and he produced a detailed report in June 1998 **[3:2]**. He found that the 1993 reorganisation had been a mistake, and that the CPS should be divided into 42 areas, coterminous with police areas. This reorganisation took place in 1999, and each area is now headed by a Chief Crown Prosecutor, and is subdivided into two or more branches.

(ii) The legal status of the CPS

The first case in which a court had to decide whether CPS decisions were subject to judicial review was *R v Chief Constable of Kent, ex p L* **[3:3]**, in which the Divisional Court explored the legal relationship between the police and the CPS. Whilst the court held that the police decision was not reviewable, in respect of juveniles, the discretion of the CPS to continue or discontinue criminal proceedings may be reviewable in limited circumstances. Watkins LJ was fearful of 'opening too wide the door of review of the discretion', but are the dangers of not opening that door not equally manifest? Despite his warning, there has been no shortage of applications for judicial review of CPS decision making. Uglow et al **[3:4]**, in their review of the implications of this case, were concerned not so much about the dangers of administrative and non-reviewable decision making, but that the courts' concentration on formal criminal justice agencies ignores the increasingly important informal approaches.

Whilst the decision to prosecute is very difficult to challenge, it may be easier to challenge a decision not to prosecute. In *R v DPP, ex p C* [1995] 1 Cr App Rep 136, the Divisional Court allowed an application by a wife for judicial review of a decision by the DPP not to prosecute her husband for buggery, contrary to section 12 of the Sexual Offences Act 1956. The court held that the prosecutor had not followed the Code for Crown Prosecutors, and remitted the case to the DPP for further consideration. The case was cited in the famous decision of the House of Lords (supported by the European Court of Human Rights) in *R (on the application of Pretty) v DPP* [2002] 1 AC 800, upholding the DPP's refusal to undertake not to prosecute Mrs Pretty's husband if he helped her to die.

R v Croydon Justices, ex p Dean **[3:5]** reveals a trial judge's control over the actions of the CPS by their power to discharge a case for abuse of process (and see also *Townsend, Dearsley and Bretscher* [1998] Crim LR 126). Neither side can challenge the order of the judge: the House of Lords decided in *R v Manchester Crown Court, ex p DPP* [1993] 2 All ER 663 that the decision of a Crown Court to stay an indictment as an abuse of process is not open to judicial review. This decision may prevent delays, but it also means that the CPS has no power to challenge a decision to stay which it believes to be wrong.

(iii)   The Code for Crown Prosecutors

When the CPS receives a set of papers from the police, a Principal Crown Prosecutor will allocate the case to one of their team. As we saw in the previous chapter, much effort is being directed towards involving the CPS in the case as early as possible. The CPS has a duty to keep the evidence continually under review. Thus, in our case, a Crown Prosecutor should have been consulted by the police before Gerry was charged. Someone from the CPS will have been sent to the magistrates' court for the bail hearing the morning after Gerry was charged, and would return with the file to the CPS branch office at the end of the day. The case will be allocated to a Crown Prosecutor, but any decision to discontinue proceedings will only be taken by a Principal. The basic guide is to be found in the Code for Crown Prosecutors **[3:6]**, amplified by the CPS policy manual, which is not published. The DPP has a duty under the Prosecution of Offences Act 1985, s 10 **[3:1]** to issue the code, but this does not mean that the code amounts to delegated legislation. The DPP's guidance must cover three areas: the decision to prosecute; the selection of the appropriate charges; and the representations to be made to magistrates about where the defendant should face trial in either-way offences. The current version of the code, the fourth since 1985, was published in 2000. By simplifying the language, the CPS hoped that it was also clarifying the code. Is it now so simple and lacking in detail that it says very little? Hoyano et al **[3:7]** interviewed CPS personnel even before this latest simplification and concluded that the impact of the code had had a very limited effect on actual case decisions.

In deciding whether to continue a prosecution, the Crown Prosecutor or designated caseworker considers two questions. First is the question of the sufficiency of the evidence. The evidential threshold is a 'realistic prospect of conviction'. This is an objective test: is it more likely than not that the defendant will be convicted? The evidence must be admissible and reliable. We will see in Chapter Seven that there are no clear rules on admissibility of evidence – the judge has a wide discretion under PACE to decide what should be admitted. This element, therefore, is very difficult to predict. It may be even more difficult to predict how the jury or magistrates will decide questions of fact. They will have the benefit of hearing both the prosecution and defence cases before they make their decision. Ashworth (1998, at page 182) questions whether this predictive test is more appropriate than an 'intrinsic merits' test of the evidence, and Sanders (1994) is clear that he believes a better test would be whether a particular jury or bench ought to convict. The CPS does not review the case only once, but must keep the decision to carry on with a case continually under review – should a single test of 'a realistic prospect of conviction' be applied at whatever stage in the criminal process? Ashworth (1998, at page 184) suggests, for example, that the 'realistic prospect of conviction' test is inappropriate when remand decisions are made.

The second task for the Crown Prosecutor is to apply the 'public interest' criterion. The code **[3:5]** was revised to list more clearly the factors which tend in favour of, and those which tend against, a prosecution. Could the required balancing act be more clearly expressed? Ashworth and Fionda (1994), commenting on the subtle relationship between the code and the Home Office circular on the cautioning of offenders **[2:20]**, concluded that '[i]t is desirable that all parts of the system should have a coherent policy, but who should call the tune?' (at page 903). Narey's answer was that the police should – he concluded that 'the scope to discontinue cases in the public interest on the grounds that the offence is not serious or the likely penalty is trivial should be removed' in order that the decision on what type of offending behaviour is suitable for prosecution would be once again one for the police (1997, at page 14). However, Glidewell **[3:2]** advised that this was too sweeping a reform. The tension between the respective roles of police and prosecutor therefore lives on.

The CPS relies on the police for its information. This is a particular problem where the defendant intends to plead guilty. The file may be very small and the CPS have little information on which to assess the factors relevant to the public interest criterion. The file may also exaggerate the police construction of the case against the suspect – for example, the extent to which the suspect confessed. One way to alleviate this problem is to provide the CPS with material from other sources. In the early 1990s, the Probation Service (see Chapter Ten) introduced Public Interest Case Assessment (PICA) units in a number of areas. These units provided information for the CPS in cases where there might be personal or other circumstances that might justify the discontinuance of a prosecution on the public interest factors in the Code for Crown Prosecutors. Whilst Crisp, Whittaker and Harris (1995) suggested that such schemes are very useful in providing the CPS with verified and relevant information about a defendant's version of events, their research also reveals the difficulty in assessing cost-effectiveness in criminal justice initiatives. In his review of an interesting book by Drakeford, Haines, Cotton and Octigan, Morgan **[3:8]** uses the decline of PICA units to show how funding issues in a 'non-joined-up' criminal justice system lead to misguided decision making.

The CPS has a duty to disclose to the defence unused material. What happens if it doesn't wish to do so? The Criminal Procedure and Investigations Act 1996 introduced a statutory scheme whereby the prosecution must make primary disclosure of all previously undisclosed material which, in the prosecution's view(!), might undermine the case for the prosecution. The defendant must then give a defence statement to the prosecution and the court, setting out in general terms the nature of the defence and the matters on which the defence take issue with the prosecution. The prosecution must then make a 'secondary' disclosure of 'all previously undisclosed material which might reasonably be expected to assist the accused's defence as disclosed by the defence statement'. Clearly, any failure to disclose relevant evidence undermines the right to a fair trial, and it can be argued that if relevant evidence has to be excluded in the public interest, then the prosecution should not be sustained (see also Lord Justice Scott's report into the Matrix Churchill ('arms to Iraq') trial, which collapsed for this reason (HCP 1995–96 115) and *Rowe and Davis v United Kingdom* (2000) 30 EHRR 1).

In Gerry Good's case, the Crown Prosecutor reviews the evidence to be found in the file received from the police. She believes that the witness statements and Gerry's own unsatisfactory statements to the police are sufficient evidence against him, though she does ring to ask the police to continue their investigations, particularly looking for the knife or evidence of blood stains. Applying the factors in the Code **[3:6]**, the CPS decides that the public interest suggests that the prosecution should proceed. Paragraph 6.4 states that 'a prosecution is likely to be needed' where a weapon is used or if the defendant's previous convictions are relevant to the present offence. What does this mean? Gerry has previous convictions: in what way might they be relevant? In Gerry's case, none of the common public interest factors against prosecution is relevant, and so the case will proceed to trial.

The Crown Prosecutor must also review whether the defendant has been charged with the right offence. In Gerry's case, they may not necessarily decide to continue with the section 18 charge and will consider whether section 20 would be more appropriate. Note that the code specifically warns against proceeding with a more serious charge simply to encourage the defendant to plead guilty to a lesser charge, an issue we will return to in Chapter Five when discussing plea bargaining.

In our story, Gerry was granted bail by the magistrates. The Crime and Disorder Act 1998, section 51, provides that indictable cases will be 'sent' automatically for trial at the Crown Court, and Gerry Good will not have to return to the magistrates' court for committal proceedings, although he will be able to apply to have the case dismissed. Before the case is listed for trial, there will be a 'plea and directions' hearing (PDH) in the Crown Court, within three or four weeks of the transfer. Whilst it will be the Crown Prosecutor who conducts proceedings in the magistrates' court, the CPS has not yet been granted rights of audience in the Crown Court (except in bail applications and other non-jury matters), and so has to brief counsel (instruct a barrister). This has been a longstanding sore with the CPS, which has maintained that both recruitment and performance standards would improve if it could conduct its own cases. The tide is slowly turning in its favour: in 1993 the Lord Chancellor's Advisory Committee on Legal Education and Conduct approved part of the Law Society's application for rights of audience by extending them to suitably qualified solicitors in private practice, but employed barristers and solicitors still do not have the right to appear in the higher courts. The argument against granting the CPS rights of audience is based on the view that the Bar needs to be composed of those who prosecute and those who defend. To give rights of audience to the CPS would fundamentally change the 'independent' Bar. Block, Corbett and Peay **[3:9]** were critical of counsel's performance in many of their cases, and certainly the current system of last-minute briefing of counsel does suggest that the CPS should have greater responsibility at the trial stage. Block et al recommended that counsel should be obliged in the Bar Code of Practice to give advice to the CPS on receipt of the brief, and that Crown Prosecutors of a certain specified degree of seniority should have rights of audience in the Crown Court and the right of judicial appointment. Narey (1997) stated that PDHs would become more effective if conducted by Crown Prosecutors, who should therefore be given rights of audience at PDHs. We return to the subject of the proper role of the CPS in the next section.

(iv)   Evaluation

For Lord Justice Auld **[1:5]** an essential in preparing for trial is 'a strong, in-dependent and adequately resourced prosecutor in control of the case at least from the point of charge'. How can we measure whether Crown Prosecutors live up to this? Initially, we could consider whether the CPS is inclined to pursue weak cases, or whether it drops too many cases that should have been pursued. Whilst there can be no cut-and-dried measure of success, we can try to measure it in a number of different ways (see Ashworth (1998) for a more detailed analysis). First, the acquittal rate: perhaps those who are acquitted should not have been prosecuted.

Crown Court acquittals

	Acquittals of those who plead not guilty	Acquittals by the jury after trial
1993	58%	42%
1997	60%	40%
2001	66%	43%

Source: Criminal Statistics 1997, 2001, paragraphs 6.32 and 6.34 (Cm 5696)

But as we saw in section (i) above, it is difficult to predict the outcome of cases, especially without a clear knowledge of the defence case. These figures do not necessarily mean that all those acquitted by a jury after a trial should not have been tried in the first place. We will attempt to evaluate jury decision making in Chapter Eight.

Secondly, we can look at the discontinuance rate. Crisp and Moxon (1994) found a termination rate of between 10% and 20%. Glidewell **[3:2]**, pointing out a discontinuation rate of 12% of cases, states that there is evidence that the discontinuance rate varies greatly with types of offence, with (worryingly) the highest discontinuance rates for charges of violence against the person and criminal damage. It is not clear whether these 'terminations' are 'successes' or 'failures' – is the CPS successfully weeding out weak cases or should they have been weeded out sooner? Since the public interest factors specified for police cautioning **[2:20]** are similar to those in the Code for Crown Prosecutors **[3:6]**, it is curious that so many cases remain in the system to be able to be discontinued by the CPS. Whether the CPS adequately manages the discontinuance process is another question – Cretney and Davis (1996), for example, found evidence of a tendency to blame women who withdraw their complaints against their violent partners, concluding that there is a serious dislocation between the interests of domestic assault victims and the goals pursued by the CPS.

A third measure of success (or failure) is the number of judge-directed acquittals in the Crown Court. Here we must distinguish between directed acquittals (where the judge rules that the prosecution has not established a case to answer) and ordered acquittals (where the prosecution offers no evidence). As Block, Corbett and Peay (1993) (and [3:9]) made clear, neither measure is straightforward. However, they are able to conclude that three-quarters of directed acquittals were definitely or possibly foreseeable, and some criticism of the CPS was clearly merited.

The relationship of the CPS with the police remains problematic. At exactly what point does the CPS take over? Should it become involved earlier in the prosecution process – for example, supervising the interviewing of suspects? Under the Prosecution of Offences Act 1985, s 3(2)(e) [3:1] it is the duty of the DPP to give advice to police forces on matters relating to criminal offences. However, the police seem reluctant to seek advice in specific cases. Moxon and Crisp (quoted in the Royal Commission on Criminal Justice (1993) at page 72) suggested that the police asked for prior advice in only 4% of cases. The Royal Commission concluded that guidelines should be formulated to ensure that advice is sought consistently in more complex or serious cases.

Is it feasible to involve the CPS at the beginning of investigations? As part of the recent reorganisation, CPS teams within each area are being aligned to one or more identified police divisions, or courts, in order to provide continuity and a consistent point of contact for police divisions and courts. This informal supervisory role may be all that is possible. Because the CPS was superimposed upon the pre-existing police system, there remains a considerable overlap of functions. Should the CPS have greater control over the provision of information? Should they be able to compel further investigations? The Royal Commission on Criminal Justice (1993), with one dissent, fudges the issue by deciding that better and more formal consultation, and earlier liaison with the police, will resolve the problems. The Glidewell Report [3:2] recommended a single integrated unit, a 'Criminal Justice Unit' – a CPS unit with some police staff – so that the CPS could assume responsibility for 'the prosecution process immediately following charge'. Yet Auld [1:5] recommended that the CPS should determine charge in all but minor, routine offences. This has resulted in a pilot scheme to test new arrangements for charging suspects, evaluated by PA Consulting Group who suggested in their report (2003, available from CPS) that the provision of early charging advice led to improved case-building and more effective and efficient use of time. They found that, in one area, discontinuances fell by 90%, overall conviction rates improved by 15% and there was a 59% reduction in the number of ineffective trials. But whilst putting the CPS back into the police station may lead to a more effective system, it raises other concerns. For example, since the police remain in control of the information that reaches the CPS, will the CPS lose much of the 'independence' which is also crucial?

This discussion has concerned the early involvement of the CPS in investigations. It is also interesting to consider its involvement in the later stages of a prosecution. Should the CPS have a role at the sentencing stage, perhaps presenting a 'victim impact statement' and/or suggesting an appropriate sentence? Should the CPS continue to brief barristers to prosecute trials in the Crown Court on its behalf? Revised guidelines on the role and responsibilities of the prosecution advocate were published in 2002 (see www.cps.gov.uk).

In Chapter Two we mentioned the police involvement in juvenile liaison bodies and multi-agency panels. These are often dominated by the police. Gelsthorpe and Giller **[3:10]** questioned the relationship of the CPS with multi-agency panels, arguing that it should move 'from operational philosophy to professional ideology' – it needed an articulated set of objectives that could be measured and monitored. The first step towards this was taken in 1993 when the CPS issued its Statement of Purpose and Values. Since then many initiatives have been taken to strengthen its profile in the criminal justice system. Yet the CPS cannot breach police control unless it has real powers. As McConville et al **[3:11]** argued, the CPS is a 'police-dependent body'. Sanders (1987) commented on the difficulties of grafting an inquisitorial element onto an adversarial system.

The next chapter looks at those prosecutions that are not initiated by the police. It raises the question whether greater consistency would be achieved if prosecutions initiated by such bodies as the Benefits Agency were brought under the CPS umbrella. However, not only do financial considerations suggest that this will not happen, but perhaps the CPS has not yet established enough credibility within the criminal justice system to be entrusted with a wider role. In any case, such an extension would involve a huge injection of resources.

Further reading

Annual Reports of the Crown Prosecution Service, and of HM Inspectorate of the Crown Prosecution Service
Ashworth, A *The Criminal Justice Process: an evaluative study* (2nd edition, 1998) OUP
Ashworth, A and Fionda, J 'The New Code for Crown Prosecutors: Prosecution, Accountability and the Public Interest' [1994] Crim LR 894
Block, B, Corbett, C and Peay, J 'Ordered and Directed Acquittals in the Crown Court' (1993) RCCJ Research Study No 15 HMSO
Cretney, A and Davis, G 'Prosecuting 'Domestic Assault' [1996] Crim LR 162
Crisp, D and Moxon, D 'Case screening by the CPS: How and why are cases terminated' (1994) HORS No 137 HMSO

Crisp, D, Whittaker, C and Harris, J 'Public Interest Case Assessment Schemes' (1995) HORS No 138 HMSO

Hall Williams, J E *The Role of the Prosecutor* (1988) Aldershot: Avebury

Hilsom, C 'Discretion to Prosecute and Judicial Review' [1993] Crim LR 739

Home Office 'An Independent Prosecution Service for England and Wales' (1983) HMSO, Cmnd 9074

Mansfield, G and Peay, J *The Director of Public Prosecutions: Principles and Practices for the Crown Prosecutor* (1987) Tavistock

Mills, B 'The Code for Crown Prosecutors' (1994) 144 NLJ 899

Sanders, A 'Constructing the Case for the Prosecution' (1987) 14 Journal of Law & Society 229

Sanders, A 'The Silent Code' (1994) 144 NLJ 946

Documents

[3:1] Prosecution of Offences Act 1985, sections 1–3; 10; 16

1 The Crown Prosecution Service

(1)   There shall be a prosecuting service for England and Wales (to be known as the "Crown Prosecution Service") consisting of—

(a)   the Director of Public Prosecutions, who shall be head of the Service;

(b)   the Chief Crown Prosecutors, designated under subsection (4) below, each of whom shall be the member of the Service responsible to the Director for supervising the operation of the Service in his area; and

(c)   the other staff appointed by the Director under this section.

(2)   The Director shall appoint such staff for the Service as, with the approval of the Treasury as to numbers, remuneration and other terms and conditions of service, he considers necessary for the discharge of his functions.

(3)   The Director may designate any member of the Service who has a general qualification (within the meaning of section 71 of the Courts and Legal Services Act 1990) for the purposes of this subsection, and any person so designated shall be known as a Crown Prosecutor.

(4)   The Director shall divide England and Wales into areas and, for each of those areas, designate a Crown Prosecutor for the purposes of this subsection and any person so designated shall be known as a Chief Crown Prosecutor.

(5)   The Director may, from time to time, vary the division of England and Wales made for the purposes of subsection (4) above.

(6)   Without prejudice to any functions which may have been assigned to him in his capacity as a member of the Service, every Crown Prosecutor shall have all the powers of the Director as to the institution and conduct of proceedings but shall exercise those powers under the direction of the Director.

(7) Where any enactment (whenever passed)—
    (a)   prevents any step from being taken without the consent of the Director or without his consent or the consent of another; or
    (b)   requires any step to be taken by or in relation to the Director;
any consent given by or, as the case may be, step taken by or in relation to, a Crown Prosecutor shall be treated, for the purposes of that enactment, as given by or, as the case may be, taken by or in relation to the Director.

2 The Director of Public Prosecutions

(1)   The Director of Public Prosecutions shall be appointed by the Attorney General.

(2)   The Director must be a person who has a 10 year general qualification, within the meaning of section 71 of the Courts and Legal Services Act 1990.

(3)   There shall be paid to the Director such remuneration as the Attorney General may, with the approval of the Treasury, determine.

3 Functions of the Director

(1)   The Director shall discharge his functions under this or any other enactment under the superintendence of the Attorney General.

(2)   It shall be the duty of the Director, subject to any provisions contained in the Criminal Justice Act 1987—
    (a)   to take over the conduct of all criminal proceedings, other than specified proceedings, instituted on behalf of a police force (whether by a member of that force or by any other person);
    (b)   to institute and have the conduct of criminal proceedings in any case where it appears to him that—
        (i)   the importance or difficulty of the case makes it appropriate that proceedings should be instituted by him; or
        (ii)   it is otherwise appropriate for proceedings to be instituted by him;
    (c)   to take over the conduct of all binding over proceedings instituted on behalf of a police force (whether by a member of that force or by any other person);
    (d)   to take over the conduct of all proceedings begun by summons issued under section 3 of the Obscene Publications Act 1959 (forfeiture of obscene articles);
    (e)   to give, to such extent as he considers appropriate, advice to police forces on all matters relating to criminal offences;
    (f)   to appear for the prosecution, when directed by the court to do so, on any appeal under—
        (i)   section 1 of the Administration of Justice Act 1960 (appeal from the High Court in criminal cases);
        (ii)   Part I or Part II of the Criminal Appeal Act 1968 (appeals from the Crown Court to the criminal division of the Court of Appeal and thence to the House of Lords); or
        (iii)   section 108 of the Magistrates' Courts Act 1980 (right of appeal to Crown Court) as it applies, by virtue of subsection (5) of section 12 of the Contempt of Court Act 1981, to orders made under section 12 (contempt of magistrates' courts); and

(g)   to discharge such other functions as may from time to time be assigned to him by the Attorney General in pursuance of this paragraph.

(3)   In this section—

"the court" means—
    (a)   in the case of an appeal to or from the criminal division of the Court of Appeal, that division;
    (b)   in the case of an appeal from a Divisional Court of the Queen's Bench Division, the Divisional Court; and
    (c)   in the case of an appeal against an order of a magistrates' court, the Crown Court;

"police force" means any police force maintained by a police authority under the Police Act 1996, the National Crime Squad and any other body of constables for the time being specified by order made by the Secretary of State for the purposes of this section; and

"specified proceedings" means proceedings which fall within any category for the time being specified by order made by the Attorney General for the purposes of this section.

(4)   The power to make orders under subsection (3) above shall be exercisable by statutory instrument subject to annulment in pursuance of a resolution of either House of Parliament.

10   Guidelines for Crown Prosecutors

(1)   The Director shall issue a Code for Crown Prosecutors giving guidance on general principles to be applied by them—
    (a)   in determining, in any case—
        (i)   whether proceedings for an offence should be instituted or, where proceedings have been instituted, whether they should be discontinued; or
        (ii)   what charges should be preferred; and
    (b)   in considering, in any case, representations to be made by them to any magistrates' court about the mode of trial suitable for that case.

(2)   The Director may from time to time make alterations in the Code.

(3)   The provisions of the Code shall be set out in the Director's report under section 9 of this Act for the year in which the Code is issued; and any alteration in the Code shall be set out in his report under that section for the year in which the alteration is made.

16   Defence costs

(1)   Where—
    (a)   an information laid before a justice of the peace for any area, charging any person with an offence, is not proceeded with;

(b)   a magistrates' court inquiring into an indictable offence as examining justices determines not to commit the accused for trial;

(c)   a magistrates' court dealing summarily with an offence dismisses the information;

that court or, in a case falling within paragraph (a) above, a magistrates' court for that area, may make an order in favour of the accused for a payment to be made out of central funds in respect of his costs (a "defendant's costs order").

(2) Where—

(a)   any person is not tried for an offence for which he has been indicted or committed for trial; or

(aa)   a notice of transfer is given under a relevant transfer provision but a person in relation to whose case it is given is not tried on a charge to which it relates; or

(b)   any person is tried on indictment and acquitted on any count in the indictment;

the Crown Court may make a defendant's costs order in favour of the accused.

(3) Where a person convicted of an offence by a magistrates' court appeals to the Crown Court under section 108 of the Magistrates' Courts Act 1980 (right of appeal against conviction or sentence) and, in consequence of the decision on appeal—

(a)   his conviction is set aside; or

(b)   a less severe punishment is awarded;

the Crown Court may make a defendant's costs order in favour of the accused.

(4) Where the Court of Appeal—

(a)   allows an appeal under Part I of the Criminal Appeal Act 1968 against—

(i)   conviction;

(ii)   a verdict of not guilty by reason of insanity; or

(iii)   a finding under the Criminal Procedure (Insanity) Act 1964 that the appellant is under a disability, or that he did the act or made the omission charged against him;

(aa)   directs under section 8(1B) of the Criminal Appeal Act 1968 the entry of a judgment and verdict of acquittal;

(b)   on an appeal under that Part against conviction—

(i)   substitutes a verdict of guilty of another offence;

(ii)   in a case where a special verdict has been found, orders a different conclusion on the effect of that verdict to be recorded; or

(iii)   is of the opinion that the case falls within paragraph (a) or (b) of section 6(1) of that Act (cases where the court substitutes a finding of insanity or unfitness to plead); or

(c)   on an appeal under that Part against sentence, exercises its powers under section 11(3) of that Act (powers where the court considers that the appellant should be sentenced differently for an offence for which he was dealt with by the court below);

the court may make a defendant's costs order in favour of the accused.

(4A) The court may also make a defendant's costs order in favour of the accused on an appeal under section 9(11) of the Criminal Justice Act 1987 (appeals against orders or rulings at preparatory hearings).

(5)   Where—
  (a)   any proceedings in a criminal cause or matter are determined before a Divisional Court of the Queen's Bench Division;
  (b)   the House of Lords determines an appeal, or application for leave to appeal, from such a Divisional Court in a criminal cause or matter;
  (c)   the Court of Appeal determines an application for leave to appeal to the House of Lords under Part II of the Criminal Appeal Act 1968; or
  (d)   the House of Lords determines an appeal, or application for leave to appeal, under Part II of that Act;
the court may make a defendant's costs order in favour of the accused.

(6)   A defendant's costs order shall, subject to the following provisions of this section, be for the payment out of central funds, to the person in whose favour the order is made, of such amount as the court considers reasonably sufficient to compensate him for any expenses properly incurred by him in the proceedings.

(7)   Where a court makes a defendant's costs order but is of the opinion that there are circumstances which make it inappropriate that the person in whose favour the order is made should recover the full amount mentioned in subsection (6) above, the court shall—
  (a)   assess what amount would, in its opinion, be just and reasonable; and
  (b)   specify that amount in the order.

(8)   ...

(9)   Subject to subsection (7) above, the amount to be paid out of central funds in pursuance of a defendant's costs order shall—
  (a)   be specified in the order, in any case where the court considers it appropriate for the amount to be so specified and the person in whose favour the order is made agrees the amount; and
  (b)   in any other case, be determined in accordance with regulations made by the Lord Chancellor for the purposes of this section.

(10) Subsection (6) above shall have effect, in relation to any case falling within subsection (1)(a) or (2)(a) above, as if for the words "in the proceedings" there were substituted the words "in or about the defence".

(11) Where a person ordered to be retried is acquitted at his retrial, the costs which may be ordered to be paid out of central funds under this section shall include—
  (a)   any costs which, at the original trial, could have been ordered to be so paid under this section if he had been acquitted; and
  (b)   if no order was made under this section in respect of his expenses on appeal, any sums for the payment of which such an order could have been made.

(12) In subsection (2)(aa) "relevant transfer provision" means—
  (a)   section 4 of the Criminal Justice Act 1987, or
  (b)   section 53 of the Criminal Justice Act 1991.

[3:2] *Review of the Crown Prosecution Service,* chaired by Sir Iain Glidewell, 1998 (at page 4 of the summary):

How the prosecution process works at present

13   In order to present the case for the prosecution in court the CPS needs to have a file containing the evidence and other relevant information, including any criminal record the defendant may have. While it is for the police to obtain the evidence as part of the process of investigation, in our view the assembly of the file is part of the conduct of the proceedings for which the CPS is, or should be, responsible. Until now, however, the police have continued to compile prosecution files in a special unit often called an Administrative Support Unit (ASU). The most critical point in the flow of case papers between the investigating officer and the CPS prosecutor in court is at the interface between the ASU and the CPS Branch office.

14   Another cause of discord between the police and the CPS stems from the power of the CPS to discontinue a prosecution. One of a CPS lawyer's most important tasks is to review the evidence in the file in order to decide whether it justifies the charge laid by the police, applying criteria set out in the 'Code for Crown Prosecutors'. If the evidence is not sufficient, the lawyer may either substitute a lesser charge ('downgrading') or discontinue the prosecution altogether. The exercise of this power, which was newly-given in 1986, was resented at that time by some police officers, but most now recognise and accept that it is a valuable provision which should ensure that only those prosecutions proceed to court in which there is an appropriate chance of a conviction in accordance with the Code. This is a safeguard not only for defendants who should not have been charged but also for the public purse.

How the CPS has performed

15   Our Terms of Reference require us to 'assess whether the CPS has contributed to the falling number of convictions for recorded crime'. One thing is clear: the CPS is not concerned with the vast majority of recorded crime. The CPS is responsible for the conduct of all criminal proceedings after there has been a charge by the police or a summons. In 1996, of the crimes recorded by the police (nearly 5 million), only one in every nine (576,000) resulted in a charge or summons. Recorded crimes do not include the large number of motoring offences, so the CPS is concerned with only one out of nine recorded crimes.

16   From there onwards our task becomes more difficult. To carry out such an assessment we have had to examine the available statistics, which has not proved an easy matter. The Home Office, the Court Service and the CPS each produce statistics relating to criminal prosecutions and often the figures within apparently similar parameters are inconsistent with each other. It was to be expected that when the CPS came into existence convictions would fall as a proportion of total cases simply as a result of the CPS properly exercising their new power to discontinue some cases. However, figures produced by the CPS have shown that in recent years the proportion of cases in the Crown Court resulting in conviction has increased, but this trend differs from that shown by the figures published in the Judicial Statistics produced by the Court Service, which show a decline in convictions over the period 1985 to 1996. We have tried but failed to find an explanation for the disparity in the two sets of statistics. We cannot

therefore say that the CPS figures are wrong. We have recommended that attempts are made to agree one set of figures.

17 Overall the CPS discontinues prosecutions in, on average, 12% of cases where the police have charged. The CPS Inspectorate have found, in their consideration of Branch performance, few decisions to discontinue which they considered wrong. However, there is some evidence that the average rate of discontinuance varies greatly between types of offence, with the highest discontinuance rates being for charges of violence against the person and criminal damage, and the lowest for motoring offences. This is clearly a matter for concern, the reasons for which must be investigated.

18 We have been specifically asked to comment on the proposal in the Narey Report that the CPS should no longer have the power to discontinue cases on certain public interest grounds, namely that the court is likely to impose a nominal penalty or that the loss involved is small. We have recommended that the proposal should not be adopted but that the incidence of discontinuance on these grounds should be rare. To that end we have also recommended a small amendment to the Code for Crown Prosecutors.

19 Charges are sometimes downgraded and such few statistics as are available seem to show that this happens most frequently with those which relate to serious crime, public order offences and road traffic accidents causing death. We have no evidence which proves that downgrading happens when it should not. Nonetheless, we suspect that inappropriate downgrading does occur and have recommended that cases of downgrading are specifically examined by the Inspectorate during visits to CPS Units. Both the police and the CPS are helped by the existence of guidance in the form of Charging Standards and whilst we approve their existence we have raised questions about the content of some of the standards. More information is needed about the reasons why charges are downgraded. We have recommended research to consider both this matter and discontinuance.

20 The CPS figures show that the proportion of those pleading Not Guilty in the Crown Court who were convicted increased between 1991–92 and 1996–97 to about 40%. We have, however, given particular consideration to the statistics relating to acquittals in the Crown Court. Both the CPS statistics and Judicial Statistics agree that in 1996 less than half of these were acquittals by a jury. In other words, more than half of all acquittals in the Crown Court resulted from an order or direction of the judge. There are often good reasons why such an order or direction should be made – a vital witness may not appear to give evidence or may prove unreliable in the witness box – but nevertheless the statistic is a cause for concern. In our view, when the CPS has decided to proceed with a case after review, it is reasonable to expect that, unless a major witness is absent, the case will be strong enough to be put before a jury. We conclude that the performance of some parts of the CPS in this respect is not as good as it should be, and improvement is needed.

21 The overall conclusion from this study of the available statistics is that in various respects there has been the improvement in the effectiveness and efficiency of the prosecution process which was expected to result from the setting up of the CPS in 1986. Where the statistics show a recent improvement, that is often a recovery from a deterioration which took place in the years immediately after 1986. We do not place responsibility for this situation wholly on the CPS; in large part it stems from the failure of the police, the CPS and the courts to set overall objectives and agree the role and the responsibility of each in achieving those objectives.

22   Also under the heading 'How the CPS has performed' the Report contains a chapter describing the present state of the relationships between the CPS and the other agencies with whom it works and to whom it relates in the criminal justice system. The tensions between the police and the CPS which existed in the early years have been greatly eased, but in some places have not disappeared. There is still a tendency for each to blame the other if a prosecution file is incomplete or some other essential document missing, and, as a result, a case has to be adjourned. In order to establish their independence from the police after 1986, many in the CPS became isolationist, creating a rift in communication. In addition, many police ASUs are not functioning as effectively as they did when they were first created. As a result the CPS finds that it has to duplicate some of the work the ASU staff have done, in order to prepare a satisfactory prosecution file. It is important to seek a remedy for both problems.

23   There are frequent complaints by both magistrates and judges of inefficiency in case preparation or delay on the part of the CPS. Often the CPS is not the cause of the delay, but sometimes it properly has to accept the blame. Part of the problem lies with court listing practices, into which the CPS at present has no input. Timeliness is a most important aspect of the fair and effective prosecution of crime, but at present the magistrates' courts and the CPS have different, and often inconsistent, performance indicators for timeliness.

24   In the Crown Court, all cases are at present prosecuted by members of the Bar. Both judges and the Bar raised several issues on which action, either by the CPS or by government departments, is needed. They include a considerable disparity between the higher fees paid to defence counsel under the Legal Aid Scheme and those paid to prosecuting counsel briefed by the CPS; the issue of briefs being returned by counsel; problems arising from a shortage of CPS staff in the Crown Court, and a difficulty in Counsel obtaining fresh instructions while in court. These are all matters we address.

25   Finally in this part of the Report we consider the proper role of the CPS in relation to victims and witnesses, particularly its obligations arising out of the Victim's Charter.

26   Our assessment of the CPS is that it has the potential to become a lively, successful and esteemed part of the criminal justice system, but that, sadly, none of these adjectives applies to the Service as a whole at present. If the Service – by which we mean all the members of its staff – is to achieve its potential, it faces three challenges. Firstly, there must be a change in the priority given to the various levels of casework; the 'centre of gravity' must move from the bulk of relatively minor cases in the magistrates' court in order to concentrate on more serious crime, particularly the gravest types, in the Crown Court. Secondly, the overall organisation, the structure and the style of management of the CPS will have to change. Government has started this process by deciding that the CPS should in future be divided into 42 Areas, each headed by a Chief Crown Prosecutor. Each of these CCPs should be given as much freedom as possible to run his area in his own way, and he should suggest his staff to enable them to get on with the core job of prosecuting. Thirdly, the CPS must establish more clearly its position as an integral part of the criminal justice process. It is no longer the 'new kid on the block'.

The future of the CPS in the criminal justice system

27   The role of the CPS within the criminal justice system has not until now been spelt out and put into the context of its key objectives and related performance indicators. Nor have the relationships with the police and the courts been properly defined. At present neither the police nor the CPS have overall responsibility for the preparation of the case file. We have therefore recommended that the CPS should take responsibility for:

- the prosecution process immediately following charge;
- arranging the initial hearing in the Magistrates' Court;
- witness availability, witness warning and witness care.

...

The future organisation of the CPS

36   On coming into office in 1997 the Government announced that the CPS was to be reorganised into a structure of 42 Areas, each to be coterminous with a police force. Our Terms of Reference include that reorganisation as the basis for our work. It would be possible to make a change to a 42 Area structure with minimal disturbance to the current Branch and Headquarters organisation. However, this would not achieve the devolution which we believe is essential. Our view is that the reorganisation should be taken as an opportunity for a genuinely new start, building on the achievements of the past 12 years but creating a form of management at both national and local levels which is different in both structure and style.

37   The objectives of the changes that we propose are to:

- set up a 'decentralised national service' through the genuine devolution of as much responsibility and accountability as possible to the CCPs in the new Areas;
- redefine the role of the Headquarters organisation;
- ensure that all but the most senior lawyers in the CPS, including CCPs, spend much more of their time prosecuting;
- improve the career structure for all staff;
- give each CCP responsibility for managing the administrative support and services in his Area, subject only to the constraints of nationally based accounting and data processing systems;
- reduce the bureaucracy by prioritising the information flows and limiting the Headquarters' support functions to a few key advisory services.

...

63   In the past two years the CPS has established an Inspectorate, which publishes reports both on standards of casework in Areas or Branches, and on specific themes. We are impressed by the quality of these reports, but we believe and recommend that the Inspectorate should be made more independent by having a lay Chairman appointed by the Attorney-General and a number of lay members, and that its remit should be widened. We make proposals to achieve these aims.

[3:3] *R v Chief Constable of Kent County Constabulary, ex p L; R v DPP, ex p B*
[1993] 1 All ER 756

Two separate cases were decided together. The applicant L was a 16-year-old boy who was charged with assault occasioning actual bodily harm. Although the criteria for cautioning were made out in his case, it was decided that the circumstances of the case were too serious for a caution to be appropriate. The applicant B was a 12-year-old girl who was charged with theft. She had not been cautioned as she had not admitted the offence. Both applicants unsuccessfully sought judicial review of the decision to prosecute them.

Watkins LJ (at page 767):

The point has not previously arisen for determination. That probably is because the CPS are comparatively new to the prosecution process. They have unquestionably the sole power to decide whether a prosecution should proceed. They are entirely dominant in that very important respect and all the erstwhile corresponding power of the police has been stripped away. The CPS are the prosecutor and the police are the initiators of criminal proceedings which may, or may not, dependent upon the decision of the CPS, be disposed of by the courts. The power of the CPS includes that of referring a case back to the police for a caution to be substituted for the continuance of proceedings.

I have come to the conclusion that if judicial review lies in relation to current criminal proceedings, in contrast to a failure to take any action against a person suspected of a criminal offence, it lies against the body which has the last and decisive word, the CPS.

A refusal to prosecute or even possibly to caution by the police is another matter. In that event the police may be vulnerable to judicial review, but only upon a basis which, as the cases show, is rather severely circumscribed.

The extent of that basis appears in the well-known judgments of Lord Denning MR, Salmon and Edmund Davies LJJ in *R v Metropolitan Police Comr, ex p Blackburn* [1968] 1 All ER 763, [1968] 2 QB 118. In a later case, *R v Metropolitan Police Comr, ex p Blackburn (No 3)* [1973] 1 All ER 324 at 331, [1973] QB 241 at 254, Lord Denning MR, referring to a failure to enforce the law, stated: '... the police have a discretion with which the courts will not interfere. There might, however, be extreme cases in which he [the commissioner] was not carrying out his duty. And then we would'.

In *R v General Council of the Bar, ex p Percival* [1990] 3 All ER 137 at 152, [1991] 1 QB 212 at 234, in giving the judgment of the court, I stated having quoted from, inter alia, *ex p Blackburn* [1968] 1 All ER 763, [1968] 2 QB 118:

'Reference was also made by counsel ... to a passage in de Smith's Judicial Review of Administrative Action 94th edn, 1980 pp 549–550, to the effect that the discretion of a prosecuting authority though broad is not unreviewable. In our view such discretion is plainly reviewable but the question is whether the limits of review should be as strict as those contended for by the Bar Council. Much will depend, we think, on the powers of the body subject to review, the procedures which it is required to follow and on the way in which a particular proceeding has been conducted; there is potentially an almost infinite variety of circumstances.

We do not think it right that strict defined limits should be set to the judicial review of a body which can broadly be described as a prosecuting authority. Each case must be considered with due regard to the powers, functions and procedures of the body concerned and the manner in which it has dealt (or not dealt) with the particular complaint or application'.

That was obviously not intended to indicate a lesser limitation for judicial review of the police than appears in *ex p Blackburn*. The statement relates to other bodies with very different responsibilities and discretions to which perhaps a less rigorous approach to judicial review might apply.

In the present cases it is not inaction by the police which is complained of but the positive action of charging the two applicants and thus commencing criminal proceedings instead of in L's case cautioning him and in the case of B taking no action against her whatsoever, as well, of course, as the failure of the CPS to discontinue proceedings in both cases.

It seems to me that a decision to discontinue proceedings by the CPS can be equated with a decision by the police not to prosecute and is, therefore, open to judicial review only upon the restricted basis available to someone, assuming he has locus standi, seeking to challenge a decision by the police. Accordingly, that situation does not require further to be addressed in this judgment.

I have come to the conclusion that, in respect of juveniles, the discretion of the CPS to continue or to discontinue criminal proceedings is reviewable by this court but only where it can be demonstrated that the decision was made regardless of or clearly contrary to a settled policy of the Director of Public Prosecutions evolved in the public interest, for example the policy of cautioning juveniles, a policy which the CPS are bound to apply, where appropriate, to the exercise of their discretion to continue or discontinue criminal proceedings. But I envisage that it will be only rarely that a defendant could succeed in showing that a decision was fatally flawed in such a manner as that.

The policy of cautioning, instead of prosecuting, has for some time now been well settled and plays a prominent part in the process of decision-making both by the police and by the CPS when consideration has properly to be given to whether, in any individual case, there should be (a) no action taken or (b) a caution delivered or (c) a prosecution and thereafter (d) a continuance or discontinuance of criminal proceedings.

That policy applied, obviously, to the case of L. It did not apply to the case of B because cautioning was not for her an option. The policy, which can, I think, rightly be so called, which is applicable to her is another. It is that which is far more generally expressed, that is to say that a prosecution should not occur unless it is required in the public interest, regard being given to the stigma of a conviction which can cause irreparable harm to the future prospects of a young person and to his previous character, parental attitude and the likelihood of the offence being repeated: see the Attorney-General's 1983 guidelines.

I find it very difficult to envisage, with regard to that policy, a circumstance, fraud or dishonesty apart possible, which would allow of a challenge to a decision to prosecute or to continue proceedings unless it could be demonstrated, in the case of a juvenile, that there had been either a total disregard of the policy or, contrary to it, a lack of inquiry into the circumstances and background of that person, previous offences and general character and so on, by the prosecutor and later by the CPS. But here too I envisage the possibility of showing that such disregard had happened as unlikely. Therefore, although the CPS decision may in principle be reviewed, in practice it is rarely likely to be successfully reviewed.

I have confined my views as to the availability of judicial review of a CPS decision not to discontinue a prosecution to the position of juveniles because, of course, the present cases involve only juveniles. My view as to the position of adults, on the other hand, in this respect is that judicial review of a decision not to discontinue a prosecution is unlikely to be available. the danger of opening too wide the door of review of the discretion to continue a prosecution is manifest and such review, if it exists, must, therefore, be confined to very narrow limits. Juveniles and the policy with regard to them are, in my view, in a special position.

[3:4]   Uglow, S, Dart, A, Bottomley, A and Hale, C '*Cautioning Juveniles – Multi-Agency Impotence*' [1992] Crim LR 632 (at page 640):

This article discusses the role of the less formal parts of the criminal justice system, here Kent's local multi-agency Juvenile Offender Liaison Team (JOLT), in the light of the decision in *R v Chief Constable of Kent, ex parte L* (see **[3.2]**).

For those interested in juvenile justice, this case could be significant for a different set of reasons. The Home Office guidelines on cautioning can be seen as combining legal criteria, such as an admission of guilt, sufficiency of evidence and the seriousness of the offence, with concerns about the welfare of the offender and presumptions against the prosecution of juveniles and the likely consequences should they be convicted. The Home Office guidelines encourage consultation with agencies such as JOLT largely to enable the police better to evaluate the issues about the welfare of the offender. What is interesting about this case is the extent to which those issues went largely unmentioned. The arguments presented in court as well as Watkins LJ's judgment concentrated on the legal relationship between the decision making agencies (who has 'the last and decisive word?') and the reasonableness of the interpretation of one of the criteria, namely the seriousness of the offence.

The presumption against prosecution provided the background to the applicant's ability to challenge the decision to prosecute. However, the decision itself was defended by the police and the CPS arguing that the procedures followed allowed for separate decision making processes and a full examination of the criteria laid down in the Home Office guidelines. This concentration on the processes used to come to the decision rather than on the consequences of the decision (which is symptomatic of judicial review in general) can be seen as making the welfare of the juvenile secondary to the considerations of due process. It is interesting to note that the one agency most directly concerned with welfare and least involved with legal process, namely JOLT, was considered by the court only insofar as its actions affected those of the police and the CPS. The decision and power to prosecute was left in the hands of those agencies most closely associated with criminal justice than juvenile welfare.

This situation should not be surprising. The role of the CPS in the prosecution process is governed by statute and the police have a well-established duty to protect the public against crime. JOLT and similar agencies across the country have no statutory basis and owe their existence to the co-operation of many agencies involved with juveniles and juvenile offenders at a local level. Thus their basis cannot be derived from the so-cial services; or education departments' concern for the welfare of minors, the police concern with crime prevention or the probation service's concern for the rehabilita-tion of offenders. Rather multi-agency groups work within the spaces between and within the overlapping interests of the agencies involved with juveniles, playing a vital co-ordinating role. However, the indeterminacy of their position could be seen as a contributory factor in marginalising their role in the eyes of the law. It would appear that depending on circumstances, multi-agency teams are seen as appendages of the agencies with more clearly defined roles or with a statutory basis. In this case JOLT was seen merely as a part of the police and the CPS decision-making process, notwithstand-ing the high congruence rates between JOLT recommendations and subsequent police decisions. This concentration on the more formal criminal justice agencies could be in need of revision as informal approaches to criminal justice become increasingly com-mon; for adults as well as for juveniles in reparation and mediation as well as simple diversion.

[3:5]   R v Croydon Justices, ex p Dean [1993] 3 All ER 129

The applicant and two others were arrested on suspicion of murdering a man who had been stabbed and killed in woodland. The applicant did not take part in the actual killing, but after it had taken place, he went to the scene of the crime with the others and helped them destroy the victim's car. He was interviewed by the police, agreed to be a prosecution witness and was released without charge. He was subsequently inter-viewed again and was told that he was a prosecution witness and had the protection of the police. After a conference with the police, the CPS decided that he should be charged under section 4 of the Criminal Law Act 1967 with assisting in the destruction of the victim's car, knowing it was evidence, with intent to impede the apprehension of the other defendants. He was charged and committed for trial, and then applied for judicial review to quash his committal to the Crown Court.

The Divisional Court held that, whereas ordinarily an application to quash a committal ought to be made to the Crown Court before the start of a trial, exceptionally a commit-tal to stand trial which took place in breach of a promise that the defendant would not be prosecuted could be quashed where there was, as in this case, an abuse of process.

Staughton LJ (at page 135):

It is submitted on behalf of the Crown Prosecution Service that they alone are entitled, and bound, to decide who shall be prosecuted, at any rate in this category of case; and that the police had no authority and no right to tell Dean that he would not be prosecut-ed for any offence in connection with the murder; see the Prosecution of Offences Act 1985, s 3(2). I can readily accept that. I also accept that the point is one of constitutional importance. But I cannot accept the submission of Mr Collins that, in consequence, no such conduct by the police can ever give rise to an abuse of process. The effect on George Dean, or for that matter on his father, of an undertaking or promise or repre-sentation by the police was likely to have been the same in this case whether it was or was not authorised by the Crown Prosecution Service. It is true that they might have asked their solicitor whether an undertaking, promise or representation by the police was binding; and he might have asked the Crown Prosecution Service whether it was made with their authority. But it seems unreasonable to expect that in this case. If the Crown Prosecution Service find that their powers are being usurped by the police, the remedy must surely be a greater degree of liaison at an early stage.

[3:6] *Code for Crown Prosecutors* (4th edition, 2000)

1 Introduction

1.1 The decision to prosecute an individual is a serious step. Fair and effective prosecution is essential to the maintenance of law and order. Even in a small case a prosecution has serious implications for all involved – victims, witnesses and defendants. The Crown Prosecution Service applies the Code for Crown Prosecutors so that it can make fair and consistent decisions about prosecutions.

1.2 The Code helps the Crown Prosecution Service to play its part in making sure that justice is done. It contains information that is important to police officers and others who work in the criminal justice system and to the general public. Police officers should take account of the Code when they are deciding whether to charge a person with an offence.

1.3 The Code is also designed to make sure that everyone knows the principles that the Crown Prosecution Service applies when carrying out its work. By applying the same principles, everyone involved in the system is helping to treat victims fairly and to prosecute fairly but effectively.

2 General Principles

2.1 Each case is unique and must be considered on its own facts and merits. However, there are general principles that apply to the way in which Crown Prosecutors must approach every case.

2.2 Crown Prosecutors must be fair, independent and objective. They must not let any personal views about ethnic or national origin, sex, religious beliefs, political views or the sexual orientation of the suspect, victim or witness influence their decisions. They must not be affected by improper or undue pressure from any source.

2.3 It is the duty of Crown Prosecutors to make sure that the right person is prosecuted for the right offence. In doing so, Crown Prosecutors must always act in the interests of justice and not solely for the purpose of obtaining a conviction.

2.4 It is the duty of Crown Prosecutors to review, advise on and prosecute cases, ensuring that the law is properly applied, that all relevant evidence is put before the court and that obligations of disclosure are complied with, in accordance with the principles set out in this Code.

2.5 The CPS is a public authority for the purposes of the Human Rights Act 1998. Crown Prosecutors must apply the principles of the European Convention on Human Rights in accordance with the Act.

3 Review

3.1 Proceedings are usually started by the police. Sometimes they may consult the Crown Prosecution Service before starting a prosecution. Each case that the Crown

Prosecution Service receives from the police is reviewed to make sure it meets the evidential and public interest tests set out in this Code. Crown Prosecutors may decide to continue with the original charges, to change the charges, or sometimes to stop the case.

3.2 Review is a continuing process and Crown Prosecutors must take account of any change in circumstances. Wherever possible, they talk to the police first if they are thinking about changing the charges or stopping the case. This gives the police the chance to provide more information that may affect the decision. The Crown Prosecution Service and the police work closely together to reach the right decision, but the final responsibility for the decision rests with the Crown Prosecution Service.

4 Code Tests

4.1 There are two stages in the decision to prosecute. The first stage is **the evidential test**. If the case does not pass the evidential test, it must not go ahead, no matter how important or serious it may be. If the case does meet the evidential test, Crown Prosecutors must decide if a prosecution is needed in the public interest.

4.2 This second stage is **the public interest test**. The Crown Prosecution Service will only start or continue with a prosecution when the case has passed both tests. The evidential test is explained in section 5 and the public interest test is explained in section 6.

5 The Evidential Test

5.1 Crown Prosecutors must be satisfied that there is enough evidence to provide a 'realistic prospect of conviction' against each defendant on each charge. They must consider what the defence case may be, and how that is likely to affect the prosecution case.

5.2 A realistic prospect of conviction is an objective test. It means that a jury or bench of magistrates, properly directed in accordance with the law, is more likely than not to convict the defendant of the charge alleged. This is a separate test from the one that the criminal courts themselves must apply. A jury or magistrates' court should only convict if satisfied so that it is sure of a defendant's guilt.

5.3 When deciding whether there is enough evidence to prosecute, Crown Prosecutors must consider whether the evidence can be used and is reliable. There will be many cases in which the evidence does not give any cause for concern. But there will also be cases in which the evidence may not be as strong as it first appears. Crown Prosecutors must ask themselves the following questions:

Can the evidence be used in court?
a   Is it likely that the evidence will be excluded by the court? There are certain legal rules which might mean that evidence which seems relevant cannot be given at a trial. For example, is it likely that the evidence will be excluded because of the way in which it was gathered or because of the rule against using hearsay as evidence? If so, is there enough other evidence for a realistic prospect of conviction?

Is the evidence reliable?

b Is there evidence which might support or detract from the reliability of a confession? Is the reliability affected by factors such as the defendant's age, intelligence or level of understanding?

c What explanation has the defendant given? Is a court likely to find it credible in the light of the evidence as a whole? Does it support an innocent explanation?

d If the identity of the defendant is likely to be questioned, is the evidence about this strong enough?

e Is the witness's background likely to weaken the prosecution case? For example, does the witness have any motive that may affect his or her attitude to the case, or a relevant previous conviction?

f Are there concerns over the accuracy or credibility of a witness? Are these concerns based on evidence or simply information with nothing to support it? Is there further evidence which the police should be asked to seek out which may support or detract from the account of the witness?

5.4 Crown Prosecutors should not ignore evidence because they are not sure that it can be used or is reliable. But they should look closely at it when deciding if there is a realistic prospect of conviction.

6   The Public Interest Test

6.1 In 1951, Lord Shawcross, who was Attorney General, made the classic statement on public interest, which has been supported by Attorneys General ever since: 'It has never been the rule in this country – I hope it never will be – that suspected criminal offences must automatically be the subject of prosecution'. (House of Commons Debates, volume 483, column 681, 29 January 1951.)

6.2 The public interest must be considered in each case where there is enough evidence to provide a realistic prospect of conviction. A prosecution will usually take place unless there are public interest factors tending against prosecution which clearly outweigh those tending in favour. Although there may be public interest factors against prosecution in a particular case, often the prosecution should go ahead and those factors should be put to the court for consideration when sentence is being passed.

6.3 Crown Prosecutors must balance factors for and against prosecution carefully and fairly. Public interest factors that can affect the decision to prosecute usually depend on the seriousness of the offence or the circumstances of the suspect. Some factors may increase the need to prosecute but others may suggest that another course of action would be better.

The following lists of some common public interest factors, both for and against prosecution, are not exhaustive. The factors that apply will depend on the facts in each case.

Some common public interest factors in favour of prosecution

6.4 The more serious the offence, the more likely it is that a prosecution will be needed in the public interest. A prosecution is likely to be needed if:

a   a conviction is likely to result in a significant sentence;

b   a weapon was used or violence was threatened during the commission of the offence;

c   the offence was committed against a person serving the public (for example, a police or prison officer, or a nurse);

d   the defendant was in a position of authority or trust;

e   the evidence shows that the defendant was a ringleader or an organiser of the offence;

f   there is evidence that the offence was premeditated;

g   there is evidence that the offence was carried out by a group;

h   the victim of the offence was vulnerable, has been put in considerable fear, or suffered personal attack, damage or disturbance;

i   the offence was motivated by any form of discrimination against the victim's ethnic or national origin, sex, religious beliefs, political views or sexual orientation, or the suspect demonstrated hostility towards the victim based on any of those characteristics;

j   there is a marked difference between the actual or mental ages of the defendant and the victim, or if there is any element of corruption;

k   the defendant's previous convictions or cautions are relevant to the present offence;

l   the defendant is alleged to have committed the offence whilst under an order of the court;

m   there are grounds for believing that the offence is likely to be continued or repeated, for example, by a history of recurring conduct;

n   the offence, although not serious in itself, is widespread in the area where it was committed.

Some common public interest factors against prosecution

6.5   A prosecution is less likely to be needed if:

a   the court is likely to impose a nominal penalty;

b   the defendant has already been made the subject of a sentence and any further conviction would be unlikely to result in the imposition of an additional sentence or order, unless the nature of the particular offence requires a prosecution;

c   the offence was committed as a result of a genuine mistake or misunderstanding (these factors must be balanced against the seriousness of the offence);

d   the loss or harm can be described as minor and was the result of a single incident, particularly if it was caused by a misjudgement;

e   there has been a long delay between the offence taking place and the date of the trial, unless:
  - the offence is serious;
  - the delay has been caused in part by the defendant;
  - the offence has only recently come to light; or
  - the complexity of the offence has meant that there has been a long investigation;

f   a prosecution is likely to have a bad effect on the victim's physical or mental health, always bearing in mind the seriousness of the offence;

g   the defendant is elderly or is, or was at the time of the offence, suffering from significant mental or physical ill health, unless the offence is serious or there is a real possibility that it may be repeated. The Crown Prosecution Service, where necessary, applies Home Office guidelines about how to deal with mentally disordered offenders. Crown Prosecutors must balance the desirability of diverting a defendant who is suffering from significant mental or physical ill health with the need to safeguard the general public;

h   the defendant has put right the loss or harm that was caused (but defendants must not avoid prosecution solely because they pay compensation); or

i   details may be made public that could harm sources of information, international relations or national security.

6.6   Deciding on the public interest is not simply a matter of adding up the number of factors on each side. Crown Prosecutors must decide how important each factor is in the circumstances of each case and go on to make an overall assessment.

The relationship between the victim and the public interest

6.7   The Crown Prosecution Service prosecutes cases on behalf of the public at large and not just in the interests of any particular individual. However, when considering the public interest test Crown Prosecutors should always take into account the consequences for the victim of the decision whether or not to prosecute, and any views expressed by the victim or the victim's family.

6.8   It is important that a victim is told about a decision which makes a significant difference to the case in which he or she is involved. Crown Prosecutors should ensure that they follow any agreed procedures.

Youths

6.9   Crown Prosecutors must consider the interests of a youth when deciding whether it is in the public interest to prosecute. However Crown Prosecutors should not avoid prosecuting simply because of the defendant's age. The seriousness of the offence or the youth's past behaviour is very important.

6.10 Cases involving youths are usually only referred to the Crown Prosecution Service for prosecution if the youth has already received a reprimand and final warning, unless the offence is so serious that neither of these were appropriate. Reprimands and final warnings are intended to prevent re-offending and the fact that a further offence has occurred indicates that attempts to divert the youth from the court system have not been effective. So the public interest will usually require a prosecution in such cases, unless there are clear public interest factors against prosecution.

Police Cautions

6.11 These are only for adults. The police make the decision to caution an offender in accordance with Home Office guidelines.

6.12 When deciding whether a case should be prosecuted in the courts, Crown Prosecutors should consider the alternatives to prosecution. This will include a police caution. Again the Home Office guidelines should be applied. Where it is felt that a caution is appropriate, Crown Prosecutors must inform the police so that they can caution the suspect. If the caution is not administered because the suspect refuses to accept it or the police do not wish to offer it, then the Crown Prosecutor may review the case again.

7   Charges

7.1   Crown Prosecutors should select charges which:
a   reflect the seriousness of the offending;
b   give the court adequate sentencing powers; and
c   enable the case to be presented in a clear and simple way.

This means that Crown Prosecutors may not always continue with the most serious charge where there is a choice. Further, Crown Prosecutors should not continue with more charges than are necessary.

7.2   Crown Prosecutors should never go ahead with more charges than are necessary just to encourage a defendant to plead guilty to a few. In the same way, they should never go ahead with a more serious charge just to encourage a defendant to plead guilty to a less serious one.

7.3   Crown Prosecutors should not change the charge simply because of the decision made by the court or the defendant about where the case will be heard.

8   Mode Of Trial

8.1   The Crown Prosecution Service applies the current guidelines for magistrates who have to decide whether cases should be tried in the Crown Court when the offence gives the option and the defendant does not indicate a guilty plea. (See the 'National Mode of Trial Guidelines' issued by the Lord Chief Justice.) Crown Prosecutors should recommend Crown Court trial when they are satisfied that the guidelines require them to do so.

8.2   Speed must never be the only reason for asking for a case to stay in the magistrates' courts. But Crown Prosecutors should consider the effect of any likely delay if they send a case to the Crown Court, and any possible stress on victims and witnesses if the case is delayed.

9   Accepting Guilty Pleas

9.1   Defendants may want to plead guilty to some, but not all, of the charges. Alternatively, they may want to plead guilty to a different, possibly less serious, charge because they are admitting only part of the crime. Crown Prosecutors should only accept the defendant's plea if they think the court is able to pass a sentence that matches the seriousness of the offending, particularly where there are aggravating features. Crown Prosecutors must never accept a guilty plea just because it is convenient.

9.2   Particular care must be taken when considering pleas which would enable the defendant to avoid the imposition of a mandatory minimum sentence. When pleas are offered, Crown Prosecutors must bear in mind the fact that ancillary orders can be made with some offences but not with others.

9.3   In cases where a defendant pleads guilty to the charges but on the basis of facts that are different from the prosecution case, and where this may significantly affect sentence, the court should be invited to hear evidence to determine what happened, and then sentence on that basis.

10   Re-starting a Prosecution

10.1 People should be able to rely on decisions taken by the Crown Prosecution Service. Normally, if the Crown Prosecution Service tells a suspect or defendant that there will not be a prosecution, or that the prosecution has been stopped, that is the end of the matter and the case will not start again. But occasionally there are special reasons why the Crown Prosecution Service will re-start the prosecution, particularly if the case is serious.

10.2 These reasons include:
a   rare cases where a new look at the original decision shows that it was clearly wrong and should not be allowed to stand;
b   cases which are stopped so that more evidence which is likely to become available in the fairly near future can be collected and prepared. In these cases, the Crown Prosecutor will tell the defendant that the prosecution may well start again; and
c   cases which are stopped because of a lack of evidence but where more significant evidence is discovered later.

[3:7]   Hoyano, A, Hoyano, L, David, G and Goldie, S *'A Study of the Impact of the Revised Code for Crown Prosecutors'* [1997] Crim LR 556 (at page 557):

In a detailed critique of the revised Code, published in tandem with a response from the CPS, Andrew Ashworth and Julia Fionda generally welcomed the revisions to the Code, but also expressed a number of concerns. For example, they suggested that there had been a change of emphasis in the direction of a greater propensity to prosecute, particularly in relation to young defendants, and they questioned whether the independence of the CPS may not have been compromised by apparent submission to politically inspired changes of policy.

The CPS commissioned two research studies to gauge the impact of the revised Code. The first of these was conducted 'in-house' and examined police views of the revised Code in terms of its clarity, accessibility, and relevance to their work. Secondly, the CPS commissioned us to ascertain whether the evidential and public interest tests were being implemented in line with the guidance contained in the revised Code, and to discover what impact, if any, the revision had had upon prosecutors' case decisions. The terms of reference provided that the research was to be completed in a six-month period beginning September 1995 and that it was to be conducted by way of 80 interviews with CPS personnel in four CPS areas. Four branch offices were selected from within each area. The interview sample included all grades of personnel, from caseworkers to Branch Crown Prosecutors. The interviews, which were tape-recorded, included discussion of specific case scenarios.

Is the revised Code an improvement?

One aim of the revisions was to make the Code more easily understood outside the CPS. Almost all the prosecutors whom we interviewed considered that the Code had been rendered more accessible to the police and to members of the public. That still of course leaves the question of whether a simplified document is of assistance to prosecutors themselves.

(and at page 564):

The role of the CPS as a filter for evidentially weak cases and for cases which it would not be in the public interest to pursue is important and demanding in equal measure. Our impression from meeting prosecutors is that it is a responsibility which they take very seriously; but equally many of them feel that factors limiting their discretion are not understood by the public, and that they are often unfairly criticised as a result.

It is our overall impression, based on this survey, that prosecutors in the four areas which we examined adopt a common approach in terms of the way they view cases and the factors which they consider. There was no discernible variation in response by area to any of the issues and questions which we raised in our interviews. This of course cannot be taken as proof that *case decisions* are consistent on a national basis; that is beyond the scope of a study based on interviews with CPS staff, but such interviews do at least provide an indicator. At the same time one must acknowledge that the Code itself guides decision-making only at a very basic level. It is a signpost rather than a map, indicating a general direction rather than providing a detailed route.

According to the Attorney-General, the review of the Code was designed:
(1) to make it more easily understood by the police and members of the public;
(2) to clarify the evidential criterion and the requirement that there be a realistic prospect of conviction; and
(3) to bring out more clearly the public interest factors in favour of a prosecution.

Our interviewees were almost unanimous in their view that the first aim has been achieved. However it is apparent that the revised Code has not been so successful in achieving the other two objectives. Prosecutors appeared uncertain as to whether the revisions were intended to send a strong signal that they should be prosecuting more cases, whether in fact any change of direction was desired, or whether there was perceived to be some inconsistency in prosecutorial decision-making which needed to be corrected. In particular it would seem that the CPS has not adequately explained to its own prosecutors why the phrase 'more likely than not' was inserted into the evidential criterion in the revised version of the Code.

Whatever the purpose of the changes to the Code, the impact upon prosecutors' decisions seems to have been fairly marginal. This is mainly because the Code tests are not susceptible to precise gradations and so prosecutors rely to a large extent on experience, both their own and that of their colleagues. The clarifications and guidance in the revised Code did not represent, for most prosecutors, a strong enough distinction to override this. Detailed policy directives relating to specific offences and problems *do* however make a difference. If changes in decision-making are required, it is clear that specific directives are more effective than altering the language of the Code in ways which do not convey – or at least, do not convey in forthright terms – a specific change of direction. This does not derogate from the value of the Code as a tool for training prosecutors who have recently joined the CPS.

[3:8]   Morgan, R Review of Drakeford, M, Haines, K, Cotton, B and Octigan, M *Pre-trial Services and the Future of Probation* (2002) BJ of Criminology 224

Given the pace of contemporary events, there is seldom an ideal time to write and publish a policy-focused book. Do it before a major structural change and the published analysis is, or appears to be, out of date. Wait to start writing until the new structure is in place and one risks missing the priority-setting tide. Drakeford and his co-authors must have faced this dilemma. They presumably collected most of their data (though their research methodological note is somewhat opaque on chronology) at about the time it became apparent that there was to be a National Probation Service, in place since April 2001 as a result of the Criminal Justice and Court Services Act 2000. But they pressed ahead with their text without waiting to see what form the national service was to take. In retrospect it seems a less than happy choice. One cannot but feel that their core fieldwork material – an account of pre-trial services in three probation areas – and their relatively timeless policy objective – furthering the expansion of probation-led pre-trial services – would have been better served had they waited until they could formulate recommendations welded to the current realities of governance. As it is, we are presented in Chapter 5 with reportage of largely irrelevant outdated opinion as to whether there *should* be a national service, and the reader is offered no guidance as to how the authors' project might best be pursued within the new tripartite framework comprising a National Probation Directorate, and 42 local Probation Boards and Chief Officers. This is a pity. A well-timed and linked article or two would have done the job better. The authors' data and argument are nevertheless worthy of close attention.

Pre-trial probation-led services largely comprise bail information and support (including accommodation) schemes. That is, ways of collecting information about accused persons' community ties, and where a remand in custody might be justified, putting in place arrangements which might satisfy the interests of justice and public protection without resort to custody or excessive restriction. There is a powerful case for linking these efforts with information and support for victims – something Drakeford and his colleagues do not discuss – because, as a good deal of evidence makes clear, victims, particularly victims of violence, are often very concerned as to where 'their' offender is during the pre-trial phase of criminal proceedings.

The authors briefly trace the legal framework for the granting and withholding of bail and describe the expanding remand population and the haphazard history of bail information and support schemes in England and Wales from the 1970s onwards. In the first half of the 1990s bail information schemes were extended to most magistrates' courts and some remand prisons by means of a hypothecated Home Office grant which was withdrawn in 1995. Thereafter the funding of pre-trial services was transferred to mainstream probation budgets, which coincidentally were substantially cut back. It is a feature of an unjoined-up criminal justice system that the principal financial beneficiaries of bail information and support services are the CPS and the courts (who are thereby better able to make informed and speedy decisions) and the Prison Service (who are required to accommodate fewer or more short-term remand prisoners), whereas the bail service provider, the Probation Service, incurs increased costs and pressures. It was no surprise, therefore, that when put under budgetary pressure after

1995, bail information and support services declined in number and in some probation areas disappeared altogether.

Are bail information and support services effective? Drakeford and his colleagues suggest that this question can be answered in a variety of ways. Are accused persons who would otherwise have likely been remanded in custody given conditional or unconditional bail, or accused persons who would otherwise have been granted conditional bail subject to no or fewer bail conditions? If so, do these defendants (a) attend court as required and/or (b) not commit further offences or commit fewer or less serious offences and/or (c) retain their employment or maintain their family and other responsibilities and/or (d) address the criminogenic factors underlying their offending behaviour so as to reduce their offending in the future? The authors' review of the research literature suggests that the answer to the effectiveness question is generally positive and that bail services are cost-effective. Remands in custody are reduced as a result of both court and prison based bail information schemes and reoffending rates among the additional bailees appear to be no higher than among bailees generally. The picture regarding the expensive use of probation hostels for bailees is more equivocal because the evidence suggests that a significant proportion would probably not have been remanded in custody.

The authors' survey of pre-trial services in three probation areas indicates that it is currently very variable in character. It is usually the bottom-up product of enthusiastic local managers, often dependent on partnerships with voluntary agencies and, because focused on unconvicted suspects, reminiscent of 'old' as opposed to 'new' probation – that is, a client-centred focus on individuals' social problems – though there are examples of a more top-down emphasis on targets, crime reduction and cost effectiveness.

The big question, however, is how to take matters forward in the new world of a single minister for probation and prisons, a joint probation and prisons Correctional Services Strategy Board (which the minister chairs), a National Probation Directorate and 42 Probation Boards empowered by s.5 of the CJCSA to ensure that there is sufficient provision (including contracted-out provision) locally to protect the public and reduce offending, including 'giving assistance to persons remanded on bail' and 'providing accommodation in approved premises for persons who have any time been charged with an offence'. The fact that this brave new world does not figure in a book entitled *The Future of Probation* should prompt someone, perhaps the author, to pick up the baton in a mainstream journal article.

[3:9] Block, B, Corbett, C and Peay, J *'Ordered and Directed Acquittals in the Crown Court: A Time of Change?'* [1993] Crim LR 95 (at page 100):

Foreseeability and avoidability: how accountable are the CPS?

Of the sample of 100 non-jury acquittals, there were 71 ordered acquittals, 28 directed acquittals and one mixed acquittal, where there were two indictments and one was acquitted by order and one by direction. Although fewer than half of ordered acquittals were considered definitely or possibly foreseeable, three-quarters of directed acquittals were so classified. This supports our view, derived from the study, that directed acquittals result largely from weak cases that should have been discontinued, whereas ordered acquittals often result from unforeseeable circumstances. This may be considered to challenge Zander's assertion that ordered acquittals represent an even weaker category of case than where the judge directs an acquittal.[1] Our study shows that in fact there are at least two categories of ordered acquittals: those weak cases that are spotted by the CPS immediately after committal, and others – seemingly good cases – which weaken unpredictably before committal or trial. Of all ordered acquittals in our sample (71), 14 were listed for mention (the former category) and 37 weakened nearer or on the day of trial (the latter category).

Use of the term 'weak cases' implies criticism of the CPS, but this is misleading. The real basis for criticism is the distinction between predictably weak cases which the CPS fail to spot and unpredictably weak cases. Of fundamentally weak cases, the CPS may be held responsible for those resulting in ordered acquittals that should have been spotted even before committal, and for those ending in directed acquittals due to weaknesses not spotted at all. Any analysis of the national statistics which is used as a basis for assessing the performance of the CPS needs to take account of these distinctions.

Accordingly, the increase in the proportion of ordered to directed acquittals could be interpreted as reflecting the increasing ability of the CPS to identify weak cases, which then result in ordered rather than directed acquittals. Consistent with this would be the numbers of ordered acquittals due to witnesses or victims not turning up at trial – a feature of the unforeseeably weak ordered acquittal group – possibly being due to police not chasing up witnesses rather than CPS inaction. The results of this study, however, equally suggest that many weak cases could have been identified and discontinued before committal. Such action would have prevented the inclusion of these cases in the national statistics of non-jury acquittals completely. These avoidable non-jury acquittals constitute between 15% and 43% of this sample of cases – the 15% figure representing the lowest level of prosecutorial inefficiency (those cases foreseeably weak pre-committal) and 43% the highest (including all those possibly foreseeable cases which might have been identified at or immediately after committal). Moreover, it is surprising that some weak cases, where the weakness was foreseeable (and agreed as such by the CPS assessor), were allowed to proceed to directed acquittals. Although small in number (five), it is an indictment of the CPS that these cases were not converted into ordered acquittals by earlier CPS action, or prevented from becoming acquittals at all by even earlier discontinuance.

(and at page 105):

The results of this inquiry show that of a sample of 100 non-jury acquittals, although 45 were unavoidable due to entirely unforeseen and unforeseeable circumstances, the remainder could or might have been avoided, and in 22 cases even the CPS assessor said that the acquittal was foreseeable and arguably therefore ought to have been avoided. In a minimum of 15%, where it was assessed that a directed or ordered acquittal could have been foreseen prior to committal, the case should have been terminated or manifest deficiencies in the evidence rectified. These acquittals were clearly the responsibility of the CPS in the first instance. Once the case had been committed, blame could more properly be laid with counsel, who did not always advise the CPS that a case was weak or that certain evidence was lacking. Other acquittals too were not attributable to the CPS but stemmed from the intervention of the trial judges, or lack of intervention by counsel.

---

[1]   This includes those acquitted by the judge where no evidence is offered (for example, because of the refusal of a witness to testify). Zander, M 'What the Annual Statistics Tell Us about Pleas and Acquittals' (1991) Crim LR 252.

In view of the limited sample size, it would be unwise to make too many claims on the basis of the findings of the present study. However, as there is no reason to believe that the sample was in any way typical of non-jury acquittals some limited observations and recommendations for change will be advanced. It is suggested that, if implemented, the following modifications to the system could reduce substantially the proportion of non-jury acquittals.

First, the powers of the CPS need enhancing. It is all too easy for a case to seem watertight at committal yet to become manifestly unsafe between committal and trial. A further review of the evidence may reveal it to be not so strong as previously believed, or counsel can point out deficiencies that were missed. Where this occurs, all that the CPS can do at present is to list the case for mention; they cannot discontinue. At the beginning of the trial counsel can offer no evidence and the judge can order an acquittal. Since Grafton, however, the judge cannot interfere with counsel's decision not to offer any further evidence and must direct an acquittal. It is anomalous that the CPS cannot discontinue before trial when they have full discretion to offer no further evidence at the trial up to the end of the prosecution case. Clearly, ordered acquittals of this type could be eliminated if section 23 of the Prosecution of Offences Act 1985 were amended so that the CPS were able to discontinue at any time up to the beginning of Crown Court trial.

[3:10]   Gelsthorpe, L and Giller, H *'More Justice for Juveniles: Does More Mean Better?'* [1990] Crim LR 153 (at page 161):

Dissent and independence

The Crown Prosecution Service was set up as an 'independent' service to 'promote consistency and fairness' and to 'reduce the proportion of cases pursued despite lack of sufficient evidence' amongst other things. Indeed, one of the underlying themes in the setting up of the Service was that it should be an important counterbalance to the increased police powers provided by the Police and Criminal Evidence Act 1984.

Despite this, the Crown Prosecution Service remains dependent upon the police for information. Since the raison d'être of the police is to detect and prevent crime we might reasonably expect a presumption in favour of prosecution with respect to those cases they refer to the Crown Prosecution Service. Andrew Sanders has shown how information from the police is constructed in such a way as to suggest that prosecution is both expedient and desirable. He refers to the potential for discounting evidence, to the fact that the police do not actively seek information that could establish innocence and to the fact that the police do not see their role extending to checking the defence story if doing so would be difficult, even when, for example, following up the story is beyond the resources of the defence. Sanders establishes that cases are not simply about sets of objective facts which can be ascertained once and for all. The police try to construct strong cases by eliminating ambiguity and removing features which undermine cases. Those cases which they present to the Crown Prosecution Service are generally only those cases which they want to prosecute. The Crown Prosecution Service has inquisitorial power to vet cases, to screen them and to halt those which are evidentially insufficient, but it has more sources to explore the cases in depth. The Crown Prosecution Service remains dependent upon the police for the carefully constructed accounts it receives. Indeed, many Crown Prosecutors we interviewed resisted the idea of receiving information from any source other than the police, or at least, resisted the idea of unlimited information.

What is of interest here in the context of juvenile cases, is that we found the police used the same set of conceptual categories as Crown Prosecutors in their decisions to divert or refer cases to court. For those recommended for prosecution the police 'construction' of the cases provides the basis for Crown Prosecution Service assessment and review. The Crown Prosecutors depend on the police for a core of information which could be quickly and routinely checked. Information on offenders and their offences is transmitted to the Crown Prosecution Service with the tacit understanding that these are all cases which deserve to go to court. There was a commonality in their approach and use of their conceptual categories. But the question remains, if the police and Crown Prosecutors use similar conceptual categories in their approach to decision-making, why is it that disagreements occur? A superficial analysis here might be to suggest that the police and Crown Prosecutors have different tolerance levels of 'trouble', different standards or different policies. This is not the case. Rather, it is that perceptions of 'trouble' need to be redefined by the Crown Prosecution Service in the context of its own organisational goals. Thus despite Crown Prosecutors' reliance on police constructions of cases, they do assess cases in the light of the exigencies of everyday organisational practice and it is these which shape their 'operational philosophy'.

At its simplest an organisational priority of the Crown Prosecution Service is to effect a smooth-functioning of the prosecution process. The chief 'problem relevance' in pursuing this is the limitation on available time and human resources. The 'operational philosophy' adopted is one which tests out whether the case as presented by the police is 'routine' or 'potentially problematic'. This is done by assessing the case for the factors we have identified. This assessment is a two-fold process: first the case is assessed by reference to technical considerations – evidential sufficiency, previous referrals, procedural soundness, seriousness of the offence. Where potential problems arise in this assessment reference is made to secondary considerations – agency intervention, personal circumstances, tariff-guessing and the ability to bide one's time.

In the majority of cases the police provide sufficient technical information and there is little (if any) reference to secondary material. In routine cases there is little in the way of 'character assessment'. The more problematic the information to substantiate the first-order technical considerations, however, the more pressure there is to rebut the presumption in favour of prosecution. The presence of problematic technical considerations in a case potentially threatens the smooth-functioning of the prosecution process. In these circumstances, prosecutors examine the information around the secondary considerations to determine whether a potentially problematic prosecution should be given an organisational priority. 'Independence', therefore, emerges not from some Olympian platform of values nor from some discrete professional ideology but from the organisational context – from what we have termed the 'operational philosophy'.

From operational philosophy to professional ideology

Interestingly, the recent Crown Prosecution Service report on Juvenile Proceedings (1989) envisages change in the organisational context of prosecution decisions. One of the main recommendations states that:

The Crown Prosecution Service should be seen to be promoting multi-agency panels. If properly constituted they offer the best method of achieving the correct decision in individual cases (paragraph 6.4, our emphasis)'.

The Report notes the following points in their favour:
(i) they provide a structures forum where all agencies can make their views known;
(ii) a better decision should be reached if all interested parties are involved;
(iii) the Crown Prosecution Service should only receive cases where a prosecution is deemed to be necessary;
(iv) the Crown Prosecution Service should not be open to the accusation that it was simply rubber stamping a police decision to prosecute. (paragraph 6.1, our emphasis).

The recommendation begs a number of questions: why does the Crown Prosecution Service want information from other agencies? What information is required? Would this information be filtered through to the Crown Prosecution Service independently of the Police? How would the information be used? Does more information necessarily mean better decisions?

Clearly, more information from agencies is expected to lead to 'better' decision-making and to the enhancement of the independent status of the Crown Prosecution Service. But this does not address the fact that organisational priorities and constraints currently 'drive' practice considerations. On the one hand the Crown Prosecution Service appears to function on the basis of an 'operational philosophy' – the smooth functioning of the prosecution process – on the other, it appears resistant to the development of a 'professional ideology' which would, above all other things, mark its independent status.

The development of a 'professional ideology' would involve an explicit declaration of beliefs, principles and objectives. Secondly, strategies would have to be adopted to achieve the objectives. Thirdly, the objectives would have to be translated into measurable criteria and targets set. Fourthly, monitoring would have to be carried out to assess whether or not targets had been met. Lastly, policies and practices would have to be evaluated in the light of data derived from monitoring processes.

Such a development would bring both advantages and difficulties. Positively, such an approach would reinforce the central position of the Crown Prosecution Service in the criminal justice system. But areas of difficulty include the issue of accountability and the problem of the lack of coherence and consistency. To whom would the Crown Prosecution Service be accountable, central government or local government? What if the Crown Prosecution Service were to develop objectives based on a percentage usage of custodial sentences per court and local government declared itself a 'custody-free zone'? With regard to the issue of coherency and consistency it is not at all clear how objectives would be set. Given that there is presently a wide variation in views amongst juvenile specialists in the Crown Prosecution Service, who would determine the values and principles to be used? While the current Code for Crown Prosecutors does provide a general statement of intent with respect to the diversion of juveniles from court, it does not provide specific objectives. Sanders makes much the same point in his discussion of the 'public interest'.[2]

2   Sanders, A 'Incorporating the 'Public Interest' in the Decision to Prosecute', in Hall Williams (ed) *The Role of the Crown Prosecutor* (1988).

'[There is an] absence of any clearly stated view of the public interest ... Even the existence, let alone the content, of one universal 'public interest' is far from self-evident. If any concept of public interest is to have legitimacy, it must be based on specific, clearly articulated and publicly debated values'.

The analogy is clear: an articulated set of objectives which can be measured and monitored would enable the Crown Prosecution Service to develop a professional ideology and with it a pivotal position in the criminal justice system. The current practice of an 'operational philosophy' does not achieve this.

[3:11] **McConville, M, Sanders, A and Leng, R** *The Case for the Prosecution* (1991) Routledge (at page 124):

All cases which are either charged or reported for summons are subject to review both within the police and by the Crown Prosecution Service. Since the CPS was superimposed upon the pre-existing policy system rather than replacing any part of it, there is considerable duplication and overlap of functions. For both organisations the grounds of review are the same and involve consideration of whether the public interest is best served by prosecution or some other disposal, whether the evidence establishes a realistic prospect of conviction and whether the proposed charge is appropriate in law. Although the CPS, like the police reviewer, is isolated from operational policing, the prosecutor may seek to influence the investigation process by requesting that specific further inquiries be made. However, certain functions are exclusively the preserve of one or other organisation. The police have total control over which cases enter the system and only the police caution or informally warn an offender. In juvenile cases it is the job of the police to solicit the views of other agencies with responsibility for the welfare of children. On the other hand, the CPS has responsibility for the conduct of the case in court, may drop or amend charges and has ultimate veto of prosecution.

All forces have instituted special procedures to enable agencies with responsibility for the welfare of children to take part in the juvenile decision-making process. The official purpose of these juvenile liaison procedures is to ensure that public interest factors including the welfare of the child are considered on an individual basis. The police are under a statutory duty to notify Social Services if they are going to prosecute a juvenile (s 5(8) Children and Young Persons Act 1969). The systems in operation vary considerably ranging from permanent multi-agency bureaux as pioneered by Northampton to less elaborate systems in which the views of the other agencies are solicited by post or telephone. In the forces which we researched, one force relied upon home visits conducted by specialist police officers to obtain information about the circumstances of juvenile suspects, with the views of the other agencies obtained by post or telephone. One force considered juvenile cases at a regular juvenile liaison meeting convened by the police and attended by representatives of Social Services and the Probation Service. In the third force a specialist juvenile liaison officer collected information and views from the other agencies, with the option of convening a 'panel' in the event of persistent disagreement about a particular case.

Conventional explanations for the development of the CPS and juvenile liaison procedures can be traced to the argument of the objectivity required in prosecution and the need to take a broader view when applying public policy criteria to prosecution decisions. Under this view, CPS and juvenile liaison provide effective scrutiny of earlier police decisions because the individuals involved are independent of the police and operate according to the skills and values of their own professions.

Another interpretation is that such agencies and procedures are simply doing the state's job for it more efficiently than previously, albeit in a 'welfare disguise' – whether by 'winning by appearing to lose' in the case of the CPS or by adopting a 'corporatist approach' in the case of juvenile liaison. Corporatism refers, in Pratt's words, to the tendencies found in advanced welfare societies whereby the capacity for conflict and disruption is reduced by means of the centralisation of police, increased government intervention, and the co-option of various professional and interest groups into a collective whole with homogenous aims and objectives. (Pratt, 1989,[3] citing Unger, 1976).

Under corporatism, the legal process takes on the form of bureaucratic-administrative law, blurring the boundary between the public and private realms, and increasingly concerned to develop routinised criteria in order to enable dispositions to be effected according to an extra-judicial tariff in the most efficient manner. We shall argue, especially in relation to juvenile liaison bureaux, that this corporatist tendency is apparent in the dominant position occupied by the police in all decisions, in the co-option of other professionals into police ideologies and in the routinisation of extra-judicial decision making.

As we described in earlier chapters, constructing the case is not simply an exercise in collecting together and marshalling all relevant information. Rather the selection, creation and presentation of the evidence is geared towards the objective which the police seek to achieve, and effectively dominates later review procedures. Because the police expect case review and understand the ground rules which govern it, they can anticipate it. Thus, the 'seriousness' of an offence may be manipulated by description: an attack may be 'vicious', 'unprovoked', or premeditated; a shop theft may be 'motivated by pure greed'; a suspected shoplifter may have 'looked round furtively'; emphasis on the suspect's own words may be used to convey the officer's view of the case, as by stressing that a shoplifter said 'it just seemed easy' thereby perhaps negating a doubt the reviewer might have about the offence being rooted in forgetfulness, illness or stress. Construction by omission is equally significant. Thus in one case a store detective had suggested to a suspect that she had forgotten to pay. This was criticised by the CPS reviewer who requested the police to advise the store detective not to make such suggestions when questioning shoplifters in future. Case construction may also be a means of co-opting non-police reviewers into police ideology and values or may convey a more general message about local policing imperatives. Thus, the offence in question may be 'rife' in that part of town, the suspect may be described as a 'football hooligan'.

The rhetoric of prosecution decision making emphasises objectivity, impartiality and individualisation. Police influence over a case is said to be confined to the investigation and case preparation stages with ultimate decision making by the prosecutor applying rigorous tests of public interest and evidential sufficiency. The reality is a system of routinised decision-making embodying an overwhelming propensity to prosecute, bolstered by the presumption that earlier decisions were properly made and should not be overturned. The system is dominated throughout it stages by the interests and values of the police, with the CPS playing an essentially subordinate and reactive role.

---

[3]   Pratt, J 'Corporatism: the third model of juvenile justice', 29 BJ of Criminology 236.

(and at page 147):

In the welfarist rhetoric of the criminal justice process, no individual is charged until after the case has been thoroughly reviewed, not only within the police but also ultimately by an independent and impartial prosecuting agency divorced from the investigatory functions of the police. This review process, it is claimed operates to overcome the danger that 'case commitment' by arresting and case officers may lead to unjustified charging, and, generally, to ensure that individuals are brought to court only where there is a realistic prospect of conviction on the basis of the evidence and where it is also in the public interest to deal with the matter by way of prosecution. The special position of juveniles has led to the creation of juvenile liaison bodies where representatives of the caring agencies can give further impetus to non-prosecution by bringing to the forefront non-police values and ideologies.

In reality, the system of review is corporatist in nature: marked by continued police dominance of decision making, a propensity to prosecute, extra-judicial tariffs, routinisation rather than individualised judgment and the broad rejection of public interest criteria. Police dominance is primarily secured by their control over how cases are constructed, a function which enables them to anticipate and thus control review. Although the police have been required to involve other agencies in decision-making, this has been done within police structures (juvenile liaison bureaux) and on police terms but surrounded by a welfarist rhetoric which masks a structure whose objectives appear to be the opposite of its rubric. The CPS, far from being an independent agency, is a police-dependent body, confining review to evidence-sufficiency questions, eschewing public interest criteria, utilising the contradictory and malleable nature of the principles in the codes to further narrowly conceived objectives and, at its worst, adopting an uncritical support-the-police mandate.

CHAPTER FOUR

Non-Police Investigations

Although defendants are most likely to be introduced to the criminal justice system by the victim and a police investigation, there are other, contrasting, routes to prosecution that merit a separate chapter, since different prosecuting authorities have very different policies and priorities. As much as a quarter of all prosecutions of adults for non-motoring offences are not initiated by the police. Every year hundreds of people are prosecuted for tax and customs offences, thousands for social security frauds, for failing to purchase a TV licence, or for failing to hold a valid motor vehicle excise licence (tax disc). Every year hundreds of people die at work, and many more are severely injured. Disasters such as the sinking of a ferry or a fire in a public place often reveal corporate incompetence and criminality. The amount of tax evaded by companies and individuals every year is huge. Levi (1992) estimated that one particular case being investigated by the Serious Fraud Office involved a sum equal to the total annual losses from vehicle-related crime. Non-police prosecutions are even more important if we look at the number of offences rather than the number of offenders. In fact, the scale of crimes committed other than by ordinary people on the street is so vast that we often find it easier to ignore it.

Lidstone et al [4:1] carried out a wide-scale study for the 1981 Royal Commission on Criminal Procedure. Although now 20 years old, it is still a useful starting point, highlighting the wide range of factors which may influence the number of prosecutions an agency undertakes. The ten most common types of non-police prosecutions in that study were (in descending order of their use by the courts): the Post Office (including TV licence cases); the British Transport Police; the Department of the Environment (vehicle excise licences); local authorities; retail stores; the Department of Health and Social Security (as it then was); London Transport; Customs and Excise; private individuals; and Regional Traffic Commissioners. In this chapter we will examine some of these.

(i) Taxation frauds

The Commissioners of Inland Revenue and of Customs and Excise are probably the most selective of the non-police agencies. Their policies are set out in the *Report of the Committee on Enforcement Powers of the Revenue Departments* **[4:2]**. This policy is still followed today, and the decision to prosecute continues to be taken by officials at Under Secretary or Deputy Secretary level in order to maintain some kind of independent review of the decision to prosecute **[4:3]**. Following the report of the Keith Committee, the range of sanctions available to the Revenue Departments was extended. Compounding, which enables them to force compliance as well as a financial penalty, is today widely used as an alternative to taking legal proceedings for an offence under the Customs and Excise Acts. Other non-judicial penalties include seizure of goods, vehicles or equipment used in smuggling or revenue offences. Civil fraud procedures were introduced for VAT by the Finance Act 1986 and were extended to excise duty frauds and customs duties frauds by sections 7–14 and Schedule 4 and 5 of the Finance Act 1994. This is part of a process of decriminalisation of many (often strict liability) offences.

The Inland Revenue's policy of selective enforcement was unsuccessfully challenged in *R v IRC, ex p Mead and Cook* **[4:3]** (see also *R v IRC, ex p Allen* [1997] STC 1141). The court appears to accept without difficulty a policy that leaves the discretion to prosecute challengeable only when it is proved to be 'irrational'. In practice, the Inland Revenue and Customs officers work closely with the police. The Divisional Court in *R v Stafford Justices, ex p Customs and Excise Commrs* [1991] 2 QB 339 unsurprisingly rejected an argument that once a custody officer in a police station had charged the applicant with an offence under the Drug Trafficking Offences Act 1986, the Customs and Excise Commissioners were no longer entitled to prosecute her. The charging process is neutral in this context: proceedings are only instituted on behalf of a police force when it is the police who have investigated, arrested and brought the arrested person to the custody officer. *R v Okafor* [1994] 3 All ER 741 is an interesting example of the Court of Appeal applying the PACE Code of Practice C: The Detention, Treatment and Questioning of Persons by the Police **[2:10]** to the behaviour of Customs officers questioning suspects at Heathrow Airport.

The emphasis of this section has been on the prosecution policy of the taxation authorities, which is so much more selective than that of the police. However, McBarnet (1992) goes further, pointing out that social control through law is challenged not just by those who abuse the law but also by those who use it. She stresses the manipulability of the law in this area and the scope for bending it to specific interests so that 'economic elites with the resources to buy legal creativity can also buy immunity from the law' (at page 266). Roording **[4:3]** offers a different (Dutch) perspective, but also criticises the 'huge and institutionalised pressure' on taxpayers to confess and to co-operate. Should the system be less informal?

(ii)   Social security frauds

The Benefits Agency and Employment Service (now part of JobCentrePlus) are agencies of, respectively, the Department of Social Security and the Department of Work and Pensions. The Benefits Agency normally investigates those in receipt of Income Support and the Employment Service has responsibility for investigating 'working and signing', Giro cheque and collusion fraud committed by those registered as unemployed. Collusion fraud occurs where an employer, together with someone who is registered as unemployed, defrauds the National Insurance fund, and both the employer and the unemployed person may be prosecuted. Until 1988, these agencies tended to concentrate on the benefit office operations, but now there are more employer-based drives looking at certain types of employment where fraud is thought to be prevalent. There is much greater investigation into the hidden economy, especially in areas of the UK that are most economically active, such as London and the South East.

Dee Cook **[4:5]** analyses the different responses to tax and social security frauds. She found that in 1986–87, when 457 tax evaders were prosecuted, 8,000 people were prosecuted for falsely claiming Supplementary Benefit (the predecessor of Income Support). Cook suggests that the differences can be explained in terms of the different histories of taxation and welfare and, subsequently, the ideological construction of taxpayers as 'givers' to, and benefit claimants as 'takers' from, the state. McKeever's **[4:6]** review of recent changes in the law highlights the possibility of fraud arising from claimant confusion rather than dishonesty.

In reaching the decision whether to prosecute, the agencies will consider:
(a)   the nature of the offence;
(b)   the social, domestic and medical circumstances of the alleged offender and their family; and
(c)   the amount of overpayment involved.

Following section 67 of PACE **[2:8]**, on codes of practice – which provides, at subsection (9), that '[p]ersons other than police officers who are charged with the duty of investigating offences or charging offenders shall, in the discharge of that duty, have regard to any relevant provision of such a code' – the Home Office agreed the Code of Practice for the Treatment and Questioning of Persons by Department of Social Security and Department of Employment staff, which corresponds closely with the original PACE Code C **[2:10]**. Would the next logical step be to bring these prosecutions under the CPS?

(iii)   Regulatory agencies

Numerous bodies are empowered to regulate our lives. Examples include government departments – such as consumer protection departments, local authorities – and other public bodies, such as the Health and Safety Executive, the National Rivers Authority, the Pollution Inspectorate and the Factory Inspectorate. To what extent are these agencies accountable? Many are obliged to submit an annual report to Parliament, but apart from that their decisions may be made in secret, making it difficult to gain any overall view of their various prosecuting policies. The supermarket chain Tesco failed in its attempt to challenge the decision of a local authority to prosecute only large, nationally recognised stores in respect of Sunday trading contrary to the Shops Act 1950: *see R v Kirklees Metropolitan Borough Council, ex p Tesco Stores Ltd* (1993) Times, 26 October. Many 'regulatory offences' do not require the prosecution to prove fault, and the relevance of this strict liability to enforcement practices is discussed by Richardson **[4:7]**. She raises the problem of the usurpation of the criminal trial by administrative discretion.

Research such as Hutter's fascinating analysis of the work of Environmental Health Officers in *The Reasonable Arm of the Law?* (1988) explores how the criminal law is used to regulate business activities. Where the offender is seen as basically 'good and respectable' the enforcement agency concerned tends to adopt what is often described as an accommodative approach, seeking compliance through negotiation. Only where the alleged offender is seen as 'bad' does the agency need to enforce compliance. Compliance is also necessary since, if the regulator does not have the co-operation of the offender, they will often not discover offending until 'accidents' happen. The aim of this compliance strategy is prevention, not punishment. The agencies concerned will negotiate with the firms against whom they are enforcing the law, in a way that cannot happen between the police and a small-time crook, who has no bargaining counters with which to negotiate. Sanders **[4:8]** shows how this approach of selective enforcement and selective charging leads to class bias.

Are these regulatory bodies right to give priority to compliance over prosecution? For the sake of consistency, should all prosecutions be brought under the CPS umbrella? The cost implications and the reputation of the CPS as an independent review body mean that this is unlikely. But is there a difference in principle between these offences and police cases that explains why they should be treated differently?

(iv) The Serious Fraud Office

The Serious Fraud Office (SFO) was established by the Criminal Justice Act 1987 **[4:9]**, following the report of the Roskill Committee on Fraud Trials. The Committee's most controversial recommendation – that in some complex fraud cases the trial should take place not before a judge and jury but before a 'fraud trials tribunal' comprising a judge and two members with financial expertise – was rejected by the government. However, many of its other proposals on fraud trials were acted upon.

The SFO, which started operations in 1988, investigates and prosecutes the most serious frauds in England, Wales and Northern Ireland (eight trials in 2001–02, involving thirteen defendants: ten were convicted and three acquitted). It is accountable through its director to the Attorney-General and so to Parliament. Investigations are conducted by interdisciplinary teams of lawyers, police officers and accountants. Most of the police officers are members of the Metropolitan Police or the City of London police.

The investigatory and prosecution roles were combined in one office, just after they had been separated in the case of other criminal offences by the creation of the CPS in 1985. Does the special and complex nature of some frauds make continuity of investigation and prosecution desirable – is fraud necessarily more difficult than other crime? It is not clear exactly where the line between serious fraud and other fraud is drawn, and many serious frauds continue to be dealt with by the CPS. Another difficult line to draw is that which separates the work of the SFO from that of the Financial Services Authority, created by the Financial Services Act 1986. It has now, following the Financial Services and Markets Act 2000, taken over responsibility for the 'detection, investigation and prosecution' of some financial crime. Roording **[4:3]** would argue that a more integrated approach is advisable.

Note the Criminal Justice Act 1987, s 2 **[4:8]**: the SFO has wide powers of investigation as well as of prosecution. Its powers to compel a suspect to answer questions or otherwise to furnish information, and to require the production of documents, were examined by the House of Lords in *R v Director of Serious Fraud, ex p Smith* **[4:9]**. The European Court of Human Rights in *Saunders v United Kingdom* (1996) 23 EHRR 313 held that the admission in evidence at the applicant's trial of transcripts of interviews with Department of Trade and Industry inspectors violated article 6(1) of the European Convention on Human Rights (see **[1:8]**). Article 6(1) presupposes that the prosecution must prove its case without resort to evidence obtained through methods of coercion. As a result of this decision, section 59 (together with Schedule 3) of the Youth Justice and Criminal Evidence Act 1999 now restricts the use that can be made of answers obtained under compulsory powers of questioning in legislation such as the Companies Act 1985. Are there implications here for the provisions of the CJPOA 1994 **[2:10]** restricting the right to silence?

We saw in Chapter Three how the CPS is handicapped in providing an independent review of police decisions by not having its own powers of investigation. Since the SFO has its own investigators, it should perhaps have a high record of success. However, as Levi (1993) makes clear, measuring the success or otherwise of the SFO is not easy. It is impossible to tell whether non-prosecutions are due to political or other extra-legal factors, and prosecution policies can undergo significant shifts if large funds are made available – this happened, for example, with the special Treasury 'votes' for the Bank of Credit and Commerce International investigation. Levi argues that many prosecutions go ahead despite foreseeable weaknesses in the case, and proposes greater judicial involvement before the trial. On the other hand, he fears that prosecution decisions in cases of white-collar crime will become driven almost entirely by cost considerations, a risk exacerbated by the media and the political tendency to look at the huge costs of the individual trial, ignoring the huge dimensions of the misconduct to which they relate (at page 196). If the prosecution of serious frauds proves so difficult, and so expensive, perhaps there is an argument for leaving these cases to the civil law or to administrative regulation. But would this be letting the affluent, white-collar criminal off too lightly? What price are we prepared to pay?

(v)   Private prosecutions

Traditionally, the right of the individual to institute a private prosecution was seen as a valuable constitutional safeguard **[4:11]**. However, this right should not be exaggerated. Legal aid is not available to a private prosecutor, and in any case the right is in effect controlled by the Attorney-General, who may take over the prosecution and, if he thinks fit, enter a plea of *nolle prosequi* ('we do not wish to prosecute'). It is not unusual for the Attorney-General to make clear that if a private prosecution were to be launched, he would stop it. This happened in the case of a priest who threatened to prosecute the doctors who, having sought authority from the House of Lords [1993] AC 789, 'killed' Tony Bland, a patient in a persistent vegetative state. Thus the Attorney-General in effect has a veto on law enforcement.

Further reading

Cranston, R *Regulating Business: law and consumer agencies* (1979) Macmillan
Croal, H *White-Collar Crime* (1992) Open University Press
Hawkins, K *Environment and Enforcement* (1984) Oxford University Press
Hawkins, K and Thomas J M (eds) *Enforcing Regulation* (1984) Boston: Kluwer-Nijhoff

Hutter, B *The Reasonable Arm of the Law?* (1988) Oxford University Press
Jones, K *Law and Economy: the legal regulation of corporate capital* (1982) Academic
    Press
Kirk, D N and Woodcock, A J J *Serious Fraud: Investigation and Trial* (1992)
    Butterworths
Levi, M *The Phantom Capitalists* (1981) Heinemann
Levi, M *The Investigation, Prosecution and Trial of Serious Fraud* RCCJ Research
    Study No 14 (1993) HMSO
McBarnet, D 'It's not What You Do but the Way You Do It: Tax Evasion, Tax
    Avoidance and the Boundaries of Deviance' in Downes, D (ed.) *Unravel-
    ling Criminal Justice* (1992) Macmillan
Nelken, D 'White-Collar Crime' in Maguire, Morgan, Reiner (eds) *The Oxford
    Handbook of Criminology* (3rd edition, 2002)
Pearce, F *Crimes of the Powerful: Marxism, crime and deviance* (1976) Pluto Press
Richardson, G, Ogus, A and Burrows, P *Policing Pollution* (1982) Clarendon
    Press
Wells, C *Corporations and Criminal Responsibility* (1993) Oxford UP

Documents

[4:1]   Lidstone, K W, Hogg, R, Sutcliffe, F *Prosecutions by Private Individuals
and Non-Police Agencies* (1980) HMSO (at page 180):

The prosecuting policies and statistics of nine agencies were considered in some detail
– these were the DHSS, The Post Office, the NTVLRO (television licence evasion),
the DVLC (vehicle excise licence cases), the Inland Revenue, Customs and Excise, and
Health and Safety Executive, the Department of Trade and the Ministry of Agriculture
Fisheries and Food. These agencies were selected on the basis of several considerations: we sought to include those agencies which have a large prosecutorial workload
as well as those other agencies which, although prosecuting infrequently, fulfil important public functions within which the investigation and/or prosecution of criminal
offences plays a significant part. It was found that there were considerable differences
in policy between (and sometimes within) agencies. For example, among the revenue-
collecting agencies, NTVLRO and DVLC prosecuted far more readily than did the
Inland Revenue; within the DHSS, non-compliance with national insurance payments
was treated a great deal more lightly than social security fraud; within the Department
of Trade there were important differences in policies and types of arrangements for
investigation and prosecution in respect of company registration cases, companies
investigations, bankruptcy cases and company frauds. A further marked feature of this
study of major agencies was the vast potential for further prosecution clearly available
in many instances. This was most obvious in agencies which saw their primary task as
securing compliance with legislation through persuasion and education (such as the
Health and Safety Executive) or through negotiated settlements and penalties short of
prosecution (such as the Inland Revenue). Even agencies which prosecuted relatively
frequently, such as NTVLRO and DVLC, had considerable further potential for prosecution. Further investigation showed that in nearly all cases the role and extent of
prosecution was related to the perceived primary task of the agency. Only the DHSS

(in social security cases) and the Post Office tended to see infractions as unambiguously 'criminal', to be pursued through the deterrent and retributive mechanisms of the criminal law; in the case of the DHSS this policy presented the agency with a problem in reconciling this stance with its primary role as a dispenser of welfare benefits.

In Chapter 4 some of the minor agencies were considered, and a group of particular interest here were the 'voluntary agencies' such as the RSPCA, the RSPB and Friends of the Earth. In general they tended to be reluctant prosecutors, deploring the relative inactivity of the police and other law enforcement agencies concerning their special area of interest; lacking resources themselves to prosecute to any great extent and therefore largely dependent on the police (though here the RSPCA was something of an exception); and only mounting their own prosecutions where the police were unwilling to act.

The court study had given a picture of prosecutorial activity by non-police bodies in 12 courts. The bulk of these were agency prosecutions, rather than prosecutions by private individuals, firms or voluntary bodies. (Some of the latter, such as retail stores and the RSPCA, were in any case reluctant prosecutors.) Among the agencies, however, further investigation revealed vast differences in the numbers of prosecutions, and in prosecution policy. It may be helpful finally to set out in schematic form some of the factors (not all previously mentioned in this summary) which may influence the number of prosecutions an agency undertakes:

(a) The population at risk of offending. Some agencies (like DVLC, NTVLRO and the Inland Revenue) potentially affect nearly every household in the country; others (like to Law Society and the General Nursing Council) will because of their restricted populations at risk never be major prosecutors. But not all 'large risk' agencies prosecute widely; the Inland Revenue is a notable example.

(b) The availability of alternative measures short of prosecution. Some agencies have such methods as formal alternatives, and tend to use them extensively: examples are Inland Revenue, Customs and Excise, and Health and Safety Executive; and the methods include compounding, seizure of goods, enforcement notices and cautions.

(c) The resources available to investigate offences. Several agencies have to restrict their investigative activities because of lack of resources (for example DVLC, Department of Trade and some local authorities). When one metropolitan Passenger Transport Executive set up a squad of plain clothes inspectors to police fare evasion, it was so successful in discovering evaders that a second squad and set up, and the numbers prosecuted soared on each occasion.

(d) The difficulty of proof. Agencies such as the Inland Revenue and the Department of Trade face severe tests of proof in large-scale fraud cases. The subject matter of the charges is often complex, and the prosecutor has to prove intention or at least recklessness. The defendants are often sophisticated and well advised. If a guilty plea is unlikely then prosecution may well be discouraged, especially if, as in the case of Inland Revenue, other courses are open to the agency. This does not apply to offences of strict liability such as using a motor vehicle without a vehicle excise licence, but even here there is often great difficulty in identifying the user of the vehicle.

(e) Political pressure. Both DHSS (markedly) and the Wages Inspectorate (marginally) have increased their prosecutorial work in recent years, in response to different kinds of direct political pressure.

(f) The perception of the primary task of the agency. Agencies which perceive their primary task as educative and persuasive have particularly low prosecution rates in relation to known offences (for example Health and Safety, local authorities). Even quite extensive prosecutors, like NTVLRO and DVLC, will be found not to prosecute in a sizeable proportion of cases if compliance can be secured through other means: for them, revenue collection, not prosecution, remains the primary goal. Conversely, agencies like the larger special police forces tend to see their activity as primarily law enforcement, and therefore use prosecution as a first rather than last resort.

(g)   The perception of the offence. A widespread view in many agencies was that the offences involved were not really crime in the proper sense, and therefore not appropriate for automatic prosecution; such a view obviously encourages the use of other methods to secure compliance. A view of this kind may be challenged by outsiders (as it is, for example, by critics of the minimal prosecution policies of the Inland Revenue and the Health and Safety Executive), but this still may not affect the agency's perception. Varying perceptions of different offences may produce markedly different enforcement policies within a single agency, for example social security fraud as against non-compliance cases within the DHSS.

(h)   Police reluctance to be involved. Retail stores and electricity boards in London would not themselves prosecute at all if the police would do so; the voluntary agencies also tend to prosecute only because of the perceived reluctance or of inaction by other law enforcement agencies, especially the police. The DHSS may in future be forced to seek wider investigative powers for its officers, and perhaps take on some cases currently prosecuted by the police, if a projected reduction in police co-operation occurs.

[4:2] *Keith Committee Report of the Committee on the Enforcement Powers of the Revenue Departments* (1983) Cmnd 8822, HMSO

Department views

22.1.4   The Inland Revenue explained and justified their prosecution policy to us in the same terms as they had used to the Royal Commission on Criminal Proceedings. They noted first, that the tax legislation contains (civil) money penalties for many offences, up to and including fraud. As they said, 'It clearly envisages that severe money penalties will be the common punishment of the tax evader'. They also fully acknowledged 'the practical consideration that the burden of preparing a large number of prosecutions to the required standard and of seeing them through the courts would require many more trained and qualified staff'. They stressed the importance of prosecution as a deterrent, and that there should be no categories of offence where the weapon was never deployed 'because it is the possibility of prosecution which prevents the spread of tax fraud to unacceptable limits'. They pointed out that 'simple objective criteria such as the amount of tax evaded' might be used to set de minimis limits to exclude the smaller cases, but were unsuited to be the sole basis of decisions to prosecute. While recognising, therefore, the possible pitfalls in selectivity, the Department sought to avoid them by reserving the decision to prosecute to officials at Under Secretary or Deputy Secretary level.

Discussion and conclusions

22.1.5   We had no hesitation in rejecting the extreme alternatives of 'prosecute all or none'. We found no reason to disturb the settled practice of over 50 years of Inland Revenue taking civil money penalties for the overwhelming majority of detected offences of tax evasion. We regard as justified the Department's view that an ultimate sanction of prosecution is essential to protect the integrity of a tax system which is primarily dependent upon the accuracy of information passed to it by its tax payers and others. When asked to sign a declamation on a tax return, the taxpayer is faced with the admonitory statement 'false statements can result in prosecution'. It follows that, if the deterrent is to retain its credibility, prosecution ought to follow in, as the Department put it, 'some examples of all classes of tax fraud'.

(and at paragraphs 22.1.7–8):

22.1.7   The presence of one of the badges of heinousness as viewed by the Department makes a case more likely to be selected for prosecution. Bearing in mind that the presence of intention to deceive is crucial we find it difficult to find anything to object to in the Department's selection as criteria of (b) evidence of collusion between the taxpayer and others; (c) evidence that documents have been forged with intent to deceive the Revenue; or (d) evidence of other irregularities which are denied on challenge. We likewise endorse the Department being more ready to initiate criminal proceedings against individuals who (category (f)) have already enjoyed the benefit of negotiated settlement following a previous investigation or who, (category (e)) while making a show of co-operation, withhold significant information leading to a materially incomplete disclosure in a current investigation.

22.1.8   The remaining indicia of heinousness are more subject in that they require the Board to take a view about either the status of the potential offender (category (a)) or about particular exceptional circumstances in relation to the offence itself, for example, the amount of tax at risk in absolute terms or where the nature of the fraud is particularly ingenious (category (g)). This amounts to selecting a case for prosecution for exemplary purposes, both as a warning to others who might be minded to do likewise and as a reminder to the general public that the 'big' offender in any sense cannot escape the public disgrace of a criminal trial.

[4:3]   Roording, J *'The Punishment of Tax Fraud'* [1996] Crim LR 240 (at page 240):

In this article I intend to explore the field of punishment of tax fraud in the United Kingdom. I will make use of information I gathered with the Inland Revenue, inter alia through discussions with certain officials. As a Dutch lawyer I will necessarily take a continental view, and I shall introduce a perspective which has gained some popularity in the Netherlands recently. In this perspective the criminal law is seen as a system of punishment (a sanctions system) which, together with other such systems (especially the administrative sanctions system), is part of a wider field of law which could be called the law of sanctions. It is thought that these sanctions systems have much in common (ie the same purposes), and that all are governed by the same basic principles (for which reference is often made to Article 6 of the European Convention for the Protection of Human Rights and Fundamental Freedoms (ECHR)), so that a more integrated approach is advisable. This perspective provides a framework which makes possible a critical assessment of law enforcement practices of regulatory agencies from the point of view of the rights of suspects and offenders. At the same time it also focuses on alternative ways of punishment which could relieve the overburdened criminal justice system.

The sanctions systems in the field of tax

This sketch of the sanctions systems in the field of tax is limited to the procedures of the Inland Revenue (IR), which is responsible for the administration of direct taxes, such as income tax and corporation tax, in the United Kingdom. (I do not propose to deal with Customs and Excise, who are responsible for the administration of customs, excise and VAT and to that end have separate enforcement powers at their disposal; Customs and Excise have a fundamentally different approach from that of the Inland Revenue.) Two ways of punishment are open to the Inland Revenue: imposition of a civil penalty, and prosecution. Penalties (see Chapter X of the Taxes Management Act (TMA) 1970) are usually imposed by an officer of the Board of Inland Revenue, but in certain cases by an independent body called the (General or Special) Commissioners and in certain cases by the court. Statute either sets the maximum penalty at a fixed amount (for example in case of a simple failure to deliver a return; TMA 1970, s 93 (1)(a): maximum penalty 300) or at 100 per cent of the tax due (in case of a more serious offence, where there is fraud or negligence; see for example s 95 (incorrect return or account)). From a determination of a penalty by an officer of the Board appeal lies, first, to the Commissioners (s 100B(2)) and then to the High Court (s 100B(3)).

Besides imposing a civil penalty the Inland Revenue can also choose to initiate criminal proceedings. Usually the IR will not leave this to the police and the Crown Prosecution Service but bring a prosecution itself. Several charges are available: offences under the general criminal law, such as false accounting (s 17 of the Theft Act 1968), or cheating the public revenue, an offence under the common law. In contrast with Customs and Excise the Inland Revenue has no power to compound criminal proceedings. Theoretically the IR can impose a civil penalty and at the same time institute a prosecution for the same offence. It is however settled practice not to impose a penalty for an offence which has already been dealt with by the criminal court.

(and at page 248):

In my view the way tax fraud is punished in the United Kingdom is not satisfactory. My main criticism concerns the huge and institutionalised pressure which is exerted on taxpayers to make them confess and co-operate. It is true that there will be pressure in any system in which the criminal law operates as an alternative to another, less 'heavy' sanctions system (heavy both in terms of sanctions and in terms of procedures). However, in the English system of punishment of tax fraud the pressure is extra strong, because the Inland Revenue seeks to keep the case in the informal sphere as long as possible. There the IR can dictate its own rules, and the formal procedures become a 'big stick'. By contrast, taxpayers have more protection in the Netherlands. There the tax department must choose between prosecution and the imposition of an administrative penalty. There is no third, informal way. In addition, the criminal and administrative spheres seem to be more clearly demarcated with respect to one another. This will be even more so when a current Bill is enacted which goes so far as to determine that once a prosecution or a penalty procedure has reached a certain point, there is no return; the other way is closed then. Further safeguards, which apply in penalty procedures, are a right of access to court, the right to be informed about the grounds of the accusation, and a duty on the Revenue to prove the mental element of the offence (fraud or negligence). The new Bill mentioned above even acknowledges the right to silence with regard to administrative penalty procedures.

The root of the problem seems to me that in the English legal system, systems of punishment outside the criminal law hardly get any attention, whether from the courts or from academics.[1] It is not yet recognised that these sanctions systems show big similarities to the criminal law: in practice they operate as a very important alternative to the criminal sanctions system, with the same purpose, ie to enforce the law) and with the same means (eg fines). Unless and until this is recognised, grey areas such as that of the settlement of tax fraud will continue to exist and they will be governed by practical rules rather than legal principles.

[4:4]   *R v IRC, ex p Mead and Cook* [1992] STC 482

In November 1990, the Commissioners of Inland Revenue ordered the prosecution of the applicants for criminal offences in connection with tax evasion, and in March 1991, summonses were served an them. The prosecution had arisen out of the Revenue's investigation of the tax affairs of an accountant who had acted as the accountant to the applicants and to other taxpayers. The applicants sought judicial review of the decision to prosecute them, claiming that a comparison of the applicants' cases should have been made with those of the other taxpayers and only if there were distinguishing features which made the applicants' cases more serious than the others was the decision to prosecute them justified.

The application was dismissed.

Stuart-Smith LJ (at page 492):

The crucial factor in the present case is that the Revenue operate a selective policy of prosecution. They do so for three main reasons: first their primary objective is the collection of revenue and not the punishment of offenders; second they have inadequate resources to prosecute everyone who dishonestly evades payment of taxes; and third and perhaps most importantly they consider it necessary to prosecute in some cases because of the deterrent effect that this has on the general body of taxpayers, since they know that they behave dishonestly they may be prosecuted. It is inherent in such a policy that there may be inconsistency and unfairness as between one dishonest taxpayer and another who is guilty of a very similar offence. Nevertheless while not challenging the validity of the policy Mr Beloff submits that there must be grafted on to it requirement to treat all dishonest taxpayers guilty of similar offences for two reasons. First it is inconsistent with the policy and cannot be operated consistently with it, you cannot be both selective and treat every case alike. Second it seems to be quite impracticable. How are the Revenue to decide what cases are like? What is to be the basis of the group of cases that has to be considered? Over what period of time are the group to be considered? Are all cases involving forgery to be in one group? Or those involving forgery and false accounting? Are those who make a full disclosure to be in the same group as those who deny that they have acted dishonestly, although the Revenue consider that there is evidence that they have? These questions only have to be posed to demonstrate that it is quite impossible to answer them; and certainly in my judgment Mr Beloff was quite unable to proffer any convincing answer. What he did say was that there is an

---

[1]   Professor Ashworth clearly is an exception to this. Cf A Ashworth, op cit, especially Chapter 5. Yet the limitations of a textbook did not allow him to pursue an analysis of alternative sanctions-systems into much detail.

identifiable group of taxpayers here who were all clients of Mr Scannell. That appears to me to be a wholly adventitious and irrelevant consideration. It does not affect the nature or gravity of the offence; it only arises because in the course of investigation Mr Scannell's tax affairs the Revenue have uncovered alleged dishonest tax evasion on the part of a number of his clients, he is simply the common source from which the inquiry springs and the information flows.

There may be other dishonest taxpayers who have been advised by dishonest accountants and who have embarked on similar schemes; why should they not be part of the group? Does the group consist only of the six other taxpayers referred to in Mr Bunker's affidavit or the much larger number who are still being investigated and may turn out to have indulged in similar practices?

In my judgment the requirement of fairness and consistency in the light of the Revenue's selective policy of prosecution is that each case is considered on its merits fairly and dispassionately to see whether the criteria for prosecution was satisfied; there is no dispute that the applicants' cases were so considered. The decision to prosecute must then be taken in good faith for the purpose of fulfilling the Revenue's objectives of collecting taxes and not for some ulterior, extraneous or improper purpose, such as the pursuit of some racialist bias, political vendetta or corrupt motive. This again is not in dispute.

The principle that a public body must not frustrate a citizen's legitimate expectation takes the case no further. The only legitimate expectation that a dishonest taxpayer can have is that he may be selected for prosecution in accordance with the Revenue's stated policy; and that in considering whether to do so the decision-maker will act fairly in the sense that I have just defined.

Only if that policy could be attacked on the grounds of irrationality could the applicants succeed. They do not attempt to do so. It was a policy that was approved by the Keith Committee and it seems to me, for the three reasons that I have given earlier, not only a rational policy but very probably the only workable policy.

For these reasons, in my judgment, this application must be dismissed.

[4:5] **Cook, D** *Rich Law, Poor Law* (1989) Open University Press (at page 116):

On tax investigations

Cost-effectiveness and pragmatism are the apparent rationales which underlie Revenue investigation policy, but the effective rationale is, rather, a desire to seek the compliance of the taxpayer. Therefore, in effect Revenue policy implicitly acknowledges the primacy of the coercive view of personal taxation and, ultimately, enables empathy for the tax evader. This is evident in the view expressed by a former Enquiry Branch officer who described the Revenue's financial settlement policy as 'The only sensible way to carry on' because 'after all, we have all sinned!' (ITV World in Action 7 February 1983). It is also evident in the emphasis on financial settlement which characterises most Revenue investigations, whether conducted in local offices or by specialist units.

The analysis of enforcement policy and practice has shown that official discourses which centre on cost-effectiveness and the pragmatism of tax collection are problematic. For example, cost-effectiveness does not result if (as under current policies) insufficient staff and resources are directed to counter-evasion work, and so vast amounts of tax remain unpaid. At the same time, the counter-evasion initiatives which have been undertaken in recent years have centred upon relatively 'easy' targets which demand the least time and money to investigate. Thus the richer pickings which are available through the investigation of highly paid taxpayers, directors and trading accounts are largely ignored in favour of the type of investigations which are quick (and cheap) to undertake, with fewer lower-level staff. In the longer term cost-effectiveness is not served by such policies. Furthermore, the emphasis on cost-effectiveness may be open to serious criticism on the grounds that equality as well as efficiency should be a principle underpinning the work of any enforcing department.

The dominance of 'pragmatism' in the justificatory rhetoric of policy-makers is also more apparent than real: beneath this justification is, once again, the desire to 'spare the taxpayers' feelings'. Although, it could be argued, there are indeed practical difficulties in mounting successful Revenue prosecutions, these practical difficulties cannot alone explain a policy which advocates financial penalty in all but a very few of the 'most serious' of fraud cases, while around 20 times as many individuals are likely to be prosecuted for supplementary benefit fraud, despite the DHSS's non-prosecution policy. The effective discourse shaping such policy therefore reflects the coercive view of tax – as an intolerable inquisition – and so implicitly reflects the ideology of the free market rather than social justice.

Nevertheless, the notion of citizenship may still be invoked (even at a time of New Right ideological dominance) in order to maintain the integrity and legitimacy of the tax system: hence the Thatcher government, though committed to the New Right free market economic policies, must implicitly invoke the citizenship view of personal taxation when launching compliance initiatives. Moreover those initiatives are (even for those who see tax as an 'intolerable inquisition') necessary: first, to maintain the legitimacy of the Revenue as an equitable enforcing department and, second, to collect additional revenue which is essential (even for a minimalist) state in a time of economic stringency. It is misleading, therefore, to see 'the state' as immutable or monolithic: its policies are moulded by specific material considerations under which it may be possible to invoke entirely contradictory discourses, particularly concerning the two issues of taxation and welfare. It is from such contradictions that differential responses to tax and benefit fraud are both produced and justified.

(at page 142):

On supplementary benefits investigations

Supplementary benefit fraud investigations take place within a social context shaped by contradictory views of the modern Welfare State and its benefit recipients. On the one hand, the Welfare State's main function can be seen to be the payment of benefits as of right and the relief of need, with due attention to the dignity of the individual claimant. On the other hand, the Welfare State's main function can be seen in terms of protecting the public purse, discouraging 'avoidable' dependency and paying benefits to those who demonstrate need. Patrick Jenkin argued, according to this view, that:

'The *honest* and the *innocent* have nothing to fear from the enquiries of our officials … Helping *genuine* claimants to get their benefits remains the main function of the Social Security organisation.' (*Hansard* 6 May 1981, vol 4, no 97, my emphasis added)

The pursuit of supplementary benefit fraud may serve to reinforce notions of the dishonest claimant, and ultimately reinforce nineteenth-century distinctions between the deserving and undeserving poor.

Since the mid-1970s economic recession has promoted the dominance of (monetarist) political policies stressing a curbing of public expenditure. It is in this context that the Welfare State has overcome a crucial target for cost-cutting initiatives. Between 1979 and 1984 DHSS staffing was cut by 8,000, yet at the same time extra staff and resources were being directed against fraud and abuse. In this chapter such contradictions have been attributed to three main policy aims of the DHSS.

1. The aim of cutting overall DHSS costs by using fraud staff to obtain 'savings' of benefit through their investigatory efforts and in effect also achieving 'savings' by deterring individuals from claiming benefits to which they may be entitled, through the publicising of fraud drives (Beltram 1984a; R Smith 1985).
2. The aim of promoting the ideal of a 'go-getting' entrepreneurial society: for there to be winners there must be losers, and those losers are labelled and stigmatised as such (see Chapters 1 and 8). Equally, in such a society, self-reliance should be stressed, hence an ambivalence to mounting official take-up campaigns (NCASSC 1985).
3. The aim of undermining faith in the Welfare State by exposing its wastefulness in paying benefits to the undeserving and the 'scroungers'. These policy goals, taken together, signal the end of any 'Welfare State consensus' and instead pose alternative social market principles in the provision of relief for the poor.

Underlying these policy aims are the vocabularies of the free market, effort and individualism. New Right political philosophy has therefore intensified earlier critiques of welfare; for example, the notion of the underserving poor has been utilised to incorporate additional claimant groups who are reconstituted as 'avoidable' dependent. Single-parent families are thus represented as 'undeserving' if they have 'chosen' not to be members of a patriarchal nuclear family. The New Right's version of morality encompasses other culpable poor groups – young people who 'do not want to work or unemployed people who place an excessive burden on the state by having 'too many' children …

… such moralising attitudes towards the poor have a long history. But the crucial importance of such ideas is that they have been successfully incorporated into a political philosophy of the 1980s. In this way the New Right has not only tapped into a vast historical reservoir of ideas about the 'underserving poor', but also hijacked the vocabularies of 'freedom' and 'individualism'. The former has been used to justify curbs on the freedom of the poor in the name of freedom from excessive taxation for the better-off, and the latter to justify the dismantling of collective social provisions in the name of greater individual responsibility. For the time being, at least, social policy is dominated by the ideologies of the free market (rather than social justice) and individualism (rather than collectivism). But, there are possibilities for change through challenging what is now regarded as the 'common sense' of New Right ideology. One means of effecting such a challenge is through exposing the inconsistencies and contradictions of New Right discourse: these contradictions are realised in the differential social, political and judicial responses to tax and supplementary benefit fraud.

(at page 167):

On different responses

This chapter has examined the official policy discourses relating to the prosecution and punishment of tax and supplementary benefit fraud. In addition, the practical outcome of these policies has been analysed and several contradictions have emerged. For example, although the DHSS at present officially operates a policy designed to reduce numbers of prosecutions and seek 'benefit savings', effectively it still prosecutes over 8,000 supplementary benefit claimants per year; this is in stark contrast to the official 'selective' approach to Revenue prosecutions which effectively resulted in only 459 prosecutions in 1986–87. Moreover, the justificatory rationale behind both policies – deterrence – is not applied equally to tax and benefit fraudsters.

Judicial responses (and sentencing practice) towards tax and supplementary fraud are based on entirely different premises: the analysis of discourses used in court demonstrated crucial differences in the assumptions being made about claimant and taxpayer. In some cases it seemed that tax evaders were presumed to be victims – either of the ethos of the business and corporate world, or victims of the disgrace of their fellow citizens – as a result of Revenue prosecution. According to magistrates observed in this study, in cases of supplementary benefit fraud the victim is the taxpayer (who was seen to finance benefit payments), not the benefit fraudster. The tax fraudster is represented as at best folk-hero, at worst a victim of the taxman.

At the heart of the contradictions in policy and in practice which have been analysed here is the ideological representation of the taxpayer as a 'giver' to the state and the supplementary benefit claimant as a 'taker' from the state (and thus, ultimately, from the compliant taxpayer). These representations are the product of the particular histories of tax and welfare. These histories are characterised by a traditional resistance to taxation, save in times of national crises (for instance, during war or post-war reconstruction), and a parallel struggle over the collective welfare provision, which was similarly and grudgingly accepted after the crises of two world wars. Specific economic, social and political pre-conditions therefore underpin attitudes to tax and welfare at particular times. Contradictions in the political, social and judicial responses to tax and welfare rest upon combinations of beliefs about the nature of the relationship between the state and the individual, and the desirability of social justice or economic growth as the primary goal of modern mixed economies.

[4:6] McKeever, G *'Detecting, Prosecuting and Punishing Benefit Fraud: The Social Security Administration (Fraud) Act 1997'* (1999) 62 MLR 261

Social security fraud is currently estimated at £7 billion per year out of an annual social security budget of £90 billion. The social security system is hugely bureaucratic and administrative, leaving it wide open to abuse. Obviously there are individuals keen to exploit such vulnerability, but many innocent claimants also fall foul of its rules, quite inadvertently. In 1997, the Conservative government declared that its anti-fraud initiatives would save taxpayers £7 billion over the next three years. The main plank in the Conservatives' anti-fraud strategy, which has now been implemented by the Labour government, was the Social Security Administration (Fraud) Act 1997, designed to make the detection, prosecution and punishment of benefit fraud more effective.

(and at page 269):

The reforms introduced by the 1997 Act are obviously designed to save money and punish social security fraudsters, a policy endorsed by both sides of the party political divide. With losses from fraud at such high levels, obviously action is required. Nevertheless the problem of social security fraud needs to be put in perspective. The majority of fraud committed is as a result of organised crime yet there is a disproportionate emphasis in the 1997 Act on minor fraudsters. The view of the Social Security Committee on Housing Benefit Fraud and the evidence of the local authorities before it was that the prosecution of individual minor fraud achieves little. This view is not maintained by the 1997 Act. Data matching provisions, arguably created at the expense of certain basic human rights, assume not just that each claimant is *potentially* a fraudster but that he/she is *probably* so. Such an assumption is unfounded. Given the complexity of social security legislation, the provision of incorrect information or failure to report a change of circumstances is more likely to be due to innocent error than to fraud. Cuts in benefit administration can only contribute to this problem. Pointing the finger at those claiming disability benefits in particular, where the facts do not bear out the original assumptions, contributes again to this anti-claimant culture.

The obligations of citizenship for social security claimants have been made very clear but little attention has been paid to any corresponding rights. Efforts to improve public awareness of fraud have not been matched with measures to improve the take-up of benefits, something which remains a problem. Yet, as Ogus, Barendy and Wikeley point out, the indications are that underpayments exceed overpayments. Cuts in benefit administration are likely to result in cuts in service standards, which may mean more claimants losing out on benefit entitlements through bad advice or lack of information. Claimants become further disadvantaged as restrictions on the back-dating of benefits come into play. Dealing with the problem of fraud is entirely necessary and savings procured in this way are certainly preferable to those obtained by cutting benefit levels and entitlement. However, cuts in benefits also look likely, with benefit entitlement once again under threat.

More importantly, however, the 1997 Act does not address the underlying problems which can be said to lead to benefit fraud. As regards serious, organised fraud, the 1997 Act looks likely to improve matters for fraud investigators and prosecutors, although potentially at the expense of supposedly fundamental civil liberties. Individual claimant fraud, however, does not follow the same pattern as organised fraud and therefore demands a different approach. Dean and Taylor-Gooby suggest that a claimant's 'willingness to "fiddle" the system may primarily be a reflection of [their] adverse experiences or frustrations with that system'. An examination of the structure of the benefits system reveals that there are perverse incentives within the system which enforce benefit dependency and encourage claimants to either commit minor fraud or face substantial financial insecurity. Despite recent improvements, such as working benefits, the system is not flexible enough to cope with the modern day realities of employment, or to accommodate rapid shifts in eligibility for means-tested benefits. As a result, in order to remain financially secure claimants are forced to withhold information about their changing circumstances, particularly where those changes are of a temporary nature. In addition, much of what is currently perceived as fraud is simply straightforward claimant error. Claiming social security has become an increasingly complex business, with the rules and regulations governing the administration of benefits growing steadily. Consequently, the potential for claimant error is endless. The pressure on claimants to get completed claim forms in on time can only add to the problem, and typically results in either delay for the claimant, or in the provision of inconsistent and inaccurate information thus giving rise to a suspicion of fraud. This note has emphasised the possibility of fraud arising from claimant confusion rather than dishonesty. The danger with the 1997 Act is that the distinction between the two will no longer be valid.

[4:7]   **Richardson, G** *'Strict Liability for Regulatory Crime: the Empirical Research'* [1987] Crim LR 295 (at page 303):

In an article chiefly concerned with the debate surrounding the use of strict liability in the regulatory context, Richardson raises the thorny issue of the usurpation of the criminal trial by administrative discretion.

To an extent the empirical data, by emphasising the practical relevance of the offender's intent, might suggest that the concern over the propriety of strict liability is irrelevant. Such a conclusion is not inevitable, however. In the first place, although the data indicate that 'blameless innocents' are rarely prosecuted, the traditionalist is unlikely to be satisfied since the determination of 'blame' is made privately by an administrative agent rather than publicly with the full procedural protection of a criminal trial. Secondly, there is still the argument, referred to briefly above, that the use of strict liability serves both to detract from the significance of regulatory offences and to distinguish them from the main body of the criminal law. The introduction of strict liability into early factory legislation, for example, is thought to have placed a part in the marginalisation of early factory crime. In this sense, strict liability can be said to further the interests of the regulated by reducing the significance of non-compliance.

To some extent the first problem, the usurpation of the criminal trial by administrative discretion, can be met by the introduction of civil penalties in place of strict criminal liability. The device is common in the United States where crimes of strict liability are rare. But the mere removal of the criminal label provides no real solution to the problem of administrative discretion and must serve further to marginalise the prohibited activity. Arguably, the question of liability for corporate offences is not a 'problem' to be tackled in isolation but must be seen as merely one element of the regulatory scheme.

Whether or not regulatory offences constitute 'real' crime, the majority can be readily distinguished from the mass of traditional street crime as currently regarded. The distinction does not, however, rely on the narrow argument that regulatory crime is different because it is less serious and therefore strict liability is acceptable because penalties are low. It springs instead from the nature of the regulatory objective.

Legislative schemes regulating corporate conduct are primarily designed to prevent particular harms and are certainly seen in that light by those responsible for their enforcement. In large part, therefore, the overall legitimacy of any regulatory scheme and of the separate elements within it will flow from their combined ability to prevent harm. Each element will both contribute to and reflect the legitimacy of the whole.

In the first place protective regulation must provide for the proper definition of the prohibited event and the closer the relationship between the event and the harm, the more justifiable will be the prohibition. In addition, the research suggests that the more evidently justifiable or rational the prohibition the more assiduous will be the enforcement. In such a context, if the prohibition event is potentially harmful irrespective of the offender's mental state as classified by current criminal law principles, then there can be little instrumental justification for demanding the presence of fault as defined by those principles. Further, the corporate actor typically behaves in a particular way, installs a certain plant, for example, or markets a given drug, because of the anticipated benefits. To place 'properly' defined restrictions on such 'voluntary' behaviour and to penalise non-compliance is not to persecute the innocent even in the absence of any legally recognised degree of fault.

Secondly, if as is claimed here, the primary justification for regulatory prohibition rests on the need to prevent harm, then arguably the sanctions imposed on non-compliance should be designed with that end in view. This question inevitably raises highly contentious issues within the field of penal theory which go far beyond the scope of this article. Nonetheless, the proper role of the penal sanctions cannot be ignored in any consideration of regulatory crime.

With regard to traditional offences the prevention of future harm as the justification for criminal punishment has been severely challenged. In relation to regulatory offences, however, the argument may carry less weight. In the first place corporate offending is often regarded as less intractable than traditional criminality: the application of criminal sanctions might successfully deter, incapacitate, or even rehabilitate. Secondly, with regard to the problem of inequality of treatment, which is often linked to the preventative use of criminal sanctions, Braithwaite has argued that complete equality for regulatory offenders is beyond the scope of any criminal justice system and that the need to prevent serious harm, Thalidomide or Bhopal for example, should take priority over strict equality of treatment.[2] Finally the rearrangement of a company's practices and procedures in order to ensure that it operates without causing harm is not open to the same moral considerations as the coerced rearranging of a psyche. In the light of these considerations most commentators identify harm prevention constrained by the principles of retribution as the primary rationale for the punishment of corporate offences in general and regulatory offences in particular.

It would appear, therefore, that the sanction has considerable potential to further the objectives of the regulatory scheme, and indeed in the United States a variety of sanctioning options have been tried or considered including: equity fines, adverse publicity, redress facilitation through plea bargaining, the integration of civil and criminal claims, community service orders and corporate probation. However, in the United Kingdom, despite widespread doubts as to its efficacy, the fine remains the most common sanction. Arguably, more effort is required to devise alternatives which effectively exploit the supposed susceptibility of corporate offenders to deterrence, incapacitation and rehabilitation.

In sum, the routine enforcement of regulatory offences typically exposes strict liability as merely one element within a regulatory scheme, the overall thrust of which is preventative. The extent to which the use of strict liability in particular is justified, it is claimed, will depend on the acceptability of the whole scheme which will itself be derived from the outcome of a number of policy choices. The principles of traditional criminal law and penology should not be applied automatically to the regulatory context.

---

[2] J Braithwaite, 'Challenging Just Desserts: Punishing White-Collar Criminals,' (1982) 73 Journal of Criminal Law and Criminology 723 and J Braithwaite, Corporate Crime in the Pharmaceutical Industry (1984), Chap 9.

[4:8] Sanders, A *'Class Bias in Prosecutions'* [1985] Howard Journal of Criminal Justice 176 (at page 194):

This article has sought to demonstrate first, that prosecution patterns exhibit class bias. Second that bias is a product of the divergent policies and procedures of different law enforcement agencies. Third, that these divergent practices and contrasting outcomes cannot be justified by conventional explanations. To explain these processes would involve considerations of political economy that are beyond the scope of this article. However, some tentative lines of future enquiry can be suggested ... this, as is common in this field, begs the question of why one class of people who commit crime is not seen as criminal whereas another class of people is.

A different starting point would be to compare the roles of the police and non-police agencies (in this instance the HMFI). Let us take seriously the idea that HMFI practice is aimed at enforcing, rather than mystifying, the law. Since higher standards of health and safety, and this a broad compliance with the law, is the aim of the HMFI the methods used would obviously be those that effect the most satisfactory compromise between (i) doing that job most effectively; (ii) using HMFI resources effectively and (iii) not disrupting normal business activity. HMFI policy can be seen to balance (i) against (ii) and (iii). This is not surprising. All that is contestable under current social arrangements is the weight given to either (i) or to (ii) and (iii).

The police are in a quite different position, as indeed is the DHSS Inspectorate. If they do their job effectively – that is, suppress crime – they will not disrupt normal business activity. Their offenders' economic activities are either non-existent or easily done by others. Resources are a potential consideration, but the use of arrest and detection rates to measure police officers' effectiveness actually pushes police activity away from concern to use resources in a cost effective manner.

Moreover, crime suppression can be seen simply as an extension of the police's primary role. Historically, order maintenance was their primary role, and the prosecution of offenders constituted one way of maintaining order. As we have seen, public order charges are a resource for the police officer, but only if those charges can be translated easily into prosecutions. Prosecution then, is an essential weapon in the armoury of the police. For a government wishing to spend less on social security, prosecution has a similar function in relation to possible DHSS offenders. Arrest and charge procedures evolved to process public order offences speedily. Most police prosecutions – primarily but not wholly working class – now also get processed by these procedures, which do not facilitate non-prosecution dispositions. Middle class offenders rarely get caught in these processes since middle class persons rarely disrupt middle class order.

The police and HMFI are not directed in the ways described. Having decided to take some action against a suspect, their decisions are not determined by structural or instrumental imperatives. They will be guided, however, by numerous considerations that flow from these structural conditions. For the HMFI the disruption to business caused by prosecution will indeed be a consideration, the welfare of the workers often being a part of this. Another consideration will be Levi's positive stereotype of the businessman. The historical background to the HMFI's relationship with industry is one of conflict avoidance, and there is also a cultural and class affinity between professionals – in this case factory inspectors and businessmen. This all contributes to prosecution avoidance. Between the police and large sections of the working class there is a history of conflict, no cultural and class affinity, and a negative stereotype. Indeed, the police are said to see themselves as stopping society slipping into chaos. These different sets of conditions create propensities. Whether a particular prosecution decision will conform to a particular propensity will still be dependent, in part, upon the law enforcer's decision how best to enforce the law.

Prosecution can be seen as an ultimate sanction: the end result if the suspect and law enforcer cannot strike a bargain. What, in other words, will the suspect give in exchange for a caution? Factory managers can offer better behaviour, plus jobs and a concrete economic activity; enforcement notices represent a way of holding them to that bargain. But working class and unemployed people have little to offer. Racketeers are an exception for they have money to offer and have made some very advantageous bargains in the past. The promise of good future behaviour is all that most offenders apprehended by the police can offer. Here again stereotyping and cultural and class affinity plays its part. Accepting this promise entails assessment of the suspect's creditability, his moral character. the HMFI, as we have seen, also has to assess this. The plausibility of the suspect's future intentions, in the structural context outlined, as assessed by particular law enforcement agencies, is on trial. Shoplifting sales managers and negligent production managers are bound to be more credible in this context than most suspects whom the police encounter.

It could be argued that this is irrelevant, as if the HMFI prosecuted a high percentage of cases they would be in court so much that their work would grind to a halt. The HMFI therefore adapts its law enforcement practice to its level of resources. The pattern of resource allocation does clearly show government to be, predictably, more concerned about 'normal' crime than about factory crime. But institutions are not totally passive in these matters... If the HMFI wish to draw attention to its under-resourcing by government, tying itself up in court through prosecution would be a very effective strategy. The important question is not 'why don't the HMFI prosecute more?', but 'why don't the HMFI seek more resources which could enable them to prosecute more?'

I hope that this demonstrates that law enforcement activity can be related to socio-economic structure without resorting to conspiracy theory. I have also sought to show that bias need not be explained by police dishonesty, rule breaking, or prejudice. As all the victim surveys show, crime abounds in modern Britain, making selective crime processing necessary. The criminal law allows almost absolute discretion in prosecutions. Thus patterned class bias is produced by the police operating a legally proper positive propensity to prosecute, whilst agencies dealing with the middle classes operate an equally legally proper propensity to not prosecute. Whilst this is the mechanism through which bias occurs, its source lies in the economic and social differences between different types of 'crime' and 'criminal'. To understand prosecution patterns the micro-processes of law enforcement need to be situated in their concrete socio-economic and legal context.

[4:9]   Criminal Justice Act 1987 sections 1–3

1   The Serious Fraud Office

(1)   A Serious Fraud Office shall be constituted for England and Wales and Northern Ireland.

(2)   The Attorney General shall appoint a person to be the Director of the Serious Fraud Office (referred to in this Part of this Act as "the Director"), and he shall discharge his functions under the superintendence of the Attorney General.

(3)   The Director may investigate any suspected offence which appears to him on reasonable grounds to involve serious or complex fraud.

(4)   The Director may, if he thinks fit, conduct any such investigation in conjunction either with the police or with any other person who is, in the opinion of the Director, a proper person to be concerned in it.

(5)   The Director may—
    (a)   institute and have the conduct of any criminal proceedings which appear to him to relate to such fraud; and
    (b)   take over the conduct of any such proceedings at any stage.

(6)   The Director shall discharge such other functions in relation to fraud as may from time to time be assigned to him by the Attorney General.

(7)   The Director may designate for the purposes of subsection (5) above any member of the Serious Fraud Office who is—
    (a)   a barrister in England and Wales or Northern Ireland;
    (b)   a solicitor of the Supreme Court; or
    (c)   a solicitor of the Supreme Court of Judicature of Northern Ireland.

(8)   Any member so designated shall, without prejudice to any functions which may have been assigned to him in his capacity as a member of that Office, have all the powers of the Director as to the institution and conduct of proceedings but shall exercise those powers under the direction of the Director.

(9)   ...

(10) ...

(11) ...

(12) Any member so designated who is a barrister in Northern Ireland or a solicitor of the Supreme Court of Judicature of Northern Ireland shall have—
    (a)   in any court the rights of audience enjoyed by solicitors of the Supreme Court of Judicature of Northern Ireland, and in the Crown Court in Northern Ireland, such additional rights of audience as may be given by virtue of subsection (14) below; and
    (b)   in the Crown Court in Northern Ireland, the rights of audience enjoyed by barristers employed by the Director of Public Prosecutions for Northern Ireland.

(13) Subject to subsection (14) below, the reference in subsection (12)(a) above to rights of audience enjoyed by solicitors of the Supreme Court of Judicature of Northern Ireland is a reference to such rights enjoyed in the Crown Court in Northern Ireland as restricted by any direction given by the Lord Chief Justice of Northern Ireland under section 50 of the Judicature (Northern Ireland) Act 1978.

(14) For the purpose of giving any member so designated who is a barrister in Northern Ireland or a solicitor of the Supreme Court of Judicature of Northern Ireland additional rights of audience in the Crown Court in Northern Ireland, the Lord Chief Justice of Northern Ireland may direct that any direction given by him under the said section 50 shall not apply to such members.

(15) Schedule 1 to this Act shall have effect.

(16) For the purposes of this section (including that Schedule) references to the conduct of any proceedings include references to the proceedings being discontinued and to the taking of any steps (including the bringing of appeals and making of representations in respect of applications for bail) which may be taken in relation to them.

(17) In the application of this section (including that Schedule) to Northern Ireland references to the Attorney General are to be construed as references to him in his capacity as Attorney General for Northern Ireland.

2 Director's investigation powers

(1) The powers of the Director under this section shall be exercisable, but only for the purposes of an investigation under section 1 above, or, on a request made by an authority entitled to make such a request, in any case in which it appears to him that there is good reason to do so for the purpose of investigating the affairs, or any aspect of the affairs, of any person.

(1A) The authorities entitled to request the Director to exercise his powers under this section are—
    (a)   the Attorney-General of the Isle of Man, Jersey or Guernsey, acting under legislation corresponding to section 1 of this Act and having effect in the Island whose Attorney-General makes the request; and
    (b)   the Secretary of State acting under section 4(2A) of the Criminal Justice (International Co-operation) Act 1990, in response to a request received by him from an overseas court, tribunal or authority (an "overseas authority").

(1B) The Director shall not exercise his powers on a request from the Secretary of State acting in response to a request received from an overseas authority within subsection (1A)(b) above unless it appears to the Director on reasonable grounds that the offence in respect of which he has been requested to obtain evidence involves serious or complex fraud.

(2) The Director may by notice in writing require the person whose affairs are to be investigated ("the person under investigation") or any other person whom he has reason to believe has relevant information to answer questions or otherwise furnish information with respect to any matter relevant to the investigation at a specified place and either at a specified time or forthwith.

(3) The Director may by notice in writing require the person under investigation or any other person to produce at such place as may be specified in the notice and either forthwith or at such time as may be so specified any specified documents which appear to the Director to relate to any matter relevant to the investigation or any documents of a specified description which appear to him so to relate; and—

    (a)   if any such documents are produced, the Director may—
        (i)   take copies or extracts from them;
        (ii) require the person producing them to provide an explanation of any of them;
    (b)   if any such documents are not produced, the Director may require the person who was required to produce them to state, to the best of his knowledge and belief, where they are.

(4)   Where, on information on oath laid by a member of the Serious Fraud Office, a justice of the peace is satisfied, in relation to any documents, that there are reasonable grounds for believing—
    (a)   that—
        (i)   a person has failed to comply with an obligation under this section to produce them;
        (ii) it is not practicable to serve a notice under subsection (3) above in relation to them; or
        (iii) the service of such a notice in relation to them might seriously prejudice the investigation; and
    (b)   that they are on premises specified in the information,
he may issue such a warrant as is mentioned in subsection (5) below.

(5)   The warrant referred to above is a warrant authorising any constable—
    (a)   to enter (using such force as is reasonably necessary for the purpose) and search the premises, and
    (b)   to take possession of any documents appearing to be documents of the description specified in the information or to take in relation to any documents so appearing any other steps which may appear to be necessary for preserving them and preventing interference with them.

(6)   Unless it is not practicable in the circumstances, a constable executing a warrant issued under subsection (4) above shall be accompanied by an appropriate person.

(7)   In subsection (6) above "appropriate person" means—
    (a)   a member of the Serious Fraud Office; or
    (b)   some person who is not a member of that Office but whom the Director has authorised to accompany the constable.

(8)   A statement by a person in response to a requirement imposed by virtue of this section may only be used in evidence against him—
    (a)   on a prosecution for an offence under subsection (14) below; or
    (b)   on a prosecution for some other offence where in giving evidence he makes a statement inconsistent with it.

(8AA)   However, the statement may not be used against that person by virtue of paragraph (b) of subsection (8) unless evidence relating to it is adduced, or a question relating to it is asked, by or on behalf of that person in the proceedings arising out of the prosecution.

(8A) Any evidence obtained by the Director for use by an overseas authority shall be furnished by him to the Secretary of State for transmission to the overseas authority which requested it.

(8B) If in order to comply with the request of the overseas authority it is necessary for any evidence obtained by the Director to be accompanied by any certificate, affidavit or other verifying document, the Director shall also furnish for transmission such document of that nature as may be specified by the Secretary of State when asking the Director to obtain the evidence.

(8C) Where any evidence obtained by the Director for use by an overseas authority consists of a document the original or a copy shall be transmitted, and where it consists of any other article the article itself or a description, photograph or other representation of it shall be transmitted, as may be necessary in order to comply with the request of the overseas authority.

(8D) The references in subsections (8A) to (8C) above to evidence obtained by the Director include references to evidence obtained by him by virtue of the exercise by a constable, in the course of a search authorised by a warrant issued under subsection (4) above, of powers conferred by section 50 of the Criminal Justice and Police Act 2001.

(9) A person shall not under this section be required to disclose any information or produce any document which he would be entitled to refuse to disclose or produce on grounds of legal professional privilege in proceedings in the High Court, except that a lawyer may be required to furnish the name and address of his client.

(10) A person shall not under this section be required to disclose information or produce a document in respect of which he owes an obligation of confidence by virtue of carrying on any banking business unless—
   (a)   the person to whom the obligation of confidence is owed consents to the disclosure or production; or
   (b)   the Director has authorised the making of the requirement or, if it is impracticable for him to act personally, a member of the Serious Fraud Office designated by him for the purposes of this subsection has done so.

(11) Without prejudice to the power of the Director to assign functions to members of the Serious Fraud Office, the Director may authorise any competent investigator (other than a constable) who is not a member of that Office to exercise on his behalf all or any of the powers conferred by this section, but no such authority shall be granted except for the purpose of investigating the affairs, or any aspect of the affairs, of a person specified in the authority.

(12) No person shall be bound to comply with any requirement imposed by a person exercising powers by virtue of any authority granted under subsection (11) above unless he has, if required to do so, produced evidence of his authority.

(13) Any person who without reasonable excuse fails to comply with a requirement imposed on him under this section shall be guilty of an offence and liable on summary conviction to imprisonment for a term not exceeding six months or to a fine not exceeding level 5 on the standard scale or to both.

(14) A person who, in purported compliance with a requirement under this section—
   (a)   makes a statement which he knows to be false or misleading in a material particular; or
   (b)   recklessly makes a statement which is false or misleading in a material particular,
shall be guilty of an offence.

(15) A person guilty of an offence under subsection (14) above shall—
    (a)   on conviction on indictment, be liable to imprisonment for a term not exceeding two years or to a fine or to both; and
    (b)   on summary conviction, be liable to imprisonment for a term not exceeding six months or to a fine not exceeding the statutory maximum, or to both.

(16) Where any person—
    (a)   knows or suspects that an investigation by the police or the Serious Fraud Office into serious or complex fraud is being or is likely to be carried out; and
    (b)   falsifies, conceals, destroys or otherwise disposes of, or causes or permits the falsification, concealment, destruction or disposal of documents which he knows or suspects are or would be relevant to such an investigation,
he shall be guilty of an offence unless he proves that he had no intention of concealing the facts disclosed by the documents from persons carrying out such an investigation.

(17) A person guilty of an offence under subsection (16) above shall—
    (a)   on conviction on indictment, be liable to imprisonment for a term not exceeding 7 years or to a fine or to both; and
    (b)   on summary conviction, be liable to imprisonment for a term not exceeding 6 months or to a fine not exceeding the statutory maximum or to both.

(18) In this section, "documents" includes information recorded in any form and, in relation to information recorded otherwise than in legible form, references to its production include references to producing a copy of the information in legible form; and "evidence" (in relation to subsections (1A)(b), (8A), (8B) and (8C) above) includes documents and other articles.

(19) In the application of this section to Scotland, the reference to a justice of the peace is to be construed as a reference to the sheriff; and in the application of this section to Northern Ireland, subsection (4) above shall have effect as if for the references to information there were substituted references to a complaint.

3 Disclosure of information

(1)   Where any information subject to an obligation of secrecy under the Taxes Management Act 1970 has been disclosed by the Commissioners of Inland Revenue or an officer of those Commissioners to any member of the Serious Fraud Office for the purposes of any prosecution of an offence relating to inland revenue, that information may be disclosed by any member of the Serious Fraud Office—
    (a)   for the purposes of any prosecution of which that Office has the conduct;
    (b)   to any member of the Crown Prosecution Service for the purposes of any prosecution of an offence relating to inland revenue; and
    (c)   to the Director of Public Prosecutions for Northern Ireland for the purposes of any prosecution of an offence relating to inland revenue,
but not otherwise.

(2)   Where the Serious Fraud Office has the conduct of any prosecution of an offence which does not relate to inland revenue, the court may not prevent the prosecution from relying on any evidence under section 78 of the Police and Criminal Evidence Act 1984

(discretion to exclude unfair evidence) by reason only of the fact that the information concerned was disclosed by the Commissioners of Inland Revenue or an officer of those Commissioners for the purposes of any prosecution of an offence relating to inland revenue.

(3)   Where any information is subject to an obligation of secrecy imposed by or under any enactment other than an enactment contained in the Taxes Management Act 1970, the obligation shall not have effect to prohibit the disclosure of that information to any person in his capacity as a member of the Serious Fraud Office but any information disclosed by virtue of this subsection may only be disclosed by a member of the Serious Fraud Office for the purposes of any prosecution in England and Wales, Northern Ireland or elsewhere and may only be disclosed by such a member if he is designated by the Director for the purposes of this subsection.

(4)   Without prejudice to his power to enter into agreements apart from this subsection, the Director may enter into a written agreement for the supply of information to or by him subject, in either case, to an obligation not to disclose the information concerned otherwise than for a specified purpose.

(5)   Subject to subsections (1) and (3) above and to any provision of an agreement for the supply of information which restricts the disclosure of the information supplied, information obtained by any person in his capacity as a member of the Serious Fraud Office may be disclosed by any member of that Office designated by the Director for the purposes of this subsection—

    (a)   to any government department or Northern Ireland department or other authority or body discharging its functions on behalf of the Crown (including the Crown in right of Her Majesty's Government in Northern Ireland);

    (b)   to any competent authority;

    (c)   for the purposes of any prosecution in England and Wales, Northern Ireland or elsewhere; and

    (d)   for the purposes of assisting any public or other authority for the time being designated for the purposes of this paragraph by an order made by the Secretary of State to discharge any functions which are specified in the order.

(6)   The following are competent authorities for the purposes of subsection (5) above—

    (a)   an inspector appointed under Part XIV of the Companies Act 1985 or Part XV of the Companies (Northern Ireland) Order 1986;

    (b)   an Official Receiver;

    (c)   the Accountant in Bankruptcy;

    (d)   the Official Receiver for Northern Ireland;

    (e)   a person appointed under—

        (i)   section 167 of the Financial Services and Markets Act 2000 (general investigations),

        (ii)   section 168 of that Act (investigations in particular cases),

        (iii)   section 169(1)(b) of that Act (investigation in support of overseas regulator),

        (iv)   section 284 of that Act (investigations into affairs of certain collective investment schemes), or

        (v)   regulations made as a result of section 262(2)(k) of that Act (investigations into open-ended investment companies),

to conduct an investigation;

(f)　　a body corporate established in accordance with section 212(1) of the Financial Services and Markets Act 2000 (compensation scheme manager);

(l)　　any body having supervisory, regulatory or disciplinary functions in relation to any profession or any area of commercial activity; and

(m)　　any person or body having, under the law of any country or territory outside the United Kingdom, functions corresponding to any of the functions of any person or body mentioned in any of the foregoing paragraphs.

(7)　An order under subsection (5)(d) above may impose conditions subject to which, and otherwise restrict the circumstances in which, information may be disclosed under that paragraph.

[4:10]　*R v Director of Serious Fraud Office, ex p Smith* [1993] AC 1

The applicant had been charged with an offence under the Companies Act 1985. Subsequently he was served with a notice to attend the SFO to answer questions. He sought judicial review of the Director's decision to enforce compliance with the requirements of the notice.

The House of Lords held that although there was a strong presumption against interpreting a statute as taking away the right to silence, it was the plain intention of the Criminal Justice Act 1987 that the powers of the Director of the SFO should not come to an end when the person under investigation had been charged.

Lord Mustill (at page 44):

In conclusion I wish to emphasise that if this appeal is allowed the House will not thereby have chosen to re-establish in relation to a limited class of offence an inquisitorial method of ascertaining the truth in criminal cases which English law has long since repudiated in favour of an adversarial process. We were much pressed in argument with submissions that, although fraudulent conduct has become a serious social evil, there are other evils just as grave, or even graver, which have not attracted any special powers; that if the reason for giving exceptional powers to the Serious Fraud Office is that many frauds involve complicated transactions which are difficult to unravel, then the same could be said of the long and complex trials (for instance arising from charges of affray, or of the importation and supply of prohibited drugs) to which no such powers have been applied; and that, moreover, the powers of the Office are made available even where the transactions in question are not complicated, since the Act applies to 'serious or complex fraud' – not 'serious and complex fraud.'

Now these and similar comments would require careful scrutiny if the thrust of the argument were to the effect that Parliament could not have intended to establish an inquisitorial regime of this kind in relation to serious or complex fraud alone. But in fact no such argument is or could be made, for it is indisputable and undisputed that this is just what Parliament set out to do, and has effectively done. In truth the adverse comments are criticisms, not of the Director's contention that the powers created by the Act apply in the situation now under review, but of the policy and scope of the Act itself. These we may not entertain. As Windeyer J said in *Rees v Kratzmann* (1965) 114 CLR 63, 80:

'If the legislature thinks that in this field the public interest overcomes some of the common law's traditional considerations for the individual, then effect must be given to the statute which embodies this policy,'

In the present case the only issue is whether there is something in the language of the Act or by necessary implication, to show that the policy embodied in the Act should not be given effect as regards the questioning of a suspect who has been charged. Being of the opinion that there is not. I would allow this appeal.

[4:11] *Gouriet v Union of Post Office Workers* [1978] AC 435

The plaintiff sought injunctions against trade unions who were refusing to handle mail to South Africa, and a declaration that the Attorney-General, by refusing his consent to relator proceedings, was acting improperly and had wrongfully exercised his discretion. The House of Lords held that the plaintiff had no legal rights in the matter since he had suffered no damage.

Lord Wilberforce (at page 477):

Mr Gouriet's claim has been narrowed and made specific. His only claim now is that he, as all other members of the public, has an interest in the enforcement of the law which entitles him to access to the courts from which he cannot be 'immunised' by the Attorney-General's refusal to allow the use of his name. It is this claim which is at the centre of the case, and it requires first some discussion of the phrase 'enforcement of the law'. The phrase is an emotive one, and one that attracts rhetoric, so we must see what it means in the context.

When Parliament decides to prohibit certain conduct (eg delaying the mail) it enacts legislation defining the prohibited act (eg Post Office Act 1953, sections 58, 68). To violation or disregard of the prohibition it attaches a sanction – prosecution as for a misdemeanour with a possible sentence of two years' imprisonment. Enforcement of the law means that any person who commits the relevant offence is prosecuted. So it is the duty either of the Post Office itself, or of the Director of Public Prosecutions or of the Attorney-General, to take steps to enforce the law in this way. Failure to do so, without good cause, is a breach of their duty (for a recent formulation of this duty see the statement of Sir Henry Shawcross A-G (1951) in Edwards, The Law Officers of the Crown (1964), p 223). The individual, in such situations, who wishes to see the law enforced has a remedy of his own: he can bring a private prosecution. This historical right which goes right back to the earliest days of our legal system, though rarely exercised in relation to indictable offences, and though ultimately liable to be controlled by the Attorney-General (by taking over the prosecution and, if he thinks fit, entering a *nolle prosequi*) remains a valuable constitutional safeguard against inertia or partiality on the part of authority. This is the true enforcement process and it must be clear that an assertion of a right to invoke it is of no help to Mr Gouriet here. His case is not based on the committal of offence plus a refusal to prosecute, it is based on a right to take preventive action in a civil court which could have been taken but was not taken by the Attorney-General in relator proceedings. This involves consideration of the 'relator action' and of the Attorney-General's part in it.

A relator action – a type of action which has existed from the earliest times – is one in which the Attorney-General, on the relation of individuals (who may include local authorities or companies) brings an action to assert a public right. It can properly be said to be a fundamental principle of English Law that private rights can be asserted by individuals, but that public rights can only be asserted by the Attorney-General as representing the public. In terms of constitutional law, the rights of the public are vested in the Crown, and the Attorney-General enforces them as an officer of the Crown. And just as the Attorney-General has in general no power to interfere with the assertion of private rights, so in general no private person has the right of representing the public in the assertion of public rights. If he tries to do so his action can be struck out.

CHAPTER FIVE

Defence Lawyers

The pivotal role of lawyers in the criminal justice system is often overlooked. In an adversarial system, those who assess the criminal justice system too often concentrate on the system weighed against the defendant. Yet the most effective due process safeguard is a strong defence team. Lord Justice Auld [1:5] identified two essentials to balance the prosecution: 'an experienced, motivated defence lawyer or lawyers who are adequately paid for pre-trial preparation' and 'ready access by defence lawyers to clients in custody'. In England most defendants tried for the more serious offences are legally represented, usually at taxpayers' expense. We should therefore examine the impact and quality of this legal advice.

The legal profession is still divided into two branches. Solicitors are the first port of call for legal advice, while a barrister may advise on legal problems when briefed by a solicitor, and will normally represent defendants at trial in the Crown Court. Of course, many of those who work in solicitors' offices are not legally qualified or may hold other qualifications, such as those of the Institute of Legal Executives (ILEX). The Courts and Legal Services Act 1990 granted to the Lord Chancellor's Advisory Committee on Legal Education and Conduct (ACLEC) the right to make new rules to allow solicitors rights of audience in the higher courts. The Access to Justice Act 1999 has replaced ACLEC by a 'smaller and less expensive' committee, the Legal Services Consultative Panel, with the aim of reducing the barriers between the different branches of the profession; and section 36 of the Act specifically grants rights of audience to every barrister and solicitor in relation to all proceedings (subject to the rules of conduct of the professional bodies and their training requirements). The Lord Chancellor is given vast powers to change professional rules and to appoint the members of the Consultative Panel. A discussion of whether or not the public is best served by a divided legal profession is beyond the scope of this book, but Kerridge and Davis (1999) caution against 'the drift towards unification'. However, the blurring of the traditional distinctions between the two sides of the profession that is taking place may well lead to fusion of some sort in the near future. For the moment, it remains usual for solicitors, who may well present their own cases in the magistrates' courts, to brief counsel to represent their clients in the Crown Court or on appeal.

More important than the structure of the legal profession is the provision of adequate funds to enable good lawyers to work in the field of criminal justice. In 2001 the Criminal Defence Service (CDS), administered by the Legal Services Commission (LSC), took over from the Legal Aid Board the provision of public funding for criminal defence work (see the Access to Justice Act 1999). The CDS was created 'for the purpose of securing that individuals involved in criminal investigations or criminal proceedings have access to such advice, assistance and representation as the interests of justice require' (section 12(1)). The most radical innovation has been the new Public Defender Service, where salaried lawyers provide legal representation. This service has been launched only in a few pilot sites, which are being monitored.

The vast majority of legal services therefore continue to be provided by private practitioners. Private firms must hold a General Criminal Contract to carry out publicly funded criminal defence work. Funding issues predominate: not only the level of fees but their structure too. 'Standard fees' for magistrates' court work were introduced in 1993, despite strong opposition from the solicitors' profession. The danger of paying solicitors a standard, or fixed, fee is that they may either cut corners or turn away difficult cases.

The extract [5:1] from McConville et al's hard-hitting analysis of solicitors' firms in England and Wales in the early 1990s reveals the importance of due process safeguards in an adversarial legal system. The deficiencies highlighted by this research led the authors to question the effectiveness of recent reforms, with their emphasis on managerialism and cost-effectiveness. The authors propose a cultural transformation in criminal defence work and a reassertion of defendants' rights within an adversarial system. However, the extracts included here reflect the research conclusions rather than the reality ahead. Auld [1:5] argued that the current fee structure was 'fundamentally flawed' in that it does not provide an adequate reward or incentive for preparatory work. The fee structure should instead encourage efficient preparation of cases.

Recent years have seen a decrease in the number of solicitors' firms accepting criminal work. The latest decline is revealed in the LSC's annual report 2001–02: the number of firms offering criminal defence services declined from 3,500 prior to April 2001 to 2,909 firms under contract a year later. Quality assurance and value for money have driven many firms away. An extra chapter in this book could usefully have studied the decision making in the LSC and the Lord Chancellor's Department, but for present purposes we will concentrate on two areas where the lawyer's role may be crucial.

(i)   Legal advice at police stations

In our scenario, Gerry Good was arrested by the police and taken to the police station. As we saw in Chapter Two, the police have a duty to inform him of his right, under section 58 of PACE, to obtain legal advice at the police station free of charge regardless of his means. The decision of the Court of Appeal in *Samuel* [1988] QB 615 shows how seriously the courts take this right, though there are other cases, such as *Alladice* (1988) 87 Cr App Rep 380, where the conviction has been upheld despite a breach of section 58. We saw in Chapter Two that, in response to the European Court of Human Rights decision in *Murray* (1996) 22 EHRR 29, section 58 of the Youth Justice and Criminal Evidence Act 1999 prevents any inference being drawn from a suspect's silence prior to consulting a solicitor. This right to free legal advice is not exercised by all suspects. Sanders et al's (1989) study showed that about a quarter of all arrested people asked for a solicitor. Brown, Ellis and Larcombe [5:2] suggest that the 1991 revision of PACE Code C (on the detention, treatment and questioning of suspects) led to a small increase in the proportion of suspects receiving legal advice. They concluded that, in the early 1990s, three-quarters of suspects were being informed of the right, and of the fact that the legal advice was free, and just over half were told that the legal advice was independent, but very few were told that the consultation would be in private. They suggested a scheme under which legally qualified personnel are present at main police stations on a round-the-clock basis to avoid the problem of local variations in the provision of legal advice. The cost implications of this, however, suggest that it is highly unlikely.

At present, where suspects do not choose their 'own' solicitor, they may choose from a list of local solicitors, which the police will provide (or by ringing a centralised telephone number). When a duty solicitor is requested under the '24-hour scheme', a telephone referral service is contacted. The telephone call system to duty solicitors required at police stations has been contracted out since 1994 (the Automobile Association won the first contract).

Gerry Good was arrested in the morning and might have found someone from his solicitors less willing to come if he had been arrested at night. As we saw in Chapter Two, he rang the firm of solicitors who had represented him before. It was, as is often the case, an employee with no legal qualifications who came to the police station to represent him. The inadequacy of legal advice at police stations is a significant problem. The most striking point to emerge from Baldwin's recordings of police interviews [5:3] was the general passivity of legal representatives at the interviews. There are even striking examples in the case law, such as *Miller, Paris and Abdullahi* [5:4] where judges have expressed strong and well-deserved criticism of legal advisers.

McConville and Hodgson [5:5], too, considered that many advisers lacked adequate legal knowledge and confidence, and that sometimes they seemed to identify more with the police than with the suspect. Their conclusions are all the more striking in view of the removal of the unqualified right to remain silent under police questioning and at trial (by the CJPOA 1994 [2:10], discussed in Chapter Two). Good quality legal advice is essential. For example, McConville and Hodgson [5:5] found that many legal advisers left the police station before the formal interview took place, and others only gave advice by telephone. The Law Society introduced regulations in 1995 preventing solicitors' representatives who have not passed an accredited examination in police station skills from giving advice in police stations. It would be interesting to know whether courses such as ILEX's six-week home study Police Station Representatives Accreditation Scheme (now the Criminal Litigation Accreditation Scheme) have led to improvements in the standard of advice offered.

(ii)   Role of defence lawyers before and at trial

Let us return to Gerry's case. Ian Brown, an employee of the firm, was present at his interview. Once Gerry had been charged by the police, he was refused bail. The next morning he was represented by Mary Chapman, a solicitor with the firm, at his successful bail application in the magistrates' court. Whilst there he filled in the necessary forms to apply for legal representation, and his application was processed by court staff. In Gerry's case, there is no question that he qualifies for legal aid – he is facing a charge of wounding, his liberty is at stake, and so he falls within the 'interests of justice' criteria. There is no means test here, but at the end of the trial the judge may order defendants, depending on their means, to contribute to the costs of the case.

How do solicitors decide what work is necessary in preparing a defence? Clearly, solicitors have an enormous influence on the outcome of a case. Their decisions about interviewing alibi witnesses, checking police summaries or commissioning independent medical or forensic experts can make all the difference to the strength of a defendant's case. But whether defence solicitors take such actions may well depend on whether their pay structure rewards such work. Although Gerry's solicitor represented him at the bail application, she decides to brief counsel to represent him at his trial. Gerry's first meeting with his barrister may well be at the Crown Court shortly before the trial is due to begin. Zander and Henderson (1993) found that 44% of defence barristers said that the brief had previously been returned by someone else. No fewer than 25% of defence barristers in contested cases had received the brief later than 4 pm on the day before the trial. Perhaps this is not so surprising: barristers, being self-employed, are likely to hold onto a brief until the last minute in case their present case finishes earlier than expected. The Royal Commission on

Criminal Justice (1993) commented (at page 118) on the need to reconstruct the scale of fees to encourage counsel to give adequate priority to pre-trial preparation. This is the message reinforced by Auld **[1:5]**.

An accused person has to make two vital decisions pre-trial: first, with offences triable either way, whether to opt for trial by jury in the Crown Court; and, secondly, whether to plead guilty or not guilty. The two will often be considered together (though the government proposes to abolish a defendant's right to choose trial by jury) and the advice given first by solicitors and later by barristers may be decisive. Hedderman and Moxon **[5:6]** studied the reasons for the decisions leading to Crown Court trial. Most of those who chose to be tried at the Crown Court were influenced by the prospect of acquittal, although 82% ended up pleading guilty. Again, more than half of those who elected trial by jury said that the possibility of a lighter sentence at the Crown Court influenced their decision, even though judges were three times more likely to impose a custodial sentence and the sentences that they imposed were much longer. Riley and Vennard **[6:5]** suggest that one reason for defendants opting for the Crown Court is that they themselves have greater confidence at a hearing in that court. The fact that 82% ended up pleading guilty, despite having opted for jury trial because of its higher rate of acquittal, is not really surprising: in many cases, the prosecution agrees to accept a guilty plea to a lesser charge only at the last minute. It may well be that it is only when they meet their barrister at the door of the court that defendants finally realise that an acquittal may be unlikely.

Zander and Henderson (1993) found that 26% of defendants changed their plea to guilty at a late stage, thus causing trials to 'crack'. Is this because people who want to plead not guilty are persuaded to change their minds, or because people who really always planned to plead guilty 'play the system'? If the defendant is confident that ultimately he will be sent to prison, he may seek to delay the fateful day as long as possible. Narey (1997) commented that 'a substantial proportion of elections are little more than an expensive manipulation of the criminal justice system and are not concerned with any wish to establish innocence in front of a jury' (at page 2).

The substantial sentence discount given for guilty pleas must have a strong influence on many defendants. As we will see in Chapter Seven, defendants who plead guilty normally receive a sentence discount of some 25–30%. Baldwin and McConville's (1977) study concluded: 'It is at least possible that what barristers, in good faith, perceive as no more than advice being offered to their clients, may be perceived by their clients themselves as pressure to change their plea'. Zander and Henderson's Crown Court study for the Royal Commission (1993) has controversially led some to argue that perhaps 1,400 innocent people plead guilty every year. Bargains as to plea are often distinguished from bargains as to sentence. Sentence bargains necessarily involve the judge, and will therefore be examined in Chapter Seven, although the questions concerning the legitimacy of such bargains are the same as those discussed here. The Royal Commission's reasons for recommending that judges should be able to indicate sentence are included at **[7:3]**.

Should there be such pressure on people to plead guilty? The Royal Commission concluded that as long as people were adequately advised and that they were in fact guilty, there was nothing wrong with a system of inducements to encourage them to plead guilty. Following this, the CJPOA 1994 **[2:10]** put the discount for guilty pleas on a statutory footing. Sanders and Young **[7:7]** are highly critical, arguing that a system of plea bargaining undermines the rule of law by allowing the state to secure convictions based on vague and unsubstanti-ated allegations. As they put it, 'defence lawyers spend more time negotiating away defendants' rights than they do in upholding them' (at page 267). This encouragement of guilty pleas is hard to reconcile with adversarial principles. As Sanders and Young say elsewhere, 'Covertly to tolerate plea bargaining is hypocritical; but to approve its legality smacks of totalitarianism' (Young and Sanders, 1994).

In Gerry's case, a bargain as to plea might involve an agreement that, in return for his pleading guilty to the less serious charge of section 20, the prosecution will drop the more serious charge under section 18. This can be done without any involvement on the part of the judge, although it is possible for the judge or magistrates to insist that the prosecution proceeds with the more serious charge. Thus, in the trial of Peter Sutcliffe (the 'Yorkshire Ripper') in 1981 the judge insisted that the charges of murder were proceeded with, even though the Attorney-General was willing to accept a plea of guilty to manslaughter by reason of diminished responsibility. Gerry maintains with his solicitor that he will plead not guilty and so she does not attempt to negotiate a pre-trial plea bargain. On the morning of the trial, there is some informal negotiation in the robing room between counsel for both sides, but the prosecution decide to continue with the charge under section 18, largely because of the evidence that Rosa Bottles was pursued for half a mile from the pub, which they argue suggest that Gerry intended to wound her. His criminal record may also influ-ence their decision.

Defence counsel's role at the trial itself is, of course, vital. In conjunction with the solicitor, many tactical decisions have to be made: which witnesses to call, whether the defendant should give evidence, exactly what questions to ask, and whether to cross-examine or re-examine. In Gerry's case, the barrister, Tim Moffat, is a fiery young man with whom Gerry feels little sympathy when he meets him briefly in court before the trial, but he seems to know his job. The personal performance of counsel is likely to have an impact on the jury. Lawyers may have a split loyalty: should they argue fully every point in their client's case or should they think of the public interest in, for example, a brief trial? Their own career prospects may lead them at times to leave some aspects of their client's case unexplored, especially if they think that the judge is unsympathetic. If a solicitor or barrister considers the client to be undeserving, they may provide a poorer service. The eloquence of counsel inevitably affects the verdict: a persuasive barrister will be more effective than a poor one. The Royal Commission on Criminal Justice (1993) recommended limiting the length of opening and closing speeches to 15 and 30 minutes, respectively. Would this be appropriate? After conviction, defence counsel has the stage again, making a speech in mitigation on behalf of the offender, to give to the court the defendant's explanation of the offence and any other matters going in the defendant's favour.

What happens if lawyers are incompetent? Paying clients may vote with their feet and change solicitors, but when the taxpayer is footing the bill, it is more difficult to keep adequate control over incompetence, and the Lord Chancellor's Department continues, as we have seen, to work on ways of monitoring performance. Poor performance by barristers should mean that solicitors do not brief them again, but is this adequate quality control, since solicitors themselves will rarely be in court to carry out effective monitoring (often sending less senior members of staff instead)? In *Ensor* [5:7] the Court of Appeal confirmed an earlier ruling to the effect that a mistaken or unwise decision by counsel could not normally be regarded as a proper ground of appeal. The Royal Commission (1993) was critical of this narrow test: 'It cannot possibly be right that there should be defendants serving prison sentences for no other reason than that their lawyers made a decision which later turns out to have been mistaken'. Malleson [5:8], in her review of grounds for appeal, found that in 9 out of 300 cases, lawyers' errors were cited as grounds of appeal. Not surprisingly, all these defendants were either unrepresented or had changed legal advisers, and none were granted leave to appeal. The Royal Commission concluded that vast improvements were needed in the provision of advice: 'We recommend that both branches of the profession take all necessary steps to ensure that practitioners not only perform their duty to see the client at the end of the case, as most do, but also give preliminary advice both orally and in writing'.

The European Court of Human Rights ruling in *Boner v United Kingdom, Maxwell v United Kingdom* (1994), that the refusal of legal aid for an appeal was a breach of a prisoner's rights under article 6(3) European Convention on Human Rights [1:9], may have encouraged the authorities to be more ready to grant legal representation. But Plotnikoff and Woolfson's [5:9] conclusions on the quality of legal advice confirm the view that, within an adversarial system, good quality representation is essential. The fallacy in the argument that since defendants are frequently legally represented there is now less of a need to keep due process safeguards within the system, is obvious. Low pay deters good lawyers moving into publicly funded legal work.

Further reading

Abel, R L *The Legal Profession in England and Wales* (1988) Basil Blackwell

Boon, A and Levin J *The Ethics and Conduct of Lawyers in England and Wales* (1999) Oxford: Hart

Curran, P 'Discussion in the Judge's Private Room' [1992] Crim LR 79

Justice *The Judiciary in England and Wales* (1992)

Kerridge, R and Davis, G 'Reform of the Legal Profession: Alternative Way Ahead' (1999) 62 MLR 807

McConville, M and Mirsky, C 'Looking through the Guilty Plea Glass: The Structural Framework of English and American State Courts' [1993] 2 Social and Legal Studies 173

Morrison, J and Leith, P *The Barrister's World and the Nature of Law* (1992) Open University Press

Pannick, D *Advocates* (1993) Oxford Paperbacks

Sanders, A, Bridges, L, Mulvaney, A and Crozier, G *Advice and Assistance at Police Stations and the 24-Hour Duty Solicitor Scheme* (1989) Lord Chancellor's Department

Young, R and Sanders, A 'Plea Bargaining and the next Criminal Justice Bill' (1994) 144 NLJ 1200

Zander, M and Henderson, P *Crown Court Study* RCCJ Research Study No 19 (1993) HMSO

Documents

[5:1]   McConville, M, Hodgson, J, Bridges, L and Pavlovic, A Standing Accused: The Organisation and Practice of Criminal Defence Lawyers (1994) Clarendon Press

(From Chapter 5: Advisers at Interrogation, at page 126):

Until recently, routine police interrogation methods were well-hidden from courts, solicitors and researchers. Interrogations were essentially police-citizen encounters with outsiders barred from access, accounts of which were police constructions. The accounts attested to the probity of police character, their honesty of purpose, and the reasonableness of their questioning. Clients' accounts, by contrast, were presumptively illegitimate and the official (police) accounts undermined what little credibility suspects might otherwise have enjoyed. The legal profession accepted an element of wrongdoing by the police and misconduct was sometimes established at court but, by and large, the products of interrogation were under police control and collectively they portrayed a system which operated with correctness, restraint and regularity.

Following PACE, the police are presented with a new problem in that they no longer have exclusive control over accounts of interrogations. This has caused a seismic change in the nature of those accounts, with contemporaneous records bearing practically no relation to the world created by the police in their pre-PACE evidence. Whilst this in itself ought to be a matter of concern, it is clear that police goals remain unchanged, although their capacity to instantiate those goals is now imperfect. None the less, the police continue to try to enhance their own credibility and undermine that of the suspect. In this process, rules relating to admissibility are not of central concern to them and they are prepared to bring to bear dubious methods of inquiry.

Although the police are now more frequently than before forced to carry out interrogations in the presence of defence advisers, this has not proved a major restraint. Despite gaining access, the legal profession has no thought out strategy of how to use that access. In part, this is because they have been socialised into accepting as legitimate methods which are objectionable or dubious. In part, they have such a narrow definition of what they *can* do, that they end up by making no objections to police practices. And in part, there has been such insufficient thought given to interrogation, that they do not know what is or is not proper.

It is not simply a question of know-how and technical competence, however, but rather a question of attitude and values. Looked at as a whole, advisers who attend police stations accept uncritically the propriety and legitimacy of police action, even where what they witness themselves, what they hear from clients, and what they suspect goes on, leaves them convinced that the police break the rules and in other ways are beyond the law. The reason for this is that many advisers, like the police, instinctively believe, without requiring substantiation through evidence, that there is a case to answer, and that it is the client who must give the answer. This in turn springs from a working assumption that the client is probably factually guilty. In line with these ideologies, advisers permit the police free rein in interrogations and thereby legitimate dubious police methodologies.

(From Chapter 8: The Solicitor at Court: Plea and Mitigation, at page 210):

The routine nature of work in most solicitors' offices is more than matched by the routinisation of their plea settlement and mitigation practices. For the most part, solicitors do not see magistrates' courts as trial venues but as places where defendants can be processed through guilty pleas without, in general, any risk of severe sanction. The idea that the prosecution should be 'put to the proof' – required to establish a case against the defendant – is not accepted as 'valid' or 'realistic' by defence solicitors. Whilst it would be misleading and unfair to argue that solicitors do not care about their client, so strong is their presumption of guilt and their faith in the prosecution's case, that they fail to see their own role in the production of pleas, and their implication in ambiguous or inconsistent pleas of guilt. But it is not right to argue that solicitors are socialised, through court and prosecutorial inspired disciplinary mechanisms, into non-adversarial practices: they join hands with prosecutors not out of fear of sanction but because they share similar social and crime control values. Whether they like it or not, solicitors, by routinising pleas and mitigation, invite the state to see them as delivering standard services.

(From Chapter 10: Solicitors, Barristers and the Crown Court, at page 267):

In organisational terms, Crown Court cases occupy a regraded position in the structure of the typical firm of solicitors. One or two firms were exceptional in employing competent and experienced clerks and legal executives. Here, the case was prepared well in advance and a real effort made to engage in proactive defence work. Witnesses were sought and pursued until contacted; enquiry agents were sent to draw up plans of the scene of the crime; and forensic experts were employed in response to the client's assertion of inaccurate or fabricated evidence. However, these individuals were quite exceptional even within the firms in which they were employed. In the majority of practices much preparatory work is undertaken by non-qualified staff, and solicitors themselves have little contact with routine Crown Court cases. Lack of care in the preparation of these cases may be partially remedied if there is a case conference with counsel in advance of the court hearing, but reliance on this risks loss of witnesses and other information, and routinely results in the collection of evidence whose value is reduced by its staleness. In an unacceptably high number of cases, evidence is still being gathered long after the time when it was first available, sometimes during the trial itself.

In these cases, solicitors view the tasks of their staff, particularly in attending court, as undemanding and insignificant. The role definition applied to staff, leads solicitors to employ junior, casual or part-time individuals who are not otherwise involved in the case at all. The fact that the rates of remuneration are so low shows that it is not just solicitors who undervalue these tasks but the state itself.

The confidence that solicitors have in the system for handling of Crown Court cases is not based upon a rigorous evaluation of the process. With occasional outstanding exceptions, the average solicitor has little involvement in preparing these cases, and what work is done is often too little and too late. Whilst case conferences can make good some of the earlier shortcomings, these do not occur in most cases. At best, conferences can stimulate clerks to set in train investigative tasks that should have taken place much earlier with the increased risk of loss of information or a reduction in its value. In addition to this, cases are routinely vulnerable to changes of counsel and the late delivery of briefs, in several instances being put into the hands of barristers on the day of the hearing itself. With only inexperienced or casual staff from firms in attendance and without a record of what took place at conferences, solicitors themselves are in no position to evaluate the performance of counsel or any subsequent complaint from the client. Given this context, the trust the solicitors repose in counsel can be based only in images they have of barristers as experts possessing recipe knowledge revealed to 'insiders' as part of the process of Crown Court decision-making.

Whilst our observations confirmed that some barristers are strongly committed to cases, understanding of the need for a sympathetic approach, and careful to test the underlying basis of a guilty plea, counsel in general do not exhibit these positive characteristics. Strikingly, on the hearing day at court, but also in conferences in chambers, barristers evince little interest in scrutinising the evidence or in attempting to convince the defendant of its weight and probative value. Rather, conferences are treated as 'disclosure interviews', the purpose of which is to extract a plea of guilty from the client. In this process, what the prosecution alleges, what witnesses may say, and what the client wishes to say, are not discussed. In place of forensic testing, 'the evidence' is reified, set up as a totality, and invested with a force which irresistibly points to guilt. In place of evidence, a whole gamut of persuasive tactics is deployed against clients enabling barristers to take control of cases and to prevent most clients from becoming, in any real sense, defendants.

If the logic of this process is towards a guilty plea, the precise details of the final arrangements are high contingent. In some cases, barristers act to restrain complaint individuals from pleading to any and all charges, but in other cases the client's will is given free and unsupervised rein. A small proportion of defendants may resist pressure to capitulate but, deprived of support from solicitors' representatives, few can successfully hold out for long. Compliance is made more likely by the 'offers' which percolate through following prosecution counsel's review of the worth of the prosecution. Whilst the result of this prosecution review is usually a scaling down of the charges in predictable ways, it sometimes appears to have nothing to do with a rational assessment of the evidence but instead is an attempt to get a plea to *something*. When barristers introduce into discussions sentencing and charge propensities of particular judges and dark suggestions of backstairs' dealings, the contingent nature of the outcome is beyond measurement and can only be stated.

[5:2]   Brown, D, Ellis, T and Larcombe, K *Changing the Code: Police Detention under the Revised Codes of Practice* HO Research Study No 129 (1992) HMSO (at page 96):

The right to legal advice is only an effective right if the legal profession are able to deliver that advice adequately. The increase in demand for their services among suspects inevitably places additional strain on the profession. This comes at a time when there is already considerable debate among solicitors about the system of remunerating them for attendance at the police station. At one station in the present study, duty solicitors went on strike during phase two of the observational study (although this did not cause any obvious difficulties securing the attendance of solicitors).

There is clear evidence from the research that the coverage of advisory work at the police station by the legal profession is variable in the extreme and that this has suffered in some respects, almost certainly on account of rising demand. While more suspects are consulting legal advisers and they are attending the station more often, they are remaining for interviews between police and suspect far less frequently. Furthermore, a suspect's prospects of seeing a legal adviser at the police station and of having one present at interview vary considerably. Someone arrested at Peterborough or Wednesfield, for example, could virtually depend on seeing a legal adviser at the police station; however, someone taken to Weston Favell or Wellingborough would be fortunate to receive anything other than advice over the telephone. At the latter two stations, suspects would be even luckier to have a legal adviser present at a police interview: they attended only 11% and 20% of interviews at these stations in cases in which advice was requested. At Peterborough and Wednesfield, on the other hand, legal advisers were present at nearly two-thirds and 84% of such interviews. There is some evidence to suggest, too, that suspects' decisions about legal advice may be affected by its availability. It is probably no coincidence that, at Peterborough, the proportion of suspects requesting solicitors was high and at Wellingborough low.

This variation in the provision of advice probably owes much to different local arrangements for providing advice: for example, the strength of the duty solicitor scheme, the proximity of firms to police stations, the number of firms prepared to carry out advisory work there and whether representatives are widely employed to provide such advice. Whatever the reason for the variation, it raises, as with juveniles, issues about equitable treatment of criminal suspects and equality of access to legal advice. The revised Code has gone a considerable way towards ensuring that suspects (adults in particular) are treated equally in the provision of information about rights and providing the facility to request those rights. It is unable to ensure that the right to legal advice is implemented equitably. How this could be achieved is beyond the scope of the report. The answer may rest with some form of scheme under which legally qualified personnel are present at main police stations on a round-the-clock basis. As reported in Chapter 3, this might overcome the reservations of many about requesting a solicitor, as long as those who staffed the scheme did not become too closely identified with the police. It would also ensure that those who did want advice could depend on it being delivered without delay and in person, with the option of requesting attendance at police interviews if desired. It would also ensure that appropriate adults in cases involving juveniles would not be confronted with further delay after they arrived if they did opt for legal advice.

The giving of legal advice at the police station through the consistent presence of a solicitor would also eradicate a major difficulty with present arrangements, namely the provision of much advice by telephone and in conditions of considerable lack of privacy. Sanders et al (1989)[1] have pointed out that suspects tend to find telephone advice of lesser utility than advice at the station. Stations also do not generally possess dedicated facilities for private telephone consultations. Ad hoc arrangements were sometimes made, but conversations between solicitor and client were usually conducted in the custody area within the hearing of anyone in the vicinity, including investigating officers. The level of noise sometimes made such consultations extremely difficult, and police present often tended to make little effort to minimise the disruption. Bearing in mind that nearly one-third of all legal advice is given over the telephone, this is clearly an unsatisfactory state of affairs and detracts heavily from the value of this right.

[5:3]   Baldwin, J *The Role of Legal Representatives at the Police Station* RCCJ Research Study No 3 (1992) HMSO (at page 52):

As noted earlier in this report, a critical question is whether lawyers should be acting more forcefully on their clients' behalf at the police station. There is a good deal of scope for them to do so, and there were only a few lawyers on the video tapes who demonstrated that they could wield much authority in the interview room if the need arose. Some lawyers were more tolerant than were others of police officers who adopted harrying tactics, who persisted doggedly with certain lines of questioning or who made crude assumptions of guilt. Searching questions need to be asked, therefore, about how far legal representatives – who are in most instances unqualified legal personnel – can be said to be providing adequate protection to their clients in the police station.

The lawyers' view of their role at the police interviews reflects the way that their attitudes have been moulded by the history of their relations with the police. The interview takes place on police territory and it is police officers who are in charge of it. Officers often describe it as 'their' interview, and the lawyers contacted in this study did not commonly see it in other terms. Although police attitudes towards the presence of solicitors have shifted in the course of the past decade – reflecting to a considerable extent the changes brought in by the PACE legislation – lawyers continue to be treated with circumspection and suspicion. While they are no longer regarded as gatecrashers at interviews, they are nonetheless only tolerated at police stations if they behave appropriately. Advising clients not to answer questions or intervening at interviews are not seen by police as reasonable forms of behaviour. It is only if they toe the line that lawyers are regarded as acceptable participants at police interviews.

[1]   See Further reading section.

Passivity and compliance on the part of lawyers are therefore the normal, the expected, almost the required responses at the police station. Solicitors are conditioned by their history, their experience, even their own professional training and guidance, to be passive in the police interview room, and the existing rules reinforce this by giving police officers the upper hand. The lawyers' role in the interview room remains a precarious one, and it is no real surprise to note that the junior staff who mainly turn up to police stations are more inclined to facilitate police questioning than they are to challenge it.

[5:4] *R v Paris, Abdullahi and Miller* (1993) 97 Cr App Rep 99

The three appellants were convicted of the murder of a Cardiff prostitute. There was no forensic evidence against them. Against Miller, the prosecution case rested on the evidence of two discredited witnesses, Miller's own admissions and admissions he made to two visitors when in prison. After hearing part of the confession evidence on tape, the trial judge ruled it admissible. On appeal, it was contended that Miller's confession was unreliable, having been obtained by oppression.

The Court of Appeal, in quashing the convictions, held that it was undoubtedly oppressive within the meaning of section 76(2) of PACE to shout at a suspect what they wanted him to say after he had denied involvement over 300 times, particularly since the person in question was on the borderline of mental handicap. The Lord Chief Justice was critical of both the police and the suspect's solicitor.

Lord Taylor CJ (at page 109):

Before parting with this case, we should comment on the apparent failure of the provisions in the Police and Criminal Evidence Act 1984, to prevent evidence obtained by oppression and impropriety from being admitted. In our judgment, the circumstances of this case do not indicate flaws in those provisions. They do indicate a combination of human errors.

First, the police officers adopted techniques of interrogation which were wholly contrary to the spirit and in many instances the letter of the codes laid down under the Act. In our view, those responsible for police training and discipline must take all necessary steps to see the guidelines are followed.

Secondly, although we did not hear what his instructions were, the solicitor who sat in on the interviews, seems to have done that and little else. Guidelines for solicitors on 'advising a suspect in the police station' were first published by the Law Society in 1985 with second and third editions in 1988 and 1991. The current edition provides under paragraph 6 as follows, inter alia:
'6.3.2   you may need to intervene if the questions are: ... (c) oppressive, threatening or insulting;
6.3.3   you should intervene if the officer is not asking questions but only making his/her own comments ...
6.4.1   if questions are improper or improperly put, you should intervene and be prepared to explain your objections ...
6.4.2   if improprieties remain uncorrected or continue, advise the suspect of his/her right to remain silent.'

It is of the first importance that a solicitor fulfilling the exacting duty of assisting a suspect during interviews should follow the guidelines and discharge his function responsibly and courageously. Otherwise, his presence may actually render disservice. We can only assume that in the present case the officers took the view that unless and until the solicitor intervened, they could not be criticised for going too far. If that is so, they were wholly wrong.

Finally, it is most regrettable that the worst example of the police excesses (tape 7) was not played in full to the learned judge before he ruled on admissibility.

Despite this combination of errors, it must be pointed out that the record of timings and the tape recordings of the interviews required by the Act, have enabled this Court to review what took place and, albeit belatedly, to allow these appeals. At the conclusion, we now direct the learned Registrar to send copies of tape 7 to the Chief Inspector of Constabulary, to the Director of Public Prosecutions and to the Chairman of the Royal Commission on Criminal Justice.

[5:5]   McConville, M and Hodgson, J *Custodial Legal Advice and the Right to Silence* RCCJ Research Study No 16 (1993) HMSO (at page 16):

2.2   All the firms that we examined had established their own in-house system for responding to requests for advice at any time of day or night. To service demand, firms had established rota systems, to which most members of staff were allocated. In addition, some firms regularly contracted out work to individuals on a piece-work basis or used the services of outside agencies to handle night and weekend calls or, in some cases, any and all calls which came to the firm. A very prominent pattern in high volume criminal defence firms was the employment of former police officers to discharge police station advice work as well as to undertake other tasks such as the interviewing of witnesses. In the present study, which replicates the findings of the long-term study in which the authors have been engaged for the past three and a half years, some 47% of firms employed former police officers for police station work. In addition to this, outside agencies, staffed by former police officers, had grown up to service the needs of several firms in respect of own solicitor requests, and two of the firms of solicitors studied (as well as others in the same localities) regularly contracted out work to such agencies.

Who attends police stations to give legal advice

2.3   Whilst earlier research cited above has indicated recourse to representatives in 'own solicitor' cases at a rate exceeding 40%, the findings of our study show that the true rate is much higher. Our study suggests that the rate of recourse to representatives may well be as high as three-quarters as Table 2.1 shows.

Table 2.1 The status of advisers attending police stations in response to requests from suspects

Status of Adviser	n	%
Admitted solicitor	44	24.4
Articled clerk	28	15.6
Clerk on staff	56	31.1
Former police officer	38	21.1
Non-staff clerk	8	4.4
Outside agency	6	3.3
Totals	**180**	**99.9**

The figures disclosed in Table 2.1 if anything overstate the frequency with which solicitors acting on their own account respond to requests for advice since on some of the occasions where solicitors went to the police station they did so in their capacity as duty solicitors. Moreover, where a solicitor attended with a non-qualified member of staff (n=6) we classified the status of the adviser as 'solicitor' even though, in such cases, it was usual after the initial client consultation, for the solicitor to leave the non-qualified member of staff to handle alone the interrogation and any subsequent advice sessions.

The overall figures hide some differences between firms: whilst, as we have seen, many firms used the services of former police officers, a majority did not, some expressing themselves to be shocked at the practices of their colleagues; and, in a few firms, it was clear, not only from the cases we observed but also from our conversations with firms' personnel, that solicitors made strenuous efforts to attend police stations.

(and at page 199):

It has become increasingly evident that the low level of personnel utilised in the provision of legal advice at police stations and the resultant poor quality of that advice is unlikely to be amenable to immediate reform. Rather, it is a product of the overall structure of the private solicitors' profession, its ideologies, and the way in which it is currently organised to provide criminal defence services as a whole. This is not simply a function, as spokespersons for the profession often claim, of the financial restrictions imposed under legal aid, although it is likely that the problem of poor quality advice will be exacerbated if the proposed introduction of standard fees (instead of hourly rates of payment) for magistrates' court criminal defence work goes ahead. However, there are no plans to alter the current hourly basis for payment under legal aid for police station advice, and the rates for which such payments are made are already among the highest available to the profession for any form of legal aid work. As a result, the overall income derived by solicitors for this one aspect of their criminal defence work now amounts to over £50m per annum, or the equivalent of more than a quarter of the total amount they receive for representation of defendants in all stages of magistrates' court proceedings. In the light of this and the political context of even greater government pressure to control growth in legal aid expenditure, there is likely to be very little scope for improving rates of payment for police station advice work.

Nor is there any evidence that higher rates of payment would, in themselves, bring about any real improvements in the quality of advice, or of advisers, at police stations. For example, duty solicitors already receive enhanced payments, one-third higher than those paid to other solicitors, for attending police stations during unsocial hours.

Yet research (Sanders et al, 1989) has shown that, despite this extra financial incentive, duty solicitors consistently provide telephone advice to suspects in police stations, rather than attending on them personally, far more frequently than do 'own' solicitors for equivalent types of case. Nor have recent rule changes to the official duty solicitor arrangements, designed to encourage more attendance at police stations, had any visible effect in reducing rates of telephone advice by duty solicitors.

By contrast, the greater frequency with which other solicitors do ensure that an adviser attends personally on suspects at police stations is without doubt related to the wider licence they have, compared with duty solicitors, to employ unqualified staff to undertake this work. Our research indicates that the rate of use of non-qualified staff by 'own' solicitors may in fact be considerably higher than shown in previous studies. And, again, the fact that this practice is of doubtful legality under the formal rules governing payments out of legal aid funds, certainly where firms routinely use outside agents to carry out police station visits on their behalf, does not seem to deter them in any way. Nor should this be surprising, given the lack of any systematic means of monitoring solicitors' behaviour in this respect, and of enforcing the rules on non-delegation to outside agents and, even more so, the fact that the downgrading of police station advice work is now deeply ingrained in the general organisation of solicitors' criminal defence practices.

Indeed, the reality of these practices is that criminal defence solicitors have come increasingly to rely on their firms being able to undertake ever larger volumes of routine representation in magistrates' courts (solicitors being excluded, at least at present, from most forms of advocacy in the higher criminal courts). The central organising principle of solicitors' criminal defence practices, therefore, is to ensure the maximum deployment of qualified staff on in-court advocacy, with the result that most out-of-court and non-advocacy services are delegated to other staff. In this context, it may be important to solicitors, for the purposes of customer satisfaction and retention, to ensure that established clients at least receive an attendance at the police station by some personal 'representative' of the firm, even though the status of the person is often deliberately left vague so far as the police and especially clients are concerned. On the other hand, as solicitors currently perceive the organisational imperatives of criminal defence work, it is considered not viable, both in financial and social/personal terms, for qualified staff to be deployed routinely on police station work and thereby diverted, directly or indirectly (because of the out-of-hours work it entails), from regular magistrates' court advocacy.

The result is that police station advice, far from being given the central role in an adversarial process that both the law and sociological analysis would assign to it, has been effectively redefined by solicitors in essentially non-adversarial terms, as at best carrying out an administrative 'watching brief' over police interrogations and hardly involving advocacy on behalf of the client at all. Altering this situation would require a major re-focusing of solicitors' criminal defence practices as a whole, with much greater importance being attached to the less visible, out-of-court aspects of the work. Such a restructuring may be impossible within the present organisation of the profession and of legal aid, and it is certainly difficult to see how it could be achieved in the face of even tighter budgetary restrictions on legal aid expenditure as a whole.

'Ideological drift' and law reform

11.17 The logic of our findings is that the right to silence should be strengthened rather than further weakened or attenuated. The collective effect of 'reforms' in this area has been to adversely change the position of the accused in the criminal justice process without any empirical grounding or proper philosophical justification. In fact, the criminal justice process has been reshaped without attention being paid to its foundational principle, namely, that it has grown out of the duty upon the state to demonstrate its right to punish those believed to be involved in criminal activity. It is this principle which ultimately imposes strict standards of proof upon the Crown and prevents it from compelling the suspect to co-operate in the investigation or to testify. Whilst the Crown may, in seeking to discharge its burden of proof, utilise information voluntarily provided by the suspect, those who rely upon silence do no more than ask the state to discharge the burden imposed on it by law.

In this context, the integrity, autonomy and right to self-respect of individuals arrested by the police, so vigorously defended by the Royal Commission on Criminal Procedure (1981) is already at risk in the practice and ideology of criminal justice today. The police have moved historically from a position in which they had no access to detain persons to one today in which they have unmediated access. Alongside this, citizens have moved from a position in which they were asked if they had *anything* to say, to one in which they may be held in detention until the police are satisfied that they have *nothing* left to say (Code C, para 16.1). Nothing could better symbolise the primacy given in policing to arrest over information-gathering, and the subversion of a 'right' to silence into a legal requirement to remain in police detention and interrogation until the police decide that no more can be wrung out of the arrestee.

[5:6] Hedderman, C and Moxon, D *Magistrates' Court or Crown Court?* *Mode of Trial Decisions and Sentencing* HORS No 125 (1992) HMSO

(from the Summary, at page vi):

In recent years there has been a large increase in the proportion of triable-either-way cases which have been committed to the Crown Court for trial. This has contributed to an increase in the remand population and the sentenced prison population. It also has substantial resource implications for the Crown Prosecution Service, the courts and the legal aid fund.

There is only very limited information as to why magistrates and defendants take the mode of trial decisions they do. Apart from the extra burdens which Crown Court trials impose on the criminal justice system, comparisons of published statistics suggest that Crown Court trials are much more likely to lead to custodial sentences being imposed. However, there has not hitherto been a study comparing severity of sentence at the two venues while controlling the main case factors. The present study sought to remedy this omission and confirms that those dealt with at the Crown Court are at much greater risk of custody, even after allowing for differences in case characteristics. The study was concerned with the way in which convicted offenders were dealt with at the two venues, and the reasons for the decisions leading to Crown Court trial, not with the trial process itself. Acquitted defendants were not, therefore, included.

The main findings are:

- Almost 60% of cases dealt with in the Crown Court were sent there because magistrates declined jurisdiction. Yet magistrates' sentencing powers would have been sufficient to deal with a majority of these cases.
- Nearly three quarters of those denied a choice of venue would have chosen to be dealt with at a magistrates' court (mostly in the expectation of a lighter sentence and/or a quicker trial).
- Most of those who chose to be dealt with at the Crown Court were influenced by the prospect of acquittal; yet the majority (82%) ended up pleading guilty to all charges on which they were convicted.
- There was little evidence that the considerable variation in sentencing practice between individual courts has any systematic influence on defendants' decisions as to venue.
- More than half of those who elected Crown Court trial said that the possibility of a lighter sentence at the Crown Court influenced their decision. Yet the Crown Court made far more use of custody than magistrates' courts, irrespective of the area. This remained true when courts were matched on a number of factors. This analysis showed that judges were three times as likely to impose immediate custody, and sentences were on average two and a half times as long. Overall, therefore, they imposed more than seven times as much custody in comparable cases.
- One third of defendants who elected trial would, in retrospect, have preferred to have been dealt with at a magistrates' court.
- 70% of those who elected Crown Court trial had done so on the advice of a barrister or solicitor. Only five per cent had been advised to opt for summary trial.
- A substantial number of defendants, including some who intended to plead guilty from the outset, chose to be dealt with at the Crown Court because they did not trust magistrates to give due weight to their case, often feeling that they would be biased in favour of the police; in almost one quarter of cases where solicitors advised their client to plead guilty from the outset they nevertheless favoured Crown Court trial.
- Late changes of plea were often associated with late changes in the offences charged, and it is possible that if charges could have been agreed prior to the mode of trial decision more defendants would have been content to accept summary trial.
- Even where magistrates declined jurisdiction, well over half the defendants received sentences that could have been imposed by magistrates.
- For all types of offence, victims were much more likely to receive compensation if the case was dealt with by a magistrates' court. This remained true even after allowing for the greater use of custody (which usually precludes a compensation order) at the Crown Court.
- Social inquiry reports appeared most influential in diverting offenders away from fines and towards probation-based disposals; there was no evidence that they had a significant influence on courts' use of custody.

(from Discussion and Conclusions, at page 38):

The decision of magistrates or defendants in relation to mode of trial has a particularly strong and wide-ranging influence on other agencies, with very substantial cost implications. For example, in 1988–89 the cost of a contested case in a magistrates' court was £295 as compared with £3,100 at the Crown Court; average prosecution costs were £50 at magistrates' courts compared with £460 at the Crown Court. And defendants dealt within the Crown Court are much more likely to have a social inquiry report prepared on them, at a cost (in 1988–89 of £210). Legal aid costs too, were several times higher though comparative figures are currently not available.

Differences in the costs of the various disposals, however, make the biggest overall difference to the cost of trials at the two venues. The high cost of imprisonment makes the largest contribution to this, but community service orders (£25 per week with an average duration of 35 weeks) also contribute to the difference, albeit with some offsetting benefits for the community. By contrast fines, which were used far more by magistrates' courts than the Crown Court, were estimated in 1989 to have yielded an average of £77 per either way case, after allowing for collection costs (see Magistrates' Courts' Scrutiny, 1989). Magistrates' courts were also much more likely to compensate victims.

High standards of justice and public confidence in the criminal justice system are, of course, of fundamental importance. Such considerations have ensured the survival of jury trial in a very wide range of cases, and the freedom to have offences tried at the Crown Court is increasingly exercised. So what is achieved by having such a large number of cases dealt with in the Crown Court?

Whilst the extra financial costs of Crown Court trial are clear enough, the benefits are less easily measured. No one can say with confidence which venue is more successful at convicting the guilty and acquitting the innocent, but since the Crown Court acquits more defendants than do magistrates' courts some defendants clearly benefit from a Crown Court trial. The benefits for those convicted are harder to discern. Some feel that they have had 'a fairer trial', and this perceived benefit cannot be lightly dismissed. Nevertheless, for many defendants the decision to take their case to the Crown Court has meant time in prison – whether on remand or under sentence – which might otherwise have been reduced or avoided altogether. Subjective feelings about fairness are seemingly at odds with the practical consequences of the mode of trial decision which are often simply that the defendant received a more severe penalty.

The defendants' choice

Those who *choose* to be tried at the Crown Court do so for two main reasons, often based on misconceptions. First, Crown Court trial is seen as offering a better prospect of acquittal, second, as securing a lighter sentence (often through negotiations over charges). Although the chances of acquittal are better at the Crown Court, for many this is nullified by their eventual guilty plea. The Justices' Clerks' Society commented:

> 'Defendants will elect and lawyers will advise clients to elect jury trial in cases where there exists no credible defence in the hope there will be returned a perverse verdict.'

The finding that a majority of those interviewed who elected did eventually admit their guilt, usually on legal advice (presumably as hopes of a perverse verdict fade) makes it difficult to refute the substance of this claim – namely that guilty defendants with weak cases frequently opt for the Crown Court.

The finding that so many people believe that they will receive a lighter sentence at the Crown Court is puzzling, though expectations of lesser charges and the greater likelihood of a social inquiry report may influence this view. Whilst there are no doubt instances where the Crown Court imposes a less severe sentence than a magistrates' court would have, the study provides overwhelming evidence that as a general rule the decision to go to the Crown Court carries with it a far greater risk of a custodial sentence and of a much longer sentence when custody is imposed.

If there were stronger incentives for resolving decisions relating to charge and plea *before* the mode of trial decision is taken, this could play a part in redistributing cases to the magistrates' courts. From the point of view of those sentenced, venue is likely to be much more important than plea or, in most cases, charge, in terms of the eventual penalty. This point perhaps needs to be taken more fully into account when defendants are advised about mode of trial.

It was perhaps disappointing to find that so many defendants (and solicitors) gave as a reason for electing Crown Court trial that they would learn more about the prosecution case. When advance disclosure was introduced it had been hoped that it would lead to more cases being dealt with at magistrates' courts since it would no longer be necessary to opt for Crown Court trial in order to secure details of the prosecution case. However, it would seem that the information available to the defence, which may be only a brief summary, is often felt to be insufficient.

Directed committals

From interviews with prosecutors, justices' clerks and magistrates it was clear that elections for trial were widely regarded as the major reason why so many cases were committed to the Crown Court. It is therefore important to bear in mind that magistrates themselves were responsible for sending three-fifths of the cases in the study to the Crown Court – a proportion that has grown in recent years, and continues to do so. (However, it should be borne in mind that some interviewees said that in committing for trial magistrates were sometimes anticipating the known preference of the accused. It is not known how often this occurs.)

Under the Magistrates' Courts Act 1980 magistrates should, when considering whether or not to decline jurisdiction, 'have regard to whether the circumstances make the offence one of serious character, whether the punishment they have the power to inflict would be adequate and ... any other circumstances which appear to the court to make it more suitable for the offence to be tried one way rather than the other'. At first sight, it is not clear how 'serious character' can be considered separately from consideration of whether sentencing powers are adequate. However, a relatively serious offence may sometimes attract a sentence which a lower court could have imposed, for reasons which have no bearing on the mode of trial decision. There may, for example, be exceptional mitigating factors such as severe stress; or the offender may have made restitution to the victim since the committal decision was taken.

In some respects the 1990 national mode of trial guidelines seek to strengthen the presumption in favour of summary trial. For example, many courts have a threshold of £2,000 for property offences and this has been raised to £4,000. Also, although many domestic burglaries will continue to be seen as unsuitable for summary trial, the guidelines make it clear that this should not be automatic.

The guidelines list aggravating factors that may be associated with particular offences, such as 'professional hallmarks' in a burglary or handling case, or 'use of a weapon of a kind likely to cause serious injury' in an ABH or GBH case. It is stated that cases should be tried summarily unless one or more of the listed features is present and that its sentencing powers are insufficient. However, general observations are made, which include: 'the defendant's antecedents and personal mitigating circumstances are irrelevant for the purpose of deciding mode of trial'. Given the influence of such factors in the sentencing process it is difficult to see how courts can divorce consideration of whether their sentencing powers are sufficient from consideration of factors relating to the offender. It would seem that factors which in the abstract are regarded as serious do not always lead to more severe sentences being imposed. As an example, the Home Office study of Crown Court sentencing (Moxon)[2] found that theft involving breach of trust attracted unsuspended custody rather less often than the 'other theft' category.

Given that some of the factors affecting sentence are regarded as irrelevant to the mode of trial decision, it is inevitable that Crown Court sentences will sometimes be less severe than those available to magistrates. But the scale on which this occurs does raise a number of questions. For example, are magistrates being asked to take decisions without sufficient information, and therefore forming an exaggerated view of the seriousness of the case? Are magistrates too often being asked to take mode of trial decisions on the basis of charges which have not been finalised?

One consequence of the Criminal Justice Act 1991 will be to remove antecedents as a factor to be considered when committing a defendant for sentence. Magistrates will therefore be able to commit any defendant for sentence, which should make it easier for them to try borderline cases as they will no longer run the risk of having to pass sentence on a first offender when the case turns out to be much more serious than they had anticipated.

In conclusion, the high cost of Crown Court trial, both in terms of direct costs and the indirect costs of more severe sentences and a higher remand population, seems to offer few tangible benefits, least of all for defendants. The fact that magistrates' courts in some areas manage to deal with a much higher proportion of either way cases than others, with no obvious difficulties, suggests that the scope for the CPS and magistrates to agree on summary trial in many more cases is very considerable. This view is supported, too, by the fact that far more either way cases were dealt by way of summary trial in the past. And the fact that magistrates rarely find it necessary to use their sentencing powers to the full – only one in ten defendants received custodial sentences, with an average duration of only 2.8 months – also suggests that they could take a more robust view of the suitability of cases for summary trial. Defendants and their legal advisers, for their part, should be in no doubt that if they do not have the evidence to sustain a not guilty plea they would, in many instances, be well advised to opt for summary trial.

If the recent trend could be reversed, the rewards would be considerable. Pressure on the Crown Court, the Crown Prosecution Service, the legal aid fund and prisons could be eased, and many defendants would avoid custody or receive shorter terms of imprisonment.

---

[2] Moxon, D *Sentencing Practice in the Crown Court* HORS 103 (1988) HMSO.

[5:7]   R v Ensor [1989] I WLR 497

The appellant was tried on two counts of rape, each of a different woman. He wanted an application for severance to be made. Counsel concluded that an application would fail, and that some advantage would accrue from having the counts tried together and no application for severance was made. The appellant was convicted on both counts. The Court of Appeal dismissed the appeal.

Lord Lane CJ (at pages 501):

We must look a little more closely at the extent to which this court will concern itself with what passes between an accused person and his legal representatives.

Mr Escott Cox contends that in a criminal trial defending counsel is only obliged to seek specific instructions from his client in relation to two matters: first, as to plea; and, secondly, as to whether the client himself wishes to give evidence. All other decisions are for counsel, and it is for him to decide, as a matter of discretion, which matters, if any, needed to be discussed with the accused. The discretion is one, he submits, which this court will not attempt directly to review, although it might, for example, in a wholly exceptional case be prepared to consider whether compelling evidence which was available but which defence counsel for no good reason refused to lead renders the conviction unsafe and unsatisfactory.

Mr Jeffreys relied heavily on *R v Irwin* [1987] 1 WLR 902, decided by another division of this court on 19 February 1987. That was a case in which at a retrial counsel for the defence decided not to call alibi witnesses who had given evidence at the earlier trial which had ended in a disagreement. On appeal it was said, at p 905G, that the question was not whether counsel was right in thinking that the witnesses should not be called but whether he was entitled to bind his client. The court held that he was not entitled to do so, asserting at p 906H, that on this topic there is no authority to be found in any criminal case.

It seems that the court in *R v Irwin* [1987] 1 WLR 902 was not referred to the decision of this court in *R v Novac* (1976) 65 Cr App Rep 107. There the court was concerned with the topic we have to consider in the present case, namely, the question of severance. A number of defendants each faced a conspiracy count and counts alleging specific offences, and one defendant, Raywood, applied for the specific offence count against him to be severed from the conspiracy count. The application was refused but his appeal succeeded on the basis that the application ought to have been allowed, and Bridge LJ giving the judgment of the court, continued at p 112:

> 'It is surprising that no application similar to that made on behalf of Raywood should have been made on behalf of Novac or Andrew-Cohen to sever the specific offence counts against them. [Counsel] for Novac told us that he thought it pointless to make such an application after the application on behalf of Raywood had been refused. But we can see no basis which would have justified him in assuming that the one application must necessarily be determined in the same way as the other. It was for him to make an application to sever on his own client's behalf if thought appropriate. *No such application having been made there can be no basis for complaint in this court that the conspiracy and related counts were heard together in Novac's case with the specific offence counts.*' (Our emphasis).

In *Novac* the court does not seem to have considered it necessary to inquire whether counsel in refraining from making an application to sever acted with or without the express authority of his client, no doubt because generally speaking this court will always proceed upon the basis that what counsel does is done with the authority of the client who has instructed counsel to conduct his case.

In *R v Gaultam*, (1987) Times, 4 March, which was decided by this court on 27 February 1987, a few days after the appeal in *R v Irwin* had been heard, Taylor J said:

'It should be clearly understood that if defending counsel in the course of his conduct of the case makes a decision, or takes a course which later appears to have been mistaken or unwise, that generally speaking has never been regarded as a proper ground for an appeal.'

That was a shoplifting case in which counsel, for what were patently good reasons, had declined to lead medical evidence at the trial until after the jury had returned a verdict.

On 12 March 1987 another division of this court heard the appeal of Alan John Swain who contended, with apparent justification, that his counsel, by incompetent cross-examination, had introduced evidence which was prejudicial to his case, which was then amplified by the witness in answer to a question put to him by the judge. In an attempt to circumvent the difficulties which he faced arising out of what was said in *R v Gaultam*, counsel at the hearing of the appeal sought to rely mainly on the intervention of the judge, but the court found that what was said in answer to the judge added nothing to what had already been said by the witness to counsel. Various other points were considered with which we need not now be concerned, but O'Connor LJ, giving the judgment of the court, said that, if the court had any lurking doubt that the appellant might have suffered some injustice as a result of flagrantly incompetent advocacy by his advocate, then it would quash the convictions, but in that particular case it had no such doubts.

We consider the correct approach to be that which was indicated by this court in *R v Gaultam* subject only to the qualification to which O'Connor LJ referred in *R v Swain* (unreported). We consider further that the decision in *R v Irwin* [1987] 1 WLR 902, even if it can be reconciled with *R v Novac* – which we doubt – should be regarded as being confined to its own facts. This ground of appeal accordingly fails, because counsel's carefully considered decision not to apply to sever the charges, even if erroneous, cannot possibly be described as incompetent, let alone flagrantly incompetent, advocacy.

[5:8] **Malleson, K** *Review of the Appeal Process* RCCJ Research Study No 17 (1993) HMSO (at page 38):

Taken together the findings from these two comparative studies indicate that when compared with legally assisted applications unassisted applications are:
(i) Poorly presented and ill-informed.
(ii) More frequently based on substantive issues concerning the justice of their conviction rather than technical or legal grounds.

(iii) More commonly based on the alleged errors of counsel as grounds for appeal despite the fact that the Court will very rarely hear such an appeal.
(iv) Dealt with in very brief judgments by the single judge and the full Court.
(v) Very unlikely to be granted leave to appeal.

The findings of this research lend support to the concern that unassisted applications are at a disadvantage in the appeal system so that there may be cases with merit which are not identified. Without a detailed study of a large number of individual unassisted cases it is difficult to estimate how many cases with merit are wrongly weeded out by the present 'two tier' system and how best they could in future be identified.

In addition to concern about the nature and treatment of unassisted applications which enter the system, this research highlights the danger that there may be meritorious cases without legal support which do not enter the system in the first place. An unknown number of unassisted convicted persons whose cases have merit may be deterred from appealing because they are aware that unassisted applications are very rarely successful and because they believe that they will serve a longer sentence if their application fails despite the fact that the single judge and the full Court very rarely apply the time loss rules.

Recommendations

Appellants should have a right to legal assistance in presenting an application for leave to appeal for consideration by the single judge and renewing a refused application to the full court.

The findings of the research are such that consideration should be given as to whether the present 'two tier' system needs to be reformed. It is accepted as a basic principle of justice that persons accused of serious offences with limited resources should have legal assistance to defend themselves however weak that defence may be in the view of their legal advisers. We do not expect counsel to decline to present a person's defence in Court because he has determined that it is unlikely to succeed. On this principle we should expect that each convicted person has a similar right to assistance in preparing and presenting an appeal. Just as an accused person instructs his or her solicitor on a defence or provides information for mitigation in a guilty plea so a convicted person should, if he or she wishes, after receiving legal advice, instruct a solicitor in the preparation of an appeal. Counsel may advise that the grounds will be unlikely to succeed, but that decision should be for the single judge alone.

Under the present system an appellant with a meritorious case but without legal assistance must have substantial financial, intellectual, and psychological resources if their appeal is to succeed. If they are in custody, they are particularly reliant on the support and goodwill of others outside. This means that people with limited abilities and resources, such as mentally disordered or handicapped people, young people, or those whose spoken or written English is poor are most disadvantaged. These are also the people who, as miscarriages of justice cases over the years have highlighted, are most likely to be the victims of injustice in the legal system and thus may have most need of the appeal system. The right to legal assistance on appeal would particularly help these vulnerable groups.

If the single judge was retained, this change would not amount to the introduction of a right to appeal, but rather a right to legal assistance in preparing an application for leave to appeal. If all applications were drafted by counsel and submitted by solicitors we could be confident that they would be judged equally on their merits alone.

This reform should not add any great cost to the legal aid bill because the overall numbers affected would be relatively small. Under the present system counsel must advise on appeal, and will draft grounds of appeal in many cases. The change would only affect those few cases where counsel has not provided advice on appeal or advises against appealing where the convicted person still wishes to appeal and requests that grounds be drafted on his or her behalf. While the cost of this change would be small, the potential benefit would be great in that the appeal system would be seen to be more open, accessible and fair at a time when its public credibility is at a particularly low point.

[See also extract at **[9:5]**]

[5:9]   Plotnikoff, J and Woolfson, R *Information and Advice for Prisoners about Grounds for Appeal and the Appeal Process* RCCJ Research Study No 18 (1993) HMSO (at page 115):

This chapter discusses the results of the research and proposes some changes at improving the quality of advice and information provided to potential appellants in custody. The objective of these is to specify the commitment on the part of the legal profession and the prisons to providing a defined level of service to inmates and to ensure that the nature of the service is made known to all.

With one exception, none of the recommendations made lends itself to a simple costing exercise and this has not been attempted.

The legal profession

The nature and extent of the service provided to clients by lawyers in the 28 days following conviction or sentence are very variable. There is widespread ignorance both of some aspects of the law on appeal and of the guidelines to good practice on the responsibilities of legal advisers during this period. The first findings and recommendations relate to the guidelines themselves.

The Bar GGP[3], Law Society GGP[4] and CACD Guide[5] are inconsistent and contain a number of omissions. Specific areas where inconsistencies occur are the length of time that counsel should take to provide written grounds to the solicitor and the powers that exist to order loss of time in the case of frivolous appeals. None of the guidance documents currently reflects both the legal position relating to loss of time and the actual practice in recent years. The Law Society GGP wrongly states that the maximum that

---

3   *The Crown Court Guide – A Guide to Good Practice* General Council of the Bar.
4   *The Crown Court Guide – A Guide to Good Practice* The Law Society.
5   *A Guide to Proceedings in the Court of Appeal Criminal Division* pronounced by the Criminal Appeals Office.

can be forfeited is 90 days and omits to mention that the single judge as well as the full Court has the power to issue such an order. None of the documents reflects the infrequency of time loss awards or that the maximum lost in recent years is 28 days.

Over half the solicitors who responded were unaware that the CACD cannot impose a sentence of greater severity than that awarded by the Crown Court. The legal position is not mentioned in any of the guides.

The CACD Guide stipulates that immediately after the conclusion of the case a client should be given a written note of counsel's view, even if this is only provisional, on the advisability of an appeal. Such a note does not constitute written advice but it does provide the client with a record of counsel's view, however provisional, on the advisability of an appeal. This is not mentioned in either the Bar GGP or the Law Society GGP. Responses to the questionnaires sent out during the study revealed that 89% of solicitors and 99% of counsel never hand over anything written at this meeting. No-one did so as a matter of course.

The Law Society GGP makes no mention of including in the brief to counsel a request to furnish written advice on appeal in the event of a conviction. When solicitors were asked whether counsel provide signed grounds without being specifically asked to do so, only 22% said they always did so. Eight per cent said this never happens.

The duty of solicitors to provide advice and keep clients and their families informed is interpreted in differing ways. One quarter of prisoners said they received no appeals advice from their lawyers at any point during the 28 days following conviction or sentence. Only 39% of inmates claimed to have received appeals advice from a lawyer since coming to prison. This situation may be due, at least in part, to confusion over exactly what costs can reasonably be claimed under the trial legal aid order, an issue not covered in any of the guideline documents. Twenty per cent of solicitors said that they do not charge at all for work done in this period and over a third who do charge said that they had had payments refused or reduced.

Recommendation 1: The appeals sections in The Law Society and Bar Guides to Good Practice produced by the Standing Commission on Efficiency and the Guide to Proceedings in the Court of Appeal Criminal Division need to be revised. The revision process should be co-ordinated to ensure that the recommendations in these documents are harmonised.

The following specific areas need to be addressed during this exercise:
(i) whether it is realistic to expect the solicitor to be present at call visits at court following conclusion of the case and, if not, the consequences that flow from delegation of this duty to a representative
(ii) the completion and handing over at the end of the case of the form at Appendix 1 in the CACD Guide, indicating counsel's view on the advisability of appeal
(iii) the time limit within which counsel should provide the professional client with written advice on the advisability of an appeal and, where appropriate, signed grounds
(iv) the time limit within a copy of counsel's opinion should be forwarded to the client
(v) the rules and practice relating to loss of time orders
(vi) the activities and costs, including prison visits, relating to advice and assistance on appeals that it is reasonable to fund under the trial legal aid order.

None of the guides contains any provision for the specific problems of clients who do not speak English. Thirty-nine per cent of solicitors and 23% of barristers indicated in their responses that they did not feel able to provide an adequate service to such clients. The following recommendation is a first step towards improving the situation.

Recommendation 2: All forms and written guidance relating to the appeals process should be translated into other languages. The solicitor should include in the brief to counsel a copy of the check-off from Appendix 1 both in English and in the first language of the client where this is different. Counsel should complete both forms at the conclusion of the case. This practice should be included in the guidance documents.

Although many clients are visited in the cells at court immediately following the case, there is no absolute right to such a visit. Both lawyers and prisoners complained of the consultation being cut short by prison or police authorities keen to transport the convicted person to prison. The defendant is often confused and in a state of shock or distress at this time, it may be the last meeting between lawyer and client and time must be made available to allow a written note on counsel's view of an appeal to be handed over and explained.

Recommendation 3: Convicted or sentenced defendants who are legally represented should have a right to a 15 minute meeting with their lawyers at Crown Court following the end of the case for the purpose of discussing counsel's opinion of prospects for an appeal.

Revision of policy documents can only play a limited part in rectifying practices that deny convicted defendants full access to the appeals process. Only through a process of education can there be any real expectation that best practice will become standard practice. For many criminal practitioners, proceeding with an appeal is a relatively infrequent occurrence. Nevertheless, initial procedures relating to provision of advice on appeals apply to all cases that result in a conviction and should form part of the continuing education for lawyers in criminal practice.

Recommendation 4: The Law Society and the Bar Council should take steps to ensure that the guidance they provide on good practice is reflected in the programmes of continuing education for legal practitioners and their representatives working on criminal cases.

CHAPTER SIX

Magistrates

One of the most surprising aspects of the English criminal justice system is the vast role given to lay magistrates. Questions of both guilt and sentence in about 98% of all criminal prosecutions are decided by magistrates.

Number of offenders sentenced in the magistrates' courts

1993	1,357,800
1997	1,860,000
2001	1,280,000

Source: Criminal Statistics 1993, 1997, 2001, paragraph 7.18 (Cm 5696)

The bulk of these prosecutions were for purely summary offences, which can only be tried in a magistrates' court, and include many minor motoring offences (though not the most minor, which are dealt with by fixed penalty notices issued by the police). The remainder (20% in 2001) were offences triable either way, which may be tried either in a magistrates' court or in the Crown Court. Even in a case such as Gerry Good's, where he will eventually be tried before a jury, some key decisions are taken in the magistrates' court. Magistrates' justice is cheap and relatively fast – but is amateur justice fair? This question is all the more important given the general shift towards transferring more cases to the magistrates' courts. It is also important to note the increasing use of legally qualified stipendiary magistrates, now known as district judges (magistrates' courts), who sit alone. Is this fairer than a tribunal of lay magistrates? How can we tell?

(i) Role of the lay magistracy

The almost 30,000 lay magistrates in England and Wales sit in magistrates' courts, co-ordinated under 96 Magistrates' Courts Committees (MCCs). Until

1992 the Home Office controlled the organisation of magistrates' courts, whilst the Lord Chancellor appointed and dismissed magistrates. This inconsistency led to the transfer of the management of magistrates' courts to the Lord Chancellor's Department. Meanwhile, new funding arrangements were introduced, putting cash limits on all courts, in effect penalising those that failed to process cases speedily enough. The reorganisation of MCCs proposed in the White Paper *A New Framework for Local Justice* was achieved in the Police and Magistrates' Courts Act 1994. Section 69 gave the Lord Chancellor the power to replace two or more MCCs with a single MCC. Local MCCs, with a Justices' Chief Executive as chief administrative officer, manage the courts, and the pressure seems to be on them to reduce the numbers both of courts and of MCCs. The Access to Justice Act 1999 added more flexibility to the rules, allowing alteration of the various territorial units that make up the magistrates' courts service and allowing summary cases to be heard outside the commission area in which they arose.

Now more change is afoot: the Courts Bill 2002 imposes on the Lord Chancellor a duty to ensure 'an efficient and effective' system to support the courts. The Bill is short on detail (most changes will be made by delegated legislation) but it is clear that the new Court Administration Councils will centralise the organisation of the courts. It replaces commission areas and petty session areas with local justice areas. In the future, the Lord Chancellor will not only appoint and dismiss magistrates, but he will also give directions as to places at which magistrates' courts may sit and as to the distribution of court business. He will specify local justice areas and may make orders altering them. Lord Justice Auld [1:5] recognised the importance of local justice and indeed suggested (at page 272) that 'all members of the judiciary, whether lay or professional, should be brought within the responsibility of the local Resident Judge and the judicial hierarchy of which he is part'. He pointed out the difficulty of identifying what precisely it is that is to be valued in 'local justice': he distinguishes geographical locality from the locality of those dispensing justice. These issues are explored in depth by Seago et al [6:1] in their research into the expanded use of district judges. Morgan [6:2] argues for greater use of lay magistrates in the criminal justice process.

Will the Court Administration Councils create regional bureaucracies, too large to be adequately responsive to local needs? Already the managerialist and cost-cutting priorities of the Magistrates' Courts Inspectorate have led to concerns that the magistrates' courts are so 'managed' that justice and due process become poor relations to economy. Does it matter if the magistracy is becoming less of a 'local' body?

Lay magistrates are appointed by the Lord Chancellor from names submitted by local advisory committees. Until 1992 the names of those on the committees were usually kept secret, but now they are published. Most are senior or recently retired magistrates, themselves appointed by the Lord Chancellor. Following the recommendations of the Home Affairs Select Committee on

Judicial Appointments (1996), the Lord Chancellor revised the procedures for appointing lay magistrates. The changes, in the form of a Direction to Advisory Committees in 1998, should result in a more standardised approach to the appointment of magistrates. At present, magistrates have to live within 15 miles of their commission area, and they have no jurisdiction outside that area. Thus, if they move to another part of the country, they cannot automatically arrange to sit on another bench (this will change with the enactment of the Courts Bill 2002). They have to retire at 70. They may be dismissed by the Lord Chancellor, who, controversially, does not have to give reasons for a dismissal. In 1986 Kathleen Cripps, a Derbyshire magistrate, unsuccessfully sought judicial review of the Lord Chancellor's decision to dismiss her after she had demonstrated on behalf of CND (the Campaign for Nuclear Disarmament) outside her courthouse.

The key characteristics of the lay magistracy are that they are unpaid and non-lawyers. Nowadays, they receive expenses, but the possibility of lost earnings inevitably deters many potential applicants. A magistrate is expected to sit for 26 days a year, normally on a bench of three. For the self-employed this is a hefty commitment, and for those in employment, job and promotion prospects, as well as pay, may suffer. It is not surprising that the social balance of the bench is often criticised. A classic account of the merits of the lay magistracy is provided by Skyrme [6:3]. It is worth comparing his analysis with, for example, the more critical approach of Gifford (1986), who recommended a much more proactive search for magistrates, and suggested that magistrates should only serve limited terms of office in order that they should not become case-hardened. Unfortunately he did not attempt to evaluate the financial implications of his recommendations. Darbyshire (1997) is critical of the class, political, ethnicity and age profile of the magistracy.

Since 1966 magistrates have had to attend compulsory training courses on law and procedure, and on how to act judicially, but these courses are necessarily brief. During their time as magistrates they will also attend sentencing conferences and undergo continuing training of twelve hours every three years. But to criticise them because they are not trained is to miss the point: they are chosen as lay people, and advised on the law by a professional clerk.

Most of the magistrates' work is done in open court, though they may sign arrest and search warrants and emergency protection orders at home. They also issue licences to sell alcohol and have a role in family law, sitting in the Family Proceedings Court, dealing with maintenance, residence and contact orders, as well as questions concerning children in need of care. Criminal cases involving children (under 14) and young persons (14–17 inclusive) are normally dealt with in the Youth Court, where hearings are in private and should be more informal than those before the adult court. There must be at least one magistrate of each sex sitting on the panel of three in the Youth Court. They exercise very different sentencing powers from those available in the adult court.

A significant recent development has been the increasing number of district judges (or stipendiary magistrates as they were known until 1999). 'Stipes', as they are still sometimes colloquially known, are qualified lawyers, who must have a seven-year general qualification (ie have held rights of audience in relation to any class of proceedings for at least seven years).

Numbers of district judges (magistrates' courts) and stipendiary magistrates

1990   64 stipendiaries (48 of them in London)
1994   78 full-time stipendiaries (supported by 90 acting stipendiaries)
1998   78 full-time stipendiaries (supported by 90 acting stipendiaries)
2003   105 DJ (MC) and 150 Deputies

District judges sit alone. Although in theory they share the workload with lay magistrates, in practice they will hear cases that are likely to last more than one day or which involve difficult points of law. Both Metropolitan district judges, sitting in London, and provincial District judges, who may preside in courts over a wide area, are likely to wield a strong influence in their courts. This was encouraged in both the Royal Commission (1993) – which suggested (at page 142) a 'more systematic approach' to the role of stipendiary magistrates, and their deployment on a slightly wider scale – and in the Police and Magistrates' Courts Act 1994, which provides in section 72 that 'the chief Metropolitan stipendiary magistrate shall by virtue of his office be the chairman of any magistrates' courts committee for an area which consists of or includes the whole of the inner London area'. As Rozenburg (1994) pointed out, 'Elsewhere in our criminal justice system the initial finding of guilt or innocence is made by ordinary people – juries or magistrates. But a stipendiary magistrate decides the facts as well as the law: he or she is given less pay than a circuit judge for more responsibility. Any move towards the greater use of stipendiaries should be resisted' (at page 341).

District judges are also more likely to become case-hardened and judicially 'burnt out' than lay magistrates. The Lord Chancellor set up a working party in 1994 to produce guidelines identifying more clearly the respective roles of district judges and the lay bench. Narey (1997), whilst noting that stipendiaries were 'vastly more effective' in managing the parties in any given case, rejected the possibility of a substantial increase in the number or proportion of stipes. The most recent detailed research on magistrates is Morgan and Russell's 2000 report **[6:4]**, commissioned on behalf of the Lord Chancellor's Department and Home Office to explore the relationship between law and professional magistrates. Do you agree with their emphasis on the importance of 'active citizens in an active community'? This report clearly influenced Auld [1:5] in his recommendation that magistrates and district judges should continue to exercise their established summary jurisdiction. The student of the magistrates' courts should, however, watch closely the evolving relationship between professional and lay magistrates.

The justices' clerk, a barrister or solicitor of not less than five years standing, also has a somewhat ambiguous role. Under the Justices of the Peace Act 1968, their role is to provide legal advice to lay magistrates and to manage the courts. Since the line between advice and instruction is a thin one, it is difficult to measure whether clerks overstep their purely advisory role. Clerks should, for example, advise on the admissibility of evidence (a question of law) but not on the credibility of a witness (a question of fact). They should advise on appropriate sentences but not on the actual sentence. In recent years, they have also been granted more administrative powers: Narey (1997) went so far as to suggest that the presumption should be that cases should not be put before magistrates until they are ready to proceed. As this administrative role grows, there are concerns that justice's clerks may start to usurp the proper role of the magistrates. In their management role, the clerks already have a great influence, since they control the listing of cases. The post of justices' chief executive was introduced in 1994 and every MCC has appointed one to manage its area. The Access to Justice Act 1999 removed the requirement for justice's chief executives to be qualified lawyers, and transferred responsibility for certain administrative functions from justices' clerks to justices' chief executives. Does this cause you any concern?

Riley and Vennard [6:5] suggested that defendants have less faith in the magistrates' courts than they do in jury trials. Even the supposed cost advantages need to be properly evaluated. Of course, minor offences should be processed quickly, cheaply and uniformly. Thus, few object to fixed penalties for minor motoring offences. However, more serious offences such as assault occasioning actual bodily harm and criminal damage up to a value of £5,000 are now triable only by magistrates. Is the line between summary jurisdiction and trials on indictment drawn in the right place? Do you think that Auld's recommendation of a third, intermediate, tier (a judge and two lay magistrates) should have been explored further?

(ii) Legal aid decisions

We saw in Chapter Two how all suspects in a police station are entitled to free legal advice. The same is not true in the magistrates' courts. Duty solicitor schemes in magistrates' courts exist, but within tight constraints, funded under either the Advice and Assistance or the Advocacy Assistance rules of the Criminal Defence Service. A duty solicitor may not give advice on a not guilty plea: this is provided instead under the legal representation scheme. Nor is the duty solicitor scheme applicable in most non-imprisonable offences, ie minor offences.

Thus, in our case, Gerry Good will have completed a form and the solicitor will send it on to his local magistrates' court. What criteria do court staff apply in deciding whether an applicant requires financial assistance in meeting the costs of his case? There is no longer a means test, but at the end of the trial the judge may issue a Recovery of Defence Costs order, depending on the defendant's means. The merits test, or 'interests of justice' test, is still based on the so-called 'Widgery criteria' laid down by a committee chaired by the then Lord Chief Justice, Lord Widgery in 1966. These criteria are complex and imprecise. Factors to be taken into account in deciding 'the interests of justice' include: the likelihood of a custodial sentence; the legal difficulty of the case; the defendant's ability to understand the proceedings; and the nature of the defence case. If these criteria are adequate, do the courts take them seriously in considering applications? Only about 5% of those tried for summary offences in the magistrates' courts are legally aided, a figure which rises to 71% for those charged with either-way offences, and 94% of those tried in the Crown Court (and 82% of those appearing for sentence in the Crown Court) were legally aided in 2001. Over 78% of those before the Youth Court obtained legal aid (Source: Judicial Statistics, 2001). A greater cause for concern than national statistics may be, as with the granting of bail applications (see below), regional variations in the granting of legal aid.

Where court clerks refuse to make an order, they will give reasons and defendants can renew their application. On a renewed application, the clerk must either grant it or refer it to the magistrates. In the case of a summary offence, the defendant may make a further application – as the court has power to grant legal representation at any stage of the proceedings – or may seek judicial review in the High Court; but neither course is likely to be successful.

(iii) Bail decisions

Since the accused is presumed innocent until proved guilty, it is hardly surprising that under the provisions of the Bail Act 1976 **[6:6]** there is a general right to bail. As Raifeartaigh (1997) puts it, 'the presumption of innocence forbids liberty depriving measures which are premised on the view that the accused is guilty of a crime unless he has been duly convicted by a court of that offence' (at page 18). Does the Bail Act 1976 pass this test? The Criminal Justice and Public Order Act 1994 curtailed the right to bail by introducing two exceptions. Under section 25, a person charged with, or convicted of, murder or attempted murder, rape or attempted rape, or manslaughter, was to be automatically remanded in custody if they had previous convictions for any of those offences. Similarly, under section 26, those accused or convicted of an indictable offence, or one triable either way which appeared to have been committed when the defendant was on bail, 'need not' be granted bail. Imprisonment without trial sits uncomfortably alongside the presumption of innocence, and the European Court of Human Rights found in *Caballero v United Kingdom* (2000) 30 EHRR 643 (followed in *SBC v United Kingdom* (2001) 34 EHRR 619) that the automatic denial of bail was an infringement of the European Convention on Human Rights, art 5 [1:9]. Meanwhile, the government had already anticipated this finding: section 25 was amended by the Crime and Disorder Act 1998, s 56, and bail may now be granted 'in exceptional circumstances'.

However, the reality is that many suspects are indeed existing offenders and cannot responsibly be left in the community pending their trial. The right of the public to protection and the rights of the suspect thus clash dramatically.

Numbers of remand prisoners

	Average remand population in prisons
1992	10,100
1998	12,600 (higher than ever before)
2000	11,270 (a 10% decrease from the year before)

Source: Prison Statistics 1998, 2001

Conditions in remand prisons are some of the worst in British prisons, and some 15 year-olds may find themselves in Prison Service custody because of the shortage of local authority secure accommodation. The thematic review of conditions for unsentenced prisoners, carried out by HM Chief Inspector of Prisons [6:7], makes uncomfortable reading. The extract here covers simply the strategic issues and recommendations, but the whole report is worth reading. It reminds readers of the miserable conditions for many remand prisoners, of the enormous social and economic dislocation caused by a period of imprisonment. For example, 41% of unsentenced women are held more than 50 miles from home. This figure rises to 44% for young women. Before custody, one-third of men and one-quarter of women had been in employment, but only 18% of men and 11% of women expected to have a job to go to on release.

As a group, remand prisoners tend to be anxious, socially isolated, victimised and disturbed. Particularly shocking are the results of two surveys: one sent to the governors/directors of the 53 prisons holding unsentenced prisoners, the other the results of questionnaires completed by 711 prisoners. There was a clear mismatch between the facilities that governors believed they were providing and what prisoners claimed to be their actual experience. For example, according to the governors' survey, outside exercise was available in most prisons (81%) for a period of about an hour every day. However, the prisoner survey showed that over one-third of young prisoners and 17% of adults had no outside exercise at all, and only just over one-third had anything approaching the figure that was quoted in the governors' survey. Governors of all but one prison were confident that a set of legal reference books was available for the use of remand prisoners, but only 11% of men and 12% of women prisoners said they had such access. Fewer than half of the 63% of prisoners who wanted to see a bail information or legal services officer, had in fact been able to do so.

Could more of these people have been safely left in the community? Two contrasting figures should be looked at: offending rates by those on bail; and the acquittal rate of those who have been remanded in custody. Morgan (1992) showed the difficulties involved in assessing the rates of offending while on bail, though the proportion of defendants convicted of offences committed whilst on bail is about 10–12%. The acquittal rate of those who have been remanded in custody has been remarkably constant over the last few years: 23% for men and 21% women (this figure includes those whose cases are not proceeded with); another one-fifth receive community sentences, and a further one-fifth of men and one-third of women remand prisoners receive a fine, discharge or other non-custodial sentence.

Percentage of remand prisoners who ultimately receive a custodial sentence

	Men	Women
1992	41	26
1998	46	33
2000	48	36

Source: Prison Statistics 1992, 1998, 2000

Schedule 1 of the Bail Act 1976 **[6:6]** provides three grounds for refusing bail – where the court has substantial grounds for believing that if a defendant were remanded on bail, they would: (i) fail to surrender to custody; (ii) commit an offence while on bail; or (iii) interfere with witnesses or otherwise obstruct the course of justice. All turn on questions of predicting risk.

Let us apply the test to Gerry Good. How can we know if he will turn up for trial, or whether he will commit an offence while on bail? He has a criminal record, but he is meant to be presumed innocent of his present offence until proved guilty. Are magistrates adequately equipped to evaluate dangerousness? We noted in Chapter Three the lack of information available to the courts in deciding bail applications. In the early 1990s, there were significant efforts to improve the quality of this information. In 1992 Lloyd **[6:8]** analysed the impact of various bail information schemes and tried to assess whether such information is best presented to the court direct, or via the CPS or defence solicitors. Morgan and Henderson [6.9] reported on the Bail Process Project, set up in 1992 in five court areas to improve the quality of information available to magistrates. Their conclusion that reducing waiting times for trials would reduce the rate of offending on bail can have come as no surprise! Yet, as we saw in [3:8], funding cuts have meant that much less is being done.

A key question is whether it is just to remand someone in custody because of a statistical risk that they will re-offend. Eaton [6:10] usefully pointed out the added hurdle faced by women who are not tied into typical family models: they are less likely to be granted bail. Her conclusion was stark: 'In applications for bail, we have more than a description of an acceptable model of the family and its associated gender roles: we have an acknowledgement that such a family structure may offer a form of control comparable to that offered by the prison system'. Worrall [6:11] developed this analysis of women as 'socially constructed within the discourses of domesticity, sexuality and pathology' when she contrasted the attitudes of women magistrates to women defendants with the attitudes of their male colleagues on the bench. With regard to magistrates' treatment of defendants from different ethnic groups, Brown and Hullin (1993) studied contested bail applications in Leeds in 1989 and did not uncover any significant differences in treatment.

In Gerry Good's case, the bail application lasts less than 20 minutes. The magistrates grant him bail subject to two conditions: one that he does not go within 500 yards of the Black Bull public house, and the second that he reports to the police station three times a week. They lecture him on the need to avoid his victim, and their decision is clearly influenced by the fact that they are convinced by his solicitor, Mary Chapman, that he has a permanent home. The Probation Service has an important role in ensuring that the court is provided with information about places in bail hostels and other supervised lodging arrangements: see Chapter Ten. Where the magistrates are doubtful about releasing a defendant on bail, they may attach conditions, or require security or sureties. Hucklesby (1994) explored the inconsistent use of conditional bail by magistrates. Security involves the deposit of a thing of value, normally a passport, to stop someone leaving the country. Sureties are people who know the defendant and are prepared to put up a sum of money, a recognisance, against the risk that the defendant will fail to appear. Doubts whether it is just to put this pressure on families and friends to act as informal janitors means that sureties are asked for rarely in English courts, and they do not pay the money over in advance. (However, this did not stop the government making parents liable for their children's fines in the Criminal Justice Act 1991). Motivated by a desire to reduce the number of adjournments in criminal proceedings, the government introduced three measures in the Crime and Disorder Act 1998, which may result in the increased use of sureties:

(i) section 54(1) enables the police and the courts to require a surety in any case where it is believed that the deposit of a security will 'increase the likelihood of a bailed defendant appearing in court when required'. Thus, the court may take the view that an up-front payment, in the form of a surety, will be more effective in securing the defendant's attendance than the availability of a surety with the means to enter into a recognisance for a more substantial sum;

(ii) section 54(2) introduces a new power to require a defendant, as a condition of bail, to seek an interview with a legal representative. This addressed the concern that many adjournments are granted simply for the purpose of sorting out legal representation; and

(iii) section 55 strengthens existing procedures for the forfeiture of recognisances in bail cases to encourage sureties to make greater efforts to ensure that the defendant appears in court.

It is perhaps surprising that it was not until the Bail (Amendment) Act 1993 **[6:12]**, which came into force in 1994, that the prosecution first gained a right of appeal where a court granted bail to someone charged with a serious offence. CJPOA 1994, s 30 also strengthened the courts' powers to reconsider a bail decision at any time in indictable cases if information comes to light that was not available to the police or the court when the original bail decision was taken. Ashworth (1998, at page 239) suggests other basic improvements to the bail application process, such as the development of bail guidelines for magistrates to apply.

Under the Magistrates' Courts Act 1980, s 128 a magistrates' court has power to remand a defendant in custody for up to eight days in the first instance, but thereafter may remand them for up to 28 days, provided that the defendant is present in court and has previously been remanded for the same offence. On conviction but pending appeal, the offender may apply for bail. Reproduced at **[6:13]** is the Practice Direction: Bail Pending Appeal. Whether a person should be kept in custody pending an appeal against conviction, or indeed between conviction and the time sentence is passed, raises similar questions to those discussed above.

(iv) Mode of trial

Indictable offences are tried by judge and jury in the Crown Court; summary offences in the magistrates' court. For the last 20 years, in cases involving either-way offences, the venue for trial was determined following a procedure laid down by the Magistrates' Courts Act 1980, ss 19, 20. If the magistrates decided that the case was suitable to be dealt with summarily, they informed the defendant that they might either consent to be tried in the magistrates' court or elect to be tried before a jury. The list of offences which are triable either way is hardly logical. For example, defendants can elect jury trial if they are found with a small amount of cannabis, or are charged with minor shoplifting, whereas the more serious offence of assaulting a police officer can only be tried summarily. The categorisation of offences makes sense only if one looks at the nineteenth-century origins of much of the criminal law, and the piecemeal way in which some offences have been re-classified downwards in recent years in order to avoid the costs of trial by jury. National Mode of Trial Guidelines, designed to help magistrates decide whether to commit a case for trial, were issued in 1990 by the Lord Chief Justice, and have been revised by the Criminal Justice Consultative Council. The Home Office consultation paper *Determining Mode of Trial in Either-Way Cases*, published in July 1998, laid the ground for the Home Secretary's announcement in May 1999 that magistrates, rather than defendants, should decide whether an either-way case should go to jury trial. In 1999 the government introduced the Criminal Justice (Mode Of Trial) Bill in the House of Lords, which sought to remove defendants' rights to choose trial by jury, but this was defeated. The government, undeterred, reintroduced the Bill in the House of Commons but was met by a similar revolt. Once the Criminal Justice Bill 2002 becomes law, magistrates deciding on mode of trial will be told of a defendant's previous convictions.

Hedderman and Moxon's research [5:6] showed that magistrates sent for trial a large number of cases that they could have tried themselves, and that defendants often opt for trial on the basis that they are going to plead not guilty, but then end up pleading guilty. Riley and Vennard [6:5] stressed the need to examine magistrates' reasons for declining to hear a case. At the time of that research, magistrates had no knowledge of defendants' circumstances or previous convictions in making their decision. Riley and Vennard found that magistrates only disagreed with the prosecutor's proposal that the case was suitable for summary trial in 23 out of 663 cases. The Royal Commission on Criminal Justice (1993) looked at the position in Scotland, where the mode of trial decision rests with the prosecuting authority, but concluded that this would not be acceptable in England, at least for the time being. It recommended that, if the prosecution and defence could reach agreement on the mode of trial, that should be legally binding. If they are unable to agree, the decision should remain with the court. It proposed that a defendant's right to elect trial by jury should be abolished: in effect, a dramatic way of making more offences triable only by magistrates. Narey (1997) agreed, concluding that magistrates would be well able to distinguish those defendants who, because of potential loss of reputation or for other reasons, were justified in seeking a Crown Court hearing. Auld [1:5] considered that it might be more appropriate for district judges to make the allocation decision. A decision on whether Parliament's fierce offensive on the defendant's right to elect jury trial is well placed must wait until Chapter Eight.

(v) Pre-trial hearings

It is important that weak cases be filtered out. Until 1967, all cases to be tried by jury went through a preliminary hearing in the magistrates' court (committal proceedings) where the magistrates took oral evidence to decide whether the prosecution had made out a *prima facie* case. From 1967 the vast majority of cases were dealt with as 'paper committals'. Where an accused person was legally represented, magistrates' courts could, with defendants' agreement, commit for trial to the Crown Court without any consideration of the evidence. In other cases, the court examined the strength of the evidence and decided whether it warranted committal for trial. However, the CJPOA 1994 sought to abolish committal proceedings: the prosecution was now simply to give a notice of transfer to the defendant and to the court, and unless the defendant applied to have the case dismissed, the notice of transfer would take effect automatically. These provisions, which were hastily added to the Bill, proved unworkable and were never brought into force. Narey (1997) concluded that indictable-only cases should start their life in the Crown Court rather than spending half their life in the magistrates' courts, and this was enacted in the Crime and Disorder Act 1998, s 51 **[2:21]**. Offenders charged with indictable offences will now be 'sent' to the Crown Court for trial. How are weak cases to be filtered out? Defendants may apply for the dismissal of any charge at any time before they are arraigned (see Schedule 3 to the Act).

Meanwhile, the Criminal Procedure and Investigations Act 1996 introduced a new 'plea before venue' system, which means that defendants who intend to plead guilty to either-way offences are automatically dealt with summarily. Since sentences imposed by magistrates are significantly less severe (see **[5:6]**), this must seem unproblematic for those who wish to take the benefit of this, and of the discount for guilty pleas. But it puts further pressure to plead guilty on those who genuinely wish to contest their guilt, and who have not yet seen or heard the prosecution case against them. It has also resulted in an extraordinary increase in the number of people committed by magistrates for sentence in the Crown Court.

An important function of committal proceedings used to be that it gave the defendant a preview of the case against him. The Magistrates' Courts (Advance Information) Rules 1985 (SI 1985/601) required the prosecution to disclose a summary of the case in either-way cases. Because these summaries were often inadequate, or even misleading, in the 1990s it became standard practice to disclose all witness statements. The position was revolutionised by the Criminal Procedure and Investigations Act 1996. The police now have a 'primary' duty to disclose to the defence only such prosecution material which 'in the prosecutor's opinion might undermine the case for the prosecution'. The defence then has a duty to disclose a statement of the defence, including the reasons why the defence takes issue with the prosecution case. Secondary prosecution disclosure should then reveal material 'which might be reasonably expected to assist the accused's defence'. There is clearly a huge danger where the primary duty of the prosecution is so subjective, and where adverse inferences may be drawn where the defence fails to disclose a line of defence or changes tack at trial (see section 11). The Criminal Justice Bill 2002 in Part V seeks to make the test for primary prosecution an objective one, and will also require more to be included in defence statements. The issue of disclosure in our adversarial system inevitably remains a thorny and difficult area of law.

(vi)   Trial and sentencing

In summary trials, if the defendant appears, the court clerk will read out the charge(s) and ask the defendant whether he pleads guilty or not guilty. If the defendant pleads guilty, the court may convict him without hearing the evidence.

Proportion of defendants in magistrates' courts pleading guilty

	Either-way offences	Summary non-motoring offences	Summary motoring offences
1985	65%	70%	76%
1992	48%	52%	61%
1997	50%	47%	57%
1998	54%	45%	59%
2000	54%	42%	54%

Source: Criminal Statistics 1997, 2001, Table 6.4

In the early 1990s, as more defendants made use of their right to plead not guilty, so greater pressures were put on them to plead guilty, thus further undermining due process safeguards. If a defendant pleads not guilty, the magistrates will hear the evidence from both parties, and either convict the defendant or dismiss the case. Many researchers have suggested that magistrates are 'prosecution-minded' and 'conviction-minded'. Thus, Parker, Sumner and Jarvis (1985) concluded that magistrates reinterpret legislation and court reports in order to make a moral assessment of each offender; and that local sentencing traditions are maintained by local training, by the apprenticeship model – whereby a magistrate spends several years as a 'winger' before taking the chair in court – and by the local selection process. Brown **[6:14]** interviewed many magistrates in six different courts, carrying out a 'sociological study in the construction of knowledge in organisational life', leading her to conclude that magistrates deal with cases according to depersonalised routines, which takes away the individuality of defendants.

If the accused fails to appear, the court may, on proof of service of summons, proceed in their absence, or they may adjourn the hearing. The Magistrates' Courts Act 1980, s 12 allows defendants to plead guilty by post for certain minor offences. Where they are convicted, the court may proceed to sentence immediately, or it may adjourn the case if further information is required before sentencing. If magistrates decide that their sentencing powers are inadequate they may commit the convicted offender to the Crown Court for sentence. As a result of the plea before venue introduced in 1997 (see above), there has been a significant increase in the number of cases being committed for sentence. Until recently, cases committed to the Crown Court for sentence were heard by a judge sitting with between two and four magistrates. The Access to Justice Act 1999, s 79 removed the requirement for magistrates to sit on committals for sentence. Whilst this change may have been economical, it removed a useful mechanism for developing consistency in magistrates' sentencing practice.

Governments seem to enjoy changing the law on sentencing. The Powers of the Criminal Courts (Sentencing) Act 2000 (PCC(S)A 2000) was a welcome attempt to codify these provisions. It built on the Criminal Justice Act 1991, which had introduced a new framework for sentencing. The underlying message of the 1991 Act was that the sentence should be in proportion to the seriousness of the offence of which the offender was convicted. At the time, it was not clear what effect the Act would have on sentencers: at one level, it appeared to reproduce in a convoluted and complicated way much of what sentencers were already doing. However, it was not long before the government panicked and 'toughened up' the message – by means of the Criminal Justice Act 1993 – in what Ashworth and Gibson (1994) called 'one of the most remarkable volte-faces in the history of penal policy in England and Wales' (at page 101). Whilst the original Act had provided that a sentencer – in deciding whether a case was so serious that only a custodial sentence could be justified, or whether a case was serious enough to warrant a community sentence – could look at only one other associated offence, now the court may look at 'one or more' associated offences.

Another example of 'toughening up' was the replacement of the original section 29, which required the court to ignore previous convictions unless they demonstrated aggravating features of the offence for which sentence was being passed. This section made little sense, but probably only meant that a bad record should not lead to a disproportionate sentence. However, the Home Secretary feared that the section might be being interpreted as meaning that courts were no longer allowed to take notice of previous convictions. The replacement section (now section 151 of the PCC(S)A 2000) allows courts to take into account previous convictions and 'failure to respond to previous sentences' in considering seriousness, and makes it compulsory for courts to treat offending while on bail as an aggravating feature.

The third part of the 1993 volte-face was the abolition of unit fines. The vast majority of offenders are fined: even for those sentenced in the magistrates' courts for either-way offences, more than 40% were fined. Unit fines, introduced in 1992, were designed to enable the court to deprive offenders of a proportion of their disposable weekly income for a number of weeks, and so to be fairer between offenders of different wealth. They were abolished after less than a year, largely because the individual units had been inappropriately valued and because defendants were reluctant to fill in the means form. No attempt was made to improve the unit fines system: it was abruptly dumped. Magistrates now simply follow the advice of the Magistrates' Association (a voluntary association to which most magistrates belong): 'if imposing a fine, remember to increase or decrease the amount according to the financial circumstances of the offender'. Surprisingly, the Association encourages courts to build on the many different local means forms currently in existence as a way of acquiring adequate information about the offender. A guideline means form might be more useful. The current statutory maximum fine in the magistrates' court is £5,000. Flood-Page and Mackie (1998), in their study of sentencing practice in magistrates' courts in 1994–95, found a wide range of methods used to calculate the size of a fine. They also found a decline in the use of fines (and compensation orders), concluding that 'if some probation schemes require greater resources but achieve more, as some evidence suggests, then there may be a case for reversing the decline in the use of fines partly in order to release resources for more effective intervention with fewer offenders' (at page 129).

The Criminal Justice Act 1991 also strengthened the range of community sentences and provided that a community sentence may be imposed only if the offence is 'serious enough' to warrant it. No guidance is laid down as to the meaning of 'serious'. The main community penalties are: community rehabilitation orders (until 2000 known as probation orders); community punishment orders (previously community service orders); community punishment and rehabilitation orders (previously combination orders); curfew orders; and drug treatment and testing orders. Magistrates also have the power to send offenders to prison for up to six months for one offence, or up to twelve months in total. All this will change when the Criminal Justice Bill 2002 becomes law: there will then be a single generic 'community order'; judges and magistrates will decide what requirements to attach to this order from a long list of options, including unpaid work, participation in various programmes, curfew, exclusion from certain areas, etc.

Numbers of people received into prison

	Total	Sentenced by magistrates' courts
1992	69,832	36,962
1998	91,282	48,910
2000	129,700	50,380

Source: Prison Statistics 1992, 1998, 2000, paragraphs 1.20–1.21

Because of the short sentences that they serve, those sentenced by magistrates' courts account for only about 10% of the prison population, but it is a strikingly high figure, accounting sometimes for half of those sent to prison in any one year.

Guidance to magistrates on sentencing has been available for a number of years. As long ago as 1966, the Magistrates' Association produced 'Suggestions for Road Traffic Penalties', and in 1989 a 'Sentencing Guide for Criminal Offences (other than Road Traffic)', together with a table of suggested compensation levels. The guidelines are set out in a clear diagrammatic form. Reproduced at **[6:15]** is the most recent version of the guidelines for three common offences. They give an 'entry point' for each offence, as a guide for an offence of average seriousness, based on a first-time offender pleading not guilty. Some of these are surprisingly high: for example, custody is the entry point for possessing an offensive weapon. The guidelines advise that a 'timely' guilty plea should be regarded as a mitigating factor for which a sentencing discount of approximately one-third might be given. This advice was put on a statutory basis by the CJPOA 1994, s 48 **[2:10]**, which provides that a court must take into account the stage in proceedings when the offender indicated his intention to plead guilty, and the circumstances in which that indication is given. Whilst many people have argued that the discount contravenes human rights – the presumption of innocence, the privilege against self-incrimination and the right to a fair hearing – Henham's **[6:16]** research reveals more practical concerns.

The guidelines have no legal status, and justices' clerks and local liaison judges may well play a role in deciding the extent to which the guidelines are adopted in individual courts. Whilst fixed penalties for some minor offences are widely accepted, so is the need to individualise them at a more serious level. The law on sentencing is one thing; questions of principle still need to be explored (see Walker and Padfield (1996) or Ashworth (2000)).

The role of the higher courts in laying down sentencing guidelines for magistrates is minimal, since most appeals are heard by the Crown Court, whose decisions receive little publicity. Thus, magistrates' discretionary powers are in many ways wider than those of judges in the Crown Court. Magistrates have the power to correct their errors within 28 days, under the Magistrates' Courts Act 1980, s 142, although it is a power rarely used. Until 1990, magistrates, although indemnified out of public funds, were personally liable for acting in excess of jurisdiction. Fear that too many claims would lead to defensive judging, which is not in the public interest, led to the amendment of the Justices of the Peace Act 1979, ss 44, 45 by the Courts and Legal Services Act 1990, s 108. This put magistrates on the same footing as judges, and they are now only liable where they act in bad faith, even when acting outside their jurisdiction.

A final but important discretionary power of magistrates relates to costs, under the Prosecution of Offences Act 1985, s 16 **[3:1]**. If a defendant is acquitted, they are not automatically entitled to costs from the prosecution, and even if an order as to costs is made, it may be for a lesser sum than the amount that was actually spent.

Further reading

Ashworth, A *The Criminal Process* (2nd edition, 1998) Oxford

Ashworth, A Sentencing and Criminal Justice (3rd edition, 2000) Butterworths

Ashworth, A and Gibson, B 'The Criminal Justice Act 1993: Altering the Sentencing Framework' [1994] Crim LR 101

Brown, I and Hullin, R 'Contested Bail Applications: the treatment of ethnic minority and white offenders' [1993] Crim LR 107

Carlen, P *Magistrates' Justice* (1976) Martin Robertson

Gifford, T *Where's the Justice?* (1986) Fontana

Darbyshire, P 'An Essay on the Importance and Neglect of the Magistracy' [1997] Crim LR 627

Darbyshire, P 'For the New Lord Chancellor – Some Causes for Concern about Magistrates' [1997] Crim LR 861

Flood-Page, C and Mackie, A *Sentencing Practice: an examination of decisions in magistrates' courts and the Crown Court in the mid-1990s* (1998) HORS No 180 HMSO

Hucklesby, A 'Bail in Criminal Cases' in McConville, M and Wilson, G (eds) *The Handbook of the Criminal Justice Process* (2002), OUP

King, M and May, C *Black Magistrates* (1985) Cobden Trust

Morgan, R and Jones, S 'Bail or Jail?' in Stockdale, E and Casale, S (eds) *Criminal Justice under Stress* (1992) Blackstone

Morgan, P M *Offending While on Bail: A Survey of Recent Studies* HORPU Paper No 65 (1992) HMSO

Parker, H, Sumner, M and Jarvis, G *Unmasking the Magistrates* (1989) Open University Press

Rozenburg, J *The Search for Justice* (1994) Hodder & Staughton

Walker, N and Padfield, N *Sentencing: Theory, Law and Practice* (2nd edition, 1996) Butterworths

Documents

[6:1]   Seago, P, Walker, C and Wall, D 'The Development of the Professional *Magistracy in England and Wales*' [2000] Crim LR 631 (at page 648):

Stipendiary magistrates as out-of-towners

Judicial independence might be compromised in a third, primarily geographical, sense if power is centralised through the expansion of stipendiaries. On this ground, there is the fear that local justice will erode as the links with local communities, as reflected through the backgrounds, experience and outlooks of lay justices, are diluted. Public confidence in the judiciary, in part generated by the judiciary being identifiable with the society which it judges, might then be dented. According to the Home Affairs Committee Report, the Lord Chancellor's Department makes a clear distinction between lay and professional magistrates in terms of how far they should represent the community, but it accepts that in order to ensure confidence, the public should see people like themselves on the bench.[1]

One might begin to explore this allegation in the same way as the previous allegation, in other words, to consider whether stipendiaries should be viewed as unreflective of local interests and then to consider the ways in which the lay magistracy might avoid this charge. However, the furtherance of local justice may, unlike the previous sites for debate, be itself a contested value, the justifiability of which must also be explored.

The localism of lay and professional magistrates

The concept of geographically sensitive justice is troublingly vague, but such a lay 'bench ethos' can be constructed from what Carlen calls a 'mass of situationally evolved knowledge'.[2] Lay magistrates do seem to view themselves as the 'custodians of the community', representing and understanding the locality and its customs and values, so that a 'threat to the community becomes a threat to the magistracy and vice versa.'[3] In addition, the rules of appointment expressly state that magistrates must live within 15 miles of the boundary of the commission area.[4] By contrast, as already described, stipendiary magistrates will have a nation-wide commission throughout England and Wales under section 78 (1) of the Access to Justice Act 1999, as opposed to their present appointment to a commission area, although they will still be allocated to a base court. The expectation is that they will become more mobile, which could provide some support for the supposition that stipendiary magistrates are less socially reflexive than lay magistrates.

---

1   *Home Affairs Committee Report*, para. 11; *Hansard*, H. L. Debs, Vol. 573, col. 1122, June 27, 1998, Lord Irvine.
2   P. Carlen, *Magistrates' Justice* (Martin Robertson, London, 1976), p.75.
3   S. Brown, *Magistrates at Work* (Open University Press, Buckingham, 1991), pp. 111-112.
4   Justices of the Peace Act 1997, s. 6. The Lord Chancellor requires that candidates should have a reasonable degree of knowledge of the area to which they wish to be appointed and generally expects them to have lived in that area for a minimum of 12 months.

A counter-argument to the claims of lay localism is that localism is itself much diluted in contemporary times. There are, for example, far fewer magistrates' courts sites than in the past, so that any local attachments will be less strong for all justices, whether lay or professional. This trend was given a boost by a Home Office Consultation Paper on *The Size of Benches*[5] which pressed for both the abolition of benches with fewer than 12 magistrates and also a reduction in the number of petty sessional areas. Consequently, the number of benches has been reduced from nearly 650 to under 400 as a result. The administrative squeeze has also been backed by cash limits from 1992 onwards, all of which prompted the closure of smaller court-houses in favour of larger inner-city court buildings. This combination of changes could be said to remove the physical and symbolic link between localities and magisterial justice,[6] though one might argue that the socio-geographical bounds of 'localities' are now considerably wider, so that the alteration of the court boundaries is in correspondence with the expansion of, for example, manageable drives to work, shops or entertainment. The logical next step would be to rationalise further in terms of the provision of judicial administration. In this way, as justice becomes less localised, why should magistrates' courts buildings be distinct from Crown Court buildings? Why should there be a separation of the staff working within them? And most controversial of all, in the absence of any practical need for, as opposed to abstract ideology of, localism, why is there a need for lay justices to reflect local connections?[7]

Local justice as a desirable justice

Even if local justice is a characteristic of lay magistrates more so than stipendiary magistrates, is it consistent with good quality justice?[8] The arguments for it seem to revolve around concepts such as trial by one's peers, as well as the benefits of local knowledge and sensitivity to local needs. More generally, all recent major studies have supported the continuance of a fundamentally lay and local system as a democratic and educative 'bridge' between the public and the courts.[9]

Yet criticism arises whenever local differences do markedly emerge, on the grounds that localism infringes concepts of justice in the sense of treatment as an equal.[10] For example, the pressure group Liberty complained in their report, *Unequal Before the Law*, in 1992[11] that like cases were not being treated alike in terms of magisterial custodial

---

5   (1986). See J. W. Raine and M. J. Wilson, *Managing Criminal Justice* (Harvester Wheatsheaf, Hemel Hempstead, 1993), p. 106.

6   Concern on this ground is expressed by the *Home Affairs Committee Report*, para. 198.

7   J. W. Raine and M. J. Wilson, *Managing Criminal Justice* (Harvester Wheatsheaf, Hemel Hempstead, 1993), p. 116.

8   See Z. K. Bankowski, N.R. Hutton and J. J. McManus, *Lay Justice?* (T & T Clark, Edinburgh, 1987).

9   *Home Affairs Committee Report*, para. 198.

10   C. Alugo, J. Richards, G. Wise and J. Raine, 'The magistrates' court and the community' (1996) 160 J.P. 329.

11   Custodial sentences made up 4.96 per cent of the total in 1990, but individual petty sessional divisions varied from 17.44 per cent to 0 per cent. See also: R. Hood, *Sentencing in Magistrates' Courts* (Stevens, London, 1962); R. Tarling, *Sentencing Practice in Magistrates' Courts* (Home Office Research Study 56, London, 1979); D. Acres, 'Consistency and sentencing' (1987) 151 J.P. 343, H. Parker, M Sumner and G. Jarvis, *Unmasking the Magistrate* (Open University Press, Milton Keynes, 1989), p. 16.

sentencing differentials. Disproportionate legal aid grants/refusals are also treated as problematic.[12] The Lord Chancellor adverted to the dilemma in a speech in 1999:

'Local diversity is your unique strength – the factor which can take into account the idiosyncrasies of local culture and behaviour. But society can be hard in its judgment on what it perceives as inconsistency. The public, and the media, look critically at the decisions of bench against bench. They can interpret differences as proof that the magistrates are uncertain amongst themselves, and that nature of justice that you get depends on where you live.'[13]

Conversely, a professional, non-local background may actually assist independence by ensuring greater standardisation which will engender consumer confidence in judicial standards. One response has been the introduction of training for lay justices since 1966,[14] which might be said to blur the lay/professional boundary.

Conclusion: judicial independence and local accountabilities

Salaried judges predominate in the summary criminal courts of many other common law jurisdictions – including Scotland, Northern Ireland and the Republic of Ireland, as well as Australia, Canada, New Zealand and the USA.[15] However, the wholesale replacement of the lay magistracy is not, and never has been, government policy for England and Wales. The exclusive employment of stipendiary magistrates would be more expensive, and the fundamental principles of citizenship, democracy and the protection of individual rights call for representative, and therefore predominantly lay and local, involvement at all levels of justice whether achieved by a jury or lay magistrates.[16] Though the Criminal Courts Review being conducted by Lord Justice Auld[17] has the authority to reconsider this balance between lay and professional, there are few signs that the demise of the laity in justice, even if recommended, would be politically acceptable.

Equally, the extinction of stipendiary magistrates seems highly impracticable and improbable. In the first place, a significant number of Benches find it difficult to appoint sufficient lay justices, and our calculations suggest that it would probably require thousands of extra volunteers completely to replace the stipendiary magistrates, which would also mean unwieldy Benches of over 700 in the larger City courts. So, the consensus seems to be a compromise between legality and local laity. A strong rhetorical emphasis at the summary level rests upon 'community', as articulated through lay involvement: lay magistrates are 'a bridge between the public and a court system which might otherwise seem remote'.[18] But the lay judiciary must work within a framework of legal formality and have training and professional assistance through clerks – and so

12   See R. Young and D. Wall, *Access to Criminal Justice* (Blackstone Press, London, 1996), Chap. 7.
13   Speech to the Council of the Magistrates' Association (http://www.open.gov.uk/lcd/speeches/1999/25-3-99.htm; 1999).
14   See *The Training of Justices of the Peace in England and Wales* (Cmnd. 2856, HMSO, London, 1965).
15   See Sir T. Skyrme, *History of the Justices of the Peace* (Barry Rose, Chichester, 1991) Vol. 3.
16   See *Hansard*, H. L. Debs. Vol. 582, cols 1066, October 29, 1997, Lord Irvine.
17   http://www.criminal-courts-review.org.uk/.
18   *Home Affairs Committee Report*, para. 198.

they are turned into, what Burney calls, 'half-baked professionals'.[19] One might then depict the stipendiary as a further form of complementary compromise to community involvement – dealing with cases or case-loads which lay justices find too hot or too heavy to handle. In order to achieve this supportive role, there seems to be broad support for an 'integrationalist' approach whereby there is a greater presence of stipendiaries, but their function is 'to support rather than supersede lay magistrates'.[20] Consistent with this approach, the increase in the number of stipendiaries has been significant but remains very modest and not enough to ensure continuous national coverage in areas without a permanent stipendiary by 'semi-attached' stipendiaries.[21] Nor has the work of stipendiaries been clearly differentiated from that of the lay bench, despite suggestions along these lines by the *Venne Report*[22] and the *Narey Report*.[23]

Alongside independence, another important agenda for the future is accountability with regard to the magistracy, though the tensions between judicial independence and judicial accountability are here evident. One would expect accountability in a system which vaunts its localism, but in what senses, if any, do local judges make themselves accountable for their judicial work? First, there is legal accountability, such as through the giving of reasons (more by stipendiaries than lay justices),[24] through public access to court-rooms, through appeals to the Crown Court or by legal review in the Divisional Court. But legal decisions are not discussed in advance or endorsed after delivery by the general local public. One might argue that judicial independence would be compromised if they were, but these arguments have been faced down in regard to constabulary independence, in respect of which periodic local liaison committee meetings allow for consultation, report and complaint, though not direction or censure, by the public.[25] So, if handled correctly, 'accountability can in fact enhance the public's respect for independence.'[26] Secondly, there is still little obvious accountability in political terms, from individual clerks to the MCCs and from the MCCs to the 'paying authority'.[27]

Why are these major issues of accountability not addressed in any of the policy papers we have discussed? One might conclude that the genuine motivation for the growth of the professional magistracy is driven by the bureaucratic objectives of the New Public Managerialism, which pictures the public, including local offenders, as consumers of services rather than active citizens. The opposition, from lay magistrates, has been pitched at an ideological level, but it is equally an ideology in which the relationship with the community is one way and paternalistic rather than reflexive. Nevertheless, the insertion of a professional magistracy does call into question the justifiability and working of local justice and may, along with other changes expose at the same time the strength of the ideology as well as the weaknesses of its application. If mechanisms of accountability were to be instituted, then the position of the stipendiary in local justice might actually become less anomalous, for there would be a link between professionals and community not currently provided for. Thus, all justices, both lay and

---

[19]   E. Burney, J.P: *Magistrate, Court, and Community* (Hutchinson, London, 1979), p. 216.
[20]   *Home Affairs Committee Report*, para. 196.
[21]   See *Venne Report*, paras 8.4, 8.6.
[22]   *Venne Report*, para. 5.3.
[23]   *Narey Report*, para. 14.
[24]   *R. V. Harrow Crown Court, ex p. Dawe* (1994) 158 J.P. 250.
[25]   See the Police and Criminal Evidence Act 1984, s. 106.
[26]   M. L. Friedland, *A Place Apart* (Canada Communications Group, Ottawa, 1995), p.xiii.
[27]   In relation to a MCC, the 'paying authority' means any responsible local authority whose area comprises all or part of the area to which the MCC relates. The paying authority provides 20% of MCC funding, with the Lord Chancellor's Department responsible for 80%, subject to a cash limit. See the Justices of the Peace Act 1997, ss. 55, 57.

professional, would be able to claim that they represented community wishes, and the harmony of judge and judged could be achieved by a more objective conduit than a feeling in the bones of the magistrate.

[6:2] Morgan, R *'Magistrates: The Future According to Auld'* (2002) 29 J Law and Society 308 (at page 314):

The problem with Auld's dismissive stance [to public opinion] is that it assumes that the judges, and the politicians they advise, are the best and sole arbiters of what system is fair and efficient and suggests that the public must then be persuaded that what what the judges have decided is ideal. I consider that position mistaken.

Of course it might be argued that since Auld has endorsed the jurisdiction and role of the lay magistracy, what is the fuss about? There are threee ripostes to this. First, Auld's dismissal of public opinion also underpins some of his more radical proposals (regarding access to jury trial, for example). Secondly, it is not clear to me that Auld has endorsed the position of the lay magistracy. Thirdly, Auld has chosen to ignore what the public, were they aware of the fact, would almost certainly find objectionable about the operation of the magistrates' courts as currently constituted, shortcomings which will be exacerbated if Auld's proposals are implemented. I will consider the latter points in reverse order.

1. *An aspect of post-code justice ignored?*

It is currently a matter of chance whether a defendant in magistrates' court proceedings has his or her case dealt with by lay magistrates or a district judge. It will depend on the court in which the defendant appears (some courts have a full-time district judge, most do not) and the luck of the draw if the defendant appears in a court in which a full-time district judge does sit. There are no allocational rules. There are only general allocational practices, and they vary. Does it matter whether a defendant appears before a district judge sitting alone or lay magistrates sitting as a panel of two or three? The answer, as we have seen, is yes. We do not know if the chances of acquittal are different: the number of trials in our survey were too small to test the proposition. But it makes a substantial difference when it comes to the likelihood of being remanded in custody or sentenced to immediate imprisonment. In cases where there is a possibility of that outcome our defendant is roughly twice as likely to end up in custody if he or she appears before a district judge.

What has Auld to say on this? Very little, save to say that if there is sentencing disparity between lay magistrates and district judges then the district judges are more likely to have got their decisions right:

'I believe that District Judges are more likely to follow national practice and sentencing policy guide-lines in this respect than magistrates, with their individual traditions and training, and history of disparate sentencing.'

He fails to point out that disparity may be just as much a feature of sentencing by the professional judiciary, something which the professional judiciary, supported by the Lord Chancellor's Department, has taken care to ensure is not investigated. Further, to ensure that lay magistrates are brought into sentencing line Auld proposes that in future their training be organized by the Judicial Studies Board. But he offers no other remedy. He makes no suggestion that lay magistrates and district judges should do other than continue to sit separately in his proposed Magistrates' Division and, as we have noted, he recommends that lay magistrates be excluded from sentencing decisions in his proposed District Division.

The present situation represents the very opposite of what most people think justice demands should be the case. Provision for panel decision making in more serious cases where issues of liberty are at stake is a safeguard for which there appears to be widespread support. It is significant that since the Auld Report has been published a minister has described the present arrangement as 'odd' and 'arbitrary'.

2. Endorsement of the role of lay magistrates?

Between and on the lines of the Auld Report are several reasons for doubting that the lay magistracy should feel that their role is to be safeguarded.

First, there is Auld's recommendation that in future 'the Lord Chancellor should be more ready to take the initiative to assign a District Judge to an area where, having consulted as appropriate, he is of the view that local justice in the area requires it.' That is, the initiative should not be left to the localities but seized by the centre. Auld's intervention on this issue was prompted by evidence of local benches successfully delaying the appointment of a district judge where the Magistrates' Courts Inspectorate (MCSI) and the Lord Chancellor's Department thought it desirable:

'such parochialism demeans the otherwise worthy contribution magistrates make
  to the running of the criminal justice system, and it should no longer hold sway.'

It seems certain that he had in mind the case of Bristol where the recent appointment of a district judge resulted not from a recommendation from the local Lord Chancellor's Advisory Committee but from the MCSI. Senior lay magistrates locally resented the proposition, and following his appointment, the professional incumbent, an experienced stipendiary who had previously worked in London was reputedly given cases to deal with which his lay colleagues considered to be undemanding and probably beneath his dignity – vehicle parking infractions and the like. That is, the lay magistrates delivered a studied insult and asserted their determination not to relinquish to the judge those more serious cases which we must assume they saw his arrival as intending to cream off.

Whatever the rights and wrongs of the Bristol case, it seems likely that Auld's recommendation will be seized on and additional district judges appointed, particularly in areas where there is evidence of delay, where the lay magistrates prove to be less flexible and where there are difficulties recruiting suitable lay magistrates: these conditions are most likely to arise in the metropolitan centres.

Secondly, though Auld says that he sees no case for altering the present balance of lay magistrates and district judges he also says that 'the position may be different' if his recommendation that there be a unified court with an intermediate tier is adopted. There would then be only a compelling case for retaining 'a sizeable lay magistracy' – how sizeable, Auld does not say, though he notes that having many more district judges would 'require a major programme of change' and would take time. It is significant that the relevant Home Office minister has already stated that:

'if the District Division becomes a reality, it will be necessary for District Judges to be available throughout the country (which, of course, they are not at the moment). If this happens, there may be a case for looking again at the distribution of work within the Magistrates' Division.'

I think it is also clear that, in order to pave the way for his District Division, Auld favours substantially increasing the number of district judges who he observes often sit also as recorders and that appointment as a district judge is 'emerging as the first step on a judicial rung that may lead to a permanent appointment as a Circuit Judge and, possibly, beyond'. The vertical integration of the criminal courts implies the further development of judicial careers, both of which I expect to be encouraged. All these developments would have significant implications for the role of the lay magistracy.

Thirdly, it is for above reasons that I doubt lay magistrates should feel greatly reassured by Auld's recommendation that there be no extension of justice's clerks' case management jurisdiction. What is being safeguarded is less the prerogative of lay magistrates and more the developing role of the professional judiciary. Note, for example, that Auld concludes that district judges have no need of a legally qualified clerk to sit with them in court – an anomalous provision to which we drew attention – and that it will be for district judges, not lay magistrates or justices' clerks, to determine the appropriate venue for the hearing of either-way cases in the event of the defence and prosecution disagreeing.

Fourthly, Auld's report has one or two telling comments to make about costs. Auld has practically nothing to say on costs, which makes it all the more striking that he is prepared to suggest that our attempt to estimate the cost implications of employing more district judges in place of lay magistrates is at best incomplete and at worst flawed. We found that:

- estimates of the direct costs to the LCD alone of using two types of magistrate show, not surprisingly, that lay magistrates are far cheaper. A lay justice: we estimated costs £495 per annum compared to £90,000 for a stipendiary, which translates to £3.59 compared to £20.96 per case;
- however, when overheads are loaded into the equation, the difference is far smaller – £52.10 compared to £61.78 per appearance; and
- if opportunity costs are added – a controversial issue in which fairly courageous assumptions have to be made – we estimated that lay magistrates are more expensive – £70.80 compared to £61.78 per court appearance;
- further, if the cost consequences of current differential decision-making, are added, the calculations pull in different directions. Employing more district judges will lead to fewer court appearances as a result of their more robust examination of applications: this would save money. However, district judges' greater use of custody would significantly increase costs for the Prison Service.

Auld thinks, contrary to the Magistrates' Association, that we were correct to include an estimation of opportunity as well as direct costs, but he judged that our calculations were 'necessarily somewhat theoretical and speculative and ... open to criticism in a number of respects'. Of our conclusion that more district judges would likely add to the number of custodial decisions and thus costs, he says:

'Save as a cynical measure of expediency, it would be wrong to consider whether to change the present sharing of summary jurisdiction on the basis that District Judges are too hard or that magistrates are too soft in their decisions as to custody.'

In fact at no stage did we suggest that policy should be decided on the basis of costs: we simply attempted to estimate the likely cost consequences of different policy scenarios. Nevertheless, as we have seen, by saying that if there are sentencing disparities between judges and lay magistrates the district judges are correct, Auld is implicitly arguing that these are extra costs the criminal justice system *should* bear. By contrast the savings accruing from district judges granted fewer adjournments – which might as easily be challenged – Auld is content to accept. Indeed it is apparently not cynical for him to suggest that in our own research we almost certainly underestimated the savings likely to result under this head. He correctly points out, for example, that we failed to estimate – we do not do so because, as we acknowledged, we could find no firm basis on which to do it – the reduced knock-on costs of having fewer court appearances for the police, the legal aid budget, the CPS, and so on. It seems likely that the fact that savings may arise from making greater use of district judges will inevitably encourage their greater use. Indeed, as we argued in our report, if tougher sentencing is set aside (and that might be addressed in training for district judges), the greater the increase in the number of district judges and the greater the displacement of lay magistrates, the more likely it becomes that step savings (resulting from need for fewer courtrooms and a reduced supporting infrastructure, and possibly fewer courthouses) can be achieved.

The above ingredients in Auld suggest less commitment to the current balance of lay magistrates and district judges in the Magistrates' Division than at first appears. If I am correct, and the proportion of appearances in the magistrates' courts is increased, it will have implications for the relationship between two groups. In our survey of lay and stipendiary magistrates we found, not surprisingly, that whereas the stipendiaries could overwhelmingly think of several reasons for having more stipendiaries – faster, more efficient, better able to deal with legally complicated cases, and so on – the majority of lay magistrates could cite no reasons at all. Conversely whereas one or two stipendiaries conceded that there were arguments against having more stipendiaries – that it is unfair to have one person sitting in judgment, for example, the majority of lay magistrates subscribed to several negative arguments. The two groups do not see eye to eye on the possible futures of their respective contribution and since one group comprises unpaid volunteers, this is a factor to be heeded: lay magistrates might widely withdraw their unpaid labour were they to see their own status being diminished and their role reduced. In coming to the conclusion that the business in the magistrates' courts should be allocated as at present, Auld is endorsing the Venne Report which recommended a 'presumption' in favour of stipendiary magistrates, when available, undertaking 'heavier' work. The corollary of additional district judges doing this, if they sit alone, is that lay magistrates are relegated to dealing with the less interesting and challenging work, of having their lists intellectually asset-stripped. This is what the lay magistracy fears and dislikes. There is a real tension here. If lay magistrates perceive their role to be marginalized, it is doubtful whether their continued and widened recruitment can be assured.

The role of magistrates in the proposed District Division

One of Auld's answers to the difficulties in recruiting and retaining the services of a socially representative magistracy is the 'attraction' of the 'opportunity to hear more serious and interesting trials' in his proposed District Division. In answer to the practical difficulty of finding lay magistrates with the time to hear such cases, Auld suggests that the proposals he has for the introduction of more flexible magistrates' sitting patterns, combined with evidence of lay magistrates' current availability, make this problem soluble – an opinion with which the Magistrates' Association apparently agrees:

There are many magistrates who, for one reason or another, are not restricted by their employment or other commitments to sitting for half a day a week and who might well relish the opportunity to sit on longer and more substantial cases.

Setting on one side the major arguments which can be made against Auld's proposals for a District Division – arguments which mostly hinge on the great reduction in access to and consequent number of jury trials involved – how practical and logical is the scheme he proposes in terms of lay magistrates' participation?

The first point to make is that Auld's idea of a mixed (lay and professional judges) tribunal conforms broadly to what in our own survey of other jurisdictions we described as the Germano-Scandinavian model, though the arrangement is found in several jurisdictions outside that European region. Mixed tribunals were commended to auld by Sanders. There is one important difference, however. Whereas mixed tribunals in other jurisdictions, and as proposed by Sanders, collectively determine issues of both fact (though generally not law) and sentence, Auld proposes an arrangement [in which] lay magistrates play no part in sentencing. Auld offers two reasons:

- lay magistrates would, he contends, lack the necessary competence and experience: sentencing at this level of seriousness would be very different from sentencing in the summary court and would become more complicated still were the recommendations of the Halliday Report (which proposes sentence review hearings) implemented;
- it would not be practical to involve lay magistrates: following trial most cases would have to be adjourned for sentence and 'it would often be difficult to reconstitute the same panel for the purpose of passing sentence'.

Auld's objections to lay magistrates' involvement in sentencing do not seem to me to be well grounded. If it is possible to find lay magistrates willing and able to sit on trials for several days, it should hardly be difficult to get them to return for a sentencing hearing. As for the suggestion that they lack the necessary competence and experience to do the task, this is likely to be regarded as insulting by lay magistrates and scarcely squares with Auld's earlier argument that in deciding matters of fact the magistrates would not have to be given directions by the judge because of their competence and experience in structured decision making.

Indeed so disingenuous is Auld's argument for excluding magistrates from sentencing that one wonders whether it is a smokescreen for a more serious consideration, namely, that to concede panel sentencing in the proposed District Division would throw into stark relief and call into question lone sentencing in the Magistrates' and Crown Divisions, something which, as we have seen, our surveys of the public and of lay magistrates is widely considered objectionable (though I should emphasize that we canvassed opinion on this point only with regard to serious decisions in the magistrates' courts). As regards lone sentencing by judges in the Crown Court, Auld maintains that he received no proposals for change, which is odd because the case for panel decision making in the Crown Court is clearly set out in one submission from a commentator extensively cited by him. Moreover, during the course of undertaking successive research projects I have repeatedly heard barristers argue the shortcomings of lone decision making by Crown Court judges. As for lone decision making by district judges in the magistrates' courts Auld, as we have seen, repeatedly had the objections drawn to his attention, but chose to ignore them. What is clear is that if some lay magistrates have the time to sit on lengthy trials in the District Division, they would clearly have time to sit alongside district judges in the Magistrates Division. There is a gap in Auld's logic here.

Other questions remain, however. Were lay magistrates to sit with district judges in the District Division, which lay magistrates would likely do it? And how would they do it?

I have no doubt that some lay magistrates will welcome the opportunity to try contested cases alongside district judges in the District Division and will find time to do it. Our study showed that a minority of lay magistrates are able and do devote much more of their time to the task than the minimum number of twenty-six sittings a year stipulated by the Lord Chancellor. More than one-fifth of lay magistrates already sit more than once a week – that is more than twice the minimum number of sittings – in addition to attendance at meetings, training sessions, and so on. That so many are able and willing to devote so much unpaid time to the task, generally without claiming loss of earnings (86 per cent) and often without claiming expenses either (23 per cent), reflects that fact that the magistracy is overwhelmingly middle-class, two-fifths of whom are retired. We did not analyse our data to consider the socio-economic characteristics of the frequent-sitters, but it would be surprising were they not even more disproportionately from the retired and professional/managerial ranks.

There is a dilemma to be faced, therefore. If lay magistrates are to sit with professional judges in any division they must have the training, experience, and self-confidence to act as equals to challenge the professional judges. For otherwise they may be no more than what one observer has suggested the lay judiciary are generally considered in Germany, 'decorative flower pots'. Auld recognized the objection to mixed panels that they may be dominated by the professional judges. It is an issue on which there is a great deal of anecdotal but virtually no hard evidence both with regard to practice in the Crown Court (where mixed panels hear appeals from magistrates' courts decisions) and the former Quarter Sessions (where magistrates used often to sit with professional judges). The evidence from other jurisdictions is mixed. But, having reviewed that evidence, Doran and Glenn argue that 'the very presence of the lay members may in itself influence the stance adopted by the professional'. Auld is almost certainly correct, however, to doubt that foreign examples are good indicators of the likely pattern here. English and Welsh magistrates are much more highly trained and experienced than their Scandinavian and German counterparts. They sit frequently and separately from professional judges – which their Continental equivalents do not. It is unlikely that they would defer excessively to their professional colleagues.

But the outcome would be different were the sittings of lay magistrates greatly to change. If Sanders's proposal that lay magistrates sit much less frequently were adopted, for example, them mixed tribunals would probably become participative fig-leafs. By the same token, Auld's suggestion that lay magistrates sit in more flexible patterns and possibly less often so as to broaden their recruitment and social representativeness would likely turn out to be something of a sham were magistrates, once appointed, able freely to choose how often and in what court they sat. The bench might *appear* more socially representative, but it would likely be the case that most sittings, and certainly those involving the more serious cases, would involve magistrates more socially unrepresentative than benches are now. Furthermore, at which point does the frequency of sitting engender a case-hardened approach? Auld observed that the practical distinction between lay magistrates and district judges had diminished. At what point do lay magistrates cease to be lay?

There are no easy answers to this dilemma. The essence of the magistracy is that it should be lay and socially representative. But not so lay that it cannot act with justice and self-confidently challenge the professional judges when sitting with them. My own view is that it is objectionable that serious cases should be tried and sentenced by lone judges in the present magistrates' courts. Further, the question raised by Auld's proposed District Court is whether any serious case should be sentenced by a lone decision maker. Finally, I doubt that participation in serious proceedings should be left to the personal decision of individual magistrates. It is desirable that the social composition of the magistracy be broadened. For the same reason it is equally desirable that all magistrates be involved in the trial and sentencing of serious cases.

[6:3] **Skyrme, T** *The Changing Image of the Magistracy* (2nd edition, 1983) Macmillan (at page 6):

At first sight the system seems not only anomalous but indefensible and, having regard to their powers and vast field of responsibility, it is astonishing that the justices have not only survived but have flourished in an age when established institutions have been subject to ever-increasing denigration, when the amateur has been steadily replaced by the professional and when voluntary service is anachronistic in the prevailing climate of totalitarianism. The Justice of the Peace is the kind of historical legacy that one would have expected to be the first to founder in the revolutionary flood of the post-war years. It could not have survived had it not been acceptable to successive governments and to the public at large. The explanation of its acceptability, despite certain latent defects, is probably threefold: first, the depth of the roots of the lay magistracy in the British social system and the inclination of the people to honour tradition and to preserve ancient institutions; second, the ability of the justices, as evidenced in their previous history, to adjust to changing conditions; and third, the intrinsic merits of the system itself which, if exploited and developed, give it a peculiar attraction not shared by any other form of judicial machinery.

The principal defects usually attributed to lay justices are that they are too ready to accept police evidence and that they rely too much on the advice of the clerk. In some degree both criticisms are still valid, though far less so than they were 30 years and more ago, and neither defect is altogether incurable. As against these disadvantages the justices have certain unique qualities on the credit side. From the point of view of the government they have two advantages; they are cheap and they are flexible. As they received no pay they are more cost-effective than a salaried stipendiary, though the difference is not as great as is sometimes assumed because justices work more slowly than stipendiaries and if they have to sit in two or more courts to dispose of the same amount of work there will be the additional cost of extra staff and accommodation; in addition, although not remunerated, justices are entitled to allowances which can amount to a not inconsiderable sum when several of them are sitting. Nevertheless, justices are on the whole cheaper than any other effective method of administering justice than has so far been devised. In 1965, Lord Gardiner caused inquiries to be made in 20 countries to find out in each case the numbers of whole-time judges and the cost of judicial administration. The cost (excluding police and prisons) expressed as a percentage of the annual national budget ranged from 1.46 at the top of the scale to 0.16 in the case of England, Scotland and Wales, who were at the bottom. As regards the number of judges, several counties had more than 200 per million of population while Scotland with 15 and England and Wales with 8 were again at the bottom. As was to be expected, most Common Law countries were in the lowest bracket because of their single-judge systems; thus the United States had 34 judges per million population; Australia 29 and New Zealand 24. These figures should be treated with reserve as some were based on estimates, but the position of England and Wales at the bottom of the league was generally attributed to the much larger proportion of court work disposed of by their unpaid, part-time lay magistrates compared with other countries.

Justices also appeal to the government because their system is flexible; sudden fluctuations in the volume of work can be handled by calling upon justices to sit more or less often in more or fewer courts as the need arises, whereas a whole-time judge or stipendiary has little scope to expand his output if work increases, and if it diminishes he may be left partially unemployed at public expense.

These are not the only inherent merits of a properly constituted lay justice system. Two, or preferably three, heads are better than one and they are better still if they combine intimate knowledge, experience and understanding of the problems facing different sections of the local community, which can often enable them to deal with cases more justly and efficaciously than the professional courts. The collective views of a cross-section of the population, representing different shades of opinion, can be more effective in dispensing justice acceptable to the public than the decision of a single individual necessarily drawn from a fairly narrow social class and whose experience of local problems may be limited. Justices also act as a check on one another and provide a balanced conclusion, whereas there is nothing to curb the general idiosyncrasy or the spasmodic whim or irritability of a single magistrate. Furthermore, as justices attend court at intervals they approach their task with a freshness and objectivity that is lacking in a professional judge who is wholly engaged in adjudicating day after day.

The system of lay justices reflects, through citizens participation, the traditional English involvement of the layman in the administration of justice. It enables the citizen to see that the law is his law, administered by men and women like himself, and that it is not the esoteric preserve of the lawyers. Lord Hailsham, in a speech made when he was Lord Chancellor, stressed the value of the lay magistracy as a unifying factor in society as a whole, and he described their potential influence, not only on the bench but also out of court, as 'one of the characteristic institutions holding our society together'.

The identification of the ordinary citizen with the administration of justice should therefore have a popular appeal, yet when it comes to the test the average citizen seems to prefer to be tried by a professional magistrate. This is most noticeable where there is a clear choice of tribunal, as in family and adoption proceedings, and where preference is normally shown for the professionalism of the county court rather than the lay justices' court. This may be due at least in part to the erroneous view which much of the population hold of the justices today: that they are prejudiced, prosecution-minded, middle-class bigots, motivated by lust for power and totally lacking in any feeling for those who appear before them. This description might not have been far wrong a century ago, when it could have been directed with equal justification at other institutions, but the vast changes that have occurred since then are not generally realised. The detritus of the past has been washed away and the justices of today are able to exhibit some of the latent advantages of the system which were not revealed under their predecessors. A lay justice cannot equal the professional skill of a stipendiary, but the function of magistrates is largely to decide questions of fact and for this purpose to exercise common sense and sound judgment against a background of knowledge and experience of the world at large. By this criterion the quality of the average lay justice is no less than that of the professional stipendiary.

Provided that justices are carefully chosen in the light of their ability, integrity and understanding, and can be seen to be well qualified for their work, and provided also that they are given adequate training and opportunities to enable them to become and remain proficient in the performance of their duties, then it is possible for the layman, who combines experience as a magistrate with experience in other walks of like, to offer advantages which are not to be found in the professional systems; not least of these advantages being the ability to exercise a stabilising influence within the community in which he lives to an extent not open to the professional judge. It is to this end that the reforms of the past 40 years have been largely directed.

(and at page 67):

The controversy over the social composition of the magistracy usually turns upon whether benches are predominantly upper-class to the exclusion of the rest of the population. The Lord Chancellor does not seek to strike a numerical balance between representatives of each social group; there seems to be no good reason why he should do so and it would be impossible to achieve this result because of the movement of individuals from one group to another. The declared policy of each Lord Chancellor since 1945 has been to make sure that each bench is a microcosm of the local community within which it operates, and this amounts to seeing that in every petty sessional division there are at least some justices from each of the principal social and political groups in the area and that the bench is not dominated by any one group. I would claim that we have gone a long way towards attaining this object.

[6:4]   Morgan, R and Russell, N *The Judiciary in the Magistrates' Courts* HO RDS Occasional Paper No 66 (2000) Home Office (from the summary, at page vii):

This research was jointly commissioned by the Lord Chancellor's Department and the Home Office. The study was undertaken during the first nine months of 2000 by a research team comprising the University of Bristol and two commercial companies, RSGB (a division of Taylor Nelson Sofres plc) and CRG, Cardiff, specialists in market research and cost benefit analysis respectively.

Methodology

The research comprised seven types of data collection:
- baseline information on the budgets, buildings, court staff and magistrates' characteristics. Data were gathered both nationally and locally, and included information on ten magistrates' courts in London and the provinces, with and without stipendiaries
- 2,019 self-completed magistrates' diaries, spanning three-week sessions, covering activities, timings etc. from the ten courts
- 1,120 self-completed magistrates' questionnaires addressing issues of sitting arrangements, their views on balance between lay and stipendiaries etc. from the ten courts
- observations of 535 court sessions at the ten courts
- 400 telephone interviews with regular court users from the ten courts
- public opinion survey: conducted with a nationally representative sample of 1,753 members of public
- 23 responses to a letter to representatives of the Council of Europe member states.

Composition and working practices of the magistracy

Composition

At the time of the research the magistracy comprised:
- approximately 30,400 lay magistrates
- 96 full-time stipendiaries
- 146 part-time stipendiaries.

The lay magistracy:
- is gender balanced
- is ethnically representative of the population at a national level
- is overwhelmingly drawn from professional and managerial ranks
- comprises a high proportion (two-fifths) who have retired from full-time employment.

In comparison, stipendiaries:
- are mostly male and white
- tend to be younger.

Sitting patterns

Lay magistrates:
- sit in court an average 41.4 occasions annually (although many sit a good deal more frequently)
- devote (taking holidays into account) an extended morning or afternoon to the post once a week
- additionally spend the equivalent, on average, of a full working week on training and other duties.

The contracts of full-time stipendiaries require them to perform judicial duties five days a week, 44 weeks of the year. However there is some ambiguity as to what this means in terms of court sittings. Provincial stipendiaries sit more often than their colleagues do in London, but both groups sit in court closer to four days per week.

Lay magistrates usually sit in panels of three, but sometimes of two (16% of observed panels). Stipendiaries nearly always sit alone but on rare occasions sit together with lay magistrates.

Caseload allocation

While stipendiaries take on more or less the full range of cases and appearances, they tend to be allocated more complex, prolonged and sensitive cases. Unlike lay magistrates, their time is concentrated on triable-either-way rather than summary cases.

Working methods and decision-making

Speed

Stipendiary magistrates deal with all categories of cases and appearances more quickly than their lay colleagues because they retire from court sessions less often and more briefly (0.2 compared to 1.2 occasions per session, for only 3 compared to 16 minutes). They also deal with cases more quickly on average (9 minutes compared to 10 minutes). This means:

- stipendiaries hear 22 per cent more appearances than lay magistrates per standardised court session (12.2 compared to 10)
- if stipendiaries were allocated an identical caseload to lay magistrates, it is estimated that they would deal with 30 per cent more appearances.

The greater speed of stipendiaries is not achieved at the expense of inquisition and challenge; on the contrary, hearings before stipendiaries typically involve more questions being asked and more challenges being made.

Manner of working: adjournments and bail

Both lay and stipendiary magistrates are invariably judged to meet high standards in dealing with court business (attentiveness, clarity of pronouncements, courtesy, and so on). However, stipendiaries are considered to perform better in relation to those criteria that suggest greater confidence – showing command over the proceedings and challenging parties responsible for delay.

Fewer appearances before stipendiaries lead to adjournments (45% compared to 52%). This is partly because fewer applications are made to stipendiaries but also because they are more likely to resist applications for adjournments (97% compared to 93%). It is therefore likely that the employment of additional stipendiaries would lead to fewer court appearances overall.

Lay magistrates are less likely to:
- refuse defendants bail in cases where to prosecution seeks custody and the defence applies for bail (19% compared to 37%)
- make use of immediate custody as a sentence (12% of triable-either-way cases compared to 25%).

The employment of additional stipendiaries might therefore significantly increase the prison population.

Stipendiaries tend to run their courts themselves and rely very little on their court legal advisors when it comes to making and explaining decisions and announcements. This calls into question whether they need legally qualified court advisors.

The views of regular court practitioners

A sample of 400 court practitioners (court advisors, solicitors, CPS personnel, probation officers) were surveyed by telephone.

Very few court users expressed 'no' or only 'a little' confidence in either type of magistrate, but stipendiaries were more likely to inspire a 'great deal' or a 'lot' of confidence. Users found it harder to generalise about lay magistrates, indicating a greater range in their performance.

The court users expressed very similar views to the court observers when asked to rate dimensions of behaviour. Stipendiaries were widely seen as:
- more efficient, more consistent and more confident in their decision-making
- questioning defence lawyers appropriately
- giving clear reasons for decisions
- showing command over proceedings.

Lay magistrates were more often judged better at:
- showing courtesy to defendants and other court members
- using simple language
- showing concern to distressed victims.

But the majority of respondents did not think lay and stipendiary magistrates differed on these criteria.

Regular court practitioners, particularly lawyers and CPS personnel, said that they and their colleagues behave differently when appearing before lay and stipendiary magistrates. They:
- prepare better for stipendiaries
- try to be more precise and concise in their statements to them
- anticipate that they will be questioned and challenged more.

Court legal advisors on the other hand said that they prepare more for lay magistrates, because they anticipate the need to give legal advice to them.

Public opinions of the magistracy

A nationally representative sample of 1,753 members of the public were interviewed regarding their views on, and knowledge of the magistracy.

Whereas the overwhelming majority of the public is aware of the terms 'magistrate' and 'magistrates' court', only a minority have heard of 'lay' as opposed to 'stipendiary' magistrates.

When the difference between them is explained, almost three-quarters (73%) say that they were not aware of this difference.

Only a bare majority of respondents correctly identify that most criminal cases are dealt with in the magistrates' courts, and that juries do not make decisions there.

Knowledge about the qualifications and sitting practices of lay magistrates is even less accurate. Respondents who are more knowledgeable about the system tend to have greater confidence in it.

Having had the differences explained to them, most of the public thinks that:
- lay magistrates represent the views of the community better than stipendiaries (63% compared to 9% - the remaining 28% see no difference or don't know)
- lay magistrates are more likely to be sympathetic to defendants' circumstances (41% compared to 12%)
- stipendiaries are better at making correct judgements of guilt or innocence (36% compared to 11%) and managing court business effectively (48% compared to 9%)
- there is no difference between lay and stipendiaries in awareness of the effect of crimes on victims and approaching each case afresh.

In addition, when comparing single magistrates with panels:
- a small majority of respondents (53%) consider that motoring offences are suitable to be heard by a single magistrate
- a large majority think that the more serious decisions of guilty/not guilty (74%) and sending to prison (76%) should be decided by panels of magistrates.

Most respondents think that the work of the magistrates' courts should be divided equally between the two types of magistrates, or that the type of magistrate does not matter.

The direct and indirect costs of lay and stipendiary magistrates

If only directly attributable costs (salaries, expenses, training) are considered, lay magistrates are much cheaper because they are not paid directly and many do not claim loss of earnings. A sizeable minority does not even claim their allowable travelling expenses. A lay magistrate costs on average £495 per annum compared to the £90,000 per annum total employments costs of a stipendiary. These translate into a cost per appearance before lay and stipendiary magistrates of £3.59 and £20.96 respectively (Table 1). When indirect costs (premises, administration staff, etc.) are brought into the equation the gap between the two groups narrows, to £52.10 and £61.78.

Table 1   The cost of appearing before lay and stipendiary magistrates (per appearance)

	Lay Magistrates	Stipendiary Magistrates
	£	£
Direct costs (salary, expenses, training)	3.59	20.96
Indirect costs (premises, administration staff etc.)	48.51	40.82
Direct & indirect costs	52.10	61.78

The effect upon costs of substituting stipendiary for lay magistrates

There would have to be a significant increase in the use of the more productive stipendiaries to enable administrative staff and courtroom reductions to be made on any scale.

If blocks of work currently undertaken by lay magistrates were transferred to stipendiaries:

- one stipendiary would be needed for every 30 magistrates, if all lay tribunals comprised three justices
- one for every 28, if the present proportion of tribunals comprising only two lay justices were to continue.

Stipendiaries' greater tendency to resist adjournments and their greater use of custody at the pre-trial and sentencing stages means that if the number of stipendiaries were doubled (assuming present patterns were retained):

- there would be a reduction of 10,270 appearances in connection with indictable offences, giving an additional cost of £0.88 million per annum (a net increase because the reduced rates of adjournments do not overcome the higher attributable costs of stipendiaries).
- the number of remands in custody would increase by 6,200 per annum. Assuming an average remand period of 46 days, this has an associated cost of around £24 million (essentially falling on the Prison Service)
- the number of custodial sentences would increase by 2,760 per annum, costing £13.6 million. Set against this is the cost of the type of sentence that the offender would have received in the place of a prison sentence. If this is taken as some form of community penalty then the overall additional cost of this increase in custodial sentences would be around £8.5 million.

The effect upon costs of substituting lay for stipendiary magistrates

Alternatively if there were no stipendiaries, then there would be an increase in the number of appearances of 10,270, the number of remands in custody would decrease by 6,200, and the number of custodial sentences would decrease by 2,760 – with each of the consequent cost savings.

Other jurisdictions

Drawing on the 23 responses from the Council of Europe member states and enquiries to other (mostly Common Law) jurisdictions, it can be seen that there are three principal models of adjudication:

- the *professional*
- the *lay*
- the *hybrid* (mixed lay and professional).

Each of these can be refined in terms of whether decision-making is by single persons or panels, and the number of tiers into which criminal cases and courts are divided.

However there is no straightforward relationship between the degree to which democracy is embedded and lay involvement in judicial decision-making. Many longstanding democracies involve lay persons while other do not. The re-establishment of democracy in a country does not necessarily stimulate the introduction of lay involvement in judicial decision-making, sometimes the reverse occurs, depending on the cultural and political tradition.

The most common arrangements for lay involvement comprise lay persons making decisions in the lowest tier, or sitting alongside professional judges in the middle or higher tiers. However, it is also common that their decisions are restricted to minor non-imprisonable offences. More serious decisions are invariably made by professionals or hybrid panels.

England and Wales is the only jurisdiction identified in this research where such a high proportion of criminal cases, including serious cases, are decided by lay persons. In addition, the allocation of cases to either lay or stipendiary magistrates by chance, rather than by policy, is unique to this jurisdiction.

Conclusion

Though the research does not point in a particular policy direction, the findings do indicate how the public and court users are likely to react to certain proposals for change.

Although the public do not have strong feelings about the precise role of magistrates, they think that summary offences, particularly if not contested, can be dealt with by a single magistrate but that panels should make the more serious judicial decisions. Cost considerations suggest that this could only be achieved (in the short-term at least) by continuing to make extensive use of lay magistrates.

Criminal justice practitioners, while appreciative of the quality of service given by lay magistrates, have greater confidence in professional judges (stipendiaries). Furthermore governmental pressure to make the criminal courts more efficient, and to reduce the time that cases take to complete, will also tend to favour the greater efficiency of stipendiary magistrates. However, this has to be balanced against the potential increase in cost to the Prison Service.

The nature and balance of contributions made by lay and stipendiary magistrates could be altered to better satisfy these wider considerations, but should not prejudice the integrity and support of a system founded on strong traditions. Not only is the office of Justice of the Peace ancient and in an important tradition of voluntary public service, it is also a direct manifestation of government policy which encourages *active citizens* in an *active community*. In no other jurisdiction does the criminal court system depend so heavily on such voluntary unpaid effort. At no stage during the study was it suggested that in most respects the magistrates' courts do not work well or fail to command general confidence. It is our view, therefore, that eliminating or greatly diminishing the role of lay magistrates would not be widely understood or supported.

[6:5]   Riley, D and Vennard, J *Triable-either-way Offences: Crown Court or Magistrates' Court?* HORS No 98 (1988) HMSO (at page 21):

The present survey lends support to the belief that a significant proportion of either-way cases which are tried at the Crown Court are committed at the discretion of the magistrates. Such cases amounted to 40% of those dealt with at the Crown Court. There was, in addition, considerable variation among the survey courts – by a factor of three – in the rate at which magistrates declined jurisdiction, reaching as high as 63% of committals to one of the four courts. The differences between the areas was evident within offence categories, suggesting that there were systematic variations in how magistrates exercised their discretion over mode of trial.

The finding that magistrates' decisions agreed with prosecution representations concerning mode of trial in 93% of cases is open to varying interpretations. The information upon which magistrates are expected to form their view concerning mode of trial is largely confined to that presented by the prosecution at the mode of trial hearing; defence solicitors in the present survey more often than not made no representations on this matter. This, coupled with the similar criteria adopted by magistrates and prosecution, seems likely to produce agreement about where the case should be tried. On the other hand, the present results suggest that while there was consistency between prosecutors' and magistrates' views about mode of trial within areas, in similar cases courts in one CPS area more often declined jurisdiction than courts in the other area.

It is recognised that, under the present rules, not all either-way cases committed at the discretion of the magistrates would be suitable for summary trial. Quite apart from considerations of offence seriousness, section 19 of the Magistrates' Courts Act 1980 requires that, in determining which mode of trial appears more suitable, the bench has regard to 'whether the punishment which a magistrates' court would have the power to inflict' for the offence 'would be adequate'. The present study did not investigate magistrates' reasons for their mode of trial decisions, therefore the impact of this consideration is unknown. Home Office statistics indicate that more than half (55%) of those convicted at the Crown Court in either-way cases receive a sentence within the sentencing powers of magistrates' courts (*Criminal Statistics* 1986, Table 7.1), but this may simply reflect the fact that some defendants are committed by magistrates for reasons other than the seriousness of the offence or their powers of punishment – such as the practice of declining to try a defendant whose co-accused has elected trial at the Crown Court. The sentence imposed by the judge will also take into account mitigating factors not known to the magistrates when deciding mode of trial.

That said, the level of sentencing in either-way cases committed to the Crown Court, together with the variation between benches in their propensity to decline jurisdiction, indicate some scope for reducing the volume of either-way cases committed at the discretion of the bench. Questions remain, however, concerning the reasons for area variation and the influence on bench policy of guidance provided by Crown Court judges.

The effect on Crown Court workload and on the remand and sentenced prisoner populations of any change in magistrates' venue decisions or in their powers to commit, would largely depend on defendants' willingness to consent to summary trial when offered a choice of venue. Among cases in the present sample committed to the Crown Court at the initiative of the bench, there was an indication from interviews with defence solicitors that about two-fifths (24) of defendants (whose venue preferences were known) would have consented to summary trial if they had been given the option.

In either-way cases considered suitable for summary trial, defendants' venue and pleas decisions largely reflected the perceived advantages and disadvantages of trial at the different venues and the strength of the prosecution case. In most cases, mode of trial decisions and pleas were consistent with defendants' intentions before being advised on these matters by defence solicitors. There was little evidence from the survey that advance disclosure or other exchanges between prosecution and defence were substantially related to defendants' choice of venue or the pleas entered at court. Confirming the results of earlier research, defendants who wanted to plead not guilty tended to see Crown Court trial as offering the better prospect of acquittal and were apparently not deterred by longer waiting times or the chance of a more severe sentence if convicted. Differences in the prospects of acquittal between the Crown Court and magistrates' courts are presumably well known to defendants and their solicitors and this may have weighed more heavily in their choice of venue than sentence considerations. Among defendants who pleaded not guilty to all charges in the present sample, 66% tried at the Crown Court were acquitted compared with 45% at summary trial. These figures do not take into account the relative strength of the prosecution and defence evidence in cases tried at the two venues, but there is some research evidence that defendants are more likely to be acquitted in the Crown Court even having accounted for differences in the nature and strength of the evidence adduced.

For defendants who admit their guilt, there are on the face of it few advantages in Crown Court trial: cases are likely to take longer to come to court and the upper limit on Crown Court sentences exceeds that in the magistrates' court. It has been argued that the additional delay at the Crown Court represents an attraction for some defendants anxious, for example, to enhance mitigating factors (such as a stable personal relationship or employment record) or to maximise time spent remanded in custody to offset a prospective custodial sentence. The present survey provides some support for this view, but according to their solicitors, most defendants who elected intending to plead guilty were motivated by factors other than delay. The reasons most frequently cited to explain this choice of venue were the defendants' previous experience with the courts, the greater confidence in a hearing at the Crown Court than before magistrates. This is consistent with the findings that some three-fifths of those who elected and eventually pleaded guilty were, at the time mode of trial was decided, actively considering contesting their cases. The decision to plead guilty often appeared to have been taken at a later stage.

The knowledge that the Crown Court can inflict a heavier sentence than the magistrates' court would seem to be a strong disincentive to electing. Criminal Statistics 1986, (Tables S1.1(A), S2.1(A)) show that the proportionate use of custody is far higher in the Crown Court for all offence groups. For example, in 1986 58% of male defendants sentenced in the Crown Court on theft or handling charges were given custodial penalties compared with 12% of those sentenced in the magistrates' court. The advice on venue offered by defence solicitors might be expected to reflect their experience of sentencing practices at the two modes of trial. On the other hand, since the Crown Court deals by and large with the more serious either-way cases, it is to be expected that the proportionate use of imprisonment is higher there than in the lower courts. In like cases it may be that judges at some courts pass more lenient sentences than magistrates, or are no more stringent. This would explain why, according to their solicitors, some defendants in the present sample elected believing they would receive a lighter sentence than if convicted by magistrates. For others, the prospect of a fairer hearing and better chance of acquittal evidently outweighed any fears about the sentence the judge might impose on conviction.

The long-standing concern to find ways of containing the number of triable-either-way cases committed for trial at the Crown Court is likely to remain a key issue if, as seems likely on the basis of past evidence, the workload at the Crown Court and the size of the remand and sentenced prisoner populations continue to grow. The present research confirms that, for defendants wishing to contest their case and for some who intend to plead guilty, the incentives to acceptance of summary trial are few. A more promising approach may, therefore, be to encourage magistrates to accept jurisdiction in a higher proportion of either-way cases. Since, however, uncertainty remains as to magistrates' reasons for declining jurisdiction, further research might usefully examine the link between bench practices and the representations made by prosecutors, having regard to the influence on local policies of guidance handed down by liaison judges.

[6:6]   Bail Act 1976 section 4; Schedule 1

4   General right to bail of accused persons and others

(1)   A person to whom this section applies shall be granted bail except as provided in Schedule 1 to this Act.

(2)   This section applies to a person who is accused of an offence when—
    (a)   he appears or is brought before a magistrates' court or the Crown Court in the course of or in connection with proceedings for the offence, or
    (b)   he applies to a court for bail or for a variation of the conditions of bail in connection with the proceedings.

This subsection does not apply as respects proceedings on or after a person's conviction of the offence or proceedings against a fugitive offender for the offence.

(3)   This section also applies to a person who, having been convicted of an offence, appears or is brought before a magistrates' court to be dealt with under Part II of Schedule 3 to the Powers of Criminal Courts (Sentencing) Act 2000 (breach of certain community orders).

(4)   This section also applies to a person who has been convicted of an offence and whose case is adjourned by the court for the purpose of enabling inquiries or a report to be made to assist the court in dealing with him for the offence.

(5)   Schedule 1 to this Act also has effect as respects conditions of bail for a person to whom this section applies.

(6)   In Schedule 1 to this Act "the defendant" means a person to whom this section applies and any reference to a defendant whose case is adjourned for inquiries or a report is a reference to a person to whom this section applies by virtue of subsection (4) above.

(7)   This section is subject to section 41 of the Magistrates' Courts Act 1980 (restriction of bail by magistrates court in cases of treason).

(8) This section is subject to section 25 of the Criminal Justice and Public Order Act 1994 (exclusion of bail in cases of homicide and rape).

(9) In taking any decisions required by Part I or II of Schedule 1 to this Act, the considerations to which the court is to have regard include, so far as relevant, any misuse of controlled drugs by the defendant ("controlled drugs" and "misuse" having the same meanings as in the Misuse of Drugs Act 1971).

SCHEDULE 1 Persons Entitled to Bail: Supplementary Provisions

Section 4

PART I
DEFENDANTS ACCUSED OR CONVICTED OF IMPRISONABLE OFFENCES

Defendants to whom Part I applies

1   Where the offence or one of the offences of which the defendant is accused or convicted in the proceedings is punishable with imprisonment the following provisions of this Part of this Schedule apply.

Exceptions to right to bail

2   The defendant need not be granted bail if the court is satisfied that there are substantial grounds for believing that the defendant, if released on bail (whether subject to conditions or not) would—
    (a)   fail to surrender to custody, or
    (b)   commit an offence while on bail, or
    (c)   interfere with witnesses or otherwise obstruct the course of justice, whether in relation to himself or any other person.

2A   The defendant need not be granted bail if—
    (a)   the offence is an indictable offence or an offence triable either way; and
    (b)   it appears to the court that he was on bail in criminal proceedings on the date of the offence.

3   The defendant need not be granted bail if the court is satisfied that the defendant should be kept in custody for his own protection or, if he is a child or young person, for his own welfare.

4   The defendant need not be granted bail if he is in custody in pursuance of the sentence of a court or of any authority acting under any of the Services Acts.

5   The defendant need not be granted bail where the court is satisfied that it has not been practicable to obtain sufficient information for the purpose of taking the decisions required by this Part of this Schedule for want of time since the institution of the proceedings against him.

6   The defendant need not be granted bail if, having been released on bail in or in connection with the proceedings for the offence, he has been arrested in pursuance of section 7 of this Act.

Exception applicable only to defendant whose case is adjourned for inquiries or a report

7   Where his case is adjourned for inquiries or a report, the defendant need not be granted bail if it appears to the court that it would be impracticable to complete the inquiries or make the report without keeping the defendant in custody.

Restriction of conditions of bail

8(1) Subject to sub-paragraph (3) below, where the defendant is granted bail, no conditions shall be imposed under subsections (4) to (7) (except subsection (6)(d) or (e)) of section 3 of this Act unless it appears to the court that it is necessary to do so for the purpose of preventing the occurrence of any of the events mentioned in paragraph 2 of this Part of this Schedule ...

(1A) No condition shall be imposed under section 3(6)(d) of this Act unless it appears to be necessary to do so for the purpose of enabling inquiries or a report to be made.

(2)   Sub-paragraphs (1) and (1A) above also apply on any application to the court to vary the conditions of bail or to impose conditions in respect of bail which has been granted unconditionally.

(3)   The restriction imposed by sub-paragraph (1A) above shall not apply to the conditions required to be imposed under section 3(6A) of this Act or operate to override the direction in section 11(3) of the Powers of Criminal Courts (Sentencing) Act 2000 to a magistrates' court to impose conditions of bail under section 3(6)(d) of this Act of the description specified in the said section 11(3) in the circumstances so specified.

Decisions under paragraph 2

9   In taking the decisions required by paragraph 2 or 2A of this Part of this Schedule, the court shall have regard to such of the following considerations as appear to it to be relevant, that is to say—
  (a)   the nature and seriousness of the offence or default (and the probable method of dealing with the defendant for it),
  (b)   the character, antecedents, associations and community ties of the defendant,
  (c)   the defendant's record as respects the fulfilment of his obligations under previous grants of bail in criminal proceedings,

(d)   except in the case of a defendant whose case is adjourned for inquiries or a report, the strength of the evidence of his having committed the offence or having defaulted,

as well as to any others which appear to be relevant.

9A

...

Cases under section 128A of Magistrates' Courts Act 1980

9B   Where the court is considering exercising the power conferred by section 128A of the Magistrates' Courts Act 1980 (power to remand in custody for more than 8 clear days), it shall have regard to the total length of time which the accused would spend in custody if it were to exercise the power.

PART II
DEFENDANTS ACCUSED OR CONVICTED OF NON-IMPRISONABLE OFFENCES

Defendants to whom Part II applies

1   Where the offence or every offence of which the defendant is accused or convicted in the proceedings is one which is not punishable with imprisonment the following provisions of this Part of this Schedule apply.

Exceptions to right to bail

2   The defendant need not be granted bail if—
   (a)   it appears to the court that, having been previously granted bail in criminal proceedings, he has failed to surrender to custody in accordance with his obligations under the grant of bail; and
   (b)   the court believes, in view of that failure, that the defendant, if released on bail (whether subject to conditions or not) would fail to surrender to custody.

3   The defendant need not be granted bail if the court is satisfied that the defendant should be kept in custody for his own protection or, if he is a child or young person, for his own welfare.

4   The defendant need not be granted bail if he is in custody in pursuance of the sentence of a court or of any authority acting under any of the Services Acts.

5   The defendant need not be granted bail if, having been released on bail in or in connection with the proceedings for the offence, he has been arrested in pursuance of section 7 of this Act.

PART IIA
DECISIONS WHERE BAIL REFUSED ON PREVIOUS HEARING

1   If the court decides not to grant the defendant bail, it is the court's duty to consider, at each subsequent hearing while the defendant is a person to whom section 4 above applies and remains in custody, whether he ought to be granted bail.

2   At the first hearing after that at which the court decided not to grant the defendant bail he may support an application for bail with any argument as to fact or law that he desires (whether or not he has advanced that argument previously).

3   At subsequent hearings the court need not hear arguments as to fact or law which it has heard previously.

PART III
INTERPRETATION

1   For the purposes of this Schedule the question whether an offence is one which is punishable with imprisonment shall be determined without regard to any enactment prohibiting or restricting the imprisonment of young offenders or first offenders.

2   References in this Schedule to previous grants of bail in criminal proceedings include references to bail granted before the coming into force of this Act; and so as respects the reference to an offence committed by a person on bail in relation to any period before the coming into force of paragraph 2A of Part I of this Schedule.

3   References in this Schedule to a defendant's being kept in custody or being in custody include (where the defendant is a child or young person) references to his being kept or being in the care of a local authority in pursuance of a warrant of commitment under section 23(1) of the Children and Young Persons Act 1969.

4   In this Schedule—

"court", in the expression "sentence of a court" includes a service court as defined in section 12(1) of the Visiting Forces Act 1952 and "sentence", in that expression, shall be construed in accordance with that definition;

"default", in relation to the defendant, means the default for which he is to be dealt with under Part II of Schedule 3 to the Powers of Criminal Courts (Sentencing) Act 2000;

"the Services Acts" means the Army Act 1955, the Air Force Act 1955 and the Naval Discipline Act 1957.

[6:7] HM Chief Inspector of Prisons *Unjust Deserts: A Thematic Review of the Treatment and Conditions for Unsentenced Prisoners in England and Wales* (2000) (at page 123):

Strategic Issues and Recommendations for the Management of Establishments Holding Unsentenced Prisoners

12.01 This review has revealed a startling gap between what the public might reasonably expect to be in place for unsentenced prisoners and what is actually in place. More worryingly however, it also identifies a gap between the official understanding of what is being delivered as described in the replies from the *Governors' survey* and the actual experience of unsentenced prisoners; a gap largely supported by our own observations from fieldwork and inspections.

12.02 The following factors seem to be relevant to this state of affairs:
- Local prisons are overcrowded. The Prison Service has endeavoured, quite rightly, to keep the rising numbers of prisoners sent to them by the courts as close as possible to where they are to appear for trial. Also, for entirely understandable and sensible reasons the Prison Service has chosen to protect training prisons from overcrowding by concentrating this pressure on local prisons. This has resulted in the latter holding a rising number of sentenced prisoners, both short term, who increasingly serve their whole sentences in local prisons, and longer term, who can wait for extended periods to be transferred to training prisons. The sheer pressure of numbers has therefore thwarted the development of proper regimes for unsentenced prisoners.
- Prisoners in local prisons are generally compliant. Most prisoners prefer to be held in local prisons where they are closer to their homes, friends and families than in more distant training prisons. Indeed this has been such a priority for most prisoners that they have been prepared to put up with poor conditions in order to take advantage of being able to stay in their local area. The rate of turnover in the population is also such that most prisoners tolerate their conditions on the basis that they will not have to do so for a long time. Apart from the riots of the early nineties, unsentenced prisoners have not posed serious control problems. Complaints from unsentenced prisoners themselves have not therefore provided a stimulus for change.
- The diversity of prisoner needs presents difficult challenges for staff. All offenders entering the prison system do so through local prisons. Any of these establishments might hold remands awaiting trial, convicted unsentenced and sentenced prisoners, debtors, civil prisoners, deportees or immigration detainees and those on overcrowding drafts from other local prisons. Sentenced prisoners may be short or longer sentenced and include life sentence prisoners both newly sentenced, recalled from training prisons or licence revoked. Among this mixture of prisoners will be those with violent tendencies, those who are vulnerable to attack from others, those who are mentally unwell, those who are drug misusers, those who are drug dealers, those who are depressed and suicidal and, of course those who are subsequently found not guilty. Although some may be familiar to staff from previous periods in custody, many will be unknown and the uncertainty and risk inherent in this mix creates one of the biggest challenges for managers and staff.
- Local prisons have inadequate physical facilities. Many of the old local prisons were constructed for the penal policies of a different age and lack the facilities that are required to support healthy prison regimes. Until some twenty years ago when

finances for the maintenance of prison buildings became more readily available, all were in a wretched condition. Improvements have been made, notably in the abolition of 'slopping out', but most are still in need of large capital investment to make them fit for their purpose. For example, in many of the cells designed for one person but used to accommodate two, there is no suitable screen between the toilet and the living space. The Director General and his colleagues are aware of these deficiencies and are as keen as anyone else to rectify them, but do not have the necessary finance to carry out the work.

- Local prisons have a culture of disengagement with prisoners. For many decades the unspoken but unmistakable message to staff from senior Prison Service managers has been that their job is to serve the courts by taking as many prisoners as necessary, and to avoid escapes and disturbances. Given the risks associated with these tasks and the limited resources to manage them, a culture of disengagement with prisoners and risk avoidance has become established.

- Local prisons are able to resist change. The staff of local prisons become the culture carriers as they are longer serving than either the prisoners or their managers. The former pass through on short periods of remand, short sentences or on to training prisons, and the latter pass through on relatively short tours of duty as they build their careers. In these circumstances staff become disproportionately influential and without training, management and leadership for their role in a modern Prison Service, their prime motivation becomes one of making life as comfortable as possible for themselves and their colleagues, and their allegiance and commitment to the Prison Service's Statement of Purpose becomes hard to find. In such prisons there is an absence of justice and fairness in dealing with legitimate requests and complaints from prisoners, Governors appear powerless to introduce even the simplest of changes without disputes, and progress becomes impossible without a clear mandate for change from Ministers and the Prisons Board.

The Way Forward

12.03 At any time there are well over thirty thousand people held in fifty-three local prisons and remand centres in England and Wales. Some of the establishments in which they are held treat unsentenced prisoners with humanity and try to meet their individual needs; the five contracted out local prisons, for example, and most local prisons for women. Few of the suggestions for improvement in this review are entirely original in that many reflect examples of good, indeed outstanding current practice in both directly managed and contracted out establishments. One such example is the recommendation to replace the policy of separating unconvicted from convicted prisoners with an integrated approach that is based on safety and respect which has been tried and tested by at least one former Governor of a local directly managed prison. What is missing, however, is a clear unifying vision for unsentenced prisoners which details how they should be treated and the conditions in which they should be held, and a management system which ensures consistent delivery in all local prisons and remand centres.

12.04 The senior management of the Prison Service has tended to believe that the answer lies in finding capable Governors to take command of these prisons. It is true that without strong leadership nothing will change, but far more than the personal qualities of individual governors are needed if lasting change is to be achieved. I must emphasise that responsibility for this state of affairs does not lie with the current Prisons Board. Indeed, I believe that it is because of the leadership already demonstrated by the Director

General that there is now a real opportunity to tackle the culture of those establishments that have been producing poor, and in some cases, unacceptable treatment and conditions for prisoners, including those held on remand, for too many years. There is every reason to be optimistic that staff in the Prison Service will respond positively to the challenge of providing a healthy and needs based regime for unsentenced prisoners as they have done successfully in other parts of the prison estate, notably high security prisons. However, they will need re-training as well as strong leadership if they are to operate in a radically different way. Many, for example, will need help to understand the needs and rights of unsentenced prisoners and the proper role of local prisons within a joined up Criminal Justice System. They will also need to understand the complex mental health problems of unsentenced prisoners and the importance of ensuring that they have access to due process.

Recommendations

12.05 I have detailed throughout this review a number of areas where change needs to be made, and a number of recommendations are included in the text. However, I have two over-riding strategic recommendations which I detail here. Firstly, in view of the physical inadequacy of the facilities and buildings within which many unsentenced prisoners are held.

I recommend that the cost of the work required to ensure that all local prisons and remand centres have the necessary facilities to hold prisoners in decent conditions should be published and that the finance to carry it out should be provided within a five year programme.

12.06 In view of the enormity of the challenge which faces the Prison Service in bringing about cultural change in many of the establishments holding unsentenced prisoners.

I recommend that a strategy is introduced by the Prisons Board, with the full support of Ministers, for a two year programme of change to identify and deliver agreed prisoner focused outcomes as detailed in this review, for all unsentenced prisoners in local prisons and remand centres. This strategy should contain a clear sense of direction for local prisons and remand centres, detail the elements of work which they should undertake and include costed service delivery agreements. The strategy should include the introduction of a mandatory and comprehensive initial and ongoing training programme for new staff and an immediate programme to re-educate current staff. There should also be a remedial element to the strategy to identify those prisons needing to achieve fundamental change in the way that unsentenced prisoners are treated. This information can be readily gathered from inspection reports over recent years. Such identified prisons should be set clear targets, based on the delivery of agreed outcomes for unsentenced prisoners. They should also be given suitable senior managers to carry out this work, which might include nominated 'change managers' with a clear briefing and training for what is to be achieved, and time in post to carry through the required changes. Such senior management teams should also be given both practical and personal support from senior functional managers in Prison Service Headquarters, and opportunities for the regular exchange of experiences through meetings with colleagues in other similar establishments.

12.07 I intend to carry out a follow up to this review in two years time, and will continue to monitor the treatment and conditions of unsentenced prisoners within my ongoing inspection programme. I look forward to witnessing the improvements which I am confident that the Prison Service can deliver, with the full backing of Ministers.

[6:8] Lloyd, C *Bail Information Schemes: Practice and Effect* HO RPU Paper No 69 (1992) HMSO (at page 65):

How is bail information most effective?

One of the most interesting findings of this research has been the differences in the way in which bail information has its effect in the three courts studied. While the Blackpool scheme seemed to have influenced the remand decision primarily through strengthening the defence's case for bail, at the other extreme, the Manchester scheme's effectiveness relies almost entirely on its influence on the CPS. Both these findings from the data could have been predicted from the interviews with solicitors and probation officers in the field. The Manchester CPS were universally described as an independent agency, keen to make their own decisions rather than act at the bidding of the police. Interviews with prosecutors verified this opinion: they spoke positively of bail information and, for the most part, saw it as a useful adjunct to their decision-making. By contrast the CPS at Blackpool – and to a lesser extent at Hull – were more critical of the local scheme and saw bail information primarily as an aid to the defence.

Which *modus operandi* is the most effective? Taking account of the numbers interviewed, it was the Hull scheme that seemed to divert the highest proportion of interviewed defendants from a remand in custody. It would therefore appear that bail information is most effective when used fully by the CPS and the defence.

Another possible way of influencing the remand decision would be to provide information directly to the court. Jones and Goldkamp (1991)[28] have recently criticised the bail information initiative in the UK for not involving magistrates sufficiently in the development and use of bail information. The possibility of providing bail information directly to magistrates was raised in interviews with court clerks, solicitors and probation staff and received a mixed reception. Interestingly, it was a number of defence and CPS solicitors who were in favour of the provision of information direct to the court, suggesting that information would be more effective if presented in this way. However, various criticisms of this approach was made. First, it was thought possible that some magistrates might confuse bail information sheets with social inquiry reports and assume that the sheets represented probation recommendations for bail. Second, it was pointed out that if magistrates expected bail information sheets to be presented for each defendant, if a sheet was not presented for a defendant they might automatically assume that there was nothing positive to be said, although the reason for the absence of a bail information sheet might simply be that the BIO ran out of time. As long as magistrates were adequately prepared for such a scheme's introduction, the first argument would seem to carry little weight. The second argument is more persuasive. A scheme would have to ensure complete coverage of cases where the police were objecting to bail in order to prevent this process occurring. Nevertheless it seems surprising that there has been no experimentation with a scheme that provides copies of the bail information sheet to the CPS, the defence and the court. There is a sense in which information read out in court by the prosecutor or defending solicitor lacks objectivity. While defence solicitors can refer to the fact that the information was verified by a probation officer or ancillary, the context of the presentation of this information is within the defence's

---

28 Jones, P R and Goldkamp, J S 'Judicial Guidelines for Pre-trial Release' (1991) 30 Howard Journal 140.

argument for bail, and this may detract from the perceived 'independence' of the information.

(and at page 70):

Conclusions

The study reported here has added further support to the growing body of research and monitoring evidence which shows bail information schemes to be successful in diverting defendants from remands in custody. The importance of such work cannot be understated. Remand centres and local prisons remain the most crowded sector of the prison system, with Spartan regimes and high rates of suicide. The avoidance of a potential remand in custody is therefore saving the defendant from a period of imprisonment on remand in overcrowded conditions, and may also contribute to the likelihood of a non-custodial sentence. Moreover, the cost-effectiveness analysis presented here suggests that bail information schemes are also saving the criminal justice system a considerable amount of money.

Perhaps the most interesting part of the research has been the exploration of the different ways in which bail information has its effect in three courts. Unfortunately this issue could not be addressed adequately at Lincoln Prison because of the lack of information about CPS and defence applications. While national policy and previous research have tended to focus on the influence of bail information on the CPS, it is clear from the evidence presented here that bail information can also have a significant effect through influencing the number and strength of defence applications. While the sample of three court-based schemes is admittedly small, it is nevertheless interesting to note that the scheme which had the largest relative effect on remand decision was the one which exploited both paths of influence to the full.

However, it should be emphasised that the probation service and its BIOs have only limited powers in influencing the way in which other agencies utilise bail information: good working relationships can be forged between BIOs and prosecutors and defence solicitors, and senior probation managers can liaise with their counterparts in the other organisations. Nevertheless, perhaps the most important determinant of the way in which bail information works is the particular subculture or dynamics of the local magistrates' court, and in particular, the ethos of the local CPS branch. Bail information will be most effective in a court with a high rate of remanding in custody; a local CPS which is prepared to reconsider police requests and use bail information as a means to achieve more independent decision making; and defence solicitors who are prepared to make a bail application at first appearance.

[6:9] Morgan, P M and Henderson, P *Remand Decisions and Offending on Bail: Evaluation of the Bail Process Project* HORS 184 (at pages vii–x):

The aim of the Bail Process Project was to improve the quality, accuracy and timeliness of the information available to remand decision-makers so that they were better able to assess the risk of offending on bail.

Inter-agency working groups were set up in five court areas in 1992. Each group, chaired by the Justices' Clerk, studied the remand process in its own area, and identified problems that affected the information available to the police custody officers, CPS prosecutors and magistrates when they made a pre-trial decision or recommendation on bail or custody. The groups then set in hand the changes that were possible to solve these problems.

The problems that were identified are described by Burrows et al (1994) and are summarised in Appendix A of this report. The main changes that were introduced by the courts were as follows.

- In most areas, the early *availability of the defendant's criminal record* was a problem. One area was able to extend the hours of direct access to its local records from eight to twenty-four hours a day. Another negotiated access to the more detailed record held by the National Identification Service (as compared with the brief record held on the police national computer). A third area was able to establish a mechanism whereby the court was informed if the defendant was already on bail from a different police station or court within the same police force area.

- All five areas carried out some *training of magistrates in risk assessment*, and ways of improving magistrates' awareness of bail hostel facilities in the area were explored. Three areas set up *training courses for police custody officers* on the same topic to ensure greater uniformity of practice.

- Three areas amended the *wording of bail conditions of residence or curfew*, to oblige the defendant to present himself or herself in person to police officers monitoring his/her compliance. Three areas distributed *simplified bail notices* to make the terms of bail clearer to defendants, that is, the date of the next court appearance and any conditions attached. These were issued to defendants granted unconditional bail as well as those granted bail with conditions.

- In two areas, court clerks started to keep *a record of representations made in remand decisions* so that future benches would know the reasons why earlier decisions had been made.

- Two areas made changes in court listing times to allow more *time for pre-court discussion between the agencies* and, in one area, new arrangements allowed Saturday courts to have access to the probation service.

- In two areas, local steering mechanisms were established under the Court User group to ensure *better liaison between two bail information schemes in the same area*, and to ensure general understanding of how negative information (that which might work against the granting of bail) was handled by the probation service (see Appendix D).

- In single areas, the following changes were made: a *new prison-based bail information scheme* and a *trial bail support scheme* for 18- to 25-year-olds were established; a scheme was set up to provide *volunteers to act as 'appropriate adults'* during police interviews with under-17-year-olds; and arrangements were made for a *review panel for mentally disordered offenders*.

Case tracking data were collected on cases involving bail/custody decisions in the five areas over a period of three months in 1993 and three months in 1994 (before and after the improvements suggested above). Defendants released on bail in the two samples of cases were followed up at the criminal records office to find details of any offences that were committed while they were on bail.

Analyses showed that the *proportion of defendants granted court bail who were convicted of an offence committed while they were on bail* was reduced in two of the court areas, and changed only slightly or not at all in the other three. The clear decreases were in the

Horseferry Road court area (from 18% in 1993 to 11% in 1994), and in the Leicester court area (from 20% in 1993 to 12% in 1994). The proportion of persons *charged with offences committed on court bail* showed similar decreases: in Horseferry Road area from 22% to 16%, and in Leicester, from 24% to 16%.

The analyses suggest that offending on bail decreased in the Horseferry Road area because more persons were remanded in custody (the custody rates increased by six percentage points between 1993 and 1994). Leicester showed a different picture in that the custody rates went down by about five percentage points. This suggests that the reduction in offending on bail in Leicester may have been caused by some of the improvements made, such as better access to defendant's bail history, or an increased emphasis on the training of magistrates in the assessment of risk.

The analyses also showed that the rates of offending while on police bail after charge (as measured by convictions) showed a small decrease overall from 9% to 8%. There were small decreases in three areas, between two and three percentage points, no change in Newport and a small increase in Bournemouth. Bournemouth and Salford showed the lowest rates for offending on police bail (between 5% and 8%): for Salford this is probably explained by the fact that this area was found to have a much higher rate of police custody after charge (see Chapter 4).

The rates of offending on police bail as measured by charges showed a similar pattern with slightly higher figures. Over all areas, the rates changed from 12% in 1993 to 11% in 1994.

An exercise was carried out with bail decision-makers in Leicester to explore their approach to assessing risk. This established a set of factors which were held to be important, and explored how these were seen to be related to the assessment of the risk of the defendant failing to appear at court and the risk of offending while on bail (see Tables 3.1 and 3.2).

The case tracking data were analysed to explore which categories of defendant were associated with higher and lower than average rates of offending on court bail. Those with higher rates included defendants:

- with no fixed abode (42% offended on bail)
- charged with car theft or burglary (32%, 29% respectively offended on bail)
- who waited more than six months before trial (32% or more than three months (24%)
- aged 17 and under (29%)
- who had served a previous custodial sentence (28%)
- who had a previous record of breaching bail (27%)
- who were unemployed (21%).

Those with lower rates were those:

- who waited less than a month before trial (4%)
- who were in employment (7%)
- who were charged with assault (7%) or fraud (8%)
- who were 21 or over (13%).

(Rates for combinations of these factors are shown in Table 5.3.)

The Bail Process Project arose from concern about the extent of offending on bail. In 1992, there was a great deal of public discussion of the issue when three police forces published a range of figures from surveys carried out in their own areas, and the Home Office published results from its internal research. The then Home Secretary gave an undertaking to Parliament to tackle this issue by setting up pilot projects in selected local areas. The intention was to improve the quality of the information available to the courts to assist them in identifying these defendants who were most likely to offend on bail.

This commitment led to a steering committee being set up which included representatives from all the relevant criminal justice agencies, ie the police, the Crown Prosecution Service (CPS), the magistrates' courts, the probation service and the Law Society. The committee was to tackle two main tasks:

* to investigate what information was required by remand decision-makers, and in what ways the information available was judged to be deficient
* to explore ways of remedying these deficiencies and, where possible, to put these remedies into effect.

Background: who makes pre-trial decisions

In England and Wales, the majority of decisions about the granting of bail before trial arise at three points: when a suspect has been arrested by the police but the evidence available is not sufficient for charges to be brought; when a suspect has been arrested and charged with an offence; and when the court has decided to adjourn the hearing of a case to another date. The first two of these decisions are made by the police: the third is made by magistrates.

(and at page 60):

To avoid unnecessary remands in custody, and to reduce offending on bail, magistrates must target the two out of three (in the highest risk group) and the one in 16 in the lowest risk group. Such targeting might be based on information over and above the broader categories described: perhaps more detail of the current offence and how it relates to the criminal record to indicate a pattern of offending, an indication of the attitude of the defendant, and any circumstances or influences which may have a positive affect on future behaviour. However, even if such information were available, there is no guarantee that accurate predictions of offending would be possible. Another relevant factor is the waiting time before trial: the research has shown that longer waiting times are related to higher offending on bail. This suggests that, if changes in procedure or practice can be devised to reduce the waiting times for defendants on bail, there should be a corresponding reduction in offending on bail. Broad estimates suggest that a reduction in waiting times of around one month should correspond to a decrease of three per cent in offending on bail.

[6:10]   Eaton, M 'The Question of Bail' in Carlen, P and Worrall, A (eds) *Gender, Crime and Justice* (1987) Open University Press (at page 106):

Throughout the process of summary justice a model of the family is employed when dealing with both men and women defendants. This model, with a male breadwinner and a dependant woman, responsible for child-care and domestic labour, is used in pleas of mitigation and social inquiry reports. The same model also underlies current legislation on taxation and benefits and traditional policies in providing for and responding to the family. It is a model based on a sexual division of labour which has consequences for women in both waged and domestic labour. For many women it means deprivation and isolation.

In the labour market, men may expect to earn a 'family wage' since it is assumed that their earnings provide for others. Women find that the jobs available to them do not offer the same earnings. In 1982 the average full time wage for a woman was 72% of a man's wage. Women in part-time work, who constitute two-fifths of the female labour force were even worse off; their hourly rate in 1982 was, on average, 57% of the hourly rate paid to men in full-time work. As part-time workers these women have fewer rights to sick pay, holiday pay or pensions. While many married women work to keep the family above the poverty line, they are usually unable to claim for dependants if they become unemployed. Domestic responsibilities bring long hours of work for most women. One survey revealed that women with young children worked an average of seventy-seven hours a week – nearly twice as long as an industrial working week of forty hours. Child-care and housework are still assumed to be the woman's work even if she has paid employment outside the home. The choice facing many women is the 'double shift' of paid employment and domestic labour, or the isolation and lower income of full-time housework.

Isolation is not just the result of the social organisation of housework. It is also a consequence of the traditions of privacy which surround the family. The same attitude is manifest in police reluctance to respond to instances of wife assault. Those relegated to the domestic sphere are most vulnerable to the abuse of power within that sphere. Even where women do not suffer physical abuse, mental illness may be a response to the conflicting demands placed on them. Depression is more likely among women involved full-time in housework than it is among unmarried women and married women with jobs outside the home.

Within the family women are vulnerable to violence, depression and poverty and for these reasons it has been the subject of much feminist critique. Only by questioning the position of women within this structure is there any challenge to the continual subordination of women – a subordination learned and reconstituted daily within the family. Of course courts do not question the gender roles of women within the family – these are accepted as normal and natural. They are implicit in the model of family which underlies pleas of mitigation and social inquiry reports, as they are in applications for bail. But applications for bail go further than other examples of courtroom rhetoric. In applications for bail we have more than a description of an acceptable model of the family and its associated gender roles: we have an acknowledgement that such a family structure may offer a form of control comparable to that offered by the prison system.

[6:11]   Worrall, A 'Sisters in Law? Women Defendants and Women Magistrates' in Carlen, P and Worrall, A (eds) *Gender, Crime and Justice* (1987) Open University Press (at page 122):

This chapter has attempted to demonstrate that the relationship between magistrates and defendants is constructed within a discourse of common sense which, despite its inherent paradoxes and discontinuities, is represented as a consistent and coherent unity. Although magisterial common sense may appear to challenge and transgress 'expert' discourse, it is in fact a competing discourse of 'expertise'. In relation to women defendants, it is characterised by a threefold myth:

1 That magistrates can never claim to know anything about women defendants because knowledge accrues through experience and women defendants are always already invisible and inaccessible to the senses.

2 That magistrates can never generalise about women defendants *qua* women, because the law is blind to differences of gender (as of class, age, race etc.).

3 That magistrates can always reach a consensus about women defendants both because of and despite social, economic, political or, specifically, gender differences, these differences being hailed (at the point of recruitment to the Bench) and denied (at the point of judgement) in the interests of justice.

These judicial myths have been challenged, and it has been argued that magistrates construct the woman defendant within specific conditions:

1 They act 'as though' they have knowledge of women defendants, that knowledge emanating from cultural stereotypes of appropriate female behaviour and being reinforced by their own socially and discursively privileged personal life experience.

2 They invoke the ostensibly gender-neutral moral concept of *merit* to justify treating women defendants *qua* women differently from male defendants, since meritorious conduct in men and women is differentially defined.

It has been argued, additionally, that women magistrates suppress their empathetic understanding of women's positions in society (an empathy based on shared biological experience) because, having entered the masculine world of the criminal justice system by virtue of their womanhood, their ability to sustain their authority and credibility within it is dependent on their denial of that womanhood.

Nevertheless, in this chapter I have sought to demonstrate that there may exist the potential for a greater understanding of women defendants by the magistracy, if women magistrates felt more confident – and were allowed – to express their genuinely differing perspectives and opinions. The structure for such a richness and variety of contribution exists; what is lacking is the will to experience the discomfort of conflict, especially when the mechanism for achieving an apparent consensus – the appeal to, and of, common sense – is so readily available. Women magistrates, like women defendants, are socially constructed within the discourses of domesticity, sexuality and pathology. The evidence of this chapter suggests that they may indeed be 'sisters in law', subject to a common oppression but not yet able to fully recognise each other.

[6:12] Bail (Amendment) Act 1993 section 1

1 Prosecution right of appeal

(1) Where a magistrates' court grants bail to a person who is charged with or convicted of—

(a) an offence punishable by a term of imprisonment of 5 years or more, or

(b) an offence under section 12 (taking a conveyance without authority) or 12A (aggravated vehicle taking) of the Theft Act 1968,

the prosecution may appeal to a judge of the Crown Court against the granting of bail.

(2)   Subsection (1) above applies only where the prosecution is conducted—
- (a)   by or on behalf of the Director of Public Prosecutions; or
- (b)   by a person who falls within such class or description of person as may be prescribed for the purposes of this section by order made by the Secretary of State.

(3)   Such an appeal may be made only if—
- (a)   the prosecution made representations that bail should not be granted; and
- (b)   the representations were made before it was granted.

(4)   In the event of the prosecution wishing to exercise the right of appeal set out in subsection (1) above, oral notice of appeal shall be given to the magistrates' court at the conclusion of the proceedings in which such bail has been granted and before the release from custody of the person concerned.

(5)   Written notice of appeal shall thereafter be served on the magistrates' court and the person concerned within two hours of the conclusion of such proceedings.

(6)   Upon receipt from the prosecution of oral notice of appeal from its decision to grant bail the magistrates' court shall remand in custody the person concerned, until the appeal is determined or otherwise disposed of.

(7)   Where the prosecution fails, within the period of two hours mentioned in subsection (5) above, to serve one or both of the notices required by that subsection, the appeal shall be deemed to have been disposed of.

(8)   The hearing of an appeal under subsection (1) above against a decision of the magistrates' court to grant bail shall be commenced within forty-eight hours, excluding weekends and any public holiday (that is to say, Christmas Day, Good Friday or a bank holiday), from the date on which oral notice of appeal is given.

(9)   At the hearing of any appeal by the prosecution under this section, such appeal shall be by way of re-hearing, and the judge hearing any such appeal may remand the person concerned in custody or may grant bail subject to such conditions (if any) as he thinks fit.

(10)   In relation to a child or young person (within the meaning of the Children and Young Persons Act 1969)—
- (a)   the reference in subsection (1) above to an offence punishable by a term of imprisonment is to be read as a reference to an offence which would be so punishable in the case of an adult; and
- (b)   the reference in subsection (5) above to remand in custody is to be read subject to the provisions of section 23 of the Act of 1969 (remands to local authority accommodation).

(11)   The power to make an order under subsection (2) above shall be exercisable by statutory instrument and any instrument shall be subject to annulment in pursuance of a resolution of either House of Parliament.

[6:13] *Practice Direction:* Crown Court: Bail Pending Appeal [1983] 1 WLR 1292

1   The procedure is described in the *Guide to Proceedings in the Court of Appeal Criminal Division*. This is available at Crown Courts and is to be found at (1983) 77 Cr App Rep 138 and [1983] Crim LR 415.

2   The procedure is also set out in outline on Criminal Appeal Office Forms C (Crown Court Judge's Certificate of fitness for appeal) and BC (Crown Court Judge's Order granting bail), copies of which are held by the Crown Court. The court clerk will ensure that these forms are always available when a judge hears an application under these provisions.

3   The judge may well think it right: (a) to hear the application in chambers with a shorthand-writer present; (b) to invite the defendant's counsel to submit before the hearing of the application a draft of the grounds which he will ask the judge to certify on Form C.
      Counsel for the Crown will be better able to assist the judge at the hearing if the draft ground is sent beforehand to him also.

4   The first question is whether there exists a particular, and cogent, ground of appeal. If there is no such ground there can be no certificate, and if there is no certificate there can be no bail. A judge should not grant a certificate with regard to sentence merely in the light of mitigation to which he has, in his opinion, given due weight, nor in regard to conviction on a ground where he considers the chance of a successful appeal is not substantial. The judge should bear in mind that, where a certificate is refused, application may be made to the Court of Appeal for leave to appeal and for bail.

5   The length of the period which might elapse before the hearing of the appeal is *not* a ground of appeal appropriate to the judge's certificate.

6   That period, if there is otherwise good ground for a certificate, may be one factor in the decision whether or not to grant bail; but a judge who is minded to take this factor into account may find it advisable to have the court clerk contact the Criminal Appeal Office Listing Co-ordinator in order that he may have an accurate and up-to-date assessment of the likely waiting time. The Co-ordinator will require a general account of the weight and urgency of the case.

7   Where the defendant's representative considers the bail should be applied for as a matter of urgency the application should normally be made, in the first instance, to the trial judge, and the Court of Appeal may decline to treat such an application as urgent if there is no good reason why it has not been made to the trial judge.

[6:14] **Brown, S** *Magistrates at Work: Sentencing and Social Structure* (1991) Open University Press (at page 81):

The processes of classification and translation themselves both help to create and sustain a rendering of reality in which the individual case may be diagnosed, a pathology created, a 'solution' proposed, and which in its very individuality indicates a relationship with the overall corpus of unruly youth. This offender is situated in relation to that offender; this one is not a lost cause, that one is a hardened offender. Similarly one penalty implies the whole hierarchy of penalties. Through the whole business of processing juveniles, very little attention is paid by participating actors to the *validity* of the social background representations invoked.

No desire is shown to understand the meaning of the offence from the child's point of view; rather the child must account for it in the court's terms (Why did you do it? Did you know it was wrong?). Little interest is shown in whether locking children up in detention centres actually has an effect on behaviour, few questions are asked as to whether or not the whole package of an escalating penalty may not successively reinforce the likelihood of the juvenile's being re-introduced into the 'system'.

The emphasis is on describability. The individual is transposed into a set of knowledge representations which are comprehensible not with reference to the actual lived experience and actions of the individual but rather with reference to the instrumentality of those representations: what it is that they enable, and what it is that they preclude. In this sense, Shaun, and Ian, and Nicola, and Michelle themselves, are irrelevant to the juvenile court; 'social information' does not refer to them as people but to the project of the juvenile court in reconstructing them as information objects, entities amenable to processing. Social information simplifies individuals and reduces them to docile figures on sheets of paper.

Thus classification takes away the actual individuality of defendant and the circumstances of his or her life and replaces it with a spurious individuality consisting of a series of attributes capable of judgment; Law's 'docile figures'. The potentially most unruly of the resources is the juvenile her or himself, hence their particular insertion into the business of sentencing. The simultaneous enrolment and silencing of the child is both an expression of, and necessary to, the effective deployment of power.

(and at page 104):

Magistrates control a diffuse and potentially all inclusive discourse through the operation of the socialised tariff. They exercise a real power which is based on their ability to invoke social information categories in support of decisions which in the end rest upon their powers of judgment:

> It's just a question of judgment, really, you learn by experience.

> I think a lot of lady magistrates ... you do things by your intuition.

> We're not social workers. We have to use our common sense.

> It all comes down to ... judgment really in the end.

The control over imprecise concepts which the use of social information involves ensures that any challenge to that judgment is particularly difficult. The structure of the bifurcatory tariff is a distinct advantage in the successful exercise of discretionary power, because it creates a facility of categories – a continuum of salvability to incorrigibility – which justifies the use of social data. In providing the heuristic mechanism by which magistrates allocate offenders on that always already existing bifurcatory slope, control indicators are techniques of power.

(Ir)rationality and the problem of decision making in the juvenile court

Ultimately, however, the techniques of power of the socialised tariff are enabled by the fundamental irrationality which characterises the most liberal of juvenile courts. The vagueness of the decision concepts with which justices have to work (good/bad home backgrounds etc) are symptomatic of the lack of substantive rationality in the decision environment within which they work. Strictly speaking, substantive rationality ends the moment when it ceases to be possible to make a computation of the type 'if x, then y' (March and Simon 1970). Even allowing that this is an ideal type rather than something which can be fully realised in most decision situations, it is clear that the magisterial task could never remotely approximate rationality. Rationality demands that goals can be clearly defined, that the means to achieve desired goals can be spelt out and that the means to achieve the desired goals are available to the decision maker.

Magistrates are faced with a highly complex decision environment since ostensibly their goal is to alter the behaviour of human beings. The goal of 'trying to prevent re-offending', 'to protect the public' or 'to help pull him back from the edge' are so diffuse as to create a good deal of uncertainty. This is without even beginning to think about the complexities of not just stopping offending behaviour but reforming a person. Such goals defy clear definition, (What is a 'useful citizen'? What is 'normal'?) let alone the formulation of sensible means to achieve them. There is no possibility of magistrates achieving the kind of global behavioural control which is connoted by such aspirations; there is certainly no 'cure' for juvenile offending which can be achieved through magisterial powers.

[6:15] **Magistrates' Association** *Sentencing Guidelines* (2001)

Criminal Damage	Criminal Damage Act 1971 s.1 Triable either way or summarily only. Consult Clerk Penalty: Either way – Level 5 and/or 6 months Summarily – Level 4 and/or 3 months

CONSIDER THE SERIOUSNESS OF THE OFFENCE
(INCLUDING THE IMPACT ON THE VICTIM)

GUIDELINE: →   *IS DISCHARGE OR FINE APPROPRIATE?*
IS IT SERIOUS ENOUGH FOR A COMMUNITY PENALTY?
IS IT SO SERIOUS THAT ONLY CUSTODY IS APPROPRIATE?
ARE MAGISTRATES' SENTENCING POWERS APPROPRIATE?

GUIDELINE FINE – STARTING POINT C

 CONSIDER AGGRAVATING AND MITIGATING FACTORS

for example
    Deliberate
    Group offence
    Serious damage
    This list is not exhaustive

for example
    Impulsive action
    Minor damage
    Provocation
    This list is not exhaustive

If offender is on bail, this offence is more serious
If offender has previous convictions, their relevance and any failure to respond to previous
sentences must be considered – they may increase the seriousness

TAKE A PRELIMINARY VIEW OF SERIOUSNESS, THEN
CONSIDER OFFENDER MITIGATION

for example
    Age, health (physical or mental)
    Co-operation with police
    Voluntary compensation
    Evidence of genuine remorse

CONSIDER YOUR SENTENCE

Compare it with the suggested guideline level of sentence and reconsider
your reasons carefully if you have chosen a sentence at a different level.
Consider a discount for a timely guilty plea.

DECIDE YOUR SENTENCE
NB. COMPENSATION – Give reasons if not awarding compensation

Remember: These are GUIDELINES only

Theft	Theft Act 1968 s.1 Triable either way – see Mode of Trial Guidelines Penalty: Level 5 and/or 6 months May disqualify where committed with reference to the theft or taking of the vehicle

CONSIDER THE SERIOUSNESS OF THE OFFENCE
(INCLUDING THE IMPACT ON THE VICTIM)

IS DISCHARGE OR FINE APPROPRIATE?

GUIDELINE: → *IS IT SERIOUS ENOUGH FOR A COMMUNITY PENALTY?*

IS IT SO SERIOUS THAT ONLY CUSTODY IS APPROPRIATE?

ARE MAGISTRATES' SENTENCING POWERS APPROPRIATE?

 ## CONSIDER AGGRAVATING AND MITIGATING FACTORS

for example
- High value
- Planned
- Sophisticated
- Adult involving children
- Organised team
- Related damage
- Vulnerable victim
- *This list is not exhaustive*

for example
- Impulsive action
- Low value
- *This list is not exhaustive*

If racially aggravated, or offender is on bail, this offence is more serious
If offender has previous convictions, their relevance and any failure to respond to previous
sentences must be considered – they may increase the seriousness

TAKE A PRELIMINARY VIEW OF SERIOUSNESS, THEN CONSIDER OFFENDER MITIGATION

for example
- Age, health (physical or mental)
- Co-operation with police
- Voluntary compensation
- Evidence of genuine remorse

CONSIDER YOUR SENTENCE

Compare it with the suggested guideline level of sentence and reconsider
your reasons carefully if you have chosen a sentence at a different level.
Consider a discount for a timely guilty plea.

DECIDE YOUR SENTENCE
NB. COMPENSATION – Give reasons if not awarding compensation

Remember: These are GUIDELINES only

Wounding – Grievous Bodily Harm	Offences Against the Person Act 1861 s.20 Triable either way – see Mode of Trial Guidelines Penalty: Level 5 and/or 6 months

CONSIDER THE SERIOUSNESS OF THE OFFENCE
(INCLUDING THE IMPACT ON THE VICTIM)

IS DISCHARGE OR FINE APPROPRIATE?

IS IT SERIOUS ENOUGH FOR A COMMUNITY PENALTY?

IS IT SO SERIOUS THAT ONLY CUSTODY IS APPROPRIATE?

GUIDELINE: → *ARE MAGISTRATES' SENTENCING POWERS APPROPRIATE?*

 ## CONSIDER AGGRAVATING AND MITIGATING FACTORS

for example	for example
Deliberate kicking/biting	Single blow
Extensive injuries	Minor wound
Group action	Provocation
Offender in position of authority	*This list is not exhaustive*
On hospital/medical premises	
Premeditated	
Victim particularly vulnerable	
Victim serving the public	
Weapon	
This list is not exhaustive	

If offender is on bail, this offence is more serious

If offender has previous convictions, their relevance and any failure to respond to previous sentences must be considered – they may increase the seriousness

TAKE A PRELIMINARY VIEW OF SERIOUSNESS, THEN CONSIDER WHETHER THE CASE SHOULD BE COMMITTED FOR SENTENCE, THEN CONSIDER OFFENDER MITIGATION

for example
    Age, health (physical or mental)
    Co-operation with police
    Voluntary compensation
    Evidence of genuine remorse

CONSIDER COMMITTAL OR YOUR SENTENCE

Compare it with the suggested guideline level of sentence and reconsider your reasons carefully if you have chosen a sentence at a different level. Consider a discount for a timely guilty plea.

DECIDE YOUR SENTENCE
NB. COMPENSATION – Give reasons if not awarding compensation

Remember: These are GUIDELINES only

[6:16] **Henham, R** 'Bargain Justice or Justice Denied? Sentence Discounts and the Criminal Process' [1999] MLR 515 (at page 524):

Methodology

At the project's inception in 1994 it was decided to select one First Tier Crown Court Centre from each of the six Circuits, ie Nottingham (Midland and Oxford); Leeds (North Eastern); Manchester (Northern); Norwich, later replaced by Lewes (South Eastern); Cardiff (Wales and Chester); and Winchester (Western). This number represented 6.7% of the 90 Crown Court Centres (including Greater London Centres) and ensured adequate representation from each Circuit.

The Judicial Statistics for 1994 showed that overall, of the 90,759 defendants dealt with by the Crown Court, 66% (59,577) pleaded guilty. Averaged between the 90 Crown Court Centres this produced a figure of 662 cases. Over the six-month period chosen for data collection a 5% sample of the average number of guilty pleas for each Centre chosen would have necessitated a sample size of 33 cases per Centre. It was felt that greater representation of the use of sentence discounts would be achieved by this sample design rather than attempting to create Circuit or Centre sub-groups to reflect differences in guilty plea rates as between Circuits which was impractical. Furthermore, a 3% sample of the overall number of guilty pleas was unrealistic since some 2,979 cases would have required detailed examination. In the event, permission was eventually sought to increase the sample size for each Centre to 50 cases, this reflecting approximately 7.6% of the annual average number of guilty pleas for each Centre and 0.5% of the annual number of guilty pleas for defendants dealt with in all Crown Court Centres according to the 1994 figures.

Resource implications and analytical complexity suggested that a written record of the relevant decision-making process would be more reliable than verbatim notes of judicial sentencing comments obtained by a trained researcher attending selected guilty plea hearings. For these reasons it was decided to select the sample of 50 cases for each Centre retrospectively to cover the period April to September 1997, permission to access relevant court records having been obtained from the Lord Chancellor's Department. Approximately two guilty plea cases per week over the six-month period were identified on a random basis, and Form 5089 extracted from the court record was used to obtain transcripts of judicial sentencing comments direct from the court reporting firm present at sentence. Hence, the information derived from the court record together with the verbatim transcript of the judge's sentencing remarks in each case constituted the empirical input subsequently analysed. The final sample of 310 cases from the six selected Crown Court Centres where full information was available was ultimately comprised as follows: Cardiff (57), Leeds (55), Lewes (57), Manchester (29), Nottingham (50) and Winchester (62).

Conclusions and implications

It was assumed from the outset that in order to fully understand the operation of sentence discounts in the Crown Court the following (apparently) straightforward questions needed to be answered:
(1)   did the guilty plea produce a sentence discount?
(2)   what explanation was given for the sentence discount by the judge? .
(3)   how was the sentence discount actually reflected in the sentence?

As explained in the opening section, numerous studies (including most recently Flood-Page and Mackie) have dealt with the third question but no previous attempt has been made to monitor the operation and effectiveness of section 48 of the Criminal Justice and Public Order Act 1994 on the criminal process. In addition to its overtly crime control function of reducing the number of 'cracked trials', the section should have provided greater transparency to a process with fundamental due process and human rights implications, through improving our understanding of how the judiciary deal with the first two questions stated above in the actual sentence decision-making process. However, as we have seen, it appears a substantial minority of judges are not only failing to provide an explanation of the basis of the discount, they are not stating it at all.

There are also two areas of particular difficulty concerning the ambit of section 48 which need to be addressed. The first is that section 48 imposes no obligation on the sentencer to state the fact of a guilty plea or explain further the implications of this for any sentence discount. The second problem is that no obligation lies on the sentencer under section 48 to declare that *no* sentence discount has been given or to explain further the basis upon which such a decision has been reached. The consequences are that in these two situations in particular, we may have no idea of the sentencer's rationale in each case, unless he or she chooses to elaborate this further. It will be recalled that for the purposes of this research, it was suggested that failure to elaborate on the reasons for allowing a sentence discount when the sentencer had taken the positive step of stating that credit would be given for a guilty plea (but going no further) should be regarded as a breach of section 48(2). These ambiguities and anomalies and the convoluted language of the section are exacerbated by what appear as logical flaws in its conception relating to the sentence decision-making process. For example, the reference in section 48(1)(b) to 'the circumstances in which' the plea indication was given is specifically related to the timing of the plea in section 48(1)(a) rather than with wider concerns which may together be instrumental in deciding on the extent of any sentence discount allowed. The study found that other mitigating factors were present in 51 per cent of cases where circumstances other than the timing of the plea were referred to.

One approach to dealing with the difficulties referred to is to recast the wording of the section in its entirety as follows:

48. Reduction in sentences for guilty pleas

(1) In determining what sentence to pass on an offender who has pleaded guilty to an offence in proceedings before that or another court a court shall take into account:

   (a) the fact that the defendant has pleaded guilty

   (b) the stage in the proceedings when the offender indicated his intention to plead guilty

   (c) the extent to which the offender has shown remorse for the offence

   (d) the extent to which the offender co-operated with the Police and (or) the Crown Prosecution Service before he indicated his intention to plead guilty

   (e) the extent to which the guilty plea has avoided the time and expense of a trial

   (f) the extent to which the victim(s) and (or) witness(es) have been spared the ordeal of a trial

(2) If factors other than those referred to in subsection (1) above are taken into account by the court they shall be stated in open court.

(3)(a) If, as a result of taking into account any matter referred to in subsections (1) and (2) above, the court imposes a punishment which is less severe than the punishment it would otherwise have imposed, it shall state in open court that it has does so and explain its effect to the offender in ordinary language.

(b) If, having taken into account any matter referred to in subsections (1) and (2) above, the court decides not to impose a sentence which is less severe than that which it otherwise considers appropriate, it shall state this fact in open court and explain its effect to the offender in ordinary language.

It is apparent from the re-wording that the objective in section 48(1) and (2) is to ensure that the sentencer is forced to articulate the rationale for the sentence discount from a wider range of potentially relevant factors than exist under the present section, including where the discount has been given simply on the basis of the plea itself. Moreover, by virtue of the re-cast section 48(3)(b) the sentencer would be forced to state and explain why no sentence discount had been given at all.

There are, however, other areas where more specific guidance from the Court of Appeal is required. Firstly, the position regarding offences taken into consideration ('tics') and sentence discounts remains unclear, and secondly, and more importantly, it is unclear whether courts are consistently following the Court's advice in *Fearon* that a plea discount should be given irrespective of the strength of the prosecution case or continuing to apply the fifth exception in *Costen* regardless. Such guidance could, of course, follow a recommendation from the newly constituted Sentencing Advisory Panel established by section 81 of the Crime and Disorder Act 1998, but any initiative to clarify the courts approach to the application of section 48 should preferably emanate from the Court of Appeal itself which must, in any event, also have regard (inter alia) to the need to promote consistency in sentencing and the need to promote public confidence in the criminal justice system. It was, in fact, following the Government decision *not* to implement Chapter 1 of Part II of the Crime (Sentences) Act 1997 that the Lord Chief Justice issued a Practice Direction requiring sentencers to explain fully the effect of custodial sentences as part of a campaign to restore public confidence in sentencing. I would submit that the need for greater transparency in the operation of sentence discounts highlighted by this research could be adequately met by a similar practice direction from the Lord Chief Justice directed towards ensuring that sentencers not only make it clear that a sentence discount has been given, but that they also explain fully the reasons for it and state the precise effect of the discount on the sentence.

Nevertheless, Ashworth has convincingly argued that more fundamental reform of the system of sentence discounts is necessary principally on the basis that it openly contravenes a number of fundamental rights and freedoms enshrined in the European Convention of Human Rights; namely, the presumption of innocence, the privilege against self-incrimination, the right to equality of treatment and the right to a fair and public hearing. Ashworth also supports a reappraisal of the whole system of guilty pleas and suggests that either complete abolition or major changes in criminal procedure could produce a fairer system for both victims and witnesses. It is certainly true, as Fenwick points out, that victims currently have no right to participate in decisions to accept a guilty plea in return for a sentence discount or to accept a plea to a lesser charge. Hence, the victim's likely desire that the trial should proceed without the offer of a sentence discount may be ignored. Such a result may be regarded as detrimental since victims (actual and potential) clearly have an interest in seeing a true offender convicted. Further, some victims may prefer the ordeal of a court appearance to seeing the defendant receive a light sentence as a result of a sentence discount, whether graduated or not. Past support for plea discounts and the crime control ideology, with its emphasis on financial constraint, speed and finality of conviction, has been on the basis that it is broadly in the interests of victims because it spares victims the ordeal of giving evidence whilst recognising that due process rights such as the right to a fair and public hearing may be infringed and some innocent defendants may be induced to plead guilty. Fenwick is surely correct in suggesting that the perceptions of victims towards this process are actually more complex and that there is a case for establishing rights of consultation and participation in those decisions, at least for victims of serious offences.

Although cogent arguments for reform of the guilty plea system undoubtedly exist, in the short-term this research has highlighted the pressing need for increased guidance to Crown Court judges and the need for more information to be made available to defendants on the implications of the choices they make, and to victims, witnesses and the public at large, on the real consequences of the guilty plea. The research has indicated that, although the strategic policy goals of sentence discounts are being achieved, the rationale and extent of discount decisions (via section 48) are not being articulated consistently by the courts. This failure is compounded by the fact that there appear to exist unjustifiable differences between sentence discounts for different offences, differences in regional and judicial practice and cogent reasons to support a gradual reduction in the amount of the discount itself. I submit that there is consequently an urgent need for section 48 of the Criminal Justice and Public Order Act 1994 to be amended along the lines suggested to correct its manifest weaknesses; for the Lord Chief Justice to issue a practice direction on the correct approach to the use of sentence discounts by the Crown Court; for additional judicial training to reinforce the need for consistency of approach and transparency in decision-making, and for increased Court of Appeal guidance on sentence discounts (following consideration of the issue by the Sentencing Advisory Panel) to rationalise their effect as between different offences.

CHAPTER SEVEN

Trial Judges

An English judge controls a criminal trial in the Crown Court in some ways as a referee supervises a boxing match. The two sides battle it out, and he (sometimes she) stands by to check that neither side breaks the rules. But this simplistic comparison hides the fact that the judge is a powerful referee, whose decisions may often affect the outcome of the trial. In our case, Gerry Good is charged with an offence under the Offences Against the Person Act 1861, s 18 (OAPA 1861). He is to be tried before a judge and jury. The role of the judge is clearly crucial to the conduct and outcome of the proceedings.

Gerry Good has been on bail. Before the case comes on for trial there will have been a plea and directions hearing. The indictment will have been put to him by the clerk, and he lodged a plea of not guilty. The prosecution and defence (very likely not the lawyers who will appear at trial) will have helped the judge identify key issues in the case and agreed time limits for the disclosure of documents. The case will then have been listed for trial.

On the day the trial is listed to start, Gerry Good arrives at court at 9 am in order to meet his barrister, Tim Moffat. The judge that day has another short plea and directions hearing at 10 am, so Gerry's case does not come on until 11 am. Between 10 am and 11 am the lawyers involved try unsuccessfully to bargain a guilty plea (see Chapter Five). The CPS applies to add an alternative count to the indictment:

Count One

Statement of Offence

Wounding with intent, contrary to section 18 of the Offences Against the Person Act 1861.

Particulars of Offence

Gerry Good on or about the 13th day of June 2002 unlawfully and maliciously wounded Rosa Bottles with intent to do her grievous bodily harm.

Count Two

Statement of Offence

Unlawful wounding, contrary to section 20 of the Offences Against the Person Act 1861.

Particulars of Offence

Gerry Good on or about the 13th day of June 2002 unlawfully and maliciously wounded Rosa Bottles.

But Gerry maintains his not guilty plea. The jury is sworn (see Chapter Eight). The judge takes a low profile throughout the trial. Counsel for the prosecution outlines his case to the jury and calls his witnesses: Rosa Bottles, the pub landlord and two police officers. Witnesses will be examined by the prosecution counsel, cross-examined by Gerry's counsel, and re-examined by the prosecution counsel. The judge may interrupt to repeat a question or to ask the witness to go slower. He may intervene to stop inappropriate lines of questioning, but from Gerry Good's point of view, the judge seems unimportant until he makes his summing up to the jury. When he imposes the sentence, he moves to centre stage. However, in reality, he is highly influential on all the actors throughout the courtroom drama.

(i) Who are the trial judges?

The Crown Court sits at around 90 centres throughout England and Wales. For trial purposes in the Crown Court, offences are divided into four classes of seriousness. Although all those charged with indictable crimes are tried in the Crown Court, the more serious charges will be tried before a High Court judge, the least serious before a circuit judge or recorder (part-time judges, usually practising barristers or solicitors, who sit for between three and six weeks a year). The Circuit Bench was created by the Courts Act 1971 as part of a major reorganisation of the criminal courts. Most judges were previously practising barristers, although since 1971 it has been possible for solicitors to sit as judges in the Crown Court. A barrister or solicitor of ten years' standing, or a recorder who has held office for at least three years, can be appointed as a circuit judge. Thus, a solicitor may become a circuit judge after serving time as a recorder. The Courts and Legal Services Act 1990 enabled a suitably qualified solicitor to become a High Court judge, and the first was appointed in 1993.

In 1990 the Lord Chancellor's Department issued a document explaining the system for the appointment of judges, reflecting an opening up of the recruitment process and indeed a commitment to seeking out a wider pool of applicants. Sir Leonard Peach's Independent Scrutiny of the Appointment Processes of Judges and QCs, which reported in 1999, concluded that the process was thorough and competent. He recommended the creation of a Commissioner for Judicial Appointments with the duties of performing audits of procedures as well as carrying out the role of ombudsman for both judicial and Queen's Counsel appointments, and this was accepted. The annual reports of the commissioner are available on the Lord Chancellor's Department website (www.lcd.gov.uk). Uncertainty about the system of appointment was reinforced by the Scottish High Court of Justiciary's decision in *Starrs v Procurator Fiscal* [2000] HRLR 191, where it was held that the use of temporary sheriffs, who conducted as much as 25% of Scotland's criminal cases, contravened the European Convention on Human Rights, art 6 **[1:9]**. The court held that the appointment system failed to uphold judicial independence because temporary sheriffs' contracts were for only a year. They were hired and fired by the Lord Advocate, who, apart from being a member of the Scottish government responsible for the legal system, is also head of the Scottish prosecution service. Lord Reed said that that did 'not square with the appearance of independence'. In 2000, the Lord Chancellor announced that 'no useful purpose' was served by having separate offices of recorder and assistant recorder, but there remains a large number of part-time judges.

Numbers of judges

	Circuit judges	Recorders	Assistant recorders
1994	487 (28 women)	795 (42 women)	496 (51 women)
2000	561 (39 women)	907 (84 women)	446 (72 women)
2003	621 (50 women)	1,356 (50 women)	—

There are no black or Asian High Court judges, and in 2003 there were five circuit judges (0.9%) and 33 recorders from ethnic minorities. Although the appointment system leaves much to be desired, it is only partly responsible for the narrow social and educational background of English judges, analysed most famously by Griffiths (1991) (see also Pannick (1987)). The conservatism of judges is also partly explained by the conservatism of many of those who choose to become lawyers in the first place.

The holder of the office of part-time judge or circuit judge has no constitutional protection. The Lord Chancellor may, if he thinks fit, remove such a judge from office on the grounds of incapacity or misbehaviour. Whether this has any effect on a judge's performance is difficult to measure. Defendants have little protection against an incompetent or unfair judge. In many countries, litigants may complain to some sort of 'judicial performance commission' if they believe a judge has acted unjudicially. In England, the unhappy litigant has no such remedy. Section 2(5) of the Crown Proceedings Act 1947 provides that the Crown cannot be sued for the tortious conduct of any person 'while discharging or purporting to discharge any responsibilities of a judicial nature vested in him'. Lord Denning's statements in *Sirros v Moore* **[7:1]** illustrate the extent of the judge's immunity from suit. The right of appeal against an incorrect decision is not always an adequate remedy, especially since justice is thereby both delayed and often costly.

(ii) Sentence bargains

Plea or charge bargaining between prosecution and defence, which was examined in Chapter Five, can be seen as a form of sentence bargaining: if Gerry Good, or rather his counsel, had persuaded the prosecution to drop the charge under s 18, he could have been fairly confident that, on a guilty plea to a charge under s 20, he would have received a lighter sentence than if he continued to fight the case. Here we are concerned with where the bargaining process goes one stage further, and the judge himself becomes involved in the discussions.

For many years, defendants pleading guilty have been regarded as entitled to a sentence discount of some 20%–30%, although the precise amount varies from judge to judge and from case to case (see *Buffrey* (1993) 14 Cr App Rep (S) 511). The primary reason for this discount is that it encourages defendants who know that they are guilty to plead guilty, thereby saving the cost of a jury trial. In some cases, the discount may be an acknowledgment that the defendant has saved the victim from giving evidence, or a recognition of genuine remorse. In *Claydon* (1993) 15 Cr App Rep (S) 526 the Court of Appeal went so far as to say that where an offender voluntarily surrenders and confesses, a sentence discount of 50% was appropriate. The CJPOA 1994, s 48 **[2:11]** requires all courts, when passing sentence, to take account of the timing and other circumstances of a plea of guilty (see *Rafferty* [1999] 1 Cr App Rep 235). There is a danger that this discount may lead those who are not guilty to plead guilty. Zander and Henderson **[7:2]** present their findings without comment or evaluation, yet their question to the legally qualified participants in the trials they studied – on whether innocent people were pleading guilty – has led some commentators to argue that perhaps 1,400 innocent people plead guilty in the Crown Court every year. However, the Royal Commission (1993) **[7:3]** believed that there was 'little if any' evidence that innocent people had pleaded guilty because of the sentence discount. But the important question is whether those who believe themselves to be innocent should be penalised for pleading not guilty.

Sentence bargains are particularly important where the defendant stands on the cusp of prison. Often he wants to know if he can be sure that, if he pleads guilty, he will avoid prison. This might well be so in the case of Gerry Good. He has several, relatively minor, previous convictions, and is now to be tried for intentional wounding (contrary to OAPA 1861, s 18). If he pleads guilty to malicious wounding (s 20), will he escape prison? The decisions in *Turner* **[7:4]**, *Smith* **[7:5]** and *Dossetter* **[7:6]** show how the Court of Appeal discourages unnecessary visits to the judge's room. The court stresses that, if such visits do happen, there should always be a recording device or a shorthand writer present. Because of the cost, in terms of time and money, of cracked trials (those trials where the case is listed for trial before a jury, but on the day of the trial the defendant pleads guilty), the Royal Commission (1993) **[7:3]** recommended the partial reversal of *Turner*. It suggested that, at the request of defence counsel on instructions from the defendant, judges should be able to indicate the highest sentence that they would impose at that point, on the basis of the facts put to them. A request for such an indication might be made at a preparatory hearing called especially for this purpose, or at the trial itself. One danger with this approach is that the judge is being asked to speak with inadequate information, particularly when a pre-sentence report has not yet been prepared. Of even greater concern is that such a process may lead to a presumption of guilt. Any move from the courtroom to the judge's chambers smacks of secrecy and administrative convenience, and a loss of due process safeguards.

Lord Justice Auld **[1:5]** also concludes his analysis of this issue with a complex recommendation for a system of 'advance indication of sentence' for those considering pleading guilty, which should be fully recorded. Sanders and Young **[7:7]** were highly critical of what they saw as the Royal Commission's crime control mentality, which lay behind this and many of its other proposals. They would doubtless be as critical of Auld's proposal. Perhaps the only way to relieve the pressure on the innocent to plead guilty would be to abolish the sentence discount for guilty pleas altogether. A 30% discount for a plea is, after all, the equivalent of a 50% increase in sentence for unsuccessfully maintaining a plea of not guilty. For cost reasons alone, this proposal is highly improbable.

Another problem with both formal and informal systems of sentence discounting is that it is likely to be applied unevenly. The Royal Commission supported the policy recommended by Hood **[7:8]** of ethnic monitoring of all court outcomes. Hood provides evidence that the current system of sentence discounts, combined with the tendency of Afro-Caribbean defendants to plead not guilty, put them at risk of being sentenced to longer sentences than their white peers.

(iii)   The judge's discretion to exclude evidence

Most evidence in court is given orally, although agreed written statements are increasingly admitted. This section only discusses the wide discretionary power of the trial judge to exclude evidence, but it should be noted that the law of evidence are in need of much wider reform. The law of evidence is a complex mix of statute and case law. Spencer (1994) makes a plea for the courts to take a more purposive approach to the law of evidence generally: 'for many years the tendency has been to interpret [the rules of evidence] mechanically, without considering whether they help or hinder the courts in their vital task of convicting the guilty and acquitting the innocent' (at page 644). This message is taken up by Auld **[1:5]** who calls for the codification of the law of evidence. But, sadly, all that is offered in the Criminal Justice Bill 2002 is a number of hugely complex amendments to the existing law.

Judges rarely call witnesses themselves: Zander and Henderson's Crown Court study (see **[7:2]**) found that in 19% of cases judges reported that they knew of one or more important witnesses who had not been called by either side. It is a reflection on the adversarial system (see **[1:3]**) that they do not see it as their function to call even a useful witness. Perhaps, also, too much weight is given to the performance of individual witnesses, who themselves are dependent on the questions of counsel for the answers they can give.

Decisions to exclude evidence may be taken at a pre-trial hearing to avoid the waste of time and money which occurs when the jury have to be sent out during the trial for a *voire dire* ('trial within a trial'). The common law position (before PACE) on the exclusion of evidence was summed up by Lord Goddard CJ in the Privy Council decision *Kuruma v R* [1955] AC 197, at page 204:

> 'In their Lordships' opinion, the test to be applied in considering whether evidence is admissible is whether it is relevant to the matters in issue. If it is, it is admissible and the court is not concerned with how the evidence was obtained ... The judge always has a discretion to exclude evidence if the strict rules of admissibility would operate unfairly against an accused ... If, for instance, some piece of evidence, eg, a document, had been obtained from a defendant by a trick, no doubt the judge might properly rule it out'.

In that case, the Privy Council upheld the conviction of a man who had been sentenced to death for the unlawful possession of two rounds of ammunition, after having been unlawfully searched by police officers below the authorised rank. Pre-PACE, the courts usually left the disciplining of police officers to be performed through actions for damages, formal complaints procedures or by the occasional prosecution.

The present law on the exclusion of evidence is to be found in sections 76(2) and 78 of PACE **[2:9]**. At first sight, these sections appear to be contradictory: one being mandatory, and the other discretionary. Examples of excluded unfairly obtained evidence were given earlier in this book, in *Loosely* **[2:16]** and in *Paris, Abdullahi and Miller* **[5:4]**. The courts are involved in a difficult balancing act: supporting the police in the investigation of crime, yet upholding the integrity of the criminal justice system. In *Christou* **[7:9]** the evidence gained by the police officers in an undercover operation was acceptable and in *Bryce* [7:10] it was not. Can the cases be distinguished? The law reports contain many other striking examples: in *Khan* [7:11] the House of Lords upheld the trial judge's decision to admit evidence, despite the fact that the police were guilty of a civil trespass and may have infringed the defendant's right to privacy by using an electronic listening device (a decision upheld by the European Court of Human Rights in *Khan v United Kingdom* (2001) 31 EHRR 1016. See also *Chalkley and Jeffries* [9:6]).

The Royal Commission on Criminal Justice (1993) was satisfied with the way that the law was working, though Professor Zander's powerful dissent [9:1] is worth noting here. The majority of the Royal Commission thought that the Court of Appeal's power to quash convictions after breaches of PACE should be limited to cases where the jury's verdict was unsafe. But Zander stressed that the role of the Court of Appeal in promoting the observation of the crucial and complex network of the PACE rules is of the greatest importance. He believes that 'the majority would in effect be encouraging the Court of Appeal to under-cut a part of [section 78]'s moral force by saying that the issue of "unfairness" can be ignored where there is sufficient evidence to show that the defendant is actually guilty' (at page 235). In Chapter Nine we return to the changes made to the powers of the Court of Appeal by the Criminal Appeal Act 1995.

The Royal Commission was unanimous in recommending the introduction of a rule similar to Rule 403 of the United States Federal Rules of Evidence, which empowers the judge to exclude evidence if 'although relevant, its probative value is substantially outweighed by the danger of unfair prejudice, confusion of the issues, or misleading the jury, or by considerations of undue delay, waste of time, or needless presentation of cumulative evidence'. The commission believed that the introduction of such a rule would allow judges to be more 'robust' in pre-venting juries from having to sit through evidence that adds little or nothing to what is already before them. Thus, the power of the judge to control the issues that would go before the jury would be increased. Auld [1:5] points out that it is only since 1993 that the size of the problem of applying PACE has arisen: he urges not only a codification of the law of evidence but also a simplification of the rules for excluding evidence on the grounds of its unfairness.

(iv)   The summing up

After the evidence has been presented, and after the prosecution and defence have made their closing speeches, the judge sums up the case in order to help the jury in their task of reaching a verdict (the Judicial Studies Board's model directions for judges to use are freely available nowadays on its website: www.jsboard.co.uk).

Thus, the judge in Gerry Good's case, for example, will explain to the jury the burden and standard of proof and the respective roles of judge and jury. He will state that they may only convict if they are sure, or satisfied beyond reasonable doubt, of Gerry's guilt. He will then summarise the facts on which their decision is required, and give directions on relevant points of law. He will have to define to the jury the legal meaning of 'intent' in OAPA 1861, s 18 and explain the effect of Gerry's intoxication (if indeed he was intoxicated) on his 'intent'. He has to describe the relationship of s 18 with s 20 and explain the circumstances when the jury may bring in an alternative verdict. None of these factors are straightforward in English law: indeed, there has been a loud lobby for many years calling for a codification of the criminal law, but this does not catch the politicians' imagination. Even in this simple case, the summing up is likely to last at least an hour. Should the jury be given a written copy?

Should the judge be allowed to refer to the facts of the case? Even in a short case like Gerry Good's, the facts are rarely straightforward. Here, Gerry's account of his police interviews does not accord with that of the police. The jury have heard both sides of the case: can the judge present a balanced perspective to the jury? In the United States, where the summing up is known as the 'jury charge', the judge only gives the jury an explanation of the law, without reference to the facts. In England, the extent to which the judge comments on the facts is left to the discretion of the individual judge. In Gerry's case, the jury retire for a little over an hour, and return a verdict of not guilty to the section 18 offence, but guilty to the section 20 offence.

(v) Sentencing

After a jury brings in a verdict of guilty, the question of sentence is entirely decided by the judge. Where the defendant has pleaded not guilty, the facts will have been explored fully before the jury, before they reached their verdict. More difficult may be the case where the defendant has pleaded guilty, but where there is a wide divergence between the prosecution and defence on the facts. This is dramatically illustrated by the facts of *Newton* **[7:12]**, where the Lord Chief Justice explained the proper approach to be taken by a trial judge when dealing with the task of sentencing such a defendant. More often than not, the trial judge will decide to accept the defendant's view of the facts, in order to save the added costs and delays of a 'trial within a trial' to establish contested facts. This can lead to a defendant being substantially under-sentenced.

The statutory framework of judges' sentencing powers is similar to that discussed in the last chapter on magistrates' powers – consolidated in the PCC(S)A 2000 **[6:13]** but already much amended, and soon to change massively again (see Criminal Justice Bill 2002). The statutory maximum for the offence in question is normally laid down in the statute creating the offence. Gerry was charged with an offence under section 18, but convicted of an offence under section 20, of the OAPA 1861. The Act originally laid down punishments of penal servitude, but it has been amended such that the maximum penalty for wounding with intent (contrary to section 18) is life imprisonment and the maximum penalty for wounding (contrary to section 20) is five years' imprisonment. Despite this wide theoretical difference, in practice, the normal sentencing bracket even for a section 18 offence is only three to eight years' imprisonment. When Parliament increases the statutory maximum penalty for an offence (as, for example, it did in the Criminal Justice Act 1993, where the maximum penalty for causing death by dangerous driving was raised from five to ten years), it may have little practical impact.

The judge will take account of the facts of the offence, the circumstances of the offender and the plea in mitigation. In Chapter Ten we will look at the role of the Probation Service in preparing and presenting pre-sentence reports. The Criminal Justice Act 1991 made these mandatory where the court was considering a custodial sentence, though the Criminal Justice Act 1993 diluted the requirement. In Gerry Good's case, no pre-sentence report had been prepared before trial, but the judge decides to adjourn the case for two days for the expedited preparation of a report. The judge must now decide whether or not to remand Gerry in custody pending sentence (see Chapter Six for a discussion of bail). In the event, despite defence counsel having stressed the fact that Gerry has respected the terms of his conditional bail over the past few weeks, the judge remands him to a bail hostel.

At the resumed hearing, counsel for the prosecution will call a police officer (the 'antecedents officer') to give details of Gerry Good's previous convictions. The role of defence counsel in presenting a plea in mitigation, and in deciding whether to call witnesses in support of the defendant's good character, was raised in Chapter Five. The court duty probation officer will be in court to speak, if necessary, on the pre-sentence report. The report on Gerry Good is included in Chapter Ten. The judge gives Gerry Good a brief lecture on why he finds it impossible in this case to do other than impose an immediate custodial sentence. Stockdale (1967) questions the value of such homilies: it is doubtful whether they have any general or particular deterrent effect – 'a far more likely effect is a general and particular resentment, and sometimes a contempt for the court' (at page 34). The more difficult part for the judge is his duty to explain the implications of the sentence: we will look at the complex early release rules in Chapter Ten.

It was pointed out in Chapter Six that the imposition of a sentencing framework on judges by the Criminal Justice Act 1991 **[6:13]** was not particularly successful. Some parts of the Act simply reproduced existing practice in general terms, other parts were soon radically changed. This book cannot explore sentencing in detail: for an analysis of the different provisions applying to the sentencing of violent or sexual offenders, or the decline in the use of suspended sentences, for example, students are referred to texts dedicated to sentencing law and practice (eg *Thomas' Current Sentencing Practice*, much used by both judges and lawyers).

Gerry Good is sentenced to three years in prison. Since the key concept of 'seriousness' (see PCC(S)A 2000, s 79) is undefined, judges continue to choose a particular sentence by considering the 'tariff' for the offence, laid down in guideline judgments of the Court of Appeal, mostly in appeals against sentence, and by following their own instincts. The Court of Appeal will only vary the sentence imposed at trial where it is 'manifestly excessive or wrong in principle' (Criminal Appeal Act 1968, s 2 [9:4]), and so the judge's discretion is rarely interfered with.

Appeals against sentence

	Offenders sentenced in the Crown Court	Applications for leave to appeal against sentence	Successful appeals against sentence
1993	69,500	4,848	1,309
1998	80,400	6,550	1,589
2001	72,100	5,497	1,101

Source: Judicial Statistics 2001; Table 1.8; and Criminal Statistics, Chapter 7

Two recent sentencing judgments of the Court of Appeal (Criminal Division) are included ([7:13] and [7:14]) to illustrate the sort of guidance available to the trial judge. Students should browse through the Criminal Appeal Reports (Sentencing), which serve as a useful reminder of the conditions in which many offenders live, and the very repetition of these sad and often tragic pictures of life is a challenge for those who study the criminal justice system: this 'system' is dealing with very real individuals (see also [1:12] and [1:13]). Judges develop different reputations as sentencers, and doubtless the reputation of the individual judge has an important influence on the decision of the defendant whether to plead guilty. In 1980 Ashworth et al [7:15] carried out a 'pilot study' into sentencing policy and practices in the Crown Court. The Lord Chief Justice then refused permission for the work to proceed any further. Although much has changed in the intervening years, the discussion extracted remains a useful summary of the case for academic research in this area. Hood's more recent study [7:8] was the first large-scale statistical attempt to try to assess whether defendants of different ethnic origin were treated equally when sentenced in the Crown Courts. More research should be carried out into how, in practice, judges actually reach decisions.

Until 1988, only the defence had the right to appeal, but since the enactment of the Criminal Justice Act 1988, s 36 the Attorney-General may refer 'unduly lenient' sentences to the Court of Appeal. Chapter Nine raises arguments in support of a wider prosecution right of appeal, to encourage a more thorough review of sentencing decisions. Another attempt to limit discretion in this field has been the creation of the Sentencing Advisory Panel by the Crime and Disorder Act 1998. It started work in 1999 and provides advice to the Court of Appeal (see Chapter Nine). An example of the Court of Appeal building on that advice is shown at **[7:13]**. Meanwhile, the sentencing judge remains a powerful and influential actor in the criminal trial process.

Further reading

Alschuler, A W 'An Exchange of Concessions' [1992] 142 NLJ 937
Ashworth, A *Sentencing and Criminal Justice* (3rd edition, 2000) Weidenfeld & Nicolson
Devlin, P *The Judge* (1979) OUP
Griffith, J A G *The Politics of the Judiciary* (5th edition, 1997) Fontana
Home Office *Statistics on Race and the Criminal Justice System* (annual)
Pannick, D *Judges* (1987) OUP
Pattenden, R *Judicial Discretion and Criminal Litigation* (1990) Oxford
Rock, P *The Social World of the English Crown Court* (1993) Clarendon Press
Spencer, J R 'Orality and the Evidence of Absence Witnesses' [1994] Crim LR 628
Stevens, R 'Unpacking the Judges' (1993) Current Legal Problems 1
Stevens, R *The Independence of the Judiciary* (1993) Oxford
Stockdale, E *The Court and the Offender* (1967) Gollanz
Thomas, D A *Current Sentencing Practice* (constantly updated) Sweet & Maxwell
Walker, N *Sentencing: Theory, Law and Practice* (1985) Butterworths

Documents

[7:1] *Sirros v Moore* [1975] QB 118

A judge in the Crown Court heard an appeal against the decision of magistrates to recommend to the Home Secretary that the appellant be deported. The magistrates had directed that he should not be detained pending the Home Secretary's decision. Having dismissed the appeal, the judge then ordered that the appellant be held in custody. The Court of Appeal held that because the judge had not adopted the right procedure, the order on which the appellant was taken into custody was invalid and he had rightly been released on habeas corpus. However, the judge was immune from liability in a civil action for damages.

Lord Denning MR (at page 136):

(iii) The modern courts

In the old days, as I have said, there was a sharp distinction between the inferior courts and the superior courts. Whatever may have been the reason for this distinction, it is no longer valid.

There has been no case on the subject for the last one hundred years at least. And during this time our judicial system has changed out of all knowledge. So great is this change that it is now appropriate for us to reconsider the principles which should be applied to judicial acts. In this new age I would take my stand on this: as a matter of principle the judges of superior courts have no greater claim to immunity than the judges of the lower courts. Every judge of the courts of this land – from the highest to the lowest – should be protected to the same degree, and liable to the same degree. If the reason underlying this immunity is to ensure 'that they may be free in thought and independent in judgment,' it applies to every judge, whatever his rank. Each should be protected from liability to damages when he is acting judicially. Each should be able to do his work in complete independence and free from fear. He should not have to turn the pages of his books with trembling fingers, asking himself: 'If I do this, shall I be liable in damages?' So long as he does his work in the honest belief that it is within his jurisdiction, then he is not liable to an action. He may be mistaken in the fact. He may be ignorant of the law. What he does may be outside his jurisdiction – in fact or in law – but so long as he honestly believes it to be within his jurisdiction, he should not be liable. Once he honestly entertains this belief, nothing else will make him liable. He is not to be plagued with allegations of malice or ill-will or bias or anything of the kind. Actions based on such allegations have been struck out and will continue to be struck out. Nothing will make him liable except it be shown that he was not acting judicially, knowing that he had no jurisdiction to do it.

This principle should cover the justices of the peace also. They should no longer be subject to 'strokes of the rodde, or spur'. Aided by their clerks, they do their work with the highest degree of responsibility and competence – to the satisfaction of the entire community. They should have the same protection as other judges.

(iv) The Crown Court

Today we are concerned with judges of a new kind. The judges of the Crown Court. It is, by definition, a superior court of record: see section 4(1) of the Act of 1971. The judges of it should, in principle, have the same immunity as all other judges, high or low. The Crown Court is manned by judges of every rank. Judges of the High Court, circuit judges, recorders, justices of the peace, all sit there. No distinction can or should be drawn between them. Each one shares responsibility for the decisions given by the court. If the High Court judge is not liable to an action, it should be same with the circuit judge, the recorder or the justice of the peace. No distinction can be taken on the seriousness of the case. Any one of them may sit on one day on a case of trifling importance, on the next on a case of the utmost gravity. No distinction can be taken as tot he nature of the case. It may be a matter triable only in indictment, or it may be a man up for sentence, or an appeal from magistrates. If they are not liable in trials on indictment, they should not be liable on other matters. But, whatever, it is, the immunity of the judges – and each of them – should rest on the same principle. Not liable for acts done by them in a judicial capacity. Only liable for acting in bad faith, knowing they have no jurisdiction to do it.

Conclusion

The judge had no jurisdiction to detain Sirros in custody. The Divisional Court were right to release him on habeas corpus. Though the judge was mistaken, yet he acted judicially and for that reason no action will lie against him. Likewise, no action will lie against the police officers. They are protected in respect of anything they did at his direction, not knowing it was wrong: see *London Corp v Cox* (1867) LR 2 HL 239, 269. I would therefore dismiss the appeal.

[7:2]   Zander, M and Henderson, P *The Crown Court Study* RCCJ Research Study No 19 (1993) HMSO (at page 138):

4.11   'Innocent pleading guilty' cases

4.11.1   *Was this a case of an innocent person pleading guilty?*

In cases where the defendant pleaded guilty to all charges, defence barristers were asked (Db184): 'An innocent defendant sometimes decided to plead guilty to achieve a sentence discount or reduction in the indictment. Were you concerned that this was such a case?' (According to the Bar's Code of Conduct, counsel's duty in such a situation is to advise his client that he should not plead guilty unless he is guilty. But the decision as to plea is for the client.)

There were 846 substantive replies to this question – not counting 368 non-replies, most probably signifying Don't know or No view. In 793 (94%) the reply was No. But 53 (6% of the 846) the reply was Yes. These 53 cases 'grossed up' represent close to 1,400 cases a year. This appeared to be a cause for concern. It was clear that further analysis of the cases should be undertaken.

The further analysis showed that few (if any) of these cases could safely be characterised as clear examples of what Q184 in the defence barrister's questionnaire was intended to reveal – namely cases where a person, who in the view of his lawyers could have been innocent of all the charges he faced, nevertheless pleaded guilty because of the sentence discount. It was plain that in many of the 53 cases the defence barristers had misunderstood the thrust of the question – no doubt due to the imperfect drafting of the question and the absence of guidance to respondents as to what it was intended to mean.

In regard to 15 of the 53 cases, the defendant also returned a questionnaire. In six of these cases he pleaded guilty though he was not guilty of the offence. In nine he said he had been guilty of the offence(s) charged or similar offences. The other side of the same coin was the response made by defendants themselves to a somewhat similar question we put to them. We did not think we could fairly ask defendants who pleaded not guilty whether they were actually guilty of the offence. But we asked those who pleased guilty (Def38): 'Did you actually commit the offence(s) for which you pleaded guilty, or a similar offence?'

There were 269 effective replies. Of these, 71% said they had committed the offence as charged and another 17% said they had committed a similar offence.

But there were 31 cases (11%) where the defendant claimed that he had not committed the offence. In 26 of these 31 cases the defence barrister had also returned a question-naire. In 20 of the 26 cases the barrister gave no indication in answering Q184 that he took the view that his client might have been an innocent person pleading guilty because of the sentence discount.

But in six, as has been seen, the barrister did give this indication. (In none of these six cases did the defendant go to prison.)

- Case No 46 – D, aged 21, no previous convictions, charged with theft from his employer, got a community service order. He had simply helped a friend but had not done much and had not benefited from the crime. Db thought it was too trivial to warrant prosecution. Def. said 'I didn't commit the offence but pleaded guilty because of the credit factor which was explained to me because of the statement of my co-defendant'. He had confessed in a tape-recorded interview.
- Case No 50 – D, no previous convictions, charged with gross indecency, given a conditional discharge. Def. said he did not commit the offence but pleaded guilty 'to get it over as quickly as possible'. He agreed with the advice of his lawyers to plead guilty. Db said the Def. had had no faith that his evidence would be be-lieved.
- Case No 9 – D, aged 22, several previous convictions, charged with assault oc-casional actual bodily harm and theft, put on probation and ordered to pay com-pensation of £400. Db said: 'The prosecution was intending to add a charge of blackmail. D refused to run the risk.' Def. said 'I pleaded guilty because of threat to amend the charges to assault with intent to rob and blackmail, theft and actual bodily harm. I was blackmailed into pleading guilty. Disgusting. By the time you read this paper I will probably be in prison for two crimes – one of which I did not commit'.
- Case No 23 – D, female aged 49, three Class B drugs' charges, one of supplying, two of possession. Three previous convictions for similar offences in 1977, 1986, 1987. Given a suspended sentence of 12 months imprisonment. Def. said 'Knew I was guilty of the offences I was accused for. I was lucky to get away with a sus-pended sentence.' Db said a conference with the client satisfied him that hers was not a case of an innocent person pleading guilty. She was facing her first custodial penalty.
- Case No 24 – D, female aged 25, charged with theft and 1 other offence taken into consideration (TIC). Previous convictions for shoplifting in 1983, 1987 and 1991. Given a suspended sentence of 3 months. Def. said 'I was advised to plead guilty by my barrister to get it over and done with. Otherwise we would of (sic) come back for a hearing.' She agreed with this advice. Db said D's instructions revealed a good defence. Crown offered to drop a further charge currently in the magistrates' court on a similar matter of a guilty plea.'
- Case No 16 – D, male aged 25, no previous convictions, charged with shoplifting from WH Smith's and Woolworth's. His co-defendant had a string of previous convictions for shoplifting. Def. admitted the WH Smith's offence but initially denied the Woolworth's one. Pleaded guilty to both. Given conditional discharge. Def. said 'Pleaded guilty although I was not guilty – to keep myself in one piece. I decided my plea on advice from the barrister and solicitor. I did not agree with the advice. I was only being used.' He had made a confession in the police car and at the police station. He had signed it, but it was not accurate: 'I signed under the influence of drink and drugs.'

In the other 25 cases where the defendant said he was not guilty the following were typical of the reasons or explanations given:

- Case No 0014 'So I did not have to go through a trial. Also because of the advice of my barrister.' (Many previous convictions. Facing nine charges including burglary and assault occasioning actual bodily harm. Received 15 months.)
- Case No 0085 'If I had pleaded not guilty, I would have received a bigger sentence, I think.' (one previous conviction in 1988 for offences against the person. Charged with burglary. (Conditional discharge plus £75 prosecution costs.)
- Case No 0592 'I have been in prison for similar thefts. I was out to steal that day but I never actually attempted to steal what the store detective claimed. I pleaded guilty because my barrister spoke to the judge and got assurance that if I pleaded guilty I would not be sent to prison. However this guarantee did not extend if I pleaded not guilty and was found guilty.' (Many previous convictions. Charged with attempted theft. Conditional discharge.)
- Case No 0125 'Because the police bully you and it is pure hell.' (Many previous convictions. Facing four charges of burglary and theft. 9 months imprisonment.)
- Case No 0183 'I wanted to protect my co-accused.' (Many previous convictions. Charges of theft, taking a conveyance, driving whilst disqualified, driving without insurance, 6 months imprisonment on each charge concurrent.)
- Case No 0642 'Seemed easier at the time to get it over with.' Agreed with the lawyers' advice to plead guilty. (Many previous convictions. Charged with drugs and vehicle offences. 3 months imprisonment suspended.)
- Case No 0310 'Because my solicitor told me so.' (Several previous convictions. Charged with burglary. Probation.)
- Case No 0352 'To dispence (sic) with the case and lead a normal life.' (many previous convictions. Charged with theft, 3 months imprisonment, including 1 months for an activated previous conditional discharge.)
- Case No 0418 'To save time and taxpayer's money.' (Many previous convictions. Facing seven charges of burglary and theft. Three sentences of 2 years imprisonment concurrent and four of 3 months imprisonment.)
- Case No 0575 'I did not want to put the victim through a court ordeal.' (1 minor previous conviction. Charged with four counts of indecent assaults on a child. Two months imprisonment.)

[7:3] *Royal Commission on Criminal Justice* (1993) Cm 2263, HMSO (at page 111):

45   Against the risk that defendants may be tempted to plead guilty to charges of which they are not guilty must be weighted the benefits to the system and to defendants of encouraging those who are in fact guilty to plead guilty. We believe that the system of sentence discounts should remain. But we do see reason to make the system more effective. In particular we believe that a clearer system of graduated discounts would help to alleviate the problem of 'cracked' trials. The Crown Court Study showed that 'cracked' trials were 26% of all cases or 43% of cases other than those listed as guilty pleas. 'Cracked' trials create serious problems, principally for all the thousands of witnesses each year – police officers, experts and ordinary citizens – who come to court expecting a trial only to find that there is no trial because the defendant has decided to plead guilty at the last minute. This causes in particular unnecessary anxiety for victims whose evidence has up to that point been disputed.

46   At present, the sentence discount is available at any stage until the beginning of the trial but the Court of Appeal has stated in terms that, other things being equal, an earlier plea ought to attract a higher discount and that late tactical pleas should not attract the same discount:

'This court has long said that discounts on sentences are appropriate, but everything depends upon the circumstances of each case. If a man is arrested and at once tells the police that he is guilty and co-operates with them in the recovery of property and the identification of others concerned in the offence, he can expect to get a substantial discount. But if a man is arrested in circumstances in which he cannot hope to put forward a defence of not guilty, he cannot expect much by way of a discount. In between come this kind of case, where the court has been put to considerable trouble as a result of a tactical plea. The sooner it is appreciated that defendants are not going to get a full discount for pleas of guilty in these sort of circumstances, the better it will be for the administration of justice.'[1]

47   We agree with the view expressed by the Court of Appeal that, other things being equal, the earlier the plea the higher the discount. In broad terms, solicitors and barristers should advise their clients to that effect. Judges must, however, retain their discretion to deal appropriately with the particular circumstances of the individual case. Subject to these points, a system of graduated discounts might work broadly as follows:

(a)   The most generous discount should be available to the defendant who indicates a guilty plea in response to the service of the case disclosed by the prosecution.

(b)   The next most generous discount should be available to the defendant who indicates a guilty plea in sufficient time to avoid full preparation for trial. The discount might be less if the plea were entered only after a preparatory hearing.

(c)   At the bottom of the scale should come the discount for a guilty plea entered on the day of the trial itself. Since resources would be saved by avoiding a contested trial even at this late stage, we think that some discount should continue to be available. But it should be appreciably smaller than for a guilty plea offered at one of the earlier stages.

We do not think that clearer articulation of the long accepted principle that there should be greater sentence discounts for earlier pleas will increase the risk that defendants may plead guilty to offences they did not commit. We would on the other hand expect that it would lead some who would at present plead guilty to do so earlier.

48   We believe, however, that still more could be done to reduce the incidence of 'cracked' trials. As the Seabrook Committee argued, the most common reason for defendants delaying a plea of guilty until the last minute is a reluctance to face the facts until they are at the door of the court. It is often said too that a defendant has a considerable incentive to behave in this way. The longer the delay, the more the likelihood of a witness becoming intimidated or forgetting to turn up or disappearing. And, if the defendant is remanded in custody, he or she will continue to enjoy the privileges of an unconvicted remand prisoner whereas, once a guilty pleas has been entered, the prisoner enters the category of convicted/unsentenced and loses those privileges. Although this last disincentive can be removed, as we recommend below, the problem of last minute changes of plea can never be completely eradicated. We believe, however, that a significant number of those who now plead guilty at the last minute would be

---

[1]   *R v Hollington and Emmens* (1985) 82 Cr App Rep 281.

more ready to declare their hand at an earlier stage if they were given a reliable early indication of the maximum sentence that they would face if found guilty.

49   The defendant will be interested not so much in the discount on sentence that he or she might receive as the actual sentence and in particular whether it will be custodial or not. It used to be possible for defence counsel to ask the judge for an indication of the sentence that his or her client might receive if found guilty after a contested trial, as opposed to the sentence that might be passed if the plea were changed to guilty. But the discussion of likely sentences with judges is now severely constrained by the Court of Appeal's judgment in *R v Turner*.[2] According to this, judges may say that, whether the accused pleads guilty or not guilty, the sentence will or will not take a particular form. They must not, however, state that on a plea of guilty they would impose one sentence while on conviction following a plea of not guilty they would impose a severer sentence. The court took the view that this would be placing undue pressure on defendants, depriving them of that complete freedom of choice which is essential.

50   Many witnesses, particularly from the judiciary and the Bar, urged on us the desirability of reverting, in essence, to the system as it applied before the judgment in the case of *Turner*. The Crown Court Study also showed that, among the judges and barristers who responded, there was overwhelming support for change. We do not support a total reversal of the judgment in *Turner*, since we agree that to face defendants with a choice between what they might get on an immediate plea of guilty and what they might get if found guilty by the jury does amount to unacceptable pressure. But the effect of *Turner* and related judgments appears to have been to make judges reluctant to discuss sentence with counsel at all. We think that there is a case for a change of approach. We recommend that, at the request of defence counsel on instructions from the defendant, judges should be able to indicate the highest sentence that they would impose at that point on the basis of the facts as put to them. A request for such an indication might be made at a preparatory hearing, at a hearing called specially for this purpose, or at the trial itself.

51   We envisage that the procedure which we recommend would be initiated solely by, and for the benefit of, defendants who wish to exercise a right to be told the consequences of a decision which is theirs alone. Where a defendant would need the protection of an appropriate adult during inquiries carried out at a police station, the system must be operated with particular care. The sentence 'canvass', as we have called it, should normally take place in the judge's chambers with both sides being represented by counsel. A shorthand writer should also be present. If none is available a member of the court staff should take a note to be agreed immediately by the judge and both counsel. The judge may give the answer to the question 'what would be the maximum sentence if my client were to plead guilty at this stage?' but to no other. The judge's indication should be based on brief statements from prosecution and defence of all the relevant circumstances, which should include details of the defendant's previous convictions if any and, if available, any pre-sentence report required by the Criminal Justice Act 1991.

---

[2]   [1970] 2 WLR 1093. [See also **[7:4]**.]

[7:4]   *R v Turner* [1970] 2 QB 321

The defendant pleaded not guilty at his trial on a charge of theft of a car. He had previous convictions, and during an adjournment he was advised by his counsel to change his plea. Having spoken to the trial judge, counsel advised that in his opinion a non-custodial sentence would be imposed if he changed his plea, whereas if he persisted with his not guilty plea and was convicted, there was a real possibility of a sentence of imprisonment being imposed.

The Court of Appeal, in allowing the appeal, held that counsel could properly advise a defendant in strong terms to change his plea provided that it was made clear to him that the ultimate choice was freely his, but if the advice was conveyed as that of someone who had seen the judge, a defendant should be disabused of any impression that the judge's views were being repeated.

Lord Parker CJ (at page 324):

Before leaving this case, which has brought out into the open the vexed question of so-called 'plea-bargaining', the court would like to make some observations which may be of help to judges and to counsel and, indeed, solicitors. They are these:

1   Counsel must be completely free to do what is his duty, namely to give the accused the best advice he can and if need be advice in strong terms. This will often include advice that a plea of guilty, showing an element of remorse, is a mitigation factor which may well enable the court to give a lesser sentence than would otherwise be the case. Counsel of course will emphasise that the accused must not plead guilty unless he has committed the acts constituting the offence charged.

2   The accused, having considered counsel's advice, must have a complete freedom of choice whether to plead guilty or not guilty.

3   There must be freedom of access between counsel and judge. Any discussion, however, which takes place must be between the judge and both counsel for the defence and counsel for the prosecution. If a solicitor representing the accused is in the court he should be allowed to attend the discussion if he so desires. This freedom of access is important because there may be matters calling for communication or discussion, which are of such a nature that counsel cannot in the interests of his client mention them in open court. Purely by way of example, counsel for the defence may by way of mitigation wish to tell the judge that the accused has not long to live, is suffering maybe from cancer, of which he is and should remain ignorant. Again, counsel on both sides may wish to discuss with the judge whether it would be proper, in a particular case, for the prosecution to accept a plea to a lesser offence. It is of course imperative that so far as possible justice must be administered in open court. Counsel should, therefore, only ask to see the judge when it is felt to be really necessary, and the judge must be careful only to treat such communications as private where, in fairness to the accused, this is necessary.

4   The judge should, subject to the one exception referred to hereafter, never indicate the sentence which he is minded to impose. A statement that on a plea of guilty he would impose one sentence but that on a conviction following a plea of not guilty he would impose a severer sentence is one which should never be made. This could be taken to be undue pressure on the accused, thus depriving him of that complete freedom of choice which is essential. Such cases, however, are in the experience of the court happily rare. What on occasions does appear to happen however is that a judge will tell counsel that, having read the depositions

and the antecedents, he can safely say that on a plea of guilty he will for instance, make a probation order, something which may be helpful to counsel in advising the accused. The judge in such a case is no doubt careful not to mention what he would do if the accused were convicted following a plea of not guilty. Even so, the accused may well get the impression that the judge is intimating that in the event a severer sentence, maybe a custodial sentence would result, so that again he may feel under pressure. This accordingly must also not be done.

The only exception to this rule is that it should be permissible for a judge to say, if it be the case, that whatever happens, whether the accused pleads guilty or not guilty, the sentence will or will not take a particular form, eg a probation order or a fine, or a custodial sentence.

Finally, where any such discussion on sentence has taken place between judge and counsel, counsel for the defence should disclose this to the accused and inform him of what took place.

[7:5]   *R v Smith* [1990] 1 WLR 1311

The appellant, who was the subject of a probation order, was charged on indictment with assault occasioning actual bodily harm and affray. Before the arraignment at the Crown Court there was a private discussion between the judge and counsel in the judge's private room at which no shorthand writer was present and no record was made. As a result of that discussion, counsel for the appellant was under the impression that the appellant would receive a suspended sentence of imprisonment. The appellant, on counsel's advice, changed his proposed plea from not guilty to both counts to that of guilty to affray. The judge heard the facts, and ordered a report from the appellant's probation officer. When he received the report, he passed a sentence of an immediate term of imprisonment.

The Court of Appeal allowed his appeal against sentence, varying the sentence by suspending the term of imprisonment for a period of two years.

Russell LJ (at page 1314):

If nothing else, this appeal demonstrates yet again the problem inherent in out-of-court discussions between counsel and the trial judge in criminal cases. Of course, on the authority of the well known case of *R v Turner* (1970) 54 Cr App Rep 352, in some circumstances it is permissible for counsel to see the judge in his room to ascertain his reaction to possible sentencing options open to him. But that should never occur, as has been said on almost innumerable occasions in this court, in the absence of a shorthand notetaker or, alternatively, in the absence of some recording device. In this case there was neither a shorthand writer present not a recording device. What has happened here is something that from time to time does happen, namely there has arisen a dispute (not to put too fine a point on it) between the judge's account of what was said and the account that has been produced for perusal by this court in the form of affidavit evidence from both defending and prosecuting counsel. The dispute comes before this court when it is ill-equipped to resolve conflicts of recollection between counsel and the judge, and where in seeking to do justice, this court runs the real risk of not achieving it. Instead, a thoroughly unsatisfactory state of affairs is created where either the defendant has a genuine sense of grievance or the prosecution has not properly ventilated its case, or both disquieting consequences ensue.

We find it disturbing that despite frequent observations made in this court discouraging unnecessary visits to the judge's room, they appear to continue up and down the country. In the hope – we hope it is not a vain one – that some notice will now be taken of what we are about to say we remind those who have responsibility in these matters of the words of Mustill LJ in *R v Harper-Taylor and Bakker* [1988] NLJR 80. The Lord Justice said this when dealing with a case not dissimilar to the present, in the sense that there had been a prolonged discussion, ranging over a wide field in the judge's room:

'Since we regard the discussion in the judge's room as the source of all the subsequent entanglements, some general observations on the practice of meeting the judge in his private room may be appropriate. A first principle of criminal law is that justice is done in public, for all to see and hear. By this standard a meeting in the judge's room is anomalous: the essence, and indeed the purpose, being that neither the defendant nor the jury nor the public are there to hear what is going on. Undeniably, there are circumstances where the public must be excluded. Equally, the jury cannot always be kept in court throughout. The withdrawal of the proceedings into private, without even the defendant being there, is another matter. It is true, as this court stated in *R v Turner* (1970) 54 Cr App Rep, 352, 360, that there must be freedom of access between counsel and the judge when there are matters calling for communications or discussions of such a nature that counsel cannot in the interests of his client mention them in open court. Criminal trials are so various that a list of situations where an approach to the judge is permissible would only mislead; but it must be clear that communications should never take place unless there is no alternative.

Apart from the question of principle, seeing the judge in private creates risks of more than one kind, as the present case has shown. The need to solve an immediate practical problem may combine with the more relaxed atmosphere of the private room to blur the formal outlines of the trial. Again, if the object of withdrawing the case from open court is to maintain a degree of confidence, as it plainly must be, there is room for misunderstanding about how far the confidence is to extend; and, in particular there is a risk that counsel and solicitors for the other parties may hear something said to the judge which they would rather not hear, putting them into a state of conflict between their duties to their clients, and their obligation to maintain the confidentiality of the private room.

The absence of the defendant is also a potential source of trouble. He has to learn what the judge has said at second hand, and may afterwards complain (right or not) that he was not given an accurate account. Equally, he cannot hear what his counsel has said to the judge, and hence cannot intervene to correct a misstatement or an excess of authority: a factor which may not only be a source of unfairness to the defendant, but which may also deprive the prosecution of the opportunity to contend that admissions made in open court in the presence of the client and not repudiated by him may be taken to have been made with his authority.

[7:6] *R v Dossetter* [1999] 2 Cr App Rep (S) 248

The Court of Appeal, having upheld the sentence of seven years' imprisonment imposed on the appellant for conspiring to produce counterfeit US Bills to the value of $6m, commented on what had taken place in the Crown Court during the trial in June 1998.

Rose LJ (at page 252):

Before leaving this matter, it is regrettably necessary to comment on what took place on June 1 and 2, in that, on the first of those dates, no fewer than four visits were made by counsel then appearing for the defendants, of whom counsel then appearing for Dossetter was clearly in the forefront, to the judge's private room. On June 2, there were two such further visits. It is unnecessary to rehearse the detail of what transpired on those six occasions. Fortunately, it was in each case tape recorded.

What took place was the most blatant attempt, particularly by counsel on behalf of Dossetter, to engage in plea bargaining with the judge, before Dossetter decided whether or not he was going to plead guilty. For the last 30 years, this court has repeatedly said that the nature of discussions, in private, between a judge and counsel, must be limited and must be exceptional. Plea bargaining, in the sense of seeking to extract from a judge an indication of the sentence which he will give if a particular defendant pleads guilty, forms no part of English criminal jurisprudence.

In the case of *Turner* (1970) 54 Cr App R 352, the judgment of the court of which Widgery LJ was one of the members was given by Lord Parker, then Chief Justice. Lord Parker, in a passage which begins at the bottom of p 359, indicated the principles which must apply in relation to private discussions between a judge and counsel. It is unnecessary to read, though plainly it bears reading by a number of those who were involved in this case, the full text of what Lord Parker said, But the fourth principle which he enunciated is of particular materiality to this case ...

What lamentably happened in this case was that, at the outset of the first of the six occasions to which we have referred, counsel for Dossetter indicated the sort of sentence which he was advising Dossetter to expect if he pleaded guilty. The sentence which, in due course the judge passed, was within that bracket. It follows that there cannot be, in this case, any complaint that Dossetter was misled by anything that had been said in chambers. What the judge said repeatedly in, as it seems to this court, not giving any clear indication of the sentence which he would pass, was that Dossetter must take his chance.

These discussions should never have taken place. Yet again, this court emphasises that such discussions should not take place. Justice, in this country, save in the most exceptional circumstances, identified by Lord Parker in *Turner*, must be conducted in public.

[7:7]   Sanders, A and Young, R *Criminal Justice* (2nd edition, 2000)
Butterworths (at pages 477–482):

7. Conclusion

The pre-trial processes in the criminal courts exhibit many of the hallmarks of the crime control model. In a system in which all the participants understand that the majority of cases will be disposed of by guilty pleas, attention is naturally focused on case settlement rather than preparing for a fight in court. The system itself is geared towards the routine production of guilty pleas, as can be seen in the legal aid fee structure, the organisation of the legal profession, the sentence discount principle and so on. The wholesale adoption of crime control ideology by solicitors, barristers and judges up and down the country further oils the conveyor belt moving defendants inexorably towards conviction. It is undeniable that elements within the legal profession remain committed to due process, but they provide the exception to the rule of crime control. That some defendants insist on trial by jury is in some ways the most remarkable feature of the criminal justice process.

The possibility of regulating or even eradicating charge bargaining has been explored by a number of domestic writers,[3] and has been attempted, with some well-documented success, in one American jurisdiction.[4] There are good principled reasons why we should attempt such an eradication here. The due process and human rights arguments discussed in relation to the sentence discount (see section 2(e)) apply with much the same force to the practice of charge bargaining. To these we can add the victim-centred arguments against all forms of plea bargaining that were discussed in ch 1, section 10.[5]

As for the freedom model, whilst not blind to the considerable resource advantages of guilty pleas, it would not accept that sentence discounts and charge bargains are the most cost-effective and freedom-enhancing way of doing justice. It seems unlikely that all, or even a majority of, defendants would plead not guilty if we left the system as it is but eliminated discounts and bargains. For a start that should encourage the police and prosecutors to ensure that an appropriate charge is brought in the first place and that cases only come to court that satisfy the necessary evidential and public interest tests. Even under the current system many defendants readily accept their guilt and see no point in putting an unarguable case before the court.[6] The proportion of defendants who felt this way should increase under a reformed system which demanded ethical charging and prosecution practices. Many more defendants would plead guilty because of the considerable incentives to do so even in a land without plea bargaining. These incentives include less time spent inside the system (as more time is needed to prepare a contested case than a guilty plea), less time spent in court (it takes longer to

---

[3]   See D Galligan, 'Regulating Pre-Trial Decisions', in I Dennis (ed), *Criminal Law and Justice* (London: Sweet & Maxwell, 1987); and A Bottomley, 'Sentencing reform and the structuring of pre-trial discretion' in M Wasik and K Pease (eds), *Sentencing Reform,* (Manchester: MUP, 1987).

[4]   Carns and Kruse. See also Ashworth (1998) p 293 for discussion of jurisdictions which shun sentence discounts.

[5]   See generally H Fenwick, 'Charge Bargaining and Sentence Discount: the Victim's Perspective' (1997) 5 Int R Victimology 23.

[6]   See McConville et al (1994) pp 182–185 for supporting references and for a careful discussion of the extent to which this point can be pressed.

fight a case than to concede it), lower court costs, the chance to mitigate on the basis of remorse, sparing any defence witnesses (such as friends or family) the ordeal of testifying, sparing oneself the ordeal of cross-examination, and so on.[7] Some are no doubt altruistic enough (or sufficiently remorseful) to want to spare victims and other prosecution witnesses the bother of testifying. It might take some time for our system to adjust to a regime of non-bargain justice [8] but that fact has never stopped governments from implementing radical reform when they favour the prosecution, as was the case with the effective abolition of the right to silence. The fact that the elimination of bargain justice is in the interests of victims, defendants, and the promotion of human rights might yet convince a government that this strategy is worth pursuing.[9]

The strategy of simply eliminating bargain justice would represent progress, but it still leaves in place so many incentives to plead guilty that one might argue that the presumption of innocence would still effectively be undermined. A more radical proposal would be to do away with the concept of a guilty plea altogether, or to do so for Crown Court cases at least. Inquisitorial jurisdictions have traditionally functioned without a reliance on this concept.[10] Under this proposal there would in every case that fell within the no-plea regime a degree of judicial scrutiny of the prosecution case, so as to ensure that convictions were always based on sufficient, reliable, admissible and fairly obtained evidence. Defendants could be given a choice of trial by jury and judge, or trial by judge alone. Those not actively contesting guilt would be funnelled towards the latter option, whilst others could be given a more open choice[11] Schulhofer has estimated that abolishing all systemic incentives to plead guilty in this way and replacing the guilty plea system with bench trials by judges sitting alone would increase the trial rate by some 650% but with only a 20% increase needed in judicial resources at the adjudication stage.[12] That seems a small price to pay for a more victim-centred system that better protects human rights and innocent defendants.[13]

An even more radical proposal would be to replace our current system of punishment with that of restorative justice in which offender would be held accountable to victims for the harm done to them, usually through a process of mediation. This would entail a shift away from the 'battle' model of adversarial justice (whether due process or crime

---

[7]   Thus we saw in section 2(d)(i) how one solicitor stressed many benefits of pleading guilty that had nothing to do with sentence discounts or charge bargains.

[8]   We should not underestimate the extent to which plea bargaining has become an entrenched feature of the criminal justice landscape, nor forget that it has supported the growth of institutions (such as state funded defence services) which serve its cause: G Fisher, 'Plea Bargaining's Triumph' (2000) 109 Yale LJ 857. One implication of Fisher's painstaking historical analysis is that to dismantle plea bargaining will require a fundamental reappraisal and reshaping of many other aspects of the criminal justice system.

[9]   We should note that the state has an interest in retaining plea bargaining, not just as a repressive tool, but also so as to be able to 'cut deals' with police informers, particularly where a not guilty plea could lead to embarrassing revelations about the state's collusion with those involved in organised crime, or in paramilitary activity in Northern Ireland: *The Guardian* 30 September 2000. On the corrupting effect of using informers, see further ch 12, section 3.

[10]   Although more recently they have begun to succumb to the temptation to bargain away this part of their legal heritage. See Ashworth (1998) pp 267–268 and the sources cited there.

[11]   See S Doran and J Jackson. 'The Case for Jury Waiver' [1997] Crim LR 155.

[12]   S Schulhofer, 'Plea bargaining as disaster' (1992) 101 Yale LJ 1979.

[13]   The extent to which innocent defendants are better protected under a non-bargain system is, we should acknowledge, a matter of controversy: see R Scott and W J Stuntz. 'A Reply: Imperfect Bargains. Imperfect Trials and Innocent Defendants' (1992) 101 YLJ 2011.

control oriented) towards the kind of 'family model' that was advocated by Griffiths in his largely overlooked critique of Packer's models.[14] In the family model it is assumed that state officials can be trusted to carry out their duties in good faith and using their best judgement, that those found to have offended should not be stigmatised or exiled but rather censured and reintegrated into society, and that everyone should be treated with respect.[15] The fact that the interests of those found to have offended would be promoted should mean that defendants and defence lawyers would not seek to turn the criminal process into an obstacle course save in those cases where guilt was in question. Instead, offenders would much more readily accept responsibility and the real issue would concern what needed to be done to put things right. Although Griffiths did not discuss the position of victims, it is apparent that his model would promote communitarian conceptions of punishment administered by and through the mechanism of a 'community conference'.[16] This model could therefore satisfy victims' interests in public vindication, in participation, and in repair. Fenwick, who looks at plea-bargaining from the victim's perspective, has expressed tentative support for this idea.[17] It would be stupid, however, to see the 'family model' as the holy grail of criminal justice reform. Griffiths had little to say on the content of criminal procedure in cases where guilt was contested. Others have noted, however, that the assumptions of the family model are consistent with an inquisitorial mode of procedure.[18] We noted in chapter 1 that the inquisitorial model has many weaknesses of its own, whilst the implication of subsequent chapters is that state officials have not yet shown themselves worthy of the kind of trust the family model calls for. There is also a danger that community conference outcomes between victims and offenders will turn out to be inadequately regulated by state officials and just as contrary to the public interest as the plea bargains they might replace.

So what is to be done? We have raised in this conclusion the kind of thorny questions best tackled by Royal Commissions, or at least so one might think. Yet the report of the Runciman Commission dealt with the subject of charge bargaining in a single sentence: 'We see no objection to such discussions, but the earlier they take place the better; consultation between counsel before the trial would often avoid the need for the case to be listed as a contested trial.'[19] On this subject, as on many others, the Runciman Commission failed to cite any evidence or marshal any supporting arguments to justify its preference for more crime control.[20] The Runciman Commission thus represents a missed opportunity to reassess the fundamentals of our system of criminal justice and nothing has happened since to indicate that any of the reforms mooted above might find favour with policy-makers. In drawing this chapter to a close we want to reflect for a moment on this dismal episode in the formulation of criminal justice policy.

<table>
<tr><td>14</td><td>J Griffith, 'Ideology in Criminal Procedure or a Third "Model" of the Criminal Process' (1970) 79 Yale LJ 359.</td></tr>
<tr><td>15</td><td>See also J Braithwaite, Crime, Shame and Reintegration (Cambridge: CUP, 1989).</td></tr>
<tr><td>16</td><td>See ch 1, section 10.</td></tr>
<tr><td>17</td><td>Fenwick (1997) pp 23–24 and 34–35.</td></tr>
<tr><td>18</td><td>M Damaska, 'Evidentiary Barriers to Conviction and Two Models of Criminal Procedure: A Comparative Study' (1973) 121 U Penn LR 506 at pp 570–573. For a further discussion of the issues raised in this para see ch 1, section 10.</td></tr>
<tr><td>19</td><td>RCCJ (1993) p 114. Many of its recommendations were designed to guarantee earlier communication between opposing counsel. For example, a requirement that the defence disclose its case in outline was supported, in part, because this might result in 'an earlier resolution through a plea of guilty' (p 97) and see also pp 101–108 on encouraging 'pre-trial preparation'.</td></tr>
<tr><td>20</td><td>Note that none of the 22 research studies funded by the Runciman Commission was on plea bargaining.</td></tr>
</table>

As the Runciman Commission was set up in the wake of the freeing of the Birmingham Six it was widely expected that it would focus on the safeguards and reforms needed to better protect against miscarriages of justice. That these expectations proved false is partly attributable to the way in which the government set its terms of reference. These required the Runciman Commission 'to examine the effectiveness of the criminal justice system in England and Wales in securing the conviction of those guilty of criminal offences and the acquittal of those who are innocent, having regard to the efficient use of resources'.[21] It would have been open to the Runciman Commission to reject the implication in these terms of reference that all three of these matters are of equal weight. Instead it embraced this notion wholeheartedly. Thus, for example, it saw 'miscarriages of justice' as comprising both the conviction of the innocent and the acquittal of the guilty.[22] Because it regarded these matters of equal concern it saw no problem in recommending changes to the system which would both undermine the adversarial system and substantially increase the likelihood of innocent persons being convicted. For the Runciman Commission, these costs were more than offset by the prospect of convicting more of the guilty at a 'value for money'[23] price. It is this crude cost-benefit analysis that lay behind its proposals to abolish a defendant's right in either way cases to elect trial by jury[24] and to encourage greater use of all forms of plea bargaining.

To some extent, then, the Runciman Commission simply made a value choice, expressing a preference for more crime control and less due process. But as we pointed out at the start of this book, empirical evidence should play a central part in informing one's choice of values. Certainly the Runciman Commission expressed beliefs about how the system works, but its views were based on stereotypes and prejudices as much as on hard evidence. Thus, it declares its conviction, without any supporting evidence or argument, that clearer articulation of the sentence discount principle would not increase the risks of the innocent pleading guilty.[25] Again, while the Runciman Commission found it 'odd' that most of those electing trial by jury eventually pleaded guilty it was not interested in exploring the reasons for this.[26] It was simply assumed that defendants were wasting everybody's time and money by delaying their pleas of guilty until the last moment. The current Home Secretary has expressed exactly the same lazy self-serving belief in pushing ahead with his plans to abolish the right to elect trial by jury.[27] He has ignored research evidence suggesting that the problem lies with the failure of the CPS to scrutinise their evidence at an early stage, and adjust charges accordingly, in many cases.[28] In the new politics of criminal justice,[29] the great mass of criminal defendants is constructed as 'undeserving' of due process, presumed guilty, and portrayed in public as cynical manipulators of the system who warrant swifter punishment. Moreover, the process by which punishment is legitimated should spare 'innocent victims' as much further 'ordeal' as possible. Summary trial serves these ends better than Crown Court trial, but a guilty plea better still.

---

21   RCCJ (1993) p i.
22   RCCJ (1993) p 2.
23   See RCCJ (1993) pp 4–5.
24   Discussed in chapter 8.
25   RCCJ (1993) p 112.
26   See RCCJ (1993) p 86.
27   Quoted in P Duff, 'The Defendant's Right to Trial by Jury: A Neighbour's View' [2000] Crim LR 85. The Mode of Trial Bill, rejected again by the House of Lords in September 2000, is discussed in ch 8, section 5(c).
28   See discussion of mode of trial decisions in ch 8, section 5(c).
29   See McConville (1998).

This crime control line of reasoning, that guilty persons will take advantage of due process protections in order to further their own interests and in seeking to avoid their just deserts, is not borne out by research findings on the operation of the criminal process. Thus, for example, late plea changing in the Crown Court is predominantly the product of a system that simultaneously proclaims the right of defendants to call upon the prosecution to prove its case before judge and jury whilst doing its utmost to ensure that the vast majority waive that right. The mass production of guilty pleas has become a systemic imperative in the criminal courts. Defendants do not commonly play the system; the system plays with them, their rights, and their freedom.

[7:8] Hood, R *Race and Sentencing: a Study in the Crown Court* (1992) Oxford University Press

Offenders of Afro-Caribbean origin comprise over 10% of the male sentenced population, between 8 and 9 times their proportion in the population at large. Almost a quarter of female prisoners are black: a substantial number are foreigners imprisoned for importing drugs (and see **[1:11]**). This study was carried out in the Crown Court Centres which service the region covered by the West Midland Police, and was based on a sample of 2,884 male offenders sentenced in 1989 (886 black, 536 Asian, 1,443 white and 16 from other backgrounds) as well as all 433 women sentenced in these courts over the same period.

The following extracts are taken from Chapter 12: Discrimination in the Courts? (pages 179–192):

This study has confirmed what has for long been suspected, namely that, to a very substantial degree, the over-representation of Afro-Caribbean males and females in the prison system is a product of their over-representation among those convicted of crime and sentenced in the Crown Courts. The best evidence that it is possible to make from this study is that 80% of the over-representation of black male offenders in the prison population was due to their over-representation among those convicted at the Crown Court and to the type and circumstances of the offences of which black men were convicted. The remaining 20%, in the case of males but not females, appeared to be due to differential treatment and other factors which influence the nature and length of the sentences imposed: two thirds of it resulting from the higher proportion of black defendants who pleaded not guilty and who were, as a consequence, more liable on conviction to receive longer custodial sentences.

From Crown Court records it was not possible to shed much light on the circumstances and factors which might produce a higher rate of convictions amongst the black population, but there were some clues which are worthy of further investigation. A higher proportion of black people were charged with offences which could only be dealt with on indictment at the Crown Court: considerably more being charged with robbery, often of the kind normally referred to as 'mugging'. One should not minimise the distress caused by such behaviour, especially when women are the victims, nor the general sense of unease which it breeds, but as a form of violent or property crime it is often not more serious in its consequences than grievous bodily harm or housebreaking, both of which can be dealt with summarily if the court and defendant consent. This would not, of course, have meant that all of these black defendants would have accepted summary trial. The reason is that considerably more of them had, early on in the procedure, signified their intention to plead not guilty: 46% of blacks and Asians compared with 34% of whites charged with robbery. Nevertheless, the unavailability of discretion to deal with these offences either-way inevitably brings more black defendants into the arena of the Crown Court and its greater propensity to inflict a custodial penalty.

Black offenders were also disproportionately involved in the supply of drugs, usually cannabis, and these convictions regularly arose from police activity rather than from a complaint by citizens. This is not the place to open the debate about the seriousness of illegal dealings at street level in cannabis. It is only to say that if these offences were excluded the proportion of black males dealt with at the West Midlands courts would have been 13.7% rather than 17.2%, equivalent to 20% lower. By contrast, excluding such cases amongst white and Asians would have reduced their number by only 0.6% and 0.9% respectively. Of course, it is impossible to say whether these persons would have committed other offences but it is incontrovertible that the continued legal proscription of cannabis and the insistence that trading in it, even on a small or moderate scale, is an offence which should always be committed to the Crown Court for trial,[30] is a substantial factor influencing the number of black persons in the prison population.

Furthermore, black defendants were at a disadvantage both because of decisions they made and decisions made about them during the processing of cases before they appeared for sentence. They were more likely to be remanded in custody by magistrates who committed them for trial, even taking into account the seriousness of the charges against them and other factors which might legitimately have had an effect on the decision whether to give bail. They were much less likely to have had a social inquiry report prepared on their background, mainly because a considerably high proportion of them signified their intention to plead not guilty, but also because fewer who pleaded guilty were reported on, although, the reasons for this are not known.

Being already in custody, pleading not guilty, and not having a report were all associated with a higher probability of receiving a custodial sentence or with a lengthier sentence. And all of them, of course, limit the possibilities for effective pleas in mitigation. Those who have been in custody have less opportunity to show that they have been of exemplary behaviour or have sought to make amends by, say, entering regular employment since they were charged with the offence. Those who deny the offence cannot suddenly, on being found guilty, convincingly express remorse. For those without social inquiry reports there is often insufficient information on hand to put the offence in its social context, and no opportunity to take advantage of a specific proposal from a probation officer for an alternative sentence to custody. It would appear, therefore, that ethnic minority defendants were inadvertently subjected to a form of indirect discrimination at the point of sentence due to the fact that they chose more often to contest the case against them. Because of the way that the system works to encourage guilty pleas through a 'discount' on sentence, which has been shown to produce a substantial reduction, and because it is the policy of the Probation Service not generally to make social inquiry reports on those who intend to contest the case against them, black defendants obviously put themselves at greater risk of custody and longer sentences.

...

Black defendants at the Dudley courts got a sentence greater than that recommended by a probation officer much more often than did blacks at Birmingham. Moreover,

---

[30] In his *Practice Note: Mode of Trial Guidelines*, the Lord Chief Justice Lord Lane laid down that supply of, or possession of with intent to supply, a class B drug should be committed for trial 'unless there was only small-scale supply for no payment' [1990] 1 WLR 1439 at 1442.

blacks at the Dudley courts received sentences generally further up the scale of penalties; and if they were recommended for probation or community service they were more likely to get a more severe penalty than was a white defendant.

In attempting to understand what may have produced this divergent pattern, it was at once noticeable that the differences were greatest not in the mid to upper band of cases where difficult decisions were being made about whether to use custody or not, but in the range of cases at the lower end of the scale of severity. There was strong evidence to suggest that factors which would have been regarded as mitigating the seriousness of the case if the defendant was white were not given the same weight if the defendant was black in the cases dealt with at Dudley courts. Yet, they were given a similar weight for black offenders dealt with at Birmingham. For instance, blacks at the Dudley courts were sentenced to custody in a significantly higher proportion of cases whether they were employed or unemployed, whether they were under 21 or over 21, whether they had only one prior conviction or two or more, whether they pleaded guilty or not guilty.

A much higher proportion of the black offenders at the Dudley courts (amongst those in the lower band of seriousness) who had been convicted with at least one other black defendant were sentenced to custody at the Dudley courts. Here the difference between the observed and expected rate, given the nature of the cases, was so big that it explained half of the difference between the observed and expected rate of custody for all black cases at the Dudley courts. An examination of these cases failed to find any distinctive differences between them and the cases where whites had been convicted with other whites. Nor were the black cases at Birmingham, where custody was, in contrast, rarely used, substantially different in character. It appears reasonable to assume that the judges at the Dudley courts viewed these cases in a different light to those involving groups of whites. While it is true that there were slightly more black offenders who were committed with other black offenders at the Dudley courts than at Birmingham, there were substantially more white at the Dudley courts who had been convicted alongside other whites. Furthermore, blacks were sentenced more often to custody than either whites at the Dudley courts or blacks at Birmingham, when they were the sole offender. On the whole, there was nothing to suggest that the judges who dealt with the Dudley courts' cases were confronted with a worse impression of black criminality than were the far more lenient judges at Birmingham. On the contrary, black defendants were a lower proportion of the caseload of the Dudley courts, and the seriousness of the cases dealt with, as measured by their risk of custody score, was no different from the cases in Birmingham.

...

When one contrasts the overall treatment meted out to black Afro-Caribbean males one is left wondering whether it is not a result of different racial stereotypes operating on the perceptions of some judges. The greater involvement of black offenders in street crime and in the trade in cannabis, their higher rate of unemployment, their greater resistance to pressures to plead guilty, and possibly a perception of a different, less deferential, demeanor in court may all appear somewhat more threatening. And, if not threatening, less worthy of mitigation of punishment. It was significant that being unemployed increased the risk of a black male getting a custodial sentence, but not, in general, for a white or an Asian offender. In contrast, the better financial and employment status of the Asians and their more socially integrated households, when judged by white standards, as well as the fact that they were much more likely to be first-time offenders, may have meant that they were probably able to present themselves as less threatening, and more worthy of mitigation than either white or blacks. Only in respect of the length of sentences received by those who were sentenced to prison did Asian adult males fare worse. But without research which would allow the investigation of judicial attitudes towards, and perceptions of, racially related differences in crime patterns and in cultural responses to the criminal justice system, all this for the moment must remain speculation. It cannot be doubted that such a programme of research is now needed.

The findings regarding women will surprise many, especially given the very large over-representation of black women in penal institutions. The evidence in general supports the so-called 'chivalry' or 'paternalistic' hypothesis that judges give much more weight to mitigating features of the case in sentencing women offenders, whether white or black. No differences were found between the use of custody, of alternatives, or in sentence length between white and black women when variables relating to the seriousness of the offences were controlled for. Black women were just as likely as the whites to have had a social inquiry report prepared about them prior to sentence and were no more likely than the white to have been given a sentence greater than that recommended by the probation officer. Furthermore, compared with black men, black women were dealt with relatively leniently just as white women were dealt with leniently compared with white men. Nevertheless, when a particularly disadvantaged group were singled out – those who had various attributes which could be associated with failure to conform to female stereotypes – a relatively high proportion of them were sentenced to custody: yet, no more blacks than whites and no more females than males. One thing is certain. If considerations relating to their gender did not mitigate the punishment of women, and they were treated as men are, there would be many more in custody than at present.

What conclusions of a practical kind can be drawn from this study? First, that the research has revealed a complex picture of the way in which race appears to have affected the pattern of sentencing. In doing so, it has led to some uncomfortable conclusions for those whose duty it is to sentence offenders. It will not be possible any more to make the claim that all the differences in the treatment of black offenders occur elsewhere in the criminal justice system. At least some of it occurs in the courts, and more often in some localities than others. Much will be achieved if judges recognise this. One aim of studying sentencing by empirical methods is to help stimulate reassessment of attitudes and judicial responses. Previous research has shown how unaware judges may be of their own practices, let alone those of their colleagues. It may be that some are not yet sufficiently sensitive to the way in which racial views and beliefs may influence their judgment. If this research can stimulate such self-awareness and re-evaluation it will have made a modest contribution towards the positive self conscious appreciation of the need to take the question of race seriously which the Judicial Studies Board has now recognised by the setting up of its Ethnic Minorities Advisory Committee.

Secondly, this study draws attention to the way in which the criminal process may contribute to indirect discrimination against black people. There is clearly a need to consider the implications of the policy which favours so strongly those who plead guilty, when ethnic minorities are less willing to let a prosecution go unchallenged. This has implications, in particular, for the range and value of the information available to the courts in deciding whether or not to impose a custodial sentence as well as the type of non-custodial sentence. And, for the reason already mentioned, it will be necessary to monitor carefully the way in which the courts exercise their discretion, under the Criminal Justice Act 1991, to pass sentence without a pre-sentence report when the case is one triable only on indictment.

Thirdly, there are obvious implications relating to the duty placed on the Secretary of State by Section 95(1)(b) to 'publish such information as he considers expedient for the purpose of ... facilitating the performance ... [by persons engaged in the administration of criminal justice] ... of their duty to avoid discriminating against any person on the grounds of race or sex or any other improper ground.' To do this it will be essential for the Crown Courts to monitor the ethnic origin of all persons appearing before them. If the self-reflection on sentencing performance mentioned above is to be achieved, information on sentencing dispositions, analysed by ethnic origin, should be communicated to each judge and to the court as a whole annually. Only then will it be possible to detect whether sentencing patterns which might prove to be unfavourable to any ethnic minority are becoming established.

[7:9]   R v Christou [1992] QB 979

In an undercover police operation in London, a shop was set up purportedly to buy and sell jewellery. It was staffed solely by undercover officers purporting to be shady jewellers willing to buy stolen property. Discreetly sited cameras and sound equipment recorded all that occurred over the counter. The appellants who each made repeated sales at the shop pleaded not guilty to indictments charging burglary and handling stolen goods as alternatives. The trial judge ruled that the evidence obtained was not unfairly obtained,

The Court of Appeal dismissed the appeals, and held that the judge had exercised his discretion correctly.

Lord Taylor CJ (at page 989):

... the trick was not applied to the appellants; they voluntarily applied themselves to the trick. It is not every trick producing evidence against an accused which results in unfairness. There are, in criminal investigations, a number of situations in which the police adopt ruses or tricks in the public interest to obtain evidence. For example, to trap a blackmailer, the victim may be used as an agent of the police to arrange an appointment and false or marked money may be laid as bait to catch the offender. A trick, certainly; in a sense too, a trick which results in a form of self-incrimination; but not one which could reasonably be thought to involve unfairness.

In our view, although the Code extends beyond the treatment of those in detention, what is clear is that it was intended to protect suspects who are vulnerable to abuse or pressure from police officers or who may believe themselves to be so. Frequently, the suspect will be a detainee. But the Code will also apply where a suspect, not in detention, is being questioned about an offence by a police officer acting as a police officer for the purpose of obtaining evidence. In that situation, the officer and the suspect are not on equal terms. The officer is perceived to be in a position of authority; the suspect may be intimidated or undermined.

The situation at Stardust Jewellers was quite different. The appellants were not being questioned by police officers acting as such. Conversation was on equal terms. There could be no question of pressure or intimidation by Gary or Aggi as persons actually in authority or believed to be so. We agree with the judge that the Code simply was not intended to apply in such a context.

In reaching that conclusion, we should ourselves administer a caution. It would be wrong for police officers to adopt or use an undercover pose or disguise to enable themselves to ask questions about an offence uninhibited by the requirements of the Code and with the effect of circumventing it.

Were they to do so, it would be open to the judge to exclude the questions and answers under section 78 of the Act of 1984. It is therefore necessary here to see whether the questioning by Gary and Aggi was such as to require the judge in his discretion to exclude the conversation. The judge carefully reviewed the evidence on this issue. He concluded that the questions and comments from Gary and Aggi were for the most part simply those necessary to conduct the bartering and maintain their cover. They were not questions 'about the offence.' The only exception was the questioning about which area should be avoided in reselling the goods. However, even that was partly to maintain cover since it was the sort of questioning to be expected from a shady jeweller.

We are of the view that the judge's approach to the aspect of the case concerned with the Code cannot be faulted.

Before parting with the case, we should refer to a further argument mounted by Mr Thornton. He submitted that the undercover exercise, lasting as it did for some three months, was contrary to public policy. The basis for that submission was that the officers ought to have arrested offenders as soon as they had sufficient evidence. Instead, they allowed offenders such as these two appellants to return again and again with further stolen properties. Only when the shop was wound up were charges brought. The mischief alleged is that offenders were allowed to commit further offences which would or may have been obviated had they been arrested earlier. The existence of the shop was therefore facilitating, if not encouraging, the commission of crime.

Clearly, it must be a matter for policy and operational decision by the police as to how they reconcile and balance the need on the one hand to bring an individual offender swiftly to book and deter crime.

[7:10]   R v Bryce [1992] 4 All ER 567

The appellant was charged with handling stolen goods and theft. At his trial, the evidence against him included a conversation alleged to have taken place when an undercover policeman using a false name and posing as a potential buyer for a car telephoned the appellant and agreed to buy a stolen car, another conversation which took place when the two later met, and an unrecorded interview which came after a recorded interview in which the appellant had made no comments. The Court of Appeal quashed his conviction.

Lord Taylor CJ (at page 571):

[Counsel for the appellant] submits the evidence that the appellant turned up in a stolen car at Smithfield as a result of a telephone call was admissible. However, the conversation on the telephone and at Smithfield should, he submits, have been excluded because 'Pearson' asked questions which were in the nature of an interrogation. They deprived the appellant of his right not to incriminate himself by answering questions which, had they been put by a police officer acting overtly as such, would have required a caution under the code. In particular, [Counsel] points to the question and answer on the telephone: '*Pearson*. How warm it is? *Paul*. It is a couple days old' and the question and answer at Smithfield: '*Pearson*. How long has it been nicked? *Paul*. Two or three days.'

Those questions went to the heart of the vital issue of dishonesty. They were not even necessary to the undercover operation, which was designed to provide evidence of the appellant in possession of a recently stolen car offering it for sale at a knock-down price. Moreover, the second question simply invited the appellant to repeat his answer to the first in more specifically incriminating terms. On the voire dire 'Pearson' was asked in cross-examination what he would have done had the appellant said the car was not stolen. He replied:

'If he had said, "It is not stolen", I would have asked other questions, Sir. What are you doing selling a motor car like that? What is wrong with it? Is it an import? Has it come from abroad?'

In our judgment, that series of questions by an undercover officer would clearly offend against the caveat this court stated in *R v Christou*. It would blatantly have been an interrogation with the effect, if not the design, of using an undercover pose to circumvent the code.

The two questions of which [Counsel] makes strongest complaint did not go as far as that. They were single, isolated questions in separate conversations. There was no extended interrogation. However, they did go directly to the critical issue of guilty knowledge. Moreover, they were hotly disputed and there was no contemporary record. In *R v Christou* there were questions from the undercover officers as to the area where it would be unwise to resell the goods, the answers being obliquely an indication that the goods had been or may have been stolen from that area to the knowledge or belief of the suspect. However, in that case the whole interview was recorded both on tape and on film. The circumstances to be considered by the learned judge in that case in deciding whether the admission of the evidence would have an adverse effect on the fairness of the trial and how adverse where therefore quite different from those in the present case. The film and sound record eliminated any question of concoction. Not so here. The questions asked were direct, not oblique, the conversation was challenged and the appellant had no means of showing by a neutral, reliable record what was or was not said. For those reasons we consider that the learned judge erred here in admitting those answers.

We turn to the second ground. At the police station, an interview was properly set up and conducted in accordance with the code. It was tape-recorded, timed and it began with a caution. However, its only yield was a succession of 'No comment's from the appellant. It is submitted that what followed was clearly in breach of the code. The officers assert that after the tape recorder was switched off the appellant said he did not wish anything written down, but then proceeded to volunteer an account which in effect contained an admission.

Mr Thomas submits, first, that the appellant ought to have been cautioned again or reminded of the caution in accordance with para 10.5 of Code C, which provides:

'When there is a break in questioning under caution the interviewing officer must ensure that the person being questioned is aware that he remains under caution. If there is any doubt the caution should be given again in full when the interview resumes.'

The tape-recorded interview had concluded; what followed was therefore at the very least 'a break in questioning'. In our judgment, that submission is unanswerable. The failure to caution the appellant again was not just a technical breach in the circumstances of this case. According to the police, once the recorder was switched off, the appellant said he wanted nothing written down. He repeated that, saying 'If you record it, I won't say anything.' The officer's reply, 'Well, what happened then?' might reasonably have been taken as an acceptance of the appellant's terms. The appellant may well therefore have believed that what was not recorded could not be given in evidence. Hence the importance of a fresh caution or reminder of it. Significantly, as [Counsel] for the Crown fairly pointed out, the officer does not claim to have asked the question, 'Is that everything Paul?' until he was already sealing the tapes. One might have expected the question to have been asked before the recorder was switched off.

Mr Thomas further submits that the alleged admissions by the appellant were not recorded contemporaneously and, for that reason too, they should have been excluded. It was strenuously denied by the appellant that any such admissions were made and indeed that any interview, on or off the record, occurred after the tape recorder was switched off.

If this interview was correctly admitted, the effect would be to set at nought the requirements of the Police and Criminal Evidence Act 1984 and the code in regard to interviews. One of the main purposes of the code is to eliminate the possibility of an interview being concocted or of a true interview being falsely alleged to have been concocted. If it were permissible for an officer simply to assert that, after a properly conducted interview produced a nil return, the suspect confessed off the record and for that confession to be admitted, then the safeguards of the code could readily be bypassed.

In our judgment there would have to be some highly exceptional circumstances, perhaps involving cogent corroboration, before such an interview could be admitted without its having such an adverse effect on the fairness of the trial that it ought to be excluded under s 78.

Here the situation was a classic example of that suspicious sequence – a total denial or refusal to comment, followed by an alleged confession, followed in its turn by a refusal to sign the notes and a denial that the confession was made. We have no doubt that the alleged interview should in the circumstances of this case have been excluded.

Since the conversations and interviews with the police, both undercover and in uniform, formed such a major part of the prosecution case, we were bound to hold that the irregularities identified above rendered the conviction unsafe and unsatisfactory. Accordingly we quashed the conviction.

[7:11]   *R v Khan* [1997] AC 558

The appellant was charged with being knowingly concerned in the fraudulent evasion of the prohibition on the importation of a class A drug, heroin. The evidence included a record of the appellant's conversation with several people in a house to which, unknown to the occupants, the police had attached an electronic surveillance device. He appealed on the grounds that the evidence of his conversation should not have been admitted in evidence.

The appeal was dismissed.

Lord Nicholls (at page 582):

My Lords, I have had the opportunity to read in advance a draft of the speech of my noble and learned friend, Lord Nolan. I agree that this appeal should be dismissed. I add only two observations of my own. First, the appellant contended for a right of privacy in respect of private conversations in private houses. I prefer to express no view, either way, on the existence of such a right. This right, if it exists, can only do so as part of a larger and wider right of privacy. The difficulties attendant on this controversial subject are well known. Equally well known is the continuing, widespread concern at the apparent failure of the law to give individuals a reasonable degree of protection from unwarranted intrusion in many situations. I prefer to leave open for another occasion the important question whether the present, piecemeal protection of privacy has now developed to the extent that a more comprehensive principle can be seen to exist. It is not necessary to pursue this question on this appeal. Even if the right for which the appellant contended does exist, this would not lead to the consequence that obtaining evidence for the purpose of detecting or preventing serious crime was an infringement of the right or, even if it were, that the evidence was inadmissible at the trial.

Second, the discretionary powers of the trial judge to exclude evidence march and in hand with article 6(1) of the European Convention on Human Rights and Fundamental Freedoms. Both are concerned to ensure that those facing criminal charges receive a fair hearing. Accordingly, when considering the common law and statutory discretionary powers under English law the jurisprudence on article 6 can have a valuable role to play. English law relating to the ingredients of a fair trial is highly developed. But every system of law stands to benefit by an awareness of the answers given by other courts and tribunals to similar problems. In the present case the decision of the European Court of Human Rights in *Schenk v Switzerland* 13 EHRR 242 confirms that the use at a criminal trial of material obtained in breach of the rights of privacy enshrined in article 8 does not of itself mean that the trial is unfair. Thus the European Court of Human Rights case law on this issue leads to the same conclusion as English law.

[7:12]   *R v Newton* (1982) 77 Cr App Rep 13

The appellant pleaded guilty to buggery of his wife. The appellant maintained that the acts complained of were consensual, the victim that they were violent and non-consensual. The Court of Appeal allowed his appeal against sentence.

The Lord Chief Justice (at page 15):

There are three ways in which a judge in these circumstances can approach his difficult task of sentencing. It is in certain circumstances possible to obtain the answer to the problem from a jury. For example, when it is a question of whether the conviction should be under section 18 or section 20 of the Offences against the Person Act 1861, the jury can determine the issue on a trial under section 18 by deciding whether or not the necessary intent has been proved by the prosecution.

The second method which could be adopted by the judge in these circumstances is himself to hear the evidence on one side and another, and come to his own conclusion, acting so to speak as his own jury on the issue which is the root of the problem.

The third possibility in these circumstances is for him to hear no evidence but to listen to the submissions of counsel and then come to a conclusion. But if he does that, then, as Judge Argyle himself said in a passage to which reference will be made in a moment, where there is a substantial conflict between the two sides, he must come down on the side of the defendant. In other words where there has been a substantial conflict, the version of the defendant must so far as possible be accepted.

It is plain from what I have read, and indeed as accepted by learned counsel for the Crown, that the judge failed to adopt one of the three courses open to him, or the one that he did adopt was wrongly performed by him. The answer is, so far as the sentence of eight years is concerned, that that must be quashed. It is plain that in the circumstances of this case the appellant has already served too long in prison, and we propose therefore to substitute for the sentence of eight years' imprisonment such sentence as will result in his release today.

[7:13]   *R v Webbe* [2001] EWCA Crim 1217 [2002] 1 Cr App Rep (S) 82

Rose LJ: These four appeals and one renewed application for leave to appeal against sentence have been listed together to enable the Court to consider the proposal of the Sentencing Advisory Panel, in their advice to this Court in March 2001, that sentencing guidelines should be framed in relation to offences of handling dishonestly obtained goods, contrary to section 22 of the Theft Act 1968.

...

The difficulty of issuing guidelines in relation to handling arises from the enormous variety of possible sentences according to the circumstances, as pointed out by Lord Lane C.J., in *Patel* (1984) 6 Cr.App.R.(S.) 191 at pages 192-193. The offence is triable either way and can attract a penalty within the range from a conditional discharge or modest fine at one end, to many years' imprisonment, up to the maximum of 14 provided by Parliament, at the other.

The particular feature of handling which marks it out from most other offences is that it is, by definition, ancillary to another offence in a way which can conveniently be described as secondary to a primary offence. Because the primary offence may be, for example, shoplifting or armed robbery, the degree of gravity of the secondary offence can vary accordingly.

...

We have therefore concluded that, although there is, as it seems to us, no clear evidence of inconsistency in the court's current sentencing practice, it will be helpful in promoting consistency to adopt the Sentencing Advisory Panel's proposal that guidelines should be given. We stress, however, as this Court has stressed in earlier cases, that what we suggest is not to be regarded as mandatory, but is by way of guidance only.

There are a number of authorities to which reference can conveniently be made, which show the range of sentences which may be appropriate in relation to handling.

...

In *Bloomfield* (1995) 16 Cr.App.R.(S.) 221, the Court of Appeal noted that the appropriate sentencing bracket for a receiver, who dealt regularly with thieves and burglars providing a regular outlet, was between two and four years' imprisonment, although, in that particular case, which was a one-off offence, a significantly lower sentence was imposed, namely 15 months for receiving three stolen caravans, for which he, a caravan dealer, had paid £9,000.

In *Attorney-General's Reference No. 70 of 1999* [2000] 2 Cr.App.R.(S.) 28, sentences totalling 12 months' imprisonment were increased to 30 months in relation to an offender convicted of conspiracy to handle and steal computers, which he sold through his business. In the course of the judgment of the Court, reference was made, at page 30, to a number of authorities, to at least one of which we have already referred.

In that context, we turn to the advice of the Sentencing Panel with which, as will emerge, we largely although not entirely agree. Paragraph 11 of that advice, with which we agree, is in these terms:

> "The relative seriousness of a particular case of handling depends upon the interplay of different factors. One important issue is whether the handler has had advance knowledge of the original offence; or has directly or indirectly made known his willingness to receive the proceeds of the original offence, as compared with a handler who has had no connection with the original offence but who has dishonestly accepted the stolen goods at an undervalue. Where the handler has had knowledge of the original offence, the seriousness of the handling is inevitably linked to the seriousness of that original offence. The link to the original offence explains the need for the high maximum penalty of 14 years' imprisonment for handling, which might otherwise look anomalous. Sentences approaching the maximum should clearly be reserved for the most serious and unusual cases where the handler had previous knowledge of a very serious offence such as an armed robbery, which itself carries life imprisonment as its maximum."

Paragraph 12, with the terms of which we also agree, and says as follows:

> "The replacement value of the goods involved is often a helpful indication of the seriousness of the offence. (In this context the Mode of Trial guidelines suggest that cases of handling should normally be dealt with in the magistrates' court, and hence attract a maximum sentence of six months' imprisonment, if the value of the property is under £10,000.) We do not, however, believe that monetary value itself should be regarded as the determining factor."

We interpose the comment that it is important for sentencers to bear in mind that value would not be regarded as prescriptive. There is an obvious difference, for example, between the gravity of receiving in a public house £100 worth of stolen television sets, and the gravity of receiving £100 in cash from the proceeds of a robbery which has taken place in the receiver's presence. Furthermore, accurate values in relation to the property received may very often be extremely difficult to ascertain.

The Panel, in paragraph 12 of their advice, go on to identify other factors significantly affecting the relative seriousness of the handling offence, namely the level of sophistication of the handler, the ultimate designation of the goods, the criminal origin of the goods, the impact on the victim, the level of profit made or expected by the handler, and, especially in cases of actual or intended disposal of goods, the precise role played by the handler. In our judgment, those factors are rightly identified.

We also agree, in relation to paragraph 13 of the panel's advice, that handling cases at or towards the lower end of the scale are characterised by the handler having no connection with the original offence, an absence of sophistication on the part of the handler, the less serious nature of the original offence, the relatively low value of the goods and the absence of any significant profit.

The Sentencing Panel, in paragraph 14, go on to identify nine factors, which may be regarded as aggravating the offence. With each of these factors we agree. They are as follows:

1   The closeness of the handler to the primary offence. (We add that closeness may be geographical, arising from presence at or near the primary offence when it was committed, or temporal, where the handler instigated or encouraged the primary offence beforehand, or, soon after, provided a safe haven or route for disposal).
2   Particular seriousness in the primary offence.
3   High value of the goods to the loser, including sentimental value.
4   The fact that the goods were the proceeds of a domestic burglary.
5   Sophistication in relation to the handling.
6   A high level of profit made or expected by the handler.
7   The provision by the handler of a regular outlet for stolen goods.
8   Threats of violence or abuse of power by the handler over others, for example, an adult commissioning criminal activity by children, or a drug dealer pressurizing addicts to steal in order to pay for their habit.
9   As is statutorily provided by section 151(2) of the Powers of Criminal Courts (Sentencing) Act 2000, the commission of an offence while on bail.

We also agree with the mitigating factors identified as being among those relevant by the sentencing panel: namely, low monetary value of the goods, the fact that the offence was a one-off offence, committed by an otherwise honest defendant, the fact that there is little or no benefit to the defendant, and the fact of voluntary restitution to the victim.

We also agree with the Panel that other factors to be taken into account include personal mitigation, ready co-operation with the police, previous convictions, especially for offences of dishonesty and, as statutorily provided by section 152 of the Powers of Criminal Courts (Sentencing) Act 2000, a timely plea of guilty.

The Panel, in paragraph 21 of their advice, helpfully identify four possible levels of seriousness of the offence. They suggest that a distinction can be drawn between offences first, for which a fine or a discharge is appropriate; second, for which a community sentence is appropriate; third for those which cross the custody threshold and, fourth, more serious offences.

We agree that offences do fall into those four categories. We do not, however, take the view that it is always possible to draw a distinction between the first two categories of offence with quite the clarity which the Panel suggest.

In our judgment, the Panel are right to say that, where the property handled is of low monetary value and was acquired for the receiver's own use, the starting point should generally be a moderate fine or, in some cases (particularly, of course, if a fine cannot be paid by a particular defendant) a discharge. Such an outcome would, in our judgment be appropriate in relation to someone of previous good character handling low value domestic goods for his own use. By low value we mean less than four figures.

We agree that, irrespective of value, the presence of any one of the aggravating features to which we have referred is likely to result in a community sentence rather than a fine or discharge. We agree that a community sentence may be appropriate where property worth less than four figures is acquired for resale, or where more valuable goods are acquired for the handler's own use. Such a sentence may well be appropriate in relation to a young offender with little criminal experience, playing a peripheral role. But adult defendants with a record of dishonesty are likely to attract a custodial sentence.

Thus far, as we have indicated, we agree with the factors which the Panel identifies in relation to the sentencing process for less serious offences. But we do not believe that a clear dividing line is capable of being drawn between those offences which, appropriately attract, on the one hand, a discharge or fine and, on the other, a community sentence.

So far as the custody threshold is concerned, we agree that a defendant either with a record of offences of dishonesty, or who engages in sophisticated law breaking, will attract a custodial sentence. It is in relation to the length of that sentence that the aggravating and mitigating features which we have earlier identified will come into play, as will the personal mitigation of the offender, who may appropriately, in accordance with *Ollerenshaw* [1999] 1 Cr.App.R.(S.) 65, be dealt with by a somewhat shorter sentence than might, at first blush, otherwise have seemed appropriate.

We also agree with the panel that, in relation to more serious offences, there will be some for which a sentence within the range of 12 months to four years will be appropriate and there will be others for which a sentence of considerably more than four years, up to the maximum, may be appropriate. In this regard, the factors to be taken into consideration will include whether an offence is committed in the context of a business, whether the offender is acting as an organiser or distributor of the proceeds of crime and whether the offender has made himself available to other criminals as willing to handle the proceeds of thefts or burglaries.

In all of these more serious cases, according to the other circumstances, sentences in the range of 12 months to four years are likely to be appropriate if the value of the goods involved is up to around £100,000. Where the value of the goods is in excess of £100,000, or where the offence is highly organised and bears the hallmarks of a professional commercial operation, a sentence of four years and upwards is likely to be appropriate, and it will be the higher where the source of the handled property is known by the handler to be a serious violent offence such as armed robbery. As we have earlier indicated, sentences significantly higher than four years also may be appropriate where a professional handler, over a substantial period of time, demonstrated by his record or otherwise, has promoted and encouraged, albeit indirectly, criminal activity by others.

The sentences which we have indicated will, of course, be subject to discount in appropriate cases for a plea of guilty.

We should also add that a court passing sentence in handling cases should always have in mind the power to make restitution orders under sections 148 and 149 of the Powers of Criminal Courts (Sentencing) Act 2000, to make compensation orders under section 130 of the Powers of Criminal Court (Sentencing) Act 2000, and to make confiscation orders in relation to profits, under the Criminal Justice Act 1988 and the Proceeds of Crime Act 1995. A magistrates' court cannot, of course, make a confiscation order in a case of handling. But it is open to magistrates, in such a case, where appropriate, to commit to the Crown Court for sentence.

It is implicit, in what we have said, that this Court is greatly indebted to the sentencing Advisory Panel for the advice which they have tendered.

In the context of those observations, we turn to the particular cases before this Court.

Bernard Webbe, who is 33, pleaded guilty at Manchester Crown Court on December 11, 2000 to an offence of attempting to handle and an offence of handling stolen watches. He was sentenced on January 8, 2001 by his Honour Judge Owen to 15 months' imprisonment concurrently on each count. He appeals against sentence by leave of the single judge.

The offences came to light on August 17, 2000 when, in the course of a search being made at an address in Stretford, by police officers in relation to drugs offences, the officers asked to search the appellant's car. In the boot there were three watches and £250 in cash. The appellant said they were Christmas presents which he had bought the day before through his company. One of the watches was an 18 carat gold watch with a retail value of £7,700. It had, on its journey from Switzerland to a Malaysian agent in Singapore in 1996, gone missing. That was the subject of count 1. Count 2 related to two other link chronographs, each with a retail value of £1,150 which had been stolen in transit to a shop in Northern Ireland. That gave rise to count 2. In interview the appellant made no comment. But later, he said that he had paid £200 for the watches, to a man he had met in the street.

The appellant is of previous good character, and there was before the sentencing judge, as there is before this Court, a pre-sentence report which indicated the appellant's regret and that he was not a man who had criminal attitudes or a general disrespect for the law. He seemed to be genuinely ashamed and the risk of reoffending was minimal.

On his behalf, Mr Whelan submits that the sentence passed failed to take proper account of the plea of guilty, the good character of the appellant, the fact that he was unaware of the true value of the watches, and the absence of any professional hallmarks in this offence.

It is apparent that the total retail value of these goods was only slightly in excess of £10,000. It is also apparent that the appellant was not forthcoming in interview and could have provided the police with more help than he did as to the source and circumstances of his acquisitions. That being so, it seems to us that the custody threshold was passed, though the case could, in our judgment, properly have been dealt with, in all the circumstances, in the magistrates' court.

Taking into account the appellant's good character, the fact that the goods were apparently for the appellant's own use, the plea of guilty and the observations made in

Ollerenshaw, we take the view that a sentence of 15 months, was manifestly excessive. We quash it. The appeal is allowed to the extent that, in substitution for that sentence, we impose a sentence of four months' imprisonment concurrently on each count.

...

This Court takes the view that it would not be proper to differentiate between the sentences appropriate for Mitchell and Davies. Factors in relation to each of them, which we hope we have sufficiently identified, point in different directions. Not without a degree of hesitation, we take the view that the sentence of 18 months was somewhat longer than all the circumstances of this case require. It is true that these appellants could not have been closer to the primary offence than they were. It is true that the primary offence was a grave one. As against that, the benefit to either of them was small in the case of Davies and non-existent in the case of Mitchell, and the actual value of the goods taken, (albeit of course credit cards and keys are of use to the criminal fraternity) was comparatively modest. Taking into account in particular, the youth of these appellants, and the other factors to which we have referred, we quash the sentence of 18 months and substitute for it, in relation to each of them, a sentence of 12 months' detention in a young offender institution. This will lead to their release in the not too distant future. To that extent their appeals are allowed.

Robert John Moore pleaded guilty at Northampton Crown Court on September 19, 2000 to two offences of handling stolen property. He asked for 47 other offences, predominantly of burglary and theft, to be taken into consideration. He was sentenced by His Honour Judge Allen, sitting with justices, to 4 years' imprisonment concurrently on each account.

The total value of the goods in the indictment was somewhat less than £2,000. On the other hand, the value of the property involved in the other offences, almost none of which was recovered, was some £20,000.

The appellant appeals by leave of the single judge.

The facts can be very briefly stated. On the evening of February 12/13, 2000, a dwelling house in Kiln Way, Wellingborough, was entered through an open window and jewellery stolen. On the same evening, another dwelling house, not far away, was entered by breaking a rear kitchen window while the occupants were in bed and a considerable number of compact discs and computer equipment was stolen.

On February 15, that is to say a day or two after the burglary in Kiln Way, the appellant visited a pawnbrokers and presented a stolen necklace and ring, for which he was paid cash. As evidence of identity, he produced a tenancy agreement in his own name.

A few days later, on February 21, the appellant handed to his girlfriend stolen rings which she took and converted into cash at the same pawnbrokers. On March 22 the appellant went to another pawnbrokers to sell compact discs and he was arrested by police officers. His home was searched and a number of stolen items were seized. It emerged that the appellant and his girlfriend had tried to sell computer parts at other shops in Wellingborough. At about the same time, the victims of the Kiln Way burglary saw some of the stolen property in the window of the pawnshop.

The appellant was interviewed on three occasions. On the first, he claimed that the CDs were his own and the jewellery belonged to his girlfriend. He denied involvement in the Kiln Way burglary and was unable to explain the other stolen items at his premises. On the second occasion, some six weeks later, he refused to be any more forthcoming but, on April 28, he effectively admitted having carried out the burglary at Kiln Way, saying the window was open and he climbed in, went upstairs and found the jewellery.

The 47 offences which he asked to have taken into consideration included some 27 of theft and some 17 or so of burglary.

The learned judge, in passing sentence, said he gave credit for the plea and such frankness as the appellant had shown, but the handling of the stolen property, soon after the burglaries, and the other offences involving many dwelling-house burglaries, called for the sentence which he imposed.

The appellant is 26. He has 18 previous convictions involving 60 offences. He has been sentenced to immediate custody on seven previous occasions. His record includes many offences of dishonesty, including burglary, theft and handling.

The submission which is made on his behalf, by Miss Hales, is that the weight of offences taken into consideration was very much greater than the two offences to which the appellant pleaded guilty on the indictment. The learned judge, in passing the sentence which he did, inadequately reflected the credit which needed to be given by the court for the frankness which the appellant had shown in admitting these other offences, and asking for them to be taken into consideration. She submits, rightly, that the convention of taking offences into consideration, is pragmatically based and is of benefit to the police and to a defendant. It is of benefit for the police in clearing up offences. It is of benefit to the defendant because he avoids the need to have to appear on another occasion to be dealt with for offences which he now admits. Miss Hales does not submit that, if the appellant were being sentenced for the many offences of burglary which he had taken into consideration, four years would be otherwise than appropriate. But she submits that it did not adequately reflect the degree of co-operation by the appellant, in all these circumstances of this case.

In our judgment, it is not generally desirable that a very large number of offences should be taken into consideration when there are comparatively few offences in the indictment and when the offences taken into consideration are of a different kind from those in the indictment. It is a far preferable course for the indictment, so far as possible, to reflect the general level of criminality of a particular defendant.

There are, of course, cases where it is entirely appropriate for there to be many similar offences to be taken into consideration, for example, in social security frauds; and many other examples can be thought of.

That said, in the present case, all the offences taken into consideration were offences of dishonesty. They were not offences, in that sense, dissimilar from those in the indictment. Furthermore, the burglary offences were ones to which the same maximum sentence as for handling applies, that is 14 years.

In our judgment, the learned judge fully recognised that the appellant was entitled to credit, not only for his pleas of guilty, but also for the co-operation which he had shown in disclosing and admitting his part in the other offences which were taken into consideration. We have no hesitation in concluding that, had the learned judge been called upon to sentence the offender for 17 domestic burglaries, in the light of his record, the sentence would have been very considerably longer than four years' imprisonment. Despite Miss Hales' submission, therefore, we are unpersuaded that the sentence of four years failed to reflect the degree of co-operation displayed by the appellant.

So far as the receiving offences themselves are concerned, it is apparent, in relation to at least one of them, that the appellant was, to put it no higher, extremely close to the commission of the primary offence. The total sentence was not excessive. In our judgment, there is no merit in this appeal and accordingly it is dismissed.

Paul White, on June 26, 2000, changed his plea to guilty on three counts of handling stolen goods and pleaded guilty to a further count of handling which had been added by leave of the court.

On July 21, at Liverpool Crown Court, he was sentenced by His Honour Judge Trigger to 30 months' imprisonment, ordered concurrently on each count to which he had pleaded guilty but consecutively to the period of three years' imprisonment, which he was then currently serving. Verdicts of not guilty were entered under section 17 of the Criminal Justice Act, following his pleas of not guilty to offences of conspiracy to steal and to handle.

He now renews his application for leave to appeal against sentence, following refusal by the single judge.

The facts disclosed that, the applicant had admitted handling some £210,000 worth of goods. He did so in these circumstances. He leased a warehouse in Liverpool, which was searched by the police, on August 9, 1999. There were found pallets of cigarettes, wine, whiskey, gin and vermouth, which had belonged to one of two trailer loads, stolen from a haulage company in Manchester two days before. The goods recovered were worth £72,000. There were also recovered two parked trailers, which with their loads, had been stolen in the early hours of that very day from South Wales. One trailer contained 130 assorted television sets, the other 540 boxed television stands. The trailers were worth about £12,000 each. The goods still on them were worth £84,000.

Nearby there were two other trailers loaded with electrical items, cookers, tumble dryers and spin dryers. The trailer had been stolen a day or so before, between August 7 and 8, from two firms in Stoke on Trent. Of 122 items stolen, 113 were recovered from the trailers. The stolen load was valued at about £20,000. A stolen trailer was later recovered not far away. There was another trailer, containing a palette of car tyres. That came from a consignment of tyres stolen on August 2, 1999, while they were being moved from Burton on Trent to Tilbury Docks. 780 tyres had been stolen. 40 were recovered by the police; £37,000 worth of tyres were missing. The container was worth between £5,000 and £6,000.

There were other co-accused, the brothers Grego, who were sentenced to nine months' imprisonment, having each pleaded guilty to one count of theft, and two others who were acquitted.

The learned judge, in passing sentence, referred to the total value of the items as being over £100,000 and items such as television sets being readily disposable. He gave credit for the plea of guilty, but he drew attention to the fact that, at the time, the applicant had been on bail for a remarkably similar offence. That was an aggravating feature. The judge pointed out that the applicant must have been aware of others higher up in the organisation but that was not information which he had shared with the police. The judge concluded that the applicant had run a dishonest business yard, making it available to others for the disposal of dishonest goods. Without people like him, the business of thieves would be more difficult.

The applicant is 36 years of age. He has, on nine previous occasions, appeared before the courts for a variety of offences, predominantly involving motor vehicles. There is a prison report before the court, which speaks of the applicant's good behaviour, privileged position, and willingness to help inmates and staff.

The submission made by Mr Haygarth is that albeit a sentence of imprisonment was appropriate and albeit a sentence of imprisonment which would convert the existing three years to a long-term sentence was inevitable, the sentence of two-and-a-half years imposed by the learned judge was arguably excessive, and should be interfered with by this Court. That submission we are unable to accept.

This, as it seems to us, was large scale professional receiving by a man with an unpromising criminal record. Goods reached him remarkably quickly after they had been stolen. The offences were committed while he was on bail for other serious offences. In our judgment, the sentence passed upon him, albeit ordered to run consecutively to the sentence he was serving was a modest sentence. It cannot, in our judgment, be categorised as, even arguably, manifestly excessive. Accordingly this application is refused.

[7:14]   A-G's References (Nos 59, 60 and 63 of 1998) (*R v Goodwin*) [1999] 2 Cr App Rep (S) 128

Lord Bingham CJ begins his judgment by making some general observations on the approach to be adopted when sentencing young offenders for offences contrary to section 18 of the Offences Against the Persons Act 1861:

We begin by reminding ourselves of the terms of section 18 of the 1861 Act which so far as relevant provides:

> 'Whosoever shall unlawfully and maliciously by any means whatsoever wound or cause any grievous bodily harm to any person ... with intent ... to do some ... grievous bodily harm to any person ... shall be guilty of an offence, and being convicted thereof shall be liable ... to imprisonment for life ...'

An offence against this section has always been regarded as of great seriousness, reflected in the maximum penalty of life imprisonment. The reason is obvious. Not only must there be proof of grievous or serious injury, but that injury must have been caused intentionally or deliberately. There is an obvious contrast with section 20 of the same Act. Under that section the same injury must be proved, but the commission of the offence does not depend on proof of intention to cause it. The difference lies in the criminality of the defendant's intention. That is a significant difference, reflected in the maximum penalty of five years' imprisonment on conviction under section 20. The seriousness with which section 18 offences are regarded is evident not only in the severity of the potential punishment but also in the fact that a section 18 conviction ranks as 'a serious offence' for the purposes of section 2 of the Crime (Sentences) Act 1997. The consequence of that is that a second conviction of 'a serious offence' obliges the court, in the absence of exceptional circumstances, to impose a sentence of life imprisonment.

It is true to say that all offences against section 18 are serious because they involve the deliberate or intentional causing of serious injury. But as with any other crime, some instances are more serious than others: the use of a firearm, a razor, a knife, a broken bottle, a club, a baseball bat, or a pick helve, or something of that sort, has usually been held to aggravate the offence. The courts have also, however, been obliged to recognise that injuries of almost equal seriousness can be caused by kicking with a shod foot or biting. It is also of course possible to inflict serious injury with the bare fist, although this is usually regarded as less serious, partly because in that instance the offender may lack the premeditation usually shown by a defendant who has armed himself with a dangerous weapon. Perhaps the least inexcusable example of an offence against section 18 is where a defendant entitled to defend himself responds with unreasonable and excessive force directed against an aggressor. Even then a custodial sentence, probably of some length, will usually be appropriate. In any other case a custodial sentence will almost invariably follow.

In sentencing young offenders the court will of course have regard to the welfare principle expressed in section 44 of the Children and Young Persons Act 1933: the younger the offender the less the justification in any ordinary case for treating the offender exactly as if he or she were an adult. It must be recognised that an effective means of protecting the public in the future is to reform a criminal whether young or old. Sentencers must, however, always bear in mind that the welfare of the young offender is never the only consideration to be taken into account. When an offender, however young, deliberately inflicts serious injury on another there is a legitimate public expectation that such offender will be severely punished to bring home to him the gravity of the offence and to warn others of the risk of behaving in the same way. If such punishment does not follow, public confidence in the administration of the criminal law is weakened and the temptation arises to give offenders extra-judicially the punishment that the formal processes of law have not given. When we speak of the public we do not forget the victim, the party who has actually suffered the injury and those close to him. If punishment of the offender does little to heal the victim's wounds, there can be little doubt that inadequate punishment adds insult to injury.

Applying these observations to the three cases under consideration, all three sentences were increased:

In the case of an offender aged 18 who threw a beer glass into the face of another youth, causing facial injuries which would result in permanent scarring, the court found a sentence of 18 months' detention in a young offender institution to be unduly lenient. The court substituted a sentence of two years' detention in a young offender institution, indicating that apart from the element of double jeopardy, a proper sentence on a conviction would have been four years and on a plea, three years' detention in a young offender institution.

The second case concerned an offender aged 16 who, following a fist fight, attacked another youth with a bottle which he had apparently broken for the purpose, and stabbed him in the armpit, causing life threatening injuries requiring emergency surgery and leaving lasting disabilities and scarring. The court found that a combination order combined with a compensation order was unduly lenient. The court substituted a sentence of three years' detention under section 53(2) of the Children and Young Persons Act 1933, indicating that a sentence of five years' detention would have been appropriate following a contested trial.

The third case involved an offender aged 16 who became involved in a fight with another boy following an incident at school. In the course of the fight the offender produced a folding knife and stabbed the victim in the back. The victim suffered a deep wound which penetrated the lung, causing severe internal bleeding. The victim required surgery and was left with a scar on his back. The court found that a supervision order with requirements to attend a youth justice centre to participate in specified activities (made partly on the basis that the offender had spent five months on remand in a secure unit) was unduly lenient. The court substituted a sentence of detention under section 53(2) and (3) of the Children and Young Persons Act 1933 for two-and-a-half years, indicating that a term of four-and-a-half years would have been appropriate on a conviction following a trial and three-and-a-half years on a plea.

[7:15]   Ashworth, A, Genders, E, Mansfield, G, Peay, J and Player, E
Sentencing in the Crown Court: Report of an Exploratory Study (1984) Oxford Centre for Criminological Research Occasional Paper No 10 (at page 60):

All the judges whom we consulted insisted that the right to determine the form and length of sentence in each case should be theirs, and firmly opposed any suggestion of 'interference' by Parliament in the form of legislative restrictions on sentencing. 'The Judges should be trusted', as one judge put it. A wise sentencing discretion was defended as necessary to give proper effect to the varying facts of individual cases. This pre-occupation with variations of facts in individual cases leads many judges to regard sentencing as 'an art rather than a science'. It is generally thought inappropriate to require a judge to give reasons for his choice of sentence, and such 'reasons' as are given tend to consist of general references to factors taken into account rather than a detailed explanation of how the judge weighted those factors in arriving at the precise sentence. There is judicial ambivalence about the implications of the view that sentencing is 'an art rather than a science'. The grip of the maxim that 'each case depends on its own facts' leads many judges to considerable scepticism about the very enterprise of formulating and stating principles of sentencing. Indeed, even if general principles were clearly articulated, a particular judge's interpretation of the material presented to him might lead him to categorise the facts in one way whilst another judge classified them differently. On the other hand, the 'pilot study' found no shortage of judicial requests for more guidance on some issues which seem capable of resolution or which raise particular difficulties. It is elementary to point out that maxims such as 'each case depends on its own facts' do not sit comfortably with a judicial commitment to consistency and to 'uniformity of approach'. The Lord Chief Justice, in his judgment in *R v Bibi* (1980) 71 Cr App Rep 360 and in other judgments since the 'pilot study' was completed, has shown his firm belief that more guidance is necessary and, by implication, that it can be helpful to Crown Court sentencers in dealing with their cases.

Research could go much further than simply showing that the 'facts of the case' are not objective matters but are the result of a subtle reconstruction by the individual judge, and that judges do draw upon general views or propositions when arriving at sentences.

it could identify key factors which tend to be interpreted differently by individual judges, and could identify salient variations in the attitudes of judges to certain types of offence, types of offenders and types of sentence. This information could be used in framing the guidance given to sentencers at judicial seminars or by the Court of Appeal. It could make a major contribution to the development of consistency in sentencing, by ensuring not only that the guidance meets and takes account of the needs of sentencers but also that the guidance is likely to be effective. The possibility of judges interpreting similar cases in different ways ought to be reduced if clear guidance on the significance is to be found in *Bibi* (1980), where the Lord Chief Justice identified classes of case in which sentences might be lowered but made no reference to the effect on sentence of the offender's previous record, the number of offences, and so on. Is it realistic to call for 'uniformity of approach' when no reference is made to the effect on sentence of matters which sentencers clearly regard as important? Policy initiatives aimed at altering practice in a particular sphere of sentencing may meet with little success, as did the *Bibi* initiative, or have unintended side-effects, unless they are grounded upon systematic knowledge of judicial approaches to sentencing.

Some might argue that the diversity of approaches we found among the small numbers of 'experienced' judges interviewed in this 'pilot study' raises a powerful case for greater control over the use of sentencing powers by judges, whether by legislative restrictions or otherwise. That might be the correct conclusion, but it need not be. Another possibility would be to use the results of research in framing study programmes for judges. The 'pilot study' found that many judges appeared to have devoted little thought to the principles on which they act. The Judicial Studies Board might be willing to use research findings on judges' awareness of their own sentencing practices, on judges' feelings of constraint, on different interpretations of the facts of cases, and generally on judicial attitudes towards various factors in sentencing. It might be profitable if the divergent practices were discussed and debated at judicial seminars, with a view to formulating general policies on some matters and modifying attitudes. If, as the 'pilot study' suggests, one reason why guidance from Parliament or from the Court of Appeal might have limited effect lies in the resilience of individual judicial attitudes, then it might be best to tackle these individual differences directly in the context of a judicial seminar. Systematic research into Crown Court sentencing could supply the basis for such an approach.

Research findings also have implications for the concept of judicial independence. On the one hand, despite judges' opposition to any encroachment upon their independence by members of the executive such as the Home Office, some judges seem quite unaware of the influence upon the listing of cases exerted by certain administrators. Research which is able to identify influences of this kind may enhance rather than challenge the independence of the judiciary. On the other hand, there are respects in which the concept of judicial independence seems to be used inappropriately: greater contact with the probation service would not necessarily threaten, either apparently or in reality, the impartiality of the judiciary and might well improve understanding of the expectations of each party. Perhaps the most forceful manifestation of judicial independence, however, lies in the substantial autonomy of the individual judge. In theory, of course, each judge is subject to the law, to the appeal process, and to the undertaking in his judicial oath. In practice, the paucity of legal rules and principles on sentencing and the limitations of their enforcement set by the appeal system (with no prosecution appeals, and few defence appeals actually coming before the Court of Appeal) leave the individual judge with considerable room to gall into idiosyncrasies in sentencing. Whilst assistant recorders and recorders will know that their appointment to a higher judicial office may to some extent depend upon reports of their 'performance', there appear to be few controls on the approach to sentencing of a circuit judge. Sentences which are grossly out of line are likely to be corrected if the excess is one of severity rather than leniency, and there is the possibility of a 'word in the ear' from a presiding judge on the circuit, but in general judges have considerable leeway. They appear also to have developed techniques for the neutralisation of criticism. Apparent inconsistencies in sentencing are explained by reference to the facts of the particular case; the press, the public and politicians are believed to be generally ill-informed about the full facts of cases and thus their criticisms are discounted; indeed, individual judges may attempt to neutralise criticism from the Court of Appeal, in a case in which it varies a sentence passed at the trial, by maintaining that the Court is out of touch with current practice. One consequence of all this is that the principle of judicial independence may have become a cloak behind which the idiosyncrasies of an individual judge go substantially unchallenged, thus undermining the 'uniformity of approach' which the Lord Chief Justice has declared to be his aim.

At the end of our report to the Lord Chief Justice on the 'pilot study', we outlined the proposal for a full research project which would continue the attempt 'faithfully to reflect the realities of Crown Court sentencing and the system within which it takes place, and to explore the reasons why judges approach sentencing as they do'. Within the study we propose to pursue certain particular lines of enquiry:

- the attitudes of judges to certain kinds of crime and certain kinds of sentence;
- the interpretations which judges place upon evidence before them, in order to arrive at the 'facts of the case' which they consider relevant for the purpose of sentencing;
- what judges expect of the Court of Appeal and, if permission were given, how the Court of Appeal views its functions in relation to the lower courts;
- what judges seek from social enquiry reports and speeches in mitigation;
- how the practices of probation officers, counsel and court administrators can influence the course which a case takes;
- how it is that judges sometimes feel they have no alternative but to pass a particular sentence, when other judges would pass different sentences;
- how well judges understand their own sentencing practices, and whether it is possible for a judge to believe that he is passing a reduced sentence when, by his own standards, he is not.

In December 1981, the Lord Chief Justice, Lord Lane, informed us that the research would not be allowed to go ahead.

CHAPTER EIGHT

Juries

Since Gerry Good was charged with an offence under OAPA 1861, s 18, he is triable only on indictment. He will therefore be tried in the Crown Court before a judge and jury. It is the jury who decide whether or not he is guilty. Juries are often seen as the 'bulwark of our liberty', yet the reality may be very different: there is increasing scepticism about what is clearly an expensive and under-researched method of trial. Perhaps the most interesting question is how juries reach their decisions, but little is known about how juries work in practice. The Contempt of Court Act 1981, s 8 **[8:1]** effectively banned any research into jury decision making. No action has yet been taken on the recommendation of the Royal Commission on Criminal Justice (1993) that it should be possible for properly authorised research to be carried out into the way in which juries reach their verdicts and that section 8 should be amended (although Lord Justice Auld **[1:5]** was more ambivalent about the need for this). Some research into how juries actually carry out their task has been done using shadow or mock juries (see, for example, McCabe and Purves (1974)), and there have been a number of television programmes using this technique. However, since the mock jury knows that that is all it is, the value of such studies is limited. Darbyshire (2001) provides a useful review of the literature.

(i) Selecting the jury

The basic rules governing juries are found in the Juries Act 1974 **[8:2]**, though the Criminal Justice Act 1988, s 119 raised the maximum age of jurors to 70 (but jury service is voluntary after the age of 65) and CJPOA 1994, ss 40–43 amended the rules on disqualification and excusal. A jury does not necessarily reflect the community as a whole: the initial summoning is done at random from names on the electoral roll, and many people may not be registered on the roll. Of those summoned, a high proportion successfully avoid or evade service (see Darbyshire, 2001). The Royal Commission on Criminal Justice urged electoral registration officers to take every possible step to ensure that electoral rolls are as comprehensive as possible. It pointed out that it is particularly important that efforts are made to persuade people from ethnic minorities to register. How are electoral officers to achieve this? Is there any convincing alternative to using the electoral roll?

Some people are ineligible for, and others are disqualified from, jury service. Judges, those concerned with the administration of justice, the clergy and the mentally disordered are all ineligible. The people disqualified are those who have at any time been sentenced to more than five years' imprisonment; those who have served any period of imprisonment, suspended sentence or community service order within the last ten years; and those placed on probation within the last five years. CJPOA 1994, s 40 provides that a person who is on police or court bail in criminal proceedings is disqualified from serving as a juror. Those with minor criminal convictions may sit on a jury – but is it right to disqualify those on bail? The Royal Commission was not convinced that the jury service rules are the best that could be devised, but it concluded that, before they are changed, there needs to be proper research into their possible influence on jury trials. Auld [1:5] suggests the law should be amended to substitute for the condition of registration on an electoral roll 'inclusion in such a roll and/or on any one or more of a number of specified publicly maintained lists or directories, but excluding anyone listed, who, on investigation at the summons stage, is found not to be entitled to registration as an elector'.

Between the ages of 18 and 65 jury service is compulsory: this can be both inconvenient and expensive to the individual juror. When the jury summonses have been issued, many people return them, pleading a wide variety of reasons for being unable to sit on a jury on the dates in question, such as a booked holiday or an important work commitment. The Divisional Court in *R v Guildford Crown Court, ex p Siderfin* [1990] 2 QB 683 held that there was no excusal as of right on religious grounds. However, the Royal Commission's recommendation that practising members of religious societies or orders who find jury service to be incompatible with their tenets or beliefs should be excused was enacted by CJPOA 1994, s 42. A more important deterrent is the risk of loss of earnings. The Royal Commission recommended an urgent review of financial loss allowances, but this raises the bigger question of how this compulsory community service can be justified. In a typical short case like Gerry Good's, the jury will have been summoned for a two-week period. Several jurors may have sat together on a jury the day before, but much time will have been spent hanging around – the facilities are often poor: uncomfortable chairs, no TV or newspapers, chain-smokers and non-smokers squashed up together, no refreshment facilities. It is not surprising that Auld [1:5] argued strongly for improved court facilities for jurors, including facilities to enable jurors-in-waiting to conduct their own affairs. In section (iii) below some attempt will be made to assess the value of the lay jury in deciding questions of fact in certain criminal trials. An important associated question is whether twelve is too high a number – fewer people's time would be wasted if the jury had fewer members. Would a jury made up of nine, or even six, people be as satisfactory?

Are juries truly representative? Zander and Henderson's Crown Court study (1993) (and see [7:2]) found that neither women nor people from ethnic minorities were badly under-represented. Women made up 47% of all jurors (but only 22% of jury foremen) and non-white jurors made up 5% of jurors, as compared with 5.9% of the total population. Perhaps of more concern is the distribution of non-white jurors in individual cases. In 65% of cases there were no non-whites on the jury (and in one, no white jurors). The Court of Appeal held in *Ford* [8:3] that there is no right to a multiracial jury. However, the Royal Commission believed that in some cases race should be taken into account. It accepted the proposal of the Commission for Racial Equality that, before trial, the prosecution or defence should be able to apply to the judge for a multiracial jury, including up to three people from ethnic minorities. This the judge would grant only if the applicant's case was reasonable because of some special feature. Auld [1:5] also advocated a scheme for cases in which the court considers that race is likely to be relevant to an important issue in the case, for the selection of a jury consisting of, say, up to three people from any ethnic minority group.

There are other criticisms of the composition of juries. The longer a trial, the more complicated it is likely to be. Yet the longer the trial, the more jurors will find legitimate grounds for excusal, and the less representative they will be. There are those who suggest that 18 is too young a minimum age for jurors, since they will be too inexperienced. However, Zander and Henderson (1993) found that age had little or no effect on jury verdicts: if anything, older age-group juries were more likely to acquit than the younger. Should there be physical or educational tests, as recommended by Lord Denning (1982)?

Those summoned for jury service constitute the jury panel, and from the panel the jury for an individual case will be selected. The parties to the case are entitled to inspect the list, but it contains only names and addresses. From the jury panel, the jury is selected randomly in open court, by the clerk of the court reading out the names from a pile of cards. Thus, in Gerry Good's case, once he has been arraigned (asked if he pleads guilty or not guilty) perhaps 20 jurors will be led into the back of the courtroom. The clerk will read out one name at a time. As they enter the jury box, each juror may be challenged by the prosecution or the defence. Probably Gerry Good keeps his eyes down, vaguely irritated and vaguely embarrassed by the whole process. The defence used to have a right of peremptory challenge (the right to challenge prospective jurors without having to give reasons) but this was reduced from seven to three challenges per defendant by the Criminal Law Act 1977 and abolished by the Criminal Justice Act 1988. The main objection to these challenges was that they interfered with the random selection of the jury, but there was no evidence that peremptory challenges had any effect on acquittals, and they were rarely used. What peremptory challenges did allow was the exclusion of those who defendants, or their counsel, felt by their appearance were unlikely to reach a fair verdict.

Thus, today the defence only has the right to 'challenge for cause'. Since, unlike in the United States, potential jurors cannot be questioned in order to discover whether there is any ground for a challenge, challenges for cause are rare. The prosecution has the right to challenge for cause, or to require a juror to 'stand by for the Crown', which is similar to a peremptory challenge. This right was not abolished by the Criminal Justice Act 1988, but the following year the Attorney-General issued guidelines stating that the Crown should assert its right to stand by 'only sparingly and in exceptional circumstances' **[8:4]**. The guidelines allow the search of criminal records for the purpose of ascertaining whether or not a member of the panel is a disqualified person, and some further investigations of members of the panel in security or terrorist cases. This practice, known as 'jury vetting', remains controversial, perhaps mainly because it is unclear how widespread the practice is.

(ii) The function of the jury

The Court of Appeal confirmed in *H v Ministry of Defence* **[8:5]** that juries are today rarely available in civil personal injury cases. Controversy surrounds the use of juries in libel cases, where the jury not only decide liability but also award damages, often in a way which can be both unpredictable and unjust. A jury is also summoned in some inquests in coroners' courts (particularly where there has been a death in custody). In criminal cases, the jury's role is limited to determining guilt, and they have no role in sentencing. Juries have to decide issues of fact, and on those facts decide whether or not the defendant is guilty of the crime charged. They give no reasons for their decisions, with the result that it is extremely difficult to challenge a verdict. Does this undermine a defendant's right to a fair trial?

During the course of a trial the jury sit together in the jury box and listen to the evidence. In 1994 the Law Commission issued a consultation paper, *Counts in an Indictment*, seeking views on the information that should be provided to a jury at the start of a trial. It is widely acknowledged that juries are likely to perform better if they know what to expect and if they receive full, clear guidance and assistance. They therefore receive written notes explaining the procedure of jury service, and usually see an introductory video, before the case begins.

Perhaps they should be encouraged by judges to take notes if they want to? At a time when juries are increasingly being asked to study lengthy and complicated written evidence, the Royal Commission (1993) sensibly recommended that the provision of writing materials should be standard.

In Gerry Good's case, four witnesses for the prosecution are called, and none for the defence. Since 1995, the jury has been entitled to draw 'such inferences as appear proper' from a defendant's failure to testify in court (see CJPOA 1994, s 35). The Crime and Disorder Act 1998, s 35, extends this provision to allow adverse inferences to be drawn against defendants under the age of 14. Although a person cannot be convicted solely on an inference drawn from silence, this change in the law can be seen to undermine the presumption of innocence. How it works in practice can be seen in *Cowan* [1996] 1 Cr App R 1. A rather harsh example is *Friend* [1997] 2 Cr App R 231, where the jury were entitled to draw adverse inferences from the decision of a mentally disabled 15 year-old not to give evidence. However, the drawing of adverse inferences from silence in the police station is a much greater threat to due process than inferences drawn from silence at trial (see Chapter Two).

After counsel for both sides have made their closing speeches, the judge gives the summing up, the importance of which was discussed in Chapter Seven. The jury will be told that they have to reach a unanimous verdict, although they may well know that eventually a majority verdict may be permitted. At the end of the summing up they retire to a jury room to consider their verdict, and will then be kept together privately until either they reach a verdict or they are discharged because they find themselves unable to do so. Sometimes jurors wish to ask the judge questions or be reminded of a piece of evidence, in which case they will be brought back into open court. Occasionally, when the jury have been unable to reach a verdict swiftly, it has been necessary to keep them in a hotel overnight, but nowadays they will usually be permitted to separate for the night, even once they have retired to consider their verdict.

Majority verdicts, first introduced by the Criminal Justice Act 1967, are now governed by the Juries Act 1974, s 17 **[8:2]** and are becoming less rare.

Jury verdicts and majority verdicts

	Defendants convicted after a plea of not guilty	*Percentage after a majority verdict*
1993	12,460	15%
1997	11,510	20%
2001	9,694	23%

Source: Judicial Statistics 1997–2001, Table 6.11 (update)

The jury are sent out to reach a unanimous verdict and it is left to the judge's discretion whether, after at least two hours have passed, they are prepared to accept a majority verdict. If a majority verdict is guilty, the foreman must state in open court the number of jurors who agreed to, and the number who dissented from, the verdict. Are majority verdicts a dangerous inroad into the principle that no one should be convicted unless the prosecution has proved their guilt beyond reasonable doubt, or are they a sensible pragmatic compromise? Are there adequate due process safeguards? The main justification for introducing the majority verdict was said at the time to be that a majority verdict would reduce the risk of improper pressure being put on individual jurors and reduce the likelihood of 'jury nobbling'. Today the main justification would probably be the costs saved in avoiding a retrial, but the risks of corrupt influences and jury intimidation still remain.

Is the function of the jury to apply a clearly established legal definition to the facts that they have found to be proved, or do they have an additional function of introducing lay values into the administration of justice (see Andrews (1978))? Is it part of their function to prevent the unjust use of the criminal law, exercising what is sometimes called 'jury equity'? Drawing the line between the proper functions of judge and jury can be very difficult. *Brutus v Cozens* **[8:6]** is a classic example: whilst the House of Lords says that it is for the magistrates (or jury) to decide the meaning of 'insulting behaviour', the real question is whether it should be the judge or the jury who should decide whether the protester was infringing the law set out in the Public Order Act 1936. The meaning of an ordinary word may not be a question of law, but the proper construction of a statute clearly is. The criminal law reflects an ambivalence: some words – such as, for example, 'insulting' or 'dishonest' – are left for the jury to interpret according to their common sense, while others – such as 'intention', 'recklessness' or 'provocation' – have been rigidly judicially defined such that, at times, as a matter of law, they no longer mean what ordinary English suggests.

Is 'causes' in the Water Act 1989, s 107(1) a question of fact or law? The section provides that: 'a person contravenes this section if he causes or knowingly permits (a) any poisonous, noxious or polluting matter or any solid waste matter to enter any controlled waters …' In *National Rivers Authority v Yorkshire Water Services Ltd* [1995] 1 AC 444 the Divisional Court, following *Brutus v Cozens*, held that whether or not Yorkshire Water was causing pollution was a question of fact for the jury, not a matter of law for the judge as the Crown Court had suggested. The House of Lords later allowed a final appeal by the sewage company. Does the distinction between law and fact in this context make sense, or is it just a technique that allows judges to avoid ruling on difficult questions? Here the important issue is whether a sewage company who unknowingly caused pollution, because an unauthorised person had dumped iso-octanol into the sewers, should be convicted of a criminal offence as defined in Act. Is this the function of judge or jury?

(iii) Assessing the jury

A fundamental question is whether the jury or the judge is better equipped to deal with the meaning of ordinary words (or the ordinary meaning of words, as Guest (1986) prefers to put it). The jury are often said to have an important constitutional role: 'the lamp that shows that freedom lives', as Lord Devlin famously said. Certainly a jury can acquit someone against the evidence, when their conscience leads them so to do. One reason why sheep-stealing stopped being a capital offence was that juries were refusing to convict sheep-stealers, and in the 1930s Parliament was forced to introduce a new offence of causing death by reckless driving when juries showed a marked reluctance to convict for manslaughter those who killed by dangerous driving. The acquittal in 1984 of Ponting – a senior civil servant who passed secret documents to an MP and was prosecuted under the Official Secrets Act 1911 – is said to show the constitutional importance of the jury, with their freedom to disagree with both the judge and the government. Lord Devlin [8:7] describes the jury as a democratic veto on law enforcement.

But this argument is debunked by Darbyshire [8:8]. Juries are used in relatively few cases: the Crown Court deals with less than 3% of all criminal cases.

Acquittals of defendants by juries

	Acquittals (as percentage of those pleading not guilty)	Percentage of those acquitted who are acquitted by jury (as opposed to on direction of judge)
1993	58%	43%
1997	64%	35%
2001	66%	33%

Source: Judicial Statistics, Chapter 6

How can we know if these people were wrongly acquitted? It is very difficult to assess the jury. Are they too easily swayed, susceptible to rhetoric? Are they prone to leniency? Are they too doubtful nowadays of police evidence? The acquittal of Ponting can be seen as inappropriate – the proper means for amending the Official Secrets Act was through the ballot box, not via the jury room – and one has to remember that in all 'miscarriage of justice' cases it was the jury who decided to convict.

It is clear that defendants and their legal advisers prefer trial by jury and consider it fairer than trial by magistrates (see [6:2]). But is this belief justified? Zander and Henderson (1993) (and see [7:2]) asked the various participants in the trial process whether they were surprised by the jury's verdict. Prosecution barristers were surprised in 15% of cases, defence barristers and judges in

14%, defence solicitors in 18%, police in 25% and CPS in 27% of cases. They were not necessarily surprised by the same verdicts, and acquittals gave rise to surprise more frequently than convictions. The police and CPS were surprised by 44%–47% of acquittals. Judges were surprised by 25% of acquittals, though most of these were 'understandable in the light of the evidence'. However, according to judges, 29% of all acquittals were against the weight of the evidence, against the judge's direction on the law, or simply inexplicable to judges. The number of 'problematic acquittals', according to prosecution barristers, was 31%, and for defence barristers the figure was 16%. Does this suggest that a quarter of all acquittals are wrong?

Even more worryingly, judges and prosecution barristers thought that the jury's decision to convict was against the evidence or against the law in 2% of cases. For defence barristers the percentage of problematic convictions was 17% – 2% of jury convictions a year would be 250 cases; 17% would be 2,000 cases. Are juries more reliable than judges? Even if the jury are getting it wrong in some cases, the fault may be with the legal process rather than with the jury. As Griew (1985) pointed out, 'A jury without stars or a compass cannot be accused of bad navigation' (at page 346). In assessing the case, they are reliant on the information presented to them and on the performance of counsel, and are doubtless influenced by the formidable courtroom, the formal procedure and status of the trial judge.

Are juries capable of understanding the evidence and making decisions in complex cases? Stockdale (1967) questions why judge and jury are kept so rigorously separated 'and free to make their own mistakes'. Should they have their own legal adviser present to steer their deliberations? Jackson and Doran (1997) argue that the traditional division of labour between judges and juries should be redrawn in order to enable judges to take greater responsibility for areas where their fact-finding strengths are located (for example, identification and scientific evidence). As we saw in *H v Ministry of Defence* [8:5], juries are now rarely used in civil cases. The Roskill Committee on Fraud Trials [8:9] had little difficulty in concluding that juries should be abolished for complex fraud trials, and that trial should take place before a Fraud Trials Tribunal. The extract refers to a study that cast grave doubts on a jury's fact-finding ability. But if one accepts that some cases are too difficult for a jury, where should the line be drawn? Many cases hang on complicated scientific evidence, and it is difficult to argue that fraud is necessarily more 'difficult' than, say, murder or rape.

Most discussions of trial by jury conclude by looking at the alternatives – and deciding that no other system is better. Useful discussion of the alternatives are to be found in Cornish (1968), in the Roskill Committee report and in Levi's report [8:10], which summarises some of the disadvantages of the possible alternatives in fraud trials. One option, which seems to be the one preferred by governments in recent years, is to limit the number of cases for which trial by jury is available, and to transfer an increasing number of offences to the magistrates' courts. Thus, the Criminal Justice Act 1988 reduced four offences to the summary-only category (driving whilst disqualified, taking a car without the owner's consent, common assault, and criminal damage to a value less than £2,000); and CJPOA 1994, s 46 raised the upper limit in the case of criminal damage to £5,000. Part of the function of the mode of trial guidelines, discussed in Chapter Six, is to encourage magistrates to keep more either-way offences in their own courts. The heated political debate that erupted over the failed Criminal Justice (Mode of Trial) Bill 1999, which was seen by many as an erosion of a fundamental right, has recurred with the proposal in the Criminal Justice Bill 2002 to give defendants the right to trial by judge alone unless a co-defendant objects or the judge considers that the public interest requires trial by jury. Judges will also be able to order trial without jury on grounds of length or complexity, or where there is a real danger of jury tampering.

But is trial by jury in practice all that it is held up to be? What are the jury actually doing when considering their verdict? More research is needed into the methods used by juries to evaluate the evidence, although Professor Sir John Smith warns (1998, at page 105):

'Much of our law of evidence is based on assumptions about the behaviour of juries which are mere guesswork and, of course, I recognise that it is highly desirable that we should know whether these assumptions are well founded or not. But I fear that there is a price to be paid – namely the revelation that many cases are decided in consequence of material irregularities in the jury room with the consequent undermining of public confidence in jury trial. If we are to keep jury trial – and there is an overwhelming sentiment in favour of doing so – it is perhaps better not to know. Is this a case where ignorance is bliss?'

Further reading

Andrews, J A 'Uses and Abuses of the Jury' in *Reshaping the Criminal Law* Glazebrook, P R (ed.) (1978) Sweet & Maxwell
Baldwin, J and McConville, M *Jury Trials* (1979) Oxford: Clarendon
Cornish, W R *The Jury* (1968) London: Allen Lane
Denning, Lord *What Next in the Law?* (1982) Butterworths
Darbyshire, P et al 'What can the English Legal System Learn from Jury Research Published up to 2001?' (www.criminal-courts-review.org.uk)
Devlin, P *Trial by Jury* (1956) London: Stevens
Enright, S and Morton, J *Taking Liberties: The Criminal Jury in the 1990s* (1990) Weidenfeld & Nicolson

Findlay, M and Duff, P (eds) *The Jury under Attack* (1988) Butterworths

Griew, E 'Dishonesty: Objections to *Feely* and *Ghosh*' [1985] Crim LR 341

Guest, S 'Law, Fact and Lay Questions' in *Criminal Law and Justice* Dennis, I H (ed.) (1986) Sweet & Maxwell

Hastie, R *Inside the Juror: the psychology of juror decision making* (1983) Cambridge University Press

Hans, V P and Vidmar, N *Judging the Jury* (1986) New York: Plenum Press

Jackson, J and Doran, S *Judge without Jury: Diplock Trials in the Adversary System* (1995) Oxford: Clarendon

Jackson, J and Doran, S Judge and Jury: Towards a new division of labour in criminal trials (1997) 60 M.L.R. 759

McCabe, S *The Jury at Work* (1972) Blackwell: OUP RU Paper No 4

McCabe, S and Purves, R *The Shadow Jury at Work* (1974) Blackwell: OUP RU Paper No 8

Smith, J C 'Is Ignorance Bliss? Could Jury Trial Survive Investigation?' (1998) 38 Med Sci Law 98

Stockdale, E *The Court and the Offender* (1967) Gollanz

Vidmar, N (ed.) *World Jury Systems* (2000) OUP

Zander, M and Henderson, P *The Crown Court Study* RCCJ Research Study No 19 (1993) HMSO

Documents

[8:1]   Contempt of Court Act 1981 section 8

8   Confidentiality of jury's deliberations

(1)   Subject to subsection (2) below, it is a contempt of court to obtain, disclose or solicit any particulars of statements made, opinions expressed, arguments advanced or votes cast by members of a jury in the course of their deliberations in any legal proceedings.

(2)   This section does not apply to any disclosure of any particulars—
    (a)   in the proceedings in question for the purpose of enabling the jury to arrive at their verdict, or in connection with the delivery of that verdict, or
    (b)   in evidence in any subsequent proceedings for an offence alleged to have been committed in relation to the jury in the first mentioned proceedings,
or to the publication of any particulars so disclosed.

(3)   Proceedings for a contempt of court under this section (other than Scottish proceedings) shall not be instituted except by or with the consent of the Attorney General or on the motion of a court having jurisdiction to deal with it.

[8:2] Juries Act 1974 (as amended by the Criminal Justice and Public Order Act 1994) sections 1; 3; 9; 17

1 Qualification for jury service

Subject to the provisions of this Act, every person shall be qualified to serve as a juror in the Crown Court, the High Court and county courts and be liable accordingly to attend for jury service when summoned under this Act, if—

    (a)   he is for the time being registered as a parliamentary or local government elector and is not less than eighteen nor more than seventy years of age; and

    (b)   he has been ordinarily resident in the United Kingdom, the Channel Islands or the Isle of Man for any period of at least five years since attaining the age of thirteen,

but not if he is for the time being ineligible or disqualified for jury service; and the persons who are ineligible, and those who are disqualified, are those respectively listed in Parts I and II of Schedule 1 to this Act.

3 Electoral register as basis of jury selection

(1)   Every electoral registration officer under the Representation of the People Act 1983 shall as soon as practicable after the publication of any register of electors for his area deliver to such officer as the Lord Chancellor may designate such number of copies of the register as the designated officer may require for the purpose of summoning jurors, and on each copy there shall be indicated those persons on the register whom the registration officer has ascertained to be, or to have been on a date also indicated on the copy, less than eighteen or more than seventy years of age.

(2)   The reference in subsection (1) above to a register of electors does not include a ward list within the meaning of section 4(1) of the City of London (Various Powers) Act 1957.

(3)   ...

9 Excusal for certain persons and discretionary excusal

(1)   A person summoned under this Act shall be entitled, if he so wishes, to be excused from jury service if he is among the persons listed in Part III of Schedule 1 to this Act but, except as provided by that Part of that Schedule in the case of members of the forces ... a person shall not by this section be exempt from his obligation to attend if summoned unless he is excused from attending under subsection (2) below.

(2)   If any person summoned under this Act shows to the satisfaction of the appropriate officer that there is good reason why he should be excused from attending in pursuance of the summons, the appropriate officer may excuse him from so attending and shall do so if the reason shown is that the person is entitled under subsection (1) above to excusal.

(3)   Crown Court rules shall provide a right of appeal to the court (or one of the courts) before which the person is summoned to attend against any refusal of the appropriate officer to excuse him under subsection (2) above.

(4)   Without prejudice to the preceding provisions of this section, the court (or any of the courts) before which a person is summoned to attend under this Act may excuse that person from so attending.

17   Majority verdicts

(1)   Subject to subsections (3) and (4) below, the verdict of a jury in proceedings in the Crown Court or the High Court need not be unanimous if—
>   (a)   in a case where there are not less than eleven jurors, ten of them agree on the verdict; and
>   (b)   in a case where there are ten jurors, nine of them agree on the verdict.

(2)   Subject to subsection (4) below, the verdict of a jury (that is to say a complete jury of eight) in proceedings in a county court need not be unanimous if seven of them agree on the verdict.

(3)   The Crown Court shall not accept a verdict of guilty by virtue of subsection (1) above unless the foreman of the jury has stated in open court the number of jurors who respectively agreed to and dissented from the verdict.

(4)   No court shall accept a verdict by virtue of subsection (1) or (2) above unless it appears to the court that the jury have had such period of time for deliberation as the court thinks reasonable having regard to the nature and complexity of the case; and the Crown Court shall in any event not accept such a verdict unless it appears to the court that the jury have had at least two hours for deliberation.

(5)   This section is without prejudice to any practice in civil proceedings by which a court may accept a majority verdict with the consent of the parties, or by which the parties may agree to proceed in any case with an incomplete jury.

[8:3]   *R v Ford* [1989] QB 868

The appellant, who was of mixed race and preferred to be called black, was chased and arrested by a police constable, also of mixed race. He was charged with six offences arising from the unlawful use of a motor car and from his subsequent arrest. At the Crown Court he pleaded guilty to one count, and at the outset of the trial he applied to the judge, through counsel, for a multiracial jury. The judge, under the misapprehension that counsel was about to use the case as a platform for racial haranguing, refused the application. The appellant was convicted on two counts.

The Court of Appeal, allowing his appeal on other grounds, confirmed that there is no right to a multiracial jury.

Lord Lane CJ (at page 871):

At common law a judge has a residual discretion to discharge a particular juror who ought not to be serving on the jury. This is part of the judge's duty to ensure that there is a fair trial. It is based on the duty of a judge expressed by Lord Campbell CJ in *R v Mansell* (1857) 8 E & B 54 as a duty 'to prevent scandal and the perversion of justice'. A judge must achieve that for example by preventing a juryman from serving who is completely deaf or blind or otherwise incompetent to give a verdict.

It is important to stress, however, that that is to be exercised to prevent individual jurors who are not competent from serving. it has never been held to include a discretion to discharge a competent juror, or jurors, in an attempt to secure a jury drawn from particular sections of the community, or otherwise to influence the overall composition of the jury. For this latter purpose the law provides that 'fairness' is achieved by the principle of random selection.

The way in which random selection should take place is a matter not for the judge but for the Lord Chancellor, as we endeavoured to point out in the course of argument to Mr. Herbert by citing the relevant portion of the Juries Act 1974, which is section 5(1). That provides:

> 'The arrangements to be made by the Lord Chancellor under this Act shall include the preparation of lists (called panels) of persons summoned as jurors, and the information to be included in panels, the court sittings for which they are prepared, their division into parts or sets (whether according to the day of first attendance or otherwise), their enlargement or amendment, and all other matters relating to the contents and form of the panels shall be such as the Lord Chancellor may from time to time direct.'

There are several cases which give examples of this residual discretion. It may be exercised even in the absence of any objection by any of the parties. The basic position is that a juror may be discharged on grounds that would found a challenge for cause. In addition jurors who are not likely to be willing or able properly to perform their duties may also be discharged.

The most common cases which this question has arisen have involved questions of ethnic groups where it has been suggested that the jury should consist partly or wholly of members of that same ethnic group. Those applications provide particular difficulty for the judge and the present case is a very good example. They arise without warning and are usually argued without any reference to authority, as indeed was very largely the case in the present instance.

It has never been suggested that the judge has a discretion to discharge a whole panel or part panel on grounds that would not found a valid challenge. Similarly, in the absence of evidence of specific bias, ethnic origins could not found a valid ground for challenge to an individual juror. The alleged discretion of the judge to intervene in the selection of the jury does not therefore fall within any acknowledged category of judicial power or discretion.

There are, moreover, strong reasons why such a discretion should not be recognised. The whole essence of the jury system is random selection, as the passage from *R v Crown Court at Sheffield, ex p Brownlow* [1980] QB 530, from Lord Denning's judgment cited in the course of argument, shows. He said, at p 541: 'Our philosophy is that the jury should be selected at random – from a panel of persons who are nominated at random. We believe that 12 persons selected at random are likely to be a cross-section of the people as a whole – and thus represent the views of the common man... The parties must take them as they come.'

The judgment was supported by Shaw LJ, sitting with Lord Denning MR.

Secondly, it is worth noting that on occasions in the past when it has been thought desirable that the court should have a power of this kind, it has been expressly granted by statute and equally subsequently abolished by statute.

Thirdly, such an application is in effect a request to the judge either to give directions as to the constitution of the panel or to order some individual jurors to be replaced without assigning a cause, that is peremptorily. It is true that in *R v Bansall* [1985] Crim LR 151, in response to an application of this type, Woolf J did give directions that the jury panel should be selected from a particular area known to contain members of the Asian community, but the judge does not appear to have had the benefit of full argument on the point.

Responsibility for the summoning of jurors to attend for service in the Crown Court and the High Court is by statute clearly laid upon the Lord Chancellor. That is clear from section 2 and section 5 of the Juries Act 1974 which has already been cited in this judgment. It is not the function of the judge to alter the composition of the panel or to give any directions about the district from which it is to be drawn. The summoning of panels is not a judicial function, but it is specifically conferred by statute on an administrative officer. That fact may not have been drawn to the attention of the court in the cases we have cited and others which have suggested that the judge has power to give directions as to the composition of the panel of jurors.

It should also be remembered that the mere fact that a juror is, for instance, of a particular race or holds a particular religious belief cannot be made the basis for a challenge for cause on the grounds of bias or on any other grounds. If therefore a judge were to exercise his discretion to remove a juror on either of these grounds, he would be assuming bias where none was proved, Such a course is not only unjustified in law, but also indeed might be thought to be seriously derogatory of the particular juror. Further, any attempt to influence the composition of the jury on these grounds would conflict with the requirement that the jury to try an issue before a court shall be selected by ballot in open court from the panel as summoned: see Juries Act 1974, section 11.

The conclusion is that, however well-intentioned the judge's motive might be, the judge has no power to influence the composition of the jury, and that it is wrong for him to attempt to do so. If it should ever become desirable that the principle of random selection should be altered, that will have to be done by way of statute and cannot be done by any judicial decision.

[8:4] *Attorney-General's Guidelines: Juries: The Exercise by the Crown of its Right of Stand By* (1989) 88 Cr App R 124

The Attorney-General has issued the following guidelines on the exercise by the Crown in England and Wales of its right to stand by. The guidelines are to have effect from 5 July 1989, to coincide with the implementation of section 118 of the Criminal Justice Act 1988, which abolished the right of peremptory challenge. The Attorney-General has also reissued his guidelines on giving checks. These incorporate amendments made in 1986, together with a new amendment to paragraph 9 whereby the Attorney-General's personal authority is required before the right to stand by can be exercised on the basis of information obtained as a result of an authorised check.

1   Although the law has long recognised the right of the Crown to exclude a member of a jury panel from sitting as a juror by the exercise in open court of the right to request a stand by or, if necessary, by challenge for cause, it has been customary for those instructed to prosecute on behalf of the Crown to assert that right only sparingly and in exceptional circumstances. it is generally accepted that the prosecution should not use its right in order to influence the overall composition of a jury or with a view to tactical advantage.

2   The approach outlined above is founded on the principles that:
    (a)   the members of a jury should be selected at random from the panel subject to any rule of law as to right of challenge by the defence; and
    (b)   the Juries Act 1974 together with the Juries (Disqualification) Act 1984 identified those classes of persons who alone are disqualified from or ineligible for service on a jury. No other class of person may be treated as disqualified or ineligible.

3   The enactment by Parliament of section 118 of the Criminal Justice Act 1988 abolishing the right of defendants to remove jurors by means of peremptory challenge makes it appropriate that the Crown should assert its right to stand by only on the basis of clearly defined and restrictive criteria. Derogation from the principle that members of a jury should be selected at random should be permitted only where it is essential.

4   Primary responsibility for ensuring that an individual does not serve on a jury if he is not competent to discharge properly the duties of a juror rests with the appropriate court officer and, ultimately, the trial judge. Current legislation provides, in sections 9 and 10 of the Juries Act 1974, fairly wide discretions to excuse or discharge jurors either at the person's own request, where he offers 'good reason why he should be excused', or where the judge determines that 'on account of physical disability or insufficient understanding of English there is doubt as to his capacity to act effectively as a juror ...'

5   The circumstances in which it would be proper for the Crown to exercise its right to stand by a member of a jury panel are:
    (a)   where a jury check authorised in accordance with the Attorney-General's Guidelines on Jury Checks reveals information justifying exercise of the right to stand by in accordance with paragraph 9 of the guidelines and the Attorney-General personally authorises the exercise of the right to stand by; or
    (b)   where a person is about to be sworn as a juror who is manifestly unsuitable and the defence agree that, accordingly, the exercise by the prosecution of the right to stand by would be appropriate. An example of the sort of exceptional circumstances which might justify stand by is where it becomes apparent that, despite the provisions mentioned in paragraph 4 above, a juror selected for service to try a complex case is in fact illiterate.

Jury checks

1   The principles which are generally to be observed are:
  (a)   that members of a jury should be selected at random from the panel;
  (b)   the Juries Act 1974 together with the Juries (Disqualification) Act 1984 identified those classes of persons who alone are either disqualified from or ineligible for service on a jury. No other class of person may be treated as disqualified or ineligible;
  (c)   the correct way for the Crown to seek to exclude a member of the panel from sitting as a juror is by the exercise in open court of the right to request a stand by or, if necessary, to challenge for cause.

2   Parliament has provided safeguards against jurors who may be corrupt or biased. In addition to the provision for majority verdicts, there is the sanction of a criminal offence for a disqualified person to serve on a jury. The omission of a disqualified person from the panel is a matter for Court officials but any search of criminal records for the purpose of ascertaining whether or not a jury panel includes any disqualified person is a matter for the police as the only authority able to carry out such a search and as part of their usual function of preventing the commission of offences. The recommendations of the Association of Chief Police Officers respecting checks on criminal records for disqualified persons are annexed to these guidelines.

3   There are however certain exceptional types of case of public importance for which the provisions are to majority verdicts and the disqualification of jurors may not be sufficient to ensure the proper administration of justice. In such cases it is in the interests both of justice and the public that there should be further safeguards against the possibility of bias and in such cases checks which go beyond the investigation of criminal records may be necessary.

4   These classes of case may be defined broadly as:
  (a)   cases in which national security is involved and part of the evidence is likely to be heard in camera;
  (b)   terrorist cases.

5   The particular aspects of these cases which may make it desirable to seek extra precautions are:
  (a)   in security cases a danger that a juror, voluntarily or under pressure, may make an improper use of evidence which, because of its sensitivity has been given in camera;
  (b)   in both security and terrorist cases the danger that a juror's political beliefs are so biased as to go beyond normally reflecting the broad spectrum of views and interests in the community to reflect the extreme views of sectarian interest or pressure groups to a degree which might interfere with his fair assessment of the facts of the case or lead him to exert improper pressure on his fellow jurors.

6   In order to ascertain whether in exceptional circumstances of the above nature either of these factors might seriously influence a potential juror's impartial performance of his duties or his respecting the secrecy of evidence given in camera, it may be necessary to conduct a limited investigation of the panel. In general, such further investigation beyond one of criminal records made for disqualifications may only be made with the records of Police Special Branches. However, in cases falling under paragraph 4(a) above (security cases), the investigation may, additionally, involve the security services. No checks other than on these sources and no general inquiries are to be made save to the limited extent that they may be needed to confirm the identity of a juror about whom the initial check has raised serious doubts.

7   No further investigation, as described in paragraph 6 above, should be made save with the personal authority of the Attorney-General on the application of the Director of Public Prosecutions and such checks are hereafter referred to as 'authorised checks'. When a Chief Officer of Police has reason to believe that it is unlikely that an authorised check may be desirable and proper in accordance with these guidelines he should refer the matter to the Director of Public Prosecutions with a view to his having the conduct of the prosecution from an early stage. The Director will make any appropriate application to the Attorney-General.

8   The result of any authorised check will be sent to the Director of Public Prosecutions. The Director will then decide, having regard to the matters set out in paragraph 5 above, what information ought to be brought to the attention of prosecuting Counsel.

9   No right of stand by should be exercised by Counsel for the Crown on the basis of information obtained as a result of an authorised check save with the personal authority of the Attorney-General and unless the information is such as, having regard to the facts of the case and the offences charges, to afford strong reason for believing that a particular juror might be a security risk, be susceptible to improper approaches or be influenced in arriving at a verdict for the reasons given above.

10   Where a potential juror is asked to stand by the Crown, there is no duty to disclose to the defence the information upon which it was founded, but Counsel may use his discretion to disclose it if its nature and source permit it.

11   When information revealed in the course of an authorised check is not such as to cause Counsel for the Crown to ask for a juror to stand by, but does give reason to believe that he may be biased against the accused, the defence should be given, at least, an indication of why that potential juror may be inimical to their interests; but because of its nature and source it may not be possible to give the defence more than a general indication.

12   A record is to be kept by the Director of Public Prosecutions of the use made by Counsel of the information passed to him and of the jurors stood by or challenged by the parties to the proceedings. A copy of this record is to be forwarded to the Attorney-General for the sole purpose of enabling him to monitor the operation of these guidelines.

13   No use of the information obtained as a result of an authorised check is to be made except as may be necessary in direct relation to or arising out of the trial for which the check was authorised.

Annex to the Attorney-General's guidelines on jury checks; recommendations of the Association of Chief Police Officers

1   The Association of Chief Police Officers recommends that in the light of observations made in *Mason* (1980) 71 Cr App Rep 157 the police should undertake a check of the names of potential jurors against records of previous convictions in any case when the Director of Public Prosecutions or a chief constable considers that in all circumstances it would be in the interests of justice so to do, namely:

    (i)   in any case in which there is reason to believe that attempts are being made to circumvent the statutory provisions excluding disqualified persons from service on a jury, including any case when there is reason to believe that a particular juror may be disqualified;

    (ii)   in any case in which it is believed that in a pervious related abortive trial an attempt was made to interfere with a juror or jurors;

    (iii)   in any other case in which in the opinion of the Director of Public Prosecutions or the Chief constable it is particularly important to ensure that no disqualified person serves on the jury.

2   The association also recommends that no further checks should be made unless authorised by the Attorney-General under his guidelines and no inquiries carried out save to the limited extent that they may be needed to confirm the identity of a juror about whom the initial check has raised serious doubts.

3   The Association of Chief Police Officers further recommends that chief constables should agree to undertake check of jurors, on behalf of the defence only if requested to do so by the Director of Public Prosecutions acting on behalf of the Attorney-General. Accordingly if the police are approached directly with such a request they will refer it to the Director.

4   When, as a result of any checks of criminal Records, information is obtained which suggests that, although not disqualified under the terms of the Juries Act 1974 a person may be unsuitable to sit as a member of a particular jury the police or the Director may pass the relevant information to prosecuting counsel, who will decide what use to make of it.

[8:5]   *H v Ministry of Defence* [1991] 2 All ER 834

The Ministry of Defence admitted liability for personal injuries caused by negligence in the treatment of a 27-year-old soldier, who had had a major part of his penis amputated without his consent. The Court of Appeal allowed the Ministry's appeal against the trial judge's decision that a trial by jury should be allowed.

Lord Donaldson (at page 839):

Finally, Mr Sedley draws attention to the fact that it is not for this court to disturb a discretionary decision of a judge sitting at first instance, unless it is satisfied that he has misdirected himself or his decision is clearly wrong. This, of course, we unreservedly accept.

We have reluctantly, but firmly, come to the conclusion that the judge's discretionary order was wrong and we think that he basis of the error was either a failure to appreciate the significance of the shift in emphasis created by the enactment of section 69 of the 1981 Act in place of section 6 of the 1933 Act or his acceptance of the submission that the retention of a judicial discretion necessarily involved the proposition that there must be some claims for compensatory damages in personal injury cases which were appropriate to be tried by jury or both. It follows that we are entitled, and indeed bound, to exercise a fresh discretion.

There was some discussion in argument as to the propriety of an appellate court declaring a policy or guidelines for the exercise of a judicial discretion, but it was rightly accepted that this could and should be done, provided that it was made clear that every case had to be considered on its own merits and that, if the rationale of the policy was not wholly applicable, even if the case fell within the terms of that policy, a judge was always free to depart from it. This too was unreservedly accept.

The policy should be that stated in *Ward v James* [1965] 1 All ER 563; [1966] 1 QB 273, namely that trial by jury is normally inappropriate for any personal injury action in so far as the jury is required to assess compensatory damages, because the assessment of such damages must be based upon or have regard to conventional scales of damages. the very fact that no jury trial of a claim for damages for personal injuries appears to have taken place for over 25 years affirms how exceptional the circumstances would have to be before it was appropriate to order such a trial and the enactment of section 69 of the 1981 Act strengthens the presumption against making such an order.

[8:6]   *Brutus v Cozens* [1973] AC 854

During a Wimbledon tennis match the appellant ran onto the court blowing a whistle and attempted to distribute leaflets. He sat down on the court and play was disrupted. He was charged with using insulting behaviour whereby a breach of the peace was likely to be occasioned, contrary to section 5 of the Public Order Act 1936. The magistrates held that his behaviour had not been insulting and dismissed the information. The House of Lords upheld this decision, stating that the magistrates' decision was one of fact, and there was no evidence that they had misdirected themselves.

Lord Reid (at page 861):

The meaning of an ordinary word of the English language is not a question of law. The proper construction of a statute is a question of law. If the context shows that a word is used in an unusual sense the court will determine in other words what that unusual sense is. But here there is in my opinion no question of the word 'insulting' being used in any unusual sense. It appears to me, for reasons which I shall give later, to be intended to have its ordinary meaning. It is for the tribunal which decides the case to consider, not as law but as fact, whether in the whole circumstances the words of the statute do or do not as a matter of ordinary usage of the English language cover or apply to the facts which have been proved. If it is alleged that the tribunal has reached a wrong decision then there can be a question of law but only of a limited character. The question would normally be whether their decision was unreasonable in the sense that no tribunal acquainted with the ordinary use of language could reasonably reach that decision.

Were it otherwise we should reach an impossible position. When considering the meaning of a word one often goes to a dictionary. There one finds other words set out. And if one wants to pursue the matter and find the meaning of those other words the dictionary will give the meaning of those other words in still further words which often include the word for whose meaning one is searching.

No doubt the court could act as a dictionary. It could direct the tribunal to take some word or phrase other than the word in the statute and consider whether that word or phrase applied to or covered the facts proved. But we have been warned time and again not to substitute other words for the words of a statute. And there is very good reason for that. Few words have exact synonyms. The overtones are almost always different.

Or the court could frame a definition. But then again the tribunal would be left with words to consider. No doubt a statute may contain a definition – which incidentally often creates more problems than it solves – but the purpose of a definition is to limit or modify the ordinary meaning of a word and the court is not entitled to do that.

So the question of law in this case must be whether it was unreasonable to hold that the appellant's behaviour was not insulting. To that question there could in my view be only one answer – No.

But as the Divisional Court [1972] 1 WLR 484, have expressed their view as to the meaning of 'insulting' I must, I think, consider it. It was said, at p 487:

> 'The language of section 5, as amended, of the Public Order Act 1936, omitting words which do not matter for our present purpose, is: "Any person who in any public place ... uses ... insulting ... behaviour ... with intent to provoke a breach of the peace or whereby a breach of the peace is likely to be occasioned, shall be guilty of an offence." It therefore becomes necessary to consider the meaning of the word "insulting" in its context in that section. In my view it is not necessary, and is probably undesirable, to try to frame an exhaustive definition which will cover every possible set of facts that may arise for consideration under this section. It is, as I think, quite sufficient for the purpose of this case to say that behaviour which affronts other people, and evidence a disrespect or contempt for their rights, behaviour which reasonable persons would foresee is likely to cause resentment or protest such as was aroused in this case, and I rely particularly on the reaction of the crowd as set out in the case stated, is insulting for the purpose of this section.'

I cannot agree with that. Parliament had to solve the difficult question of how far freedom of speech or behaviour must be limited in the general public interest. It would have been going much too far to prohibit all speech or conduct likely to occasion a breach of the peace because determined opponents may not shrink from organising or at least threatening a breach of the peace in order to silence a speaker whose views they detest. Therefore vigorous and it may be distasteful or unmannerly speech or behaviour is permitted so long as it does not go beyond any one of three limits. It must not be threatening. It must not be abusive. It must not be insulting. I see no reason why any of these should be construed as having a specially wide or a specially narrow meaning. They are all limits easily recognisable by the ordinary man. Free speech is not impaired by ruling them out. But before a man can be convicted it must be clearly shown that one or more of them has been disregarded.

We were referred to a number of dictionary meanings of 'insult' such as treating with insolence or contempt or indignity or derision or dishonour or offensive disrespect. Many things otherwise unobjectionable may be said or done in an insulting way. There can be no definition. But an ordinary sensible man knows an insult when he sees or hears it.

Taking the passage which I have quoted, 'affront' is much too vague a word to be helpful; there can often be disrespect without insult, and I do not think that contempt for a person's rights as distinct from contempt of the person himself would generally be held to be insulting. Moreover, there are many grounds other than insult for feeling resentment or protesting. I do not agree that there can be conduct which is not insulting in the ordinary sense of the word but which is 'insulting for the purpose of this section'. If the view of the Divisional Court was that in this section the word 'insulting' has some special or unusually wide meaning, then I do not agree. Parliament has given no indication that the word is to be given any unusual meaning. Insulting means insulting and nothing else.

If I had to decide, which I do not, whether the appellant's conduct insulted the spectators in this case, I would agree with the magistrates. the spectators may have been very angry and justly so. the appellant's conduct was deplorable. Probably it ought to be punishable. But I cannot see how it insulted the spectators.

[8:7] Devlin, P 'The Conscience of the Jury' (1991) 107 Law Quarterly Review 398 (at page 402):

These are the mundane reasons for preserving trial by jury, especially in crime. It exhibits, especially in the criminal verdict, the element of popularity that is appropriate in a democracy; it will be a long time before the judiciary ceases to be associated in the public mind with the upper classes.

But the paramount reason for it is that in defiance of regularity and of the disapproval of Lord Mansfield it lets the workings of conscience into the system. Judges are sworn to uphold the law; the jury is not. Sooner or later in life a man may be confronted with a struggle between what the law demands and what conscience urges. It is not a struggle that is peculiar to the jury box.

When juries fail to punish those whom they do not believe to deserve it, who is to say that they have not done what Lord Mansfield told them to do and answered to God? It is not they who are being perverse. The perversity is in the judges and bureaucrats who are so slow to see that when a procession of different juries refuses to convict of a particular crime, there is more likely to be something wrong with the law than with the juries.

This is the situation which gives the jury its peculiar place in our Constitution. It gives it what is tantamount to a democratic veto on law enforcement.

It is true that the law is made by Parliament which is a democratic body. But the function of Parliament in modern times is to approve, reject or modify the plans of the Executive. Members of Parliament are made of the same stuff as jurors. But they operate at planning headquarters behind the lines. Juries are in the front line. They see the impact of the law on its subjects and they have to decide when to use its weapons. They exercise the discretion of the man on the spot. This is as far as military analogy can be pushed. Put into constitutional terms, the jury is invested with a dispensing power to be used when their respect for law is overridden by the conviction that to punish would be unjust.

It is not only in individual cases that they act. Though they themselves have no legislative power, they can decisively influence those who have. For it is no use making laws which juries consistently fail to enforce.

It is not our great liberties that are threatened today. If they were, they would be guarded by judges. It is the little liberties which are infringed. Since the infringements are embedded in the statute the judges are powerless; the jury is not. It respects the law but it will not put it above the justice of the case.

Is this a picture of Lord Denning institutionalised? Perhaps so, but with one very big difference. The power that puts the jury above the law can never safely be entrusted to a single person or to an institution, no matter how great or how good. For it is an absolute power and, given time, absolute power corrupts absolutely. But jurors are anonymous characters who meet upon a random and unexpected summons to a single task (or perhaps a few), whose accomplishment is their dissolution. Power lies beneath their feet but they tread on its so swiftly that they are not burnt.

[8:8] Darbyshire, P 'The Lamp that Shows that Freedom Lives – is it Worth the Candle?' [1991] Crim LR 740 (at page 741):

The symbolic function of the jury far outweighs its practical significance. I shall argue in this paper that this sentimental attachment to the symbol of the jury is dangerous. Adulation of the jury is based on no justification or spurious justification. It has fed public complacency with the English legal system and distracted attention from its evils; a systematic lack of due process pre-trial and post-trial and certain deficiencies in the trial process itself. It has distorted the truth. The truth is that for most people who pass through a criminal justice system this palladium is simply not available and for those who can and do submit themselves to its verdict, it will not necessarily safeguard their civil liberties.

A 'Constitutional Right' to jury trial

This justification for the jury is perhaps the best known and the most often served up without explanation, as a self-evident truth. Three problems arise under this heading:
(a) the supposed guarantee of a right to jury in Magna Carta;
(b) what is meant by a constitutional right to jury trial in the English legal system; and
(c) what is meant, in jurisprudential terms, by asserting that there is a right to jury trial.

(a) Magna Carta

Many writers claim that jury trial was enshrined as a constitutional right in Magna Carta 1215, clause 39, which provided for a 'trial by peers'.[1] Later authors undoubtedly derived this myth from Devlin, who perpetuated it in 1956, having taken it from Blackstone's Commentaries.

Whilst Blackstone's grandiloquent account of the English legal system in the eighteenth century is of great entertainment value, few later legal historians or constitutional lawyers would accept it as historically accurate. Some of his assertions have been used to quite an alarming extent, however, in establishing the constitutional foundations of newer common law jurisdictions.

The famous clause 39 of Magna Carta reads: 'Nullus liber homo capiatur vel imprisonetur, aut disseisiatur aut utlagetur, aut utlagetur, aut exuletur, aut aliquo modo destruatur, nec super eum ibimus nec super eum mittemus, nisi per legale judicium parium vel per legum terrae'; which Holdsworth[2] translates as: 'No freeman shall be taken or/and imprisoned, or disseised, or exiled, or in any way destroyed, nor will we go upon him nor will we send upon him, except by the lawful judgment of his peers or/and by the law of the land'.

---

[1] Eg Devlin, P *Trial by Jury* 1956 at page 164; Blake, N 'The Case For The Jury'; Brown, D and Neal, D 'Show Trials: the Media and the Gang of Twelve'; Frieberg, A 'Jury Selection in Trials of Commonwealth Offences'; all in Findlay, M and Duff, P *The Jury under Attack* (1988) Butterworths.

[2] Holdsworth, W R *A History of English Law* vol 1 (7th edition, 1903) (1956) at page 59.

Legal historians have been at pains to point out that clause 39 has nothing to do with trial by jury and, as Cornish said[3] 'It has always been bad history to trace the system back to Magna Carta.' Holdsworth acknowledges that the mis-interpretation of clause 39 has had sweeping effects on English constitutional history but explains: '... it is also clear that the words judicium parium do not refer to trial by jury. A trial by a royal judge and a body of recognitors was exactly what the barons did not want. What they did want was firstly a tribunal of the old type in which all the suitors were judges of both law and fact, and secondly a tribunal in which they would not be judges by their inferiors. Some of them did not consider that the royal judge, none of them would have considered that a body of recognitors, were their peers.'

Earlier, in his History of Trial By Jury[4] Forsyth had said that it was a common but erroneous opinion that judicium parium or trial by one's peers had reference to the jury and had misled many, including Blackstone. He explains that judicium implies the decision of a judge, not a jury verdict. I would add that it is crucial to remember that, in 1215, the jury was still a group of oathswearing witnesses, or compurgators. They did not pronounce judgment. The *pares*, suggests Forsyth, were: 'members of the county and other courts, who discharged the function of judges, and who were the peers or fellows of the parties before them.'[5]

As these and other historians have pointed out, by Magna Carta the barons simply sought to secure a deal from King John, within which they safeguarded their right to be judged by judges of no lesser rank than themselves. Liber homo has been translated as either 'freeman' or 'freeholder' and 'freeman' did not mean what it does today. As we should remember from school history, freemen were a limited class in the feudal system.

(b)   A constitutional right?

Even if one were to concede that it has become a constitutional convention, since the fourteenth century, when statute prescribed that jurors be independent, that juries be used in certain criminal trials, I balk at the concept of trial by jury's being 'more than one wheel of the constitution'.[6] Devlin and others speak as if there were an entrenched right to jury trial, as there is in the United States Constitution or the Canadian Bill of Rights. The concept of a 'constitutional right; has, historically, been so alien to British constitutional lawyers, that the phrase seldom appeared in textbooks before the 1980s and now it only appears in the context of the debate over the need for a Bill of Rights. Indeed, the call for a Bill of Rights has arisen for this very reason: the sovereignty of parliament dictates that we do not have any entrenched rights, especially in issues beyond the grasp of EC or international law. This is manifest in relation to jury trial. Parliament has almost rendered the civil jury extinct and has continually eroded the use and availability of the jury in the criminal trial.

---

3   Cornish, W R *The Jury* (1968) at page 12.
4   Forsyth *History of Trial by Jury* (1852) at page 108.
5   Forsyth *History of Trial by Jury* (1852) at page 110.
6   Devlin, P *Trial by Jury* 1956 at page 164.

(c) A right?

There is also a jurisprudential problem with those who justify the use of jury trial as a right. the term 'right' at least to 'will' theorists, implies a choice. When we speak of procedural rights in the criminal justice system, we imply a choice. For example, I do not have to exercise my right of silence. Similarly, if I am charged with an offence which is triable either way, I can choose to be tried by judge and jury or magistrates. This choice can properly be called a 'right' to jury trial. What of indictable offences? Here, I must appear before the Crown Court, where my only choice is as to plea. My only right is as to trial. I cannot choose to be tried by judge alone, as I could in the United States. Thus, it is correct to speak of a 'right to jury trial' in the United States but not to speak of jury trials being a 'right', in general terms, in the English legal system, as so many defenders of the jury are wont to do.

By reasoning thus, I am accepting that the essence of a right must be a power of waiver, MacCormick would take issue with this and argue that restricting my power of waiver does not negate my right. To this, I would repeat Simmonds' reply 'It is doubtful if paternalism of this kind is best interpreted as a protection of the part's rights'.

Not only does the concept of a right to jury trial in indictable offences fail to accord with 'will' theories of rights, it also fails to satisfy classical 'interest' theories of rights and I would extend my argument here to include triable either way offences. According to interest theories, as I would apply them here, jury trial can only be described as a 'right' if the intended beneficiary of the court's duty to provide that right is the defendant. If the purpose of jury trial is primarily ideological, as I argue here, as a symbol to legitimate the criminal justice system, then the defendant is the unintended beneficiary and thus cannot be said to have real right to jury trial.

[8:9]   *Roskill Committee on Fraud Trials* (1986) HMSO (at page 138):

The anomaly

8.21 We draw attention to an astonishing development in the administration of the law. In the vast majority of legal cases in England and Wales today the persons selected to hear them are skilled people with particular knowledge and attributes, as opposed to a random selection drawn from the public at large which is the principle on which jury trials are at present founded. By 1984 magistrates' courts were handling about 2.2 million criminal cases a year. In the same year there were over 22,000 trials in the county courts and about 2,200 trials of civil actions in the Queen's Bench Division of the High Court, and only a handful of cases was tried with a jury. Tribunals, typically composed of a legal Chairman sitting with two lay members, also deal with disputes in immigration, rates, social benefits, industrial problems and many other fields. There are now over 60 specialist tribunals dealing with hundred of thousands of cases a year. Out of all the citizens (possibly some 3 million) who, in the course of any year, find themselves in difficulty with the law, only a small proportion (32,300 in 1984) will be tried by a jury.

8.22 The underlying logic of this situation, we find puzzling in the extreme. If society believes that trial by jury is the fairest form of trial, is it too costly and troublesome to be universally applied? If so, the millions of people convicted of summary offences before magistrates' courts in recent years, some of them facing imprisonment as a result, have a legitimate grievance, since they have been denied, on grounds of expediency, what is deemed to be the fairest form of trial. But if jury trial is not inherently more fair, given its extra cost and trouble, what are the merits which justify its retention? Society appears to have an attachment to jury trial which is emotional or sentimental rather than logical.

8.23 The most important conclusion to draw from these considerations, however, is that in almost every area of the law, society has accepted that just verdicts are best delivered by persons qualified by training, knowledge, experience, integrity or by a combination of these four qualifications. Only in a minority of cases is the delivery of a verdict left in the hands of jurors deliberately selected at random without any regard for their qualifications. Thus, those who advocate that complex fraud trials should be conducted before a select, as opposed to a random, tribunal are arguing not that such cases should be treated in any special or unique fashion, but that they should be treated in a manner more akin to the way the vast majority of all other legal cases are treated today.

8.24 In our opinion the absence from the jury box in a complex fraud case, except by chance, of persons with the qualities described in the preceding paragraph seriously impairs the prospect of a fair trial. We draw attention to other impediments to justice in succeeding paragraphs.

(and at page 142):

The limits of comprehension

8.33 Because direct research on jurors' comprehension of actual fraud cases would amount to a contempt of court, we commissioned a research project of a more indirect nature from the MRC Applied Psychology Unit at Cambridge. The research was conducted with individual volunteers, not with actual members of a jury. Sometimes these volunteers were classified so as to resemble members of a jury. The detailed research findings of this project are published separately.[7] Only a broad conclusion needs to be quoted here.

8.34 The research posed the question, when complex information is communicated to individuals in a manner designed to resemble courtroom procedure, how much of it is retained? And the answer is, very little indeed. By definition, the research cannot be conclusive, since it cannot be conducted on actual jurors. Nevertheless, the research findings strongly support the view of experienced observers and the promptings of commonsense, that the most complex of fraud cases will exceed the limits of comprehension of members of a jury. We have no doubt that most ordinary jurors experience grave difficulties in following the arguments and retaining in their minds all the essential points at issued, particularly in a long hearing of a complex character. This creates the serious risk wither that the jury will acquit a defendant because they have not understood the evidence or will convict him because they mistakenly think they have understood it when they have in fact done little more than applied the maxim 'there's no smoke without fire'.

---

[7]   Improving the presentation of information to juries in fraud cases (1986) HMSO.

Conclusions on complex fraud trials

8.35 There is no accurate evidence which we have been able to obtain to suggest that there has been a higher proportion of acquittals in complex fraud cases than in fraud cases or other criminal cases generally. Nevertheless, we do not find trial by a random jury a satisfactory way of achieving justice in cases as long and complex as we have described. We believe that many jurors are out of their depth. The breadth of experience of these cases of many of our witnesses leads us to accept their evidence.

8.36 There is another factor to which we attach great importance. We made inquiries whether prosecuting authorities refrained from prosecuting in some cases because of the difficulty of presenting them to juries selected at random in a way which the juries would be able to comprehend. We were told that this was rarely the sole reason, but that it was sometimes a major contributory factor in deciding not to proceed with a prosecution. We also had evidence that the difficulty of presenting a complex case often resulted in a decision to opt for less serious charges than the facts warranted.

8.37 We regard this as a serious situation. All the available evidence indicates that, in the United Kingdom, fraud is a growth industry and attention is directed to the statistics furnished in Appendix K. Unless all fraud cases are vigorously pursued the number will increase. For example, at the end of 1984, in London alone, there were 636 cases under investigation by the Metropolitan and City Police Company Fraud Department and £776 millions at risk. The prizes for success in such criminal ventures are so large that a growing number of people are being attracted into fraudulent dealings. We have observed moreover that there is public disquiet when company failures occur under conditions which suggest fraud or wrongdoing and no prosecution follows. We hope that the gravity of this situation will not be underestimated. Fraud is posing a threat to London as a financial centre and to the considerable volume of invisible exports which represents a major factor in the economy of the country.

8.38 Elsewhere in this report we recommend improvements in the investigation and preparation of cases; changes in the remuneration structure for the Bar designed to favour proper case preparation; an alternative procedure designed to bring cases more quickly to the Crown Court pending the government's decision on the abolition of committal proceedings; further development of the pre-trial review designed to simplify cases and isolate the real grounds of difference; the abolition of the right of peremptory challenge; substantial changes in the rules of evidence; a higher standard of presentation of the hearing; the use of visual aids; and the selection of judges with special experience. In sum, these proposals represent a fundamental overhaul of the courtroom process, which most of our witnesses regard as long overdue.

8.39 These changes would be a great assistance to juries and we would expect them to result in increased comprehensibility by them. But in the light of the foregoing analysis of the nature of a complex fraud case and the uncertain quality of a jury of 12 persons selected at random, we are satisfied that a different form of tribunal is necessary to try cases which fall within the Guidelines. Any such tribunal should we think have two basic characteristics in order to ensure that it would arrive at a fair and just verdict. First, it should be comprised of persons who are able to comprehend without difficulty the kind of complex transactions which are under inquiry. Second, the persons should be chosen, like all other persons who are appointed to judicial or quasi-judicial positions in the United Kingdom in criminal, civil, and other tribunals, because they are believed to uphold a high standard of integrity and to have a general competence which fits them to discharge their responsibilities.

8.40 The numerous changes we propose are long overdue and we think they are necessary in any event, for the proper administration of justice and the conduct of the different tribunal. It is impossible to ascertain how many cases would arise each year which fall within the Guidelines. It seems inevitable that there will be an increase of complex fraud cases and in any case we have not been able to assess the increased number of cases which will come to trial as a result of the improvements we proposed. The figures in paragraph 8.30 show that there has been an average of 26 fraud trials each year lasting more than 20 working days. The magnitude of the load will become clearer when experience has been gained with improved jury trials in cases in which they will still adjudicate. But we have no doubt about the immediate need for a different tribunal for complex fraud cases.

[8:10] **Levi, M** *The Investigation, Prosecution and Trial of Serious Fraud* RCCJ Research Study No 14 (1993) HMSO (at page 190):

Though the cultural and political obstacles to jury abolition in fraud cases are powerful, it may be useful to summarise some problems with alternative modes of trial of fraud. These could take place at the election of (a) the prosecution, as in transfer proceedings; (b) the defence, as in the US, Canada, and some Australian jurisdictions; (c) both, if they agree; and (d) the judge. If defendants had the right to elect for trial without jury, there would have to be provisions should they disagree. The possible alternative modes of trial are:

(1) Trial by judge(s) alone

Judges sit alone in long civil trials – themselves a demonstration of the way in which the inherent complexity of some frauds takes a long time to examine – but in my judgment, the stress of doing so in criminal trials is enormous. Judges might benefit from the presence of people of some expertise – greater, perhaps, than those recruited as clerks in recent long cases, whom judges have found very useful – to bounce arguments against, and that is an argument for there being three (or, more riskily, two) judges. This will cost money and cause listing problems, as dual arrangements have to be made. The advantage of judicial trial is that oral prolixity will be discouraged, the hearsay rule can be abandoned, and a much more businesslike atmosphere engendered. The disadvantage is that if the moral standards of ordinary people are the baseline, how are judges to know what those standards are? Chancery judges may be viewed by some as too tolerant using practitioners' views as the standard, as allegedly happened in the trial arising out of the failure of secondary bank London and Country Securities – while 'criminal judges' may be seen as too severe (and as lacking detailed knowledge of commercial systems and values). Trial by judge alone exposes the judiciary to accusations of political bias, as may be seen from the conviction (and jailing for six years) of the Olivetti Chairman Carlo de Benedetti by the Milan court in April 1992 in connection with the Banco Ambrosiano fraud. It could be countered that judges often direct acquittals at present, and that this has not received much adverse comment: there would certainly be a greater risk of this, however, if juries were not involved at all. A further counter is that we should go for what is objectively 'the right system'.

(2)   Trial by judge with assessors

This may look like an attractive option. It would take some of the political 'heat' off the judiciary should there be an acquittal and would inject some market expertise into the judgment process. However, how are the assessors to be chosen? From a 'fit and proper' general panel, as they are at Lloyd's and other regulators' disciplinary hearings? Are the defence going to be allowed to propose persons or if not, to object for cause, and on what criteria? Will there be a voir dire of the assessors? What if the defendants disagree among themselves about the suitability of assessors, as is quite plausible, either genuinely or as a tactic? What if, in Guinness, the prosecution had wanted people from the Takeover panel, Saunders had opted for marketing people, Parnes for other 'dynamic' stockbrokers, etc?

The trial may not be shortened by the presence of expert assessors, if the experts become entangled in technical debates or argue as long as the accountancy profession have done about the correct standards in SSAPs, or how one judges what is a 'true and fair view' of accounts! How will the defendants and the general public view the objectivity of the verdicts, irrespectively of how fairly the assessors have actually approached the issues? To satisfy this populist concern, the assessors could be substituted by two or more ordinary people drawn as jurors presently are, who would sit with the judge at the end, or even during the case.

(3)   Trial by special jury

In some respects, this is more consistent that present jury trials with the original concept of the jury as persons who were familiar with the accused and the general environment in which the offence occurred. This solution suffers from the problems noted in the section on assessors, and special jurors may be no more inclined than present jurors to follow the judge's legal directions. In some respects, the legitimacy problems are even worse. Let us imagine that a jury of merchant bankers or of City folk, however distinguished, had acquitted in Blue Arrow: would the public have believed it was anything other than a 'fix' by 'the City looking after their own kind'? If they had convicted, the defendants might well have represented that it was a vendetta against them (to eliminate a competitor) or that it was an attempt to sanitise the image of the City by throwing some sacrifices to the courts. (Imagine if a special jury of Lloyd's brokers had tried Ian Posgate in his criminal trial: who would have accepted that no prejudice was involved?) Some jurors interviewed certainly took the view that trial other than by jury would be 'a fix'. To reveal that alternative proposals have problems is not to rule them out, but my object here is to make it clear that public policy should not assume that simply because judges and assessors are persons of rectitude, their decisions will be viewed with legitimacy.

(4)   Other alterations to trial by jury

One possible 'mixed' system would be to have a tribunal composed of a judge, two assessors, and two lay persons, with a requirement that at least one of each would have to agree before someone could be convicted. (Perhaps a conviction might require the agreement of the judge.) In France, the Cour d'Assises which deals with major crimes which have a maximum penalty of five years or more – currently excluding frauds, which have maxima under five years and are tried by judges alone in the Tribunal Correctionel – has a jury composed of three judges and nine persons drawn from the electoral register. An alternative, more modest, approach would not violate the essential principle of jurors being representative sample of the population: a 'quota system' would ensure a more statistically proportionate number of middle-class persons than one often observes. Given their numbers in the general population, there ought to be some five 'middle-class' persons on a jury, and there could be a special jury panel to make up that proportion of the whole. This would ensure some spread of opinion and debate, and allay the fears of the political conspiracy theorists. Despite the shake-out in the financial services industry, unless fraud trials are greatly reduced in length, there are bound to be difficulties in getting people with current commercial expertise, not least because the pay limits are so low and many of them live outside the catchment area of the major fraud trial centres.

A further possibility is to give defendants the right to elect trial without a jury, as in North America and New Zealand and some parts of Australia. It is notable that the defendants in the Equiticorp case, a New Zealand SFO prosecution which is expected to last two years, have elected trial by judge, as reportedly as common in North America in cases where defendants have technical defences and wish a verdict to be accompanied by appealable reasoning. It also offers a bulwark against jury prejudice, particularly if inflamed by the media. If defendants are given the right of electing trial without jury, there would have to be procedures for solving inter-defendant disputes. One way forward might be to allow for trial without jury only if all defendants in one trial were agreed: this would enable severed components of one 'case' to undergo different modes of trial if the defendants wished it.

Chapter Nine

Appeal and Review Decisions

The ease and speed with which a decision can be challenged in a higher court is one yardstick by which to measure a criminal justice system. In England, the role of the Court of Appeal in correcting miscarriages of justice must be scrutinised, particularly in the light of several high-profile miscarriage of justice cases in recent years. In our story, Gerry Good has now been convicted of an offence under OAPA 1861, s 20 and has been sentenced to three years in prison. This chapter will show how unlikely he is to appeal successfully against either conviction or sentence. The Court of Appeal takes a very cautious approach, reluctant to interpret its powers too widely.

The appeal process has a number of functions. First, and perhaps most obviously, it has to correct mistakes. An appeal court checks that the court of first instance reached an appropriate result, and should put the matter right if it did not. Secondly, it has a due process function. The appellate courts should quash decisions reached unfairly, in order to safeguard the integrity of the criminal justice system as a whole. Finally, it has a consistency function: it allows the judiciary to develop clear legal rules, so providing for the harmonious development of the law.

However, these functions are not always achieved, nor are they all considered to be equally important. Thus, in appeals against conviction, the Court of Appeal is reluctant to interfere with the jury's fact-finding role; and in appeals against sentence it has always held that there is no such thing as a correct sentence – only if the sentence was 'wrong in principle' will the Court of Appeal interfere. The due process function is weighted more strongly by some than by others: Zander's dissent [9:1] in the report of the Royal Commission of Criminal Justice (1993) is a strong affirmation of due process values. The consistency function is no more clear-cut, raising many of the fundamental dilemmas facing any legal system: in order to be fair, a legal system must be certain and predictable; but in order to be fair, it must also show some flexibility. Does our criminal justice system correctly balance certainty and flexibility?

(i) Usual appeal routes

(a) After summary trial

Summary appeals, from convictions in the magistrates' courts, are governed by the Magistrates' Courts Act 1980, s 108 **[9:2]** and are heard in the Crown Court. The judge will normally sit with two lay magistrates. The appeal takes the form of a rehearing, with all the witnesses being recalled. Historically, this is because the records of proceedings in the magistrates' court were inadequate, and so there was no option but to hear the case again. But, ironically, this has the effect today that an appeal from a conviction for a summary offence, which normally has less important consequences for the offender than a conviction for an indictable offence, is often dealt with more thoroughly than an appeal from the verdict of a jury. The powers of the Crown Court are governed by the Supreme Court Act 1981, s 48 **[9:3]**. The court may impose any sentence which was available to the original court. Unmeritorious appellants are deterred by the knowledge that the court may (although it rarely does) increase the sentence imposed on the offender.

Appeals in the Crown Court

	Number heard	*Percentage successful*
1993	23,722	47%
1997	16,199	23%
2001	12,679	44%

Source: Judicial Statistics

Less than 1% of cases dealt with in the magistrates' courts are appealed. Does this reflect satisfaction with summary justice, a lack of legal aid, or a fear of an increased penalty? For Auld **[1:5]** the answer is to remove appeals as of right from the magistrates' courts: but is this really necessary?

There is no further appeal from the Crown Court (except appeals by way of case stated: see (ii) below).

(b) After trial in the Crown Court

For those tried in the Crown Court, an appeal lies to the Court of Appeal (Criminal Division). A formal system of criminal appeals was introduced only in 1907. Important reforms were effected, as a result of the Tucker Report (1954), in the Criminal Appeal Act 1966 – which replaced the old Court of

Criminal Appeal with the current Court of Appeal (Criminal Division) – and in the Criminal Appeal Act 1968. This was then substantially amended in 1995 **[9:4]**. For a critique of Auld's comments **[1:5]** on the inefficient use of judicial resources in the appellate process, see Malleson and Roberts (2002).

Appeals in the Court of Appeal (Criminal Division) are normally heard by Lords Justices of Appeal and High Court judges. Curiously, these judges may have had little experience of criminal trials. The recommendation of the Royal Commission on Criminal Justice (1993) – that it would be beneficial if senior circuit judges, often with greater experience and knowledge of criminal trials, should be able to sit as members of the court – was adopted in CJPOA 1994, s 52. It is also arguable that there should be lay members of the court, an issue we will return to later in this chapter.

Initially the defendant applies to a single judge for permission (or leave) to appeal, unless the appeal raises a question of law alone. This is a written application, and there is normally no hearing. Even where there is a hearing, witnesses are rarely called. Permission is required when the appeal turns on questions of fact, because of the reluctance of the judiciary to upset jury verdicts. Since most miscarriages of justice hang on questions of fact, such as the police fabrication of evidence, is this 'permission hurdle' appropriate?

Applications for permission to appeal

	Number of applications	Granted permission	Appeals allowed
1993	2,134	601	402
1997	2,318	537	186
2001	1,943	438	135

Source: Judicial Statistics 1993, pages 11–12; 1997, pages 13–14; 2001, page 14

Thus, few defendants make an application to appeal, and even fewer are successful. The percentage of successful appeals appears to be shrinking fast. The role of lawyers is vital: Chapter Five looked at the need for good quality legal advice throughout the legal process, and an extract from Plotnikoff and Woolfson **[5:9]** described their findings and outlined their recommendations on good practice and the responsibilities of legal advisers in the 28 days following conviction. The Royal Commission (1993) gave considerable space to recommendations for improvements to the practical procedures, in order to help applicants apply for permission to appeal. What has happened?

The grounds of appeal were reformed in 1995, following the recommendations of the majority of the Royal Commission. Malleson **[9:5]** showed how the grounds of appeal overlapped confusingly. The Commission accepted that the Court of Appeal was too narrow in its approach, too heavily influenced by the role of the jury, which led it to concentrate too much on assessing errors of law or procedural irregularities. The Commission was split as to what form the new powers should take: the majority suggested that a single broad ground, that the conviction 'is or may be unsafe', would be adequate. A minority (of three) were concerned that an umbrella formula would not give the Court of Appeal sufficient guidance towards adopting a less restrictive approach. In Chapter One we noted that the managerial and efficiency concerns of the Royal Commission allowed it to avoid developing a coherent philosophy or vision. The differences of opinion within it, on reforming the powers of the Court of Appeal, is another example of the commission's failure adequately to debate fundamental principles (in this case, the function of the appeal process). Note the new wording of section 2:

Old section 2 Criminal Appeal Act 1968

Except as provided by this Act, the Court of Appeal shall allow an appeal against conviction if they think:

(a) that the conviction shall be set aside on the ground that under all the circumstances of the case it is unsafe or unsatisfactory; or

(b) that the judgment of the court of trial should be set aside on the ground of a wrong decision of any question of law; or

(c) that there was a material irregularity in the course of the trial;

and in any other case shall dismiss the appeal.

Provided that the court may, notwithstanding that they are of opinion that the point raised in the appeal might be decided in favour of the appellant, dismiss the appeal if they consider that no miscarriage of justice has actually occurred.

New section 2 Criminal Appeal Act 1968

Subject to the provisions of this Act, the Court of Appeal:

(a) shall allow an appeal against conviction if they think that the conviction is unsafe; and

(b) shall dismiss such an appeal in any other case.

What difference has the change in the law made in practice? It is, of course, very difficult for a defendant such as Gerry Good to establish that his conviction is unsafe. He will have to rely on the transcript of the trial, and he will bear a heavy burden of proof. The Court of Appeal in *Chalkley and Jeffries* [1998] **[9:6]** held that a conviction is safe if there is no possibility that the defendant was convicted of a crime of which he was in fact innocent. But the Court of Appeal in *Mullen* [1999] **[9:7]** seemed to suggest that 'unsafe' bears a meaning wider than simply factually unsafe. Surely if a defendant is convicted following grossly unfair prosecution practices, he should have his conviction quashed? The Court of Appeal in *Togher* [2001] 3 All ER 463 preferred the approach in *Mullen*.

Much controversy has surrounded the Court of Appeal's power to hear fresh evidence under the Criminal Appeal Act 1968, s 23 **[9:4]**. This section (amended by the Criminal Appeal Act 1995, s 4) gives the Court of Appeal a wide mandate, but the court remains hesitant about becoming involved. Thus, the Court of Appeal in *McIlkenny* **[9:8]**, the case of the 'Birmingham Six', set out its vision of its role. Is the Court of Appeal construing its role too conservatively? If the Court of Appeal too easily accepts fresh evidence, there is a danger that defendants might 'save up' evidence for the appeal, and the court would be usurping the role of the jury. Yet Pattenden (1996) argues that 'an appellate court genuinely concerned to avoid miscarriages of justice should admit all evidence which could be believed by a reasonable jury, which could have affected the outcome of the case [and] that has not been deliberately saved up for appeal, should the accused be convicted' (at page 138).

There have been a number of legislative attempts to encourage appellate judges to use their powers to order retrials more frequently. Section 43 of the Criminal Justice Act 1988 **[9:9]** gave them power to order a retrial where this appears to be 'in the interest of justice'. Previously, power had been restricted to cases where there was fresh evidence.

Year	Number of retrials ordered	Year	Number of retrials ordered
1989	1	1996	53
1990	3	1997	33
1991	15	1998	73
1992	12	1999	70
1993	20	2000	72
		2001	58

Source: Judicial Statistics 1995; 1997, page 12; 2001, page 14

But retrials are not a panacea: they are expensive, often impractical, and sometimes unfair. Perhaps this explains the recent downturn.

Appeals against sentence are more common than appeals against conviction, because many of those who plead guilty still seek to challenge the sentence imposed by the Crown Court. Although the Court of Appeal will only vary a sentence if it was 'wrong in principle' (and remember that defendants require permission to appeal), appeals against sentence are statistically a little more successful than appeals against conviction.

Appeals against sentence

	Applications for permission to appeal	*Permission granted*	*Appeal successful*
1993	4,848	1,597	1,309
1998	6,550	1,909	1,589
2001	5497	1,551	1,101

Source: Judicial Statistics 1993, pages 11–12; 1997, page 12; 2001, page 14

The 'loss of time' rule, developed in two practice statements – [1970] 1 WLR 663 and [1980] 1 All ER 555 – allows the Court of Appeal to order that time spent in prison pending an appeal should not count towards sentence. In *Monnell and Morris v United Kingdom* **[9:10]**, the European Court of Human Rights considered whether the rule infringed the European Convention on Human Rights, and held by a majority that there had been no such infringement. Extracts from both the majority and dissenting judgments are included in order to illustrate how the approach of the European Court of Human Rights to its task is somewhat different from the approach of a domestic appellate court. The Royal Commission (1993) considered the power to order loss of time 'to be necessary as a means of discouraging appeals that have no merit' (at page 167). In practice, it is true, the Court of Appeal rarely orders that time spent on appeal should not count towards sentence, but does this excuse such an erosion of due process rights?

(ii) Unusual methods of appeal and review

Another way in which a party may appeal is by way of case stated. Under the Summary Jurisdiction Act 1857, s 6, the Divisional Court of the Queens' Bench Division of the High Court may 'reverse, affirm or amend the determination in respect of which the case has been stated, or remit the matter to the justices, with the opinion of the court thereon'. This procedure is normally used where the magistrates made an error of substantive law or acted in excess of jurisdiction, and the prosecution states a case for the opinion of the Divisional Court in order that that court (and the House of Lords, if the decision is further appealed) can stamp on a wrong ruling on a point of law before it spreads dangerously around the lower courts.

Appeals by way of case stated

	Appeals received from magistrates' courts	Appeals received from Crown Courts	Appeals allowed from magistrates' courts	Appeals allowed from Crown courts
1993	182	34	72	13
1997	144	32	62	7
2001	112	24	40	8

Source: Judicial Statistics, 1993, page 16; 1997, page 17; 2001, page 19)

The procedure is useful for correcting inappropriate rulings on the substantive law, but it may well be time to modernise the procedure and terminology.

Judicial review by the Divisional Court of criminal justice decisions is not common:

Applications for judicial review in criminal proceedings

	Applications	Applications allowed
1993	472	68
1997	284	45
2001	330	53

Source: Judicial Statistics 1993, page 15; 1997, page 16; 2001, page 18

The importance of judicial review of criminal proceedings is not revealed by the small number of cases involved: look at the number of such cases extracted in this book, which have included reviews of decisions taken by the Home Secretary [2:3], the police, the CPS [3:3] and the Serious Fraud Office (SFO) [4:6]. Judicial review is a vital constitutional safeguard, especially where statutory rights of appeal are inadequate. A further example is provided by the case of *R v Secretary of State for Home Affairs, ex p Bentley* [9:13], which was later referred back to the Court of Appeal by the Criminal Cases Review Commission. Judicial review differs from an appeal in three important ways: first, it is a review of the law and not an investigation of the facts; secondly, judicial review results either in a decision being quashed or upheld (the reviewing court will not substitute its own decision); and thirdly, judicial review is based in common law and is not a creation of statute. Judicial review of court decisions is rare, because where an appeal procedure is available, that will be the appropriate route for the appellant to pursue.

In the past, judicial review was usually only applied for if there had been some illegality, for example, if magistrates had failed to comply with the rules of criminal procedure. Today, despite the greater willingness of the courts to review cases, it remains very difficult to succeed in challenging any alleged misuse of discretion. Lord Diplock summarised the grounds upon which judicial review can be successfully sought as 'illegality, irrationality and procedural irregularity' (*Council of Civil Service Unions v Minister for the Civil Service* [1985] AC 374). Errors of law generally create illegality, and so are challengeable. The scope of irrationality is more difficult: it is difficult to find examples in the criminal context of the High Court quashing a decision for being 'irrational'. Even procedural irregularities will not necessarily lead to the quashing of a decision, since judicial review is itself discretionary. Because in judicial review proceedings, the court is reviewing the manner in which a decision is taken, and not the merits of the decision, such proceedings are no substitute for a real appeal process.

(iii)   The role of the Attorney-General

The Attorney-General exercises ministerial responsibility for the CPS and SFO. His power to enter a plea of *nolle prosequi*, which has the effect of stopping proceedings, was noted in Chapter Four. He also has an important role in the appellate process. Generally, the prosecution has no right of appeal in English law. There is an argument for giving the prosecution a right of appeal – for example, where the acquittal is perverse and flies in the face of the evidence, or where the acquittal is due to an error on the part of the prosecution. The Royal Commission on Criminal Justice (1993) rejected such proposals, suggesting only that where it can be shown that the jury was bribed or intimidated, the prosecution should be able to apply for a retrial. However, the Criminal Justice Bill 2002 will allow the prosecution, in cases which carry life imprisonment, to ask the Court of Appeal to quash an acquittal and order a retrial where there is new evidence that makes it 'highly probable' that the person is guilty. This undermining of the double jeopardy rule (that no one should stand trial on the same facts twice) has, unsurprisingly, been very controversial.

Under the Criminal Justice Act 1972, s 36 **[9:11]**, the Attorney-General may refer an acquittal for the opinion of the Court of Appeal. Whilst the judgment of the Court of Appeal in the case has no effect on the actual trial or acquittal of the defendant, it is used as a procedure to correct inappropriate rulings on the substantive criminal law. An example is provided at **[9:12]**. Jaconelli (1981) argues that hypothetical disputes should not be a means of clarifying controversial points of law. This view should be contrasted with that of A T H Smith (1984), who suggests that the Attorney-General's reference procedure should be extended to replace appeals to the House of Lords in criminal matters (see (iv) below).

More recently, the Criminal Justice Act 1988, ss 35, 36 **[9:8]** have given the Attorney-General power to appeal against an 'unduly lenient' sentence, and in these cases the Court of Appeal may actually increase the sentence (see **[7:14]**; **[7:15]**). However, the Court of Appeal has again interpreted its role very narrowly here. As Lord Lane CJ said in *A-G's Reference (No 4 of 1989)* 11 Cr App Rep (S) 517, at page 531: 'A sentence is unduly lenient, we would hold, where it falls outside the range of sentences which the judge, applying his mind to all the relevant facts, could reasonably consider appropriate'. Little research has been done into which cases are reviewed, and it may well be that the media exert an improper influence over which cases are referred to the Court of Appeal. Henham (1994) argues that the procedure should either be abolished or replaced by a general prosecution right of appeal free from the limitations of the present system. Thomas (1972) argued that a few prosecution appeals in test cases 'would lead to a more careful articulation of principles in the area of sentencing which would lead in turn to an improvement in the performance of trial courts generally' (at page 306). Can this argument be taken so far as to suggest a mechanism for the review of all sentences, or simply that the CPS should be involved at the trial stage in suggesting a suitable sentence (see Chapter Three)?

(iv)   The Sentencing Advisory Panel

The Crime and Disorder Act 1998 created the Sentencing Advisory Panel. The panel provides informed advice to the Court of Appeal in order to help promote consistency in sentencing practice. Chaired by Professor Martin Wasik, it has produced a steady stream of consultation papers on a large number of offences. Following such consultation, the panel provides advice for the Court of Appeal: the first advice, on environmental offences, was issued in March 2000. The Court of Appeal has now issued several guideline judgments which have been based largely on the panel's advice: see **[7:13]** for an example. The existence of the panel remains somewhat contentious: to what extent should a part-time advisory panel influence sentencing practice? Under the Criminal Justice Bill 2002, a new Sentencing Guidelines Council will be established to take over responsibility for issuing sentencing guidelines. Once the Bill is in force, the panel will submit its advice to the council rather than to the Court of Appeal. Time will tell how these two bodies will co-exist.

(v)   The role of the House of Lords

The House of Lords in its judicial capacity plays a relatively minor role in the criminal justice system. Under the Criminal Appeal Act 1968, s 33 **[9:4]** there are two requirements before there can be a further appeal to the House of Lords: (a) the court from which the appeal is brought (either the Divisional Court or the Court of Appeal) must certify that the case involves a point of law of general public importance; and (b) that court, or the House of Lords itself, must give permission to appeal. The Royal Commission (1993) recommended the removal of the requirement that the Court of Appeal certifies that the case involves a point of law of general public importance, on the basis that it is unduly restrictive, but this has not happened. Having both hurdles to overcome reflects the priority given to limiting the number of cases that reach the House of Lords. Yet Auld **[1:5]** recommended that on points of law of general public importance, consideration should be given to allowing a 'leapfrog' appeal from the Crown Court to the House of Lords when the law is in such an unsatisfactory state that only the House of Lords can resolve it. Auld also recommended that distinguished academics should sometimes be invited to help the House of Lords.

Petitions to the House of Lords

	Petitions received	*Refused permission to appeal*	*Successful appeals*
1993	16	11	0
1998	12	11	2
2001	34	13	13

Source: Judicial Statistics 1993, page 9; 1998, page 9; 2001, page 10

Why do we need two levels of appeal in criminal matters? Having reviewed the House of Lords' unimpressive record in clarifying the criminal law, Glanville Williams said, in a letter published at (1981) Crim LR 581, that 'it is a nice question whether, with this sort of balance sheet, the appellate jurisdiction of the House of Lords in criminal cases is worth the expense to the community'. The question is just as pertinent today. A T H Smith (1984) also concluded that appeals to the House of Lords should be abolished, though he would continue to give the House of Lords a role by means of Attorney-General's references to consider hypothetically whether or not any particular activity is within the ambit of the criminal law.

(vi) The role of the Home Secretary

The Home Secretary, as the government minister in charge of law and order, is thoroughly involved in criminal justice decisions and policy. He is the driving force behind most legislative change. Review the mass of material emanating from the Home Office! In Chapter Two his increasing powers over the police were examined, and in Chapter Ten we will look at his involvement in early release decisions.

He also advises the Crown on the prerogative of mercy. This may take one of three forms: a free pardon, a conditional pardon or remission of all or part of the penalty imposed by the court. Although a pardon is normally granted because the guilt of the defendant can no longer be accepted beyond all reasonable doubt, the conviction itself stands. This is because only a court can quash a judicial decision. The Divisional Court has held that the courts have jurisdiction to review the exercise of the royal prerogative of mercy: *R v Secretary of State for Home Affairs, ex p Bentley* **[9:13]**. A person who has been pardoned may, however, be given compensation under the Criminal Justice Act 1988, s 133 **[9:8]**: in *R (Mullen) v Secretary of State for the Home Department* [2002] EWCA Civ 1882, [2003] 1 All ER 613 the Court of Appeal held that Mullen (see **[9:7]**) was entitled to compensation under this provision.

Perhaps the most controversial role of the Home Secretary has been in fixing the length of time that those sentenced to life sentences must serve before the Parole Board reviews their detention. There have been many rulings against these practices by both domestic courts and the European Court of Human Rights – see, for example: *V and T v United Kingdom* (1999) 30 EHRR 121; *Stafford v United Kingdom* (2002) 35 EHRR 1121 **[10:16]**; *R (Anderson) v Secretary of State for the Home Department* [2002] UKHL 46 [2003] 1 AC 837 – but the Home Secretary has been reluctant to give up these powers (and see Chapter Ten on early release rules). What is the proper role of the Home Secretary in sentencing, and in criminal justice more generally?

(vii)   The Criminal Cases Review Commission

Since the Court of Appeal has no power to entertain second applications for permission to appeal, there needs to be a mechanism to reopen cases which turn out to be miscarriages of justice. Until 1995, a procedure existed whereby the Home Secretary could refer a case back to the Court of Appeal. The Home Secretary sat on the horns of a dilemma: on the one hand, he was criticised for his reluctance to use his powers; and on the other he was also criticised, being essentially a political figure, for having a role in the court process at all. In most cases a convicted person had to attract the support of a public figure or a newspaper before the Home Secretary would refer a case back to the Court of Appeal. The power of the media was very clear.

The Royal Commission (1993) recommendation that the Home Secretary's power be given instead to a Criminal Cases Review Authority **[9:14]** was adopted in the Criminal Appeal Act 1995, s 8 **[9:15]**, and the authority was later renamed the Criminal Cases Review Commission (CCRC). The CCRC is made up of 14 members, chaired by Sir Frederick Crawford, and it started work in April 1997. Its powers are set out in the Criminal Appeal Act 1995, s 13 **[9:15]**: a case may be referred by the CCRC to the Court of Appeal if there is a 'real possibility' that the conviction will be overturned because there exists evidence/arguments which were 'not raised in the proceedings which led to it or on any appeal or application for leave to appeal'. There is a safety valve built into section 13(2) of the Act: the CCRC is not prevented from making a reference 'if it appears to [it] that there are exceptional circumstances which justify making it'.

The CCRC is given powers of investigation by sections 17–21 of the 1995 Act, but its powers are in reality controlled by its budget. The CCRC itself calculated in 1998 that it needed 60 case review managers (rather than the 26 then in place) in order to achieve break-even between case intake and output, and to reduce the number of cases accumulating. However, the Home Office rejected its application for further funding. Since then the Home Affairs Select Committee of the House of Commons has reported on the problems of case backlog and delay within the CCRC (1998–99 HC 106; see also James, Taylor and Walker (2000)). By its fifth annual report, published in 2002, the CCRC was able to report that at last increased resources were allowing it to deal with the backlog of accumulated cases. The annual reports give a clear picture of the sort of cases with which the CCRC deals, and of its working practices.

Even if the CCRC was adequately resourced, how can we measure its 'independence' and its 'efficacy'? We saw in Chapter Two the problems, in relation to the police, of maintaining a force which is simultaneously both independent and truly accountable for its actions. The same issues arise here. Another way forward would have been to enhance the powers of the judiciary to refer cases back to the Court of Appeal, and to strengthen the resolve of the Court of Appeal itself to correct miscarriages of justice.

Further reading

Criminal Cases Review Commission Annual Reports
Foot, P *Murder at the Farm: Who Killed Carl Bridgwater?* (1988) Penguin
Henham, R 'Attorney-General's References and Sentencing Policy' [1994] Crim LR 499
Jaconelli, J 'Attorney-General's References – a Problematic Device' [1981] Crim LR 543
James, A, Taylor, N and Walker, C 'The Criminal Cases Review Commission: Economy, Effectiveness and Justice' [2000] Crim LR 140
Justice *Miscarriages of Justice* (1989)
Justice *Remedying Miscarriages of Justice* (1994)
Kennedy, L *Wicked Beyond Belief: the Luton Murder Case* (1980) London
Malleson, K and Roberts, S 'Streamlining and Clarifying the Appellate Process' [2002] Crim LR 272

Mullin, C *Error of Judgement: the Birmingham Bombings* (1986) Chatto & Windus

Pattenden, R *Judicial Discretion and Criminal Litigation* (1990) Oxford: Clarendon Press

Pattenden, R *English Criminal Appeals 1844–1994* (1996) Oxford: Clarendon Press

Pattenden, R 'Prosecution Appeals' [2000] Crim LR 971

Spencer, J N 'Judicial Review of Criminal Proceedings' [1991] Crim LR 259

Smith, A T H 'Criminal Appeals in the House of Lords' (1984) 47 MLR 133

Stevens, R *Law and Politics: the House of Lords as a judicial body* (1979) Weidenfeld & Nicolson

Tregilgas-Davey, M 'Miscarriages of justice within the English legal system' (1991) 141 NLJ 668

Thomas, D A 'Increasing Sentences on Appeal' [1972] Crim LR 288

Documents

[9:1] *Royal Commission on Criminal Justice: Professor Zander's Dissent* (1993) HMSO Cmnd 2263

Professor Zander dissented on three topics: defence disclosure, pre-trial procedures and the powers of the Court of Appeal. Only the third part of his dissent is included here.

(at page 223):

III The Court of appeal's power to quash a conviction (or order a retrial) on account of error at trial or malpractice by the prosecution.

62   When convictions are quashed by the Court of Appeal it is usually because there has been some error or irregularity at the trial or some procedural or legal defect in the pre-trial process, or there has been serious malpractice by the prosecution. Typically, the trial judge misdirected the jury on the law or the evidence, or his summing up was unbalanced, or he wrongly admitted inadmissible evidence.[1] The Commission is unanimous in believing that the Court of Appeal's past practice of allowing many guilty persons to escape their just deserts simply because there has been a defect in the process leading to their conviction requires consideration. But the Commission is not unanimous as to how the problem should be addressed.

63   The majority of the Commission propose that, where there is an appeal against conviction, the conviction should be upheld unless the ground of appeal is such as to

---

[1]   See Malleson, K *Review of the Appeal Process* Royal Commission on Criminal Justice Research Study No 17 (1993) Table 1.1, which showed that 60% of successful appeals were based on errors by the trial judge.

undermine the conviction – in the sense that the Court of Appeal concludes that the verdict is no longer safe. In that event, it would quash the conviction. The gravity of the defect on its own would no longer carry any weight. The question would always be only whether the verdict was safe. If the Court of Appeal thinks the defect may make the conviction unsafe, it would order a retrial. (One of the consequences of such a change of approach would be significantly, perhaps drastically, to reduce the number of successful appeals against conviction.)

64   Two Commissioners and I would go further in regard to errors of law or procedure at the trial, other than minor errors or irregularities. As stated in chapter ten of the Report, paragraph 37, we would in addition give the Court of Appeal the power to order a retrial in such cases even though the error or defect cannot be said to make the verdict unsafe. In our view defendants should not be serving prison sentences on the basis of trials that are seriously flawed. If the court holds that the error at the trial is a serious one but that for any reason a retrial is not a practicable or desirable option, it would have to quash the conviction.

65   Where, however, the basis of the appeal is something that occurred pre-trial the view taken by the minority depends on the gravity of the defect. If the defect is minor or 'harmless' error, we agree with the majority that the appeal should fail. On this the Commission is therefore unanimous. If the defect, though not of the gravest kind, is of the level of gravity that now leads the court to quash the conviction, I and another Commissioner believe that the Court of Appeal should continue to be empowered to deal with such a defect even though it may not render the conviction unsafe. The typical case would be a serious breach of PACE or of its Codes of Practice. Since the introduction of PACE in January 1986 there have been dozens of cases that have gone to the Court of appeal where the substance of the appeal has been that the police broke one or other of the PACE rules. Many have concerned failure to comply with the rules regarding access to a solicitor, or provision of an appropriate adult or with the rules regarding recording of interviews. In a proportion of such cases the Court of Appeal has held that the defect was sufficiently serious to require that the conviction be quashed.

66   The majority would limit the Court of Appeal's power to deal with breaches of PACE to those cases where the breach rendered the jury's verdict unsafe. In my view this is insufficient because it ignores the important role that the Court of Appeal plays in upholding the PACE rules – quite apart from the question whether the breach affected the verdict. Breaches of PACE are automatically breaches of police disciplinary rules but as the Report states[2] 'there are hardly any formal disciplinary proceedings for breaches of PACE'. If any action is taken, even for serious breaches of PACE, it virtually never goes beyond mere 'advice' to the officer concerned. The role of the Court of Appeal in promoting observance of the complex and crucial network of PACE rules is therefore of great importance. The majority's approach would weaken this role. I would however wish to see the Court of Appeal, wherever possible, deal with a serious breach of PACE by ordering a retrial rather than by allowing a guilty person to go free by quashing the conviction. Retrials are not ideal[3] but where there has been a serious breach of PACE they can be preferable to allowing a guilty person to go free.

---

[2]   Chapter three, paragraph 102.
[3]   They are, however, frequent in many common law jurisdictions, including Australia, Canada, Ireland and New Zealand. Michael Knight, in *Criminal Appeals* (1970, Stevens) reports that, for instance, in Ireland in the period 1954–64 retrials were ordered in three-quarters of all quashed conviction cases.

67   If, however, the pre-trial malpractice is of the most serious kind, the Court of Appeal must be able not simply to order a retrial but to quash the conviction. This is the only appropriate response where prosecution agencies have fabricated or suppressed important evidence or where the defendant has been subjected to serious violence in the course of interrogation. Obviously, if the fabricated or suppressed evidence or the confession produced by violent means was the only or the main evidence for the prosecution, the Court of Appeal would have no difficulty in quashing the conviction. In such a case the Commission is unanimous as to the outcome. But it may be that there is other, reliable evidence showing that the defendant committed the offence. Nine of my ten colleagues believe that if there is sufficient sound evidence, even the most serious misconduct by the prosecution should not result in the conviction being quashed.

68   I cannot agree. The moral foundation of the criminal justice system requires that if the prosecution has employed foul means the defendant must go free even though he is plainly guilty. Where the integrity of the process is fatally flawed, the conviction should be quashed as an expression of the system's repugnance at the methods used by those acting for the prosecution.

69   The majority's position would, I believe, encourage serious wrongdoings from some police officers who might be tempted to exert force or fabricate or suppress evidence in the hope of establishing the guilt of the suspect, especially in a serious case when they believe him to be guilty. There have unfortunately been some gross examples of such conduct.

70   The position adopted by the majority also seems to me to risk undermining the principle at the heart of section 78 of PACE which explicitly gives the court the power to exclude evidence on the ground that it renders the proceedings 'unfair'. The word 'unfair' expresses the underlying moral principle and the Court of Appeal has repeatedly used this new statutory power very broadly to express its refusal to uphold convictions based on unacceptable police practices even when it could not be said that the misconduct had any impact on the jury's verdict.

71   Section 78 would of course remain – but the majority would in effect be encouraging the Court of Appeal to undercut a part of its moral force by saying that the issue of 'unfairness' can be ignored where there is sufficient evidence to show that the defendant is actually guilty. Any judge concerned to discourage prosecution malpractice would I believe be dismayed by the majority's position. In terms of the message sent to the police service and other prosecution agencies it could undo much of the good effect being achieved by the attitude of the judges to section 78 of PACE.

72   But the matter goes beyond discouraging prosecution malpractice. At the heart of the criminal justice system there is a fundamental principle that the process must itself have integrity. The majority suggest that the answer to prosecution wrongdoing in the investigation of crime is to deal with the wrongdoers through prosecution or disciplinary proceedings. Even were this to happen (and often in practice it would not), the approach is not merely insufficient, it is irrelevant to the point of principle. The more serious the case, the greater the need that the system upholds the values in the name of which it claims to act. If the behaviour of the prosecution agencies has deprived a guilty verdict of its moral legitimacy the Court of Appeal must have a residual power to quash the verdict no matter how strong the evidence of guilt. The integrity of the criminal justice system is a higher objective than the conviction of any individual.

[9:2] Magistrates' Courts Act 1980 (as amended) section 108

108 Right of appeal to the Crown Court

(1) A person convicted by a magistrates' court may appeal to the Crown Court—
    (a)   if he pleaded guilty, against his sentence;
    (b)   if he did not, against the conviction or sentence.

(1A) Section 14 of the Powers of Criminal Courts (Sentencing) Act 2000 (under which a conviction of an offence for which ... an order for conditional or absolute discharge is made is deemed not to be a conviction except for certain purposes) shall not prevent an appeal under this section, whether against conviction or otherwise.

(2) A person sentenced by a magistrates' court for an offence in respect of which ... an order for conditional discharge has been previously made may appeal to the Crown Court against the sentence.

(3) In this section "sentence" includes any order made on conviction by a magistrates' court, not being—
    (a)   ...
    (b)   an order for the payment of costs;
    (c)   an order under section 2 of the Protection of Animals Act 1911 (which enables a court to order the destruction of an animal); or
    (d)   an order made in pursuance of any enactment under which the court has no discretion as to the making of the order or its terms;
and also includes a declaration of relevance under ... the Football Spectators Act 1989.

[9:3] Supreme Court Act 1981 (as amended) section 48

48 Appeals to Crown Court

(1) The Crown Court may, in the course of hearing any appeal, correct any error or mistake in the order or judgment incorporating the decision which is the subject of the appeal.

(2) On the termination of the hearing of an appeal the Crown Court—
    (a)   may confirm, reverse or vary any part of the decision appealed against, including a determination not to impose a separate penalty in respect of an offence; or
    (b)   may remit the matter with its opinion thereon to the authority whose decision is appealed against; or
    (c)   may make such other order in the matter as the court thinks just, and by such order exercise any power which the said authority might have exercised.

(3) Subsection (2) has effect subject to any enactment relating to any such appeal which expressly limits or restricts the powers of the court on the appeal.

(4)   Subject to section 11(6) of the Criminal Appeal Act 1995, if the appeal is against a conviction or a sentence, the preceding provisions of this section shall be construed as including power to award any punishment, whether more or less severe than that awarded by the magistrates' court whose decision is appealed against, if that is a punishment which that magistrates' court might have awarded.

(5)   This section applies whether or not the appeal is against the whole of the decision.

(6)   In this section "sentence" includes any order made by a court when dealing with an offender, including—
  (a)   a hospital order under Part III of the Mental Health Act 1983, with or without a restriction order, and an interim hospital order under that Act; and
  (b)   a recommendation for deportation made when dealing with an offender.

(7)   The fact that an appeal is pending against an interim hospital order under the said Act of 1983 shall not affect the power of the magistrates' court that made it to renew or terminate the order or to deal with the appellant on its termination; and where the Crown Court quashes such an order but does not pass any sentence or make any other order in its place the Court may direct the appellant to be kept in custody or released on bail pending his being dealt with by that magistrates' court.

(8)   Where the Crown Court makes an interim hospital order by virtue of subsection (2)—
  (a)   the power of renewing or terminating the order and of dealing with the appellant on its termination shall be exercisable by the magistrates' court whose decision is appealed against and not by the Crown Court; and
  (b)   that magistrates' court shall be treated for the purposes of section 38(7) of the said Act of 1983 (absconding offenders) as the court that made the order.

[9:4]   Criminal Appeal Act 1968 (as amended) sections 2; 23; 33

2   Grounds for allowing an appeal under s 1

(1)   Subject to the provisions of this Act, the Court of Appeal—
  (a)   shall allow an appeal against conviction if they think that the conviction is unsafe; and
  (b)   shall dismiss such an appeal in any other case.

(2)   In the case of an appeal against conviction the Court shall, if they allow the appeal, quash the conviction.

(3)   An order of the Court of Appeal quashing a conviction shall, except when under section 7 below the appellant is ordered to be retried, operate as a direction to the court of trial to enter, instead of the record of conviction, a judgment and verdict of acquittal.

23 Evidence

(1)   For the purposes of an appeal under this Part of this Act the Court of Appeal may, if they think it necessary or expedient in the interests of justice—

- (a)   order the production of any document, exhibit or other thing connected with the proceedings, the production of which appears to them necessary for the determination of the case;
- (b)   order any witness who would have been a compellable witness in the proceedings from which the appeal lies to attend for examination and be examined before the Court, whether or not he was called in those proceedings; and
- (c)   receive any evidence which was not adduced in the proceedings from which the appeal lies.

(2)   The Court of Appeal shall, in considering whether to receive any evidence, have regard in particular to—

- (a)   whether the evidence appears to the Court to be capable of belief;
- (b)   whether it appears to the Court that the evidence may afford any ground for allowing the appeal;
- (c)   whether the evidence would have been admissible in the proceedings from which the appeal lies on an issue which is the subject of the appeal; and
- (d)   whether there is a reasonable explanation for the failure to adduce the evidence in those proceedings.

(3)   Subsection (1)(c) above applies to any evidence of a witness (including the appellant) who is competent but not compellable ...

(4)   For the purposes of an appeal under this Part of this Act, the Court of Appeal may, if they think it necessary or expedient in the interests of justice, order the examination of any witness whose attendance might be required under subsection (1)(b) above to be conducted, in manner provided by rules of court, before any judge or officer of the Court or other person appointed by the Court for the purpose, and allow the admission of any depositions so taken as evidence before the Court.

33   Right of appeal to House of Lords

(1)   An appeal lies to the House of Lords, at the instance of the defendant or the prosecutor, from any decision of the Court of Appeal on an appeal to that court under Part I of this Act or section 9 (preparatory hearings) of the Criminal Justice Act 1987 or section 35 of the Criminal Procedure and Investigations Act 1996.

(1A) In subsection (1) above the reference to the prosecutor includes a reference to the Director of the Assets Recovery Agency in a case where (and to the extent that) he is a party to the appeal to the Court of Appeal.

(2)   The appeal lies only with the leave of the Court of Appeal or the House of Lords; and leave shall not be granted unless it is certified by the Court of Appeal that a point of law of general public importance is involved in the decision and it appears to the Court of Appeal or the House of Lords (as the case may be) that the point is one which ought to be considered by that House.

(3)   Except as provided by this Part of this Act and section 13 of the Administration of Justice Act 1960 (appeal in cases of contempt of court), no appeal shall lie from any decision of the criminal division of the Court of Appeal.

[9:5]   Malleson, K *Review of the Appeal Process* RCCJ Research Study No 17 (1993) HMSO (at page 15):

From these findings, the work of the Court of Appeal can be summarised as follows. Most of its time is spent reviewing the decisions of the trial judge, considering whether his summing up was adequate, whether or not he misdirected the jury as to the application of the law or evidence, or whether he erred in exercising his discretion to include or exclude a piece of evidence. It is rare for the court to hear fresh evidence, consider the existence of a 'lurking doubt' about the conviction or order a retrial. Thus, the court performs, in practice, a relatively limited function. With the exception of the retrial, this cannot be explained as a result of the restrictions of the provisions of the CAA. The rarity of the use of a retrial must, as least party, be explained by the wording of s 7, but the courts interpretation of the grounds set out in s 2(1) and particularly the phrase 'unsafe and unsatisfactory' seems to be quite wide enough to cover a broad range of cases.

The fact that the sample did include fresh evidence cases, lurking doubt and retrial cases shows that the court is quite capable of taking a broad view of its powers and applying them to a wide range of cases if it so chooses. The evidence of both forensic experts and witnesses of fact were considered in cases involving a diverse range of issues and circumstances. The presence of a small number of such cases is evidence that the court considers that it does possess wide powers but that it is reluctant to use them very often.

There are three main explanations which may account for the fact that the court exercises the full range of its powers so infrequently:
(i)   The court is very concerned that as far as possible the jury's decision should be final and the trial should not come to be seen as an 'initial skirmish'[4] The court's anxiety not to undermine the principle of the sovereignty of the jury was referred to directly or indirectly in many of the cases reviewed. When assessing a witness's credibility or the soundness of the conviction the court appeared to be considering questions of fact and placing itself in the position of the jury, so threatening the principle which it claims to be reinforcing.
(ii)   The court is keen to limit the flow of cases into the appeal system. A number of the cases reviewed commented on the length of time which the appeal had taken to be heard and the court is conscious that delays can amount to a fresh source of injustice. In limiting the type of cases which it hears, the court contributes to the task of holding closed the 'floodgates' to keep out the tide of cases which it fears will swamp the already overstretched resources of the Court of Appeal. Lawyers and appellants know that they are very unlikely to persuade the court to hear fresh evidence or find that there is a 'lurking doubt' about the conviction. This knowledge may help to ensure that few such cases come into the appeal system. The court's decision that errors of an appellant's legal advisers are not generally valid grounds of appeal is an important example of this process of keeping down the numbers of appeals. The fact that many appeals are submitted on the basis of

---

[4]   See *R v Shields and Patrick* [1977] Crim LR 281.

lawyer's errors, despite the ruling, only to be weeded out by the single judge[5] suggests that many more are kept from appealing by the knowledge that it would be hopeless to do so. This process may also be assisted by fear of the time loss rules which keep many potential appellants out of the system. It is likely that they are so rarely applied because the threat alone is sufficient to keep down the numbers of appeals. Possibly, if it came to be widely known that this power is hardly ever exercised, causing numbers of applications for leave to appeal to rise, its use would increase.

(iii) The resources which the court has at its disposal do not equip it to review all the circumstances of alleged injustice, before during and after trial, which can be raised at appeal. From the papers provided by the CAO the court is relatively well placed to effectively assess the quality of the summing up or the judges decisions on law or procedure but is ill-equipped to look into the surrounding circumstances of the cases. Although it has the power to call for documents, exhibits or other thing connected with the case, this is rarely exercised and it has no facilities for investigating the full range of issues which may be raised at the appeal and is in a weak position to assess the actions and integrity of individuals and institutions such as the police, witnesses, lawyers or forensic experts.

The research findings indicate that the court is reluctant to exercise frequently its full range of powers. Three factors can be identified as affecting the court's approach to reviewing appeals against conviction. These are, firstly, the principle of the sovereignty of the jury which is perceived by the court to limit its role in the criminal justice process, secondly, the limited resources of the appeal system which demands that the court contributes to keeping the 'floodgates' closed and, lastly, the court's limited investigative resources for reviewing individual cases. [See also **[5:8]**]

[9:6] *R v Chalkley and Jeffries* [1998] QB 848

Police officers considered that there was a serious threat that the appellants were planning robberies involving firearms. Having obtained permission from an authorising officer, they arrested the first appellant in connection with an unrelated matter, which allowed them to take his keys and let themselves into his home without his knowledge and to install a listening device in his home. Defence counsel submitted that the evidence of the listening device had been obtained unlawfully and should not have been admitted. The trial judge ruled that the police had acted in good faith and that the evidence was therefore admissible. The appellants changed their plea to guilty. They appealed against conviction on the ground that the judge's ruling was wrong.

The Court of Appeal dismissed the appeals.

Auld LJ (at page 98):

In our view, whatever may have been the use by the Court of the former tests of 'unsatisfactor[iness]' and 'material irregularity' (see the penetrating and engaging analysis of Sir Louis Blom-Cooper QC in '*The Birmingham Six*' and other cases, *Victims of Circumstance*, 1997, Duckworth, Cap V), they are not available to it now, save as aids to determining the safety of a conviction. The Court has no power under the

---

5   See comparison of own-grounds and legally assisted applications for leave to appeal.

substituted section 2(1) to allow an appeal if it does not think the conviction unsafe but is dissatisfied in some way with what went on at the trial. The editors of the third supplement to the current edition of *Archbold* (1997) refer to this as a 'minor, but important, respect' in which the 1995 substitution has done more than just change the wording of the 1968 Act. Whilst we agree that it is an important change, it may not be 'minor', particularly in those cases where, although the Court is of the view that justice has not been seen to be done, it is satisfied that it has been done – that is, that the conviction is safe. All of this is, however, subject to what the Court will make of Article 6(1) of the European Convention on Human Rights, entitling everyone charged with a criminal offence to a fair trial, when it becomes part of our domestic law. Such European Court of Human Rights jurisprudence on the point as there is (see *Murray v United Kingdom* [1996] 22 EHRR 29; *Saunders v United Kingdom* [1996] 1 Cr App Rep 463, [1996] 22 EHRR 313, 342, para 86; *Staines and Morrissey* [1997] 2 Cr App Rep 426, and *Coyne v United Kingdom* 26 September 1997. For a helpful summary of these recent authorities and the light that they may shed on the notion and effect of unsatisfactoriness of a conviction regardless of its safety, see Sir Louis Blom-Cooper QC, op cit pp 74–77) who suggests that procedural unfairness not resulting in unsafety of a conviction may be marked in some manner other than quashing the conviction.

...

We hold that the appellants' appeals against conviction fail because, by their pleas of guilty, they intended to admit and have admitted their guilt, and that their convictions are, therefore, safe.

(and at page 107):

[W]e consider that the proper course is to make our own decision about the fairness of admitting this evidence. We have no doubt whatever about the fairness of doing so. As we have said, there was no dispute as to its authenticity, content or effect; it was relevant, highly probative of the appellants' involvement in the conspiracy and otherwise admissible; it did not result from incitement, entrapment or inducement or any other conduct of that sort; and none of the unlawful conduct of the police or other of their conduct of which complaint is made affects the quality of the evidence. In the circumstances, we can see no basis for concluding that the admission of this evidence would, in the words of section 78, have had such an adverse effect on the fairness of the proceedings that the Judge should not have admitted it. Accordingly, we would dismiss the appeals on that ground also.

[9:7]   *R v Mullen* [1999] 2 Cr App Rep 143

The defendant, who was wanted by the police in England, was brought back to England from Zimbabwe by a Zimbabwean immigration officer in 1988. He was arrested and in due course convicted of conspiracy to cause explosions and sentenced to 30 years' imprisonment. He was refused permission to appeal against sentence. In 1998, he was granted an extension of time and permission to appeal against conviction. Evidence disclosed revealed that the security services in England and Zimbabwe had colluded in order to procure the defendant's deportation from Zimbabwe in circumstances in which he was denied access to a lawyer, contrary to Zimbabwean law and internationally recognised human rights.

Although there was no complaint about the fairness of the trial itself, the Court of Appeal allowed his appeal.

Rose LJ (at page 791):

This court's jurisdiction is statutory and depends for present purposes on the meaning properly to be attributed to the word 'unsafe'. In particular, is it apt to confer jurisdiction to quash a conviction when no complaint is made about the conduct of the trial and the sole ground of appeal is that no trial should have taken place, because of the prosecution's abuse of the process of the court prior to trial?

In *R v Chalkley* [1998] QB 848, 859, Auld LJ, giving the judgment of the court, referred to the amended test as being much simpler than the old test in the Act of 1968 prior to amendment. At page 869 he expressly agreed with a passage in *Archbold, Criminal Pleading, Evidence & Practice*, 1997 edn, 3rd supplement, page 99, paragraph 7-45, which contains the following:

> 'Neither the misconduct of the prosecution, nor the fact that there has been a failure to observe some general notion of "fair play" are in themselves reasons for quashing a conviction ... "unsafe" ... is clearly intended to refer to the correctness of the conviction (ie a conviction is unsafe if there is a possibility that the defendant was convicted of an offence of which he was in fact innocent).'

At first blush, this passage in the court's judgment might be understood as precluding this court from regarding the present conviction as unsafe. But it is to be noted that *R v Horseferry Road Magistrates' Court, ex p Bennett* [1994] 1 AC 42 was not referred to and, in *R v MacDonald* [1998] Crim LR 808 Auld LJ, giving the judgment of a differently constituted division of this court, said:

> 'Before parting with the matter we express some reservation about the jurisdiction of the Court to quash a conviction where there has been an abuse of process of the *ex parte Bennett* kind, that is, where a fair trial was possible and in the event resulted in a safe conviction, but where, on a proper view of the matter, the prosecution should have been stayed as an affront to justice. The question does not arise for our determination in the light of our conclusion that a fair trial was possible and took place, that it was not unfair to try the defendants and that safe convictions resulted. And the matter was only touched on briefly in argument. However, if our view had been that it was an abuse of the *ex parte Bennett* kind, we do not know where we could have found the power to quash what we regard as a safe conviction. The court's jurisdiction is entirely statutory, and the single criterion for interference with a conviction is now – since its recent amendment of section 2 of the Criminal Appeal Act 1968 – its unsafety. The court seems to have assumed such jurisdiction in *R v Bloomfield* [1997] 1 Cr App Rep 125 and *R v Hyatt* (1977) 3 Archbold News 2, but as the editors of *Criminal Law Week* comment in their Issue 2 of 1998, it is far from obvious as to why this should be so. See the observation of Lord Lloyd in *R v Martin* [1998] AC 917, 928–929, and the judgment of this court in *R v Chalkley* [1998] QB 848, 868–870. It may be that a conviction in a trial which should never have taken place is to be regarded as unsafe for that reason. It may be that, despite the statutory basis of the court's jurisdiction, it has also some inherent or ancillary jurisdictional basis for intervening to mark abuse of process by quashing a conviction when it considers that the court below should have stayed the proceeding. Or it may be that the recent amendment to the Act of 1968 has removed the supervisory role of this court over abuse of criminal process

where the affront to justice, however outrageous, has not so prejudiced the defendant in his trial as to render his conviction unsafe. All that is for decision by another court in an appropriate case.'

In the light of these observations, *R v Chalkley* [1998] QB 848 cannot, in our judgment, properly be regarded as having concluded the matter. On the contrary, it is apparent from what he said in the passage cited in *R v MacDonald* [1998] Crim LR 808 that Auld LJ regarded the point as still open. A similar view was expressed in *R v Simpson* [1998] Crim LR 481 by Garland J in the passage cited earlier.

However, in *R v Martin* [1998] AC 917, which was referred to in *R v MacDonald* [1998] Crim LR 808 but not in *R v Simpson* [1998] Crim LR 481, Lord Lloyd of Berwick said [1998] AC 917, 928–929:

'Even if the Courts-Martial Appeal Court had been satisfied that there was an abuse of process, it would still have been necessary for the court to dismiss the appeal, unless persuaded that the conviction was unsafe. For the Courts-Martial Appeal Court is a creature of statute, and has no power to allow appeals save in accordance with section 12(1) of the Courts-Martial (Appeals) Act 1968 as substituted by section 29(1) of and paragraph 5 of Schedule 2 to the Criminal Appeal Act 1995.' (These provisions are identical to those amending section 2 of the Act of 1968 in relation to this court).'

Lord Browne-Wilkinson and Lord Slynn both agreed with Lord Lloyd's reasons for dismissing the appeal. Lord Hope of Craighead said, at page 930:

'... I do not think it can be doubted that the appeal court – in this particular case, the Courts-Martial Appeal Court – have power to declare a conviction to be unsafe and to quash the conviction if they find that the course of proceedings leading to what would otherwise have been a fair trial has been such as to threaten either basic human rights or the rule of law.'

It seems plain that these conflicting observations by Lord Lloyd and Lord Hope were obiter and formed no part of the reasoning which led to the decision in *R v Martin* [1998] AC 917. Furthermore, it does not appear that their Lordships were invited to consider what was said in Parliament when the Act of 1968 was amended or what the pre-amendment practice of this court was, as exemplified by *R v Heston-Francois* [1984] QB 278 and *Attorney-General's Reference (No 1 of 1990)* [1992] QB 630, 643–644. It is also pertinent that Sir John Smith's article in [1995] Crim LR 920 was not before the House of Lords in *R v Martin* [1998] AC 917.

In our judgment the conflicting views expressed in *R v Martin* [1998] AC 917 in themselves afford a sufficient demonstration of the ambiguity of 'unsafe' to permit this court, in accordance with *Pepper v Hart* [1993] AC 593, to have recourse to Hansard. Furthermore, if the construction of Lord Lloyd is correct, it will, with respect, lead to absurdity, which provides a further reason for recourse to Hansard: in relation to a minor offence triable by justices, abuse arguments can lead to redress by judicial review in the Divisional Court, but, in relation to a serious offence tried at the Crown Court, abuse arguments could not lead to appellate success.

Accordingly, we turn to Hansard (HC Debates), 6 March 1995, col 24, the relevant passages from which are conveniently set out in Sir John Smith's article [1995] Crim LR 920, 924. It is unnecessary to rehearse what was said on second reading and in standing committee. But it is apparent that the amended form of section 2 of the Act of 1968 was intended by the Home Secretary, by Lord Taylor of Gosforth CJ and, crucially, by Parliament, to restate the existing practice of the Court of Appeal; although there is nothing to suggest that express consideration was then given by anyone to whether 'unsafe' was apt to embrace abuse of the *Bennett* or any other type. It is common ground that *R v Heston-Francois* [1984] QB 278 and *Attorney-General's Reference (No 1 of 1990)* [1992] QB 630 show the pre-amendment practice of this court, namely that abuse can be a ground for quashing a conviction.

Furthermore, in our judgment, for a conviction to be safe, it must be lawful; and if it results from a trial which should never have taken place, it can hardly be regarded as safe. Indeed the *Oxford English Dictionary* gives the legal meaning of 'unsafe' as 'likely to constitute a miscarriage of justice'.

Sir John Smith's article does not deal with 'unsafe' in relation to abuse, though his commentary on *R v Simpson* [1998] Crim LR 481, raises directly pertinent questions. But, for the reasons which we have given, we agree with his 1995 conclusion that 'unsafe' bears a broad meaning and one which is apt to embrace abuse of process of the *Bennett* or any other kind.

It follows that, in the highly unusual circumstances of this case, notwithstanding that there is no criticism of the trial judge or jury, and no challenge to the propriety of the outcome of the trial itself, this appeal must be allowed and the defendant's conviction quashed.

[9:8]   *R v McIlkenny* (1992) 93 Cr App Rep 287

This is the famous judgment of the Court of Appeal in the 'Birmingham Six' case. In 1975 the appellants were convicted of 21 counts of murder, arising out of the IRA bombing of two pubs in Birmingham in which 21 people were killed and 162 injured. Their appeals against conviction were dismissed. In 1987 the Home Secretary referred the case to the Court of Appeal on the ground that there was fresh scientific evidence and fresh evidence that the appellants had been beaten following their arrests, and this was likewise dismissed. On a second reference in 1990, the court held that the convictions were now unsafe and unsatisfactory, as a result of both the fresh scientific evidence and the fresh investigation into the police evidence. The court stressed that they were saying nothing about the innocence or otherwise of the applicants, and indeed stressed the strengths as well as the weaknesses in the prosecution case.

Lloyd LJ (at page 310):

The Role of the Court of Appeal

Since the present appeal has given rise to much public discussion as to the powers and duties of the Court of Appeal (Criminal Division), and since the Home Secretary has set up a Royal Commission to investigate and report, it may be helpful if we set out our understanding of the present state of the law.

(1)   The Court of Appeal (Criminal Division) is the creature of statute. Our powers are derived from, and confined to, those contained in the Supreme Court Act 1981, the Criminal Appeal Act 1968 and the Criminal Justice Act 1988. We have no inherent jurisdiction apart from statute: see *Jeffries* (1968) 52 Cr App Rep 654, [1969] 1 QB 120, *R v Collins* (1969) 54 Cr App Rep 19, [1970] 1 QB 710 and *DPP v Shannon* (1974) 59 Cr App Rep 250, [1975] AC 717. Thus we have no power to conduct an open-ended investigation into an alleged miscarriage of justice, even if we were equipped to do so. Our function is to hear criminal appeals, neither more or less.

(2)   Just as we have no powers other than those conferred on us by Parliament, so we are guided by Parliament in the exercise of those powers. Thus by section 2(1) of the 1968 Act we are directed to allow an appeal against conviction if, but only if, (a) we think that the conviction is unsafe or unsatisfactory; (b) there has been a wrong decision on a question of law or, (c) there has been a material irregularity. In all other cases we are obliged to dismiss the appeal. Where we allow an appeal, we are directed by section 2(2) to quash the conviction. Where we quash the conviction, the other operates, by virtue of section 2(3) as a direction to the trial court to enter a verdict of acquittal, except where a retrial is ordered under section 7 of the Act. Nothing in section 2 of the Act, or anywhere else obliges or entitles us to say whether we think that the appellant is innocent. This is a point of great constitutional importance. The task of deciding whether a man is guilty falls on the jury. We are concerned solely with the question whether the verdict of the jury can stand.

(3)   Rightly or wrongly (we think rightly) trial by jury is the foundation of our criminal justice system. Under jury trial juries not only find the facts; they also apply the law. Since they are not experts in the law, they are directed on the relevant law by the judge. But the task of applying the law to the facts, and so reaching a verdict, belongs to the jury, and the jury alone. The primacy of the jury in the English criminal justice system explains why, historically, the Court of Appeal had so limited a function. Until 1907, there was no Court of Criminal Appeal at all. If, before then, a point of law arose in the course of a trial, the judge could 'reserve' the point, if he thought fit, for consideration by the Court for Crown Cases Reserved. In the event of the point being decided in favour of the accused, the conviction would be quashed. But there was no right of appeal as such. The Criminal Appeal Act 1907 created the right of appeal for the first time. It also enabled the Court of Criminal Appeal to receive fresh evidence. There was no power to order a retrial, except by way of the writ of venire de novo. But that writ only issued when the trial had been a nullity. There was no general power to order a retrial until the Criminal Appeal Act 1964, and then only in fresh evidence cases. The power has since been greatly extended.

(4)   The primacy of the jury in the criminal justice system is well illustrated by the difference between the Criminal and Civil Divisions of the Court of Appeal. Like the Criminal Division, the Civil Division is also a creature of statute. But its powers are much wider. A civil appeal is by way of re-hearing of the whole cases. So the court is concerned with fact as well as law. It is true the court does not re-hear the witnesses. But it reads their evidence. It follows that in a civil case the Court of Appeal may take a different view of the facts from the court below. In a criminal case this is not possible. Since justice is as much concerned with the conviction of the guilty as the acquittal of the innocent, and the task of convicting the guilty belongs constitutionally to the jury, not to us, the role of the Criminal Division of the Court of Appeal is necessarily limited. Hence it is true to say that whereas the Civil Division of the Court of Appeal has appellate jurisdiction in the full sense, the Criminal Division is perhaps more accurately described as a court of review. In the 1907 Act there was a power to set aside a verdict

if the court thought it unreasonable, or that it could not be supported having regard to the evidence. This power was very narrowly construed. The wording has now been changed. We have power to upset the verdict of a jury on a question of fact if we think a conviction unsafe or unsatisfactory under all the circumstances of the case. These words were substituted by section 4 of the Criminal Appeal Act 1966. We shall return to their meaning later.

(5) Another feature of our law, which goes hand in hand with trial by jury, is the adversarial nature of criminal proceedings. Clearly a jury cannot embark on a judicial investigation. So the material must be placed before the jury. It is sometimes said that the adversarial system leaves too much power in the hands of the police. But that criticism has been met, at least in part, by the creation of the Crown Prosecution Service. The great advantage of the adversarial system is that it enables the defendant to test the prosecution case in open court. Once there is sufficient evidence to commit a defendant for trial, the prosecution has to prove the case against him by calling witnesses to give oral testimony in the presence of the jury. We doubt whether there is a better way of exposing the weaknesses in the prosecution case, whether the witness be a policeman, a scientist or a bystander, than by cross-examination.

(6) A disadvantage of the adversarial system may be that the parties are not evenly matched in resources. As we have seen, one reason why the judge expressed his preference for Dr Skuse was that Dr Black had carried out no experiments to prove his theory. Experiments presumably cost money. Whether Dr Black could have carried out any experiments within the limitation of legal aid, or the time available, we do not know. But the inequality of resources is ameliorated by the obligation on the part of the prosecution to make available all material which may prove helpful to the defence. The later history of the present appeal shows how well the prosecution can perform that obligation.

(7) No system is better than its human input. Like any other system of justice the adversarial system may be abused. The evidence adduced may be inadequate. Expert evidence may not have been properly researched or there may have been a deliberate attempt to undermine the system by giving false evidence. If there is a conflict of evidence there is no way of ensuring the jury will always get it right. This is particularly so where there is a conflict of expert evidence, such as there was here. No human system can expect to be perfect.

(8) Just as the adversarial system prevails at the trial, so also it prevails in the Court of Appeal. It is for the appellants to raise the issues which they wish to lay before the court. Those issues are set out in the grounds of appeal. It will be remembered that at the initial application for leave to appeal, virtually the only issue before the court was the fairness of the summing-up. If the appellants had insisted on raising other issues, they could have done so. The same applies when the case was referred back to the court in 1987. A number of distinguished scientists were called on both sides. But as we have seen, the scientific issues before the court in 1987 were not the same as they are now. Thus nobody suggested in 1987 that Dr Skuse's results could have been due to nitrite contamination from the soap he was using to clean his bowls. Nobody knew that Dr Drayton would modify her view in the light of later scientific research. Nobody knew that the 'contemporaneous' notes taken by DC Woodwiss of the two McIlkenny interviews were written on four different pads of paper. So the issues were very different.

(9) For an adversarial system to work, there must be an adversary. One of our difficulties in the present appeal has been that we have listened to the fresh evidence of Dr Scaplehorn and Dr Baxendale, without the benefit of hearing any cross-examination. We say at once, and as emphatically as we can, that this is not criticism of the Director or Mr Boal. They have acted with perfect propriety. The concluding paragraphs of the Farquharson's Committee's Report on The Role of Prosecuting Counsel, May 1986 (Archbold 43rd ed para 4–47a) deals with prosecution counsel's function in the Court of Appeal in this way:

> 'If prosecution counsel has formed the view that the appeal should succeed he should acquaint the court with the view and explain the reasons for it. If the court disagrees with him counsel is entitled to adhere to his view and is not obliged to conduct the appeal in a way which conflicts with his own judgment. At the same time it remains counsel's duty to give assistance to the court if requested to do so.'

Mr Boal and the DPP had a number of very difficult decisions to take in the abnormal circumstances of the present appeal. Having decided that they could not support the scientific evidence on which the prosecution was based, or the police evidence, it was their duty to. They have since given us every possible assistance. But the effect of their decision was, inevitably, that we have not heard the other side put, if indeed there is another side.

(10) This has led us to consider whether some other system might be devised in the very exceptional class of case, of which this is one, where fresh evidence comes to light long after the conviction. In the ordinary case, not depending on fresh evidence, there is no difficulty. Nor is there any difficulty in fresh evidence cases, where the fresh evidence is discovered soon after the trial. If the evidence is incredible, or inadmissible, or would not afford a ground for allowing the appeal, we decline to receive it. If the fresh evidence surmounts that preliminary hurdle, we first quash the conviction, if we think it unsafe or unsatisfactory, and then order a retrial under section 7 of the Act, if the interests of justice so require. Where new evidence is conclusive, we quash the conviction without ordering a retrial: see *R v Flower* (1965) 50 Cr App Rep 22, [1966] 1 QB 146. There is a view, put forward notably by Lord Devlin in The Judge, that we should always quash a conviction where fresh evidence has been received, since a conviction is bound to be unsafe, or at least unsatisfactory, where it has not been based on all the evidence. But this view did not find favour with the House of Lords in *Stafford and Luvaglio v DPP* (1973) 58 Cr App Rep 256, [1974] AC 878.

The difficulty in fresh evidence cases arises where a retrial is no longer practicable, as in the present case. The difficulty becomes acute when there is no contest. For we then have to make up our own minds whether the convictions are unsafe or unsatisfactory without having the benefit of hearing the evidence tested by cross-examination. Where a retrial is still possible, the quashing of the conviction is, as it were, only the first half of a two stage process. Where a retrial is no longer possible, it is the end of the road. This is not the occasion to offer a solution to the difficulty ourselves. No doubt all these problems will be reviewed by the Royal Commission.

[9:9]   Criminal Justice Act 1988 sections 36; 133

36   Reviews of sentencing

(1)   If it appears to the Attorney General—
- (a)   that the sentencing of a person in a proceeding in the Crown Court has been unduly lenient; and
- (b)   that the case is one to which this Part of this Act applies,

he may, with the leave of the Court of Appeal, refer the case to them for them to review the sentencing of that person; and on such a reference the Court of Appeal may—
- (i)   quash any sentence passed on him in the proceeding; and
- (ii)   in place of it pass such sentence as they think appropriate for the case and as the court below had power to pass when dealing with him.

(2)   Without prejudice to the generality of subsection (1) above, the condition specified in paragraph (a) of that subsection may be satisfied if it appears to the Attorney General that the judge erred in law as to his powers of sentencing or failed to impose a sentence required by section 109(2), 110(2) or 111(2) of the Powers of Criminal Courts (Sentencing) Act 2000.

(3)   For the purposes of this Part of this Act any two or more sentences are to be treated as passed in the same proceeding if they would be so treated for the purposes of section 10 of the Criminal Appeal Act 1968.

(4)   No judge shall sit as a member of the Court of Appeal on the hearing of, or shall determine any application in proceedings incidental or preliminary to, a reference under this section of a sentence passed by himself.

(5)   Where the Court of Appeal have concluded their review of a case referred to them under this section the Attorney General or the person to whose sentencing the reference relates may refer a point of law involved in any sentence passed on that person in the proceeding to the House of Lords for their opinion, and the House shall consider the point and give their opinion on it accordingly, and either remit the case to the Court of Appeal to be dealt with or deal with it themselves; and section 35(1) of the Criminal Appeal Act 1968 (composition of House for appeals) shall apply also in relation to any proceedings of the House under this section.

(6)   A reference under subsection (5) above shall be made only with the leave of the Court of Appeal or the House of Lords; and leave shall not be granted unless it is certified by the Court of Appeal that the point of law is of general public importance and it appears to the Court of Appeal or the House of Lords (as the case may be) that the point is one which ought to be considered by that House.

(7)   For the purpose of dealing with a case under this section the House of Lords may exercise any powers of the Court of Appeal.

(8)   The supplementary provisions contained in Schedule 3 to this Act shall have effect.

(9)   In the application of this section to Northern Ireland—

(a)   any reference to the Attorney General shall be construed as a reference to the Attorney General for Northern Ireland;

(b)   the references to sections 10 and 35(1) of the Criminal Appeal Act 1968 shall be construed as references to sections 10(2) and 33(1) of the Criminal Appeal (Northern Ireland) Act 1980, respectively.

133   Compensation for miscarriages of justice

(1)   Subject to subsection (2) below, when a person has been convicted of a criminal offence and when subsequently his conviction has been reversed or he has been pardoned on the ground that a new or newly discovered fact shows beyond reasonable doubt that there has been a miscarriage of justice, the Secretary of State shall pay compensation for the miscarriage of justice to the person who has suffered punishment as a result of such conviction or, if he is dead, to his personal representatives, unless the non-disclosure of the unknown fact was wholly or partly attributable to the person convicted.

(2)   No payment of compensation under this section shall be made unless an application for such compensation has been made to the Secretary of State.

(3)   The question whether there is a right to compensation under this section shall be determined by the Secretary of State.

(4)   If the Secretary of State determines that there is a right to such compensation, the amount of the compensation shall be assessed by an assessor appointed by the Secretary of State.

(4A) In assessing so much of any compensation payable under this section to or in respect of a person as is attributable to suffering, harm to reputation or similar damage, the assessor shall have regard in particular to—

(a)   the seriousness of the offence of which the person was convicted and the severity of the punishment resulting from the conviction;

(b)   the conduct of the investigation and prosecution of the offence; and

(c)   any other convictions of the person and any punishment resulting from them.

(5)   In this section "reversed" shall be construed as referring to a conviction having been quashed—

(a)   on an appeal out of time; or

(b)   on a reference—

    (i)   under the Criminal Appeal Act 1995; or

    (ii)   under section 263 of the Criminal Procedure (Scotland) Act 1975;
       ...

    (iii)   ...; or

(c)   on an appeal under section 7 of the Terrorism Act 2000.

(6)   For the purposes of this section a person suffers punishment as a result of a conviction when sentence is passed on him for the offence of which he was convicted.

(7)   Schedule 12 shall have effect.

[9:10]   *Monnell and Morris v United Kingdom* (1987) 10 EHRR 205

The two applicants had applied unsuccessfully to the Court of Appeal for leave to appeal against both their convictions and sentences. The Court of Appeal, although neither applicant had been present or represented at the hearing, had ordered that part of the time already spent by the applicants in custody since conviction should not count towards the service of the sentences. The applicants argued that the periods of detention which the court ordered not to count towards their sentence was not covered by any of the categories of permitted detention set out in article 5(1) European Convention on Human Rights (see **[1:9]**), and that the procedure followed did not comply with articles 6(1), (3)(c) and 14. The court held, by a majority of five to two, that there had been no violation of articles 5 or 6, and unanimously that there had been no violation of article 14.

The following extract is taken from the majority judgment (at page 217):

The power of the Court of Appeal to order loss of time, as it is actually exercised, is a component of the machinery existing under English law to ensure that criminal appeals are considered within a reasonable time and, in particular, to reduce the time spent in custody by those with meritorious grounds waiting for their appeal to be heard; this is made patently clear in the 1965 report of the Interdepartmental Committee on the Court of Criminal Appeal and in the two Practice Directions issued by the Lord Chief Justice. In sum, it is a power exercised to discourage abuse of the court's own procedures. As such, it is an inherent part of the criminal appeal process following conviction of an offender and pursues a legitimate aim under sub-paragraph (a) of Article 5(1).

47   It was pointed out in argument that under the law of many of the convention countries detention pending a criminal appeal is treated as detention on remand and a convicted person does not start to serve his or her sentence until the conviction has become final. In such systems, the appellate court itself determines the sentence and, in some of them, exercises a discretion in deciding whether or to what extent detention pending appeal shall be deducted from the sentence. The Delegate of the Commission was of the opinion that such systems, unlike the English system at issue in the present case, would be compatible with Article 5(1).

The difference between the two approaches to sentencing procedures is, however, one of form and not of substance as far as the effect on the convicted person is concerned. Sub-paragraph (a) of Article 5(1), which is silent as to the permissible forms of legal machinery whereby a person may lawfully be ordered to be detailed after conviction, must be taken to have left the Contracting States a discretion in the matter. Sentencing procedures may legitimately vary from Contracting State to Contracting State, whilst still complying with the requirements of Article 5(1)(a). The court considers that the technical and formal difference in the way in which sentencing procedures are arranged in the United Kingdom as compared with other Convention countries is not such as to exclude the applicability of sub-paragraph (a) of Article 5(1) in the present case.

48   In the light of all the foregoing factors, the court finds that there was a sufficient and legitimate connection, for the purposes of the deprivation of liberty permitted under sub-paragraph (a) of Article 5(1), between the conviction of each applicant and the additional period of imprisonment undergone as a result of the loss-of-time order

made by the Court of appeal. The time spent in custody by each applicant under this head is accordingly to be regarded as detention of a person under conviction by a competent court, within the meaning of sub-paragraph (a) of Article 5(1).

49　The applicants at certain points in their pleadings appeared to be arguing that their applications for leave to appeal were not in fact hopeless or frivolous. This was a matter of appreciation coming within the discretion conferred on the Court of Appeal by the terms of section 29(1) of the Criminal Appeal Act 1968. Save in so far as is necessary to review the contested measure of deprivation of liberty for compatibility with the Convention, it is not within the province of the European Court to substitute its own assessment of the facts for that of the domestic courts.

50　More generally, the court is satisfied in the circumstances of the present case as to the lawfulness and procedural propriety of the contested periods of loss of liberty. To begin within, it has been disputed that the relevant rules and procedures under English law were properly observed by the English courts in relation to the making of the loss-of-time orders. Further, contrary to the submissions of the applicants, the court finds that these orders depriving the applicants of their liberty issued from and were executed by an appropriate authority and were not arbitrary.

The contested deprivation of liberty must therefore be found to have been both lawful and effected in accordance with a procedure prescribed by law, as those expressions in Article 5(1) have been interpreted in the court's case law.

51　There has accordingly been no breach of Article 5(1) in the present case in respect of either applicant.

(and at page 223):

In the opinion of the Court, Article 6 required that Mr Monnell and Mr Morris be provided, in some appropriate way, with a fair procedure enabling them adequately and effectively to present their case against the possible exercise to their detriment of the power under section 29(1) of the 1968 Act. The court will accordingly review the procedure followed to ascertain whether this condition was satisfied.

62　To begin with, the principle of equality of arms, inherent in the notion of fairness under Article 6(1), was respected in that the prosecution, like the two accused, was not represented before either the single judge or the full Court of appeal.

The principle of equality of arms is, however, only one feature of the wider concept of fair trial in criminal proceedings; in particular even in the absence of a prosecuting party, a trial would not be fair if it took place in such conditions as to put the accused unfairly at a disadvantage.

63　In this connection, it is to be noted that, pursuant to the legal aid scheme, Mr Monnell and Mr Morris had the benefit of free legal advice on appeal. Counsel who had represented them at the trial advised that there were no reasonable prospects of successfully appealing, but both men chose to ignore this advice and pressed ahead with applications for leave to appeal.

64   They were both also aware that, in the absence of arguable grounds of appeal, to lodge and then to renew their applications for leave to appeal might well result in loss-of-time orders. Warnings to this effect were given in the Forms AA and SJ. Nevertheless and despite the fact that the single judge had refused leave, they renewed their applications to the full court of Appeal on the same grounds as in their original applications.

65   As to the possible manner of presenting their case, the system whereby applications for leave to appeal are lodged and then renewed on official forms meant that Mr Monnell and Mr Morris, like all applicants for leave to appeal, were afforded the opportunity to submit written grounds of appeal.

Admittedly, their ancillary applications to be present before the Court of Appeal were unsuccessful, this being a matter within the discretion of the court. Consequently, neither man was able to formulate oral arguments in person before being penalised by an additional loss of liberty.

However, there is no reason why their written submissions should not have included considerations relevant to exercise of the power to direct loss of time, especially in view of the warnings given to them in Forms AA and SJ as to the importance of legal advice and the consequences of pursuing an application without arguable grounds. Indeed, arguments going to the issue of the unmeritorious character of the application will necessarily have been incorporated in their submissions in support of the grounds of appeal.

In accordance with the usual procedure, when considering Mr Monnell's and Mr Morris's applications, both the single judge and the full Court of Appeal had before them all the relevant papers, including the grounds of appeal, a transcript of the trial and, for Mr Monnell, the social inquiry and psychiatric reports prepared on him.

66   Mr Monnell and Mr Morris, like any applicant for leave to appeal, had the right to instruct counsel to appeal on their behalf and present oral argument at a hearing both before the single judge and the full Court of Appeal.

67   It can be presumed that neither Mr Monnell nor Mr Morris could afford to pay counsel out of his own pocket, and under English law they were not automatically entitled to legal aid for the preparation of the written grounds of appeal or for representation through counsel at an oral hearing. Under paragraph 3(c) of Article 6, they were guaranteed the right to be given legal assistance free only so far as the interests of justice so required. The interests of justice cannot, however, be taken to require an automatic grant of legal aid whenever a convicted person, with no objective likelihood of success, wishes to appeal after having received a fair trial in the first instance in accordance with Article 6. Each applicant, it is to be noted, benefited from free legal assistance both at his trial and in being advised as to whether he had any arguable grounds of appeal. In the court's view, the issue to be decided in relation to section 29(1) of the Criminal Appeal Act 1968 did not call, as a matter of fairness, for oral submissions on behalf of the applicants in addition to the written submissions and material already before the Court of Appeal.

68   In short, the interests of justice and fairness could, in the circumstances, be met by the applicants being able to present relevant considerations through making written submissions.

In coming to this conclusion, the court has also borne in mind that, as the power under section 29(1) is exercised in practice, the maximum loss of time risked is in the order of two months and not the whole of the period spent in custody between conviction and determination by the Court of Appeal. It is true, as the applicants' lawyers stressed before the court, that this practical restraint is not brought to the attention of prospective applicants for leave to appeal. However, in view of all the other considerations prevailing, this shortcoming cannot be decisive for present purposes.

69   Finally, the court has no cause to doubt that the Court of Appeal's decision to refuse the applicants leave to appeal and, further, to impose loss of time was based on a full and thorough evaluation of the relevant factors.

70   Having regard to the special features of the context in which the power to order loss of time was exercised and to the circumstances of the case, the court finds that neither Mr Monnell nor Mr Morris was denied a fair procedure as guaranteed by paragraphs 1 and 3(c) of Article 6. There has accordingly been no breach of either of these provisions of the Convention.

The following extract is taken from the dissenting opinion (of judges Pettit and Spielmann):

I   Article 5(1) of the Convention

As opposed to the majority, we voted for the violation of Article 5(1) of the Convention.

Quite correctly the court considered that formal differences in the judicial process for ordering detention after conviction cannot render Article 5(1) inapplicable.

In our opinion, however, the majority of the court was wrong in concluding that the aforementioned provision was not violated in the present case.

Generally speaking, it should be observed that, quite significantly, the vast majority of the member States of the Council of Europe do not possess a system of loss of time similar to the one submitted to the examination of the court.

As a matter of fact, the aforementioned system as regulated by an Act of 1968 provides that when an application for leave to appeal is rejected the single judge may order part or all of the time spent in custody awaiting the determination of the application not to count towards the prospective appellants' sentence. The same applies when the application is renewed before the full court which, moreover, may order a longer loss of time.

This entails a later date of release.

On a purely humanitarian level one may wonder about the validity of an institution which requires authorisation for the lodging of an appeal providing for sanctions in the case of refusal.

More particularly, this being the system of the respondent State, the court had to inquire whether, in the circumstances of the case, such as institution was compatible with the provisions of the Convention.

The Government submitted that the Court of Appeal merely gives directions as to the manner of execution of the sentences of those who persist in lodging an appeal, which the court itself considers as futile.

We cannot share this reasoning.

Even if we were to accept in principle the system of loss of time, it should have been hedged about with a number of elementary guarantees.

We believe that the impugned legislation is in breach of Article 5.

The time lost may comprise the entire period spent in custody between conviction and rejection of the application for leave to appeal.

Within these limits the competent authority decides according to no fixed criteria and no objective reasons.

In the two cases submitted to the court the loss of time at risk was in the range of 8 and 14 months.

The loss of time ordered was 28 and 46 days.

In practice apparently the average time lost would be 64 days.

What is more serious, however, is that the risk run in theory is of a nature to deter even an innocent person, or someone who considers himself to be innocent, from lodging an appeal.

In fact, as the Government itself recognises, the impugned system is used to dissuade convicted persons in custody from lodging appeals in order not unnecessarily to increase the workload of the court.

In our opinion it is inconceivable that the demands of the administration of the courts (shortage of judges, personnel, etc) should be given pre-eminence in a system of penalties involving deprivation of liberty.

Such a deviation, in the short or medium term, runs the risk of exposing the detained person, or anyone amenable to justice, to an instrument of a criminal policy, which is subject to political variations as to what should be, or should have been, the administration of justice.

In these conditions we concur with the opinion of the overwhelming majority of the Commission that there was a violation of Article 5(1) of the Convention.

In fact, as observed by the Commission, we consider that the period of time ordered not to count towards the applicants' sentences imposed by the trial judge cannot be regarded as forming part of their detention after conviction at first instance. The express terms of the loss of time orders exclude this hypothesis.

Quite correctly the majority of the Commission so concluded (...) bearing in mind the purpose for which the loss of time orders were made, which was unconnected with the original sentences imposed on the applicants or with the offences for which they were convicted.

In our opinion, the periods of detention which have been ordered not to count towards the service of the applicants' sentence cannot be considered as detention coming within the terms of Article 5 of the Convention.

II   Article 6 of the Convention

The court considered, quite wrongly in our opinion, that there was no violation of Article 6 of the Convention.

In fact, even if we were to admit that the impugned system was compatible with Article 5 of the Convention, the additional prison sentence imposed on the two applicants remained the consequence of the refusal of leave to appeal.

In these conditions, we consider that the principle of fair trial would require the applicants to be heard by the competent authorities to enable them to present their arguments in person.

Could one seriously support that a written submission by the applicant – composed in the isolation of a prison – could satisfy the requirements of Article 6?

The importance of an additional prison sentence at stake raises objections to such an argument.

Is it not true that on that score the requirements of Article 6, which were applied in the case of Öztürk – where only a fine was at stake – should also be afforded when several months in prison were in issue?

In accordance with the opinion of the Commission, we consider that the applicants' absence from the determination of their applications for leave to appeal, which resulted in the making of the orders that they lost time in the calculation of their service of sentence, deprived them of a fair hearing in the determination of the criminal charges against them as guaranteed by Article 6(1) and of the right to defend themselves in person as guaranteed by Article 6(3)(c) of the Convention.

We believe that where the liberty of the individual is at stake it is necessary that all decisions are taken in the presence of the person affected in the course of a fully adversarial hearing.

[9:11]   Criminal Justice Act 1972 section 36

36   Reference to Court of Appeal of point of law following acquittal on indictment

(1)   Where a person tried on indictment has been acquitted (whether in respect of the whole or part of the indictment) the Attorney General may, if he desires the opinion of the Court of Appeal on a point of law which has arisen in the case, refer that point to the court, and the court shall, in accordance with this section, consider the point and give their opinion on it.

(2)   For the purpose of their consideration of a point referred to them under this section the Court of Appeal shall hear argument—
 (a)   by, or by counsel on behalf of, the Attorney General; and
 (b)   if the acquitted person desires to present any argument to the court, by counsel on his behalf or, with the leave of the court, by the acquitted person himself.

(3)   Where the Court of Appeal have given their opinion on a point referred to them under this section, the court may, of their own motion or in pursuance of an application in that behalf, refer the point to the House of Lords if it appears to the court that the point ought to be considered by that House.

(4)   If a point is referred to the House of Lords under subsection (3) of this section, the House shall consider the point and give their opinion on it accordingly; and section 35(1) of the Criminal Appeal Act 1968 (composition of House for appeals) shall apply also in relation to any proceedings of the House under this section.

(5)   Where, on a point being referred to the Court of Appeal under this section or further referred to the House of Lords, the acquitted person appears by counsel for the purpose of presenting any argument to the court or the House, he shall be entitled to his costs, that is to say to the payment out of central funds of such sums as are reasonably sufficient to compensate him for expenses properly incurred by him for the purpose of being represented on the reference or further reference; and any amount recoverable under this subsection shall be ascertained, as soon as practicable, by the registrar of criminal appeals or, as the case may be, such officer as may be prescribed by order of the House of Lords.

(5A) Section 20(1) of the Prosecution of Offences Act 1985 (regulations as to scales and rates of payment of costs payable out of central funds) shall apply in relation to this section as it applies in relation to Part II of that Act.

(6)   Subject to rules of court made under section 1(5) of the Criminal Appeal Act 1966 (power by rules to distribute business of Court of Appeal between its civil and criminal divisions), the jurisdiction of the Court of Appeal under this section shall be exercised by the criminal division of the court; and references in this section to the Court of Appeal shall be construed accordingly as references to that division of the court.

(7)   A reference under this section shall not affect the trial in relation to which the reference is made or any acquittal in that trial.

[9:12]   A-G's Reference *(No 3 of 1994)* [1997] 3 All ER 936

The defendant stabbed a young woman, who was to his knowledge pregnant with his child. No injury to the foetus was detected and the defendant pleaded guilty to a charge of wounding the woman with intent to cause her grievous bodily harm. A few weeks after the stabbing, and as a result of it, the woman went into labour and gave birth to a grossly premature child who was considered to have only a 50% chance of survival. At the time of the birth it was clear that, contrary to earlier belief, the knife had penetrated the foetus. The child died 121 days later from a lung condition which was due to her premature birth but unconnected with the knife wound and the defendant was thereafter charged with her murder. At the trial, the judge directed an acquittal on the ground that no conviction for either murder or manslaughter was possible in law. The Attorney General subsequently referred to the Court of Appeal under s 36(1) of the Criminal Justice Act 1972 the questions, inter alia, (i) whether, subject to proof of the requisite intent, the crimes of murder and manslaughter could be committed where unlawful injury was deliberately inflicted to a mother carrying a child in utero where the child was subsequently born alive, existed independently of the mother and then died, the injuries while in utero either having caused or made a substantial contribution to the death, and (ii) whether the fact that the child's death resulted from injury to the mother rather than as a consequence of direct injury to the foetus could remove any liability for murder or manslaughter in those circumstances. The Court of Appeal answered the first question in the affirmative, on the ground that the foetus was to be treated as part of the mother until it had a separate existence of its own, but answered the second question in the negative. On the defendant's application the Court of Appeal referred the points to the House of Lords.

Held – (1) Murder could not be committed where unlawful injury was deliberately inflicted to a mother carrying a child in utero in circumstances where the child was subsequently born alive, enjoyed an existence independent of its mother and thereafter died, and where the injuries inflicted while in utero caused or contributed substantially to the death. Notwithstanding the dependence of the foetus on the mother for its survival until birth and the bond between them, the foetus could not be treated as part of the mother but was a unique organism. Accordingly, although there was no requirement that the person who died should be a person in being at the time the act causing the death was perpetrated, in the absence of an intention on the part of the defendant to injure either the foetus or the child which it would become, the required mens rea for murder was not present; it would be straining the concept of transferred malice too far to apply it in the circumstances since it would require the malice to be transferred not once but twice, namely from the mother to the foetus and from the foetus to the child.

(2) In those circumstances, however, manslaughter could be committed since the requisite mens rea to be proved in a case of manslaughter was an intention to do an act which was unlawful and which all sober and reasonable people would recognise as dangerous, ie likely to harm another person. Provided the defendant intended to do what he did, it was not necessary for him to know that his act was likely to injure the person who died as a result of it or to intend to injure that person. Since, in the instant case, the defendant intended to stab the child's mother and that was an unlawful and dangerous act, it followed that the requisite mens rea was established and although the child was a foetus at that time, on public policy grounds she was to be regarded as coming within that mens rea when she became a living person. Accordingly, the fact that the child's death was caused solely as a consequence of injury to the mother, rather

than injury to the foetus, did not negative any liability for manslaughter, provided the jury were satisfied as to causation.

Decision of the Court of Appeal, Criminal Division [1996] 2 All ER 10 affirmed in part.

Lord Mustill (at page 949):

My Lords, the purpose of this inquiry has been to see whether the existing rules are based on principles sound enough to justify their extension to a case where the defendant acts without an intent to injure either the foetus or the child which it will become. In my opinion they are not. To give an affirmative answer requires a double 'transfer' of intent: first from the mother to the foetus and then from the foetus to the child as yet unborn. Then one would have to deploy the fiction (or at least the doctrine) which converts an intention to commit serious harm into the mens rea of murder. For me, this is too much. If one could find any logic in the rules I would follow it from one fiction to another, but whatever grounds there may once have been have long since disappeared. I am willing to follow old laws until they are overturned, but not to make a new law on a basis for which there is no principle.

Moreover, even on a narrower approach the argument breaks down. The effect of transferred malice, as I understand it, is that the intended victim and the actual victim are treated as if they were one, so that what was intended to happen to the first person (but did not happen) is added to what actually did happen to the second person (but was not intended to happen), with the result that what was intended and what happened are married to make a notionally intended and actually consummated crime. The cases are treated as if the actual victim had been the intended victim from the start. To make any sense of this process there must, as it seems to me, be some compatibility between the original intention and the actual occurrence, and this is, indeed, what one finds in the cases. There is no such compatibility here. The defendant intended to commit and did commit an immediate crime of violence to the mother. He committed no relevant violence to the foetus, which was not a person, either at the time or in the future, and intended no harm to the foetus or to the human person which it would become. If fictions are useful, as they can be, they are only damaged by straining them beyond their limits. I would not overstrain the idea of transferred malice by trying to make it fit the present case.

[9:13]   R v Secretary of State for the Home Department, ex p Bentley [1993] 4 All ER 442

Bentley was hanged in 1952 for murder. The Divisional Court held that the Secretary of State's refusal to recommend a posthumous pardon was unlawful.

Watkins LJ (at page 452):

The CCSU case made it clear that the powers of the court cannot be ousted merely by invoking the word 'prerogative'. The question is simply whether the nature and subject matter of the decision is amenable to the judicial process. Are the courts qualified to deal with the matter or does the decision involve such questions of policy that they should not intrude because they are ill-equipped to do so? Looked at in this way there must be cases in which the exercise of the royal prerogative is reviewable, in our judgment. If, for example, it was clear that the Home Secretary had refused to pardon someone solely on the grounds of their sex, race or religion, the courts would be expected to interfere and, in our judgment, would be entitled to do so.

We conclude therefore that some aspects of the exercise of the royal prerogative are amenable to the judicial process. We do not think that it is necessary for us to say more than this in the instant case. It will be for other courts to decide on a case by case basis whether the matter in question is reviewable or not.

(and at page 454):

In an earlier part of the announcement of the decision, the Home Secretary, it will be recalled, stated that while he personally agreed that Derek Bentley should not have been hanged, he could not simply substitute his judgment for that of the then Home Secretary, Sir David Maxell Fyfe.

We understand the strength of the argument that, despite the fact that a free pardon does not eliminate the conviction, the grant of a free pardon should be reserved for cases where it can be established that the convicted person was morally and technically innocent. Furthermore, the policy of confining the grant of a free pardon to such cases has been followed by successive Secretaries of State for over a century. We therefore propose to set aside any question of a free (or full) pardon and look at the matter afresh.

The facts as disclosed by the contemporary papers are very striking. (1) Christopher Craig who fired the fatal shot, was not executed. (2) The jury recommended mercy in the case of Derek Bentley. (3) Both Mr Philip Allen, who wrote the memorandum dated 16 January 1953, and Sir Frank Newsam, the Permanent Under-Secretary, advised that effect should be given to the jury's recommendation for mercy. (4) The precedents established by the previous cases to which Mr Allen drew attention supported the argument for a reprieve. (5) Tests which had been carried out indicated that Bentley's mental state was 'just above the level of a feebleminded person'. He was aged 19. (6) It seems clear from the memorandum initialled by the Secretary of State dated 22 January 1953 that he consulted Lord Goddard CJ, the trial judge, before making his final decision. It will be remembered that in his letter to the Secretary of State dated 12 December 1952 Lord Goddard CJ had said that he could find 'no mitigating circumstances in Bentley's case'.

It is clear from the affidavit of Mr Wilson that one of the ways in which the prerogative of mercy can be exercised is by the grant of a conditional pardon, whereby the penalty is removed on condition that a lesser sentence is served. Had Bentley been reprieved in 1953, the substitution of a sentence of life imprisonment would have constituted a conditional pardon.

These questions, therefore, arise. (a) Is there any objection in principle to the grant of a posthumous conditional pardon? (b) Was the Home Secretary in error in failing to consider the grant of a conditional pardon in this case?

On the first question it may be objected that a conditional pardon is inappropriate where the full penalty has already been paid. The answer to this objection, however, is that it is an error to regard the prerogative of mercy as a prerogative right which is only exercisable in cases which fall into specific categories. The prerogative is a flexible power and its exercise can and should be adapted to meet the circumstances of the particular case. We would adopt the language used by the Court of Appeal in New Zealand in *Burt v Governor General* [1992] 3 NZLR 672 at 681:

'... the prerogative of mercy [can no longer be regarded as] no more than an arbitrary monarchical right of grace and favour.'

It is now a constitutional safeguard against mistakes. It follows, therefore, that, in our view, there is no objection in principle to the grant of a posthumous conditional pardon whew a death sentence has already been carried out. The grant of such a pardon is a recognition by the state that a mistake was made and that a reprieve should have been granted.

We return to the facts of the present case. We can well understand the decision of the Home Secretary in so far as it constituted a response to a free (or full) pardon. But we are far from satisfied that he gave sufficient consideration to his power to grant some other form of pardon which would be suitable to the circumstances of the particular case. It is true, as the Home Secretary pointed out in the announcement of his decision, that in 1953 the then Home Secretary was working in a different climate of opinion. But, as we have already underlined the facts of this case are very striking. There is a compelling argument that even by the standards of 1953 the then Home Secretary's decision was clearly wrong.

In these circumstances the court, though it has no power to direct the way in which the prerogative of mercy should be exercised, has some role to play. The Home Secretary's decision was directed to the grant of a free pardon. In these circumstances we do not think it would be right to make any formal order nor is this an appropriate case for the grant of a declaration. Nevertheless, we would invite the Home Secretary to look at the matter again and to examine whether it would be just to exercise the prerogative of mercy in such a way as to give full recognition to the now generally accepted view that this young man should have been reprieved.

It was submitted to the court that even a limited form of pardon might lead to a flood of other applications seeking to reopen past convictions. No doubt account has to be taken of such a risk. From our examination of the papers in this case, however, and in the light of our understanding of the broad scope of the prerogative of mercy, we are satisfied that the matter is exceptional and requires further consideration. The decision is, of course, one for the Home Secretary and not for the court, but it seems to us that it should be possible to devise some formula which would amount to a clear acknowledgement that an injustice was done.

[9:14] *Royal Commission on Criminal Justice* (1993) HMSO, Cmnd 2263
(at page 183):

Case for new body

2   In *R v Pinfold* the Court of Appeal held that it had no jurisdiction to entertain a second application for leave to appeal in the same case even where fresh evidence had emerged since the dismissal of the earlier appeal. The Court of Appeal can only

consider such a case again if the Home Secretary uses his power under section 17 of the Criminal Appeal Act 1968 to refer it to the Court of Appeal, when the case is treated for all purposes as an appeal to the court by the convicted person. The power to refer cases in this way is limited to those tried on indictment; it does not include summary convictions by magistrates' courts.

3   If, therefore, an unsuccessful appellant wishes to reopen his or her case in the courts, the Home Secretary must be persuaded to refer it to the Court of Appeal. The only alternative course is to persuade the Home Secretary to recommend to the sovereign that the Royal Prerogative of Mercy be exercised. This alternative, which is described more fully in the next paragraph, is most often used when the case involves a summary conviction in the magistrates' courts. It is very seldom exercised when the option of a reference under section 17 is available, because successive Home Secretaries have been understandably reluctant to reverse a decision of the courts, preferring instead to ask the courts to reconsider the case as the statute envisages. The use of the Royal Prerogative to override convictions on indictment is limited to cases where there are convincing reasons for believing that a person is innocent but a reference to the Court of Appeal is not practicable, for example because relevant material would not be admissible in evidence. The Home Office told us in written evidence that such cases are extremely rare.

4   If the Royal Prerogative of Mercy is exercised by the grant of a free pardon, the effect is that so far as possible the person is relieved of all penalties and other consequences of the conviction. Alternatively, a sentence can be varied so as to give special remission of all or part of the penalty imposed by the court. This may be done for compassionate purposes, for example to give early release to prisoners with terminal illnesses, or in order to reward prisoners who have given exceptional assistance to prison staff, the police, or the prosecuting authorities. The exercise of the Royal Prerogative in this way is not the same as the grant of a free pardon. Nor does the exercise of the Royal Prerogative amount to the quashing of the conviction, even if a free pardon is granted. The conviction stands and can only be quashed by a separate application to the Court of Appeal.

5   The available figures for the number of cases referred by the Home Secretary to the Court of Appeal under section 17 of the Criminal Appeal Act 1968 show that the power is not often exercised. From 1981 to the end of 1988, 36 cases involving 48 appellants were referred to the Court of Appeal as a result of the doubts raised about the safety of the convictions concerned. This represents an average of between 4 and 5 cases a year. In the years 1989–1992, 28 cases involving 49 appellants have been referred, including a number of cases stemming from the terrorist incidents of the early 1970s and inquiries into the activities of the West Midlands serious crimes squad. We were told by the Home Office that it receives between 700 and 800 cases a year which are no longer before the courts and where it is claimed that there has been a wrongful conviction. (The figure for 1992 was 790 of which 634 involved a custodial sentence). Plainly, therefore, a rigorous sifting process is applied, and only a small percentage of cases end in a reference to the Court of Appeal under section 17.

6   There is in theory no restriction on the numbers or categories of cases which the Home Secretary may refer to the Court of Appeal under section 17 since the section gives him discretion to refer cases 'if he thinks fit'. In practice, however, as Sir John May observed in his second report on the Maguire case, the Home Secretary and the civil servants advising him operate within strict self-imposed limits. These rest both upon

constitutional considerations and upon the approach of the Court of Appeal itself to its own powers. The Home Secretary does not refer cases to the Court of Appeal merely to enable that court to reconsider matters that it has already considered. He will normally only refer a conviction if there is new evidence or some other consideration of substance which was not before the trial court. Successive Home Secretaries have adopted this approach, and not only because they have thought that it would be wrong for Ministers to suggest to the Court of Appeal that a different decision should have been reached by the courts on the same facts. They have also taken the view that there is no purpose in their referring a case where there is no real possibility of the Court of Appeal taking a different view than it did on the original appeal because of the lack of fresh evidence of some other new consideration of substance.

7   The effect of this second criterion was examined in depth by Sir John May as part of his inquiry into the case of the Maguires. We cannot do better than quote his conclusion:

> '... there is no doubt that the criterion so defined was and is a limiting one and has resulted in the responsible officials within the Home Office taking a substantially restricted view of cases to which their attention has been drawn ... The very nature and terms of the self-imposed limits on the Home Secretary's power to refer cases have led the Home Office only to respond to the representations which have been made to it in relation to particular convictions rather than to carry out its own investigations into the circumstances of a particular case or the evidence given at trial ... the approach of the Home Office was throughout reactive, it was never thought proper for the Department to become proactive.'

8   Sir John May refers later in his second report on the Maguires to the evidence that he heard from Home Office officials and from a former Home Secretary, Mr Hurd, expressing views on alternative machinery for considering alleged miscarriages of justice. This evidence led him to the conclusion that some alternative machinery was indeed required in place of the existing power of the Home Secretary to refer such cases to the Court of Appeal under section 17 of the Criminal Appeal Act 1968. We set out below our view of what the alternative machinery should be. First, however, we give our reasons for recommending (as we do in paragraph 11 below) the creation of a new body independent of both the Government and the courts to be responsible for dealing with allegations that a miscarriage of justice has occurred.

9   Our recommendation is based on the proposition, adequately established in our view by Sir John May's Inquiry; that the role assigned to the Home Secretary and his Department under the existing legislation is incompatible with the constitutional separation of powers as between the courts and the executive. The scrupulous observance of constitutional principles has meant a reluctance on the part of the Home Office to enquire deeply enough into the cases put to it and, given the constitutional background, we do not think that this is likely to change significantly in the future.

10   We have concluded that it is neither necessary nor desirable that the Home Secretary should be directly responsible for the consideration and investigation of alleged miscarriages of justice as well as being responsible for law and order and for the police. The view that these two heavy responsibilities should be divided was expressed to Sir John May's Inquiry by a former Home Secretary and confirmed in oral evidence to us by the then Home Secretary and two of his predecessors.

11   We recommend therefore that the Home Secretary's power to refer cases to the Court of Appeal under section 17 of the Criminal Appeal Act 1968 should be removed and that a new body should be set up to consider alleged miscarriages of justice, to supervise their investigation if further inquiries are needed, and to refer appropriate cases to the Court of Appeal. We suggest that this body might be known as the Criminal Cases Review Authority. We refer to it in what follows as 'the Authority'.

Role of the authority

12   We recommend that the role of the Authority should be to consider allegations put to it that a miscarriage of justice may have occurred. The applicant's approach to the Authority would normally be made either after his or her conviction had been upheld by the Court of Appeal or after he or she had failed to obtain leave to appeal. In cases which seemed to the Authority to call for further investigation, it would ensure that that investigation was launched. Where the Authority instructed the police to conduct investigations, it would be responsible for supervising the investigation and would have the power to require the police to follow up those lines of inquiry that seemed to it necessary for the thorough re-examination of the case. Where the result of the investigation indicated that there were reasons for supposing that a miscarriage of justice might have occurred, the Authority would refer the case to the Court of Appeal, which would consider it as though it were an appeal referred to it by the Home Secretary under section 17 now. Where, in the Authority's view, the investigation revealed no grounds for such a reference, for example, because it revealed fresh material confirming the correctness of the conviction, an explanation with reasons would be given to the applicant.

Relationships of the authority with government and with Court of Appeal

13   We have already explained why we believe that the Authority should be independent of the Government. It will, however, be necessary for the Government to provide the resources to enable it to operate and a Government Minister will have to be responsible for appointing its members and accounting to Parliament for its activities. We recommend that the legislation which established it gives it operational independence but requires it to submit an annual report to the Minister concerned, who would in turn be required to lay the report before Parliament. The Minister would also be required to answer to Parliament for any suggestion that the Authority was inadequately resourced or not properly constituted for the task it was required to perform. We see these arrangements as necessary in order to ensure that the new system for correcting miscarriages of justice is working properly. We do not see them as compromising its independence.

14   We recommend that the Chairman of the Authority be appointed by the Queen on the advice of the Prime Minister as is done in the cases of Lords Justice of Appeal. Other members might be appointed by the Lord Chancellor. The Home Secretary, as the Minister responsible for criminal justice policy and for law and order, should be responsible for reporting to Parliament for the way in which the new arrangements are implemented.

15   We believe that there are cogent arguments for the Authority to be independent of the Court of Appeal. Their roles are different and, as we have said in the last chapter, we do not think that the Court of Appeal is either the most suitable or the best qualified

body to supervise investigations of this kind. We have recommended in chapter ten that the Court of Appeal should be empowered if it thinks fit to refer cases to the Authority for investigation, and that the Authority should be required to report the outcome of any such investigation to the Court of Appeal. But we do not see the Authority as coming within the court structure. Nor, equally importantly, would it be empowered to take judicial decisions that are properly matters for the Court of Appeal.

16   When, therefore, an investigation is completed whose results the Authority believes should be considered by the Court of Appeal, we recommend that it should refer the case to that court, together with a statement of its reasons for so referring it. It should at the same time provide the court with such supporting material as it believes to be appropriate and desirable in the light of its investigations, and which in its view may be admissible, though without any recommendation or conclusion as to whether or not a miscarriage of justice has occurred. It would be for the Court of Appeal, on receiving a case referred in this way, to treat it as an appeal from the Crown Court. That is to say, it would ensure that the defence and the prosecution received a copy of the statement of reasons and supporting material sent to it, together with any additional material (see paragraph 31) that the Authority thought fit. It would then be for the appellant to present his or her case in whatever manner seemed best. As happens with references by the Home Secretary under section 17 now, it should continue to be open to the appellant to raise before the Court of Appeal any matter of law or fact, or mixed law and fact, as he or she wishes, regardless of whether or not it was included in the papers sent to the court by the Authority. The appellant should also be free to appear before the court if he or she so wishes.

17   As we have explained, we do not see the Home Secretary as continuing to have in general any function in relation to individual cases of miscarriage of justice. We do, however, assume that he or she will retain ministerial responsibility for the exercise of the Royal Prerogative of Mercy. For the reasons that the Home Office gave in oral evidence, and to which we refer above (paragraph 6), it will seldom if ever be necessary or desirable to exercise the Royal Prerogative in cases where it is concluded that a miscarriage of justice may have taken place To do so would be to override the decisions of the courts, whose function it properly is to determine such cases. Nevertheless, we do not entirely rule out the need in the very exceptional case for the Authority to refer the results of its consideration and investigation to the Home Secretary to consider the exercise of the Royal Prerogative. This should only be where the Court of Appeal is unlikely to be able to consider the case under the existing rules.

18   The one category of case that has been drawn to our attention where this might happen is if the Court of Appeal were to regard as inadmissible evidence which seemed to the Authority to show that a miscarriage of justice might have occurred. We have been told by the Home Office in written evidence that these cases are rare and we hope that, following the outcome of the review of the rules of evidence that we have recommended in Chapter Eight, they will become rarer still in the future. We cannot envisage any other circumstances in which the courts would be so far unable to provide a remedy that it ought to be suggested to the Home Secretary that he should recommend the exercise of the Royal Prerogative. There may, however, be unforeseeable circumstances where the need might arise. We therefore recommend that the possible use of the Royal Prerogative be kept open for the exceptional case. We emphasise, however, that it is undesirable for the courts to be deprived of powers to quash a conviction where the evidence, whatever its status, seems clearly to show that the appellant is innocent. We therefore, as we have already said, attach great importance to the Law Commission's review of the rules of evidence which we have recommended.

19   The primary function of the Authority will be to consider and if necessary investigate cases which have already passed through the criminal justice system and in which the right of appeal has been exercised. An applicant who is told by the Authority that it will not intervene in his or her case should always be free to try again, although he or she is likely to need to present flesh evidence or argument to stand any better chance of success. We therefore do not believe that there should be any right of appeal from the Authority's decisions to investigate or not to investigate the cases put to it and to refer or not to refer them to the Court of Appeal. In our view, the Authority's decisions should also not be subject to judicial review. We therefore recommend that there should be neither a right of appeal nor a right to judicial review in relation to decisions by the Authority, but that it should be free to consider a case more than once if that seems in the circumstances to be an appropriate course.

Composition and accountability of the authority

20   The Authority should consist of several members, the precise numbers depending on its workload at any particular time. Not all need be full-time. We do not favour a single person, however well qualified and eminent, filling the role on the model of the ombudsman, since we believe that the consideration of possible miscarriages of justice will benefit from bringing to bear several different points of view. Both lawyers and lay persons should be represented. We recommend that the Chairman should be chosen for his or her personal qualities rather than for any particular qualifications or background that he or she may have. We recommend, however, given the importance of the Authority being seen to be independent of the courts in the performance of its functions, that the Chairman should not be a serving member of the judiciary.

[9:15]   Criminal Appeal Act 1995 sections 8; 13

8   The Commission

(1)   There shall be a body corporate to be known as the Criminal Cases Review Commission.

(2)   The Commission shall not be regarded as the servant or agent of the Crown or as enjoying any status, immunity or privilege of the Crown; and the Commission's property shall not be regarded as property of, or held on behalf of, the Crown.

(3)   The Commission shall consist of not fewer than eleven members.

(4)   The members of the Commission shall be appointed by Her Majesty on the recommendation of the Prime Minister.

(5)   At least one third of the members of the Commission shall be persons who are legally qualified; and for this purpose a person is legally qualified if—
    (a)   he has a ten year general qualification, within the meaning of section 71 of the Courts and Legal Services Act 1990, or
    (b)   he is a member of the Bar of Northern Ireland, or solicitor of the Supreme Court of Northern Ireland, of at least ten years' standing.

(6)   At least two thirds of the members of the Commission shall be persons who appear to the Prime Minister to have knowledge or experience of any aspect of the criminal justice system and of them at least one shall be a person who appears to him to have knowledge or experience of any aspect of the criminal justice system in Northern Ireland; and for the purposes of this subsection the criminal justice system includes, in particular, the investigation of offences and the treatment of offenders.

(7)   Schedule 1 (further provisions with respect to the Commission) shall have effect.

13   Conditions for making of references

(1)   A reference of a conviction, verdict, finding or sentence shall not be made under any of sections 9 to 12 unless—
- (a)   the Commission consider that there is a real possibility that the conviction, verdict, finding or sentence would not be upheld were the reference to be made,
- (b)   the Commission so consider—
    - (i)   in the case of a conviction, verdict or finding, because of an argument, or evidence, not raised in the proceedings which led to it or on any appeal or application for leave to appeal against it, or
    - (ii)   in the case of a sentence, because of an argument on a point of law, or information, not so raised, and
- (c)   an appeal against the conviction, verdict, finding or sentence has been determined or leave to appeal against it has been refused.

(2)   Nothing in subsection (1)(b)(i) or (c) shall prevent the making of a reference if it appears to the Commission that there are exceptional circumstances which justify making it.

CHAPTER TEN

Sentence Management

The sentenced offender is more vulnerable to the abuse of power than are most people. A variety of agencies, with different powers, may well be involved in the supervision and management of their sentence, usually out of the view of the public. In our case study, Gerry Good has been sentenced to three years in prison. Both the Probation and Prison Services will be involved in the management of his sentence. The purpose of this chapter is to raise questions about the powers and accountability of those who have such control over the lives of sentenced offenders. It provides only examples, not a definitive account, of the powers exercised by different bodies within the penal system. Thus, by way of example, whilst most offenders are fined, fine enforcement by magistrates' courts – which can result in a fine defaulter serving a sentence of imprisonment – is not dealt with here.

Two developments in recent years should perhaps be noted at the outset. The first is an increase in procedural openness. We will see in this chapter that sentence plans are often discussed with offenders and that procedures governing release from prisons or hospital are much more open than they were a decade or so ago. A fundamental question is whether this increased openness has led to increased substantive justice, or whether it sometimes disguises potential and real injustices. Procedural fairness does not necessarily lead to fairer outcomes.

Secondly, there is increasing co-operation between different agencies, and a commitment by government to managing criminal justice agencies through performance indicators, audits, framework and strategy documents, and a myriad of other 'performance tools'. Indeed, co-operation is inevitable at the post-sentence stage, where the different agencies are increasingly interdependent. The parole and supervision requirements of the Criminal Justice Act 1991 increased the need for a formal and standardised system of sentence planning. The importance of such co-operation was recognised in the Woolf Report [10:1], which examined the causes of riots in several prisons in 1990 and on whose recommendation a national Criminal Justice Consultative Council, and

24 area committees, were set up to discuss matters affecting more than one agency. The membership of these committees includes representatives of the police, Probation Service, CPS, Prison Service, judges, magistrates and the legal profession. From 2003 the CJCC becomes the Criminal Justice Council and the area Committees are now 42 local Criminal Justice Boards. It is difficult to assess the impact of these bodies: whilst they must indeed open up channels of communication, they may, for example, lead to a greater blurring of the lines of accountability.

Later in this chapter we highlight the unclear division of responsibility between the Probation and Prison services, which led the government to consider moving towards a fused 'correctional' service. The government published a stream of reports in 1998 and 1999 (*Joining Forces to Protect the Public*, the *Prisons Probation Review* and the *Correctional Policy Framework*, for example), which led to the creation of a National Probation Service for the first time (see **[10:6]**). The promotion of Martin Narey from director-general of the Prison Service to 'Commissioner for the Correctional Services' in 2003 may lead to much closer working practices and perhaps ultimately to fusion.

Hedderman's study of joint working in panel assessment schemes **[10:2]** provides an analysis of some of the difficulties of joint working. While, at one level, Hedderman's work is a study of best practice in inter-agency co-operation, at another level, we should be concerned to monitor the quality and accountability of the panel's own decision making since it is clearly having a significant impact on magistrates' decision making. Richardson **[10:3]** also shows the extent to which the legal process fails to protect the interests of prisoners and patients with mental disabilities. The extracts included here summarise her concerns that decisions that implement only loosely defined policies are themselves inadequately regulated. Whilst this book is not dealing in any detail with youth justice, the creation of youth offending teams and the Youth Justice Board (see the Crime and Disorder Act 1998, ss 37–42) raise similar questions: are the due process values emphasised in the first chapter of this book adequately upheld?

Three of the agencies discussed in this chapter play a significant role in implementing the early release schemes. All sentences are now in effect partially suspended sentences, served partly in prison and partly in the community, since the Criminal Justice Act 1991, s 40 **[10:4]** makes it clear that all prisoners who commit an imprisonable offence after release but before the end of their original sentences run the risk of being returned to prison to complete their sentence.

Those sentenced to less than twelve months' imprisonment are eligible for automatic unconditional release at the halfway point in their sentence. Prisoners are then at risk of being returned to serve the rest of their sentence if they are convicted of a further imprisonable offence before their original sentence has fully expired, but they are not subject to compulsory supervision. Those sentenced to between twelve months and four years are released at the halfway point on automatic *conditional* release. They are supervised on licence, by a probation officer, until the point where three-quarters of their sentence has passed. The Parole Board is only involved with the release of those prisoners sentenced to more than four years, who become eligible for *discretionary* conditional release at the halfway point. If early release is not granted, these prisoners are released automatically after two-thirds of their sentence has been served. They then remain under supervision until the three-quarters point in their sentence, as above. Some sex offenders remain on licence until the end of their sentence on the recommendation of the trial judge. The system applicable to life sentence prisoners will be described in (iii) below, which looks at the Parole Board.

(i) The Probation Service

Probation services were set up by the Probation of Offenders Act 1907. Before that, volunteer 'police court missionaries' had worked with offenders, using religion and moral education in an attempt to help people turn away from crime. The 1907 Act encouraged courts of summary jurisdiction to appoint probation officers to 'advise, assist and befriend' offenders, a service to be funded by local authorities. The Criminal Justice Act 1925 made it mandatory for every criminal court to appoint a probation officer. The duties of the 54 separate probation services were laid down in various pieces of legislation, consolidated in the Probation Service Act 1993. However, the Criminal Justice and Court Services Act 2000 **[10:5]** created a unified system, the National Probation Service, based on 42 local areas, matching police areas.

Probation officers have two main roles: the provision of a service of social information and advice to the courts (and also to the CPS); and the supervision and rehabilitation of offenders in the community.

The Criminal Justice Act 1991 required sentencers to consult a pre-sentence report before sentencing someone to imprisonment, but this requirement was watered down by the Criminal Justice Act 1993: the court has a discretion to dispense with a report where it is satisfied that it can properly pass sentence without one. A pre-sentence report provides general information about an offender's background and some general circumstances surrounding the commission of the offence. In the past, the emphasis might have been on their family circumstances, medical and psychiatric health, and employment situation, but today this information is directed towards assessing risk. A report on Gerry Good might look something like this.

PRE-SENTENCE REPORT

Prepared for: CAMFORD CROWN COURT   Date: 1 June 2003

Concerning:

Name: Gerry GOOD   Date of Birth: 20.6.60

Address: Age: 42 years

Petty Sessions Area: Camford

Offences: Grievous Bodily Harm

This is a Pre-Sentence Report as defined in the Criminal Justice Act 1991, s 3(5). It has been prepared in accordance with the requirements of the Probation Service National Standards. Its contents are confidential and have been prepared for the hearing above only.

INTRODUCTION

1   Sources of Information: In the preparation of this report I have: Interviewed Mr Good on one occasion at the Probation Office. Seen pre-sentence disclosure information. Spoken to the defence solicitor.

OFFENCE ANALYSIS

2   Mr Good was remarkably frank in discussing the circumstances surrounding the offence with me and it is my assessment that he genuinely has little recall of what actually happened. His responses struck me as confused, rather than evasive. He does deny the seriousness of the offence and, although this may indicate a failure to take responsibility, it is also a reflection of the fact that he did not think he had committed an offence. Mr Good acknowledges that the major contributory factor behind this offence is his dependency on alcohol – in particular he tells me he had been drinking for most of the day before the offence took place.

3   Clearly the court will view this offence as particularly serious, not only because of its nature, but because it was committed whilst Mr Good was already subject to a Community rehabilitation Order imposed by Bleakham magistrates' court on 6 April 1999 for offences of theft. That Order had a condition attached that Mr Good obtained treatment from the Alcohol Dependency Unit in Camford for his addiction. This offence therefore took place despite Mr Good's access to community resources relevant to his offending. It is my view that the circumstances in this case suggest that a further community disposal would not be effective in preventing re-offending. CPS information suggests that the victim required hospital treatment following the offence. CPS information could not, of course, capture the long-term psychological impact of such an offence, even though physical recovery may have been good. In my view Mr Good minimised the effect of the offence on the victim.

OFFENDER ASSESSMENT

4   Mr Good has lived in this area for two years. He has led an unsettled and chaotic life for the past seven years, since his marriage broke up, when he became homeless. Mr Good does have occasional contact with this mother and with his daughter, who still live in the north of England. He has had no contact with his ex-partner for six years. He has had occasional relationships with women in recent years. He tells me that he had hoped that the victim of the offence was going to become his new partner.

5   Mr Good's criminal record reveals that he has previous convictions for dishonesty and minor offences of violence. The court has imposed a number of disposals aimed at reducing the risk of re-offending. None of these has been successful. Mr Good acknowledges that until and unless he addresses his dependency on alcohol he remains at risk of re-offending. At this stage I have not completed a detailed assessment of his attitude to women. His response to supervision has not been positive. He has reported when required during some of the current Order but when he has been drinking heavily he has neglected to fulfil these requirements. Furthermore he has not attended all the appointments offered to him by the Alcohol Dependency Unit.

6   At the time of his arrest, Mr Good was not working and was in receipt of Job Seekers Allowance. The fact that he has not been in employment for more than four years indicates further the effect his addiction to alcohol has had on his ability to lead a responsible lifestyle. He has been offered employment advice by a partnership agency of the Probation Service but did not sustain or take up the advice he was offered.

ASSESSMENT OF THE RISK OF HARM TO THE PUBLIC AND THE LIKELIHOOD OF RE-OFFENDING

7   It is apparent that the defendant deeply regrets what happened between him and the victim of the attack that evening. He considered her a friend, and is deeply hurt that she has, in his eyes, initiated proceedings against him. Although he acknowledges his dependency on alcohol (and occasionally drugs) he failed to complete a treatment programme at the Alcohol Dependency Unit in Camford. My impression is that he has considerable long term personal issues which he attempts to disguise by consuming alcohol. The pessimism he expresses about the future is a reflection of the effects that his long term drinking patterns have had on his ability to take responsibility for his own actions. Until Mr Good addresses his addiction he remains at risk of causing serious harm to members of the public.

8   He has previous offences for violence and the Probation Service assessment system assesses him as of medium risk of re-offending. He is at high risk of causing harm if he were to be in a similar situation to the one he was in when he committed this offence.

CONCLUSION

9   The court will have little option but to give consideration to a custodial sentence given the seriousness of the offence. Such a sentence would protect members of the public from further harm for its duration but it is unlikely that Mr Good would be offered anything other than a nominal introductory programme on the subject of alcohol dependency within the custodial setting. Therefore the likelihood is that he would be released posing a similar risk of harm and re-offending to that which he poses currently.

10   Should the court wish to give consideration to a community sentence the options are as follows:

FINE OR DISCHARGE: Neither of these disposals would address the seriousness of the offence.

CURFEW ORDER: I do not think that a curfew order would substantially affect the risk of harm or re-offending.

COMMUNITY PUNISHMENT ORDER: This would enable Mr Good to pay back the community for some of the distress he has caused but it would not address his offending patterns.

COMMUNITY REHABILITATION ORDER: This is my primary proposal. If the court were able to give consideration to a community sentence my proposal is that Mr Good is made the subject of a Community Rehabilitation Order with a condition that he attend the general offending behaviour programme. In the course of that programme he would examine his own responses and attitudes to hopefully change his current methods of solving issues. Specific alcohol-related intervention could be sequenced following completion of the initial group work programme.

During this Order Mr Good would be expected to:

Report weekly to his supervising officer
Attend the group work programme
Be assessed for additional alcohol-related work
Look at victim and relapse prevention issues
Be assessed for employment/training

If a custodial sentence is inevitable then Mr Good will be assessed for suitability for this programme as part of his licence conditions on release.

The statutory responsibility for enforcing community penalties is with the Probation Service. Thus, if Gerry Good had been sentenced to a community penalty, his main contact would have been with a probation officer. The initial appointment with the supervising officer is, whenever possible, held within five working days of the making of the order, and the appointment is made before the offender leaves court. At the first meeting, the supervising officer gives the offender written information setting out what can be expected from the Probation Service, and what is expected of the offender. They are given a copy of the court order, with instructions to comply with its terms, and within two weeks a written supervision plan should have been drawn up. National Standards – first introduced in 1990, tightened in 1995 and re-issued in 2000 [10:6] – suggest that at least twelve appointments will be made within the first twelve weeks of supervision, normally scheduled to take place weekly. There will normally be a home visit made within the first twelve weeks of the order. Six appointments will be made within the second twelve weeks, after which appointments may reduce to monthly contact.

A probation officer is normally required to take breach action after no more than 'one unacceptable failure' by the offender to comply with the order (whereas the 1990 standards allowed 'three instances of failure'). This change reflects the pressure to move away from a welfare to a punishment model. The other great pressure is the financial squeeze. The average number of people supervised per main grade officer has risen every year since 1992, from 20.7 in 1992 to 34.6 in 1998, to 40.7 in 2001 (Probation Statistics, 2001). This reflects both rising caseloads and a falling or stable number of fully trained officers. A useful overview of current trends is provided in Raynor [10:7]. Worrall [10:8] argues passionately for what might be seen as 'traditional' probation values (advice, assistance and befriending), rejecting the prevalent view that community sentences are simply alternatives to imprisonment.

Probation hostels and bail hostels are normally run by probation staff, although there are also some 'approved' hostels (run by voluntary bodies, but approved by the Home Office to receive offenders), which may have no probation officers on the staff. However, the number of available beds in hostels has been declining since the early 1990s, as a number of hostels have closed. Many probation orders require the offender's full-time attendance on programmes at day centres, for up to a maximum of 60 days, mostly specifically related to drug and alcohol education schemes or to addressing offending behaviour. These raise important issues about the ideal and operation of rehabilitation. For those of us who would welcome less use of imprisonment, the shortage of probation hostels remains a constant concern.

Probation officers are increasingly involved in the management of the sentences of imprisoned offenders. In Gerry Good's case, he will be allocated to a supervising probation officer at the start of his sentence, and this officer should be fully involved in devising any sentence plan. Since Gerry comes within the automatic conditional release scheme, his supervising officer has to provide a pre-discharge report at least one month before release. This will include recommendations to the prison governor on any extra licence conditions felt to be necessary, and will give instructions to Gerry Good on reporting once he is released from custody. After release, if the supervising officer wishes to add or delete a licence condition during the supervision period, they will have to apply to the prison establishment from which Gerry was discharged. If the request is approved, the prison issues a new licence (in duplicate) to the supervising officer.

This scheme has been running since 1993, but problems with the effective flow of information between the Probation Service, Social Services departments, the police and the Prison Service remain. What happens if the different bodies disagree: if the governor imposes conditions that the probation officer believes to be unduly severe, are they obliged to bring breach proceedings? Does the court in such circumstances have to decide if the condition was reasonable? The picture has been complicated by the introduction of home detention curfew orders by the Crime and Disorder Act 1998. The prison governor may release short-term prisoners on a 'home detention' curfew licence (enforced by electronic monitoring or 'tagging'). Initially this could be for up to two months before the normal date of release, but it was later increased to three months. The Release of Short-term Prisoners on Licence (Amendment of Requisite Period) Order 2003 (SI No 2003/1602), which came into force in July 2003, increased the period of home detention curfew to 135 days. It is clear from the home detention curfew statistics that the power to release early in this way is exercised differently from prison to prison. It obviously makes a mockery of the precise calculation of short sentences by trial judges – now, anyone sentenced to, say, 18 months, may be released at some unpredictable time between five and nine months.

The probation officer is surrounded by a bewildering amount of guidance: the Probation Rules have over the years been supplemented by Home Office circulars, Chief Probation Officer (CPO) letters, letters from HM Inspectorate of Probation, letters from the Probation Training Unit, probation circulars, guides and so on. The creation of the National Probation Service is leading to greater clarity (see *A New Choreography: the Probation Service's Strategic Framework 2001–04*, which sets out six 'stretch objectives', including improving the performance management framework).

Clearly probation officers require discretionary powers: they are often managing difficult people in a problematic environment. It is not easy to monitor whether, for example, probation practice is non-discriminatory, as required by the Criminal Justice Act 1991, s 95 **[1:10]**. However, as central players within the system, they may serve to reinforce the bias evident elsewhere. For example, Chapter Six included an extract from Eaton's study of the treatment of women by magistrates **[6:10]**. Her (1986) book concludes that 'the practices of probation officers serve to disadvantage women by an endorsement of a model of family life which involves the oppression and exploitation of women' (at page 61).

The Home Office currently encourages an increased role for the voluntary and private sectors in the supervision of offenders. Whilst national standards stress the need for effective liaison with independent-sector agencies (see **[10:6]**), considerable uncertainty surrounds issues of accountability when anything goes wrong. A percentage of a probation service's annual budget (at present 5%) must be earmarked to be spent on 'private and voluntary sector' initiatives, which brings issues of accountability very much to the fore.

(ii) The Prison Service

What happens when Gerry is sent to prison? He is taken first to a local prison, where, as a short-term prisoner, he may serve the whole of his sentence. Other-wise, during the initial period of assessment, the observation, classification and allocation units of the prison decide on a classification for him, based on the crimes committed and the reports made on him by staff during the period of assessment. This determines to which prison he is allocated. Category A pris-oners are those whose escape would be highly dangerous to the public; category B are those for whom the highest degree of security is not necessary but for whom escape must be made very difficult; category C are those who cannot be trusted in open conditions but who do not have the ability or resources to make a determined effort to escape; and category D are those who can reasonably be trusted to serve their sentences in open conditions. A review of categorisation is carried out annually as part of sentence planning and as an incentive to good behaviour. Since this categorisation decision has a direct impact on the date of a prisoner's ultimate release, the Divisional Court in *R v Secretary of State for the Home Department, ex p Duggan* [1994] 3 All ER 277 held that, when catego-risation is reviewed, the gist of reports on which the decision is based should be given to the prisoner, as well as reasons for the decision. A category A prisoner may even have the right to an oral hearing (see *R (Williams) v Secretary of State for the Home Department* [2002] EWCA Civ 498 [2002] 4 All ER 872).

It is beyond the scope of this book to look in detail at the profile of the prison population, and life in prison. Students wanting a picture of prison conditions should read the inspection reports of HM Chief Inspector of Prisons. Better still, arrange to spend some time in a prison (voluntarily!). There are five main types of prison: local prisons (all closed establishments); training prisons; young offender institutions; remand centres; and dispersal prisons (high-security prisons where prisoners are sent to serve long sentences). There are currently twelve prisons for women and, of those, four hold women in only a part of the (otherwise male) prison. There are a small number of prisons with mother and baby units, but there are restrictions on how long young children can remain with their mothers in these institutions. An increasing number of prisons have several functions: not only do male prisons have small units for women, some adult prisons have a wing for young offenders, and training prisons may have a section for remand prisoners.

The riots in a number of prisons in April 1990, led to an investigation conducted by Lord Justice Woolf and Judge Stephen Tumim. Their report **[10:1]** painted a depressing picture and stressed the need for greater 'justice' within prisons. Some issues are only skimmed over by Woolf: for example, the over-representation of black prisoners in the prison populations.

Percentage of prison population from ethnic minorities

	Male	Female
1990	15%	23%
1998	18%	24%
2001	21%	26%

Source: Prison Statistics 2001, Chapter 6

An extract from Genders and Player **[10:9]** illustrates their research findings in three institutions. They looked in particular at four areas: disciplinary proceedings; the writing of assessments; the allocation of accommodation; and the allocation of jobs and training courses. They concluded by considering stumbling blocks to future improvement and suggesting reforms that may help to alleviate the most pressing problems. The problems facing women prisoners – partly caused, ironically, by their under-representation in the prison population – are not discussed in the Woolf Report, perhaps because the riots did not involve women prisoners. (See also HM Inspector of Prisons 1997 Thematic Review of Women in Prison, briefly extracted at **[1:13]**, and Eaton (1993)).

As a result of the 1990 riots and the Woolf Report that followed it **[10:1]**, there were significant changes in the complaints and disciplinary procedures in prisons. Each prison has an Independent Monitoring Board (until 2003 these were known as Boards of Visitors), composed of lay volunteers, whose prime duty is to act as a watchdog on the prison, with each member having free access to the prison, prisoners and prison records. A prisoner can now formally complain, either orally to the landing officer or the governor, or in writing to the governor or the Independent Monitoring Board. Another Woolf recommendation – that there should be an independent adjudicator at the apex of the system – resulted in the appointment of a Prison Ombudsman. He became the Prisons and Probation Ombudsman in 2001, but unsurprisingly his caseload remains dominated by complaints from those in prison rather than those under the supervision of the Probation Service.

The prison disciplinary system was also reformed in 1992. Until then, the Board of Visitors undertook adjudications over disciplinary matters within the prison. Woolf recommended that those responsible for monitoring conditions should not be responsible for discipline. Since then, the most serious offences against prison discipline, which are also serious criminal offences in themselves, are referred to the police with a view to prosecution in the criminal courts. In 1992, governors were given the power to deal with other offences themselves and to award up to 28 days' (increased to 42 in 1994) deferred release, known as ADAs, or 'additional days awarded'. The European Court of Human Rights, in *Ezeh and Connors v United Kingdom* (2002) 35 EHRR 691, held that disciplinary proceedings constituted criminal proceedings for the purposes of European Convention on Human Rights, art 6 **[1:9]**, notwithstanding their classification as disciplinary proceedings. Therefore, prisoners not only had a right to legal representation, but the governor was not an 'independent and impartial tribunal'. As a result the Prison (Amendment) Rules 2002 (SI 2002/2116) have changed the disciplinary process such that serious charges, which may result in ADAs, are referred to an independent adjudicator (normally a district judge). Also controversial are the administrative 'sanctions' available to the governor, such as the incentives and earned privileges scheme, segregation or transfer to another prison to maintain discipline.

English prisons in recent years have suffered dreadfully from overcrowding. There was some optimism in the early 1990s that the reforms of the Criminal Justice Act 1991 would lead to a reduction in the total number of prisoners. However, the changes in release procedures and the continuing pressure on judges to treat 'serious' offenders 'seriously' means that there are an increasing number of long-term prisoners serving increasingly longer sentences. The number of prisoners has risen to over 73,000 by the summer of 2003.

Average prison population

AVERAGE POPULATION IN CUSTODY

(*) Including non-criminal prisoners

Source: Prison Statistics 2001, Fig 1.1 (Cm 5743)

The Woolf Report **[10:1]** adversely commented on the poor regimes in many local prisons and remand centres: how much has this improved in the last decade? The regime within prison is often tedious and unconstructive. Prisoners are paid derisory wages and have little incentive to work productively. Educational and work facilities are squeezed in times of financial stringency. In an attempt to improve performance, the Prison Service now follows Key Performance Indicators (see the Prison Service's annual corporate plan). Of course, slavish adherence to such indicators can have a negative effect: perhaps, for example, an emphasis on unlocking prisoners without a corresponding rise in purposeful activities contributes to an increased number of assaults in prison. However, there can be no doubt that the current political emphasis on reducing offending has led to greater interest on 'what works' in prison, and much greater emphasis is being put on suitable courses, such as the Sex Offender Treatment Programme and other courses designed to encourage prisoners to confront their offending behaviour. However, the inevitable resources problem arises: budgets are limited, and the prison population goes ever upwards (see Morgan (2002)).

Clearly, prisoners are in the hands of the prison authorities (and their fellow prisoners) and are vulnerable to the abuse of power. The Prison Act 1952 **[10:10]** lays down the general duties of the prison authorities, and authorises the Home Secretary to make rules for the management of prisons. The Prison Rules for adult prisoners date from 1964, and are regularly amended; the Young Offender Institution Rules are similar to the Prison Rules. The Rules rarely lay down specific rights, but as Richardson **[10:3]** points out, they leave wide discretion to prison governors. Should breaches of the Prison Rules provide the basis for an action for breach of statutory duty? The courts have been reluctant to go this far: the House of Lords in *Hague* **[10:11]** overruled two different decisions of the Court of Appeal, which had allowed prisoners' claims for false imprisonment, based on principles of 'residual liberty' and 'intolerable conditions'. However, this does not mean that prisoners are without rights. The ordinary civil and criminal law applies in prison, even though it may be difficult to enforce. Judicial review is also an avenue available to the prisoner, though Loughlin (1993) warns that we should not assume that 'a greater degree of legalism automatically leads to a better or more enlightened system' (at page 50). Throughout the 1990s the number of applications for judicial review by prisoners has increased, though the breadth of the powers of the prison authorities has meant that the vast majority are unsuccessful. The cry for enforceable minimum standards and a new Prison Act will not disappear (see, for example, Livingston and Owen (1999) and the Prison Reform Trust). The Human Rights Act 1998 **[1:9]** is already having an impact in this area. As Lord Steyn said in *R (Daly) v Secretary of State for the Home Department* [2001] UKHL 26, [2001] 2 AC 532, the intensity of review in a public law case will depend on the subject matter in hand: 'In law, context is everything'.

The present emphasis on inter-agency co-operation, discussed above, extends into prisons. Home Office Circular 64/86 'Prison Throughcare – Shared Working' emphasised the responsibility of prison staff, and of probation officers seconded to prisons, to work in co-ordination under the leadership of their respective services with a focus on stated 'throughcare' objectives and with a commitment to co-ordination at regional level. The Prison Probation Review (1998) then signalled much closer working, and now the creation of the National Probation Service will doubtless lead to yet closer links.

In 1993 the Prison Service moved to executive agency status within the Home Office, and is now run by a management board, chaired by a director-general who is directly accountable to the Home Secretary. Whilst agency status may have devolved more decision-making powers to individual prison governors, the audit and performance culture which has developed has also led to more central control. The management team comprises governor grades, and the wider staff group may include a variety of specialist departments such as the probation department, education department, a chaplaincy and the healthcare service for prisoners. Does agency status weaken the political accountability of the Home Secretary to Parliament?

More controversial than agency status was the decision to privatise the management of individual prisons. The first privatised prison, the Wolds, a purpose-built remand prison, was opened in 1992, managed by Group 4 Remand Services Ltd. There are now a number of prisons managed by private companies on behalf of the Prison Service. While privatisation may lead to improved physical standards in prison, it raises questions of principle, discussed in Logan (1990). Should the state delegate to private companies its right to punish those who break the law? In practice, the accountability of the Prison Service for privately managed prisons continues to be unclear. The Home Office is represented in the prison by a comptroller, whilst the private company employs the governor. CJPOA 1994, ss 93–101 extended the arrangements for contracting out within the Prison Service, including prisoner escort arrangements. Under s 94, for example, where a court sentences someone too late in the day for that person to be admitted to prison, he may now be held overnight by the escort company instead of by the police. Sections 96 and 99 allow for the contracting out of part of a prison, or some of the functions within a prison, to the private sector. Is this a recipe for a well-managed prison system? What difference will it make in practice that the managers of the private prisons now report direct to Martin Narey, Commissioner for Correctional Services, and not to Phil Wheatley, Director of the Prison Service?

(iii) The Parole Board

Parole was introduced by the Criminal Justice Act 1967. There were two main objectives: to reduce the prison population, and to help in the rehabilitation of offenders by releasing them into the community at the 'right' time in their sentence, under the supervision of a probation officer to whom they were required to report regularly. Over the years various changes were made to the system, but the most major changes were introduced by the Criminal Justice Act 1991 **[10:4]**, which was amended by the CJPOA 1994: s 149 made the Board a non-departmental public body; and s 150 removed from the Board the power to recall prisoners. Until 1994 two systems of recall to custody ran in tandem: one operated by the Parole Board and one by the Home Secretary. Section 150 specifies that there will now only be one recall system, operated by the Home Secretary.

The Parole Board must include among its members: someone who is or has been a judge; a psychiatrist; a person who has knowledge and experience of the supervision or aftercare of discharged prisoners; and a person who has made a study of the causes of delinquency or the treatment of offenders. However, it may arrange for its functions to be discharged by small committees, or even by one of its members. The Parole Board is only involved with those prisoners serving four years or more. It grants parole at any point after the prisoners have served half their sentence. Those not granted parole must be released after serving two-thirds of their time, and they are then on licensed supervision until three-quarters of their sentence has elapsed, followed again by conditional release. The Criminal Justice Act 1991, s 32 **[10:4]** sets out the role of the Parole Board, although it acts subject to the Home Secretary's veto given in s 35.

The most useful account of decision making by the Parole Board, apart from its own annual reports, is given by Hood and Shute **[10:12] [10:13]**. Their 1994 work included the observation of almost 400 cases dealt with under the old system prior to its abolition, published as the first part of a study of the implementation of the new system. The task of the Parole Board obviously involves predicting and assessing risk: it has to balance the need to protect the public from serious harm and to prevent further offending with the benefits of supervision. It seems curious that, while Parliament has attempted to structure judicial discretion in sentencing, the wide powers of the Parole Board – which decides the length of a sentence in practice – should be left wide open. Even if predictions of dangerousness could be made accurately, is it morally justifiable to keep some people in prison longer than others only because of the risk that they represent?

The parole process was originally largely secret. However, the dossier of reports is nowadays disclosed to prisoners, who are also interviewed in their prison by a Parole Board member. The interview report is disclosed to the prisoner and added to the dossier. The case is then decided by a panel of three board members. It remains to be seen whether this increased openness leads to greater satisfaction with the process: as Hood and Shute point out (1994), both prisoners and staff have high expectations of the system.

Perhaps the most controversial parole procedures are those applicable to life sentence prisoners. The European Court of Human Rights in *Thynne* **[10:14]** ruled that once the 'tariff' period set by reference to the offence has expired, any subsequent detention on grounds of public protection should be capable of being challenged through proceedings in a court or tribunal that is independent of the executive. As a result, a much more open procedure has been introduced in relation to discretionary lifers. The Parole Board Rules make clear that the prisoner may be represented by anyone authorised by them for that purpose, subject to a list of ineligible representatives, such as those serving a sentence of imprisonment or those on parole (rule 6). The prisoner may make a written application to call witnesses, and must be given reasons in writing if this request is refused. There are now detailed procedural rules as to directions, preliminary hearings and the oral hearing.

The government has until recently maintained its position that mandatory life sentence prisoners are not entitled to the same procedural protections. The House of Lords in *Doody* **[10:15]** upheld the Secretary of State's power under the Criminal Justice Act 1991, s 35(2) **[10:4]** to reject the Parole Board's recommendation in the case of a mandatory life sentence prisoner, yet the European Court of Human Rights in *V and T v United Kingdom* (1999) 30 EHRR 121 held that the role of the Home Secretary in fixing the tariff of a juvenile murderer was unlawful; and in *R (Anderson) v Secretary of State for the Home Department* [2002] UKHL 46, [2003] 1 AC 837 the House of Lords decided that the same was true in the case of adult murderers. These changes were precipitated by the decision of the European Court of Human Rights in *Stafford v United Kingdom* (2002) 35 EHRR **[10:16]**.

The function of the Parole Board in either recommending or directing release remains controversial: can it be appropriate that a politician should decide when or whether to release any prisoner? This question challenges the justification for life sentences in the first place: would it be more appropriate to give all prisoners a fixed-term sentence, even a very long-term sentence, rather than an indefinite sentence? Yet the indeterminate sentence is here to stay: see the sentence of imprisonment for public protection proposed in the Criminal Justice Bill 2002.

The Secretary of State holds other powers over the release of long-term prisoners. Under s 39(2) of the Criminal Justice Act 1991, he may revoke the licence of any long-term or life prisoner and recall them to prison without a recommendation by the Parole Board. The Board now functions more like an independent 'court' than it did before 1992: should it not be this body, supported by satisfactory procedural safeguards, which makes release and recall decisions? CJPOA 1994, s 150 – which, in abolishing the Parole Board's role in recalls – reflected the government's commitment to immediate and speedy public protection where prisoners on licence are concerned. This should be contrasted with the procedure for those on automatic conditional release, where recalls have to be dealt with through the courts. In both cases, why does the Parole Board no longer have a role?

(iv) Mental Health Review Tribunals

Mentally disordered offenders should, wherever possible, receive care and treatment from health and social services rather than from the criminal justice system. Violent or dangerous mentally disordered offenders find themselves in one of the three 'special hospitals' – Ashworth, Broadmoor and Rampton – which are high security hospitals managed by the Special Hospitals Service Authority. Regional health authorities also provide regional secure units, but these are normally reserved for those who are judged likely to improve and be discharged within two years. There are no long-term medium-security hospital provisions (see Grounds (1992)). Home Office Circular 66/1990 encouraged the diversion of mentally disordered people from the prison system. The document reproduces the powers of the police, CPS and courts in relation to mentally disordered offenders. Fennell (1991), while welcoming the spirit of the circular, stressed the fragmented arrangements for the care of mentally disordered offenders, characterised by virtually unfettered discretion. A consultative exercise began in 1994 to look into updating the circular, but what is really needed is vastly increased resources for health and social services. Changes in the National Health Service and 'care in the community' have resulted in an ever-increasing proportion of mentally disordered offenders either living on the streets or being held in prison. The law itself may have little influence on practical decision making in a system starved of resources. Perhaps the legal structure of the Mental Health Act 1983 needs less reform than the attitudes of those who provide the resources and facilities for them.

The Mental Health Act 1983 **[10:17]** lays down the ground rules for the detention of mentally disordered people. Police powers under sections 135 and 136 of the Act were mentioned in Chapter Two. As Grounds (1992) says, 'the police are often a frontline agency, and may in effect act as a community psychiatric resource' (at page 287). Section 37 authorises the courts to order hospital admission or guardianship, and they may do this even without convicting the accused (see s 37(3)). In any case where it makes a hospital order under section 37, a court may also make a restriction order under s 41 (see Street (1999)). The effect of a restriction order is that the patient may not be discharged (except by a Mental Health Review Tribunal), granted leave of absence or transferred to another hospital, without the consent of the Home Secretary. Section 47 allows the transfer of sentenced prisoners who require psychiatric hospital treatment. The Crime (Sentences) Act 1997 inserted into the 1983 Act 'hospital and limitation directions', which allow the court to order that if the offender does not respond to treatment, they be transferred to prison and not simply discharged from hospital. Public (or media?) concern about the need to protect the public from the risks presented by the mentally unstable led to the Home Office's *Managing Dangerous People with Severe Personality Disorder: Proposals for Policy Development* (1999). With its focus on reducing the risks to the public, the document considers the introduction of a 'dangerous severely personality disordered' order, which could be imposed by a civil court (ie without the safeguard of the criminal burden of proof, and merely on a balance of probabilities). Controversies continued with the Department of Health's consultation of a draft Mental Health Bill 2002 (see the Department of Health's website: www.doh.gov.uk).

Under the European Convention of Human Rights, art 5(4) **[1:9]**, everyone is entitled to take proceedings 'by which the lawfulness of his detention shall be decided speedily by a court'. In *X v United Kingdom* (1981) 4 EHRR 188 the European Court of Human Rights decided that all people held because they were of unsound mind were entitled to a periodic judicial consideration of the merits of their continued detention. As a result, the role of the Mental Health Review Tribunals (MHRTs) – composed of lawyers, doctors and lay members – was strengthened by the Mental Health Act 1983. The role of MHRTs is to decide who can safely be released from hospital. They will usually meet in the hospital where the patient is detained. It is particularly difficult for a person who is or has been mentally disordered to prove to the satisfaction of the tribunal that their detention is not justified 'with a view to the protection of other persons' (see the Mental Health Act 1983, s 72(1)(a) **[10:17]**). Legal aid is available, which is rare in a tribunal: the legal aid provisions were expanded to cover MHRTs largely as a result of a high-profile campaign by the pressure group MIND. MHRTs have the advantages, over formal courts, of flexibility and informality, but as a result their performance is all the more difficult to assess. Peay (1989) conducted an important and thorough study. She is concerned by the covert dependence on the 'good sense' of tribunals: should legal criteria be taken more seriously or is the 'welfarist' approach more appropriate? Baker (1993) stressed the risks in using dangerousness as a criterion in decision making. Predictions of dangerousness, inevitably inaccurate, tend to lead to over-prediction. For this reason, if no other, it is particularly important to evolve clear legal criteria for the detention of those deemed 'dangerous'. Holloway and Grounds **[10:18]** bring the debate up to date.

An underlying concern highlighted in this book has been the need for procedural fairness and political accountability. Offenders needs real procedural safeguards from the time of their arrest onwards. Such protections remain vital in a process which allows bodies such as the Parole Board or MHRTs to predict who is fit for release from prison or who is a danger to the public. However, as Lacey (1986) pointed out, the actual and perhaps inevitable powerlessness of the offender at the post-conviction stage may often render effective use of court-like procedures an impossibility. She suggests that it makes more sense, if we are concerned principally with substantive fairness, to concentrate on ensuring fair procedures involving participation and accountability at the policy-making stage. Procedural justice is important, but real, substantive, justice even more so. This book has highlighted some of the tensions evident in the criminal justice process, but it is important to look also at fundamental principles. A system which is under constant pressure to save money is likely to take shortcuts: it is unlikely to value procedural fairness adequately, and even less likely to tackle the underlying causes of crime. The time has now come to invite the student to go back to first principles, to consider the proper functions of the criminal law and to analyse the meaning of criminal justice. Return to Chapter One, and begin a further evaluation of the criminal justice process.

Further reading

Annual Reports of HM Chief Inspector of Prisons for England and Wales, of the Probation Service, the Prison Service, the Parole Board etc

Baker, E 'Dangerousness, Rights and Criminal Justice' (1993) 56 MLR 528

Bottoms, A, Gelsthorpe, L and Rex, S *Community Penalties: change and challenges* (2001) Willan

Carlen, P *Sledgehammer: Women's Imprisonment at the Millennium* (1998) Macmillan

Council of Europe Report to the United Kingdom Government on the Visit to the UK carried out by the European Committee for the Prevention of Torture and Inhuman and Degrading Treatment (1991) Council of Europe

Eastman, N and Peay, J *Law without enforcement: integrating mental health with justice* (1999) Oxford: Hart

Eaton, M *Women After Prison* (1993) Open University Press

Gelsthorpe, L and Padfield, N (eds) Exercising Discretion: Decision-making in the criminal justice system and beyond (2003, Willan)

Grounds, A Mental Health Problems in *Criminal Justice under Stress* ed Stockdale, E and Casale, S (1992) Blackstone

Gunn, J et al Mentally Disordered Prisoners (1991) Home Office

Hood, R and Shute, S Parole Decision-Making: Weighing the Risk to the Public (2000, HO Research Findings No 114)

Lacey, N Discretion and Due Process at the Post-Conviction Stage, in *Criminal Law and Justice* ed Dennis, I H (1986) Sweet & Maxwell

Livingstone, S and Owen, T *Prison Law* (2nd edition, 1999)

Logan, R *Private Prisons: Pros and Cons* (1990) OUP

Morgan, R Imprisonment: a brief history, the contemporary scene and likely prospects, in *the Oxford Handbook of Criminology* (Oxford, 12002, 3rd edition)

Nash, M *Police, Probation and Protecting the Public* (Blackstone, 1999)

Padfield, N *Beyond the Tariff: Human Rights and the Life Sentence Prisoner* (Willan, 2002)

Padfield, N and Liebling, A, with Arnold, H An Exploration of Decision-Making at DLPs (2000, HO Research Findings No 132)

Peay, J *Tribunals on Trial: A Study of Decision making Under the Mental Health Act 1983* (1989) Clarendon Press

Polvi, N and Pease, K Parole and its problems: a Canadian-English comparison (1991) Howard Journal 218

Street, R The restricted hospital order: from court to community (1999) Home Office Research Study, No 186

Vagg, J *Prison Systems: A Comparative Study of Accountability in England, France, Germany and the Netherlands* (1994) Clarendon Press

Documents

[10:1]   *Woolf Report – Prison Disturbances April 1990* (HMSO, 1991) (at page 19):

1.167   Our programme is based on 12 central recommendations. These are that there should be:

(i)   closer co-operation between the different parts of the Criminal Justice System. For this purpose a national forum and local committees should be established;

(ii)   more visible leadership of the Prison Service by a Director General who is and is seen to be the operational head and in day to day charge of the Service. To achieve this there should be a published 'compact' or 'contract' given by Ministers to the Director General of the Prison Service, who should be responsible for the performance of the 'contract' and publicly answerable for the day to day operations of the Prison Service;

(iii) increased delegation of responsibility to Governors of establishments;

(iv)   an enhanced role for prison officers;

(v)   a 'compact' or 'contract' for each prisoner setting out the prisoner's expectations and responsibilities in the prison in which he or she is held;

(vi)   a national system of Accredited Standards, with which, in time, each prison establishment would be required to comply;

(vii) a new Prison Rule that no establishment should hold more prisoners than is provided for in its certified normal level of accommodation, with provisions for Parliament to be informed if exceptionally there is to be a material departure from that rule;

(viii) a public commitment from Ministers setting a timetable to provide access to sanitation for all inmates at the earliest practicable date not later than February 1996;

(ix) better prospects for prisoners to maintain their links with families and the community through more visits and home leaves and through being located in community prisons as near to their homes as possible;

(x) a division of prison establishments into small and more manageable and secure units;

(xi) a separate statement of purpose, separate conditions and generally a lower security categorisation for remand prisoners;

(xii) improved standards of justice within prisons involving the giving of reasons to a prisoner for any decision which materially and adversely affects him; a grievance procedure and disciplinary proceedings which ensure that the Governor deals with most matters under his present powers; relieving Boards of Visitors of their adjudicatory role; and providing for final access to an independent Complaints Adjudicator.

1.168   In the following paragraphs and in the remainder of the Report we describe these recommendations more fully. They are central to resolving the problems which have been identified from the April disturbances. They are also a package. They need to be considered together and moved forward together if the necessary balance in our prison system is to be achieved.

[10:2]   Hedderman, C *Panel Assessment Schemes for Mentally Disordered Offenders* (1993) HORPU Paper No 76 (at page iii):

Under panel assessment schemes formal arrangements are set up whereby probation officers, social workers and psychiatrists and other health professionals can meet to consider how best to provide for mentally disordered offenders. The panel convenes on a case-by-case basis to agree and recommend a treatment package to the agency – usually a magistrates' court – which has referred the case for assessment. The scheme's purpose is to ensure that magistrates' courts dealt appropriately with mentally disordered defendants and offenders, by ensuring that they were presented with co-ordinated recommendations which had been agreed by all the agencies which would be involved in caring and controlling for the mentally disordered offender. The first scheme was set up in Hertfordshire in 1985; since then similar arrangements have been set up in seven other probation areas and many other areas are in the a process of doing so.

This report describes the impact of the scheme in Hertfordshire and in two other areas (Reading and Bolton) over a one year period. It considers dealing with the mentally disordered from the perspective of health, criminal justice and social service agencies. The impact of promoting the panel assessment idea nationally is also examined. The report concludes by identifying the core elements of panel assessment arrangements and draws conclusions about best practice.

The impact of the scheme in the three project areas

Panel co-ordinators provided monitoring forms on 187 completed cases processed under the schemes in Bolton, Reading and Hertfordshire between April 1991 and April 1992. In addition, magistrates' courts records were examined in each area to investigate the impact of panel assessments on magistrates' decision-making.

Key findings from this part of the study were:

- the most common offence dealt with under the schemes was theft, but they were also used to dealing with defendants facing a range of charges, from breach of the peace to rape. Just over three-quarters of those referred to panel schemes had previous convictions, of whom 40% had previously been sentenced to immediate custody. Taken together, these results suggest that panels were not simply being used for the least serious or first time offenders, but were also employed when the courts were faced with serious and repeat offenders;

- most of those assessed were picked up either by the scheme co-ordinator or a probation service colleague. In a quarter of cases the referral was made either by the court clerk or magistrates;

- seven per cent (14) of cases were referred before charges were brought. The panel recommendation was accepted in each of these cases, with the result that six of them ended in a caution or no further action and eight were prosecuted. One hundred and sixty-three cases were prosecuted. Five of the eight defendants who pleaded not guilty were acquitted as were two of the four who did not enter a plea, representing 4% of all those prosecuted. In all, convictions were recorded in 84% of cases;

- at the courts covered in the present study between 45% and 60% of all the offenders dealt with during 1990 were fined. However, fines were only awarded to 4% of those dealt with after being assessed. Approximately equal numbers – around a fifth – of those assessed were given a discharge or bind over, probation orders or some form of medical disposal (comprising five hospital orders and 31 probation orders with conditions of treatment);

- most recommendations were accepted by the referring agency. Interestingly, the Reading assessment scheme – the area where panel meetings were held least frequently – was least likely to have recommendations rejected (7% compared to 17% in Hertfordshire and 28% in Bolton). In all but one of the cases where the assessment scheme recommendation was rejected, the sentences awarded were not dramatically more or less severe than that recommended. In the exceptional case the actual sentencing recommendation was at odds with the overall tone of the social inquiry report;

- the number of cases remanded for psychiatric reports increased at both Bolton and Reading magistrates' court once panel assessment schemes had been introduced. The proportion of defendants remanded for psychiatric reports at the Hertfordshire courts (St Albans and Dacorum) was higher than at Reading and Bolton. Taken together these findings suggest that magistrates' courts welcomed and made use of formal arrangements for assessing mentally disordered offenders and that confidence in such arrangements increases with time. However, the success of any scheme will be jeopardised if it fails to provide a regular and reliable service.

Given that panel assessment schemes take different forms in different areas and evolve over time, it is difficult to arrive at an accurate estimate of the costs which result from their operation. Another difficulty in estimating this is that one system's savings may increase another's costs. Nevertheless, using broad estimates of minimum costs, and bearing in mind that offenders processed under panel arrangements tended to be remanded in custody for shorter periods, the report shows that such arrangements will at least break even and may even represent a small saving, at least to the criminal justice system. Moreover, anecdotal evidence suggests that diversion does not increase health costs as most of those who are diverted are already known to both systems.

(and at page viii):

The report concludes that it is not possible to construct a blue-print for the ideal panel assessment scheme, as the particular form an assessment scheme takes is determined by local problems, facilities and working practices. However, a number of key features and common problems can be identified. In particular, management support and the co-operation of general psychiatrists are essential if panel assessments are to provide a consistent and useful service.

[10:3]   Richardson, G *Law, Process and Custody: Prisoners and Patients* (1993) Weidenfeld & Nicolson

(From Chapter 5: Internal Prison Decisions: Policy Formulation, at page 108):

The most outstanding feature of the policy formulation described in this chapter must surely be the sparsity of legislative involvement. The Prison Act and the Prison Rules combine to place large areas of policy formulation in the hands of the administrative authorities, on whom they impose few procedural constraints. Thus, although there have been significant changes in internal prison policy over the last two decades, these have necessitated little change to the legislative structure. The changes which have occurred have been inspired by pressure from a variety of sources, including international courts, domestic courts, senior management and public opinion. Most significantly, in recent years pressure for change has found expression through the Woolf Inquiry into the prison disturbances of April 1990. While it is still too early to assess the impact of the Woolf Report on Prison Service policy, and whatever doubts might be voiced on that subject, it is clear that the approach to its task adopted by the Inquiry, particularly at Stage II when the wider applications of the disturbances were examined, has done much to open up the process of internal prison policy formulation.

As the above discussion has illustrated, once, for whatever reason, the need for change is recognised within the Prison Service, the process of policy formulation itself is one of administrative decision making. In the past, although this process might have been informed by an 'independent' report, from the Chief Inspector for example, it was essentially internal and, typically, little systematic consultation would take place outside the Prison Service. In other words, little effort was made to facilitate the full reflection of the public interest. In marked contrast, the Woolf Inquiry made every attempt to consult widely and to respond to and initiate debate when formulating its own views and recommendations.

Whatever will prove to have been the impact of Woolf on the process of prison policy formulation, however, it must be remembered that these steps towards openness and responsiveness have been introduced administratively; Parliament has played little part. Indeed, the fate of the proposal to introduce Parliamentary monitoring with regard to overcrowding, and the form taken by the proposed code of standards, would suggest that there is considerable reluctance to involve Parliament, either as an overseer or as a policy formulator. Under our present constitutional arrangements such a position cannot be acceptable. Whatever the actual shortcomings of Parliament, and however far it falls below the demands of full process, it represents at present the primary forum for the identification of the public interest. It must therefore be involved both in the formulation of fundamental prison policy and in the creation of subsidiary structures for the evolution of detailed policies and rules. The prison system, its aims and governing principles, belong to society at large, not just to those who work and live within it.

(From Chapter 10: Decision Making within Special Hospitals: application Decisions, at page 256):

The above discussion suggests that the majority of decisions concerning the imposition of additional restrictions on a patient's freedoms while in hospital are very loosely regulated. The Mental Health Act 1983, although in many respects more detailed than its counterpart the Prison Act 1952, is designed to regulate only very specific area of hospital decision making: the administration of medical treatment, for example, and the censorship of patients' mail. Outside those areas the SHSA and the special hospitals are largely free to create their own policies and practices. The Code of Practice applies, but it has no direct legal force, and even where it is relevant, as in the case of seclusion, it is honoured, typically, in the breach. The resulting legal vacuum is filled in practice by internal policies created by management and reflecting, inevitably, the priorities of management. The experience of the visitor's policy and the procedure for granting trips out of hospital, and the practice of monitoring internal mail, all illustrate the ease with which administrative requirements and procedural hurdles can evolve internally to impose restrictions on the freedom of patients in excess of those demanded by statute. More rigorous formal regulation is required if the importance attaching to the retention by patients of areas of personal autonomy is to be adequately reflected, and each infringement specifically justified.

It is also evident that many of the practices currently prevailing allow decisions which carry significant implications for individual patients to be taken in the exercise of therapeutic discretion on the basis of few stated criteria. More rigorous regulation and the processes whereby such decisions are reached were advocated, not as an attempt to impose the requirements of sterile legalism, but as a positive step towards the improvement of the resulting decisions. With regard to disciplinary decisions specifically, it was suggested that the introduction of greater procedural rigours would be facilitative of the therapeutic goal rather than destructive of it. The open formulation of more specific rules was urged, together with proper investigation and the full participation of the patient at the application stage. Similarly, in relation to seclusion, if it is to be retained at all, greater stringency both in the specification of the criteria for its use and in the procedures for its implementation and monitoring was demanded, in order to ensure that every use of seclusion is justified and of as short a duration as possible.

[10:4]   Criminal Justice Act 1991 sections 32–45

32   The Parole Board

(1)   The Parole Board shall be, by that name, a body corporate and as such shall
    (a)   be constituted in accordance with this Part; and
    (b)   have the functions conferred by this Part in respect of long-term and short-term prisoners and by Chapter II of Part II of the Crime (Sentences) Act 1997 ("Chapter II") in respect of life prisoners within the meaning of that Chapter.

(2)   It shall be the duty of the Board to advise the Secretary of State with respect to any matter referred to it by him which is connected with the early release or recall of prisoners.

(3)   The Board shall deal with cases as respects which it makes recommendations under this Part or Chapter II on consideration of—

    (a)   any documents given to it by the Secretary of State; and

    (b)   any other oral or written information obtained by it,

and if in any particular case the Board thinks it necessary to interview the person to whom the case relates before reaching a decision, the Board may authorise one of its members to interview him and shall consider the report of the interview made by that member.

(4)   The Board shall deal with cases as respects which it gives directions under this Part or Chapter II on consideration of all such evidence as may be adduced before it.

(5)   Without prejudice to subsections (3) and (4) above, the Secretary of State may make rules with respect to the proceedings of the Board, including provision authorising cases to be dealt with by a prescribed number of its members or requiring cases to be dealt with at prescribed times.

(6)   The Secretary of State may also give to the Board directions as to the matters to be taken into account by it in discharging any functions under this Part or Chapter II; and in giving any such directions the Secretary of State shall in particular have regard to—

    (a)   the need to protect the public from serious harm from offenders; and

    (b)   the desirability of preventing the commission by them of further offences and of securing their rehabilitation.

(7)   Schedule 5 to this Act shall have effect with respect to the Board.

33   Duty to release short-term and long-term prisoners

(1)   As soon as a short-term prisoner has served one-half of his sentence, it shall be the duty of the Secretary of State—

    (a)   to release him unconditionally if that sentence is for a term of less than twelve months; and

    (b)   to release him on licence if that sentence is for a term of twelve months or more.

(2)   As soon as a long-term prisoner has served two-thirds of his sentence, it shall be the duty of the Secretary of State to release him on licence.

(3)   As soon as a short-term or long-term prisoner who—

    (a)   has been released on licence under this Part; and

    (b)   has been recalled to prison under section 39(1) or (2) below,

would (but for his release) have served three-quarters of his sentence, it shall be the duty of the Secretary of State to release him on licence.

(3A) In the case of a prisoner to whom section 44A below applies, it shall be the duty of the Secretary of State to release him on licence at the end of the extension period (within the meaning of section 85 of the Powers of Criminal Courts (Sentencing) Act 2000).

(4) ...

(5)   In this Part—
"long-term prisoner" means a person serving a sentence of imprisonment for a
term of four years or more;
"short-term prisoner" means a person serving a sentence of imprisonment for a
term of less than four years.

33A   Duty to release prisoners: special cases

(1)   As soon as a prisoner—
  (a)   whose sentence is for a term of less than twelve months; and
  (b)   who has been released on licence under section 34A(3) or 36(1) below and
        recalled to prison under section 38A(1) or 39(1) or (2) below,
would (but for his release) have served one-half of his sentence, it shall be the duty of
the Secretary of State to release him unconditionally.

(2)   As soon as a prisoner—
  (a)   whose sentence is for a term of twelve months or more; and
  (b)   who has been released on licence under section 34A(3) below and recalled
        to prison under section 38A(1) below,
would (but for his release) have served one-half of his sentence, it shall be the duty of
the Secretary of State to release him on licence.

(3)   In the case of a prisoner who—
  (a)   has been released on licence under this Part and recalled to prison under
        section 39(1) or (2) below; and
  (b)   has been subsequently released on licence under section 33(3) or (3A)
        above and recalled to prison under section 39(1) or (2) below,
section 33(3) above shall have effect as if for the words "three-quarters" there were
substituted the words "the whole" and the words "on licence" were omitted.

34A   Power to release short-term prisoners on licence

(1)   Subject to subsection (2) below, subsection (3) below applies where a short-term
prisoner ... is serving a sentence of imprisonment for a term of three months or more.

(2)   Subsection (3) below does not apply where—
  (a)   the sentence is an extended sentence within the meaning of section 85 of
        the Powers of Criminal Courts (Sentencing) Act 2000;
  (b)   the sentence is for an offence under section 1 of the Prisoners (Return to
        Custody) Act 1995;
  (c)   the sentence was imposed under paragraph 4(1)(d) or 5(1)(d) of Schedule
        3 to the Powers of Criminal Courts (Sentencing) Act 2000 in a case where
        the prisoner had failed to comply with a requirement of a curfew order;
  (d)   the prisoner is subject to a hospital order, hospital direction or transfer
        direction under section 37, 45A or 47 of the Mental Health Act 1983;
  (da) the prisoner is subject to the notification requirements of Part I of the Sex
        Offenders Act 1997;

(e)   the prisoner is liable to removal from the United Kingdom for the purposes of section 46 below;

(f)   the prisoner has been released on licence under this section at any time and has been recalled to prison under section 38A(1)(a) below;

(g)   the prisoner has been released on licence under this section or section 36 below during the currency of the sentence, and has been recalled to prison under section 39(1) or (2) below;

(h)   the prisoner has been returned to prison under section 116 of the Powers of Criminal Courts (Sentencing) Act 2000 at any time; or

(j)   the interval between—

    (i)   the date on which the prisoner will have served the requisite period for the term of the sentence; and

    (ii)   the date on which he will have served one-half of the sentence,

is less than 14 days.

(3)   After the prisoner has served the requisite period for the term of his sentence, the Secretary of State may, subject to section 37A below, release him on licence.

(4)   In this section "the requisite period" means—

    (a)   for a term of three months or more but less than four months, a period of 30 days;

    (b)   for a term of four months or more but less than eighteen months, a period equal to one-quarter of the term;

    (c)   for a term of eighteen months or more, a period that is 135 days less than one-half of the term.

(5)   The Secretary of State may by order made by statutory instrument—

    (a)   repeal the words "aged 18 or over" in subsection (1) above;

    (b)   amend the definition of "the requisite period" in subsection (4) above; and

    (c)   make such transitional provision as appears to him necessary or expedient in connection with the repeal or amendment.

(6)   No order shall be made under subsection (5) above unless a draft of the order has been laid before and approved by a resolution of each House of Parliament.

35 Power to release long-term and life prisoners

(1)   After a long-term prisoner has served one-half of his sentence, the Secretary of State may, if recommended to do so by the Board, release him on licence.

(2) ...

(3) ...

36   Power to release prisoners on compassionate grounds

(1)   The Secretary of State may at any time release a short-term or long-term prisoner on licence if he is satisfied that exceptional circumstances exist which justify the prisoner's release on compassionate grounds.

(2)   Before releasing a long-term ... prisoner under subsection (1) above, the Secretary of State shall consult the Board, unless the circumstances are such as to render such consultation impracticable.

37   Duration and conditions of licences

(1)   Subject to subsections (1A), (1B) and (2) below, where a short-term or long-term prisoner is released on licence, the licence shall, subject to ... any revocation under section 39(1) or (2) below, remain in force until the date on which he would (but for his release) have served three-quarters of his sentence.

(1A) Where a prisoner is released on licence under section 33(3) or (3A) above, subsection (1) above shall have effect as if for the reference to three-quarters of his sentence there were substituted a reference to the whole of that sentence.

(1B) Where a prisoner whose sentence is for a term of twelve months or more is released on licence under section 33A(2) or 34A(3) above, subsection (1) above shall have effect as if for the reference to three-quarters of his sentence there were substituted a reference to the difference between—

    (a)   that proportion of his sentence; and
    (b)   the duration of the curfew condition to which he is or was subject.

(2)   Where a prisoner whose sentence is for a term of less than twelve months is released on licence under section 34A(3) or 36(1) above, subsection (1) above shall have effect as if for the reference to three-quarters of his sentence there were substituted a reference to one-half of that sentence.

(3)   ...

(4)   A person subject to a licence under this Part shall comply with such conditions ... as may for the time being be specified in the licence; and the Secretary of State may make rules for regulating the supervision of any description of such persons.

(4A) The conditions so specified may in the case of a person released on licence under section 34A above whose sentence is for a term of less than twelve months, and shall in any other case, include on the person's release conditions as to his supervision by—

    (a)   an officer of a local probation board appointed for or assigned to the petty sessions area within which the person resides for the time being; or
    (b)   where the person is under the age of 18 years, a member of a youth offending team established by the local authority within whose area the person resides for the time being.

(5)   The Secretary of State shall not include on release, or subsequently insert, a condition in the licence of a long-term prisoner, or vary or cancel any such condition, except after consultation with the Board.

(6)   For the purposes of subsection (5) above, the Secretary of State shall be treated as having consulted the Board about a proposal to include, insert, vary or cancel a condition in any case if he has consulted the Board about the implementation of proposals of that description generally or in that class of case.

(7)   The power to make rules under this section shall be exercisable by statutory instrument which shall be subject to annulment in pursuance of a resolution of either House of Parliament.

37A   Curfew condition to be included in licence under section 34A

(1)   A person shall not be released under section 34A(3) above unless the licence includes a condition ("the curfew condition") which—
   (a)   requires the released person to remain, for periods for the time being specified in the condition, at a place for the time being so specified (which may be an approved probation hostel); and
   (b)   includes requirements for securing the electronic monitoring of his whereabouts during the periods for the time being so specified.

(2)   The curfew condition may specify different places or different periods for different days, but shall not specify periods which amount to less than 9 hours in any one day (excluding for this purpose the first and last days of the period for which the condition is in force).

(3)   The curfew condition shall remain in force until the date when the released person would (but for his release) have served one-half of his sentence.

(4)   The curfew condition shall include provision for making a person responsible for monitoring the released person's whereabouts during the periods for the time being specified in the condition; and a person who is made so responsible shall be of a description specified in an order made by the Secretary of State.

(5)   The power conferred by subsection (4) above—
   (a)   shall be exercisable by statutory instrument; and
   (b)   shall include power to make different provision for different cases or classes of case or for different areas.

(6)   Nothing in this section shall be taken to require the Secretary of State to ensure that arrangements are made for the electronic monitoring of released persons' whereabouts in any particular part of England and Wales.

(7)   ...

38A   Breach of curfew condition

(1)   If it appears to the Secretary of State, as regards a person released on licence under section 34A(3) above—
- (a)   that he has failed to comply with the curfew condition;
- (b)   that his whereabouts can no longer be electronically monitored at the place for the time being specified in that condition; or
- (c)   that it is necessary to do so in order to protect the public from serious harm from him,

the Secretary of State may, if the curfew condition is still in force, revoke the licence and recall the person to prison.

(2)   A person whose licence under section 34A(3) above is revoked tinder this section—
- (a)   may make representations in writing with respect to the revocation;
- (b)   on his return to prison, shall be informed of the reasons for the revocation and of his right to make representations.

(3)   The Secretary of State, after considering any representations made under subsection (2)(b) above or any other matters, may cancel a revocation under this section.

(4)   Where the revocation of a person's licence is cancelled under subsection (3) above, the person shall be treated for the purposes of sections 34A(2)(f) and 37(1B) above as if he had not been recalled to prison under this section.

(5)   On the revocation under this section of a person's licence under section 34A(3) above, he shall be liable to be detained in pursuance of his sentence and, if at large, shall be deemed to be unlawfully at large.

(6)   In this section "the curfew condition" has the same meaning as in section 37A above.

39   Recall of long-term ... prisoners while on licence

(1)   If recommended to do so by the Board in the case of a short-term or long-term ... prisoner who has been released on licence under this Part, the Secretary of State may revoke his licence and recall him to prison.

(2)   The Secretary of State may revoke the licence of any such person and recall him to prison without a recommendation by the Board, where it appears to him that it is expedient in the public interest to recall that person before such a recommendation is practicable.

(3)   A person recalled to prison under subsection (1) or (2) above—
- (a)   may make representations in writing with respect to his recall; and
- (b)   on his return to prison, shall be informed of the reasons for his recall and of his right to make representations.

(4)   The Secretary of State shall refer to the Board—
- (a)   the case of a person recalled under subsection (1) above who makes representations under subsection (3) above; and

    (b)   the case of a person recalled under subsection (2) above.

(5)   Where on a reference under subsection (4) above the Board—
    (a)   ...
    (b)   recommends in the case of any ... person,
his immediate release on licence under this section, the Secretary of State shall give effect to the ... recommendation.

(5A) In the case of a prisoner to whom section 44A below applies, subsections (4)(b) and (5) of that section apply in place of subsection (5) above.

(6)   On the revocation of the licence of any person under this section, he shall be liable to be detained in pursuance of his sentence and, if at large, shall be deemed to be unlawfully at large.

...

40A   Release on licence following return to prison

(1)   This section applies (in place of sections 33, 33A, 37(1) and 39 above) where a court passes on a person a sentence of imprisonment which—
    (a)   includes, or consists of, an order under section 116 of the Powers of Criminal Courts (Sentencing) Act 2000; and
    (b)   is for a term of twelve months or less.

(2)   As soon as the person has served one-half of the sentence, it shall be the duty of the Secretary of State to release him on licence.

(3)   Where the person is so released, the licence shall remain in force for a period of three months.

(4)   If the person fails to comply with such conditions as may for the time being be specified in the licence, he shall be liable on summary conviction—
    (a)   to a fine not exceeding level 3 on the standard scale; or
    (b)   to a sentence of imprisonment for a term not exceeding the relevant period,
but not liable to be dealt with in any other way.

(5)   In subsection (4) above "the relevant period" means a period which is equal in length to the period between the date on which the failure occurred or began and the date of the expiry of the licence.

(6)   As soon as a person has served one-half of a sentence passed under subsection (4) above, it shall be the duty of the Secretary of State to release him, subject to the licence if it is still subsisting.

41   Remand time to count towards time served

(1)   This section applies to any person whose sentence falls to be reduced under section 67 of the Criminal Justice Act 1967 ("the 1967 Act") by any relevant period within the meaning of that section ("the relevant period").

(2)   For the purpose of determining for the purposes of this Part—
>   (a)   whether a person to whom this section applies has served one-half or two-thirds of his sentence; or
>   (b)   whether such a person would (but for his release) have served three-quarters of that sentence,

the relevant period shall, subject to subsection (3) below, be treated as having been served by him as part of that sentence.

(3)   Nothing in subsection (2) above shall have the effect of reducing the period for which a licence granted under this Part to a short-term or long-term prisoner remains in force to a period which is less than—
>   (a)   one-quarter of his sentence in the case of a short-term prisoner; or
>   (b)   one-twelfth of his sentence in the case of a long-term prisoner.

42   Additional days for disciplinary offences

(1)   Prison rules, that is to say, rules made under section 47 of the 1952 Act, may include provision for the award of additional days—
>   (a)   to short-term or long-term prisoners; or
>   (b)   conditionally on their subsequently becoming such prisoners, to persons on remand,

who (in either case) are guilty of disciplinary offences.

(2)   Where additional days are awarded to a short-term or long-term prisoner, or to a person on remand who subsequently becomes such a prisoner, and are not remitted in accordance with prison rules—
>   (a)   any period which he must serve before becoming entitled to or eligible for release under this Part; and
>   (b)   any period for which a licence granted to him under this Part remains in force,

shall be extended by the aggregate of those additional days.

43   Young offenders

(1)   Subject to subsections (4) and (5) below, this Part applies to persons serving sentences of detention in a young offender institution, or determinate sentences of detention under section 91 of the Powers of Criminal Courts (Sentencing) Act 2000, as it applies to persons serving equivalent sentences of imprisonment.

(2)   ...

(3)   References in this Part to prisoners ..., or to prison or imprisonment, shall be construed in accordance with subsection (1) ... above.

(4)   In relation to a short-term prisoner under the age of 18 years to whom subsection (1) of section 33 above applies, that subsection shall have effect as if it required the Secretary of State-

    (a)   to release him unconditionally if his sentence is for a term of twelve months or less; and

    (b)   to release him on licence if that sentence is for a term of more than twelve months.

(5)   In relation to a person under the age of 22 years who is released on licence under this Part, section 37(4A) above shall have effect as if the reference to supervision by an officer of a local probation board included a reference to supervision by a social worker of a local authority social services department.

44   Extended sentences for sexual or violent offenders

(1)   This section applies to a prisoner serving an extended sentence within the meaning of section 85 of the Powers of Criminal Courts (Sentencing) Act 2000.

(2)   Subject to the provisions of this section and section 51(2D) below, this Part, except section 40A, shall have effect as if the term of the extended sentence did not include the extension period.

(3)   Where the prisoner is released on licence under this Part, the licence shall, subject to any revocation under section 39(1) or (2) above, remain in force until the end of the extension period.

(4)   Where, apart from this subsection, the prisoner would be released unconditionally—

    (a)   he shall be released on licence; and

    (b)   the licence shall, subject to any revocation under section 39(1) or (2) above, remain in force until the end of the extension period.

(5)   The extension period shall be taken to begin as follows—

    (a)   for the purposes of subsection (3) above, on the date given by section 37(1) above;

    (b)   for the purposes of subsection (4) above, on the date on which, apart from that subsection, the prisoner would have been released unconditionally.

(6)   Sections 33(3) and 33A(1) above and section 46 below shall not apply in relation to the prisoner.

(7)   For the purposes of sections 37(5) and 39(1) and (2) above the question whether the prisoner is a long-term or short-term prisoner shall be determined by reference to the term of the extended sentence.

(8)   In this section "extension period" has the same meaning as in section 85 of the Powers of Criminal Courts (Sentencing) Act 2000.

44A   Re-release of prisoners serving extended sentences

(1)   This section applies to a prisoner serving an extended sentence within the meaning of section 85 of the Powers of Criminal Courts (Sentencing) Act 2000 who is recalled to prison under section 39(1) or (2) above.

(2)   Subject to subsection (3) below, the prisoner may require the Secretary of State to refer his case to the Board at any time.

(3)   Where there has been a previous reference of the prisoner's case to the Board (whether under this section or section 39(4) above), the Secretary of State shall not be required to refer the case until after the end of the period of one year beginning with the disposal of that reference.

(4)   On a reference—
    (a)   under this section; or
    (b)   under section 39(4) above,
the Board shall direct the prisoner's release if satisfied that it is no longer necessary for the protection of the public that he should be confined (but not otherwise).

(5)   If the Board gives a direction under subsection (4) above it shall be the duty of the Secretary of State to release the prisoner on licence.

45   Fine defaulters and contemnors

(1)   Subject to subsection (2) below, this Part (except sections 33A, 34A and 35 above) applies to persons committed to prison or to be detained under section 108 of the Powers of Criminal Courts (Sentencing) Act 2000—
    (a)   in default of payment of a sum adjudged to be paid by a conviction; or
    (b)   for contempt of court or any kindred offence,
as it applies to persons serving equivalent sentences of imprisonment; and references in this Part to short-term or long-term prisoners, or to prison or imprisonment, shall be construed accordingly.

(2)   In relation to persons committed as mentioned in subsection (1) above, the provisions specified in subsections (3) and (4) below shall have effect subject to the modifications so specified.

(3)   In section 33 above, for subsections (1) to (3) there shall be substituted the following subsections—

"(1)   As soon as a person committed as mentioned in section 45(1) below has served the appropriate proportion of his term, that is to say—
    (a)   one-half, in the case of a person committed for a term of less than twelve months;
    (b)   two-thirds, in the case of a person committed for a term of twelve months or more,
it shall be the duty of the Secretary of State to release him unconditionally.

(2)   As soon as a person so committed who—
   (a)   has been released on licence under section 36(1) below; and
   (b)   has been recalled under section 39(1) or (2) below,
would (but for his release) have served the appropriate proportion of his term, it shall be the duty of the Secretary of State to release him unconditionally."

(4)   In section 37 above, for subsections (1) to (3) there shall be substituted the following subsection—

"(1)   Where a person committed as mentioned in section 45(1) below is released on licence under section 36(1) above, the licence shall, subject to—
   (a)   ...
   (b)   any revocation under section 39(1) or (2) below,
continue in force until the date on which he would (but for his release) have served the appropriate proportion of his term; and in this subsection 'appropriate proportion' has the meaning given by section 33(1) above."

[10:5]   Criminal Justice and Court Services Act 2000 sections 1–7

1   Purposes of the Chapter

(1)   This Chapter has effect for the purposes of providing for—
   (a)   courts to be given assistance in determining the appropriate sentences to pass, and making other decisions, in respect of persons charged with or convicted of offences, and
   (b)   the supervision and rehabilitation of such persons.

(2)   Subsection (1)(b) extends (in particular) to—
   (a)   giving effect to community orders,
   (b)   supervising persons released from prison on licence,
   (c)   providing accommodation in approved premises.

(3)   Regulations may extend the purposes mentioned in subsection (1) to include other prescribed purposes relating to persons charged with or convicted of offences.

2   Aims of the Service

(1)   This section applies to—
   (a)   the functions of the Secretary of State under this Chapter,
   (b)   the functions of local probation boards, and officers of local probation boards, under this Act or any other enactment,
so far as they may be exercised for the purposes mentioned in section 1.

(2)   In exercising those functions the person concerned must have regard to the following aims—
   (a)   the protection of the public,
   (b)   the reduction of re-offending,

    (c)   the proper punishment of offenders,

    (d)   ensuring offenders' awareness of the effects of crime on the victims of crime and the public,

    (e)   the rehabilitation of offenders.

3 Functions of the Secretary of State

(1)   The Secretary of State has the function of ensuring that provision is made throughout England and Wales for the purposes mentioned in section 1.

(2)   The Secretary of State may make any payment he considers appropriate towards expenditure incurred by any person for any of those purposes.

(3)   If he considers it appropriate, he may make any payment on conditions.

(4)   The conditions may (among other things)—

    (a)   regulate the purposes for which the payment or any part of it may be used,

    (b)   require repayment to the Secretary of State in specified circumstances.

4 Local probation boards

(1)   For the purpose of implementing this Chapter, England and Wales shall be divided into areas.

(2)   For each area there shall be a board (referred to in this Act as a local probation board) which is to exercise the functions conferred on it by virtue of this Act and any other enactment.

(3)   Schedule 1 (which makes provision about the constitution of local probation boards, their powers and other matters relating to them) is to have effect.

(4)   References in this Act or any other enactment to an officer of a local probation board are references to—

    (a)   any member of the staff of a local probation board appointed to exercise the functions of an officer of the board, and

    (b)   any other individual exercising functions of an officer of a local probation board by virtue of section 5(2).

(5)   The initial areas for the purpose of implementing this Chapter are—

    (a)   the police areas listed in Schedule 1 to the Police Act 1996 (areas into which England and Wales, apart from London, is divided), and

    (b)   the area comprising the Metropolitan Police District and the City of London Police Area.

(6)   The division of England and Wales into areas for that purpose may be altered from time to time by order made by the Secretary of State.

5   Functions of local probation boards

(1)   It is a function of a local probation board—

    (a)   to make arrangements for ensuring that sufficient provision is made in respect of its area for the purposes mentioned in section 1 and for ensuring the performance of any other functions conferred by virtue of this Act or any other enactment on the board,

    (b)   to make arrangements for ensuring the performance of any functions conferred by virtue of this Act or any other enactment on officers of the board,

and to implement, or ensure the implementation of, any arrangements it makes under this section.

(2)   In addition to making arrangements for provision to be made by its staff, a local probation board may (for example)—

    (a)   make arrangements with organisations for provision to be made on the board's behalf by the organisations,

    (b)   make arrangements with individuals who are not members of the board's staff under which they may perform functions of officers of the board,

and arrangements under paragraph (a) may provide for the organisations to designate individuals who may perform functions of officers of the board.

(3)   The provision that may be made in pursuance of such arrangements includes providing services to any person and, in particular—

    (a)   giving assistance to persons remanded on bail or for whom officers of the board have responsibilities,

    (b)   providing accommodation in approved premises for persons who have at any time been charged with or convicted of an offence.

(4)   A local probation board may provide for its staff to co-operate with persons in its area who are concerned with the prevention or reduction of crime or with giving assistance to the victims of crime.

(5)   Regulations may confer further functions on local probation boards or officers of local probation boards.

(6)   A local probation board may give grants or other financial assistance to any person only in pursuance of regulations.

(7)   A local probation board—

    (a)   may make an arrangement with another local probation board under which it provides on behalf of the other board, in respect of the other board's area, any services which it could provide under this section in respect of its own area, and

    (b)   may charge the other local probation board for any services it provides in pursuance of the arrangement.

(8)   It is for the Secretary of State to determine whether or not any provision made by a local probation board under this section is sufficient.

6 The inspectorate

(1)   The inspectorate, and the office of chief inspector, established under section 23 of the Probation Service Act 1993 (inspectorate of probation) shall continue in being, but—
    (a)   the members of the inspectorate are to be known as "Her Majesty's Inspectorate of the National Probation Service for England and Wales", and
    (b)   the chief inspector is to be known as "Her Majesty's Chief Inspector of the National Probation Service for England and Wales".

(2)   The power to appoint a person to be chief inspector or one of the other members of the inspectorate is exercisable by the Secretary of State.

(3)   The Secretary of State may determine—
    (a)   the number of members of the inspectorate,
    (b)   the remuneration, allowances or other amounts to be paid by him to or in respect of the members of the inspectorate.

(4)   Below in this Chapter—
    (a)   references to the chief inspector are to Her Majesty's Chief Inspector of the National Probation Service for England and Wales,
    (b)   references to the members of the inspectorate are to the chief inspector and the other members of Her Majesty's Inspectorate of the National Probation Service for England and Wales.

7 Functions of inspectorate

(1)   The chief inspector must secure that the provision made in pursuance of arrangements made by each local probation board under section 5 is inspected by a member of the inspectorate.

(2)   The Secretary of State may direct the members of the inspectorate to assess the provision made by reference to criteria specified in directions.

(3)   A report of an inspection under subsection (1) must be sent to the Secretary of State.

(4)   The Secretary of State may give directions as to—
    (a)   the information to be given in the report and the form in which it is to be given,
    (b)   the time by which the report is to be given.

(5)   The Secretary of State must lay a copy of the report before each House of Parliament.

(6)   The Secretary of State may give directions, in connection with the purposes mentioned in section 1 or any related purposes, conferring further functions on the chief inspector and the other members of the inspectorate.

[10:6] **Home Office** *National Standards of Probation Service* (2000)

This is published in loose-leaf format and the following extracts give only an idea of their content:

OFFENDER ASSESSMENT BEFORE SENTENCE

Bail information reports

B1.   The purpose of bail information provided by probation services is to assist the court by providing to the Crown Prosecution Service (CPS) verified information to add to their factual knowledge of the defendant, including on risk of harm to the public, and hence contributing to their representations on bail.

B2.   Bail information reports shall:
- be objective, factual and impartial;
- contain a front sheet which sets out the basic factual information on the defendant and list the sources used to prepare the report;
- clearly indicate the author, the date on which the report is written, the court and the date of hearing for which the information is intended and basic details about the defendant;
- include details of relevant information such as accommodation and employment;
- be presented as a written report whenever possible;
- be made orally when a written report cannot be prepared in time, and then be written up as soon as possible thereafter;
- in cases where risk of serious harm to the public is apparent, be copied to the police, social services or health authority as appropriate; and
- be made available to the court duty officer where the writer is unable to be in court.

B3.   Where a pre-sentence report or specific sentence report is ordered following conviction or at the point of committal to Crown Court, a copy of the bail information report, if available, should be passed to the officer charged with preparing the report.

Pre-sentence reports

B4.   The purpose of a pre-sentence report (PSR) is to provide information to the sentencing court about the offender and the offence(s) committed and to assist the court to decide on suitable sentence. A PSR shall:
- be objective, impartial, free from discriminatory language and stereotype, balanced, verified and factually accurate;
- be based on the use of the Offender Assessment System (OASys), when implemented, to provide a systematic assessment of the nature and the causes of the defendant's offending behaviour, the risk the defendant poses to the public and the action which can be taken to reduce the likelihood of reoffending;
- be based on at least one face-to-face interview with the offender;
- specify information available from the CPS, any hostel placement or from any other relevant source;

- be written, and a copy provided to the court, the defence, the offender and (where required by the Crime (Sentences) Act 1997) the prosecution;
- be prepared within, at most, 15 working days of request; or such shorter timescale as has been agreed in protocols with the court;
- contain the sections indicated in italics below.

Front sheet

B5. Every PSR shall contain a front sheet which sets out the basic factual information on the offender and the offence(s), and lists the sources used to prepare the report, indicating clearly which information has been verified. An approved format is at Annex B.

Offence analysis

B6. Every PSR shall contain an offence analysis which shall:
- analyse the offence(s) before the court, highlighting the key features in respect of nature and circumstances in which committed;
- assess the offender's culpability and level of premeditation;
- assess the consequences of the offence, including what is known of the impact on any victim, either from the CPS papers or from a victim statement where available;
- assess the offender's attitude to the offence and awareness of its consequences, including to any victim;
- indicate whether or not any positive action has been taken by the offender to make reparation or address offending behaviour since the offence was committed.

Offender assessment

B7. Every PSR shall contain an offender assessment which shall:
- state the offender's status in relation to:
    - literacy and numeracy;
    - accommodation;
    - employment;
- assess the implications of any special circumstances, eg family crisis, substance abuse or mental illness, which were directly relevant to the offending;
- evaluate any patterns of offending including reasons for offending and assess the outcome of any earlier court interventions, including the offender's response to previous supervision;
- where substance misuse is relevant, provide details of the nature of the misuse, and the offender's response to previous or current treatment;
- give consideration to the impact of racism on the offender's behaviour where directly relevant to the offence;
- include any relevant personal background which may have contributed to the offender's motive for committing the offence.

Assessment of the risk of harm to the public and the likelihood of reoffending

B8. Every PSR shall:

- contain an assessment of the offender's likelihood of reoffending based on the current offence, attitude to it, and other relevant information;
- contain an assessment of the offender's risk of causing serious harm to the public;
- identify any risks of self-harm.

Conclusion

B9. Every PSR shall contain a conclusion which:
- evaluates the offender's motivation and ability to change and identifies, where relevant, action required to improve motivation;
- explicitly states whether or not an offender is suitable for a community sentence;
- makes a clear and realistic proposal for sentence designed to protect the public and reduce reoffending, including for custody where this is necessary;
- where the proposal is for a probation order or combination order, includes an outline supervision plan containing:
  - a description of the purposes and desired outcomes of the proposed sentence;
  - the methods envisaged and interventions likely to be undertaken, including attendance at accredited programmes where appropriate;
  - the level of supervision envisaged (which for offenders at high risk of causing serious harm to the public is likely to be higher than the minimum required by the Standards);
- where a specific condition is proposed, sets out the requirement precisely as it is proposed to appear in any order, and gives a likely start date;
- where the proposal is for a curfew order, includes details of the suitability of the proposed curfew address and its likely effects on others living at the offender's address;
- for all serious sexual or violent offences, provides advice on the appropriateness of extended supervision;
- where custody is a likely option, identifies any anticipated effects on the offender's family circumstances, current employment or education.

Specific sentence reports

B10. The purpose of a specific sentence report (SSR) is to provide information about the offender and offence(s) so as to assist the sentencing court to determine the offender's suitability for a specific sentence envisaged by the court. It is a PSR for the formal purposes of Part I of the Criminal Justice Act 1991 and is used to speed up the provision of information to the court to allow sentencing without delay and is most likely to be used where the court envisages a community service order of up to 100 hours or probation order without additional requirements. An SSR shall:
- be based on an initial assessment of risk of serious harm and likelihood of reoffending;
- be a written report, even where presented orally to the court. An approved format is at Annex C;
- clearly set out the offender's suitability for a particular penalty as requested by the court;
- other than in exceptional circumstances, be available to the court on the day requested;

- recommend an adjournment for a full PSR if the writer believes that further investigation is required.

Where it has not been possible to complete a PSR or an SSR, for whatever season, including non-attendance by the offender at interview, the probation officer shall submit written notice to the court giving reasons why the report has not been completed.

Required levels of contact, achieving compliance and ensuring enforcement

D1. Achieving the minimum required levels of contact, and enforcing supervision rigorously, serves two main purposes:
- to satisfy the courts and the community that a credible level of disciplined supervision is taking place;
- to ensure that offenders have the opportunity to engage in effective supervision.

D2. In all cases, the Standards set the **minimum** requirements. They are likely to be exceeded for offenders who pose risks of serious harm to the public, or a higher probability of reoffending, or for those who may be subject to additional order or licence requirements.

Required levels of contact

D3. For those aged under 22 or serving 12 months or more in custody, the home probation service shall provide the offender with a supervising officer or case manager within 10 working days of sentencing. The levels and nature of contact between prisoners, prison staff and the offender's supervising (or managing) officer are not specified in these Standards. Staff are expected to use their judgement to ensure that there is sufficient contact at the pre-release stage to enable the successful resettlement of the offender and the preparation of a supervision plan.

D4. Supervising officers shall ensure that they refer to, and act in accordance with, the guidance in The Lifer Manual when dealing with arrangements for offenders sentenced to life imprisonment.

D5. If an offender has spent sufficient time on remand to be released on licence direct from the court and no supervising officer has been appointed, the court duty probation officer shall give the supervising probation area as much detail as possible about the offender and the release address, and arrange for the licence to be served.

D6. The police shall be given release, licence and address information as soon as practicable and in any case within 10 working days of release.

D7. Wherever possible the date of the first appointment for those on **community orders** should be given to the offender either by the probation service or by the bench (acting on probation service advice) before the offender leaves court. This should be arranged to take place within five working days of the order being made.

D8. The probation service shall ensure that for **all offenders**, at the first meeting the supervising officer shall:
- provide written information setting out what is expected of the offender during the period of supervision and what the offender can expect from the probation service;
- explain to the offender (and provide a copy of) instructions setting out the required standards of behaviour that apply during the period of supervision, which shall prohibit:
  - further offending;
  - violent or aggressive behaviour or threats of violence;
  - other conduct or language that might reasonably give offence to probation staff, other persons on supervision or members of the public;
  - other wilful or persistent non co-operation or behaviour designed to frustrate the purpose of the offender's or others' supervision;
- ensure that offenders sign their order or licence (where possible) and indicate that they understand its requirements.

D9. Appointments that count towards meeting the Standard are those made in connection with the supervision plan and include appointments with partnership agencies, such as for drug counselling. All such appointments are enforceable and appropriate enforcement action must be taken if any appointment is missed.

D10. Where additional requirements are attached to an order, they are implemented in line with the requirements of the court and normally commenced within 12 weeks of the order. Even where offenders attend a short intensive programme of, say, five sessions in one week within the first 12 weeks of the order, this Standard still requires weekly contact to be arranged.

Offenders released on licence

D11. The probation service shall ensure that:
- the first appointment with the offender after release shall be arranged to occur on the day of release or, if not practicable, on the next working day;
- arrangements shall be made then for a further minimum of weekly contact during the first four weeks following release, making a total of five contacts in the first four weeks. One of the contacts will normally be a home visit, which will be arranged to take place within ten working days of release;
- contact shall be arranged to take place at least fortnightly for the second and third months following release, and thereafter not less than monthly.

D12. The supervising officer shall:
- remind an offender on licence that the period of post-release supervision forms part of the original sentence;
- issue the offender with a statement explaining when and why breach action will be taken if the offender fails to comply, for the receipt of which the offender should sign in the record;
- explain to the offender that travel outside the UK is prohibited, other than in exceptional circumstances (agreed by an officer of Assistant Chief Officer or equivalent grade in the case of short-term prisoners, or by the Parole Board for long-term prisoners).

Probation orders and the probation element of combination orders

D13. At least 12 appointments shall be made within the first 12 weeks of supervision, normally scheduled to take place weekly. There will normally be a home visit made within the first 12 weeks of the order. Six appointments shall be made within the second 12 weeks, after which appointments may reduce to monthly contact.

Community service orders and the community service element of combination orders

D14. Services shall:
- have clear guidelines for liaison with beneficiaries;
- arrange the first work session to take place within ten working days of the order being made;
- ensure offenders are offered a minimum of five hours work per week;
- arrange work so as not to prevent the offender from being readily available to seek or take up employment if unemployed, nor conflict with an offender's entitlement to benefit, nor disrupt the working hours of an employed person, or the education of an offender in full-time education, and to take account of religious and cultural requirements;
- include, at the service's discretion, any travel time in excess of half an hour each way, subject to an overall limit of 10% of the hours prescribed;
- include, at the service's discretion, an allowance for completing basic literacy or other work necessary to enable the offender to gain maximum benefit from the order, or to provide qualifications directly related to work done under the order, provided the total such allowance does not exceed 10% of the prescribed hours;
- include up to half an hour where a work session spans lunchtime and the offender is required to remain on site, providing that the offender remains under the supervision of the supervising officer throughout; and
- not include any time during which bad weather prevents the performance of work, except where the supervisor requires the offender to remain, in which case time credited must not exceed more than half an hour a day;
- ensure *all* offenders are given a weekly record detailing:
  - the hours worked that week;
  - an indication of whether that work and the offender's conduct were satisfactory;
  - total hours worked under the order thus far; and
  - hours remaining to be worked.

D15. Where an offender is subject to a community service order or a combination order and where a further community service order is imposed (whether for further offences of for breach of a community order), for the purposes of these Standards, the second order shall be treated as if it were simply an extension of the first, ie no separate induction or commencement is required.

D16. Community service placements must:
- be assessed for the risks to individuals and property and the requirements of health and safety legislation;
- be available to meet the needs of specific individuals, such as those related to their gender, race, ethnicity or ability;
- not replace work that would normally be done by paid employees;
- occupy offenders fully and be physically, emotionally or mentally demanding.

Combination Orders

D17. The standards for both the probation and community service elements of combination orders apply, ie a minimum of 12 probation appointments plus one community service assessment and 11 community service work sessions shall be arranged in the first 12 weeks. They shall be managed together and, for enforcement purposes, any unacceptable absences from either the probation or community service element will be treated cumulatively.

D18. Exceptionally, line management may endorse a delay in the activation of either element of a combination order if this is desirable to achieve the overall objectives of the order.

Achieving compliance and ensuring enforcement

D19. For **all offenders** the supervising officer shall:
- when an offender seeks to change an appointment before the due date, indicate if this change is acceptable or not, and give reasons. If the change is not agreed by the officer then the offender's failure to attend will be deemed to be unacceptable;
- ensure that any apparent failure to comply with the requirements of the order or licence is followed up with the offender by an enquiry letter, interview or telephone call to determine the reason for failure within two working days;
- fully record every apparent failure within a further five working days, including whether or not any explanation was given by the offender, and if so what that explanation was and whether or not it was acceptable;
- if the explanation is not considered acceptable, or no explanation is given within the further five working days, record the incident as an unacceptable failure to comply;
- place copies of any written warning on the offender's case records along with a note of the offender's comment on the warning;
- where breach proceedings are required, instigate breach proceedings within 10 working days of the relevant unacceptable failure to comply;
- normally offer offenders further appointments or community service work pending breach or appeal against sentence, unless a decision has been recorded, with reasons, why this should not happen.

D20. For **all offenders**, breach action may be taken after one unacceptable failure, where appropriate.

D21. For offenders on **community sentences** the supervising officer shall:
- where breach action is not to be taken on the first unacceptable failure, formally warn the offender, using a 'yellow card' warning letter; and
- give only one warning in any 12-month period of supervision before commencing breach action.

D22. For **combination orders** only one warning is permitted for the probation or community service element.

D23. For offenders **released on licence** the supervising officer shall:

- where breach action is not taken after one failure to comply, give the offender a formal written warning of the consequences of further failure;
- where it is proposed not to take breach action after a second failure to comply, arrange for an officer of at least Assistant Chief Officer level, or equivalent grade, to confirm this course of action and give the offender a formal written warning. This must be copied to the Parole Unit;
- give no more than two written warnings within the total licence period before commencing breach action;
- commence breach action no later than the third failure to comply; and
- if changed circumstances suggest an enhanced risk of serious harm to the public, and the offender is subject to licence, inform the Parole Unit (Lifer Review Unit in the case of life licensees) immediately.

[10:7]   Raynor, P 'Community Penalties: Probation, Punishment, and "What Works"' in Maguire, Morgan and Reiner (eds) *The Oxford Handbook of Criminology* (3rd edition, 2002) Oxford University Press (at page 1195):

THE FUTURE OF COMMUNITY PENALTIES

Community penalties clearly have a future: they are such an important part of our sentencing system that it is not possible to imagine their disappearance under any reasonably probable or foreseeable set of criminal justice policies. That does not mean that we can expect all, or even most, of their features to continue as they are; change has occurred with unprecedented speed over the last few years and shows few signs of slowing down, despite the clear strains involved for organizations and practitioners. Some aspects of future policy and practice can be regarded as probable, based on extrapolation of firmly established current trends, while some are no more than possible, depending on the unknown outcomes of current processes or experiments.

Some of the clear candidates for inclusion in the 'probable' future are information technology, monitoring, and standardization. Although the development of the online case management system CRAMS has been fraught with expensive procurement problems, other systems are being developed and rolled out piecemeal which will eventually be part of an integrated system. The offender assessment system OASys is being made available to services during 2002 after a longer-than-planned development process, and although it is initially for use in a paper version only, it is guaranteed to generate demand for the eventual online version if only because the paper version is fairly cumbersome. 'Integrated Accredited Programme Software' is also approaching general availability and, when fully online, will greatly facilitate both tracking of offenders through programmes and auditing of the programmes' delivery and effectiveness. The same software which helps probation staff to monitor offenders can be used, when it is part of a national system, to monitor the work of probation services. In addition we can expect to see more use of electronic monitoring, including perhaps the tracking tag capable of following an offender's movements and the use of voice recognition software to verify the identity of offenders checking in by telephone. Another probable consequence of the increasing use of larger information flows to support processes such as audit (HM Inspectorate of Probation 2001) and resource allocation will be greater standardization of policies and practices, and a high degree of compliance with National Standards and any other performance indicators that are linked to funding.

Another feature of future probation services is likely to be a continuing emphasis on risk. Probation services have become increasingly conscious of their role in supervising (together where possible with other agencies) the potentially violent offender or the predatory sex offender (Kemshall and Maguire 2001), and further developments may be anticipated here: for example, intensive surveillance schemes in collaboration with the police (Walton 2001). The problem of what to offer to the 'high risk, low needs' offender is likely to receive more attention, and this is one of the areas in which electronic monitoring may have a contribution to make. One further consequence of this is likely to be an increase in 'bifurcation', or the provision of very different levels and kinds of services according to the assessed dangerousness of the offender. Partly this reflects the 'risk principle', but it is also the characteristic response to an increasing focus on dangerousness (Bottoms 1977).

Two other recent trends seem to have every prospect of becoming still more firmly established. One is the continuing extension of the 'What Works' agenda beyond programmes and community punishment orders to consider effective case management, pro-social approaches to supervision, and improved opportunities of access to 'protective factors' or social resources such as education, training, employment, accommodation, assistance with substance abuse problems, and health care. The approaches to resettlement currently being developed for people released from short-term prison sentences are often concerned with problems that many offenders face whether or not recently released from prison, and although the terms 'resettlement needs' suggests needs which are particularly characteristic of those who have recently been removed from the community, they can more usefully be thought of as 'social integration' needs or 'inclusion' needs. If unmet, they can often frustrate even a quite determined attempt to avoid re-offending.

The other clear candidate for inclusion in the 'probable' category is increasing differentiation and specialization in the Probation Service itself, together with an increasing amount of service delivery by staff who are not probation officers. New roles are increasingly underpinned by competency specifications, selection, assessment, and specialist training. These are increasingly organized into a comprehensive framework by the Criminal Justice National Training Organization (CJNTO 2001), including vocational qualifications which can potentially be shared with staff of other criminal justice services. The probation officer is no longer a semi-autonomous generalist attempting a range of roles and tasks on the basis of a broad qualification and experience; instead, he or she is deployed by management in a particular service delivery niche, and will often not be a qualified probation officer but a staff member of some other grade who has received specific training for the particular role. The consequences for industrial relations and human resources policy of a situation where people of very different grades and pay can find themselves doing the same work, or even in a supervisory relationship which reverses the normal grade seniority, have yet to be explored and confronted, but they will need to be.

KEY VARIABLES: RESEARCH AND POLITICS

Moving from probable to possible future scenarios, much will depend on two factors which are currently difficult to predict: first, the outcomes of evaluation of the current wave of 'What Works' initiatives; and secondly, the politics of law and order. Considering these in turn, the large-scale roll-out of accredited programmes to the Probation Service is not due to produce clear evidence of its effectiveness or ineffectiveness for some time. The reconviction studies which will form the final and most conclusive stage of evaluation of the original 'Pathfinder' pilot schemes will not report until 2003, and evaluation of initiatives rolled out since the Pathfinders will appear a good deal later. However, there are a number of reasons why these evaluations might not prove quite so critical in determining the future of probation as many people would naturally suppose. Obviously a clear set of negative results would lead to considerable problems, but the more likely scenario of mixed and some unclear results would probably not lead to huge changes in policy, provided that the political climate remains broadly similar to today's. Findings will probably not need to be uniformly or strongly positive to jus-tify the continuation of projects or programmes. It will be possible to argue that the evaluations reflect early or underdeveloped practice (particularly in the assessment of offenders, an acknowledged area of difficulty pending the introduction of new methods such as OASys) or that early implementation problems meant that evaluations were not based on best practice (a clear future, for example, of some of the 'resettlement' Pathfinder projects (Lewis et al 2001)).

More importantly, public and political commitments to 'What Works' creates a climate in which even limited positive findings can carry a good deal of weight, in contrast to the near invisibility of even quite substantial positive findings during the 'nothing works' era. The target which has been set for the Probation and Prison Services of a 5 per cent reduction in re-offending by offenders under their supervision presents considerable problems of measurement. In addition, the Probation Service performance indicator related to this target concentrates on the number of offenders completing accredited programs rather than on direct measurement of crime reduction (Probation Circular 92/2000). In sum, there are a number of reasons to believe that even a moderate amount of good news from the evaluations currently in progress would be seen as broad justifi-cation for the continuation of current policies, particularly as the focus of recent politi-cal statements has been more on community safety than on crime reduction. This will tend to direct scrutiny towards the effectiveness of other criminal justice agencies such as the police. Implementation of the recent sentencing review (Halliday 2001) will also tend to consolidate the position and role of probation services by substantially increas-ing the number of people under their supervision. This is likely to happen regardless of whether there is any trend to decrease the use of custodial sentences, since the new proposals for 'custody plus' involve a compulsory period of post-release supervision for almost all short-sentence prisoners.

In such a system the Probation Service may well find itself simply so central to the process of managing offenders, and so well integrated into the penal process, that it cannot easily be subjected to the kind of political attack which it experienced during the early 1990s. However, being a big player in the system does not guarantee influence and friendly policies: in the 1980s the Prison Service was a very big player, but policy was driven by the attempt to find alternatives to custody, since prisons were widely perceived as failing. A better scenario for probation would follow from a very positive set of evaluation findings, which would greatly increase the Service's capacity to influ-ence policies and events.

In addition to the unpredictable results of current evaluations, the second (and prob-ably greater) risk factor for the future of community penalties must be the political climate. As Garland has pointed out, late modern criminal justice policies are subject to frequent and sometimes extreme changes of direction (Garland 1996) as politicians seek support from anxious populations through media-friendly gestures. The Con-servative Home Secretary Michael Howard's 'prison works' speech of 1993 was just such a gesture, which had profound consequences for the Probation Service and for the principles of the 1991 Criminal Justice Act. Nobody can rule out the possibility of similar populist stunts in the future, and a continuing search for eye-catching initiatives by New Labour politicians has already been responsible for unhelpful tinkering such as changing the familiar names of the former probation and community service orders. Two factors, however, seem likely to offer some protection for community penalties: one is the strong survival instinct of senior probation managers, which historically has allowed them to embrace a wide and varied range of political and technocratic initiatives; the other is the improbability of a sustained campaign against community sentences as long as they remain a relatively cheap sentencing option for many thousands of offenders every year.

One further way in which probation services might seek to strengthen their political position and their perceived legitimacy might be to learn something from the politicians, and to find their own ways of seeking a greater degree of public support. Probation services always risk being seen as primarily existing for the benefit of the offender rather than serving the community as a whole. A probation service which could show communities how they gain from the rehabilitation of offenders would itself gain significantly in influence and in perceived legitimacy. One implication of this would be that instead of rehabilitative programmes being seen primarily as a benefit to offenders, and therefore arguably unfair to those facing similar difficulties who have not offended, probation services should try to present rehabilitation as work that offenders undertake as a consequence of a crime: work which is directed to changing their own behaviour and attitudes in a more pro-social direction, to the advantage of the communities in which they live. A rehabilitative penalty can reflect the interests and values of the wider community, and perhaps equip offenders with the skills to maintain themselves more effectively and to contribute more to society. The notion of rehabilitation as offenders working to rehabilitate themselves may be better aligned with community values, and more consistent with restorative principles, than the notion of offenders simply receiving help. It would also probably be more constructive than the attempt to improve public confidence by ever more rigorous approaches to enforcement.

A concrete way to embody these principles in practice (explored further in Raynor 2001) might be to seek to include an explicitly reparative element in a wider range of community sentences, perhaps with some community involvement, or involvement where appropriate of victims, in determining what the reparative content should be. The central point is to demonstrate that rehabilitation is itself fundamentally restorative and benefits the community as well as the offender. A probation service which could consistently achieve this shift in public perception would be a significant contributor to criminal justice policy and practice, promoting not only crime reduction but also the belief that communities can engage constructively with the problems caused by crime. However, this kind of speculation lies outside the scope of this chapter, except to illustrate the possibility that probation services may continue to explore their undoubted potential to develop some qualitatively different responses to offending: penalties which differ from other sentences not only in degree but also in kind, building on human capacities for cooperation, sympathy, and inclusion rather than hostility and division.

[10:8] **Worrall, A** *Punishment in the Community: The Future of Criminal Justice* (1997) Longmans (at page 149):

'Punishment in the Community' has been officially supplanted by the rhetoric of 'Prison Works'. Having moved from a need to demonstrate that 'alternatives to custody' are at least as effective as custody (in the early and mid-1980s) through a more optimistic phase of 'restricting liberty' to an extent 'commensurate with the seriousness of the offence' (in the late 1980s and early 1990s), community penalties (both supervisory and financial) are now actively competing for customers in a market environment in which prison is no longer viewed as the last resort but as one of a range of options. The official (if lame) exhortations to sentencers to avoid imprisonment wherever possible have finally ceased and any remaining inhibitions have been removed. The reoffending rates of those sent to prison, it is claimed, are no worse than for those placed on community penalties (Lloyd, Mair and Hough 1994; Maclean 1995). It is as though the secret fears contained in George Orwell's Room 101 had finally been unlocked and have been found to be less disagreeable than expected.

... a fully social analysis of community punishment must involve a debunking of received wisdom. We are not short of research. We have so much research on the effectiveness of rehabilitation programmes that we now have to move to 'meta-analysis' (McGuire 1995b) What we are short of is the political and professional will to take such research seriously unless it is always-already framed in terms of punishment (Maclean 1995).

...

At the beginning of this book I said that our conceptual analysis of non-incarcerative sanctions was impoverished by our inability to think of them as anything other than 'alternatives' to prison. I have attempted to show that such sanctions deserve analysis in their own right. But that analysis has not led to the conclusion that they are necessarily 'better', in their present form and content, than prison. On the contrary, to the extent that they blur the boundaries between freedom and captivity, they cease to be genuine 'alternatives' and are merely poor substitutes for the 'real thing'. Life for many offenders at the end of the century is not so good that we can make limitless demands on them in the belief that they will endure anything to avoid prison. And we must stop pretending that the criminal justice system can find the answer to crime. Playing at 'restorative justice' and 'mediation' in a society as grossly unequal as ours is, to mix the metaphors, applying no more than first aid to a gaping wound. Such approaches are *reflections* of a just and confident society but they do not create it. Only when there is a political will to invest in human, social and cultural capital and a willingness for sentencers to see custody as the alternative – the sentence of last resort – will things change.

Two things are clear from comparisons with the experiences of other countries. One is that the role of community punishment as a means of reducing the prison population is a failure. There is no relationship between the use of community punishment and the size of the prison population, *unless*, as with the 1991 Criminal Justice Act, there is a deliberate curbing of the courts' sentencing powers through legislation. Left to their own devices, in the current worldwide obsession with internal law and order, courts find it hard to resist the 'pull' of imprisonment. But it is also true that we do not need to be obsessed with what is happening in America. There are many examples elsewhere of innovative, if modest, schemes which help offenders to see the advantages of choosing not to offend.

The downsizing of the probation service in England and Wales is unlikely to be reversed in the foreseeable future. Amalgamations of services may increase in order to make savings and specific tasks (such as court duties and reports) will be increasingly casualised. Some services have already begun to put a range of services out to tender by independent organisations. Within the current punitive penal climate, it is difficult to argue in favour of such moves. But the probation service does not have a monopoly on caring for offenders and genuine partnership with other organisations that share the service's more traditional ethos must be recognised as one possible way forward.

The probation service will never achieve its ambition to be 'centre-stage' in the criminal justice system and it must stop tilting at the windmills of prison. Punishment in the Community alone will never succeed in reducing the prison population. The mechanisms of discipline 'in the community' are always-already excluded from the discourse of custody – they represent the *Other* of prison talk. Once this is faced up to, it may be possible to unhitch them, once and for all, from their unequal and subordinate relationship with custody, where they are viewed as being effective only in so far as they replicate the pains of imprisonment. They must instead be viewed as constituting a sphere of social control which is quite separate from that of the prison, based on self-government and normalising instruction (Rose 1989). Freed from the constraints of proving effectiveness in relation to prison, community punishments can be tailored to the needs of those towards whom the state has an obligation of advice, assistance or – dare it be said – friendship. Once uncoupled from custody, the accusation that such a vision merely serves to net-widen becomes irrelevant. Net-widening is only to be avoided when the net leads to exclusion from the rights and duties of citizenship. What is wrong with widening the net of skills and knowledge, including social skills and self-knowledge? What is wrong with widening the net of self-esteem, attachment and commitment to the future? What, in short, is wrong with widening the net of inclusion?

[10:9]   Genders, E and Player, E *Race Relations in Prisons* (1989) Clarendon Press

(From 'Racial discrimination in the allocation of living accommodation', at page 117):

Among the controversial issues in virtually all debates on race relations is the question of numbers: whether there should be any restrictions placed on the numbers of ethnic minorities permitted in any social context, or any attempt to concentrate or disperse them within the majority population. These concerns were present in the minds of most prison staff, particularly in relation to Black inmates. As has already been mentioned, more than half of the prison officers thought that the proportion of Black inmates should be strictly limited within individual establishments, yet only 20% of them wanted such restrictions to apply to Asian prisoners. The main argument was that when the Black population reached a certain level power struggles inevitably broke out with the White prisoners.

Prison officers have little control over the numbers of ethnic minority inmates allocated to their establishment. Where they do have considerable control, however, is in exercising their discretion to distribute the ethnic minority population between wings, and in allocating them to particular landings and cells. It was also stated at one of the prisons that the reason why they rarely had any trouble with Black inmates was because it was stemmed before it had a chance to take root. This, they said was achieved by the transfer officer shipping some of them out to other establishments as soon as their numbers were thought to have become too high. However, there was no way of gauging how often this took place.

Interviews were conducted with nine prison officers responsible for cell allocation at the five prisons, and informal discussions were held with other officers who were responsible for allocating prisoners to wings. Four of the nine officers claiming that when cells became vacant prisoners were allocated to them purely at random and that no other factors, including the inmates' racial origin, intruded upon the decision. The other five officers said that they took into account a number of criteria in reaching their decisions. Among the factors which they considered were age, offence, character, and racial origin of the inmate. For example, one officer said that he tried to locate older inmates together; and another that he exercised caution in the placement of sex offenders. At more than one establishment there was an attempt to place weaker inmates near the staff office and to keep strong or 'stroppy' ones away from powerful groups. At all of the establishments at least one officer responsible for cell allocation claimed that he dispersed ethnic minorities and, in particular, Black inmates. The reasons they gave for this however, varied at the different establishments. One allocating officer rationalised the dispersal of Black inmates on the grounds that they were 'noisy and tend to attract groups which create tensions and can only lead to trouble'. Another felt that Black inmates 'try to take over the wash-up facilities', that 'they are slow and take their time' and that 'the White inmates get fed up of it'. The allocating officer at another prison stated: 'You have to try to disperse them on the wing. We've had them together before and have had nothing but trouble ... one area once became a virtual 'no go' area for everyone, there were drugs and everything. Blacks are the main source of drugs in prison ... they have different customs too, the smell of their curries [on the wing] drives off the Whites and all but the bravest staff'.

It also emerged that racial dislike or racial prejudice on the part of inmates was, for some of these allocating officers, a sufficient reason for allowing cell changes. Five of them had been faced with objections from White inmates about their proximity to Blacks or Asians and all had acquiesced to a change of cell on the grounds of good management.

There was also some evidence to suggest that the policy of transferring prisoners between wings or to another prison in order to maintain good order and discipline could result in a degree of racial discrimination. Informal discussions with staff revealed that in situations of potential or actual conflict administrative convenience dictated that those who were least powerful or least numerous suffered the disadvantage of the transfer. It was often pointed out that the staff had no other option. Several cases came to light where ethnic minority inmates had been transferred despite the fact that it was generally acknowledged by both staff and inmates that it was the White prisoners who had initiated the conflict.

(From 'Racial discrimination in the allocation of inmates to jobs and training courses', at page 124):

For the purpose of analysis it was decided to use inmates' own ratings of the prestige of work tasks. Again these were divided into two groups: the 'best' and 'worst' jobs. All the industrial workshop tasks were rated amongst the worst jobs; the best jobs included orderly posts, kitchen work, wing cleaning, laundry, and outdoor jobs. There were no statistically significant differences in the proportion of White (42%) and ethnic minority (53%) inmates who were employed in the workshops. But ethnic minority inmates were significantly less likely than Whites to be currently employed in what were considered to be the best jobs. Indeed, only seven ethnic minority inmates (14%) were engaged on work parties which fell within the best job category, compared with 149 White inmates (45%). Moreover, the 7 ethnic minority inmates who were employed in best jobs were not evenly dispersed across the favoured tasks: 6 of them being engaged on wing cleaning and 1 in the laundry. In other words, there were no ethnic minority inmates in any of the orderly jobs, outdoor work parties, or in the kitchen.

It was striking that an examination of the previous prison jobs held by inmates over their period of stay at Littlebourne demonstrated the same pattern of work assignment. None of the ethnic minority inmates had ever been employed in orderly or outdoor work tasks. Only one Black inmate was recorded as having been employed in the kitchen and he had remained in this post for only three months. Nor was there any evidence to suggest that this situation has changed over time. Indeed, a snapshot picture taken of the racial composition of the work parties at Littlebourne in March 1985 showed that no ethnic minority inmates were employed in orderly or kitchen tasks and only one was engaged on an outdoor work party.

The most convincing evidence of racial bias in the labour allocation process was generated from the interviews conducted with 50 work supervisors from all five establishments, representing a cross-section of the work opportunities in each prison. For ease of analysis, the 50 work supervisors were divided into three broad categories: those in charge of 'popular' jobs; those in charge of 'unpopular' jobs; and instructors responsible for vocational training courses. The categorisation of a job as popular or unpopular varied to some extent between individual prisoners, staff and, establishments. The analysis was, therefore, based upon what was deemed to be the broad consensus. As a result, workshops, outdoor work parties, and wing cleaning, were classified as unpopular jobs; and orderly posts, kitchen, mess, works, and laundry parties were categorised as popular jobs.

A calculation was made of the proportion of ethnic minority inmates employed on each job in relation to their numbers in the establishment. Each supervisor was then asked whether this was the usual proportion on his party and how many ethnic minority inmates were currently employed in positions of responsibility. Of the 20 supervisors of popular jobs, only 20% had a proportionate representation of ethnic minorities in their parties. The remaining 80% had either a below-average representation or no ethnic minority inmates at all. In striking contrast, none of the 22 supervisors of unpopular jobs reported having no ethnic minority inmates in their work-force, and a third had an over-representation. Among the eight vocational training instructors there was considerable variation: three had no ethnic minorities on their courses, but two had an over-representation. When asked whether the current proportion of ethnic minority inmates on their parties represented the usual pattern for their work-forces, 82% said that it did.

It is interesting to note the types of jobs in which ethnic minorities were greatly under-represented. Not one of the orderly officers had an ethnic minority inmate on his work-force and five out of the six stated that this was the usual pattern. Furthermore, two of the five catering officers had no one from the ethnic minorities, the remaining three having a below-average representation. All these supervisors claimed that this was typical. In addition, two catering officers, one works officer, one laundry officer and two vocational training instructors stated that they usually had no ethnic minority inmates on their parties. Thus, a total of 11 officers or instructors did not usually have any ethnic minority inmates on their parties and these included 9 (45%) of the 20 supervisors of the popular jobs.

The message, it would appear, is quite clear. Racial imbalance is present within the labour allocation process. Although individual criticisms could be made about each of the sources of data which have been used, the strength of the evidence lies in the consistency of the findings. The Psychology Unit at East Bridge in its study suggested three potential causative factors: a 'systematic' bias against ethnic minority groups; a genuine difference in abilities; and different preferences of ethnic minority prisoners. From the interviews which were conducted with inmates it was possible to eliminate the last suggestion because prisoners of different racial origins had similar work preferences. The second explanation (lower abilities) is also dubious. The analysis of the outside employment records of 1,255 medium-term and long-term prisoners did not indicate that those from the ethnic minorities were less able than their White counterparts. Thus, credence must be given to the suggestion that racial bias lies at the root of the racial imbalance evidenced in labour allocation.

[10:10]   Prison Act 1952 sections 1; 47

1   General control over prisons

All powers and jurisdiction in relation to prisons and prisoners which before the commencement of the Prison Act 1877 were exercisable by any other authority shall, subject to the provisions of this Act, be exercisable by the Secretary of State.

47   Rules for the management of prisons, remand centres and young offender institutions

(1)   The Secretary of State may make rules for the regulation and management of prisons, remand centres, young offender institutions or secure training centres respectively, and for the classification, treatment, employment, discipline and control of persons required to be detained therein.

(2)   Rules made under this section shall make provision for ensuring that a person who is charged with any offence under the rules shall be given a proper opportunity of presenting his case.

(3)   Rules made under this section may provide for the training of particular classes of persons and their allocation for that purpose to any prison or other institution in which they may lawfully be detained.

(4)   Rules made under this section shall provide for the special treatment of the following persons whilst required to be detained in a prison, that is to say—
>   (a)–(c)   ...
>   (d)   any ... person detained in a prison, not being a person serving a sentence or a person imprisoned in default of payment of a sum adjudged to be paid by him on his conviction or a person committed to custody on his conviction.

(4A) Rules made under this section shall provide for the inspection of secure training centres and the appointment of independent persons to visit secure training centres and to whom representations may be made by offenders detained in secure training centres.

(5) Rules made under this section may provide for the temporary release of persons detained in a prison, remand centre, young offender institution or secure training centre not being persons committed in custody for trial before the Crown Court or committed to be sentenced or otherwise dealt with by the Crown Court or remanded in custody by any court.

[10:11] *Hague v Deputy Governor of Parkhurst Prison* [1991] 3 All ER 733

Hague was deemed to be a trouble-maker, and was transferred to another prison, where he was removed from association under rule 43 of the Prison Rules. The Court of Appeal had granted a declaration that, because of errors of procedure, the removal had been unlawful, but refused certiorari and damages. Weldon alleged that he had been forcibly dragged downstairs and detained without clothes overnight in a strip cell. The (differently constituted) Court of Appeal had refused to strike out that part of the statement of claim which was based on false imprisonment. The House of Lords in both cases was concerned not with judicial review, but only with civil actions for breach of statutory duty and false imprisonment.

Lord Bridge (at page 737):

My Lords, there are two appeals before the House. I shall refer to them as *Hague's* case and *Weldon's* case respectively. They raise important questions with respect to the rights of convicted prisoners.

Introduction

The decisions of the Court of Appeal in *R v Hull Prison Board of Visitors, ex p St Germain* [1979] 1 All ER 701, [1979] QB 425 and of this House in *Leech v Deputy Governor of Parkhurst Prison* [1988] 1 All ER 485, [1988] AC 533 established that the courts have jurisdiction to entertain applications for judicial review of disciplinary awards made by boards of visitors and by prison governors respectively under the Prison Rules 1964, SI 1964/388. In both cases it had been contended, in effect on behalf of the Home Office, that jurisdiction should be declined on the ground that any interference by the courts in the management of prisons would be subversive of prison discipline. In *Leech's* case [1988] 1 All ER 485 at 499, [1988] AC 533 at 566, as I record, Mr Laws had urged that, if jurisdiction were accepted in relation to awards by prison governors, this would 'make it impossible to resist an invasion by what he called 'the tentacles of the law' of many other departments of prison administration'. In deciding the appeal your Lordships faced that prospect without undue alarm and I believe that the circumstances of *Hague's* case now before the House show that it was right to do so. In *Hague's* case both courts below held that they had jurisdiction to entertain an application for judicial review which questioned the legality of Hague's segregation under r 43 of the Prison Rules and the Court of Appeal declared that the procedure followed pursuant to the terms of a Home Office circular issued in 1974 (Circular Instruction 10/1974) was not warranted by the terms of the rule and was accordingly unlawful. In your Lordships' House the Secretary of State, acting by Mr Laws, has chosen, very sensibly if I may say so, not to pursue any challenge either to the assumption of jurisdiction or to its exercise by the declarations granted. Instead the Home Office have issued a new circular prescribing a new procedure to be followed in future in the relevant circumstances which conforms to the requirements of r 43 as construed by the Court of Appeal. I believe this confirms the view that the availability of judicial review as a means of questioning the legality of action purportedly taken in pursuance of the Prison Rules is a beneficial and necessary jurisdiction which cannot properly be circumscribed by considerations of policy or expediency in relation to prison administration. Those considerations only come into play when the court has to consider, as a matter of discretion, how the jurisdiction should be exercised. But the issues which it is necessary to resolve in the present appeals relate neither to the scope of the courts' public law jurisdiction in judicial review nor to the exercise of discretion in that jurisdiction. The appeals raise the wholly different question whether a convicted prisoner who, in the course of serving his sentence, has been treated in a way which the rules do not permit has in any and what circumstances a cause of action in private law sounding in damages against the prison governor or the Home Office on the ground either of a breach of statutory duty or of the tort of false imprisonment.

(and at page 739):

Breach of statutory duty

It was not open to counsel for Hague in any court below your Lordships' House to advance a claim to damages for breach of statutory duty because of the decision of the Court of Appeal in *Becker v Home Office* [1972] 2 All ER 676, [1972] 2 QB 407, where one of the grounds on which it was held that the plaintiff failed was that a breach of the Prison Rules does not, per se, give rise to a cause of action. But Mr Sedley has now put the claim for damages in *Hague's* case on this alternative basis in the forefront of his argument and I think it logical to consider it first.

In *Becker v Home Office* [1972] 2 All ER 676, [1972] 2 QB 407 both Lord Denning MR and Edmund Davies LJ expressed their conclusion that a breach of the Prison Rules 1964 creates no civil liability in equally general terms. Mr Sedley submits that such a general approach is erroneous and that each provision in the rules must be considered separately. Whilst I do not accept this criticism of the earlier authorities, I do accept that we may properly be invited in asking the question whether the breach of a particular provision of the rules gives rise to a cause of action to examine that provision in its context. Adopting that course, I can find nothing in r 43 or in any context that is relevant to the construction of r 43 which would support the conclusion that it was intended to confer a right of action on an individual prisoner. The purpose of the rule, apart from the case of prisoners who need to be segregated in their own interests, is to give an obviously necessary power to segregate prisoners who are liable for any reason to disturb the orderly conduct of the prison generally. The rule is a purely preventive measure. The power is to be exercised only in accordance with the procedure prescribed by sub-r (2). But where the power has been exercised in good faith, albeit that the procedure followed in authorising its exercise was not in conformity with r 43(2), it is inconceivable that the legislature intended to confirm because of action on the segregated prisoner.

(and at page 742):

False imprisonment

The Court of Appeal in *Weldon's* case approached the question whether a prisoner serving his sentence can ever sustain a claim for false imprisonment, as they were invited to do so by Mr Laws, as a single question which must admit of the same answer irrespective of the identity of the defendant. Ralph Gibson LJ, delivering the leading judgment, with which both Fox and Parker LJ agreed, said ([1990] 3 All ER 672 at 681, [1990] 3 WLR 465 at 474): 'There is no reason, apparent to me, why the nature of the tort, evolved by the common law for the protection of personal liberty, should be held to be such as to deny its availability to a convicted prisoner whose residual liberty should, in my judgment, be protected so far as the law can properly achieve unless statute requires otherwise. If, however, as [Mr Laws] submits, the tort of false imprisonment is not available to a convicted prisoner against a prison officer, I accept his submission that it could not, for the same reasons, be available to a convicted prisoner against a fellow prisoner.'

Ralph Gibson LJ had also delivered the judgment of the Divisional Court in *Hague's* case in which he expressed the view that the segregation of a prisoner would not constitute the tort of false imprisonment if the order for segregation, although not lawfully authorised under r 43, was given in good faith. Giving the judgment in *Weldon's* case he found it unnecessary to express a final conclusion on this point since, if want of good faith were a necessary ingredient of the tort, he held that it was sufficiently alleged in the pleading against the officers concerned. The pleading, he held, also alleged circumstances capable of amounting to 'intolerable conditions of detention' such as would sustain a claim of false imprisonment on the authority of the decision of the Court of Appeal in *Middleweek v Chief Constable of the Merseyside Police* [1990] 3 All ER 662, [1990] 3 WLR 481. It was on these grounds that the Court of Appeal declined to strike out the pleading of false imprisonment in *Weldon's* case. Parker LJ, in adding his own reasons to his agreement with those given by Ralph Gibson LJ, was clearly much concerned with the problem of the rights of prisoners as against fellow prisoners or prison officers acting in bad faith. He said ([1990] 3 All ER 672 at 686, [1990] 3 WLR 465 at 480):

> 'Although the plaintiff may, in the end, fail to establish the facts, we must proceed for the moment on the basis that he was kept locked up naked overnight in a cell known as a strip cell. It is said that as he was lawfully detained in the prison this cannot amount to false imprisonment. If this be right it must I think follow that he could have had no claim for false imprisonment if his detention naked in that cell had continued for weeks. It would also seem to me to follow that if he had been locked up in a similar condition, not by prison officers, but by fellow inmates, he would have no such claim. It would follow, too, that, if a convicted criminal were confined in a prison which he and his fellows were permitted, within the confines of a perimeter fence enclosing some acres of ground, to lead normal lives he would have no such claim if he were locked up, with or without clothes, in a shed in some remote part of the grounds, whether by fellow inmates or prison officers. To hold that such treatment could not amount to false imprisonment offends in my judgment against common sense.'

In so far as the Court of Appeal's reasoning in these judgments proceeds from the premises urged upon them by Mr Laws that a prisoner's 'right to liberty' is either totally abrogated or partially retained in the form of a 'residual liberty', I think, with all respect, that it is erroneous. To ask at the outset whether a convicted prisoner enjoys in law a 'residual liberty', as if the extent of any citizen's right to liberty were a species of right in rem or a matter of status, is to ask the wrong question. An action for false imprisonment is an action in personam. The tort of false imprisonment has two ingredients: the fact of imprisonment and the absence of lawful authority to justify it. In *Meering v Grahame-White Aviation Co Ltd* (1919) 122 LT 44 at 54 Atkin LJ said that 'any restraint within defined bounds which is a restraint in fact may be an imprisonment'. Thus if A imposes on B a restraint within defined bounds and is sued by B for false imprisonment, the action will succeed or fail according to whether or not A can justify the restraint imposed on B as lawful. A child may be lawfully restrained within defined bounds by his parents or by the schoolmaster to whom the parents have delegated their authority. But if precisely the same restraint is imposed by a stranger without authority, it will be unlawful and will constitute the tort of false imprisonment.

I shall leave aside initially questions arising from the situation where a convicted prisoner serving a sentence is restrained by a member of the prison staff acting in bad faith, by a fellow prisoner or any other third party, or in circumstances where it can be said that the conditions of his detention are intolerable. I shall address first what I believe to be the primary and fundamental issue, viz whether any restraint within defined bounds imposed upon a convicted prisoner whilst serving his sentence by the prison governor or by officers acting with the authority of the prison governor and in good faith, but in circumstances where the particular form of restraint is not sanctioned by the Prison Rules, amounts for that reason to the tort of false imprisonment. The starting point is s 12 (1) of the Prison Act 1952 which provides: 'A prisoner, whether sentenced to imprisonment or committed to prison on remand pending trial or otherwise, may be lawfully confined to any prison.'

This provides lawful authority for the restraint of the prisoner within the defined bounds of the prison by the governor of the prison, who has the legal custody of the prisoner under section 13, or by any prison officer acting with the governor's authority. Can the prisoner then complain that his legal rights are infringed by a restraint which confined him at any particular time within a particular part of the prison? It seems to me that the reality of prison life demands an alternative answer to this question. Certainly in the ordinary closed prison the ordinary prisoner will at any time of day or night be in a particular part of the prison, not because that is where he chooses to be, but because that is where the prison regime required him to be. He will be in his cell, in the part of the prison where he is required to work, in the exercise yard, eating meals, attending education classes or enjoying whatever recreation is permitted, all in the appointed place and at the appointed time and all in accordance with a more or less rigid regime to which he must conform. Thus the concept of the prisoner's 'residual liberty' as a species of freedom of movement within the prison enjoyed as a legal right which the prison authorities cannot lawfully restrain seems to be quite illusory. The prisoner is at all times lawfully restrained within closely defined bounds and if he is kept in a segregated cell, at a time when, if the rules has not been misapplied, he would be in the company of other prisoners in the workshop, at the dinner table or elsewhere, this is not the deprivation of his liberty of movement, which is the essence of the tort of false imprisonment, it is the substitution of one form of restraint for another.

Mr Harris seeks to surmount these difficulties by submitting that whenever there is a breach of the rules which is sufficiently 'fundamental' this converts an otherwise lawful imprisonment into an unlawful imprisonment. This, as I understand it, is quite a different concept from that of an infringement of residual liberty. The submission is that any breach of the rules which is sufficiently far reaching in its effect on the prisoner, for example the failure to supply him with clothing 'adequate for warmth and health' pursuant to r 20(2), undermines the legality of his imprisonment. Logically this would lead to the conclusion that the prisoner who has not been supplied with proper clothing would be entitled to walk out of the prison, but Mr Harris understandably disclaims any such extravagant proposition. It follows that the authority given by s 12(1) for lawful confinement of the prisoner cannot possibly be read as subject to any implied term with respect to compliance with the Prison Rules and this is fatal to any submission which seeks to make the lawfulness of the imprisonment depend in any sense on such compliance.

In my opinion, to hold a prisoner entitled to damages for false imprisonment on the ground that he has been subject to a restraint upon his movement which was not in accordance with the Prison Rules would be, in effect, to confer on him under a different legal label a cause of action for breach of statutory duty under the rules. Having reached the conclusion that it was not the intention of the rules to confer such a right, I am satisfied that the right cannot properly be asserted in the alternative guise of a claim to damages for false imprisonment.

(and at page 745):

There remains the question whether an otherwise lawful imprisonment may be rendered unlawful by reasons only of the conditions of detention. In *R v Metropolitan Police Comr, ex p Nahar* (1983) Times, 28 May, two applicants for habeas corpus who had been remanded in custody were held pursuant to the provisions of s 6 of the Imprisonment (Temporary Provisions) Act 1980 in cells below the Camberwell Green Magistrates' Court which were designed only to enable persons to be held in custody for a few hours at a time and which were obviously deficient in many respects for the purpose of accommodating prisoners for longer periods. They sought their release on the ground that the conditions of their detention rendered it unlawful. The applications were rejected, but Stephen Brown J said in the course of his judgment: 'There must be some minimum standard to render detention lawful ...' McCullough J said: 'Despite the temporary nature of the detention there contemplated, there must be implied into s 6 of the 1980 Act some term which relates to the conditions under which a prisoner may lawfully be detained. I say so because it is possible to conceive of hypothetical circumstances in which the conditions of detention were such as would make that detention unlawful. I do not propose to offer any formulation of that term. Were it broken in any particular case I would reject emphatically the suggestion that the matter would not be one for the exercise of the court's jurisdiction to grant the writ of habeas corpus.'

These observations were considered by the Court of Appeal in *Middleweek v Chief Constable of the Merseyside Police* [1990] 3 All ER 662, [1990] 3 WLR 481. The plaintiff has been awarded damages for false imprisonment by the jury on the basis that his otherwise lawful detention at a police station has been rendered unlawful because it was unreasonable in the circumstances to keep him in a police cell. The defendant successfully appealed, but Ackner LJ, delivering the judgment of the court, said ([1990] 3 All ER 662 at 668, [1990] 3 WLR 481 at 487):

'We agree with the views expressed by the Divisional Court that it must be possible to conceive of hypothetical cases in which the conditions of detention are so intolerable as to render the detention unlawful and thereby provide a remedy to the prisoner in damages for false imprisonment. A person lawfully detained in a prison cell would, in our judgment, cease to be so lawfully detained if the conditions in that cell were such as to be seriously prejudicial to his health if he continued to occupy it, eg because it became and remained seriously flooded, or contained a fractured gas pipe allowing gas to escape into the cell. We do not therefore accept as an absolute proposition that, if detention is initially lawful, it can never become unlawful by reasons of changes in the conditions of imprisonment.'

I sympathise entirely with the view that the person lawfully held in custody who is subjected to intolerable conditions ought not be to left without a remedy against his custodian, but the proposition that the conditions of detention may render the detention itself unlawful raises formidable difficulties. If the proposition be sound, the corollary must be that when the conditions of detention deteriorate to the point of intolerability, the detainee is entitled immediately to go free. It is impossible, I think, to define with any precision what would amount to intolerable conditions for this purpose. McCollough J understandably and perhaps wisely abstained from any attempt of definition in *Ex p Nahar*. The examples given by Ackner LJ of a flooded or gas-filled cell are so extreme that they do not, with respect, offer much guidance as to where the line should be drawn. The law is certainly left in a very unsatisfactory state if the legality or otherwise of detaining a person who in law is and remains liable to detention depends on such an imprecise criterion and may vary from time to time as the conditions of his detention change.

The logical solution to the problem, I believe, is that if the conditions of an otherwise lawful detention are truly intolerable, the law ought to be capable of providing a remedy directly related to those conditions without characterising the fact of the detention itself as unlawful. I see no real difficulty in saying that the law can provide such a remedy. Whenever one person is lawfully in the custody of another, the custodian owes a duty of care to the detainee. If the custodian negligently allows, or a fortiori, if he deliberately causes, the detainee to suffer in any way in his health he will be in breach of that duty. But short of anything that could properly be described as a physical injury or an impairment of health, if a person lawfully detained is kept in conditions which cause him for the time being physical pain or a degree of discomfort which can properly be described as intolerable, I believe that could and should be treated as a breach of the custodian's duty of care for which the law should award damages. For this purpose it is quite unnecessary to attempt any definition of the criterion of intolerability. It would be a question of fact and degree in any case which came before the court to determine whether the conditions to which a detainee had been subjected were such as to warrant an award of damages for the discomfort he had suffered. In principle I believe it is acceptable for the law to provide a remedy on this basis, but that the remedy suggested in the *Nahar* and *Middleweek* cases is not. In practice the problem is perhaps not very likely to arise.

Conclusion

For the reasons I have given I conclude that a claim for damages either for breach of statutory duty or for false imprisonment is not sustainable in either of the cases before the House.

[10:12] **Hood, R and Shute, S** *Parole in Transition: Evaluating the Impact and Effects of Changes in the Parole System: Phase Two* (1994) Oxford Centre for Criminological Research No 16 (at page 46):

1 SUMMARY

(i) The new criteria

§96 From the summer of 1992 onwards, several changes in decision-making proce-dures were introduced which affected the consideration of prisoners sentenced under the 'old system'. The most important of these was the Home Secretary's announcement that the new criteria, laid down under section 32(6) of the 1991 Act to govern release under the DCR system, would, from 1 October 1992, also apply to old system cases. According to these criteria, before recommending parole, the Parole Board must be satisfied that:

'(a) the longer period of supervision that parole would provide is likely to reduce the risk of further imprisonable offences being committed. In assessing the risk to the community, a small risk of violent offending is to be treated as more serious than a larger risk of non-violent offending;

(b) the offender has shown by his attitude and behaviour in custody that he is willing to address his offending and has made positive efforts and progress in doing so;

(c) the resettlement plan will help secure the offender's rehabilitation.'

These are referred to in this report as Criteria RO, OB and RP respectively.

§97 Other changes were also introduced which affected old system cases. First, the number of Board members who sit on 'panels' which review parole applications was reduced from four to three. Second, six salaried full-time members were appointed in August 1993. Third, early in March 1994, the Board began to formulate detailed reasons in writing relating to the established criteria so that, should there be a judicial review of the decision, the reasons would be available for scrutiny. It was not intended that these reasons, which were required both for granting and for refusing parole, should yet be communicated to prisoners sentenced under the old system. But they were intended to encourage panels to frame their reasons in the form that would be necessary when, later in 1994, they were to be conveyed to all prisoners.

...

§99 From August 1993 to May 1994, we observed 24 panels at which 545 prisoners serving sentences of four years and more who had been sentenced under the old system were considered for parole. Eighteen of the panels were held before the Board began to record full reasons for its decisions in writing: these panels considered 423 long-term old system cases. Once full reasons were recorded, we attended a further six panels which dealt with 122 old system cases. In general, we have compared the base-line sample of 383 observed cases with the total 545 cases observed in phase two. However, where necessary, we have analysed the two samples separately.

§100 We received the parole dossiers in advance (as we had in the base-line study) and were privileged to have been able to take full notes – as far as possible verbatim – of all that was discussed. We were also sent copies of the 'panel result sheets', which record the decisions made and any reasons given.

§101 As in all evaluative studies which attempt to chart the outcome of change by comparing samples taken before and after that change has occurred, a fundamental question is the extent to which the samples are similar in respect of other factors which might influence the results. We were able to identify sufficient points of objective similarity between the two samples to feel confident in making comparisons between them. Using the data available we found that three variables were strongly associated with the probability of release. They were: the Local Review Committee (LRC) recommendation as 'suitable' or 'unsuitable'; our classification of a case as 'high risk' or not; and whether the case was at first or last review. We have, where appropriate, used these variables as a 'control' when comparing the decisions made by the Board in the base-line and phase two samples.

(ii)   The board at work

§102 In the report of the base-line study, we remarked on the fact that panels rarely had an even distribution of members representing the various statutory categories: judges, psychiatrists, probation officers, criminologists and independents. An obvious consequence of reducing the size of panels from four persons to three has been to dilute the contribution that could be made by the 'expert' members. Thus, whereas in the base-line period independents outnumbered 'experts' on seven of the 16 panels (44%), in phase two they did so on 16 of the 24 panels (67%). Indeed, there were three panels in phase two on which only independent members sat. However, the greater preponderance of independents did not mean that any group sharing a similar background and experience (for example, former prison officials) predominated. It was noticeable that panels less often had an input from a probation officer: they were present on only a quarter of panels in phase two compared with over half of the panels in the base-line study. No criminologist member was present at any of the panels in phase two: indeed, there were only two of them on the Board.

...

2   CONCLUSIONS

§145 Reducing the size of panels – from five or six members in the early years of the scheme, to four members, and finally to three members in 1993 – has radically altered the Board as originally conceived. It was envisaged that every case would be considered by persons drawn from each of the five categories set down in the statute. That no longer happens. The Carlisle Committee's warning – when it considered (and rejected) the possibility of a reduction in panel size from four to three – that 'the inter-disciplinary nature of panels would be impaired' has come to pass. This raises the important question of how best the Board can function effectively as a multi-disciplinary body.

§146 During the period covered by our field work, serious delays no longer appeared to be a major problem, although at first review they still occurred and in a few cases seriously disadvantaged the parole applicant. This is a matter which needs to be kept constantly under review.

§147 The requirement to give full written reasons means that the Board now takes considerably longer to reach and formulate its decisions. This may have implications for the workload of panels, especially if reasons have to be even fuller than those now given.

§148 The replacement of the former criteria for *refusal* (A–F) by criteria for *release* has inevitably shifted the focus of decision-making from considerations which could be either positive or negative to a presumption that parole will not be granted unless all three criteria are met.

§149 The pattern of parole decisions has changed. In some respects the Board is more liberal than it was prior to the introduction of the new criteria; in other respects it appears to be as restrictive on release as it was under the 'restricted policy'. The White Paper *Crime, Justice and Protecting the Public* (Cm 965, 1990) stated that the proposed new criteria 'are sufficiently stringent to replace the present restricted policy on parole'. This assessment has proved to be correct.

§150 Prisoners reviewed before they would be eligible under the DCR scheme were more likely to be released under the new criteria because of the ban on what is known as 'resentencing' (ie, insisting that those whose offences are regarded with distaste serve a longer proportion of their sentence in custody).

§151 Prisoners not released early in their sentence are less likely than formerly to be released at subsequent reviews, especially if the Board considers that they pose a high risk of committing a serious offence. This was so, even though they would not receive any supervision on release. We therefore predict that the reduction in the rate of release of 'high-risk' prisoners which has been due to the application of the new criteria will be even greater for such cases considered under the new DCR system.

§152 Nothing can be done (apart from shorter sentences being imposed) to alter the impact on the prison population of the change in the law which no longer allows DCR prisoners to be released before half their sentence has been served. We estimated, from the average number of days spent on parole licence prior to the halfway point of the sentence, by what percentage the length of prison sentences would have to be cut in order to ensure that prisoners who had earned parole before halfway under the old system would not have served longer in prison had they been sentenced under the DCR scheme and released at halfway. Our conclusion was that the sentences of such prisoners would have to be cut, on average, by 21 per cent.

§153 In relation to 'high-risk' prisoners, the way in which the Board reacts to the availability in the DCR scheme of supervision after two-thirds of the sentence may not remain constant. Everything depends on whether Board members believe that the statutory supervision provided between two-thirds and three-quarters of the sentence is sufficient to ensure that the public are protected and on how often they believe that 'the longer period of supervision that parole would provide is likely to *reduce* the risk of further imprisonable offences being committed' (Criterion RO; emphasis added). However, we know from this phase of our research that the new criteria have already had the effect of markedly reducing the proportion granted parole, even without the availability of statutory supervision after release at EDR. The Carlisle Report, on which much of the DCR scheme was based, certainly did not envisage that the extension of supervision for a period after EDR would mean that 'high-risk' cases would almost always fail to get 'parole' (ie, discretionary early release).

§154 The dossiers of prisoners considered under the DCR scheme should all contain newly calculated reconviction prediction scores, which show the probability of reconviction at monthly intervals over a two-year period separately for 'any offending' and for 'serious offending (resulting in a custodial sentence)'. In the final phase of this research it will be possible to see whether these scores are more often referred to and used as a basis for decision-making. We should also be able to gauge whether there is more consensus among Board members on how the score should be interpreted and the weight that ought to be placed on it.

§155 Prisoners' own 'reps' were not very influential in decisions whether or not to release. Nor was much attention paid to what the prisoner had told the LRC member. It remains to be seen whether the interview reports made by Parole Board members on DCR cases will prove to be more influential.

§156 When we interview prisoners and staff again in the final phase of this project, it will be interesting to see how they have responded to the rehabilitative challenge which has been introduced by the new criteria, particularly as reasons will have to be communicated to prisoners in writing.

§157 Although the reasons given for refusing parole were more detailed than they used to be, they were still rather brief. The next phase of this research should be able to show whether, in the light of judicial review, they will become more substantial and, if so, in what ways.

§158 Some interesting questions are raised by the finding that, in the majority of cases recommended for release, Board members failed specifically to record that they were satisfied that each of the three criteria had been met. This suggests that at least some prisoners are released who do not meet all three criteria and that the Board has exercised its discretion in their favour by weighing one criterion against others. In any event, Board members appear to favour an approach to reason giving which takes these criteria 'into account' rather than being bound by them. In this context, it is worth recalling that section 32(6) of the Criminal Justice Act 1991 gives the Home Secretary power to 'give to the Board directions as to the matters to be taken into account'. Some may argue that this is different from giving the Secretary of State power to *mandate* that a combination of specific criteria *must* be met before release can be recommended.

§159 The centrality of the problem of dealing with 'high-risk' prisoners under the new criteria raises the question of how accurate the Board is in predicting the likelihood of such prisoners committing very serious offences, both while on licence and in the period before the expiry of their sentence. In the base-line and in phase two of this study, 463 prisoners were having their last review, of which 148 were considered by Board members to pose a serious risk to the public. It would be valuable to follow-up the criminal records of all these prisoners, whether released on parole or not, in order to record the patterns of reconviction both for cases the Board identified as 'high risks' and those regarded as lesser risks. This would make it possible to assess to what extent the Board had correctly identified those who posed the greatest threat of committing a grave offence on release from prison. It might also be possible to assess if a period on parole lowered the risk of a 'high-risk' prisoner committing such a crime.

[10:13] Hood, R and Shute, S *Parole Decision-making: Weighing the Risk to the Public* HO Research Findings No 114 (2000) (at pages 2–4):

The research aimed to assess the effectiveness and efficiency of the parole system. It examined:

- how the Parole Board assessed applications
- whether interviews conducted by Parole Board members made a difference to the decisions reached
- the relationship between parole decisions and actuarially-based risk assessment scores
- reasons given for refusing or granting parole
- how probation officers' recommendations influenced parole decisions.

There are various stages in parole decision-making. In addition to the information in a prisoner's dossier (which includes details of the offence, previous convictions and reports from prison and probation officers), Parole Board Interviewing Members (PBIMs) visit prisons to interview prisoners about their parole application. Their reports are added to prisoners' dossiers and forwarded to the Parole Board. Three-member panels of the Board meet in London and on each occasion consider the dossiers of 24 parole applicants. Dossiers are read in advance and at the meeting members take it in turns to 'lead' the discussion, having prepared reasons for their decision which may be amended after discussion.

Research methods

The research was carried out in two linked phases:
- 151 PBIM interviews were observed in 14 prisons and the prisoners and PBIMs concerned were interviewed
- interviews with 63 seconded probation officers, 112 prison officers and 103 prisoners who had recently been refused parole
- questionnaires were sent to the prisoners' home probation officers.

In addition, 20 Parole Board panel meetings were observed where the applications of the 151 prisoners were discussed along with others. Information was gathered on decisions made about 437 prisoners. Panel members were asked about the value of the PBIM report. They were also asked to make an assessment of the risk of reconviction posed by each prisoner.

Decision-making

Members of panels rarely disagreed. The lead member's opinion was confirmed in 82% of cases. In a further 10%, the lead member's opinion was confirmed after some dissent and discussion. The final decision differed from that initially expressed by the lead member in only 8% of the cases observed. A prediction model of parole decision-making was calculated on the basis of data extracted from the prisoners' dossiers but not including the PBIM report. The model correctly predicted both Yes and No decisions in 85% of cases:
- 49% of the prisoners had a very low probability of release (between 0%–20%); only 4% of them were released
- at the other end of the scale, 17% had a very high probability of parole (80% and above); 89% were paroled
- taking these together, Parole Board decisions for 65% of prisoners were predicted by the statistical model with 94% accuracy.

With so many decisions correctly predicted from other information in the dossier, there was little room for the PBIM report to have a substantial impact on the decisions made. Indeed, those who drafted the reasons for the panel's decision said that their decision had been changed by something contained in the PBIM report in only 8% of cases.

The parole rate

Power to release on parole is now called Discretionary Conditional Release (DCR) and applies to those prisoners sentenced to four years or longer. The only valid comparison that can be made between the parole rate before and after the introduction of DCR is the proportion of prisoners in both periods who received parole at some time prior to having served two-thirds of their sentence. Of those serving four years or more who were reviewed between June 1992 and May 1995, under the old system, 69.7% were released on parole. By comparison, the latest Report of the Parole Board for 1998–99 shows that 47.7% of prisoners dealt with under the DCR system from its inception in October 1992 until March 1999 were granted parole. Thus, 22% fewer prisoners are now paroled during their sentence – equivalent to a 32% decline in the use of parole.

Reasons that might explain this decline are:
- the introduction of the Directions, which gave priority to risk, and the way that Board members have interpreted these Directions
- that under the new DCR system all prisoners are supervised after release whether paroled or not, whereas formerly prisoners only received supervision if granted parole
- that most prisoners now only get one parole review, whereas under the old system they had at least two.

Granting or refusing parole

As required by the Directions, panels, in their written reasons, placed great emphasis on risk factors and on whether or not prisoners had 'satisfactorily addressed their offending behaviour' – by completing an offending behaviour treatment course, for example.

When the panel refused parole, specific indicators of risk were mentioned in 84% of cases. These were mostly based on the prisoner's past history – factors such as the seriousness of the offence, previous history of sexual or violent offending, previous failure to respond to supervision and breaches of bail.

Progress, or lack of progress, made by the prisoner in addressing offending behaviour was the reason mentioned in 96% of refusals and 98% of cases where parole was granted. In a third of the cases refused, the panel stressed that 'more work' should be done, or should be 'consolidated' in prison, rather than while under parole supervision in the community.

Panels mentioned in their reasons that 73% of prisoners granted parole had 'satisfactory release plans'. However, in only one-third of cases where parole was granted did the panel state in their reasons that risk would be further reduced by a period on parole supervision. This perhaps suggests that members of the Board do not have a great deal of confidence in the effectiveness of parole supervision as a method of containing or reducing risk.

More than 80% of the refused prisoners who were interviewed said that the reasons they had been given were 'unfair'. Three-quarters said that the reasons given had not made them change their behaviour, and nearly all the rest said they had responded negatively to the 'knock back'.

Licence conditions

The average period of parole licence granted to the paroled prisoners was 330 days. Before the introduction of DCR, 44% of prisoners were paroled with further conditions attached to their licence (see Hood and Shute, 1994 and 1995). In this study, 87% had conditions attached. For example, of those paroled, 52% had a residence condition in comparison with 15% under the old system. 82% were released on condition they continued to deal with their offending behaviour (including drugs, alcohol, anger and sexual behaviour) in comparison with 32%. Furthermore, 44% of those paroled had three or more conditions attached. All prisoners are now supervised on release from prison whether paroled or not. 60% of those not paroled (who formerly had no conditions at all) had at least three conditions attached on release from prison. Thus, the degree of control over prisoners after release has increased and widened.

Parole related to reconviction risk

The risk of a prisoner committing further offences if released on parole licence is the main consideration of the Board. Parole decisions can be compared with actuarial, objectively determined risk of reconviction data. A risk of reconviction score (ROR) has been calculated by Copas et al., 1996, on the basis of a follow-up study of a large number of prisoners. Parole decisions in this study were analysed, separately for non-sex and sex offenders, in relation to the ROR for a serious offence (one likely to lead to imprisonment) during the period available for parole. The findings for non-sex offenders are shown in Table 1.

Table 1 Relationship between ROR for a serious offence on parole licence and parole decision (for non-sex offenders)

Actuarial risk of reconviction	No. of cases observed	Cases paroled (No.)	Cases paroled (%)	Percentage of cases in each risk group
0%–2%	52	43	83	15%
3%–7%	115	58	50	33%
Total (to 7%)	**167**	**101**	**61**	**48%**
8–16%	100	22	22	29%
17%	78	6	8	23%
Total (8%+)	**178**	**28**	**16**	**52%**

As can be seen in Table 1, there was a strong and statistically significant correlation between actuarial ROR and the parole decision so far as non-sex offenders were concerned. Although half of the sex offenders had a ROR of 7% or less (average 3.7%), 40% of them were denied parole, demonstrating the Board's considerable caution.

The Board was even more cautious in relation to sex offenders. Only 22% of those with a risk of reconviction rate of 7% or less (average 3.2%) were paroled. As the ROR was not a major factor explaining which sex offenders did and did not get parole, a different prediction score was calculated drawing on the formula devised by Dr David Thornton of HM Prison Service. This categorises prisoners into three risk levels and takes into account whether or not the prisoner has completed a Sex Offender Treatment Programme. The findings showed that the statistical risk of reconviction according to the Thornton scale was a less strong predictor of parole than whether the prisoner had successfully completed a Sex Offender Treatment Programme. Amongst those who had done so, the parole rate was virtually the same whatever their risk category.

'Clinical' assessments of risk compared with 'actuarial' risk

Panel members have to rely on their own 'clinical' assessment as the actuarially-based ROR score for each prisoner is not available to them. Their assessment of risk was compared with the actuarial risks calculated by Copas et al. The findings showed that panel members were making decisions on the basis of unduly pessimistic 'clinical' estimations of risk when compared with the actuarial risk calculation:

*   85% of prisoners had a statistical rate of reconviction of a serious offence during parole period in the 'low' category (0-19%). Half of them had a ROR of 7% or less. Yet, Board members estimated risk of reconviction to be 20% or higher for more than half the prisoners they assessed
*   73% of the sex offender cases fell into the lower Levels I and II of the Thornton sex offender predictor. Yet, Board members assessed the risk to be equivalent to Level III in more than half the cases.

Probation officers' reports

There was a strong correlation between parole decisions and the recommendations made by both seconded probation officers in the prison and home probation officers (see Table 2). If probation reports were negative the chances of getting parole were close to zero. However, over 40% of prisoners recommended by both probation officers were refused parole. This may partly explain why half of the prisoners interviewed said they found the reasons they had been given 'hard to take'.

Table 2 The relationship between probation officers' (seconded probation officers in prison and the prisoner's home probation officer) recommendations and parole decisions

Recommendation	*Paroled*		*Total*	
	No.	%	No.	%
Both recommended parole	133	54	247	56
Only one recommended parole	11	18	60	14
Neither recommended parole	3	2	131	30

Low-risk offenders and parole

The study assessed what the consequences would be if the parole rate for low risk offenders was increased. Estimates were made of what the effect would have been if the Parole Board had released on parole all prisoners who had both a low actuarial risk of reconviction (ROR of 7% or less) for a serious offence while on parole licence and a recommendation from both probation officers.

The average risk of these prisoners being reconvicted of an offence while on parole for which they would be likely to receive a further prison sentence was less than four in a 100. Because they have such a low risk of reconviction, their inclusion amongst all parolees would actually reduce the average rate of reconviction from 6.2% to 5.7%.

If this group of prisoners had been released, the parole rate in the sample would have risen from 33.6% to 43.2%, which is equivalent to an increase of 29%. Translating this into a national estimate, this would mean that approximately 550 more prisoners would be released on parole annually. Of these, about 500 could be expected to complete parole without a conviction of any kind. Given the expense of imprisonment compared with supervision in the community, the cost of not granting parole to these low risk offenders is considerable.

Policy implications

Procedural implications
- Both the degree of unanimity in decision-making and the ease of predicting parole decisions on the basis of recorded information raise the question of whether a formal meeting of three Board members in London is necessary for every case and, if not, how best the resources available might be used.
- The time and expense involved in the use of Parole Board Interviewing Members could be reassessed in view of the marginal role played by their reports in decision-making. Perhaps the prisoner's case could be communicated to the Board in a different way.
- There appears to be a strong argument for including an updated ROR score in parole dossiers. In a system that gives priority to risk, it is essential that risk should be assessed as accurately as possible, both to protect the public and to ensure that the liberty of low-risk prisoners is not unnecessarily restricted.

Wider implications

The 1988 Parole Review Committee (Carlisle Committee), whose recommendations led to the reform of the system by the 1991 Act, expected that, by moving the eligibility date forward from one-third to a half a sentence, and by providing supervision for all prisoners whether paroled or not, a higher, not a lower, proportion of prisoners would be granted parole. This has not happened. While the findings of this research show that parole decisions are in line with the Home Secretary's Directions, these Directions, together with the Board's interpretation of them, have undoubtedly created a more risk-averse approach than originally expected by the Carlisle Committee.

It will always be necessary to strike a balance between the risk to the public and the liberty that might be accorded the individual prisoner. These findings question whether the right balance has been found.

References

Copas, J.B., Marshall, P. and Tarling, R. (1996) *Predicting reoffending for Discretionary Conditional Release*. Home Office Research Study No. 150. London: Home Office.

Hood, R.G. and Shute, S.C (1994, 1995) *Evaluating the impact and effects of changes in the Parole System*. University of Oxford, Centre for Criminological Research. Occasional Papers Nos. 13 and 16. Oxford: University of Oxford.

[10:14] *Thynne, Wilson and Gunnell v United Kingdom* (1990) 13 EHRR 666

The three applicants had been separately convicted of serious offences and sentenced to discretionary life sentences. All three applicants complained about the lack of regular judicial scrutiny of the lawfulness of their detention and, in the cases of the second and third applicants, re-detention. The court held, by a majority of 18 to 1, that there had been a violation of article 5(4) European Convention on Human Rights, and in the case of the third applicant, also a violation of article 5(5).

(at page 693):

73   As regards the nature and purpose of the discretionary life sentence under English law, the Government's main submission was that it is impossible to disentangle the punitive and 'security' components of such sentences. The court is not persuaded by this argument: the discretionary life sentence has clearly developed in English law as a measure to deal with mentally unstable and dangerous offenders; numerous judicial statements have recognised the protective purpose of this form of life sentence. Although the dividing line may be difficult to draw in particular cases, it seems clear that the principles underlying such sentences, unlike mandatory life sentences, have developed in the sense that they are composed of a punitive element and subsequently of a security element designed to confer on the Secretary of State the responsibility for determining when the public interest permits the prisoner's release. This view is confirmed by the judicial description of the 'tariff' as denoting the period of detention considered necessary to meet the requirements of retribution and deterrence.

74   The court accepts the Government's submissions that the 'tariff' is also communicated to the Secretary of State in cases of mandatory life imprisonment; that the Secretary of State in considering release may not be bound by the intimation of the 'tariff'; and that in the assessment of the risk factor in deciding on release the Secretary of State will also have regard to the gravity of the offences committed.

However, in the court's view this does not alter the fact that the objectives of the discretionary life sentence as seen above are distinct from the punitive purposes of the mandatory life sentence and have been so described by the courts in the relevant cases.

75   It is clear from the judgments of the sentencing courts that in their view the three applicants, unlike Mr Weeks, had committed offences of the utmost gravity meriting lengthy terms of imprisonment. Nevertheless, the court is satisfied that in each case the punitive period of the discretionary life sentence has expired.

In the case of Mr Thynne, it was accepted that by the end of 1984 risk was the sole remaining consideration in his continued detention.

In addition to the life sentence imposed on him for the offence of buggery, Mr Wilson was sentenced in 1972 to seven years' imprisonment for each of the nine other counts to be served concurrently. In the circumstances of his case it would seem reasonable to draw the conclusion that the punitive period of his life sentence has expired when he was released in 1982 and that thereafter his re-detention pursuant to that sentence depended solely on the risk factor.

In Mr Gunnell's case, too, it may be taken that, notwithstanding the gravity of his offences on which the courts laid particular emphasis, the applicant had served the punitive period of his sentence by March 1982, the date fixed for his provisional release.

76   Having regard to the foregoing, the court finds that the detention of the applicants after the expiry of the punitive periods of their sentences is comparable to that at issue in the *Van Droogenbroeck* and *Weeks* cases – the factors of mental instability and dangerousness are susceptible to change over the passage of time and new issues of lawfulness may this arise in the course of detention. It follows that at this phase in the execution of their sentences, the applicants are entitled under Article 5(4) to take proceedings to have the lawfulness of their continued detention decided by a court at reasonable intervals and to have the lawfulness of any re-detention determined by a court.

(and at page 695):

79   Article 5(4) does not guarantee a right to judicial control of such scope as to empower the 'court' on all aspects of the case, including questions of expediency, to substitute its own discretion for that of the decision-making authority; the review should, nevertheless, be wide enough to hear on those conditions which, according to the Convention, are essential for the lawful detention of a person subject to the special type of deprivation of liberty ordered against these three applicants.

80   The court sees no reason to depart from its finding in the *Weeks* judgment that neither the Parole Board nor judicial review proceedings – no other remedy of a judicial character being available to the three applicants – satisfy the requirements of Article 5(4). Indeed, this was not disputed by the Government.

C   Recapitulation

81   In conclusion, there has been a violation of Article 5(4) in respect of all three applicants.

[10:15] *Doody v Secretary of State for the Home Department* [1993] 3 All ER 92

The four applicants were separately convicted of murder and received mandatory sentences of life imprisonment. Under the procedure adopted by the Secretary of State for the exercise of his discretionary power under section 61(1) of the Criminal Justice Act 1967 to decide the date on which a person serving a mandatory life sentence for murder could be released on licence, the trial judge and the Lord Chief Justice were invited to express their views on the period which the prisoners should serve for the purpose of retribution and deterrence (the 'tariff' period). The four applicants had each been told the date of the first review of their cases by the Parole Board, and considered that the Secretary of State had increased the tariff periods recommended by the judiciary. They sought declarations that:

(i) the Secretary of State was required to adopt the judicial view of the penal element of the sentence;

(ii) the prisoner was entitled to make representations before the Secretary of State set the date for the first review and, for that purpose, the right to be told of any information on which the Secretary of State would make his decision; and

(iii) the prisoner was entitled to be told the judicial view of the penal element of his sentence, the reasons for the recommendations of the judiciary and for any departure by the Secretary of State from that recommendation.

The House of Lords held that, whilst it was the Secretary of State, not the judges, who was entrusted with the task of deciding on prisoners' release, and that he was entitled to depart from the judge's advice, prisoners were entitled to be treated fairly.

Lord Mustill (at page 105):

Once it is concluded that the judicial opinion is not conclusive, and that it is the decision of the Home Secretary that matters, the opinion of the judges becomes no more than a component of the entire body of material in the light of which that decision is made.

Thus, although it is tempting to approach the question of disclosure and reasons as if it were the judges' opinions to which the applications for judicial review are directed this is mistaken. It is the decision of the Home Secretary which vitally affects the future of the prisoner, and it is the openness of this decision which is essentially in dispute. Although the shape of the arguments presented in the courts below led those courts to begin the inquiry with the judges' opinions, and hence to progress to the reasons for those opinions, and finally to a consideration of whether the reasons of the Home Secretary for departing from the judges' opinions should be disclosed, I prefer to go directly to the opposite end of the process to consider the prisoner's rights in relation to the decision by the Home Secretary. I emphasise once again that the court is not being asked to review and could not with any hope of success be asked to review this scheme in its entirety, the more so since the judges have themselves being playing an important part in it for the past ten years. Nor of course is it the task of the court to say how it would choose to operate the scheme if given a free hand. The only issue is whether the way in which the scheme is administered falls below the minimum standard of fairness.

What does fairness require in the present case? My Lords, I think it unnecessary to refer by name or to quote from, any of the often-cited authorities in which the courts have explained what is essentially an intuitive judgment. They are far too well known. From them, I derive the following. (1) Where an Act of Parliament confers an administrative power there is a presumption that it will be exercised in a manner which is fair in all the circumstances. (2) The standards of fairness are not immutable. They may change with the passage of time, both in the general and in their application to decisions of a particular type. (3) The principles of fairness are not to be applied by rote identically in every situation. What fairness demands is dependent on the context of the decision, and this is to be taken into account in all its aspects. (4) An essential feature of the context is the statute which creates the discretion, as regards both its language and the shape of the legal and administrative system within which the decision is taken. (5) Fairness will very often require that a person who may be adversely affected by the decision will have an opportunity to make representations on his own behalf either before the decision is taken with a view to producing a favourable result, or after it is taken, with a view to procuring its modification, or both. (6) Since the person affected usually cannot make worthwhile representations without knowing what factors may weigh against his interests fairness will very often require that he is informed of the gist of the case which he has to answer.

(and at page 111):

Before leaving this question, I wish to make it absolutely clear that if your Lordships are in agreement with this conclusion this will not be a signal for a flood of successful applications for judicial review. I repeat for the last time that Parliament has left the discretion on release with the Home Secretary, and that he has done nothing to yield it up. So long as this remains the case, prisoners should not deceive themselves into believing that they can obtain leave to move for judicial review simply by pointing to a difference between the opinion of the judges and the decision of the Home Secretary. Only if it can be shown that the decision may have been arrived at through a faulty process, in one of the ways now so familiar to practitioners of judicial review, will they have any serious prospect of persuading the court to grant relief.

This will result in an order in the following form:

'It is declared that: (1) The Secretary of State is required to afford to a prisoner serving a mandatory life sentence the opportunity to submit in writing representations as to the period he should serve for the purpose of retribution and deterrence before the Secretary of State sets the date of the first review of the prisoner's sentence. (2) Before giving the prisoner the opportunity to make such representations, the Secretary of State is required to inform him of the period recommended by the judiciary as the period he should serve for the purposes of retribution and deterrence, and of any other opinion expressed by the judiciary which is relevant to the Secretary of State's decision as to the appropriate period to be served for these purposes. (3) Secretary of State is obliged to give reasons for departing from the period recommended by the judiciary as the period which he should serve for the purpose of retribution and deterrence.'

[10:16] *Stafford v United Kingdom* (2002) 35 EHRR 1121

This case concerned the power of the Home Secretary not to accept a recommendation of the Parole Board to release on licence an offender subject to a mandatory life sentence whose previous licence had been revoked. The court accepted that all life sentences are made up of two parts: the first, the punishment element of the sentence, is a sentencing exercise, not the administrative implementation of the sentence of the court. The second part, imposed for the protection of the public because of the offender's dangerousness, should be reviewed regularly by a body with a power to release, and under a procedure with the necessary judicial safeguards, including, for example, the possibility of an oral hearing. The court held unanimously that there had been a violation of both article 5(1) and article 5(4) of the European Convention on Human Rights in the case before it. The Home Secretary should not have the power to detain post-tariff lifers against the recommendation of the Parole Board. The Court acknowledged that the Convention is a dynamic tool.

58   The applicant disputed that the true objective of the mandatory life sentence was life-long punishment. He remained the only mandatory life prisoner who had been detained post-tariff on the basis that the Secretary believed that he might commit a non-violent offence if released. Different considerations might apply where a risk of drug trafficking was concerned as such activity was clearly capable of causing physical or psychological harm to others. To justify indefinite imprisonment by reference to a belief that he might on release commit a non-violent crime involving no conceivable physical harm to others, was arbitrary, encompassing matters wholly unrelated in nature and seriousness to the reasons for the prisoner being within the power of the State in the first place.

2. The Government

59   The Government submitted that the imposition of a mandatory life sentence for murder satisfied Article 5(1) of the Convention. In its view, this continued to provide a lawful basis for his detention after the expiry of the six-year sentence for fraud offences as his life licence had been revoked. It rejected the applicant's argument that this detention, on the basis of a concern that he might commit serious non-violent offences of dishonesty bore no proper relationship to the object of the original mandatory life sentence. It argued that the original sentence was imposed because of the gravity of the offence of murder. A mandatory life sentence for murder fell within a distinct category, different from the discretionary life sentence, as it was imposed as punishment for the seriousness of the offence. It was not governed by characteristics specific to a particular offender which might change over time, factors such as dangerousness, mental instability or youth. A trial judge was required by Parliament to impose a life sentence for murder whether or not the offender was considered dangerous.

60   The object and purpose of the punishment was to confer power on the Secretary of State to decide when, if at all, it was in the public interest to allow the applicant to return to society on life licence and to empower the Secretary of State to decide, subject to the applicable statutory procedures, whether it was in the public interest to recall the applicant to prison at any time until his death. Whether or not the concern was about risk of further offences of violence or further non-violent offences, a refusal to release on life licence, or a decision to revoke the life licence, was closely related to the original mandatory life sentence by reason of the gravity of the offence and to ensure that the prisoner could only be released when the public interest made it appropriate to do so. The sentence also provided flexibility since it allowed reconsideration of the tariff if such had been set in ignorance of relevant factors, a possibility not available to a judge.

61   The Government submitted that, in deciding whether it was in the public interest to release the applicant, the Secretary of State was therefore entitled to have regard to the risk of serious non-violent offending. It would not be logical or rational if he was

unable to refuse to order the release of a prisoner where there was an unacceptable risk of his committing serious non-violent offences such as burglary or trafficking in heroin, which attracted far longer prison sentences than some offences of a violent nature and which caused far more harm to the public interest. The Government referred to the previous case law of the Court which found that continued detention of life prisoners was justified by their original trial and appeal proceedings. The fact that the applicant had been released on life licence and had been living for some time at liberty had no relevance to the lawful basis of his detention after revocation of that licence. Nor had there been any relevant developments in either domestic or Convention case law which altered the statutory basis of the mandatory life sentence or its proper meaning and effect.

B.   The Court's assessment

1.   *Preliminary considerations*

62   The question to be determined is whether, after the expiry on 1 July 1997 of the fixed term sentence imposed on the applicant for fraud, the continued detention of the applicant under the original mandatory life sentence imposed on him for murder in 1967 complied with the requirements of Article 5(1) of the Convention.

63   Where the 'lawfulness' of detention is in issue, the Convention refers essentially to national law and lays down the obligation to conform to the substantive and procedural rules of national law. This primarily requires any arrest or detention to have a legal basis in domestic law but also relates to the quality of the law, requiring it to be compatible with the rule of law, a concept inherent in all the Articles of the Convention. In addition, any deprivation of liberty should be in keeping with the purpose of Article 5, namely to protect the individual from arbitrariness.

64   It is not contested that the applicant's detention from 1 July 1997 was in accordance with a procedure prescribed by English law and otherwise lawful under English law. This was established in the judicial review proceedings, where the Court of Appeal and House of Lords found that the Secretary of State's decision to detain the applicant fell within his discretion as conferred by section 35(1) of the 1991 Act. This is not however conclusive of the matter. The Court's case law indicates that it may be necessary to look beyond the appearances and the language used and concentrate on the realities of the situation.[5] In the case of Weeks v. United Kingdom, which concerned the recall to prison by the Secretary of State of an applicant who had been released from a discretionary life sentence for robbery, the Court interpreted the requirements of Article 5 as applying to the situation as follows: The lawfulness required by the Convention presupposes not only conformity with domestic law but also, as confirmed by Article 18, conformity with the purposes of the deprivation of liberty permitted by the sub-paragraph (a) of Article 5(1) (see as the most recent authority the Bozano judgment of 18 December 1986, Series A No. 111, p. 23 (54)). Furthermore, the word 'after' in sub-paragraph (a) does not simply mean that the detention must follow the 'conviction' in point of time: in addition, the 'detention' must result from, 'follow and depend upon' or occur 'by virtue' of the 'conviction' (ibid., pp. 22-23, (3), and the Van Droogenbroeck judgment ... p. 19, (35)). In short, there must be a sufficient causal connection between the conviction and the deprivation of liberty at issue (see the abovementioned Van Droogenbroeck judgment, p. 21 (39)).

65   The Court recalls that in the Weeks case it was found that the discretionary life sentence imposed on the applicant was an indeterminate sentence expressly based on considerations of his dangerousness to society, factors which were susceptible by their very nature to change with the passage of time. On that basis, his recall, in light of concerns about is unstable, disturbed and aggressive behaviour, could not be regarded as arbitrary or unreasonable in terms of the objectives of the sentence imposed on him and there was sufficient connection for the purposes of Article 5(1)(a) between his conviction in 1966 and recall to prison in 1977.

66   Much of the argument from the parties has focused on the nature and purpose of the mandatory life sentence as compared with other forms of life sentence and whether the detention after 1 July 1997 continued to conform with the objectives of that sentence. And since the procedures applying to the varying types of life sentences have generated considerable case law, both on the domestic level and before the Convention organs, there has been extensive reference to the judicial dicta produced as supporting the arguments on both sides.

67   Of particular importance in this regard is the Wynne case decided in 1994, in which this Court found that no violation arose under Article 5(4) in relation to the continued detention after release and recall to prison of a mandatory life prisoner convicted of an intervening offence of manslaughter, the tariff element of which had expired. This provides strong support for the Government's case while the applicant sought to argue that this decision did not succeed in identifying the reality of the situation for mandatory life prisoners which subsequent developments have clarified still further. The Court in Wynne was well aware that there were similarities between the discretionary life and mandatory life sentences, in particular that both contained a punitive and a preventive element and that mandatory life prisoners did not actually spend the rest of their lives in prison. The key passage states: However the fact remains that the mandatory life sentence belongs to a different category from the discretionary life sentence in the sense that it is imposed automatically as the punishment for the offence of murder irrespective of considerations pertaining to the dangerousness of the offender. (p. 14, (35))

68   While the Court is not formally bound to follow any of its previous judgments, it is in the interests of legal certainty, foreseeability and equality before the law that it should not depart, without cogent reason, from precedents laid down in previous cases. Since the Convention is first and foremost a system for the protection of human rights, the Court must however have regard to the changing conditions in Contracting States and respond, for example, to any emerging consensus as to the standards to be achieved. It is of crucial importance that the Convention is interpreted and applied in a manner which renders its rights practical and effective, not theoretical and illusory. A failure by the Court to maintain a dynamic and evolutive approach would risk rendering it a bar to reform or improvement.

69   Similar considerations apply as regards the changing conditions and any emerging consensus discernible within the domestic legal order of the respondent Contracting State. Although there is no material distinction on the facts between this and the Wynne case, having regard to the significant developments in the domestic sphere, the Court proposes to re-assess 'in the light of present-day conditions' what is now the appropriate interpretation and application of the Convention.

2. Legal developments

70 The mandatory life sentence is imposed pursuant to statute in all cases of murder. This position has not changed, though there has been increasing criticism of the inflexibility of the statutory regime, which does not reflect the differing types of killing covered by the offence from so-called mercy killing to brutal psychopathic serial attacks.

71 The inflexibility of this regime was, from a very early stage, mitigated by the approach of the Secretary of State, who in all types of life sentences-- mandatory, discretionary and Her Majesty's pleasure detention adopted a practice of setting a specific term known as the 'tariff' to represent the element of deterrence and retribution. This was generally the minimum period of detention which would be served before an offender could hope to be released. It was never anticipated that prisoners serving mandatory life sentences would in fact stay in prison for life, save in exceptional cases. Similarly, the decision as to the release of all life prisoners also lay generally with the Secretary of State. The tariff-fixing and release procedures applicable to life sentences have however been modified considerably over the past 20 years, to a large extent due to the case law of this Court. It is also significant that the domestic courts were frequently called upon to rule on lawfulness issues arising out of the Secretary of State's role in fixing the tariff and in deciding the appropriate moment for release, the courts requiring the establishment of proper and fair procedures in his exercise of those functions. Between Strasbourg and the domestic courts, a steady erosion on the scope of the Secretary of State's decision-making power in this field may be identified.

72 The first examination of the Court in this area focused on the situation of discretionary life prisoners. In the cases of Weeks and Thynne, Gunnell and Wilson, the Court analysed the purpose and effect of the discretionary life sentence, imposable for very serious offences such as manslaughter and rape. It was held that since the grounds relied upon in sentencing to a discretionary life term concerned risk and dangerousness, factors susceptible to change over time, new issues of lawfulness could arise after the expiry of the tariff which, in the context of Article 5(4), necessitated proper review by a judicial body. As a result, the Criminal Justice Act 1991 provided that the question of release, after expiry of tariff of a discretionary life prisoner, was to be decided not by the Secretary of State but by the Parole Board in a procedure with judicial safeguards. The same Act also gave statutory force to the Secretary of State's policy of accepting the judicial view of the tariff in discretionary life cases. The judges then took on the role, in open court, of setting the punishment element of the sentence. Though no significant changes were made by statute to the regime of mandatory life sentences, the procedure whereby the tariff was fixed was shortly afterwards modified following the House of Lords decision in the Doody case, where it was found that procedural fairness required that mandatory life prisoners be informed of the judicial view of the tariff in order that they could make written representations to the Secretary of State before he reached his decision. This reflected a growing perception that the tariff-setting function was closely analogous to a sentencing function.

73 It was at this stage that the Court directly addressed the position of mandatory life prisoners in the Wynne case and took the view that the mandatory life sentence was different in character from the discretionary life sentence. In reaching that decision, it concentrated on the automatic imposition of the mandatory life sentence, which was perceived as pursuing a punitive purpose.

74   Not long afterwards, the situation of post-tariff juvenile murderers (Her Majesty's pleasure detainees) was the subject of applications under the Convention. Though this type of sentence, as with the adult mandatory life sentence, was imposed automatically for the offence of murder, the Court was not persuaded that it could be regarded as a true sentence of punishment to detention for life. Such a term applied to children would have conflicted with United Nations instruments and raised serious problems under Article 3 of the Convention. Considering that it must be regarded in practice as an indeterminate sentence which could only be justified by considerations based on the need to protect the public and therefore linked to assessments of the offender's mental development and maturity, it therefore held that a review by a court of the continued existence of grounds of detention was required for the purposes of Article 5(4).

75   The issues arising from the sentencing process for juvenile murderers at the tariff-fixing stage were then examined both in the domestic courts and in Strasbourg. In Ex parte T and V the House of Lords made very strong comment on the judicial nature of the tariff-fixing exercise and quashed a tariff fixed by the Home Secretary which, inter alia, took into account 'public clamour' whipped up by the press against the offenders in the case. This Court found that Article 6(1) applied to the fixing of the tariff, which represented the requirements of retribution and deterrence and was thus a sentencing exercise. The fact that it was decided by the Secretary of State, a member of the executive and therefore not independent, was found to violate this provision.

76   By this stage therefore, there were further statutory changes, which assimilated the position of juvenile murderers to that of discretionary life prisoners in giving the courts the role of fixing the tariff and providing the Parole Board with decision-making powers and appropriate procedures when dealing with questions of release.

77   While mandatory life prisoners alone remained under the old regime, the coming into force on 2 October 2000 of the Human Rights Act 1998 provided the opportunity for the first direct challenges to the mandatory life regime under the provisions of the Convention in the domestic courts. In the case of Lichniak and Pyrah the prisoners' arguments that the mandatory life sentence was arbitrary due to its inflexibility were rejected. It may be observed, as pointed out by the applicant, that the Government in that case contended that the mandatory life sentence was an indeterminate sentence by which an individualised tariff was set and that after the expiry of the tariff the prisoner could expect to be released once it was safe to do so. They expressly departed from the position that the mandatory life sentence represented a punishment whereby a prisoner forfeited his liberty for life. On that basis, the Court of Appeal found that there were no problems of arbitrariness or disproportionality in imposing mandatory life sentences. Then in the case of Anderson and Taylor, which concerned a challenge under Article 6(1) to the role of the Secretary of State in fixing the tariffs for two mandatory life prisoners, the Court of Appeal was unanimous in finding that this was a sentencing exercise which should attract the guarantees of that Article, following on from clear statements made by the House of Lords in the cases of Ex parte T and V and Ex parte Pierson.

78   The above developments demonstrate an evolving analysis, in terms of the right to liberty and its underlying values, of the role of the Secretary of State concerning life sentences. The abolition of the death penalty in 1965 and the conferring on the Secretary of State of the power to release convicted murderers represented, at that time, a major and progressive reform. However, with the wider recognition of the need to develop and apply, in relation to mandatory life prisoners, judicial procedures reflecting standards

of independence, fairness and openness, the continuing role of the Secretary of State in fixing the tariff and in deciding on a prisoner's release following its expiry, has become increasingly difficult to reconcile with the notion of separation of powers between the executive and the judiciary, a notion which has assumed growing importance in the case law of the Court.

79   The Court considers that it may now be regarded as established in domestic law that there is no distinction between mandatory life prisoners, discretionary life prisoners and juvenile murderers as regards the nature of tariff-fixing. It is a sentencing exercise. The mandatory life sentence does not impose imprisonment for life as a punishment. The tariff, which reflects the individual circumstances of the offence and the offender, represents the element of punishment. The Court concludes that the finding in Wynne that the mandatory life sentence constituted punishment for life can no longer be regarded as reflecting the real position in the domestic criminal justice system of the mandatory life prisoner. This conclusion is reinforced by the fact that a whole life tariff may, in exceptional cases, be imposed where justified by the gravity of the particular offence. It is correct that the Court in its more recent judgments in T and V, citing the Wynne judgment as authority, reiterated that an adult mandatory life sentence constituted punishment for life. In doing so it had, however, merely sought to draw attention to the difference between such a life sentence and a sentence to detention during Her Majesty's pleasure, which was the category of sentence under review in the cases concerned. The purpose of the statement had therefore been to distinguish previous case law rather than to confirm an analysis deriving from that case law.

[10:17]   Mental Health Act 1983 sections 37; 41; 42; 47–49; 70–74; 118

37   Powers of courts to order hospital admission or guardianship

(1)   Where a person is convicted before the Crown Court of an offence punishable with imprisonment other than an offence the sentence for which is fixed by law or falls to be imposed under section 109(2) of the Powers of Criminal Courts (Sentencing) Act 2000, or is convicted by a magistrates' court of an offence punishable on summary conviction with imprisonment, and the conditions mentioned in subsection (2) below are satisfied, the court may by order authorise his admission to and detention in such hospital as may be specified in the order or, as the case may be, place him under the guardianship of a local social services authority or of such other person approved by a local social services authority as may be so specified.

(1A)   In the case of an offence the sentence for which would otherwise fall to be imposed under subsection (2) of section 110 or 111 of the Powers of Criminal Courts (Sentencing) Act 2000, nothing in that subsection shall prevent a court from making an order under subsection (1) above for the admission of the offender to a hospital.

(1B)   For the purposes of subsections (1) and (1A) above, a sentence fails to be imposed under section 109(2), 110(2) or 111(2) of the Powers of Criminal Courts (Sentencing) Act 2000 if it is required by that provision and the court is not of the opinion there mentioned.

(2)   The conditions referred to in subsection (1) above are that—

    (a)   the court is satisfied, on the written or oral evidence of two registered medical practitioners, that the offender is suffering from mental illness, psychopathic disorder, severe mental impairment or mental impairment and that either—

        (i)   the mental disorder from which the offender is suffering is of a nature or degree which makes it appropriate for him to be detained in a hospital for medical treatment and, in the case of psychopathic disorder or mental impairment, that such treatment is likely to alleviate or prevent a deterioration of his condition; or

        (ii)   in the case of an offender who has attained the age of 16 years, the mental disorder is of a nature or degree which warrants his reception into guardianship under this Act; and

    (b)   the court is of the opinion, having regard to all the circumstances including the nature of the offence and the character and antecedents of the offender, and to the other available methods of dealing with him, that the most suitable method of disposing of the case is by means of an order under this section.

(3)   Where a person is charged before a magistrates' court with any act or omission as an offence and the court would have power, on convicting him of that offence, to make an order under subsection (1) above in his case as being a person suffering from mental illness or severe mental impairment, then, if the court is satisfied that the accused did the act or made the omission charged, the court may, if it thinks fit, make such an order without convicting him.

(4)   An order for the admission of an offender to a hospital (in this Act referred to as "a hospital order") shall not be made under this section unless the court is satisfied on the written or oral evidence of the registered medical practitioner who would be in charge of his treatment or of some other person representing the managers of the hospital that arrangements have been made for his admission to that hospital ..., and for his admission to it within the period of 28 days beginning with the date of the making of such an order; and the court may, pending his admission within that period, give such directions as it thinks fit for his conveyance to and detention in a place of safety.

(5)   If within the said period of 28 days it appears to the Secretary of State that by reason of an emergency or other special circumstances it is not practicable for the patient to be received into the hospital specified in the order, he may give directions for the admission of the patient to such other hospital as appears to be appropriate instead of the hospital so specified; and where such directions are given—

    (a)   the Secretary of State shall cause the person having the custody of the patient to be informed, and

    (b)   the hospital order shall have effect as if the hospital specified in the directions were substituted for the hospital specified in the order.

(6)   An order placing an offender under the guardianship of a local social services authority or of any other person (in this Act referred to as "a guardianship order") shall not be made under this section unless the court is satisfied that that authority or person is willing to receive the offender into guardianship.

(7)   A hospital order or guardianship order shall specify the form or forms of mental disorder referred to in subsection (2)(a) above from which, upon the evidence taken into account under that subsection, the offender is found by the court to be suffering;

and no such order shall be made unless the offender is described by each of the practitioners whose evidence is taken into account under that subsection as suffering from the same one of those forms of mental disorder, whether or not he is also described by either of them as suffering from another of them.

(8) Where an order is made under this section, the court

shall not—

    (a)   pass sentence of imprisonment or impose a fine or make a probation order in respect of the offence,

    (b)   if the order under this section is a hospital order, make a referral order (within the meaning of the Powers of Criminal Courts (Sentencing) Act 2000) in respect of the offence, or

    (c)   make in respect of the offender a supervision order (within the meaning of that Act) or an order under section 150 of that Act (binding over of parent or guardian),

but the court may make any other order which it has power to make apart from this section; and for the purposes of this subsection "sentence of imprisonment" includes any sentence or order for detention.

41   Power of higher courts to restrict discharge from hospital

(1)   Where a hospital order is made in respect of an offender by the Crown Court, and it appears to the court, having regard to the nature of the offence, the antecedents of the offender and the risk of his committing further offences if set at large, that it is necessary for the protection of the public from serious harm so to do, the court may, subject to the provisions of this section, further order that the offender shall be subject to the special restrictions set out in this section, either without limit of time or during such period as may be specified in the order; and an order under this section shall be known as "a restriction order".

(2)   A restriction order shall not be made in the case of any person unless at least one of the registered medical practitioners whose evidence is taken into account by the court under section 37(2)(a) above has given evidence orally before the court.

(3)   The special restrictions applicable to a patient in respect of whom a restriction order is in force are as follows—

    (a)   none of the provisions of Part II of this Act relating to the duration, renewal and expiration of authority for the detention of patients shall apply, and the patient shall continue to be liable to be detained by virtue of the relevant hospital order until he is duly discharged under the said Part II or absolutely discharged under section 42, 73, 74 or 75 below;

    (aa)   none of the provisions of Part II of this Act relating to after-care under supervision shall apply;

    (b)   no application shall be made to a Mental Health Review Tribunal in respect of a patient under section 66 or 69(1) below;

    (c)   the following powers shall be exercisable only with the consent of the Secretary of State, namely—

        (i)   power to grant leave of absence to the patient under section 17 above;

> > > (ii) power to transfer the patient in pursuance of regulations under section 19 above or in pursuance of subsection (3) of that section; and
> > > (iii) power to order the discharge of the patient under section 23 above; and if leave of absence is granted under the said section 17 power to recall the patient under that section shall vest in the Secretary of State as well as the responsible medical officer; and
> > (d) the power of the Secretary of State to recall the patient under the said section 17 and power to take the patient into custody and return him under section 18 above may be exercised at any time;

and in relation to any such patient section 40(4) above shall have effect as if it referred to Part II of Schedule 1 to this Act instead of Part I of that Schedule.

(4) A hospital order shall not cease to have effect under section 40(5) above if a restriction order in respect of the patient is in force at the material time.

(5) Where a restriction order in respect of a patient ceases to have effect while the relevant hospital order continues in force, the provisions of section 40 above and Part I of Schedule 1 to this Act shall apply to the patient as if he had been admitted to the hospital in pursuance of a hospital order (without a restriction order) made on the date on which the restriction order ceased to have effect.

(6) While a person is subject to a restriction order the responsible medical officer shall at such intervals (not exceeding one year) as the Secretary of State may direct examine and report to the Secretary of State on that person; and every report shall contain such particulars as the Secretary of State may require.

42 Powers of Secretary of State in respect of patients subject to restriction orders

(1) If the Secretary of State is satisfied that in the case of any patient a restriction order is no longer required for the protection of the public from serious harm, he may direct that the patient cease to be subject to the special restrictions set out in section 41(3) above; and where the Secretary of State so directs, the restriction order shall cease to have effect, and section 41(5) above shall apply accordingly.

(2) At any time while a restriction order is in force in respect of a patient, the Secretary of State may, if he thinks fit, by warrant discharge the patient from hospital, either absolutely or subject to conditions; and where a person is absolutely discharged under this subsection, he shall thereupon cease to be liable to be detained by virtue of the relevant hospital order, and the restriction order shall cease to have effect accordingly.

(3) The Secretary of State may at any time during the continuance in force of a restriction order in respect of a patient who has been conditionally discharged under subsection (2) above by warrant recall the patient to such hospital as may be specified in the warrant.

(4) Where a patient is recalled as mentioned in subsection (3) above—
> (a) if the hospital specified in the warrant is not the hospital from which the patient was conditionally discharged, the hospital order and the restriction

order shall have effect as if the hospital specified in the warrant were substituted for the hospital specified in the hospital order;

(b)   in any case, the patient shall be treated for the purposes of section 18 above
as if he had absented himself without leave from the hospital specified in
the warrant, and, if the restriction order was made for a specified period,
that period shall not in any event expire until the patient returns to the
hospital or is returned to the hospital under that section.

(5)   If a restriction order in respect of a patient ceases to have effect after the patient
has been conditionally discharged under this section, the patient shall, unless previously recalled under subsection (3) above, be deemed to be absolutely discharged on
the date when the order ceases to have effect, and shall cease to be liable to be detained
by virtue of the relevant hospital order accordingly.

(6)   The Secretary of State may, if satisfied that the attendance at any place in Great
Britain of a patient who is subject to a restriction order is desirable in the interests of
justice or for the purposes of any public inquiry, direct him to be taken to that place;
and where a patient is directed under this subsection to be taken to any place he shall,
unless the Secretary of State otherwise directs, be kept in custody while being so taken,
while at that place and while being taken back to the hospital in which he is liable to be
detained.

47 Removal to hospital of persons serving sentences of imprisonment, etc

(1)   If in the case of a person serving a sentence of imprisonment the Secretary of State
is satisfied, by reports from at least two registered medical practitioners—

(a)   that the said person is suffering from mental illness, psychopathic disorder, severe mental impairment or mental impairment; and

(b)   that the mental disorder from which that person is suffering is of a nature
or degree which makes it appropriate for him to be detained in a hospital
for medical treatment and, in the case of psychopathic disorder or mental
impairment, that such treatment is likely to alleviate or prevent a deterioration of his condition;

the Secretary of State may, if he is of the opinion having regard to the public interest and
all the circumstances that it is expedient so to do, by warrant direct that that person be
removed to and detained in such hospital … as may be specified in the direction; and a
direction under this section shall be known as "a transfer direction".

(2)   A transfer direction shall cease to have effect at the expiration of the period of 14
days beginning with the date on which it is given unless within that period the person
with respect to whom it was given has been received into the hospital specified in the
direction.

(3)   A transfer direction with respect to any person shall have the same effect as a
hospital order made in his case.

(4)   A transfer direction shall specify the form or forms of mental disorder referred
to in paragraph (*a*) of subsection (1) above from which, upon the reports taken into
account under that subsection, the patient is found by the Secretary of State to be
suffering; and no such direction shall be given unless the patient is described in each

of those reports as suffering from the same form of disorder, whether or not he is also described in either of them as suffering from another form.

(5)   References in this Part of this Act to a person serving a sentence of imprisonment include references—

(a)   to a person detained in pursuance of any sentence or order for detention made by a court in criminal proceedings (other than an order under any enactment to which section 46 above applies);

(b)   to a person committed to custody under section 115(3) of the Magistrates' Courts Act 1980 (which relates to persons who fail to comply with an order to enter into recognisances to keep the peace or be of good behaviour); and

(c)   to a person committed by a court to a prison or other institution to which the Prison Act 1952 applies in default of payment of any sum adjudged to be paid on his conviction.

48   Removal to hospital of other prisoners

(1)   If in the case of a person to whom this section applies the Secretary of State is satisfied by the same reports as are required for the purposes of section 47 above that that person is suffering from mental illness or severe mental impairment of a nature or degree which makes it appropriate for him to be detained in a hospital for medical treatment and that he is in urgent need of such treatment, the Secretary of State shall have the same power of giving a transfer direction in respect of him under that section as if he were serving a sentence of imprisonment.

(2)   This section applies to the following persons, that is to say—

(a)   persons detained in a prison or remand centre, not being persons serving a sentence of imprisonment or persons falling within the following paragraphs of this subsection;

(b)   persons remanded in custody by a magistrates' court;

(c)   civil prisoners, that is to say, persons committed by a court to prison for a limited term (including persons committed to prison in pursuance of a writ of attachment), who are not persons falling to be dealt with under section 47 above;

(d)   persons detained under the Immigration Act 1971 or under section 62 of the Nationality, Immigration and Asylum Act 2002 (detention by Secretary of State).

(3)   Subsections (2) to (4) of section 47 above shall apply for the purposes of this section and of any transfer direction given by virtue of this section as they apply for the purposes of that section and of any transfer direction under that section.

49   Restriction on discharge of prisoners removed to hospital

(1)   Where a transfer direction is given in respect of any person, the Secretary of State, if he thinks fit, may by warrant further direct that that person shall be subject to the special restrictions set out in section 41 above; and where the Secretary of State gives a transfer direction in respect of any such person as is described in paragraph (a) or (b) of section 48(2) above, he shall also give a direction under this section applying those restrictions to him.

(2)   A direction under this section shall have the same effect as a restriction order made under section 41 above and shall be known as "a restriction direction".

(3)   While a person is subject to a restriction direction the responsible medical officer shall at such intervals (not exceeding one year) as the Secretary of State may direct examine and report to the Secretary of State on that person; and every report shall contain such particulars as the Secretary of State may require.

70   Applications to tribunals concerning restricted patients

A patient who is a restricted patient within the meaning of section 79 below and is detained in a hospital may apply to a Mental Health Review Tribunal—

    (a)   in the period between the expiration of six months and the expiration of 12 months beginning with the date of the relevant hospital order, hospital direction or transfer direction; and

    (b)   in any subsequent period of 12 months.

71   References by Secretary of State concerning restricted patients

(1)   The Secretary of State may at any time refer the case of a restricted patient to a Mental Health Review Tribunal.

(2)   The Secretary of State shall refer to a Mental Health Review Tribunal the case of any restricted patient detained in a hospital whose case has not been considered by such a tribunal, whether on his own application or otherwise, within the last three years.

(3)   The Secretary of State may by order vary the length of the period mentioned in subsection (2) above.

(4)   Any reference under subsection (1) above in respect of a patient who has been conditionally discharged and not recalled to hospital shall be made to the tribunal for the area in which the patient resides.

(5)   Where a person who is treated as subject to a hospital order and a restriction order by virtue of an order under section 5(1) of the Criminal Procedure (Insanity) Act 1964 does not exercise his right to apply to a Mental Health Review Tribunal in the period of six months beginning with the date of that order, the Secretary of State shall at the expiration of that period refer his case to a tribunal.

(6)   For the purposes of subsection (5) above a person who applies to a tribunal but subsequently withdraws his application shall be treated as not having exercised his right to apply, and where a patient withdraws his application on a date after the expiration of the period there mentioned the Secretary of State shall refer his case as soon as possible after that date.

72   Powers of tribunals

(1)   Where application is made to a Mental Health Review Tribunal by or in respect of a patient who is liable to be detained under this Act, the tribunal may in any case direct that the patient be discharged, and—
- (a) the tribunal shall direct the discharge of a patient liable to be detained under section 2 above if they are not satisfied—
  - (i) that he is then suffering from mental disorder or from mental disorder of a nature or degree which warrants his detention in a hospital for assessment (or for assessment followed by medical treatment) for at least a limited period; or
  - (ii) that his detention as aforesaid is justified in the interests of his own health or safety or with a view to the protection of other persons;
- (b) the tribunal shall direct the discharge of a patient liable to be detained otherwise than under section 2 above if they are not satisfied—
  - (i) that he is then suffering from mental illness, psychopathic disorder, severe mental impairment or mental impairment or from any of those forms of disorder of a nature or degree which makes it appropriate for him to be liable to be detained in a hospital for medical treatment; or
  - (ii) that it is necessary for the health of safety of the patient or for the protection of other persons that he should receive such treatment; or
  - (iii) in the case of an application by virtue of paragraph (g) of section 66(1) above, that the patient, if released, would be likely to act in a manner dangerous to other persons or to himself.

(2)   In determining whether to direct the discharge of a patient detained otherwise than under section 2 above in a case not falling within paragraph (b) of subsection (1) above, the tribunal shall have regard—
- (a) to the likelihood of medical treatment alleviating or preventing a deterioration of the patient's condition; and
- (b) in the case of a patient suffering from mental illness or severe mental impairment, to the likelihood of the patient, if discharged, being able to care for himself, to obtain the care he needs or to guard himself against serious exploitation.

(3)   A tribunal may under subsection (1) above direct the discharge of a patient on a future date specified in the direction; and where a tribunal do not direct the discharge of a patient under that subsection the tribunal may—
- (a) with a view to facilitating his discharge on a future date, recommend that he be granted leave of absence or transferred to another hospital or into guardianship; and
- (b) further consider his case in the event of any such recommendation not being complied with.

(3A) Where, in the case of an application to a tribunal by or in respect of a patient who is liable to be detained in pursuance of an application for admission for treatment or by virtue of an order or direction for his admission or removal to hospital under Part III of this Act, the tribunal do not direct the discharge of the patient under subsection (1) above, the tribunal may—

(a)   recommend that the responsible medical officer consider whether to make a supervision application in respect of the patient; and

(b)   further consider his case in the event of no such application being made.

(4)   Where application is made to a Mental Health Review Tribunal by or in respect of a patient who is subject to guardianship under this Act, the tribunal may in any case direct that the patient be discharged, and shall so direct if they are satisfied—

(a)   that he is not then suffering from mental illness, psychopathic disorder, severe mental impairment or mental impairment; or

(b)   that it is not necessary in the interests of the welfare of the patient, or for the protection of other persons, that the patient should remain under such guardianship.

(4A)   Where application is made to a Mental Health Review Tribunal by or in respect of a patient who is subject to after-care under supervision (or, if he has not yet left hospital, is to be so subject after he leaves hospital), the tribunal may in any case direct that the patient shall cease to be so subject (or not become so subject), and shall so direct if they are satisfied—

(a)   in a case where the patient has not yet left hospital, that the conditions set out in section 25A(4) above are not complied with; or

(b)   in any other case, that the conditions set out in section 25G(4) above are not complied with.

(5)   Where application is made to a Mental Health Review Tribunal under any provision of this Act by or in respect of a patient and the tribunal do not direct that the patient be discharged or, if he is (or is to be) subject to after-care under supervision, that he cease to be so subject (or not become so subject), the tribunal may, if satisfied that the patient is suffering from a form of mental disorder other than the form specified in the application, order or direction relating to him, direct that that application, order or direction be amended by substituting for the form of mental disorder specified in it such other form of mental disorder as appears to the tribunal to be appropriate.

(6)   Subsections (1) to (5) above apply in relation to references to a Mental Health Review Tribunal as they apply in relation to applications made to such a tribunal by or in respect of a patient.

(7)   Subsection (1) above shall not apply in the case of a restricted patient except as provided in sections 73 and 74 below.

73   Power to discharge restricted patients

(1)   Where an application to a Mental Health Review Tribunal is made by a restricted patient who is subject to a restriction order, or where the case of such a patient is referred to such a tribunal, the tribunal shall direct the absolute discharge of the patient if—

(a)   the tribunal are not satisfied as to the matters mentioned in paragraph (b)(i) or (ii) of section 72(1) above; and

(b)   the tribunal are satisfied that it is not appropriate for the patient to remain liable to be recalled to hospital for further treatment.

(2)   Where in the case of any such patient as is mentioned in subsection (1) above—
- (a)   paragraph (a) of that subsection applies; but
- (b)   paragraph (b) of that subsection does not apply,

the tribunal shall direct the conditional discharge of the patient.

(3)   Where a patient is absolutely discharged under this section he shall thereupon cease to be liable to be detained by virtue of the relevant hospital order, and the restriction order shall cease to have effect accordingly.

(4)   Where a patient is conditionally discharged under this section—
- (a)   he may be recalled by the Secretary of State under subsection (3) of section 42 above as if he had been conditionally discharged under subsection (2) of that section; and
- (b)   the patient shall comply with such conditions (if any) as may be imposed at the time of discharge by the tribunal or at any subsequent time by the Secretary of State.

(5)   The Secretary of State may from time to time vary any condition imposed (whether by the tribunal or by him) under subsection (4) above.

(6)   Where a restriction order in respect of a patient ceases to have effect after he has been conditionally discharged under this section the patient shall, unless previously recalled, be deemed to be absolutely discharged on the date when the order ceases to have effect and shall cease to be liable to be detained by virtue of the relevant hospital order.

(7)   A tribunal may defer a direction for the conditional discharge of a patient until such arrangements as appear to the tribunal to be necessary for that purpose have been made to their satisfaction; and where by virtue of any such deferment no direction has been given on an application or reference before the time when the patient's case comes before the tribunal on a subsequent application or reference, the previous application or reference shall be treated as one on which no direction under this section can be given.

(8)   This section is without prejudice to section 42 above.

74   Restricted patients subject to restriction directions

(1)   Where an application to a Mental Health Review Tribunal is made by a restricted patient who is subject to a limitation direction or restriction direction, or where the case of such a patient is referred to such a tribunal the tribunal—
- (a)   shall notify the Secretary of State whether, in their opinion, the patient would, if subject to a restriction order, be entitled to be absolutely or conditionally discharged under section 73 above; and
- (b)   if they notify him that the patient would be entitled to be conditionally discharged, may recommend that in the event of his not being discharged under this section he should continue to be detained in hospital.

(2)   If in the case of a patient not falling within subsection (4) below—

(a) the tribunal notify the Secretary of State that the patient would be entitled to be absolutely or conditionally discharged; and

(b) within the period of 90 days beginning with the date of that notification the Secretary of State gives notice to the tribunal that the patient may be so discharged,

the tribunal shall direct the absolute or, as the case may be, the conditional discharge of the patient.

(3) Where a patient continues to be liable to be detained in a hospital at the end of the period referred to in subsection (2)(b) above because the Secretary of State has not given the notice there mentioned, the managers of the hospital shall, unless the tribunal have made a recommendation under subsection (1)(b) above, transfer the patient to a prison or other institution in which he might have been detained if he had not been removed to hospital, there to be dealt with as if he had not been so removed.

(4) If, in the case of a patient who is subject to a transfer direction under section 48 above, the tribunal notify the Secretary of State that the patient would be entitled to be absolutely or conditionally discharged, the Secretary of State shall, unless the tribunal have made a recommendation under subsection (1)(b) above, by warrant direct that the patient be remitted to a prison or other institution in which he might have been detained if he had not been removed to hospital, there to be dealt with as if he had not been so removed.

(5) Where a patient is transferred or remitted under subsection (3) or (4) above the relevant hospital direction and the limitation direction or, as the case may be, the relevant transfer direction and the restriction direction shall cease to have effect on his arrival in the prison or other institution.

(6) Subsections (3) to (8) of section 73 above shall have effect in relation to this section as they have effect in relation to that section, taking references to the relevant hospital order and the restriction order as references to the hospital direction and the limitation direction or, as the case may be, to the transfer direction and the restriction direction.

(7) This section is without prejudice to sections 50 to 53 above in their application to patients who are not discharged under this section.

118 Code of practice

(1) The Secretary of State shall prepare, and from time to time revise, a code of practice—

(a) for the guidance of registered medical practitioners, managers and staff of hospitals, independent hospitals and care homes and approved social workers in relation to the admission of patients to hospitals and registered establishments under this Act and to guardianship and after-care under supervision under this Act; and

(b) for the guidance of registered medical practitioners and members of other professions in relation to the medical treatment of patients suffering from mental disorder.

(2)   The code shall, in particular, specify forms of medical treatment in addition to any specified by regulations made for the purposes of section 57 above which in the opinion of the Secretary of State give rise to special concern and which should accordingly not be given by a registered medical practitioner unless the patient has consented to the treatment (or to a plan of treatment including that treatment) and a certificate in writing as to the matters mentioned in subsection (2)(a) and (b) of that section has been given by another registered medical practitioner, being a practitioner appointed for the purposes of this section by the Secretary of State.

(3)   Before preparing the code or making any alteration in it the Secretary of State shall consult such bodies as appear to him to be concerned.

(4)   The Secretary of State shall lay copies of the code and of any alteration in the code before Parliament; and if either House of Parliament passes a resolution requiring the code or any alteration in it to be withdrawn the Secretary of State shall withdraw the code or alteration and, where he withdraws the code, shall prepare a code in substitution for the one which is withdrawn.

(5)   No resolution shall be passed by either House of Parliament under subsection (4) above in respect of a code or alteration after the expiration of the period of 40 days beginning with the day on which a copy of the code or alteration was laid before that House; but for the purposes of this subsection no account shall be taken of any time during which Parliament is dissolved or prorogued or during which both Houses are adjourned for more than four days.

(6)   The Secretary of State shall publish the code as for the time being in force.

[10:18]   Holloway, K and Grounds, A 'Discretion and the Release of Mentally Disordered Offenders' in Gelsthorpe, L and Padfield, N (eds) *Exercising Discretion: Decision-making in the criminal justice system and beyond* (2003) Willan (at page 158):

Conclusions and proposals for reform

The results of this research raise questions about the quality of Mental Health Review Tribunal decision-making in restricted cases and suggest that Tribunals are failing in their fundamental duty to safeguard some patients from unjustified detention in hospital. This failure, however, is not solely a response to the current climate of heightened concern for public safety. The majority of problems were observed in the decision-making *process*, but problems were also noted with the Tribunals' powers, the rules governing the Tribunal process, and the evidence upon which their decisions were to be based.

Although many doubtful practices were evident, the broad approach to decision-making was generally highly conscientious. Tribunal panels could spend hours ensuring that reasons were accurately and appropriately phrased. Medical members were heard persuading patients to try new courses of treatment in an effort to help them make progress. Annoyance and frustration were observed because of Tribunals' inability to transfer patients out of maximum security and efforts were regularly made to help improve the patient's situation. It was notable that the Tribunal members experienced real pleasure when granting discharges. Successful patients were usually invited back to the hearing room to be told the good news in person and to be congratulated on their success. In cases where no discharge was authorized the Tribunals endeavoured to emphasise progress that had been made rather than highlighting problems and failures. The members were anxious not to damage a patient's future chances of discharge or transfer.

In September 1998 the government appointed an Expert Committee to conduct a review of the Mental Health Act 1983. The Committee, chaired by Professor Genevra Richardson, was commissioned to inquire into 'how much mental health legislation should be shaped to reflect contemporary patterns of care within a framework which balances the need to protect the rights of individual patients and the need to ensure public safety' (Department of Health 1999a). In response to the Expert Committee's report a Green Paper was issued outlining the government's initial proposals for reform of the Mental Health Act (Department of Health 1999b). Following a consultation period the government published a White Paper in December 2000 (Department of Health 2000). These proposals have important and far-reaching implications, particularly for the Mental Health Review Tribunal system.

One of the main recommendations is to establish a new Tribunal system. This would extend the Tribunal's function to include the task of confirming an initial compulsory treatment order[1] and for renewing that order at regular intervals.[2] Patients would also be entitled to apply to the new Tribunals for a review of their case once during the currency of each order. The new system would, therefore, require Tribunals to review the need for a compulsory order that in some cases they themselves had confirmed.

As noted above, the White Paper does not remedy the lack of Tribunal powers to effect hospital transfers in restricted cases. It also appears possible that the influence of Tribunals will be further restricted by limitations in their ability to order deferred conditional discharges. Whilst a Tribunal would be able to order discharge from hospital that is conditional on co-operation with a community care plan, such an order could only be made if the necessary forms of care are available.

In addition to the change in the Tribunals' fundamental role, proposals are also made for an alteration in the composition of the Tribunal panel. The medical member's role as both an expert adviser and a decision-maker is viewed as incompatible and contrary to natural justice. Recommendations have therefore been made to separate these roles, so that the patient is assessed by a medical member of an independently appointed expert panel. The White Paper does not make clear, however, whether the patient would have access to this assessment. The Tribunal would have a clinical member (not necessarily medical). The loss of medical members from the Tribunal panels may have serious consequences for the quality of Tribunal decision-making. The observational research demonstrated that the medical members were crucial in the deliberations of Tribunals: they guided the members through the medical evidence, they explained key concepts and terms, and helped in the formulation of reasons that accurately described patients' conditions. It is likely, therefore, that the absence of a medical member would result in even greater reliance on the views of the patient's consultant or clinical supervisor, thereby compromising the 'independence' of the Tribunal system still further.

---

[1] Offender patients would be subject to compulsory care and treatment on the decision of the court rather than the new Tribunal.

[2] The new Tribunals would be required to renew orders after six months, after a second six months and thereafter annually.

Index